Lecture Notes in Computer Science   13789

More information about this series at https://link.springer.com/bookseries/558

Roberto Moreno-Díaz · Franz Pichler ·
Alexis Quesada-Arencibia (Eds.)

Computer Aided Systems Theory – EUROCAST 2022

18th International Conference
Las Palmas de Gran Canaria, Spain, February 20–25, 2022
Revised Selected Papers

Editors
Roberto Moreno-Díaz
University of Las Palmas de Gran Canaria
Las Palmas de Gran Canaria, Spain

Franz Pichler
Johannes Kepler University
Linz, Oberösterreich, Austria

Alexis Quesada-Arencibia
Department of Computer Science
and Institute of Cybernetics
University of Las Palmas de Gran Canaria
Las Palmas de Gran Canaria, Spain

ISSN 0302-9743   ISSN 1611-3349 (electronic)
Lecture Notes in Computer Science
ISBN 978-3-031-25311-9   ISBN 978-3-031-25312-6 (eBook)
https://doi.org/10.1007/978-3-031-25312-6

This Springer imprint is published by the registered company Springer Nature Switzerland AG
The registered company address is: Gewerbestrasse 11, 6330 Cham, Switzerland

Preface

The Eurocast Conferences are particularly unique among the European Scientific-Technical Congresses because it is one of the few periodic meetings that is promoted and organized exclusively by university and socio-cultural institutions, without the tutelage, direction or funding of associations, professionals or companies. It is currently the oldest of those. It is celebrated every two years. Initially, alternating Las Palmas de G.C. and a university in continental Europe, and since 2001, always in Las Palmas de G.C.

The idea of the first Eurocast was developed in 1988 by Prof. Franz Pichler, of the University of Linz and Prof. Roberto Moreno, at a meeting in Vienna promoted by the past Honorary President, the late Dr. Werner Schimanovich. The first meeting, Eurocast 1989, took place in February of that year, in Las Palmas School of Industrial Engineers, promoted by the Faculty of Informatics of Las Palmas and the Institute of Systems of the University of Linz. The Opening Session took place in the town of Gáldar, February 26th, 1989.

Science, and especially Technology, have moved in an almost vertiginous way, driven by the need and the promotion of consumerism, associated with the change of values that has been printed in the new generations. And Eurocast, within what we understand as a certain freedom, and with prudence, has been adapting the profile of its organization from a meeting of very specific specialists, to a practically multidisciplinary, flexible and changing conference, which in each event try to attract the experts and especially young researchers, facilitating the interaction between them, which is a generator of creativity.

The key to the success of Eurocast for 33 years has been in the quality of the contributions of its participants. This has to be recognized in the first place. They have made possible, with the help of the Springer Verlag publications in Computer Science, the worldwide distribution of the most important effect of Eurocast: that of joining together for many years, scientists and engineers of ages, training, interests and from very different European and non-European institutions. And that they could share their experiences in the design and analysis of systems using the most advanced mathematical methods to make efficient models and algorithms in computers. And this from the socio-economic, biological, medical technologies and sciences and information and communication engineering topics. All in a multidisciplinary atmosphere, which has facilitated the appearance and discussion of new and creative ideas and developments.

Selected papers from previous editions have been published as Springer Lecture Notes in Computer Science volumes 410, 585, 763, 1030, 1333, 1798, 2178, 2809, 3643, 4739, 5717, 6927, 6928, 8111, 8112, 9520, 10671, 10672, 12013 and 12014 and in several special issues of Cybernetics and Systems: An International Journal. EUROCAST and CAST meetings are definitely consolidated, as shown by the number and quality of the contributions over the years.

In this open multidisciplinary spirit, the 2022 Conference is composed of three plenary lectures by distinguished international Professors and 11 major thematic workshops, which sweep a broad spectrum of cutting-edge research in computer and systems sciences and technologies, including theory and applications of metaheuristic algorithms, model-based system design, verification and simulation, applications of signal processing technology, artificial intelligence and data mining for intelligent transportation systems and smart mobility, computer vision, machine learning for image analysis and applications, computer and systems based methods and electronic technologies in medicine, systems in industrial robotics, automation and IoT, systems thinking and relevance for technology, science and management professionals, cybersecurity and indoor positioning systems, as shown in the organization pages.

In this conference, as in previous ones, most of the credit for the success lays in the right proposals of subjects for Workshops, their resonance and impact, their diffusion and their strict selection of the many intended contributions. From 110 accepted and presented papers, 77 revised papers were selected to be included in this volume. The reviews of papers and their selection was made by the agreement of at least two members of the Program Committee, listed in the following pages, by a double blind peer review process.

The editors would like to express their thanks to all the contributors, many of whom are already Eurocast participants for years, and particularly to the considerable interaction of young and senior researchers, as well as to the invited speakers, Prof. Grossmann from the University of Vienna, known expert in Mathematics and Statistics; Prof. Affenzeller, from the Applied Sciences University of Upper Austria, one of the first European experts in algorithm development in the field of metaheuristic algorithms; Prof. Nikos Makris from Harvard University and Boston General Hospital, known expert in the field of neuroanatomy of the human brain and in neuroimaging. We would also like to thank the director of the Elder Museum of Science and Technology, D. José Gilberto Moreno, and the museum staff. Special thanks are due to the staff of Springer in Heidelberg for their valuable support.

October 2022

Roberto Moreno-Díaz
Franz Pichler
Alexis Quesada-Arencibia

Organization

Organized by

Instituto Universitario de Ciencias y Tecnologías Cibernéticas
Universidad de Las Palmas de Gran Canaria, Spain
Johannes Kepler University Linz
Linz, Austria
Museo Elder de la Ciencia y la Tecnología
Las Palmas de Gran Canaria, Spain

Conference Chairman

Roberto Moreno-Díaz, Las Palmas

Program Chairman

Franz Pichler, Linz

Organizing Committee Chairman

Alexis Quesada Arencibia
Instituto Universitario de Ciencias y Tecnologías Cibernéticas
Universidad de Las Palmas de Gran Canaria
Campus de Tafira
35017 Las Palmas de Gran Canaria, Spain
Phone: +34-928-457108
Fax: +34-928-457099
e-mail: alexis.quesada@ulpgc.es

Supporter Institutions

Universidad de Las Palmas de Gran Canaria

Johannes Kepler University Linz

University of Applied Sciences Upper Austria

Museo Elder de la Ciencia y la Tecnología

Fundación Universitaria de Las Palmas

Eurocast 2022

18th International Conference on Computer Aided Systems Theory
Museo Elder de la Ciencia y la Tecnología
Las Palmas de Gran Canaria, Spain
20–25 February 2022

To the Memory of Werner de Pauli Schimanovich

https://eurocast2022.fulp.ulpgc.es/

Plenary Lectures

Werner de Pauli Schimanovich – Inventor, Scientist and Spiritus Rector of EUROCAST

Wilfried Grossmann

University Vienna, Austria

Abstract. Werner de Pauli Schimanovich was in many respects an outstanding person. His scientific activities range from Logic, Artificial Intelligence, and Philosophy, up to Politics, Urban Planning, Transportation, and design of innovative solutions for everyday life. In unorthodox ways he analyzed problems and his brilliant intellect allowed him to identify central questions and he often presented surprising answers.

But not only his intellectual capacity made him an exceptional person. His open personality and his excellent communication skills allowed him to build a network of close friends from different disciplines all over the world and he attracted a number of eminent students.

Based on personal memories and his six volume Opus Magnum EUROPOLIS we will try to capture this multifaceted personality. Unfortunately, most of the contents of EUROPOLIS is available only in German. A synoptic English edition was under preparation but not finished due to health problems. A central aspect of the presentation will be Werner's close relation to Spain and the Canary Islands, which he considered as his second home country. This close relation was a main motive for establishing the EUROCAST conferences and in his last years Werner De Pauli Schimanovich considered EUROCAST as one of his most important achievements.

Prescriptive Analytics: Optimization Meets Data- and Simulation-Based Systems Modeling

Michael Affenzeller

Applied Sciences University of Upper Austria, Austria

Abstract. Prescriptive Analytics is an interdisciplinary topic in an interdisciplinary field, or put another way it is a synergistic hybridisation of various methods and algorithms from statistics, computer science, artificial intelligence, mathematics and operations research. Its aim is to provide optimized recommendations for action in various application areas. In this way, knowledge gained in the digital world is brought back to the real world, providing better and more efficient procedures, designs and processes.

This talk will introduce prescriptive analytics into the broader context of analytics and show the relationship between prescriptive analytics and artificial intelligence with a special focus on industrial AI.

From a system theoretic point of view, new possibilities arise in the interplay of data-based and simulation based system modeling. In particular, when it comes to finding a compromise between accuracy and efficiency of system descriptions in the field of simulation-based optimization, the combination of data and knowledge-based approaches opens up new possibilities.

The presentation will include methodological research topics that are currently being pursued in the HEAL research group 1 led by Affenzeller as well as concrete project results that have already found their way into economic and industrial applications.

The Impact of Computer Processed Neuroimaging in Modern Clinical Neuroscience: Some Implications for Psychiatry and Neurology

Nikos Makris

Research Institute for Symbolic Computation (RISC), Harvard University
and Boston General Hospital, USA

Abstract. Magnetic resonance Imaging (MRI) has revolutionized medical practice, especially in diagnosis and treatment monitoring. The in vivo and non-invasive nature of MRI has been critical in this regard. Neuroimaging in particular has been of great importance in localizing brain structure, function and metabolism in normal and clinical conditions. Current neuroscience embraces renaissance ideals of growth in knowledge, culture and economy and has achieved to a large extent in integrating recent technological discoveries with humanities and, especially behavioral sciences and medicine. Neuropsychiatry has been arguably one of the principal beneficiaries of modern Neuroscience, which is a matter of great social and financial relevance, given its relationship with mental and physical well-being.

Contents

Model-Based System Design, Verification and Simulation

**Computer Vision, Machine Learning for Image Analysis and
Applications**

**Computer and Systems Based Methods and Electronic Technologies
in Medicine**

Systems Thinking. Relevance for Technology, Science and Management Professionals

Systems Theory and Applications

Transdisciplinary Software Development for Early Crisis Detection

Kerstin Albrecht[1], Christian Nitzl[1], and Uwe M. Borghoff[1,2(✉)]

[1] Center for Intelligence and Security Studies (CISS), Munich, Germany
{ciss,uwe.borghoff}@unibw.de
[2] Institute for Software Technology, Bundeswehr University Munich,
Neubiberg, Germany
https://www.unibw.de/ciss

Abstract. Transdisciplinarity between law, psychology, political science, historical science, sociology and computer science is the central idea in our research. This paper describes how software engineering approaches, especially the software development life-cycle (SDLC) and similar ideas in intelligence and security studies, such as the so-called intelligence cycle (IC), can benefit substantially from each other and even help to pave the way for new insights into the world of early crisis detection. This setting serves as a real-life testbed for transitions of particular decisions on the way from the (software) analyst to the political decision maker.

Keywords: Transdisciplinarity · Software engineering methods · Intelligence cycle · Political decision making · Early crisis detection · Requirement engineering

1 Transdisciplinary Research

The topic of early crisis detection is becoming increasingly important in the context of security policy developments and rapid technological progress. The data sources, which over time can no longer be limited to databases but with the digitalization of all processes in everyday life have given rise to the term big data, offer never-ending possibilities but also lead to countless problems, from data management to the interpretation and validation of data volumes. For several years, the management and use of big data has occupied research and industry in a wide variety of business areas. From social sciences to economics to natural sciences, data are collected, managed and evaluated. However, the collection and processing of big data far exceeds human capabilities. As a result, numerous information technology methods have been and are being developed to ensure both quantitative and qualitative use. However, a processor processes data by means of digital signals, compilers and algorithms, as well as programming languages, according to machine logic steps, and the interpretability must accordingly be specified by the programmer. A machine can therefore deliver a

R. Moreno-Díaz et al. (Eds.): EUROCAST 2022, LNCS 13789, pp. 3–10, 2022.
https://doi.org/10.1007/978-3-031-25312-6_1

corresponding result based on a given structure with syntax and semantics, but ultimately the user has control. Therefore, with new technology such as artificial intelligence (aka machine learning, deep learning, neural networks, etc.), computing power is being developed to adapt human learning behaviour. Consequently, it is again the user or developer who determines in what way or with what goal the machine should learn and what data are used. Accordingly, artificial intelligence aims to optimize value networks and requires corresponding predetermined data, through which independent learning becomes possible. In the first instance, a human trains the machine to process a data set in a defined way; the user must therefore know what result is expected from the machine. Consequently, the same problems always arise regarding the application of artificial intelligence in the context of prediction. Among other considerations, how are the data interpreted? What types of data are processed and in what ways? How are the data weighted? What filters should be used in convolutional neural networks?

The presented challenges show that mere consideration of a single and particular scientific discipline or the combination of two scientific disciplines is not sufficient to address the challenges. What is needed is **transdisciplinary research** that breaks free from (inter-)disciplinary boundaries and takes on the challenges that are characterized by a high degree of interaction [6]. We view transdisciplinary software development as a potential approach that combines different research fields for concrete problem solving, as depicted in Fig. 1.

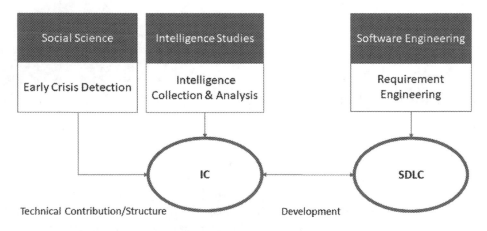

Fig. 1. Transdisciplinary software development

2   Research and Criticism

This problem also dominates research on early crisis detection. The literature describes algorithms and methods that process values on the basis of databases by means of artificial intelligence. The focus is on conflicting data from the past to the present and the use of appropriate methods to create a pattern that generates a prediction. As a result of this methodology, which is often based on time- and location-dependent variables, the limits of these models quickly become apparent in the context of the interpretability of the procedure. Thus, often only facts and figures (hard factors) are considered, and the soft factors, which play a decisive role in the development of the situation up to the crisis for the fully interdisciplinary topic, are neglected. Conflicts, risks and resulting crises can reach their origin and ultimate climax even without armed conflicts. The consideration regarding the development of a situation cannot and must not arise from the perspective of violent or armed conflicts. The origin can be a minimal development in politics, the economy or social and health care, which focuses on one subject area but also overlaps with violent effects of the final crisis.

Due to the necessity of the transdisciplinary view, the inventory and representation of the relations of knowledge areas is indispensable for the development of a transparent model for early crisis detection. Thus, before a model for prediction can be developed, a database for early crisis detection must be created. In the following, we use the Covid 19-crisis as an example.

3   Transdisciplinary Software Development

The year 2020 was marked by Covid-19, a virus that in December 2019 was reported as a pulmonary disease with unknown causes to the WHO (World Health Organization) from the Chinese city of Wuhan. In March 2020, the Director-General of the WHO officially declared the outbreak of the virus a pandemic. Since then, we have seen daily reports in the media about the so-called Corona Crisis, necessary countermeasures and the global impact.

Consequently, in the context of the pandemic, numerous questions have arisen, such as whether the crisis could have been predicted and how goal-oriented measures and prevention decisions are made by governments. A prerequisite for crisis prediction is that the occurrence probability of a devastating event and its level of impact should it materialize can be predicted to a certain degree. Particularly challenging are so-called creeping crises, which emerge gradually, become self-reinforcing in a complex system, and suddenly emerge as a rarely occurring event [4]. The prerequisites of statistical methods is that information is codified and social phenomena are operationalized [5]. Borghoff et al. [2] describe a latent variable model in conflict research, while Johansen [7] exploits a morphological analysis of scenario modelling. The 2016 German government Weißbuch [3] explains the need for early detection of crises, with a focus on sound prevention and stabilization of crises and conflicts that will best position governance in the decision-making process.

In October 2020, the Federal Ministry of Defense (BMVg) founded the Competence Center for Early Crisis Detection within the Center for Intelligence and Security Studies (CISS) at the Bundeswehr Univ. Munich. CISS organizes and coordinates the master's program in Intelligence and Security Studies (MISS) and advises political leaders in the field of security studies.[1]

Research on early crisis detection associated with the term *crisis* is pursued in numerous individual sciences with different definitions of the term. These include the social sciences and economics in the sense of a content-related or subject-related focus, and the engineering sciences and structural sciences in terms of the development of digital support. Within the framework of early crisis detection research, it is therefore necessary to specify the interdisciplinary topic initially and to distinguish it from numerous other fields of knowledge to structure the procedure of early detection and to forecast and evaluate the technical feasibility. The current research on strategic early warning of crises refers predominantly to armed conflicts (databases) and neglects the overall picture and thus numerous important interdisciplinary influencing factors. Furthermore, there is often no transparency with regard to data processing, which leads to problems in the final comprehensible evaluation of the results. Comprehensibility of how the results are obtained is crucial from the perspective of the demand carriers and decision makers. In the context of software engineering, a detailed requirement analysis is necessary for the production of a goal-prominent supporting system, which considers an interdisciplinary technical evaluation and weighting of the factors. The user or demand carrier thus plays a decisive role in the requirement analysis. The users include any analyst who addresses country-specific developments. In addition, the decision maker must be able to be comprehensibly advised by the analyst in the event of a possible crisis.

3.1   Approach

The basic focus of this work consider the terminology in the field of social sciences/political sciences around country-specific and cross-national development of crises that endanger stability and/or security from an interdisciplinary perspective of the country/region with possible effects on further countries/regions. However, the influencing factors leading to a crisis are not limited to events from the perspective of political science but can also originate from other individual sciences, such as business administration or human sciences. Consequently, methods of processing or evaluating data can also be taken from other sciences without having to redefine the term crisis from a political science perspective. Based on the definition of the situation and the consideration of the all-encompassing influencing factors, engineering sciences and structural sciences are used to structure these data and to convert them into a supporting system. However, from a

---

[1] Many colleagues have asked us how we can provide an environment where all players speak a common *working language* even when they come from different fields of expertise and study domains. This is a conditio sina qua non if you target trans-disciplinary research. The **trans**disciplinarity stems from people interacting with one another over field/domain boundaries while they influence each other. Here, the MISS is key because it not only teaches this common working language but also creates an intelligence community within the German intelligence services and the Bundeswehr. Refer also to https://www.unibw.de/ciss/miss and [1,8].

technical perspective, the weighting and relationships of the data do not come from the engineering and structural sciences. Accordingly, the procedural model for the method of early crisis detection must be given to the developers within the framework of software engineering. This can be achieved via the description and creation of a process model with the tools of software engineering and intelligence for process mapping in early crisis detection.

3.2 Intelligence Cycle and Software Development Life Cycle

The intelligence cycle is primarily not directly related to the term crisis, but in the field of military and civil intelligence, it is the precursor of an assessment of the development of a situation into a crisis. The basic model of the intelligence cycle is also used in the economic and organizational sector. Furthermore, the intelligence cycle in the basic model is often questioned, and the realistic application possibility is refuted. In our opinion, this is due to the serial process representation. As a basic model of an analysis procedure and for the preparation of a requirement analysis in the subprocess of the intelligence cycle, this is, however, completely sufficient.

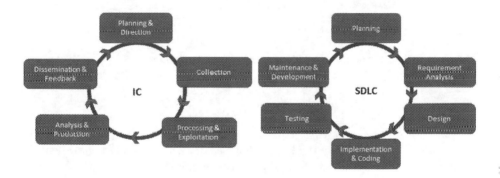

Fig. 2. Intelligence cycle and software development life cycle

As Fig. 2 shows, the cycle consists of five phases, starting with *Planning and Direction*, where an individual inquires about a field of interest or specific topic. Then, a directional plan is created, and in the second phase of *Collection*, data on the defined topic are transferred. In the subsequent phase *Processing and Exploitation*, the collected data are sorted and processed for the next step. In the phase *Analysis and Production*, the analyst's task is to evaluate the processed data to create recommendations for a political decision maker. This phase also includes the prediction of relevant trends and the evaluation of the vulnerability of certain systems for critical developments—the basis for early crisis detection. Finally, the phase *Dissemination and Feedback* is used to decide whether the intelligence cycle should be started again or whether the decision maker's information situation has been satisfied.

Procedure models in software engineering describe the entire process used to produce a software-based application and are organized into a so-called software development life cycle. Regarding our research w.r.t. early crisis detection, we limit our focus to the phases *Planning* and *Requirement Analysis*. Accordingly, a procedure model is not provided for all six phases of the software development life cycle but only for the *Requirement Analysis*, which includes the *Planning* of the requirement engineering, as shown in Fig. 3. Therefore, the goal is to use a case example to represent the basis of planning and the requirement analysis in a procedure model based on the methods of software engineering and intelligence studies.

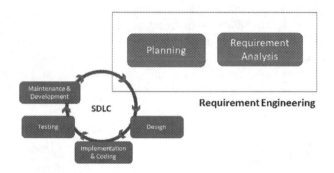

Fig. 3. Intelligence cycle and software development life cycle

3.3   Case Study

Let software developers create a permanent specific information base for the health care system, whereby the link to politics and the economy is represented. Furthermore, let several analysts address the medical situation, including the health care system, politics, and the economic situation. Depending on the subject area in question, particular dashboards visualize results on a day to day basis. We all remember Esri's dashboard filled with Covid 19-data by the Robert Koch Institute in Berlin, Germany.

The analysts run through the intelligence cycle in their respective areas of expertise to inform the political decision maker on a daily basis about relevant developments. Thus, in phase *Planning and Direction*, the area of expertise of each analyst is defined. In regular operation, the collection, sifting, sorting and analysis of data refers to daily news within the knowledge area without considering a specific topic. However, in the current situation, there is an additional mandate from the policy maker to specifically cover the development of Covid-19 from the perspective of the aforementioned topics.

In the second phase *Collection*, the analysts collect information about their intelligence disciplines. In the phase *Processing and Exploitation*, the collected data are sifted, sorted, and put into context. In the phase *Analysis and Production*, the various information is coordinated, condensed, and analysed, and a corresponding document is prepared for submission to the political decision maker. The decision maker can then choose to use the document as is or to invoke an additional round of refinement in the intelligence cycle.

4 Requirement Engineering for Early Crisis Detection

Requirement engineering lays the foundation for goal-oriented software development and therefore also for transparent early crisis detection. The software development life cycle is implemented with different process models depending on the project. We use a transdisciplinary process model, which is based on the rational unified process, to present the requirement engineering for early crisis detection. It starts with the phases *Planning* and *Requirement Analysis*. Requirement elicitation, analysis, and specification is complemented by the analyst requirement document. Likewise, the requirement specification is created from a pure technical perspective.

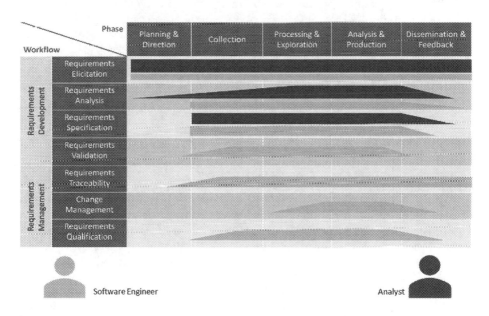

Fig. 4. Transdisciplinary process model

Figure 4 shows, on the vertical axis, the requirement engineering workflow and, on the horizontal axis, the phases of the intelligence cycle. There are three documents generated with the transdisciplinary process model: first, the analyst requirement document; second, the requirements specification represents the basic document for processing or implementing the further phases of the software development life cycle; and third, the system specification, which is necessary for the software development life cycle phase of design and coding.

The analyst requirement document is part of the requirement specification and supports communication with the software development team.

For the requirements analysis, a requirements catalog (analyst requirement document) is created from the perspective of the analyst, and thus the intelligence cycle, to represent the structure of the information required for the overall situation and consequently provides the basis for predictive models.

The phases of the process model represent the intelligence cycle, where the workflow comprises the requirement engineering. Each analyst creates a document for their area of expertise. In the first instance, all phases and the requirements of the analysts are documented at the macro level for the requirements elicitation workflow.

5   Conclusion

In our view, requirement engineering for early crisis detection must be modelled as a transdisciplinary process, integrating the intelligence cycle to capture the **overall transdisciplinary view**. Accordingly, requirements are created as the foundation for modelling predictive algorithms through direct collaboration of both technical and domain experts. If required, the requirement validation workflow can be supported with technical expertise. However, the requirement management workflow remains the full responsibility of the software engineering team.

References

1. Borghoff, U.M., Dietrich, J.-H.: Intelligence and security studies. In: Bode, A., Broy, M., Bungartz, H.-J., Matthes, F. (eds.) 50 Jahre Universitäts-Informatik in München, pp. 113–121. Springer, Heidelberg (2017). https://doi.org/10.1007/978-3-662-54712-0_9
2. Borghoff, U.M., Matthews, S., Prüßing, H., Schäfer, C.T., Stuke, O.: A latent variable model in conflict research. In: Moreno-Díaz, R., Pichler, F., Quesada-Arencibia, A. (eds.) EUROCAST 2019. LNCS, vol. 12013, pp. 36–43. Springer, Cham (2020). https://doi.org/10.1007/978-3-030-45093-9_5
3. Bundesregierung: Weißbuch. Berlin, Germany (2016)
4. Chadefaux, T.: Conflict forecasting and its limits. Data Sci. 1(1–2), 7–17 (2017)
5. Hair, J.F., Howard, M., Nitzl, C.: Assessing measurement model quality in pls-sem using confirmatory composite analysis. J. of Bus. Res. 109, 101–110 (2020)
6. Hirsch-Hadorn, G., et al.: Handbook of Transdisciplinary Research. Springer-Verlag, Heidelberg (2008). https://doi.org/10.1007/978-1-4020-6699-3
7. Johansen, I.: Scenario modelling with morphological analysis. Norwegian DefeResearch Establishment, FFI, Pb 25, 2027 Kjeller Norway Technol.Forecast. Soc. Change 126, 116–125 (2018)
8. Scheffler, A.C., Jeraj, B., Borghoff, U.M.: The rise of intelligence studies: A model for Germany? Connections: Q. J. 15(1), 79–106 (2016). https://doi.org/10.11610/Connections.15.1.06

Uncertainty and Ambiguity: Challenging Layers in Model Construction

Margaret Miró-Julià(✉)🆔, Monica J. Ruiz-Miró, and Irene García Mosquera🆔

Departament de Ciències Matemàtiques i Informàtica, Universitat de les Illes Balears,
07122 Palma de Mallorca, Spain
{margaret.miro,monica.ruiz,irene.garcia}@uib.es

Abstract. When building models that causally explain observed data
and predict future data, quantifiable uncertainty and unquantifiable
uncertainty (ambiguity) should be considered. Every decision and action
that we take in life is associated with a degree of doubt, whether it be
uncertainty or ambiguity: whether we turn right or left at an intersection,
what research idea we follow, ... and the thousands of other decisions
that we make on a daily basis. In decision making, doubt can manifest
itself in a variety of ways: one could have ... doubts about the data itself;
doubts about what data is needed; doubts about the available processes
and transformations; doubts about the possible models; doubts about
the decision criteria; ... or even doubts on one's own preferences for any
of these options.

This contribution will reflect on model construction and provide some
answers. We propose that uncertainty and ambiguity are factors that
must be considered in model construction. Machine learning within
health care and medical fields is becoming popular and proving incredibly fruitful in the areas of predicting diseases and analyzing transmission of diseases. A major class of problems in medical science involves
the diagnosis of disease, based upon various tests performed upon the
patient. The evaluation of data taken from patients and complex decision
making are the most important factors in diagnosis. A publicly available
database for breast cancer prediction will be used to study ambiguity
and uncertainty in model construction.

Keywords: Uncertainty · Ambiguity · Model construction

1 Model Construction in Data Mining

When building models that causally explain observed data and predict future
data, uncertainty (quantifiable) and ambiguity (unquantifiable) should be considered. Every decision and action that we take in life is associated with a degree
of doubt. Doubt, whether ambiguity or uncertainty affect decisions in different
and sometimes opposite ways. In [1], we pinpointed how doubt could arise in
Data Mining.

R. Moreno-Díaz et al. (Eds.): EUROCAST 2022, LNCS 13789, pp. 11–18, 2022.
https://doi.org/10.1007/978-3-031-25312-6_2

The need of efficient methods to search for knowledge in data, and thus generate models, has favored the development of a lot of Data Mining algorithms and Data Mining tools. When modeling a data set, different situations can be considered. From a theoretical point of view, data is used to build models that causally explain observed data and predict future data. The models hope to predict the change, usually averaged over the population, in the outcome variable due to a change in the causal variables. Whereas, from an algorithmic perspective, data is used to build statistical models which hopefully will allow making predictions about the properties of unobserved individuals (or missing attributes of observed individuals) who are assumed to be from the same population that generated the data.

Models describe the overall shape of the data [2], and can be thought of as "global" descriptive summaries of data sets. Pattern discovery is a "local" structure in a possibly vast search space. Patterns describe data with an anomalously high density compared with that expected in a baseline model. Patterns are usually embedded in a mass of irrelevant data [3]. Most apparent patterns in data are due to chance and data distortion, and many more are well known or uninteresting.

The study of uncertainty and ambiguity in the Knowledge Discovery process is complex and challenging. There are different factors that affect decision making process. Why do some researchers avoid ambiguity when others do not? A better understanding of what drives the researcher's behavior when dealing with ambiguity and uncertainty is essential. Research papers provide a wide variety of opinions and experiences of different researchers in model construction. There is not a single "correct" answer; answers are multiple and often contradictory. Should a full spectrum of possible models be somehow used to generate the final model? How can we know what makes a good model? It depends on the research question asked and how it is answered. Should these factors be incorporated in the process in order to construct a more personalized model?

Model formulation assumes the existence of a "true" model in a pre-specified known form. In practice, model ambiguity has received little attention. Furthermore, we are modeling uncertain data with traditional techniques. Modern computing allows a large number of models to be considered and data-dependent specification searches have become the norm to obtain a good fit. Uncertainty can be incorporated into the model using: a) Probabilistic approach: it is assumed that the input parameters of the model are random variables with a known probability density function. b) Possibilistic approach: the input parameters of the model are described using the membership function of input parameters.

A very popular model used in everyday life is regression. In statistics, multiple linear regression is a linear approach for modelling the relationship between a scalar response (dependent variable) and one or more explanatory variables (independent variables). In multiple linear regression, the relationships are modeled using linear predictor functions whose unknown model parameters are estimated from the data. Such models are called linear models. Multiple linear regression focuses on the conditional probability distribution of the response given the values of the predictors, rather than on the joint probability distribution of all of these variables. When the response variable takes two values such as true/false, yes/no, win/lose, ... we are considering a logistic regression model. Logistic regression has become an important tool in Data Mining, algorithms used in machine learning applications classify incoming data based on historical data. As additional relevant data comes in, the algorithms get better at predicting classifications within data sets.

2   Logistic Regression

Essentially, logistic regression is an extension of multiple regression model applied to situations in which the response is a categorical (or discrete) variable rather than a continuous or quantitative variable. More specifically, logistic regression defines the likelihood of specific outcomes (such as true or false) for each individual. As a result, logistic regression analysis generates a regression equation that predicts the probability of each outcome falling into one of two categories: values 0 (often meaning "no" or "failure") or 1 (often meaning "yes" or "success"). The goal of logistic regression is to use the dataset to create a predictive model of the binary outcome variable.

By far, the logistic model is the most widely used model for binary outcomes. However, it still implies strong assumptions about the relationship between outcome risk and the co-variables. The model specifies a linear relationship between the logarithm of the odds of the outcome and the co-variables, expressed on a transformed scale referred to as the "logit" transformation of the outcome probability.

2.1   The Mathematical Model

Logistic Regression models essentially represent a mathematical equation that approximates the interactions between the different variables being modeled. The mathematics of logistic regression rely on the concept of the "odds" of the event, which is the probability of an event occurring divided by the probability of an event not occurring. Just as in linear regression, logistic regression has parameters (weights) associated with dimensions of input data. Contrary to linear regression, the relationship between the parameters and the output of the model (the "odds") is exponential, not linear.

Given a dataset containing n data points (individuals). Each point i consists of a vector of p input variables $\mathbf{x_i}$, $i = 1, \ldots, n$, (also called covariates, independent variables, explanatory variables, features, or attributes), and a binary outcome variable y_i (also known as a dependent variable, response variable, output variable, or class). As in linear regression, the outcome variables y_i are assumed to depend on the explanatory variables $\mathbf{x_j}$. Also, let $\beta = (\beta_1, \ldots, \beta_p)^t$ be the parameter vector associated with the covariates $\mathbf{x_j}$.

The general logistic regression model is defined by:

$$y_i = \begin{cases} 1 & \text{with probability } \pi_i \\ 0 & \text{with probability } 1 - \pi_i \end{cases}$$

with

$$\pi_i = P(y_i = 1|\mathbf{x_i}) = \frac{e^{\mathbf{x_i}^t \beta}}{1 + e^{\mathbf{x_i}^t \beta}}.$$

The parameters of a logistic regression model can be estimated using different estimators. Two frameworks will be considered: the classical approach based on the maximum likelihood methodology; and the Bayesian approach that allows for the introduction of prior information about the phenomenon under study.

2.2 Parameters Estimation Using Classical Approach

Under the classical framework, a probability distribution for the outcome variable must be assumed and then a likelihood function defined. The likelihood function calculates the probability of observing the outcome given the input data and the model. This function can then be optimized to find the set of parameters that results in the largest sum likelihood over the training dataset.

The maximum likelihood approach to fitting a logistic regression model both aids in better understanding the form of the logistic regression model and provides a pattern that can be used for fitting classification models more generally. This is particularly true as the negative of the log-likelihood function used in the procedure can be shown to be equivalent to cross-entropy loss function.

For this classical framework, the likelihood function for estimating the parameters is defined as:

$$L(\beta) = \ln{(\beta)} = \ln \prod_{i=1}^{n} \pi_i^{y_i} (1 - \pi_i)^{1-y_i}$$

$$= \sum_{i=1}^{n} \left[y_i \mathbf{x_i^t} \beta - \ln{(1 + e^{\mathbf{x_i^t} \beta})} \right].$$

The model parameters ($\{\beta_i\}_{i=1}^n$) are usually estimated by means of classical procedures, such as the Maximum Likelihood Estimator (MLE). However, since $\frac{\partial}{\partial \beta} L(\beta) = 0$ is non-linear, some iterative techniques are needed to find a solution. Sometimes the convergence of the iterative process may fail, especially when small samples or anomalous distributions are observed.

2.3 Parameters Estimation Using Bayesian Approach

Bayesian framework is an alternative that can be considered. The method allows the introduction of prior information about the phenomenon under study. In a Bayesian statistics context, prior distributions are normally placed on the regression coefficients, usually in the form of Gaussian distributions.

If y represents the known data and θ the unknown data (model parameters), we introduce the likelihood function $f(y|\theta)$ and the prior density function $f(\theta)$. It follows that the posterior density is represented by:

$$f(\theta|y) \propto f(y|\theta) \cdot f(\theta).$$

The equation above describes the general concept behind Bayesian estimation.

An example of a possible prior for this model is a $Beta(a, b)$ prior for π, with known a and b. Then, the posterior density will be $Beta$. Generally, obtaining the posterior distribution in closed form is only possible in particular cases which usually represent simple models. In the others cases, it is necessary to use numerical methods or asymptotic results to solve the problems associated with its calculation. Currently, the use of these approximation tools is not necessary because simulation methods are available to obtain pseudo-samples from the posterior distribution on a computer. Of course, these samples must meet certain convergence criteria that allow estimated probabilistic properties. These methods introduce a level of randomness into the analysis, they are also known as Monte Carlo Markov Chain (MCMC).

The goal of MCMC methods is to find a Markov chain in the parameter space such that the equilibrium or stationary distribution of the chain coincides with the posterior distribution. Nowadays, MCMC is used in most mainstream Bayesian methods to estimate the parameters. A more detailed explanation of these aspects of Bayesian logistic regression can be found in [4].

3   Comparative Study of the Models in Breast Cancer Diagnosis

A typical problem found in the medical environment considers the diagnosis of disease using the results of various tests performed upon the patient. The analysis of data taken from patients and complex decision making are the most important factors in diagnosis. Breast cancer is a fatal disease causing high mortality in women. Constant efforts are being made for creating more efficient techniques for its early and accurate diagnosis.

Mammographic results are often used to make an early diagnosis of breast cancer. An effective diagnostic procedure is dependent upon high levels of consistency between physicians' ratings of screening and/or automatic methods (supervised and unsupervised) used as computer-aided systems.

The classification of mammographies using a binary categorical scale (diseased or not diseased) is highly susceptible to interobserver variability and human errors, resulting in a suitable problem for examining how uncertainty and ambiguity might play an influential role on the consistency of predictions.

3.1   The Data

A publicly available database https://data.world/uci/mammographic-mass [5] was used to examine accuracy and disagreement between the two learning methods.

The features reported in the database are: *"Score"*: BI-RADS assessment with values 0 (not enough information), 1 (no tumor), 2 (benign), 3 (tumor probably benign), 4 (suspicious abnormality, biopsy should be considered), 5 (tumor highly suggestive of malignancy, proper actions should be adopted) and

6 (previous biopsy with cancer); "*Age*": Patient's age in years; "*Shape*": Mass shape with values 1 (round), 2 (oval), 3 (lobular), 4 (irregular); "*Margin*": Mass margin with values 1 (circumscribed), 2 (micro lobulated), 3 (obscured), 4 (ill-defined and 5 (spiculated); "*Density*": Mass density with values 1 (high), 2 (iso), 3 (low) and 4 (fat-containing). The outcome is "*Malignant*": biopsy result with values 0 (benign), 1 (malignant).

In order to correctly interpret the results obtained by the model the levels (values taken by the categorical variables) need to be ordered relative to risk of the mass being malignant.

The database contains 961 mammograms with 516 benign cases and 445 malignant cases. The database is randomly split in training set (70% of the data) and test set (30%).

3.2 The Logistic Regression Model

The logistic regression model is used to predict the malignancy of the mass. Therefore, "*Malignant*" is the response variable (output) and, "*emphAge*", "*Shape*", and "*Margin*" are predictors (inputs). A new model expressing the probability of a malignant mass as a function of the predictor variables is required.

The logistic regression model expresses the *logit* of the probability p_i, $i = 1, \ldots, n$ as a linear function of the predictor variables:

$$logit(p_i) = \log\left(\frac{p_i}{1 - p_i}\right) = \beta_0 + \beta_1 Age + \beta_2 Shape + \beta_3 Margin$$

By using the *logit* function, one sees that the regression coefficients β_p with $p = 0, 1, 2, 3$ are directly related to the log of odds $\log\left(\frac{p_i}{1-p_i}\right)$.

In particular, the intercept β_0 is the log of odds $\log\left(\frac{p_i}{1-p_i}\right)$ for the ith woman when all predictors take values of 0. The slopes β_p with $p \neq 0$ refer to the change in the expected malignant log of odds status when the value of the i predictor increases in one unit. Specifically, β_1 refers to the change in the expected malignant log of odds of a woman who has an additional year of age.

By rearranging the previous logistic regression equation, the regression model can be considered as a nonlinear equation for the probability of success p_i:

$$p_i = \frac{exp(\beta_0 + \beta_1 Age + \beta_2 Shape + \beta_3 Margin)}{1 + exp(\beta_0 + \beta_1 Age + \beta_2 Shape + \beta_3 Margin)}$$

3.3 Parameter Estimation

The estimation of the parameters (weights) using both the classical and Bayesian framework were calculated using R, a free software environment for statistical computing and graphics (https://www.r-project.org/).

Table 1. Estimation of β_i using Classical and Bayesian Frameworks

Parameters	Classical	Bayesian
β_0	-7.044555	−7.133707
β_1	0.068578	0.06929638
β_2	0.523260	0.5273072
β_3	0.562376	0.5693969

Table 1 provides the estimation of the weights obtained from the training set for the Classical and Bayesian frameworks.

Regardless of the complexity in parameter estimation using the Bayesian framework, the values of the estimated parameters are very similar. The binary response "*Malignant*" is assumed to follow a Bernoulli distribution with probability of success p_i. The task is to construct a prior on the vector of regression coefficients $\beta = (\beta_0, \beta_1, \beta_2, \beta_3)$. Two values of the predictor x_1^* and x_2^* are considered and independent Beta priors for the corresponding probabilities of success are constructed. In the Bayesian framework, multiple, simultaneously running Markov chains that use priors to inform posteriors and posteriors to inform new posteriors are used until all of the chains converge. That is, all chains agree on what the model parameters should be. Because of the intensive nature and built-in flexibility of Bayesian modeling, Bayesian models end up being very precise and useful.

Why bother with Bayes? After all, our coefficients are almost identical. What is important is the way in which Bayesian models are constructed and the fact that the interpretation of the credible intervals is more useful than the interpretation of the classical confidence intervals. Also, probability calculations using parameters calculated in the Bayesian framework are more precise.

3.4   Interpretation of the Results

The interpretation of the previous results is very challenging and surprising. If we consider the Classical framework and calculate $P(malignant = 1)$ at the mean value of "*Age*" and at the mode for the qualitative variables "*Shape*" and "*Margin*", we obtain that the probability that the mass be malignant is about 53% (0.5300242). The prediction is not conclusive.

Furthermore, the coefficients for each covariates indicate that a one-unit change (1 year) around the mean value of "*Age*" (56 years), results in a 17.4% change in the probability that the mass will be malignant if the other covariates remain constant. A one-unit change (from one level to next) around the median value of "*Shape*" results in a 12.5% change in the probability of malignant mass if the other covariates remain constant. A one-unit change (from one level to next) around the median value of "*Margin*" results in a 13.4% change in the probability of malignant mass if the other covariates remain constant.

If the Bayesian framework is considered and we calculate $P(malignant = 1)$ at the mean value of "Age" and at the mode for the qualitative variables "$Shape$" and "$Margin$", we obtain that the probability that the mass be malignant is 86% (0.8581909). A value greater that the one obtained using Classical logistic regression. The prediction states that the mass is malignant.

Summarizing, for the same logistic regression model, the estimation of the parameters is similar but probability calculations differ greatly depending on the framework used. Is this another type of ambiguity?

4   Conclusions and Future Work

Model construction is a challenging task that we encounter daily. When building a model, decisions must be taken at every level. And with each decision made, there is a degree of doubt. The choice of the model and of the methods used to fit, learn, search the parameters include uncertainty and ambiguity.

In this paper, a logistic regression model has been considered to model breast cancer diagnosis. The parameters of the model have been estimated (learned) using different frameworks and the same training set. The values of the parameters are practically identical, but when used to predict the malignancy of new examples give different outputs. How is this possible? Making predictions also involves uncertainty and/or ambiguity that should be seen as a way to enhance research. Methods that accommodate uncertainty and ambiguity at all layers of model construction are required.

Which is the next step? Does a "true" model really exist? Or is it an illusion? What is important? The model or its predicting capabilities? Are we searching for knowledge or decision making criteria? There is a shift in society's priorities and therefore there is not a single "correct" answer; answers are multiple and often contradictory.

References

1. Miró-Julià, M., Ruiz-Miró, M.J., García Mosquera, I.: Knowledge discovery: from uncertainty to ambiguity and back. In: Moreno-Díaz, R., Pichler, F., Quesada-Arencibia, A. (eds.) EUROCAST 2019. LNCS, vol. 12013, pp. 20–27. Springer, Cham (2020). https://doi.org/10.1007/978-3-030-45093-9_3
2. Hand, D.J.: Principles of data mining. Drug Saf. **30**(7), 621–622 (2007)
3. Pattern Recognition and Machine Learning. ISS, Springer, New York (2006). https://doi.org/10.1007/978-0-387-45528-0_9
4. Congdon, P.: Bayesian Models for Categorical Data. Wiley Series in Probability and Statistics (2005)
5. Elter, M., et al.: The prediction of breast cancer biopsy outcomes using two CAD approaches that both emphasize an intelligible decision process. Med. Phy. **34**(11), 4164–4172 (2007)

George J. Boole

A Nineteenth Century Man for the Modern Digital Era

Radomir S. Stanković[1]([✉]), Milena Stanković[2], Jaakko Astola[3], and Claudio Moraga[4,5]

[1] Mathematical Institute of SASA, Belgrade, Serbia
`Radomir.Stankovic@gmail.com`
[2] Faculty of Electronic Engineering, Niš, Serbia
[3] Tempere University of Technology, Tampere, Finland
[4] Faculty of Computer Science, Technical University of Dortmund, Dortmund, Germany
[5] Department of Informatics, Technical University "Federico Santa María", Valparaíso, Chile

Abstract. It is entirely justified to use the attribute digital in describing contemporary era due to omnipresence of digital technologies and devices based on them and their strong influence to almost all aspects of human activities. The present paper is a tribute to a man whose work in logic and mathematics, leading to the mathematical logic, set theoretical foundations for the development and establishing of digital era.

Keywords: Mathematical logic · Boolean functions · Boolean algebra

1 Introduction

The current epoch in the development and evolution of humanity can with full justification be called the digital era due to the omnipresence of various kinds of digital devices ranging from many essentially important and extremely useful to the enormous number of various gadgets. Whatever aimed at deep space or micro cosmos exploring, or intended to simplify and facilitate performing of everyday tasks, they are all based on the same principles.

We are in the era characterised by the laboratory-on-chip, network-on-chip, Internet-of-Things, etc., and all this is possible just because we, humans, have learned to represent data and information encoded in them by binary sequences, and then we have learned the basic laws how to manipulate this knowledge in order to detect relationships, interconnections, similarities or differences, and afterwards derive conclusions, make decisions, and act accordingly. In other words, we have learned how to represent, model, and interpret, after some simplification and approximation, the basic laws of human thinking in terms of binary sequences and operations over them. Exactly this was the subject of study of George J. Boole already in the mid of nineteenth century.

This paper is a yet another tribute to the work of George Boole. We first shortly present his professional biography to set the circumstances under which he was working and understand where from his motivations and selection of research subject were coming. Then, we briefly discuss his three principal works [1–3] concerning the subject of the

R. Moreno-Díaz et al. (Eds.): EUROCAST 2022, LNCS 13789, pp. 19–26, 2022.
https://doi.org/10.1007/978-3-031-25312-6_3

present paper. We also discuss his communication with contemporary scholars, notably with Augustus De Morgan based on the collected 90 letters that they exchanged and which are still preserved [22], which highlights a bit the style of work and the attitude towards the research subjects of these two and some other scholars at that time [9]. The intention is to provide a piece of information that can possibly be useful for understanding how the mathematical foundations of modern digital era have been formulated and established by starting from the work of George Boole and then many others which have followed the same ideas.

2 Personal Education of George J. Boole

Life circumstances forced Boole towards a hard and tedious, but interesting way of personal schooling and education.

George Boole was oriented towards an academic education and development by his father John Boole, who, although being a professional shoemaker, have had a passionate interest in science and mathematics, as well as for making scientific and optical instruments. It is recorded that the father and the son together built cameras, kaleidoscopes, microscopes, telescopes, and a sundial. As a very young kid, Boole joined first a school for the children of tradesmen, then a commercial school, and after that, in the age of seven, a primary school, where it was noticed his talent for languages. Due to that, his father arranged additional lectures in Latin for him given by William Brooke, a book seller and printer in Lincoln where the family Boole lived at that time. After mastering Latin, Boole continued to teach himself Greek and, at the age of 14, translated a poem by Meleager, entitled "Ode to the Spring", which translation his proud father had published. The translation was so deep, mature, and profound that some scholars refused to believe this is the work of a 14 years old man. The word teenager" had not yet been coined.

In 1828, Boole joined Bainbridge Commercial Academy in Fish Hill in Lincoln, but continued his study in Latin, Greek, and algebra, as well as thought himself French, German, and later Italian.

Since in 1831, the business of his father was ruined, George Boole become the main provider for his family. To achieve the task, he has to abandon the wish of becoming a clergyman, and accepted the position of an assistant teacher first in Doncaster and then Liverpool. This was the beginning of his career as an outstanding teacher.

Together with teaching work, Boole carried out an ambitious self-education program in mathematics, by starting reading the book *Calcul Différentiel* by Lacroix in French. Boole continued his self-education by studying the work of Lagrange, Laplace, and Newton including reading of *Principia*. It can be observed that Boole followed a specific approach in his self-learning by taking advantage of his broad knowledge of languages. Boole used to persistently read a work in the original language many times, until he finally completely understood and mastered the contents.

3 Professional Biography of Boole

As noticed above, the professional career of Boole started already in his young days in 1831 while accepting the position of a teaching assistant. Then, in 1833, Boole was working at the Hall Academy at Waddington, near Lincoln, and then in 1834 opened his own school in Free School Lane, Lincoln. In 1838, Boole worked in the Waddington Academy and in 1840 opened this own Boarding School for Young Gentlemen at Pottergate, Lincoln.

In 1849, Boole joined the Queen's College in Cork, Ireland, as the first professor in mathematics, thanks to testimonials in support by leading mathematicians at that time including Augustus De Morgan, Philip Kelland, Arthur Cayley, and William Thomson.

On May 30, 1851, Boole was elected Dean of the Science Division of the Faculty of Arts, and was re-elected for the next mandate. In the same year, Boole was awarded an honorary LLD by the University of Dublin, most probably by the suggestion from his friend Reverend Charles Graves, who was at that time a Professor of Mathematics at Trinity College Dublin.

Boole was renown as a devoted teacher with a lot of patience and understanding for all his students expressing great willingness to help them in learning. This aspect of his personality is further highlighted by pointing out his engagement and activity in the Cuverian Society for the Cultivation of the Sciences, the goal of which was to provide public education in the sciences in the city of Cork. Boole was elected to full membership of the Society on November 6, 1850, then on September 19, 1851, to the Council, and further in the same year to the Sectional Committee on Statistics and Political Economy. The same year, Boole joined the Dublin Statistical Society. The following year, Boole become a Vice President of the Cuverian Society, and on May 24, 1854, the President of the Cuvcrian Society. It is important to notice that on June 11, 1857, Boole was awarded the great honour of membership of the highly prestigious Royal Society of London.

The biography of Boole is presented and discussed in an excellent way in the first book devoted to this subject by MacHale [14] published in 1985. The second edition of the book is published in 2014 under the title *The Life and Work of George Boole - A Prelude to the Digital Age* [15].

In the book [14], Boole is presented as a reserved and somber person but warm human. Boole expressed a strong sense of purpose and duty regarding institutional and civic levels. From the respect of religion, Boole shared elements of Unitarianism and Judaism, and in time became inclined towards agnosticism.

In the review of the book by MacHale, the reviewer Jongsma wrote [12] *Early employment as a schoolteacher, his development into an independent research mathematician and logician, and his sometimes-turbulent career as a conscientious and well-respected professor of mathematics at Queen's College in Cork, Ireland (now University College, where MacHale used to teach mathematics, and presently he is a professeur emeritus) are all fleshed out in detail unavailable anywhere else.*

4   Boolean Algebra

Major scientific contribution by George J. Boole, which provided for him such a prominent position in history of sciences, is certainly the mathematical concept that is presently called the Boolean algebra. Besides its importance as a mathematical object, it served as the key concept, which transformed the design process of switching circuits from an art to a science, based on the idea of describing both the functions performed and the circuits themselves realizing them in terms of the Boolean algebra. These fundamental observations were proposed by C. E. Shannon first in his master thesis [20], and then in a related very influential publication [21]. It is worth noticing that before discussing the problem of relay and contact switching circuits synthesis, Shannon attended at the Michigan University a course in mathematic where the Boolean algebra was among the topics.

In March 1941, the Japanesse engineer and scholar, Akira Nakashima, concluded that the algebra he has been developing from 1935 [17], through a thorough analysis of many examples of relay circuits and networks is identical to the Boolean algebra and put the reference to the work by Boole [18]. For further details, see [23].

It can be observed that already in 1910, Paul Ehrenfest [8] in a review of the book *Algebra of Logic* by Louis Couturat [6], wrote *Is it right, that regardless of the existence of the already elaborated algebra of logic, the specific algebra of switching networks should be considered as a utopia?*, see [24].

In former USSR, Gellius Nikolaevich Povarov, pointed out the remark by Ehrenfest and suitability of Boolean algebra for solving such tasks to V. I. Shestakov who defended a PhD thesis in the physic-mathematical sciences on September 28, 1938 at the State University Lomonosov, Moscow [25] where the references to the work of Soviet logicians Glivenko, Zhegalkin, and Sludskaja were given. For more details on this topic, see [24].

Table 1. A correspondence between logical and algebraic expressions.

Logical	Algebraic
Every X is Y	$x(1 - y) = 0$
No X is Y	$xy = 0$
Some X is Y	$xy \neq 06$
Some X is not Y	$x(1 - y) \neq 06$

The main idea of Boole which led to the definition of the Boolean algebra, can be shortly formulated as developing a symbolizing scheme for symbolizing logical relationships as algebraic relationships in a way allowing that logical deductions could be achieved by algebraic manipulations. Thus, in practice, the approach of Boole consists of the three steps

1. Express the logical data as equations in terms of suitably defined operations,
2. Solve these equations by algebraic techniques,
3. Translate the solution, if possible, into the original logical language.

Table 1 shows examples illustrating a correspondence between logical an algebraic expressions in the context of the Boolean algebra.

The related mathematical work by Boole is reported in his three important publications [1–3], and it was favorably estimated by many scholars. For instance, Tarski [26] wrote *The development of mathematical logic began at the time when Boole published his works on logic. Laws of Thought is Boole's principal work.* In [13], Lewis and Langford said *The work of Boole is the basis of the whole development [of mathematical logic].* More recently, Corcoran [5] stated *Boole did the first mathematical treatment of logic.* Similar statements can be found at many places in the literature.

5 The Boole - De Morgan Correspondence

The correspondence between these two mathematicians provides a good insight into their work in logic, but also highlights some other aspects of their personalities, various personal interests, and mutual topics to discuss. The correspondence started in late 1842 after the Boole published his first works in logic, and De Morgan noticed and commented. The book [22] contains 90 letters that are still preserved, 64 letters written by Boole and 26 by De Morgan, with a draft of a letter by De Morgan, the parts of which were not included in the corresponding letter to Boole.

The mathematical concepts discussed are certain topics of calculus, differential equations, mathematical logic, and probability. Among social and personal topics, they discussed homeopathic medicine, the plight of the Jews, psychic phenomena and theories (spiritualism), family matters, etc.

In the book by [22] the letters are arranged first chronologically, and then grouped into periods related by general themes. At the beginning of each group of letters, the author provided a brief summary of the contents and at some places the transitional material were used and shortly commented in order to provide necessary explanatory comments which is very useful for the readers. Some of the remarks and conclusions by G. C. Smith are commented and slightly corrected in the reviews of the book, as for example by Hailperin [10], and Jongsma [11].

Boole and De Morgan were in friendly personal relations as can be seen from their mutual correspondence where they besides scientific considerations, comments, and thought, also exchanged personal and family matters and general thoughts about certain contemporary affairs, literature, etc.

They worked in the same field and on the identical subjects and then discussed them. For instance, the first works in logic by Boole [1] and De Morgan [7] were published in November 1847. In his letter dated on November 28, 1847, the letter 12 in [22], De Morgan points *remarkable similarities* in these their works by adding also that he did not use the algebraic notation in his system which *employed mechanical modes of making transitions.*

An insight into the Boole De Morgan correspondence raises some interesting questions about their attitude towards particular concepts. We briefly point out three of them.

In a letter dated on February 24, 1845, Boole is answering to De Morgan to acknowledge receiving of his memoir containing already at the first page a discussion of associativity of triples that de Morgan invented by an analogy with quaternions defined by W. R. Hamilton. Thus, Boole was aware of the associativity, and it is an interesting question why he did not even mention this mathematical property in connection with either logical addition or multiplication, discussed in his work.

As pointed out in [10], by referring to the letter by De Morgan dated on April 3, 1849, letter 16 in [22], as well as a comment at the page 149 in [7], both Boole and De

Morgan allowed the possibility of a three-valued logic. In [10], it is quoted a statement at the page 149 in [7], where De Morgan states *But we should be led to extend our system if we consider propositions under three points of view, as true, false, or inapplicable. We may confine ourselves to single alternatives either by introducing not-true (including both false and inapplicable) as the recognized contrary of true: or else by confining our results to universes in which there is always applicability, so that true or false holds in every case. The latter hypothesis will best suit my present purpose.*

Continuing the discussion of the subject, on the side of Boole, Hailperin [10] quotes the following statement at page 51 in [3].

Now if the equation in question [i.e., $x^2 = x$] *had been of the third degree, still admitting of interpretation as such* [in a footnote on the preceding page Boole argues against being able to interpret $x - x^3 = x(l - x)(l + x) = 0$ in logic], *the mental division must have been threefold in character, and we must have proceeded by a species of trichotomy, the real nature of which it is impossible for us, with our existing faculties, adequately to conceive, but the laws of which we might still investigate as an object of intellectual speculation.*

Hailperin concludes it is curious that Boole makes no mention of De Morgan in that respect.

Another interesting discussion is related to the question if Boole and De Morgan considered the concepts as Nothing and Universe. Nothing is represented by Boole by the symbol 0 and Universe by 1, and they are considered as classes. De Morgan however follows the traditional syllogistic forms and excludes the extreme names but recognizes that these can be given formal treatment. The letters enumerated by 79 and 80 in [22] explain the difference between their understanding of these concepts. See also a brief discussion of this subject in [10].

6 Instead of Conclusions

There are several reasons supporting the presented point of view that George J. Boole can be viewed as a nineteenth century man for the modern digital era. We point out two of them

1. In contemporary computer science and engineering practice there are several fundamental concepts bearing the name of George J. Boole. For instance, the following concepts are widely used *Boolean algebra, Boolean ring, Boolean variables, Boolean functions, Boolean circuits, Boolean networks, Boolean difference, Boolean Operators, Boolean filtering, Boolean data type*, etc.
2. The way of learning, the self-education programs that Boole created forhimself, selection of topics to learn, manner of teaching others, which fits well with the present way of teaching and learning taking into account various modes of e-learning, distance learning, on-line courses, and other forms of self-education in the digital era.

References

1. Boole, G.J.: Mathematical Analysis of Logic, being an Essay Towards a Calculus of Deductive Reasoning. Spring, London and Cambridge, 82 p. (1847). Reprinted in P. E. B. Jourdain, (ed.) George Boole's Collected Logical Works, Vol. 1, Chicago and London 1916
2. Boole, G.J.: The calculus of logic. The Cambridge and Dublin Mathematical Journal, vol. 3, 183–198 (1848). Reprinted in P. E. B. Jourdain, (ed.) George Boole's Collected Logical Works, Vol. 1, Chicago and London, 1916
3. Boole, G.J.: An Investigation of The Laws of Thought, on Which are Founded the Mathematical Theories of Logic and Probabilities, v+iv+424 p. (1854). Reprinted in P.E.B. Jourdain (ed.) George Boole's Collected Logical Works, Vol. 2, Chicago and London, 1916. Reprinted by Dover Publications, Inc., New York, USA, 1954
4. Corcoran, J.: Review of the Book G. C. SMITH, The Boole-De Morgan Correspondence 1842–1864, Oxford Logic Guides, Clarendon Press, Oxford University Press, Oxford and New York, vii+156 pp. (1982). History and Philosophy of Logic, Vol. 7, No. 1, 1986, 65–75
5. Corcoran, J.: Aristotle's prior analytics and boole's laws of thought. Hist. Philos. Logic **24**, 261–288 (2003)
6. Couturat, L.: L'algebre de la logique, Gauthier-Villars collection Scientia, vol. 24, Paris 1905, 2nd edn., Paris 1914, 100 p.
7. De Morgan, A.: Formal Logic, or, The Calculus of Inference, Necessary and Probable, Taylor and Walton, London, November 1847
8. Ehrenfest, P.: Review of Couturat's Algebra logiki, Zurnal Russkago Fiziko-hemičeskago Obščestva, Fizičeskij otdel, Otdel vtoroj, vol. 42, pp. 382–387 (1910)
9. Grattan-Guinness, I.: The correspondence between George Boole and StanleyJevons, 1863–1864. Hist. Philos. Logic **12**(1), 15–35 (1991)
10. Hailperin, T.: Review of the book G. C. Smith, The Boole-De Morgan correspondence 1842–1864. Oxford logic guides. Clarendon Press, Oxford University Press, Oxford and New York 1982, vii+156 pp. The Journal of Symbolic Logic, Vol. 49, 1984, 657–659
11. Jongsma, C.: Review of the book G. C. Smith, The Boole-De Morgan correspondence 1842–1864. Oxford logic guides. Clarendon Press, Oxford University Press, Oxford and New York 1982, vii+156 pp. Historia Mathematica, Vol. 12, No. 2, 1985, 186–190
12. Jongsma, C.: Review of the book George Boole - His Life and Work by Desmond MacHale. ISIS **77**(3), 544–545 (1986)
13. Lewis, C.I., Langford, C.H.: Symbolic Logic, New York, Century (1932). Reprinted, New York, Dover, 1959
14. MacHale, D.: George Boole – His Life and Work, (Profiles of Genius Series, 2), xiii+304 p. Boole Press, Dublin (1985). ISBN 0-906783-05-4
15. MacHale, D.: The Life and Work of George Boole: A Prelude to the Digital Age, Cork University Press (2014). ISBN-10 1782050043. ISBN-13 987-1782059949
16. MacHale, D., Cohen, Y.: New Light on George Boole. Attic Press Ltd. (2018). ISBN-10 1782052906, ISBN-13 978-1782052906
17. Nakashima, A.: Theory and practice of relay circuit engineering (Number five). Nichiden Geppo **12**(4), 1–13 (1935)
18. Nakashima, A., Hanzawa, M.: Expansion theorem and design of twoterminal relay networks (Part 1). Nippon Electr. Commun. Eng. **24**, 203–210 (1941)
19. Povarov, G.N.: Matrix methods of analyzing relay-contact networks in terms of the conditions of non-operation. Avtomatika i Telemekhanika **15**(4), 332–335 (1954)
20. Shannon, C.E.: A symbolic analysis of relay and switching circuits, MSc thesis at MIT (1940)
21. Shannon, C.E.: A symbolic analysis of relay and switching circuits. Trans. Am. Inst. Electr. Eng. **57**, 713–723 (1938)

22. Smith, G.C. (ed.): The Boole - De Morgan Correspondence, 1842–1864, vii+156 p. Oxford University Press (1982)
23. Stanković, R.S., Astola, J.T. (eds): Reprints from the Early days of Information Sciences - On the Contributions of Akira Nakashima to Swithching Theory, Tampere International Center for Signal Processing TICSP series # 40 (2008). ISBN 978-952-15-1980-2, ISSN 1456-2774. https://ethw.org/w/images/2/2f/Report-40.pdf
24. Stanković, R.S., Astola, J.T. (eds.): Reprints from the Early days of Information Sciences - Paul Ehrenfest - Remarks on algebra of Logic and Switching Theory, Tampere International Center for Signal Processing TICSP series # 54 (2010). ISBN978-952-15-2419-6, ISSN 1456-2774. https://ethw.org/w/images/f/f5/Report-54.pdf
25. Sestakov, V.I.: Some mathematical methods for construction and simplification of two-element electrical networks of class a, Ph.D. dissertation, Lomonosov State University, Moscow, Russia (1938)
26. Tarski, A.: Introduction to Logic and to the Methodology of Deductive Sciences, Translation by O. Helmer, New York 1941. Oxford University Press (1946)

Improvement of Electromagnetic Systems by Werner Von Siemens

Heinz Schwaertzel[1] and Franz Pichler[2]([⊠])

[1] TU Munich, Munich, Germany
`heinz.schwaertzel@t-online.de`
[2] JKU Linz, Linz, Austria
`telegraph.pichler@aon.at`

1 Introduction

Werner Von Siemens, the famous German inventor and international entrepreneur is considered as one of the most important persons for the development of the field of Electrical Engineering and Communications Engineering in the 19th century. He had the great talent to make important inventions and at the same time to have the ability to establish a company, the company Siemens & Halske in Berlin, Germany, of international reputation. Many articles and books have been written in the past to document his life and his scientific and commercial success [1]. He himself published by his book "Lebenserinnerungen" the story of his most interesting life and the adventures and struggles to get the proper acknowledgement for his work [2]. His scientific publications and technical reports have been collected in two volumes by a special book which got also a translation into English [3]. In this paper we focus on a specific topic of his research and practical work, namely to his important inventions to improve the electro-magnetic system of magneto-electric machines (1856), of Morse- telegraph registers (1853,1859) and the telephone of Bell (1878). Certainly, these inventions of Werner Von Siemens have already been documented earlier in different publications. Our point is to show, that he had in all the cases just to apply his scientific knowledge how the magnetic force can be improved.

2 Magneto-Electric Machines

By the important invention of induction by the British professor.

Michael Faraday in 1831 it became possible to generate electrical current by mechanical means. The first machine for it is contributed to the french physicist Pixii. This machine consisted of a pair of coils and a turning horse-shoe magnet beneath. The alternating current generated by the coils was transformed "mechanical" by a turning commutator to get the wanted direct current. The Pixii machine was immediately improved by different inventors. We mention Saxton and Clark in England, Page in the United States, Stoehrer in Germany and Von Ettingshausen and Petrina in Austria. All this "magneto-electric machines" served mainly for scientific demonstrations, however soon practical application followed. We like to mention the "Alliance machine"

R. Moreno-Díaz et al. (Eds.): EUROCAST 2022, LNCS 13789, pp. 27–41, 2022.
https://doi.org/10.1007/978-3-031-25312-6_4

in France which provided electrical power for the arc lamps of the light-houses at the Atlantic coast.

The "Siemens armature".

The development of magneto-electric machines found interest by Werner Von Siemens. However, for the applications he had in mind the existing machines had not the necessary electrical power which was needed. One of the reasons was the loose inductive coupling of the turning coils with the battery of permanent magnets. As an improvement Werner Von Siemens proposed in 1856 the use of the "Double-T-armature" (H-armature), later called the "Siemens armature". It was realized by a coil wound in a double-T-shaped iron core of cylindrical form which turned close embedded to the battery of permanent magnets (Fig. 1).

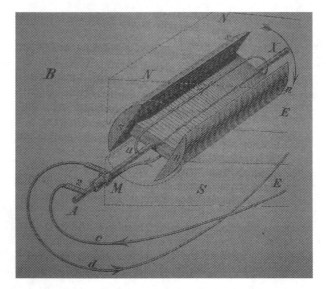

Fig. 1. Double-T-armature of Werner Von Siemens

The different "magnet inductors" of Siemens & Halske using the Siemens armature have been successfully applied for the control of mechanical driven bells at railway crossings (Fig. 2), for the electrical ignition of mines [4] and for the generation of signals in pointer-telegraphy [5]. After the discover of the "electro-dynamical principle" by Werner Von Siemens and independently by Charles Wheatstone in 1867 [6], the "Trommelanker" (drum-armature) constructed in 1872 at Siemens & Halske by Hefner-Alteneck, which can be seen as a multiple arrangement of the Siemens armature, found many applications in dynamos and electrical motors. Also the first dynamos of Edisonmade use of this type of armature.

Fig. 2. Magnet-inductor, Siemens & Halske, ca 1858

3 Morse-Telegraphy

The "Vail register" as shown in Fig. 3 constructed 1844 by Alfred Vail for the first Morse-line from Washington D.C. to Baltimore served as the construction model afterwards built by the different American makers and workshops such as Clark (Philadelphia), Phelps (Troy,N.Y.) and Chubbock (Utica, N.Y.).In Europethis model was also used by the different companies, which were engaged in the area of Morse-telegraphy. We mention here Siemens & Halske (Berlin) and Lewert (Berlin) in Germany, Breguet (Paris) in France and Ekling (Vienna) in Austria. The main parts of a Morse-register consists, as we know, of two coils which realize a strong electro-magnet, the armature with a lever to write the received Morse-signal on a strip of paper and the clock-work driven by a weight or a spring, to move the paper strip.

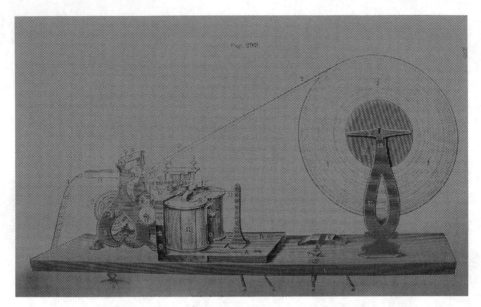

Fig. 3. Vail register as used in the first Morse-line 1844

As it is shown in the following, Werner Von Siemens, was successful in improving this model in two cases: (1) for a new telegraph system for the Russian empire, (2) for the use in submarine telegraphy.

Automatic rapid telegraph for Russia.

In 1853 S & Halske Berlin got the chance to contribute to the extension of the telegraph network in Russia. The task was, to erect a Morse-telegraph line from Warsow to Kronstadt on the Baltic Sea and to St. Petersburg, the capital. Then from St. Petersburg to Moscow and further on to the south of the Russian empire to Odessa and to the Sewastopol on the peninsular Krim (Fig. 4). Werner Von Siemens designed for this line a completely new type of telegraph system which made use of his "automatic rapid telegraphy [7]. The signals in Morse-code were first punched by a special perforator in a paper strip and afterwards transmitted by a fast working device over the line. For receiving the fast signals it was necessary to construct a new type of register which is shown in Fig. 5. In this register Werner Von Siemens improved the magnetic system of the armature by using a rotating core together with a lever with pole-pieces. This register allowed a speed of about 300 letters per minute.

Telegraphy.

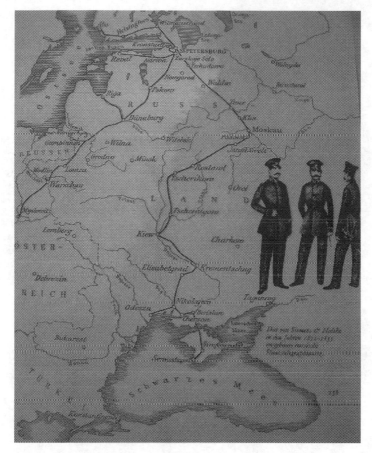

Fig. 4. Telegraph-network of the Russian Empire 1853

Submarine telegraph.

In 1859 Werner Von Siemens got from the British cable company Newell & Co the invitation to develop for the planned submarine telegraph line trough the Red Sea from Suez to Aden the telegraph system..

Fig. 5. Telegraph from Siemens & Halske for automatic rapid

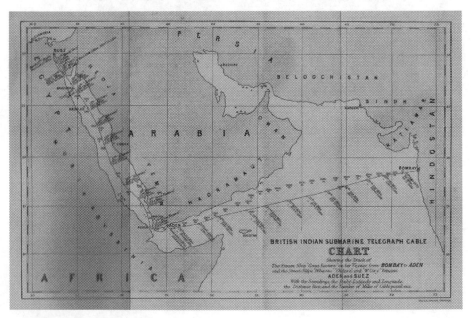

British-Indian submarine cable Suez to Aden to Bombay.

Similar to the already existing systems for submarine telegraphy Werner Von Siemens designed a system which made use of sending the Morse-signals in polarized form [8]. By the help of a special key, the Morse-signals consisting of dots and dashes were sent by a voltage of negative polarity. During the time between a positive voltage was given to the cable-line. For the receiving a polarized relay was used which was connected to a special register, the "polarized ink-writer" which recorded the received message (Fig. 6). To get a high sensitivity the magnetic system of this register was constructed similar to a polarized relay. The moving contact piece got the function of the recording lever (Fig. 7).

Fig. 6. Polarized telegraph of Siemens & Halske 1859

Fig. 7. Magnetic system of the polarized telegraph

The system working with a polarized telegraph was designed for working on long submarine cables, but it could be also used for shorter cables, for example to reach the islands which are close to the German coast. In this case, the system could also work without the polarized relay. This telegraph by Werner Von Siemens which was established for submarine telegraphy was an alternative to the already existing submarine systems which made use of the siphon-recorder of Thomson or the undulator of Lauritzen.

Indo-European Telegraph.

For the British Empire it was important to have a efficient telegraphic connection to India. From 1859 on a connection from London to Calcutta existed, taking the route by crossing the Red Sea and the Indian Pacific to Karachi and further on by a land line to Calcutta. In 1862 a landline via Turkey and Persia followed. Both connections did not operate satisfying. Therefore a new land line, the "Indo European Telegraph" was planned. As shown in Fig. 8 the route was from London to Emden (Germany) and further on via Russia and the Black Sea to Tbilisi and to Tehrani and Büsher in Persia.

Fig. 8. Indo-European Telegraph from Londonto Calcutta

For the construction of the line the companies Siemens Brothers, London, and Siemens & Halske, St. Petersburg got the responsibility. The design and manufacturing of the necessary apparatus had to be done under the leadership of Werner Von Siemens by Siemens & Halske Berlin. Based on the already existing automatic telegraphy of Wheatstone and his own experience with his system of rapid telegraphy in Russia Werner Von Siemens designed a system in which first the message was punched by a special perforator on a paper strip (Fig. 9) followed by a rapid transmission of alternating current signals generated by a Siemens magneto-inductor shown in Fig. 10 [9]. As receiver

Fig. 9. Perforator

Fig. 10. Magneto-inductor

Fig. 11. Telephone of Bell 1876

again a polarized telegraph register, similar to the register of the submarine telegraph, was used [10]. The Indo-European Telegraph stayed from 1870 to 1931 in operation.

4 Bell Telephone

The invention of the telephone by Graham Bell needed several steps. The final step in 1876 was the invention of the "magneto telephone" (Fig. 11, 12). This telephone could be used as a receiver but also as a transmitter.

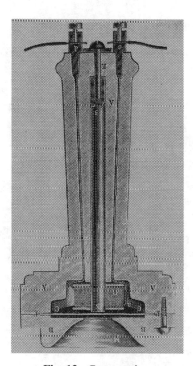

Fig. 12. Construction.

In Europe the invention of Bell found great interest, so also at Siemens & Halske in Berlin. At first it was considered as a kind of curiosity and as a physical toy. But soon its importance for practical use was discovered. However, since the microphone was not known at the beginnings, the distance which could be bridged by speech was only a few Miles. Werner Von Siemens discovered soon, that an improvement of its performance was possible. In 1878 he replaced the bar-magnet of the Bell telephone by a horse-shoe magnet and mounted on both ends the coils together with pole-pieces. The result was the "Siemens telephone" as shown in Fig. 13 and Fig. 14 which could be used for the transmission of speech for a distance more than 70 Miles.

Fig. 13. Telephone of Siemens 1878

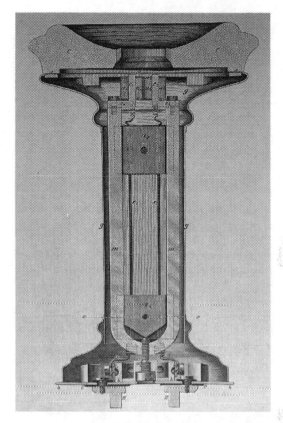

Fig. 14. Construction

The Siemens telephone found application in the first telephone apparatus of the Reichspost as shown in Fig. 15. With the invention of the carbon-microphone (Hughes 1876, Edison 1877, Berliner 1877) the magneto telephone lost its role for being used as a transmitter. For the receiver however, the invention of Werner Von Siemens to use a permanent horse-shoe magnet together with pole pieces found international acceptance and is present until today in our electro-dynamical head-phones (Fig. 16).

Fig. 15. Reichspost 1881

Fig. 16. Headphone of Blaupunkt ca 1924.

5 Conclusion

Werner Von Siemens, autodidact in science, a brilliant entrepreneur and succesful founder of a company of international reputation can be considered as one of the most important personalities for the field of Electrical- and Communications Engineering. In this paper his contribution to the improvement of magneto-electric machines (Siemens armature 1856), to telegraphy (rapid telegraph 1863, polarized telegraph 1859) and to telephony (Siemens telephone 1878) have been discussed. In all this inventions he just had to apply his knowledge how the flux in the relevant magnetic system could be improved.

References

1. Feldenkirchen, W.: Werner von Siemens. Ohio State University Press, Inventor and International Entrepreneur (1994)
2. Von Siemens, W.: Personal Recollections. Translated by W. C. Coupland. Asher & Co, London (1893)
3. Werner Von Siemens: Scientific and Technical Papers. John Murray, London 1, 2 (1895)
4. Werner Von Siemens: Siemens & Halskes dynamo-electric aparatus for mine exploding and other purposes in which a strong short current was a requisite [3], 2, pp.258–262
5. Werner Von Siemens: Application for a patent for a new magneto- electric dial telegraph. The first use of the double-T-armature (Siemens armature) in [3], 2, pp.126–131
6. Werner Von Siemens : On the conversion of mechanical energy into electrical current without the use of permanent magnets. In: [2], 2, pp.255–258
7. Werner Von Siemens: Automatic Telegraph System for the Russian State Telegraph in [3]2, pp.97–99
8. Werner Von Siemens: Siemens & Halskes apparatus for working long submarine cables in [3], 2, pp. 151–178
9. Werner Von Siemens: The automatic telegraph system intended for the Indo-European line. In: [3], 2, pp. 281–298
10. Werner Von Siemens: Morse writer for alternating currents with automatic release and translation arrangement for the Indo-European telegraph line. In: [3], 2, pp. 316–323

Theory and Applications
of Metaheuristic Algorithms

Multi-criteria Optimization of Workflow-Based Assembly Tasks in Manufacturing

Florian Holzinger[(✉)] and Andreas Beham

Heuristic and Evolutionary Algorithms Laboratory, School of Informatics, Communications and Media, University of Applied Sciences Upper Austria, Softwarepark 11, 4232 Hagenberg, Austria
`florian.holzinger@fh-hagenberg.at`

Abstract. Industrial manufacturing is currently amidst it's fourth great revolution, pushing towards the digital transformation of production processes. One key element of this transformation is the formalization and digitization of processes, creating an increased potential to monitor, understand and optimize existing processes. However, one major obstacle in this process is the increased diversification and specialisation, resulting in the dependency on multiple experts, which are rarely amalgamated in small to medium sized companies. To mitigate this issue, this paper presents a novel approach for multi-criteria optimization of workflow-based assembly tasks in manufacturing by combining a workflow modeling framework and the HeuristicLab optimization framework. For this endeavour, a new generic problem definition is implemented in HeuristicLab, enabling the optimization of arbitrary workflows represented with the modeling framework. The resulting Pareto front of the multi-criteria optimization provides the decision makers a set of optimal workflows from which they can choose to optimally fit the current demands. The advantages of the herein presented approach are highlighted with a real world use case from an ongoing research project.

Keywords: ADAPT · Multi-objective optimization · Decision making · Assembly task optimization

1 Background and Motivation

The latest industrial revolution, called Industry 4.0, bundles a multitude of different trends and technologies towards the ongoing digital transformation of industrial manufacturing. This transformation is due to various aspects such as increasing product variety and short product life cycles, triggered by consumer demands and the economic interest of manufacturers. The manufacturing industry reacts accordingly by either focusing on highly automated assembly lines, or highly customized manual assembly following the economy of scope. This situation is especially challenging for small and medium-sized manufacturers,

R. Moreno-Díaz et al. (Eds.): EUROCAST 2022, LNCS 13789, pp. 45–52, 2022.
https://doi.org/10.1007/978-3-031-25312-6_5

whose small batch size production and limited funds inhibits an amortization of a higher grade of automation, excluding them from many benefits of the ongoing digital transformation. The FELICE project[1] aims to provide a new solution for digitized and flexible assembly lines to increase both the level of automatism and the ability to react to a dynamic and changing environment. Premise of this solution is a formal representation of any given workflow containing all necessary assembly tasks executed during manufacturing, for which the ADAPT[2] modeling approach [6] is utilized. This formal representation of a workflow provides the opportunity for computational parsing, monitoring, execution and optimization. This formalization further allows the integration of adaptive elements (such as height-adaptable workstations improving the ergonomics for human workers [4]) and *collaborative robots*, or in short *cobots* (which are tasked to reduce the physical strain of human workers), in workflows. These additional assets can be utilized at various degrees by manipulating the given, formalized workflows. The inclusion or exclusion of adaptive elements results in a change of different, often rivaling key performance indicators (KPIs), such as the total duration of the workflow execution (makespan), ergonomic penalty, or physical strain of the human worker. As the available adaptive elements and the corresponding KPIs are use case dependent, the need for a generic approach arises. This paper aims to provide such generic framework for the multi-objective optimization of ADAPT workflows based on generic user-defined optimization criteria.

2   Methodology and Technologies

In the scope of the herein presented approach, the problem of optimizing workflows is treated as a multi-objective optimization problem [1], utilizing ADAPT [6] for the formal representation of workflows and the HeuristicLab framework [9] for the optimization of such workflows. For this purpose we employ implementations of a set of suitable algorithms, such as NSGA-II [2] and NSGA-III [11]. The resulting Pareto front and the corresponding models can be seen as a prescriptive solution that provides the assembly line operator with different optimal suggestions for fine-tuning of the assembly line according to current demands. For example, a tight deadline might result in the prioritization of a minimal makespan, while normally the minimization of the resulting physical strain of the workflow on the human worker might be the highest priority. Depending on the number of different optimization criteria, the problem might also transmute into the domain of many-objective optimization [5], which is generally the case as soon as four or more objectives are present. In this scenario, other algorithms such as the NSGA-III are better suited. As HeuristicLab includes optimization algorithms for both of these categories, the approach is agnostic of the underlying number of optimization criteria.

---

[1] FlExible assembLy manufacturIng with human-robot Collaboration and digital twin modEls, see https://www.felice-project.eu/.

[2] ADAPT: Asset-Decision-Action-Property-RelaTionship.

2.1 ADAPT Modeling Approach

Basis for any optimization is a formal representation of the underlying problem. For workflows, e.g. representing assembly tasks, BPMN [10] is a well established standard and the theoretical origin of other approaches, such as the ADAPT [6] modeling approach. An overview of the core elements is illustrated in Fig. 1 and a more detailed explanation is given as follows.

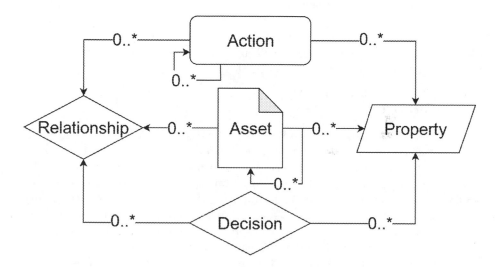

Fig. 1. An overview of the ADAPT elements and their interconnection.

- The **action**-element is used to model tasks (such as grab, move, screw, ...), which can also be seen as skills [3] being required from the current executing entity (human worker, robot, ...). Actions can also be combined into composite actions.
- An **asset** describes accompanying information which can be both produced (documents) or consumed (positional data, robot instructions, ...) by a workflow.
- A **decision** element extends workflows with the capability to react according to environmental conditions by creating a fork point for conditional workflows. Although decisions are modeled offline, they can access connected *assets* and react according to present conditions (camera data, positional data, input from user, ...).
- **Relationship**-elements are used to define existing relationships between the previously defined elements. They usually include successor-relationships between *actions* (order of execution) and include/produce-relationships between *actions* and *assets*.
- **Properties** allow the definition of additional, generic information for the elements *decision, asset* and *action*.

By defining such an ADAPT meta-meta-model, domain-specific workflows can be created and reused for various business processes. Although not strictly limited to a specific field of application, the primary use case for the ADAPT modeling approach is the design of workflows representing assembly tasks for production lines. The ADAPT modeling approach is further accompanied by three tools[3], called WORM (Workflow Modeler, a graphical WYSIWYG-frontend), HCW4i Runtime (Engine for workflow execution) and HCW4i Visualisation (Frontend for the visualisation of workflow execution and accompanying information, including visual feedback and input for decisions). The underlying workflows themselves are persisted as xml files and therefore human-readable and platform-independent which allows for simple transferal between different frameworks such as WORM and HeuristicLab.

2.2 HeuristicLab

HeuristicLab is an open source framework for heuristic optimization[4]. The developers focused on the creation of a paradigm-independent, flexible and extensible design, mainly achieved with a generic plugin-infrastructure. It features a variety of optimization algorithms and problem definitions for different domains. The available optimization algorithms encompass different types such as trajectory and population based, classification and regression, and single and multi-/many-objective. Of particular interest for the proposed solution are three core components of the HeuristicLab plugin-infrastructure, namely the problems, encodings, and multi-/many-objective algorithms. As indicated by the very name of the plugin-infrastructure, new problems can be defined and included in HeuristicLab, as long as they are derived from the predefined, generic interface called IProblem. Besides the generic IProblem, several more specific, but easier to use base classes are available, such as the MultiObjectiveBasicProblem, which can be implemented to create new multi-objective problems with a specific encoding such as binary vector or permutation encoding. One especially interesting feature with regard to encoding is the availability of a class called MultiEncoding, which acts as a wrapper for a list of encodings, providing the ability to utilize several potentially different encodings for a problem.

2.3 Integration

Foundation of the multi-criteria optimization of ADAPT workflows is the creation of a new problem definition in HeuristicLab, named ADAPTOptimization-Problem, which is derived from MultiObjectiveBasicProblem<MultiEncoding>. In addition to this problem definition, a new set of interfaces is introduced, which must be implemented according to a given use case. An overview of these interfaces is depicted in Fig. 2, a detailed explanation is given as follows.

---

[3] https://sar.fh-ooe.at/index.php/de/downloads/category/3-hcw4i.
[4] https://github.com/heal-research/HeuristicLab.

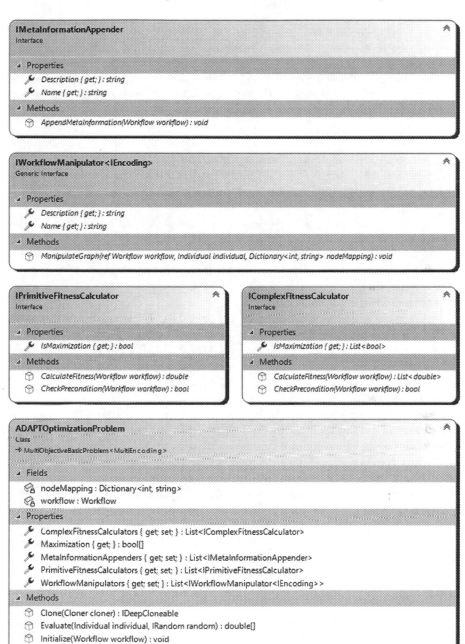

Fig. 2. An overview of the new classes and interfaces within the proposed framework.

- IMetaInformationAppender: The purpose of the IMetaInformationAppender
  is to embed additional (meta-)information into a given workflow. The recommended way is to add new properties to the existing set of actions, assets
  and decisions. Although there are no restrictions in terms of quantity of properties, each implementation of IMetaInformationAppender should preferably
  add only one specific property, which is indicated by the Name and explained
  in the Description.
- IWorkflowManipulator<IEncoding>: The IWorkflowManipulator manipu-
  lates a workflow according to a given instance of an IEncoding. The manipulation can range from simple property manipulation (change value of properties according to RealVectorEncoding) up to a complete reordering of the
  whole workflow (permutation of the execution order of actions by changing
  relationships according to a permutation encoding). Similar to the IMetaInformationAppender, the IWorkflowManipulator should also only represent a
  single concern which is again indicated in the Name and Description. As an
  implementation of this interface potentially alters the elements of the workflow, a mapping between the initial enumeration of the actions in the original
  workflow and their ID is provided.
- IPrimitiveFitnessCalculator: Represents a fitness/objective of a workflow,
  which is calculated with the CalculateFitness method. The IsMaximization
  defines whether the objective should be minimized or maximized. The method
  CheckPrecondition can be used to validate if a workflow is eligible for fitness
  calculation (implementations of IWorkflowManipulator might create infeasible workflows).
- IComplexFitnessCalculator: Each IPrimitiveFitnessCalculator traverses the
  workflow and calculates a fitness, but sometimes a single workflow traversal is sufficient to calculate a number of fitness values. To improve runtime
  performance, the IComplexFitnessCalculator is defined, allowing to return a
  number of fitness values at once.
- ADAPTOptimizationProblem: The ADAPTOptimizationProblem bundles
  all relevant information for the optimization of workflows, including a list
  of the previously defined interfaces. As the problem adheres to the required
  interfaces, it can be easily integrated in HeuristicLab and solved with any of
  the available and compatible algorithms.

The general procedure of ADAPTOptimizationProblem starts by initializing
the four previously defined lists of interfaces. Afterwards, the Initialize method
is called, which initializes the workflow and enumerates all action nodes, creating
a mapping between the initial order and the ID. The corresponding encodings
of the IWorkflowManipulator implementations are used to initialize the Multi-
Encoding of the problem. After this initialization, the workflow is manipulated
by calling the AppendMetaInformation method from each IMetaInformation-
Appender. As soon as these steps are executed, the optimization can start and
guides the search for optimal solutions. Solution candidates are generated by
executing the ManipulateGraph methods of the IWorkflowManipulator implementations on the workflow. Finally, the fitness is calculated by executing the

IPrimitiveFitnessCalculator and IComplexFitnessCalculator implementations on the manipulated workflow.

3   Use Case

A major goal of the aforementioned FELICE project is the utilization of collaborative robots to reduce the amount of physical strain on the human worker. One of the basic assumptions is that each of the defined actions can be executed by either the human worker or the cobot, each with different implications. As the cobot has to ensure the safety of the human workers, the maximum velocity of movements is limited, hence most actions will take longer when executed by the cobot. In contrast to the presumably slower cobot, the human worker experiences fatigue, especially during execution of unergonomic actions. Both of these aspects, duration and ergonomic impact, can be quantified by various methods. In the scope of the FELICE project, we focus on the Methods-time measurement (MTM) system [7] for the estimation of the duration of each action in seconds and the MURI Analysis [8] for the ergonomic penalty expressed as ordinal values (one, two or three, the higher the better). In accordance with the proposed interfaces and this simple but illustrative use case, we can now define four new IMetaInformationAppender classes, appending properties called ExecutionTime-Human, ErgonomicPenaltyHuman, CobotExecutionTime and IsCobotUtilized, representing the aforementioned metrics including a flag on whether a cobot is utilized or not. A new IWorkflowManipulator<BinaryVectorEncoding> (length of the encoding equals to the number of actions in the workflow) class is designed to alter the IsCobotUtilized flag. An implementation of the IComplexFitnessCalculator interface traverses the workflow and aggregates the corresponding execution times from either the human worker or cobot and the ergonomic penalty or zero (depending on whether the IsCobotUtilized flag is set to false for the corresponding action). This results in a set of pareto-optimal solutions in terms of makespan and ergonomic penalty. We're currently in the process of integrating the proposed framework in a real world assembly line setup, allowing us to gather data and to validate the framework in the near future.

4   Discussion and Conclusion

This paper presents a new, generic approach for the multi-criteria optimization of workflows representing assembly tasks. The novelty of the approach lies within the combination of two existing frameworks for workflow creation and optimization. As shown in the use case, this approach can be used to model multi-criteria optimization problems in manufacturing and is utilized in the FELICE project. One current limitation is the absence of precedence rules within the IMetaInformationAppender and IWorkflowManipulator interfaces. This might lead to unintended behaviour if the same property is manipulated more than once in one iteration. The currently fixed-length encoding and enumeration according to the original elements hinders insertion and removal of elements and requires workarounds in the code. These issues are currently under investigation and the solution will be improved in the scope of the FELICE project.

Acknowledgments. This project has received funding from the European Union's Horizon 2020 research and innovation programme under grant agreement No 101017151.

References

1. Deb, K.: Multi-objective optimization. In: Burke, E.K., Kendall, G. (eds.) Search Methodologies, pp. 403–449. Springer, Boston (2014). https://doi.org/10.1007/0-387-28356-0_10
2. Deb, K., Pratap, A., Agarwal, S., Meyarivan, T.: A fast and elitist multiobjective genetic algorithm: NSGA-II. IEEE Trans. Evol. Comput. **6**(2), 182–197 (2002)
3. Ferreira, P., Lohse, N., Razgon, M., Larizza, P., Triggiani, G.: Skill based configuration methodology for evolvable mechatronic systems. In: IECON 2012–38th Annual Conference on IEEE Industrial Electronics Society, pp. 4366–4371. IEEE (2012)
4. Froschauer, R., Kurschl, W., Wolfartsberger, J., Pimminger, S., Lindorfer, R., Blattner, J.: A human-centered assembly workplace for industry: challenges and lessons learned. Procedia Comput. Sci. **180**, 290–300 (2021)
5. Ishibuchi, H., Tsukamoto, N., Nojima, Y.: Evolutionary many-objective optimization: a short review. In: 2008 IEEE Congress on Evolutionary Computation (IEEE World Congress on Computational Intelligence), pp. 2419–2426 (2008). https://doi.org/10.1109/CEC.2008.4631121
6. Lindorfer, R., Froschauer, R., Schwarz, G.: Adapt-a decision-model-based approach for modeling collaborative assembly and manufacturing tasks. In: 2018 IEEE 16th International Conference on Industrial Informatics (INDIN), pp. 559–564. IEEE (2018)
7. Maynard, H.B., Stegemerten, G.J., Schwab, J.L.: Methods-time measurement (1948)
8. Papoutsakis, K., et al.: Detection of physical strain and fatigue in industrial environments using visual and non-visual low-cost sensors. Technologies **10**(2), 42 (2022)
9. Wagner, S., et al.: Architecture and design of the HeuristicLab optimization environment. In: Advanced Methods and Applications in Computational Intelligence, Topics in Intelligent Engineering and Informatics, vol. 6, pp. 197–261. Springer, Heidelberg (2014). https://doi.org/10.1007/978-3-319-01436-4_10
10. White, S.A.: Introduction to BPMN. IBM Cooperation **2**(0) (2004)
11. Yuan, Y., Xu, H., Wang, B.: An improved NSGA-III procedure for evolutionary many-objective optimization. In: Proceedings of the 2014 Annual Conference on Genetic and Evolutionary Computation, pp. 661–668 (2014)

Lightweight Interpolation-Based Surrogate Modelling for Multi-objective Continuous Optimisation

Alexandru-Ciprian Zăvoianu[1,2(✉)], Benjamin Lacroix[1,2], and John McCall[1,2]

[1] School of Computing, Robert Gordon University, Aberdeen, Scotland, UK
{c.zavoianu,b.m.e.lacroix,j.mccall}@rgu.ac.uk
[2] National Subsea Centre, Aberdeen, Scotland, UK

Abstract. We propose two surrogate-based strategies for increasing the convergence speed of multi-objective evolutionary algorithms (MOEAs) by stimulating the creation of high-quality individuals early in the run. Both offspring generation strategies are designed to leverage the fitness approximation capabilities of light-weight interpolation-based models constructed using an inverse distance weighting function. Our results indicate that for the two solvers we tested with, NSGA-II and DECMO2++, the application of the proposed strategies delivers a substantial improvement of early convergence speed across a test set consisting of 31 well-known benchmark problems.

Keywords: Surrogate modelling · Multi-objective continuous optimisation · Evolutionary algorithms · Run-time convergence analysis

1 Introduction and Motivation

A multi-objective optimisation problem (MOOP) over a multi-dimensional space (i.e., $x \in V^d \subset \mathbb{R}^d$) can be defined as:

$$\text{minimize } F(x) = (f_1(x), \ldots, f_m(x))^T, \tag{1}$$

with the understanding that the $m \in \{2, 3\}$ real-valued objectives of $F(x)$ need to be minimized simultaneously. The general solution of a MOOP is given by a Pareto optimal set (PS) that collects all solutions $x^* \in V^d$ that are not fully dominated – i.e., $\nexists y \in V^d : f_i(y) \leq f_i(x^*), \forall i \in \{1, \ldots, m\}$ and $F(y) \neq F(x^*)$. The true Pareto front (PF) is the objective space projection of the PS.

Multi-objective evolutionary algorithms (MOEAs) have emerged as very popular MOOP solvers due to their ability to discover high-quality PS approximations called Pareto non-dominated sets (PNs) after single optimisation runs [1,19]. The successful application of MOEAs to increasingly complex industrial MOOPs ranging from product design [10] to calibration [6] and quality assurance [16] has also helped to highlight that when the process of evaluating

R. Moreno-Díaz et al. (Eds.): EUROCAST 2022, LNCS 13789, pp. 53–60, 2022.
https://doi.org/10.1007/978-3-031-25312-6_6

$F(x)$ is computationally-intensive[1], the effectiveness of the solver can be severely impacted as far fewer candidate solutions/individuals $x \in V^d$ can be evaluated during the optimisation run. One of the most promising approaches for alleviating the effect of expensive $F(x)$ formulations is to replace the original fitness functions with an easy to evaluate surrogate formulation [9, 11]. However, the task of constructing accurate (non-linear) surrogate models is non-trivial and can itself be computationally intensive, especially when performed on-the-fly (i.e., during the optimisation process) [14].

The present work aims to contribute to on-the-fly surrogate construction by exploring the lightweight modelling[2] capabilities of the recently introduced multi-objective interpolated continuous optimisation problem (MO-ICOP) formulation [15] based on inverse distance weighting.

2   Research Focus and Approach

2.1   Lightweight Interpolation-Based Surrogate Model

Let us denote with $e(x, y)$ the Euclidean distance between two individuals x and y and with $X = \{x_1, ..., x_N\}$ the set containing all the N individuals evaluated by a MOEA till a given stage of its execution. Using Shepard's inverse distance weighting function [12], we can estimate the fitness of any new solution candidate $y \in V^d$ across each individual objective f_i from Eq. 1 as:

$$g_{X,f_i,k}(y) = \begin{cases} \dfrac{\sum_{j=1}^{N} \frac{f_i(x_j)}{e(y,x_j)^k}}{\sum_{j=1}^{N} \frac{1}{e(y,x_j)^k}} & \text{if } e(y,x_j) \neq 0 \text{ for all } j \\ f_i(x_j), & \text{if } e(y,x_j) = 0 \text{ for some } j \end{cases}, \forall 1 \leq i \leq n \quad (2)$$

where k is a positive real number called the power parameter. The final lightweight multi-objective surrogate for $F(x)$ is obtained by simply aggregating the individual interpolation-based models:

$$g_{X,F,k}(y) = (g_{X,f_1,k}(y), ..., g_{X,f_m,k}(y))^T, \forall 2 \leq m \leq 3. \quad (3)$$

We propose two offspring generation strategies that leverage the lightweight interpolation-based surrogate model from Eq. 3 to discover high-quality individuals during the MOEA evolutionary cycle and thus reduce the number of fitness evaluations necessary for producing high-quality PN approximations. This will translate directly into a reduction of the prohibitive run-times observed when applying MOEAs on MOOPs with computationally-intensive fitness evaluations.

It is noteworthy that across all the optimisation runs we carried out, both subsequently described strategies were mostly beneficial in the early and middle stages of convergence. Therefore, our recommendation is to only apply them during the first $gTh\%$ generations, where gTh is a control parameter.

---

[1] As it is based on numerical simulation(s) or even human-in-the-loop experiment(s).
[2] Modelling that requires virtually no training.

2.2   Offspring Generation Strategy 1: Pre-emptive Evaluation (PE)

The first strategy aims to improve any MOEA-specific approach of generating a new individual (i.e., **EvolveNextOffspring**) by using a (very fast) surrogate-based pre-emptive evaluation of fitness to stimulate the creation of offspring that have high quality - i.e., a very high likelihood of improving the current PN stored by the MOEA. If a new *offspring* does not pass the high-quality test, it will generally be disregarded. However, if the number of failed consecutive attempts to generate a high-quality offspring exceeds a certain threshold (i.e., $|solverPop| \cdot \frac{gTh}{100}$), a default acceptance criterion is triggered. In order to pass the high-quality test (lines 9 to 24 in Algorithm 1), when comparing with at least one member of the parent population, the new offspring must simultaneously:

- be better by at least $minImprTh\%$ on at least one objective;
- not be worse by more than $simTh\%$ on any objective;

Algorithm 1. The pre-emptive evaluation (PE) strategy

1: **function PreEvalOffspring**($solverPop$, $G_{X,F,k}$, $simTh$, $minImprTh$, gTh)
2: $\quad passed \leftarrow false \wedge rejections \leftarrow 0$
3: $\quad$ **while** $\neg passed$ **and** $rejections < |solverPop| \cdot \frac{gTh}{100}$ **do**
4: $\quad\quad rejections \leftarrow rejections + 1$
5: $\quad\quad offspring \leftarrow$ **EvolveNextOffspring**($solverPop$)
6: $\quad\quad$ **for** $i = 0$ **to** m **do**
7: $\quad\quad\quad offspring.\mathbf{obj}(i) \leftarrow g_{X,f_i,k}(offspring)$
8: $\quad\quad$ **end for**
9: $\quad\quad$ **for all** p **in** $solverPop$ **do**
10: $\quad\quad\quad simObj \leftarrow 0$
11: $\quad\quad\quad domObj \leftarrow 0$
12: $\quad\quad\quad$ **for** $i - 0$ **to** m **do**
13: $\quad\quad\quad\quad$ **if** $p.\mathbf{obj}(i) \cdot (1 + simTh) > offspring.\mathbf{obj}(i)$ **then**
14: $\quad\quad\quad\quad\quad simObj \leftarrow simObj + 1$
15: $\quad\quad\quad\quad$ **cnd if**
16: $\quad\quad\quad\quad$ **if** $p.\mathbf{obj}(i) \cdot (1 - minImprTh) > offspring.\mathbf{obj}(i)$ **then**
17: $\quad\quad\quad\quad\quad domObj \leftarrow domObj + 1$
18: $\quad\quad\quad\quad$ **end if**
19: $\quad\quad\quad$ **end for**
20: $\quad\quad\quad$ **if** $domObj \geq 1$ **and** $simObj = m$ **then**
21: $\quad\quad\quad\quad passed \leftarrow true$
22: $\quad\quad\quad\quad rejections \leftarrow rejections - 1$
23: $\quad\quad\quad\quad$ **break**
24: $\quad\quad\quad$ **end if**
25: $\quad\quad$ **end for**
26: $\quad$ **end while**
27: $\quad$ **return** $\langle offspring, passed \rangle$
28: **end function**

The result of calling the **PreEvalOffspring** function is an ordered pair containing a newly generated *offspring* and a Boolean flag indicating if it has *passed* the high-quality test (or, conversely, has been accepted by default). The Boolean data is used to dynamically adjust the evolutionary pressure exerted by the pre-emptive evalution strategy. Thus, whenever observing more than gTh default accepts / generation, the required objective improvement threshold for subsequent offspring is reduced using the formula:

$$minImprTh = minImprTh \cdot \left(1 - \frac{gTh}{100}\right) \tag{4}$$

We highlight that successive reductions of $minImprTh$ using Eq. 4 can rapidly lead to a situation where $minImprTh < simTh$. This signals that the evolutionary search is at a stage where the lightweight interpolation-based surrogates cannot easily identify offspring that are likely to bring major improvements to the current PN stored by the MOEA. As such, we opted to reduce our application of both surrogate strategies during the first $gTh\%$ generations to instances where $minImprTh \geq simTh$.

2.3   Offspring Generation Strategy 2: Speculative Exploration (SE)

Algorithm 2 describes our second approach for providing any (generational) MOEA with a simple means of creating high-quality offspring.

Here, the idea is to construct a (surrogate) multi-objective interpolated continuous optimisation problem ($MO - ICOP$) that mirrors the definition of the original *problem* to be solved (line 3 in Algorithm 2). The only difference is that the surrogate MO-ICOP uses the model from Eq. 3 as its fitness function (instead of the original from Eq. 1). An internal solver is then applied on the surrogate MO-ICOP and an elite subset of individuals, randomly extracted from the final population of the internal solver, will form the final result of the speculative exploration of the search space using the surrogate models. Finally, the $|solverPop| \cdot \frac{gTh}{100}$ surrogate-based elites returned by the **SpecExploreOffspring** function will be subsequently treated like regular offspring inside the evolutionary cycle of the main MOEA.

Algorithm 2. The speculative exploration (SE) strategy

1: **function SpecExploreOffspring**($solverPop,\ gTh,\ problem,\ G_{X,F,k}$)
2:      $eliteSetSize \leftarrow |solverPop| \cdot \frac{gTh}{100}$
3:      $MO - ICOP \leftarrow$ **CreateSurrogateProblem**($problem, G_{X,F,k}$)
4:      $offspringPop \leftarrow$ **InternalSolver**($MO - ICOP$)
5:      $offspringPop \leftarrow$ **RandomFilter**($offspringPop, eliteSetSize$)
6:      **return** $offspringPop$
7: **end function**

2.4   Tentative Parameterisation of Proposed Strategies

In order to control the two proposed surrogate-based offspring creation strategies, one needs to parameterise three thresholds (gTh, $simTh$, $minImprTh$) and k – the power parameter from Eq. 2.

gTh can be seen as a general control parameter for surrogate usage and current experiments indicate that the setting $gTh = 10$ produces good results for all tested MOEAs across a wide range of problems.

Given that an ideal characteristic of any PN is to provide a well-spread approximation of the true PF, a reasonable setting for the similarity threshold is $simTh = \frac{1}{|solverPop|}$. In order to increase the chances that the PE strategy identifies high-quality offspring despite the high uncertainty associated with light-weight surrogate estimations (especially in the first few generations), the value of the minimal improvement threshold should be a multiple of $simTh$. We recommend the setting $minImprTh = gTh \cdot simTh + \epsilon$ as it generally yields competitive results and reduces the parameterisation overload.

Higher values of k produce interpolation models with wider attraction basins around the seed points (i.e., X in Eq. 2). Our experiments indicate that surrogate fitness landscapes obtained with the setting $k \geq 10$ work better than those generated by $1 \leq k < 10$ across both offspring generation strategies. All the results from Sect. 4 were obtained with the setting $k = 20$.

3   Exprimental Setup

We've integrated and tested the PE and SE strategies with two solvers. The first one is the well-known NSGA-II [2] - a multi-objective evolutionary algorithm that relies on a highly Pareto elitist two-tier selection for survival (i.e., filtering) operator to obtain the population of generation $t + 1$ from the population of generation t and the offspring generated at generation t. The first filtering criterion aims to retain Pareto non-dominated individuals whilst the second one (used for tie-breaking) aims to avoid overcrowding in objective space.

The second solver we experimented with is DECMO2++ [17]. It's main characteristic is the ability to converge fast across a wide range of MOOPs when using a fixed parameterisation. This is achieved by integrating and pivoting between three different multi-objective evolutionary paradigms (Pareto elitism, differential evolution [13], and decomposition [5,18]) via coevolved sub-populations. It is noteworthy to mention that the PE and SE strategies were independently integrated in each of the three sub-populations.

Across all[3] experiments, we fixed $|solverPop| = 200$ and used the standard / literature recommended parameterisation for both MOEAs. As a stopping criterion, we fixed the total number of fitness evaluations (nfe) per run to 50.000.

---

[3] Given that results from [15] indicate that NSGA-II has a competitive advantage on MO-ICOP instances where $k \geq 6$, NSGA-II was also used as the internal solver of the speculative exploration strategy (i.e., line 4 in Algorithm 2).

We performed experiments on a comprehensive test set containing 31 bench-mark problems: all[4] the DTLZ[3], LZ09 [8], WFG[4] and ZDT[20] problems plus KSW10 – Kursawe's function [7] with 10 variables and 2 objectives. We carried out 50 independent optimisation runs for each MOEA-MOOP combination.

As a performance measure, we use the normalised hyervolume [21] to track the quality of the PN stored by the solvers at each stage of the optimisation. The normalised hypervolume indicates the size of a PN-dominated objective space relative to the size of the objective space dominated by the PF.

4   Results - Comparative Performance

In Fig. 1 we plot the average convergence performance of the two baseline MOEAs and their surrogate-enhanced versions across the benchmark test set.

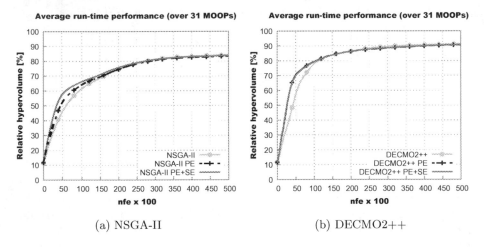

(a) NSGA-II   (b) DECMO2++

Fig. 1. Comparative convergence performance of the surrogate-enhanced and standard versions of NSGA-II and DECMO2++.

The results indicate that the usage of the pre-emptive evaluation (PE) and the speculative exploration (SE) strategies for creating (up to) the first 5000 offspring is successful in increasing the converge speed of both NSGA-II and DECMO2++. While in the case of NSGA-II, the two strategies that use lightweight interpolation-based surrogates have a compounding effect, only the pre-emptive evaluation strategy benefits DECMO2++. Furthermore, the increased selection pressure at the start of the optimisation runs prompted by the use of these strategies seems to only have a minor impact on middle and late stage MOEA performance.

The achieved improvements in terms of early convergence are noteworthy for both solvers. For example, in the case of NSGA-II, a benchmark-wide average

---

[4] Except ZDT5 which is not real-valued.

relative hypervolume of 60% can be reached with $\approx$ 50% fewer fitness evaluations when using both the SE and PE strategies. In the case of DECMO2, when using the PE strategy, a benchmark-wide average relative hypervolume of 70% can be reached with $\approx$ 33% fewer fitness evaluations.

5 Conclusions and Future Work

The present work shows how surrogate models can be easily derived from well-known interpolation functions and subsequently used inside two complementary offspring generation strategies to substantially improve the early convergence speed of MOEAs. The main advantage of the proposed interpolation-based approach is that it can be easily deployed in MOEA application scenarios where on-the-fly surrogate modelling is required.

Future work will revolve around extending the testing to more solvers, experimenting with different interpolation functions, and limiting the parameterisation requirements of the surrogate-based offspring generation strategies.

Acknowledgments. This work has been supported by the COMET-K2 "Center for Symbiotic Mechatronics" of the Linz Center of Mechatronics (LCM) funded by the Austrian federal government and the federal state of Upper Austria.

References

1. Coello Coello, C.A., Lamont, G.B.: Applications of multi-objective evolutionary algorithms. World Scientific (2004)
2. Deb, K., Pratap, A., Agarwal, S., Meyarivan, T.: A fast and elitist multiobjective genetic algorithm: NSGA-II. IEEE Trans. Evol. Comput. **6**(2), 182–197 (2002)
3. Deb, K., Thiele, L., Laumanns, M., Zitzler, E.: Scalable multi-objective optimization test problems. In: IEEE Congress on Evolutionary Computation (CEC 2002), pp. 825–830. IEEE Press (2002)
4. Huband, S., Barone, L., While, L., Hingston, P.: A scalable multi-objective test problem toolkit. In: Coello Coello, C.A., Hernández Aguirre, A., Zitzler, E. (eds.) EMO 2005. LNCS, vol. 3410, pp. 280–295. Springer, Heidelberg (2005). https://doi.org/10.1007/978-3-540-31880-4_20
5. Jaszkiewicz, A.: On the performance of multiple-objective genetic local search on the 0/1 knapsack problem - A comparative experiment. IEEE Trans. Evol. Comput. **6**(4), 402–412 (2002)
6. Kaji, H.: Automotive engine calibration with experiment-based evolutionary multi-objective optimization. Ph.D. thesis, Kyoto University (2008)
7. Kursawe, F.: A variant of evolution strategies for vector optimization. In: Schwefel, H.-P., Männer, R. (eds.) PPSN 1990. LNCS, vol. 496, pp. 193–197. Springer, Heidelberg (1991). https://doi.org/10.1007/BFb0029752
8. Li, H., Zhang, Q.: Multiobjective optimization problems with complicated Pareto sets, MOEA/D and NSGA-II. IEEE Trans. Evol. Comput. **13**(2), 284–302 (2009)
9. Loshchilov, I., Schoenauer, M., Sebag, M.: A mono surrogate for multiobjective optimization. In: Proceedings of the 12th annual Conference on Genetic and Evolutionary Computation (GECCO), pp. 471–478. ACM (2010)

10. Oyama, A., Kohira, T., Kemmotsu, H., Tatsukawa, T., Watanabe, T.: Simultaneous structure design optimization of multiple car models using the K computer. In: IEEE Symposium Series on Computational Intelligence (2017)
11. Pilát, M., Neruda, R.: Hypervolume-based local search in multi-objective evolutionary optimization. In: Proceedings of the 2014 Annual Conference on Genetic and Evolutionary Computation, pp. 637–644. ACM (2014)
12. Shepard, D.: A two-dimensional interpolation function for irregularly-spaced data. In: Proceedings of the 1968 23rd ACM National Conference, pp. 517–524 (1968)
13. Storn, R., Price, K.V.: Differential evolution - a simple and effcient heuristic for global optimization over continuous spaces. J. Global Optim. **11**(4), 341–359 (1997)
14. Zăvoianu, A.C., Bramerdorfer, G., Lughofer, E., Silber, S., Amrhein, W., Klement, E.P.: Hybridization of multi-objective evolutionary algorithms and artificial neural networks for optimizing the performance of electrical drives. Eng. Appl. Artif. Intell. **26**(8), 1781–1794 (2013)
15. Zăvoianu, A.-C., Lacroix, B., McCall, J.: Comparative run-time performance of evolutionary algorithms on multi-objective interpolated continuous optimisation problems. In: Bäck, T., et al. (eds.) PPSN 2020. LNCS, vol. 12269, pp. 287–300. Springer, Cham (2020). https://doi.org/10.1007/978-3-030-58112-1_20
16. Zăvoianu, A.C., Lughofer, E., Pollak, R., Eitzinger, C., Radauer, T.: A softcomputing framework for automated optimization of multiple product quality criteria with application to micro-fluidic chip production. Appl. Soft Comput. **98**, 106827 (2021)
17. Zăvoianu, A.C., Saminger-Platz, S., Lughofer, E., Amrhein, W.: Two enhancements for improving the convergence speed of a robust multi-objective coevolutionary algorithm. In: Proceedings of the Genetic and Evolutionary Computation Conference, pp. 793–800. ACM (2018)
18. Zhang, Q., Li, H.: MOEA/D: A multi-objective evolutionary algorithm based on decomposition. IEEE Trans. Evol. Comput. **11**(6), 712–731 (2007)
19. Zhou, A., Qu, B.Y., Li, H., Zhao, S.Z., Suganthan, P.N., Zhang, Q.: Multiobjective evolutionary algorithms: A survey of the state of the art. Swarm Evol. Comput. **1**(1), 32–49 (2011)
20. Zitzler, E., Deb, K., Thiele, L.: Comparison of multiobjective evolutionary algorithms: Empirical results. Evol. Comput. **8**(2), 173–195 (2000)
21. Zitzler, E.: Evolutionary Algorithms for Multiobjective Optimization: Methods and Applications. Ph.D. thesis, Swiss Federal Institute of Technology (1999)

Analysis and Handling of Dynamic Problem Changes in Open-Ended Optimization

Johannes Karder[1,2]($\boxtimes$) , Bernhard Werth[1,2] , Andreas Beham[1] ,
Stefan Wagner[1] , and Michael Affenzeller[1,2]

[1] Josef Ressel Center for Adaptive Optimization in Dynamic Environments, Heuristic and Evolutionary Algorithms Laboratory, University of Applied Sciences Upper Austria, 4232 Hagenberg, Austria
johannes.karder@fh-hagenberg.at

[2] Institute for Symbolic Artificial Intelligence, Johannes Kepler University, 4040 Linz, Austria

Abstract. Changes in dynamic optimization problems entail updates to the problem model, which in turn can result in changes to the problem's fitness landscape and even its solution encoding. In order to yield valid solutions that are applicable to the current problem state, optimization algorithms must be able to cope with such dynamic problem updates. Furthermore, depending on the optimization use case, changes occurring in real-world environments require an optimizer to adapt to changing process conditions and yield updated, valid solutions within a short time frame. In this paper, dynamic problem changes and their effects on an optimizer's algorithmic behavior are studied in the context of crane scheduling. Three open-ended versions of RAPGA, a relevant alleles preserving genetic algorithm, are evaluated, some of which include self-adaption and a special treatment of certain events that require domain knowledge to be recognized. The proposed extensions affect the algorithm behavior as desired. On the one hand, the algorithms converge faster after a loss in solution quality is detected. On the other hand, new genetic material is introduced, making it possible to reach high quality areas of the search space again.

Keywords: Open-ended optimization · Dynamic optimization · Crane scheduling · Evolutionary algorithm

1 Introduction and Related Work

In the domain of open-ended multi-crane scheduling, where an ever-changing set of crane moves must be assigned to a specified number of cranes, optimization algorithms need to continuously yield valid crane schedules that can be applied in real-world warehouse operations. More or less frequently, new moves are added to the set, and moves that are executed by the cranes are removed. Moves can be classified into various types:

© The Author(s), under exclusive license to Springer Nature Switzerland AG 2022
R. Moreno-Díaz et al. (Eds.): EUROCAST 2022, LNCS 13789, pp. 61–68, 2022.
https://doi.org/10.1007/978-3-031-25312-6_7

- pickup moves: move incoming items from handover locations onto storage locations inside the warehouse
- dropoff moves: move outgoing items from storage locations inside the warehouse to handover locations
- relocation moves: move items within the warehouse
- other moves, e.g. move items from one handover location to another.

Static crane scheduling problem formulations have been extensively researched, however, to the best of our knowledge, much fewer papers in the context of dynamic crane scheduling operations have been published [2]. To deal with a dynamic set of jobs, an optimization algorithm can be restarted over and over again to yield valid crane assignments and schedules for the current set of moves. This results in algorithm restarts for every change to the move set, which in turn leads to loss of optimization progress, as already optimized solutions are not transferred between algorithm invocations. When optimizing dynamic problems, open-ended algorithms are a better fit, as they do not need to be restarted per se and only ever stop once terminated manually. As the problem data (e.g. the number of moves) changes over the course of the optimization, an open-ended algorithm's problem state must be synchronized and existing solutions must be updated accordingly. Depending on the implemented solution update strategy, the loss of optimization progress is reduced, as solutions continue to exist and no algorithm restart is necessary. This reduces the time it takes to provide valid solutions with acceptable quality. When optimizing ongoing processes, decisions must be made in a timely manner and providing good (and valid) solutions is desirable. Again, in the context of crane scheduling, operators should not be forced to wait until a restarted optimizer has converged to be given a meaningful schedule.

Various literature tries to answer specific questions in the context of dynamic optimization, e.g. "What algorithm should be used to solve problem X?" [4], "How well does algorithm X perform compared to algorithm Y?" [3] or "How well is algorithm X currently performing?" [5]. By using some form of dynamic fitness landscape analysis or other techniques, at least partial answers to these questions have been obtained. Based on these observations, it is a worthwhile endeavor to further analyze the effect of dynamic changes on an optimization algorithm's behavior and solution qualities. The quality of solutions that were optimized for a previous problem state will almost certainly decline when updated for a new problem state. Therefore, introduced optimization potential should be exploited rather quickly. This can be achieved by e.g. steering the algorithm's convergence rate using parameter adaption. For genetic algorithms, Affenzeller and Wagner [1] introduced a special selection scheme called offspring selection, which can be used to influence the selection pressure that is exerted on the population during the evolutionary cycle.

The goal of this contribution is to track various properties such as selection pressure, population size and solution qualities, of an open-ended version of the relevant alleles preserving genetic algorithm (RAPGA) [1], and analyze the effects of dynamic problem changes during optimization. Furthermore, a strategy to quickly recover from an eventual loss of solution quality caused by disruptive events is proposed. A simulated crane scheduling environment is used, which models two gantry cranes that share a single crane lane and where moves are generated over time. Changes within this simulated environment are propagated to the schedule optimizer, where the algorithm's problem model is updated. In addition, existing solutions are upgraded to be compatible with the current state of the environment. This synchronization is done in each generation of the genetic algorithm. Furthermore, the aforementioned algorithm and solution properties are recorded. It is likely that e.g. solution quality decreases (i.e. the schedule makespan increases) when new crane moves are generated within the simulation and added to the move set. Last but not least, the algorithm is extended in such a way that it switches between two algorithm modes, depending on the current state of the environment. The explorative mode exerts lower selection pressure and leads to a slower convergence rate, while an exploitative mode creates higher selection pressure and lets the algorithm converge faster. Different selection pressures can, on the one hand, be created by switching parent selection operators (proportional selection $\leftrightarrow$ tournament selection) and, on the other hand, by adjusting the comparison factor $c \in [0, 1]$ used during offspring selection. Furthermore, the algorithm is able to use problem-specific knowledge to react to certain events, i.e. when a switch from a single-crane to a dual-crane scenario happens, it will mutate the population to reintroduce lost genetic material.

2   Open-Ended Optimization and Self-adaption

Many well-studied optimization problems such as the knapsack or traveling salesman problems are static, meaning that they do not change over the course of the optimization. In the context of evolutionary optimization, such static problems are primarily solved with classic optimization algorithms that terminate whenever some kind of stopping criterion has been met, e.g. when a maximum number of generations has been created or a maximum wall-clock time has been reached. Different solution approaches are needed when systems that change over time have to be optimized. On the one hand, it is possible to restart an optimizer using an updated optimization problem that reflects the system changes, but is still static. Another option is to stray away from static optimization problems to dynamic optimization problems and open-ended optimization. Optimization becomes open-ended if it runs alongside the system to be optimized and continually yields solutions that can then be implemented in the system. Contrary to static optimization algorithms, an open-ended optimizer usually does not use termination criteria such as a maximum number of generations to stop execution, but only ever ends if requested to do so manually. Furthermore, such open-ended algorithms are well-suited for dynamic optimization problems that change over time. They incorporate update mechanisms to reflect dynamic changes in existing optimizer solutions, e.g. within the population of an open-ended genetic algorithm.

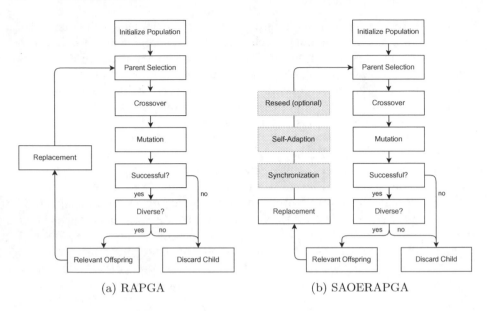

(a) RAPGA   (b) SAOERAPGA

Fig. 1. The evolutionary cycles of both standard (a) and self-adaptive open-ended (b) versions of RAPGA.

The evolutionary cycle of RAPGA can be seen in Fig. 1a. The algorithm features offspring selection, elitism and varying population sizes. Offspring is only accepted, i.e. successful, if it outperforms its parents, depending on a specified comparison factor. For a minimization problem, success $\mathcal{S}$ is defined as

$$\mathcal{S}(f_o, f_{p_1}, f_{p_2}, c) = \begin{cases} \texttt{true}, & \text{iff } f_o < \max(f_{p_1}, f_{p_2}) - c \cdot |f_{p_1} - f_{p_2}| \\ \texttt{false}, & \text{otherwise} \end{cases}$$

where f_o, f_{p_1} and f_{p_2} are the fitness values of the offspring o, parent p_1 and parent p_2, respectively, and c is the comparison factor, usually $c \in [0, 1]$. Setting $c = 0$ results in offspring being successful if it outperforms the worse parent, while setting $c = 1$ specifies that offspring must be fitter than the better parent. The algorithm also accepts diverse offspring only, i.e. all distinct offspring makes up the new population.

The extended loop of the self-adaptive, open-ended version, SAOERAPGA in short, is shown in Fig. 1b. In addition to standard RAPGA, it synchronizes its problem model and solutions according to the changes in the system to be optimized. If necessary, the algorithm self-adapts to accommodate for a loss in solution quality and finally reinitializes its population once it converged and no successful offspring could be created anymore. Depending on the chosen solution update strategy, which defines how new problem data is incorporated into existing solutions, the individuals in the population almost certainly change with respect to their overall quality. In the case of crane scheduling, the quality of existing solutions changes when new moves are added or removed over time, or when cranes go offline or back online. Therefore, in addition to updating existing solutions, it can also proof beneficial to adapt specific algorithm parameters given certain occurring changes. The first idea pursued in the paper at hand is to switch SAOERAPGA between two different operating modes: an explorative mode with lower selection pressure and an exploitative mode with higher selection pressure. When the system is calm and occurring changes do not negatively affect solution qualities, the algorithm should run in explorative mode, giving it more time to cover a broader range of solution candidates. However, as soon as a disruptive change occurs, i.e. a change which negatively impacts solution quality, the algorithm should switch to a more aggressive search behavior to quickly recover from a loss in solution quality. With these two algorithm modes, a tradeoff between fast response time and solution quality is made. Furthermore, some changes do not manifest themselves in a change in solution quality. Given the situation that only one of two cranes is conducting work, e.g. because the other crane is in maintenance or on a break, all existing moves are assigned to this single active crane. Once the second crane becomes available again, the problem data reflects that two cranes are available, however, if no mutation or reseeding is done by the optimizer, the second crane will never be utilized. Therefore, the algorithm must be able to react to changes that do not disrupt solutions, but which rather expand the search space and therefore increase the optimization potential. This requires domain/problem knowledge. By tracking the number of available cranes, SAOERAPGA is able to react accordingly. Once it notices that the number of available cranes increased, i.e. the system switches from single-crane to dual-crane mode, mutation is carried out on all but the best solution in the population. To reintroduce necessary genetic material, the assignment part of the solutions is mutated using bitflip mutation.

3   Experiments and Results

Table 1 lists the parameter settings that have been used for all tested algorithm configurations. The explorative modes use proportional selection and a low comparison factor of 0.0, whereas the exploitative modes switch to tournament selection and a high comparison factor of 1.0. This leads to increased selection pressure in exploitative mode. Optionally, bitflip mutation with a mutation strength of 0.5, meaning that, on average, every second bit is flipped, which distributes the set of moves evenly among cranes, is used.

Table 1. The parameter configurations used in all experiments.

Parameter	Explorative	Exploitative
Selector	Proportional	Tournament (GS = 5)
Comparison factor	0.0	1.0
Effort	1000	1000
Population size	500	500
Elites	1	1

As can be seen in Fig. 2, specific events have certain effects on solution qualities and algorithm behaviors. At the top, the best, average and worst quality (i.e. schedule makespan) in the population at time t is shown. The chart area below shows the population size and selection pressure. Events are marked along the x-axis of the plots. Lines with numbers indicate at which point in time and how many new crane moves were added to the system. Red shaded areas indicate phases where only one of two cranes was available. When inspecting Fig. 2, one can observe that at around 60 s, 11 new moves were generated in the simulation, which led to increased makespans. A crane first went offline at around 120 s. This also led to rapidly decreasing successful offspring, decreasing population size and increasing selection pressure. This is explained by a reduced search space. Furthermore, no particular improvement is visible after a crane that was offline goes online again. Genetic material that encodes moves for the second crane is completely lost at the start of the single crane phase and not actively reintroduced by the algorithm afterwards when using the static configuration.

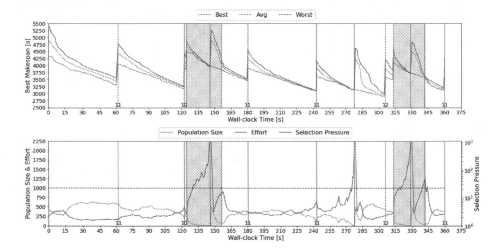

Fig. 2. Test run showing the algorithm behavior when using a static configuration.

It should be noted that given the interactions between optimizer and simulation, the course of the simulation, and also the timing of when events are recognized by the optimizer, depends on the crane actions which are taken in the simulation and dictated by the optimizer. Once the optimizer suggests a crane move that should be conducted in the simulation, and the simulation starts this move, it cannot be canceled. This means that, for example, points in time when cranes go offline and are therefore unavailable are not necessarily equal across runs.

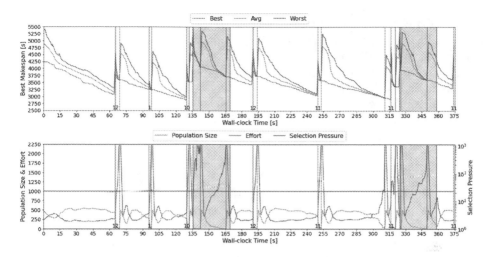

Fig. 3. Test run showing the algorithm behavior of the self-adaptive algorithm configuration α.

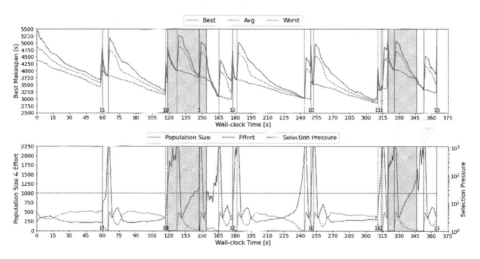

Fig. 4. Test run showing the algorithm behavior of the self-adaptive algorithm configuration β.

Figure 3 shows the quality history and algorithm behavior in case of SAOE-RAPGA. It can be seen that after disruptive events, selection pressure increases rapidly. This is explained by the switch from explorative mode to exploitative mode, which exerts much higher selection pressure on the population, leading to a rapid decrease in makespan. Just like the static configuration, the first self-adaptive configuration α also does not conduct bitflip mutation when cranes go online.

Finally, Fig. 4 shows the behavior of SAOERAPGA using self-adaptive configuration β, where in addition to self-adapting parameters, the algorithm now also reacts to cranes going online by mutating existing assignments via bit-flip mutation. This way, essential building blocks that allow the algorithm to find high quality solutions again are generated. Using explorative mode, SAOE-RAPGA can then provide valid high quality solutions in a short amount of time.

4   Conclusion and Outlook

In this paper, open-ended versions of RAPGAs, one using a static configuration and another using self-adaptive configurations, were used to optimize schedules for crane scheduling simulations. The self-adaptive versions were able to quickly recover from a loss in solution quality caused by disruptive events, as changed algorithm parameters result in higher selection pressure and faster algorithm convergence. The algorithm switches back to explorative mode once no successful offspring can be created and the population is reseeded. Single crane phases led to a loss of genetic material, more specifically the loss of genes that encode moves to be assigned to a second crane. To recover from this situation and reintroduce the necessary genetic material, bitflip mutation is carried out once the algorithm recognizes that an additional crane is operational. This allows work to be split among cranes again, which significantly decreases the makespan of schedules. Building upon these findings, it would be interesting to extend SAOERAPGA in such a way that two or more populations are evolved simultaneously for specific scenarios, e.g. single and dual crane scenarios.

Acknowledgments. The financial support by the Austrian Federal Ministry for Digital and Economic Affairs and the National Foundation for Research, Technology and Development and the Christian Doppler Research Association is gratefully acknowledged.

References

1. Affenzeller, M., Wagner, S., Winkler, S., Beham, A.: Genetic Algorithms and Genetic Programming: Modern Concepts and Practical Applications. CRC Press (2009)
2. Boysen, N., Briskorn, D., Meisel, F.: A generalized classification scheme for crane scheduling with interference. Eur. J. Oper. Res. **258**(1), 343–357 (2017)
3. Nakib, A., Siarry, P.: Performance analysis of dynamic optimization algorithms. In: Alba, E., Nakib, A., Siarry, P. (eds.) Metaheuristics for Dynamic Optimization, pp. 1–16. Springer, Heidelberg (2013). https://doi.org/10.1007/978-3-642-30665-5_1
4. Richter, H.: Dynamic fitness landscape analysis. In: Yang, S., Yao, X. (eds.) Evolutionary Computation for Dynamic Optimization Problems, pp. 269–297. Springer, Heidelberg (2013). https://doi.org/10.1007/978-3-642-38416-5_11
5. van der Stockt, S.A., Pamparà, G., Engelbrecht, A.P., Cleghorn, C.W.: Performance analysis of dynamic optimization algorithms using relative error distance. Swarm Evol. Comput. **66**, 100930 (2021)

Dynamic Vehicle Routing with Time-Linkage: From Problem States to Algorithm Performance

Bernhard Werth[1,2]([envelope]) [ID], Erik Pitzer[1], Johannes Karder[1,2], Stefan Wagner[1], and Michael Affenzeller[1,2]

[1] Josef Ressel Center for Adaptive Optimization in Dynamic Environments Heuristic and Evolutionary Algorithms Laboratory, University of Applied Sciences Upper Austria, 4232 Hagenberg, Austria
bernhard.werth@fh-hagenberg.at
[2] Institute for Formal Models and Verification, Johannes Kepler University, 4040 Linz, Austria

Abstract. Dynamic optimization problems are of significant practical relevance, but suffer from a lack of analysis. The characteristics of time-linked problems are especially difficult to capture as future problem states depend on the optimizer's performance. By tracking numeric features along the optimization process, information about the problems characteristics can be obtained, which can then be used to analyse algorithmic performance. We demonstrate this approach on a dynamic vehicle routing problem combining domain specific and fitness landscape features that can be applied to any optimization problem.

Keywords: Dynamic optimization · Vehicle routing · Evolutionary algorithm · Fitness landscape analysis

1 Introduction and Related Work

Dynamic optimization problems in a meta-heuristic context are black-box problems that change over time, while retaining enough stability that knowledge obtained from the optimization effort before the change can be used to aid with further optimization. In many cases, solutions with good performance will perform similarly well after the change event, allowing for an effective "tracking" of the optimum [8]. For many academic dynamic optimization benchmarks like the *Generalized Moving Peaks* [12] or the *dynamic NK landscapes* [4] the dynamic changes are independent of the performance of the algorithm. This has significant advantages as it allows for easier comparisons between algorithms and the notion of if and when the optimizer needs to make a decision can be separated from the optimization problem itself. In many real-world applications (e.g. *dynamic stacking* or dynamic vehicle routing [11]) the main reason to perform optimization is to influence the considered system. This causes the objective function(s)

© The Author(s), under exclusive license to Springer Nature Switzerland AG 2022
R. Moreno-Díaz et al. (Eds.): EUROCAST 2022, LNCS 13789, pp. 69–77, 2022.
https://doi.org/10.1007/978-3-031-25312-6_8

to become dependent on the previous decisions of the optimizer (i.e. a time-linkage) [2, 9]. Bosman [2] coined the term *time-linkage* and in the same paper noted the ability of time-linked problems to be deceptive: the "optimal" solution that presents the best performance at time t might negatively impact the system in the future.

Because of the increased complexity of time-linked optimization problems the analysis and monitoring of meta-heuristic solver-problem systems is even more desirable, however, rigorous theoretical analysis is sparse and confined to academic problems and simple algorithms [13]. We believe that empirical analysis of problem and optimizer in the vein of exploratory landscape analysis [5] is applicable to the real world problems giving rise to the need for dynamic optimization in the first place. In this paper we demonstrate a small benchmark problem displaying several of the rarer features of academic dynamic optimization problems, we employ techniques from both domain-specific and black-box (i.e. fitness landscape) analysis and derive a new way to quantify (problem-specific) algorithmic performance from the analysis results.

2   Open-Ended Dynamic Vehicle Routing

In this section we introduce a dynamic vehicle routing problem (DVRP) with several aspects of dynamic optimization problems that are not present in many academic benchmarks. Based upon the well-studied *multiple traveling salesman problem* (MTSP) [1] the DVRP deals with optimally routing a fixed number of vehicles in a distance graph. As the problem is designed open-ended there is no need for the vehicles to return to their depot.

Instead of needing to visit all sites once like in the static MTSP, all sites are ascribed an activation state. Vehicles visit active sites and can deactivate them after a certain service time. Sites reactivate *randomly* and the mean and standard derivation of the time-to-activation after a deactivation are constant and specific to each site. Future (re-)activations are hidden from the algorithm, this eliminates the possibility of offline-optimization and forces the optimizer to operate *online*.

The *time-linkage* of the problem is trivially given, as both current vehicle positions and activated sites are the combined result of external (the re-activation process) and internal (the decisions of the optimizer where to send the vehicles) influences.

For better illustration, Fig. 1 shows a snapshot of a DVRP instance. The vehicles $v1$ and $v2$ are currently en route to the endpoints of their past moves. The next moves, as preferred by the optimizer, are shown as dashed lines and a new activation in the top right corner of the map has caused the optimizer to discard its previously selected move for $v2$ (dotted line).

The problem is designed to be open-ended which changes the objective from finding the shortest Hamiltonian cycle (TSP) to minimizing the cumulative time of active sites. Which course of actions leads to a minimal cumulative active time for any future point in time is not trivially calculable due to stochastic effects

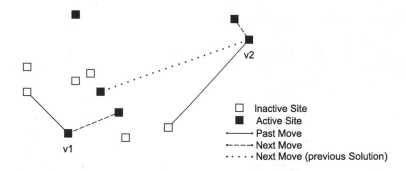

Fig. 1. Snapshot of the dynamic vehicle routing problem

and hidden information. Therefore, an approximate objective function for the current time t is used, that assumes that no more sites reactivate and minimizes cumulative active time starting from t under this premise. It is noted here that for white-box or gray-box solvers the construction, selection or parametrization of the approximate objective function is within the purview of the solver itself and not part of the problem definition.

Solutions are communicated to the problem as Permutations of length $s+v-1$ where s is the total number of sites (active or not) and v is the number of vehicles. A permutation $(1, 2, 3, 7, 8, 5, 6, 4)$ with $s = 6$, v $= 3$, current vehicle positions $(2, 1, 3)$ and current activation $(1, 0, 0, 1, 1, 1)$ would be interpreted in the following way: Vehicle 1 is currently present at site 2 and has sites $(1, 2, 3)$ in its route. Usually, site 3 would be the next target, but since it is deactivated, Vehicle 1 wraps around in its tour and will drive towards site 1. Permutation entries that are larger than s denote new route borders and the consecutive entries of 7 and 8 cause the route for vehicle 2 to be empty and the vehicle idles where it currently stands (here site 1). Note, that the algorithm has the ability to let a vehicle idle and although site 1 is active, vehicle 2 will not deactivate it. Vehicle 3 has route $(5, 6, 4)$, but its current position is not on the route. We will therefore choose the nearest active city in its tour (depending on the distance matrix). While the interpretation of such permutation encodings is somewhat complex and contains genetic *introns* (the inactive sites), it allows for an encoding that does not change dynamically in length. Solutions do not require repair after dynamic changes and the continuous application of the same solution, which might be required if the evaluation budget between dynamic changes is less than 1, still leads to each site being serviced eventually.

Lastly, to increase realism, the evaluation budget of the algorithm is usually equal in every epoch (e.g. many instantiations of the moving peaks [7]). Here, the evaluation budget is linearly scaled with the time that passes in the problem. In special cases it might be beneficial for the optimizer to send all vehicles on longer moves to allow itself more time to converge.

3   Experiments and Results

For the numerical experiments a genetic algorithm was chosen to operate on the DVRP and after every dynamic change (e.g. activation, deactivation, vehicle arrival), a vector of 33 numeric features, describing the current problem state and its immediate past, was calculated. This data collection was performed over various problem difficulties. The difficulty value d controls the speed of the reactivation of sites $\mu_s(d) = \mu_s(1) * d^{-1}$ and $\sigma_s(d) = \sigma_s(1) * d^{-1}$ with $\mu_s(1)$ and $\sigma_s(1)$ being the mean and standard deviation of the time-to-reactivation for site s. All other parameters, i.e. distance matrix, service times, number of vehicles and sites, were kept constant.

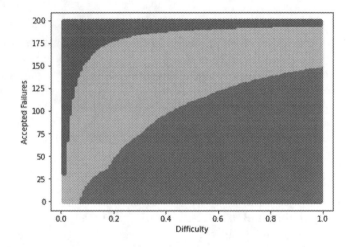

Fig. 2. Theoretical boundaries

By assuming the best and worst performing algorithm (one that always drives along the shortest and longest routing edge respectively) we can identify the relevant regions for optimization as theoretical limits. Noting that a currently active site can not activate again until deactivated, one can assume that a problem is "solved", if the expected number of sites for $t = \infty$ is below an accepted failure rate. Figure 2 shows these regions for the scenario chosen in this work (the 200 largest power stations in Upper Austria). Green areas are "too easy" for optimization, because even an impossibly bad algorithm will always achieve this performance. Red areas are "too difficult", as even an impossibly good algorithm will never meet the accepted number of activated sites.

Table 1 in the appendix lists all features used. Some of them are generated by performing different kinds of walks (i.e. random walks, neutral walks, up-down walks). For a more detailed explanation the reader is kindly referred to the work of Pitzer et al. [10]. Some measures are obtained by random sampling or performing local searches started from these random samples in the spirit of Branke et al. [3] only on a per-snapshot basis as opposed to a per-problem basis. Additionally, the feature set was expanded by incorporating domain-specific features that utilize non-hidden information.

Figure 3 shows a two-dimensional embedding of these numeric vectors achieved via t-SNE [6]. Note that t-SNE is a non-parametric embedding and neither absolute values of the x- and y-axes nor the rotation of the image have meaning. However, the neighborhood structure and separation of the individual snapshots can be interpreted. Snapshots taken from difficult and later instances cluster in the lower left corner while snapshots pertaining to easier instances are grouped in the upper right corner regardless of time.

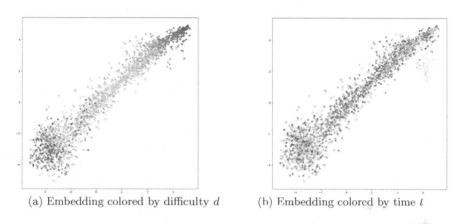

(a) Embedding colored by difficulty d (b) Embedding colored by time l

Fig. 3. Two-dimensional embedding of the collected feature vectors

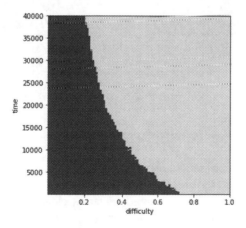

Fig. 4. Critical border

By clustering the numeric vectors via feature reduction through Principal Component Analysis (PCA) and k-means clustering ($k = 2$) we can see a clearer picture of the algorithms' performance. Figure 4 shows the separation between easier and earlier states from later and more difficult ones over difficulty and time. The border between "well-performing" and "ill-performing" system states is defined quite clearly. Up to a difficulty of 0.25 the algorithm can keep up with the speed of reactivations. Above this threshold, the problem changes into the red system region after a certain grace period that shortens with increasing difficulty. This indicates that the speed of the problem overwhelms the algorithm. We call this threshold the "critical border" of the algorithm.

Special care has to be given to the selection of the numeric features. Figure 5 shows the analysis of a smaller (51 sites) problem instance. The left Subfig. 5a shows the critical border obtained by using only domain specific features and Subfig. 5b shows the critical border obtained by using only fitness landscape features. Both feature sets agree roughly on the shape and position of the border, however if the comparison of two algorithms is ever required the feature set and machine learning models for cluster assignment need to be standardized.

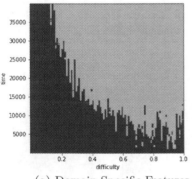
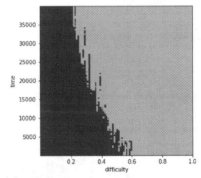

(a) Domain Specific Features   (b) Fitness Landscape Features

Fig. 5. Disparity of the critical border depending on feature selection

4   Conclusion and Outlook

The collection of information about problem characteristics as numerical features for time-linked dynamic optimization problems was demonstrated on a dynamic vehicle routing problem. The extracted features clearly separated easier from more difficult problem states and allow researchers to trace the behavior of the optimizer-problem system. Additionally, this information could be used to compare algorithmic performance by comparing critical borders, even if two algorithms never operate on the same system state.

For more complex optimization problems with more than one parameter that influences system behavior, this critical border will take on much more complex and gradual shapes, so future endeavors will expand the methodology to extract algorithm performance from feature information. Also, significant effort will need to be invested in the design, selection and evaluation of new and meaningful problem descriptors with the goal to allow automatic algorithm selection and parametrization.

Acknowledgments. This research was funded in part by the Austrian Science Fund (FWF) [I 5315-N]. The financial support by the Austrian Federal Ministry for Digital and Economic Affairs and the National Foundation for Research, Technology and Development and the Christian Doppler Research Association is gratefully acknowledged.

Appendix 1

Table 1. Problem features

Feature	Description
Random Walk	
Autocorrelation	(See [10])
Correlation Length	See [10]
Peak Information Content	See [10]
Peak Information Content Quality Delta	See [10]
Information content value	See [10]
Diversity value	See [10]
Regularity value	See [10]
Neutral Walk	
Average Neutral Neighbor Fraction	See [10]
Average Neutral Walk Length	Scc [10]
Up-Down Walk	
Auto Correlation	See [10]
Correlation Length	see [10]
Up Walk Length	See [10]
Down Walk Length	See [10]
Up Walk Length Variance	See [10]
Down Walk Length Variance	See [10]
Random Sampling	
Random Min	Minimum quality
Random Average	Average quality
Random Max	Maximum quality
Multiple Local Searches	
Local Search Min	Minimum quality after local search
Local Search Average	Average quality after local search
Local Search Max	Maximum quality after local search

(*continued*)

Table 1. (*continued*)

Feature	Description
Static Domain Specific Features	
Active Sites	How many sites are currently active
Mean Distance between Active Sites	Average Distance of all active sites to each other
Mean Distance to the Nearest Vehicle	Average Distance of all active sites to their nearest vehicle
Nearest Neighbor Disparity	How uneven the site-nearest vehicle relationships are distributed between vehicles
Mean Distance Between Vehicles	
Domain Specific Features (in the last n time units)	
Activations	How many sites activated
Average Move Distance	Average edge distance
Average Path Distance	Average per vehicle distance
Travel Utilization	How much time was spent traveling
Service Utilization	How much time was spent servicing
Waiting Utilization	How much time was spent waiting
Serviced Sites	How many sites were deactivated

References

1. Bektas, T.: The multiple traveling salesman problem: an overview of formulations and solution procedures. Omega **34**(3), 209–219 (2006)
2. Bosman, P.A.: Learning, anticipation and time-deception in evolutionary online dynamic optimization. In: Proceedings of the 7th Annual Workshop on Genetic and Evolutionary Computation, pp. 39–47 (2005)
3. Branke, J., Salihoğlu, E., Uyar, Ş.: Towards an analysis of dynamic environments. In: Proceedings of the 7th Annual Conference on Genetic and Evolutionary Computation, pp. 1433–1440 (2005)
4. Eriksson, R., Olsson, B.: On the performance of evolutionary algorithms with life-time adaptation in dynamic fitness landscapes. In: Proceedings of the 2004 Congress on Evolutionary Computation (IEEE Cat. No. 04TH8753), vol. 2, pp. 1293–1300. IEEE (2004)
5. Kerschke, P., Preuss, M., Wessing, S., Trautmann, H.: Low-budget exploratory landscape analysis on multiple peaks models. In: Proceedings of the Genetic and Evolutionary Computation Conference 2016, pp. 229–236 (2016)
6. Van der Maaten, L., Hinton, G.: Visualizing data using t-SNE. J. Mach. Learn. Res. **9**(11), 2579–2605 (2008)
7. Moser, I., Chiong, R.: Dynamic function optimization: the moving peaks benchmark. In: Alba, E., Nakib, A., Siarry, P. (eds.) Metaheuristics for Dynamic Optimization, pp. 35–59. Springer, Heidelberg (2013). https://doi.org/10.1007/978-3-642-30665-5_3
8. Nguyen, T.T., Yang, S., Branke, J.: Evolutionary dynamic optimization: a survey of the state of the art. Swarm Evol. Comput. **6**, 1–24 (2012)

9. Nguyen, T.T., Yao, X.: Dynamic time-linkage problems revisited. In: Giacobini, M., et al. (eds.) EvoWorkshops 2009. LNCS, vol. 5484, pp. 735–744. Springer, Heidelberg (2009). https://doi.org/10.1007/978-3-642-01129-0_83

10. Pitzer, E., Affenzeller, M.: A comprehensive survey on fitness landscape analysis. In: Fodor, J., Klempous, R., Suáirez Araujo, C.P. (eds.) Recent advances in Intelligent Engineering Systems, vol. 378, pp. 161–191. Springer, Heidelberg (2012). https://doi.org/10.1007/978-3-642-23229-9_8

11. Rios, B.H.O., Xavier, E.C., Miyazawa, F.K., Amorim, P., Curcio, E., Santos, M.J.: Recent dynamic vehicle routing problems: a survey. Comput. Ind. Eng. **160**, 107604 (2021)

12. Yazdani, D., et al.: Generalized moving peaks benchmark. arXiv preprint arXiv:2106.06174 (2021)

13. Zheng, W., Chen, H., Yao, X.: Analysis of evolutionary algorithms on fitness function with time-linkage property (Hot-off-the-Press track at GECCO 2021). In: Proceedings of the Genetic and Evolutionary Computation Conference Companion, pp. 47–48 (2021)

Dynamic Fitness Landscape Analysis

Erik Pitzer[1,2(✉)], Bernhard Werth[1,2], and Johannes Karder[1,2]

[1] Department Software Engineering, University of Applied Sciences Upper Austria,
Softwarepark 11, 4232 Hagenberg, Austria
{erik.pitzer,bernhard.werth,johannes.karder}@fh-hagenberg.at
[2] Institute for Formal Models and Verification, Johannes Kepler University,
Altenbergerstr 68, 4040 Linz, Austria

Abstract. Dynamic optimization problems pose a big challenge for classic optimization algorithms. They could simply be viewed as a series of related optimization problems. In particular the aspect of time-linkage has not been well studied yet. In this work we are analyzing an artificial problem based on real-world data to elucidate the potential of fitness landscape analysis methods to discover problem difficulty and follow along the changes of dynamic problems and how these changes can be measures and might be exploited by enabling algorithm introspection.

Keywords: Fitness landscape analysis · Dynamic optimization · Dynamic vehicle routing

1 Introduction

The suitability of automatic fitness landscape analysis (FLA) for the comparison of static optimization problem instances [14] and for the characterization of static problem classes [15,16] has been demonstrated in the past. Moreover, it has been used to help with algorithm selection and parameter tuning. However, for static optimization problems the usual approach is to determine (with or without FLA) a suitable algorithm and suitable parameters for the given problem class and use it solve new problems as well. Dynamic optimization problems (DOPs) [1] pose an additional challenge: The problems can and do change over time, and therefore also the suitability of optimization methods. In this paper we are analyzing the extent to which such dynamic changes are reflected in fitness landscape analysis measurements.

Dynamic optimization problems themselves have already been researched previously [1,4,10] and even their fitness landscape characteristics have been analyzed [17]. Mostly, the aspect of time-linkage, however, has not been explicitly studied [10]. Therefore, this paper will study a problem with time-linkage, i.e. where previous decision have an impact on the later development of the problem and, hence on the available choices later during the optimization. Many real-world applications exhibit similar characteristics and this paves the way for transfer of theoretical knowledge towards more practical examples.

© The Author(s), under exclusive license to Springer Nature Switzerland AG 2022
R. Moreno-Díaz et al. (Eds.): EUROCAST 2022, LNCS 13789, pp. 78–86, 2022.
https://doi.org/10.1007/978-3-031-25312-6_9

The Dynamic Vehicle Routing Problem (DVRP) is a well studied optimization problem [6] and makes for an excellent benchmark problem, as it is both flexible and simple [9]. Additionally, we have added an aspect of time linkage in our application scenario: The simulation assumes fixed locations that have to be serviced, and once serviced will need servicing again, drawing from a known but random distribution. In this case the mean time between failures (MTBF) is a tunable, than can be used to simulate scenarios of varying difficulties to study the effect on various fitness landscape measures. Time-linkage is achieved by linking subsequent service requirements to the previous service time, so that locations that have been serviced sooner, will also require re-servicing sooner, on average.

In this work we are aiming to establish a base-line of what can be seen with the help of generic fitness landscape analysis on these dynamic problems. In particular, we are going to examine the effect of difficulty on these measures as this has been an important intention for the design of many FLA measures. This information could in the future be used to give algorithms some more leverage for introspection and determine whether they are still well tuned to the current situation or need to change parameters or switch to another algorithm entirely.

2   State of the Art

2.1   Fitness Landscape Analysis

Fitness Landscape Analysis takes a very generic view on optimization problems. Only the bare minimum, that any optimization problem has to have, is used [5]. The fitness landscape $\mathcal{F}$ can be defined as a triple consisting of the following:

- solution space S
- fitness function, e.g. $f : S \to \mathbb{R}$
- neighborhood, e.g. $N : S \to \mathrm{P}(S)$ or distance, e.g. $d : S \times S \to \mathbb{R}$

Surprisingly, a large number of possible measurements can be taken with this simple formulation [15] and allow deep insights into problem classes and also allow comparison of instances. Several studies have been performed to completely understand the fitness landscape, most notably, e.g. in [18], and in [2] by elementary decomposition, or in [3] by exhaustively determining local optima and analyzing their structure. On the other hand, quick and even superficial analysis can also be a good source of information, supporting algorithm and parameter decisions by offering a glimpse into the landscape and its characteristics pertaining to optimization algorithms as detailed e.g. in [5] or [15]. These methods usually sample only a tiny fraction of the solution space, most often using trajectory based sampling in the form of different "walks". Best-known is the random walk that selects a random neighbor and provides an unbiased view of what a trajectory-based algorithm might observe. However, most algorithms do not "walk" randomly and therefore other walk types have been devised, such as an up-down walk, that alternatively maximizes towards a local maximum and

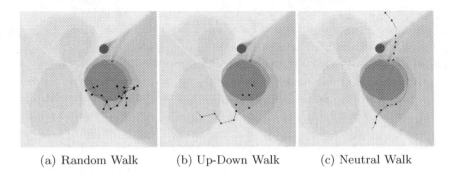

(a) Random Walk   (b) Up-Down Walk   (c) Neutral Walk

Fig. 1. Different walk types (based on [13])

then minimized towards a local minimum (ideally avoiding going back and forth) or a neutral walk that tries to stay within an equal or similar fitness range to estimate the size of (quasi) plateaus. Figure 1 illustrates some examples. Based on the obtained samples different measures have been defined. Mostly with the aim to quantify aspects of a problem's "difficulty". Most prominently, the autocorrelation [22] tries to capture the self-similarity of consecutive samples in a walk and is used to measure a trajectory's *ruggedness*. A more complex approach introduced in [20] describes several measures for a trajectory's entropy, or more informally, its "interestingness" by calculating different combinations of consecutive slope frequencies. Using other walk types other aspects can be described, such as, measures for a problem instance's basin size using up-down walk lengths or frequencies of plateaus using neutral walk lengths and neutral neighbor fractions, i.e. the average number of neighbors with the same (or similar) fitness.

2.2 Dynamic Vehicle Routing Problems

A dynamic optimization problem [1] is defined as a problem that can change over time. In its simplest interpretation, this can be seen as series of problems over time. It a more complex view, the previous optimization decisions can have an influence on future problem states (time-linkage). On the other hand, this series of problems often does have a correlation to previous problem states which can be exploited by algorithms that have a long-term state, such as e.g. a population.

In this work, we selected a well studied dynamic optimization problem, the Dynamic Vehicle Routing Problem (DVRP) [6] to test the applicability of fitness landscape analysis and elucidate the potential for dynamic control on optimization algorithms. In its simplest formulation, the Vehicle Routing Problem (VRP) [19], can be defined as the problem to find the shortest path for l vehicles, to service n locations $\{v_1, \ldots v_n\}$ starting from a depot location v_0, given a distance matrix D with driving times between all locations. Many other variants exist, e.g. adding capacity restrictions to the vehicles or a time window to the visit time at each location [7]. The Dynamic Vehicle Routing Problem (DVRP) as a simple extension can be seen as a series of VRPs where each VRP has a certain lifetime before being replaced with the next instance. In realistic scenarios these consecutive VRPs are often closely related differing, e.g. only in a single location that has been added or removed.

3   Materials and Methods

3.1   Dynamic Servicing of Power Grid Facilities

We chose to implement a variant of the uncapacitated DVRP, modeling the servicing of power grid facilities which adds an interesting aspect to DVRP that gives rise to time-linkage between consecutive states influenced by the choices of the algorithm and allows efficient pre-calculation of travel cost between locations: Fig. 2 shows the distribution of power grid facilities in Upper Austria. In our simulation, these locations are activated and re-activated based on their own normal distribution, each of these normal distributions is, in turn, parameterized by a discrete distribution to allow different characteristics between locations but giving rise to clustering as the parameters are drawn from a limited set of possibilities. The range of these parameters can be manually tuned to give a predictable amount of *difficulty*. The influence of difficulty on the distribution of failure probabilities is calculated as $\mu_{\mathrm{eff}} = \mu/\mathrm{difficulty}$, effectively elongating the times between failures for lower difficulties.

Fig. 2. Power grid facilities in Upper Austria

The sooner locations are re-activated, the harder it will be to service them in a timely manner or at all. Moreover, each location has a certain service time the vehicle needs to remain at rest. The quality is then defined as the cumulative waiting time between the need of service and the completion of service over all locations. The evaluation budget is determined by the driving time between locations. Only when a vehicle becomes available, the new situation has to be considered, so the time in between can be seen as the evaluation budget.

The interesting aspect arising here is that previous choices indirectly influence the future service demand, as the time between failures is relative to the previous service time. Moreover, the evaluation budget for the algorithm is also indirectly influenced by the past choices, depending on the driving times of all vehicles.

This scenario was selected as an artificial problem with real data to examine the propensities of FLA in the context of dynamic optimization problems. In particular, we were interested in knowing a-priori a relative difficulty of the scenarios and wanted to see whether this is reflected in the measurements and how it changes over time.

3.2   Experimental Setup

To obtain realistic data we retrieved power grid facilities from Open Street Map[1] using the Overpass API [11] for querying public data. We created several different scenarios with different distributions: once in Upper Austria (query shown in Listing 1) and once in and around Vienna. We limited the locations to the 200 largest facilities (by area) in the respective regions. We used a local instance of the Openrouteservice[2] to calculate the distance matrix using a snapshot of Open Street Maps provided by geofabrik.de[3]. The simulation was implemented inside HeuristicLab [21] and is described in more detail in a second publication in this series.

```
area[name="Oberösterreich"]->.a;
(way(area.a)[power=station];
 way(area.a)[power=substation];
 way(area.a)[power=generator];
 way(area.a)[power=plant]; );
```

Listing 1: Overpass Query for Power Grid Facilities in Upper Austria

After each change in the dynamic problem, a "snapshot" of the current state was created with the help of persistent data structures [12] to limit the required memory. These snapshots were then subjected to a whole array of fitness landscape analysis methods. The obtained measurements where then further analyzed and visualized using Jupyter and Pandas [8]. Here, an additional "smoothing" step was introduced, in particular to facilitate later clustering as the individual time series had noticeable variation due to different evaluation points in time. Therefore, each time series has been smoothed using neighbor regression with a fixed radius.

---

[1] https://openstreetmap.org.
[2] https://openrouteservice.org by HeiGIT.
[3] https://geofabrik.de.

4   Results and Analysis

While the snapshots of the runs with different difficulties occur at different times, we have plotted them on a homogeneous time scale which coincidentally also represents the current evaluation budget. Figure 3 shows the results of some very basic FLA measures. The horizontal axis contains the various difficulties while the vertical axis shows time and evaluation budget. Points in between the actual snapshots are simply filled in with the value of the previous snapshot. Furthermore, as stated earlier, the values have been smoothed along the vertical axis using a fixed-radius neighbor regression to account for small variations. It is important to note that this smoothing can also be applied during an active run as the required information is limited to data available in a single execution. As can be seen in Fig. 3, however, the classic auto correlation and its derived correlation length [22] show hardly any systematic difference over time and neither over varying difficulty levels.

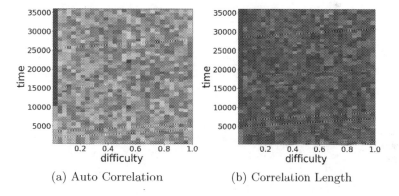

(a) Auto Correlation   (b) Correlation Length

Fig. 3. Basic FLA values

When turning to the analysis of neutrality and theoretic analysis the picture changes. Figure 4 shows several promising insights into the fitness landscape that could be obtained. Figure 4a shows the neutral neighbor fractions, i.e. the number of neighbors at any sample point that have the same fitness. This clearly shows the areas where optimization does hardly make any difference, which in this case indicates areas of little interest because they are "too easy" or not worth optimizing. On the other hand, Fig. 4b shows the quality delta at which the information content is maximized, or in other words at which scale "interesting" changes occur. Here interesting changes can only be observed at very large scale which can indicate that the problem becomes hard. Finally, Fig. 4c show the information content of random walks at minimum scale and, therefore, the "interestingness" for an optimization algorithm. Which coincidentally is also the area where an optimization makes most sense and has most potential. The area to the left is too easy to make a difference, while the area to the upper right is

too difficult, so new locations need servicing while all vehicles are still occupied
and the number of requests keeps increasing.

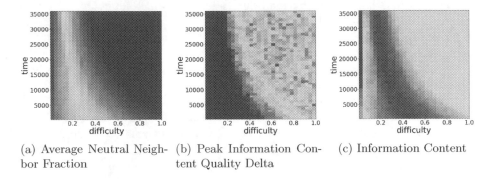

(a) Average Neutral Neigh- (b) Peak Information Con- (c) Information Content
bor Fraction   tent Quality Delta

Fig. 4. FLA values characterizing optimization potential

5   Conclusions and Future Work

While the level of these experiments is still very basic, knowing what to measure and being able to observe the development over time seem to be possible
given the right FLA techniques. It should be noted, however, that for different problems, other measures could be necessary as the problem characteristics
change. We could observe that with simple FLA measures we were able to see
boundaries between situations where optimization is appropriate. This seems a
promising perspective for further algorithm introspection which is important for
dynamic problems. It could enable an algorithm to make more informed decisions about evaluation budget, or an outcry for help if it is able to detect that
the problem is becoming increasingly more difficult and optimization alone will
not be able to handle the situation. In the future we will focus on more complex
dynamic effects such as varying failure probabilities over time and determining whether this effect remains observable by FLA. Moreover, a more complex
interplay between failures will be studied, e.g. one power outage could lead to
another. Finally, more advanced FLA measures can be applied such as measuring
isotropy or distribution of FLA values over the landscape.

References

1. Branke, J.: Evolutionary Optimization in Dynamic Environments. Springer, New
   York (2002). https://doi.org/10.1007/978-1-4615-0911-0
2. Chicano, F., Whitley, L.D., Alba, E.: A methodology to find the elementary landscape decomposition of combinatorial optimization problems. Evol. Comput. **19**(4),
   597–637 (2011)
3. Herrmann, S., Ochoa, G., Rothlauf, F.: PageRank centrality for performance prediction: the impact of the local optima network model. J. Heuristics **24**, 243–264
   (2018)

4. Jin, Y., Branke, J.: Evolutionary optimization in uncertain environments - a survey. IEEE Trans. Evol. Comput. **9**, 303–317 (2005)
5. Jones, T.: Evolutionary algorithms, fitness landscapes and search. Ph.D. thesis, University of New Mexico, Albuquerque, New Mexico (1995)
6. Khouadjia, M.R., Sarasola, B., Alba, E., Talbi, E.G., Jourdan, L.: Metaheuristics for dynamic vehicle routing. In: Alba, E., Nakib, A., Siarry, P. (eds.) Metaheuristics for Dynamic Optimization, vol. 433, pp. 265–289. Springer, Heidelberg (2013). https://doi.org/10.1007/978-3-642-30665-5_12
7. Liu, R., Jiang, Z.: A hybrid large-neighborhood search algorithm for the cumulative capacitated vehicle routing problem with time-window constraints. Appl. Soft Comput. **80**, 18–30 (2019)
8. McKinney, W.: Data structures for statistical computing in Python. In: van der Walt, S., Millman, J. (eds.) Proceedings of the 9th Python in Science Conference, pp. 56–61 (2010)
9. Morrison, R.: Designing Evolutionary Algorithms for Dynamic Environments. Springer, Heidelberg (2004). https://doi.org/10.1007/978-3-662-06560-0
10. Nguyen, T., Yang, S., Branke, J.: Evolutionary dynamic optimization: a survey of the state of the art. Swarm Evol. Comput. **6**, 1–24 (2012)
11. Olbricht, R.M.: Data retrieval for small spatial regions in OpenStreetMap. In: Jokar Arsanjani, J., Zipf, A., Mooney, P., Helbich, M. (eds.) OpenStreetMap in GIScience. LNGC, pp. 101–122. Springer, Cham (2015). https://doi.org/10.1007/978-3-319-14280-7_6
12. Pitzer, E., Affenzeller, M.: Facilitating evolutionary algorithm analysis with persistent data structures. In: Moreno-Díaz, R., Pichler, F., Quesada-Arencibia, A. (eds.) EUROCAST 2017. LNCS, vol. 10671, pp. 416–423. Springer, Cham (2018). https://doi.org/10.1007/978-3-319-74718-7_50
13. Pitzer, E., Affenzeller, M., Beham, A.: A closer look down the basins of attraction. In: UK Conference on Computational Intelligence (2010, in press)
14. Pitzer, E., Affenzeller, M., Beham, A., Wagner, S.: Comprehensive and automatic fitness landscape analysis using heuristiclab. In: Moreno-Díaz, R., Pichler, F., Quesada-Arencibia, A. (eds.) EUROCAST 2011. LNCS, vol. 6927, pp. 424–431. Springer, Heidelberg (2012). https://doi.org/10.1007/978-3-642-27549-4_54
15. Pitzer, E., Beham, A., Affenzeller, M.: Generic hardness estimation using fitness and parameter landscapes applied to the robust taboo search and the quadratic assignment problem. In: Proceedings of the Genetic and Evolutionary Computation Conference (GECCO 2012). ACM (2012)
16. Pitzer, E., Beham, A., Affenzeller, M.: Automatic algorithm selection for the quadratic assignment problem using fitness landscape analysis. In: Middendorf, M., Blum, C. (eds.) EvoCOP 2013. LNCS, vol. 7832, pp. 109–120. Springer, Heidelberg (2013). https://doi.org/10.1007/978-3-642-37198-1_10
17. Richter, H.: Dynamic fitness landscape analysis. In: Yang, S., Yao, X. (eds.) Evolutionary Computation for Dynamic Optimization Problems. Studies in Computational Intelligence, vol. 490, pp. 269–297. Springer, Heidelberg (2013). https://doi.org/10.1007/978-3-642-38416-5_11
18. Stadler, P., Wagner, G.: The algebraic theory of recombination spaces. Evol. Comput. **5**, 241–275 (1998)
19. Toth, P., Vigo, D.: The Vehicle Routing Problem. SIAM, Philadelphia (2002)
20. Vassilev, V.K., Fogarty, T.C., Miller, J.F.: Information characteristics and the structure of landscapes. Evol. Comput. **8**(1), 31–60 (2000)

21. Wagner, S., et al.: Architecture and design of the heuristiclab optimization environment. In: Klempous, R., Nikodem, J., Jacak, W., Chaczko, Z. (eds.) Advanced Methods and Applications in Computational Intelligence. Topics in Intelligent Engineering and Informatics, vol. 6, pp. 197–261. Springer, Heidelberg (2014). https://doi.org/10.1007/978-3-319-01436-4_10
22. Weinberger, E.: Correlated and uncorrelated fitness landscapes and how to tell the difference. Biol. Cybern. **63**(5), 325–336 (1990)

A Relative Value Function Based Learning Beam Search for the Longest Common Subsequence Problem

M. Huber$^{(\boxtimes)}$ and G. R. Raidl

Algorithms and Complexity Group, Institute of Logic and Computation, TU Wien,
Vienna, Austria
{mhuber,raidl}@ac.tuwien.ac.at

Abstract. Beam search (BS) is a well-known graph search algorithm frequently used to heuristically find good or near-optimal solutions to combinatorial optimization problems. Its most crucial component is a heuristic function that estimates the best achievable length-to-go from any state to a goal state. This function usually needs to be developed specifically for a problem at hand, which is a manual and time-consuming process. Building on previous work, we propose a Relative Value Function Based Learning Beam Search (RV-LBS) to automate this task at least partially by using a multilayer perceptron (MLP) as heuristic function, which is trained in a reinforcement learning manner on many randomly created problem instances. This MLP predicts the difference of the expected solution length from a given state to the expected average solution length of all states at a current BS level. To support the training of the MLP on the longest common subsequence (LCS) problem, a compact fixed-size encoding of the distribution of differences of remaining string lengths to the average string length at the current level is presented. Tests show that a MLP trained by RV-LBS on randomly created small-size problem instances is able to guide BS well also on larger established LCS benchmark instances. The obtained results are highly competitive to the state-of-the-art.

Keywords: Longest common subsequence problem · Beam search · Machine learning

1 Introduction

Beam search (BS) is a prominent incomplete tree search frequently applied to find heuristic solutions to hard combinatorial optimization problems, e.g., packing [1], and string-related problems [2,4]. Starting from an initial state r, BS traverses a state graph in a breadth-first-search manner seeking a best path from

This project is partially funded by the Doctoral Program "Vienna Graduate School on Computational Optimization", Austrian Science Foundation (FWF), grant W1260-N35.

r to a goal state t. To keep the computational effort within limits, BS selects at each level only up to β most promising states to pursue further and discards the others. The selected subset of states is called the *beam* and parameter β the *beam width*. To do this selection, each state v obtained at a level is usually evaluated by a function $f(v) = g(v) + h(v)$, where function $g(v)$ represents the length of the path from the root state to state v and $h(v)$, called the heuristic function, is an estimate of the best achievable length-to-go from state v to the goal state. The β states with the best values according to this evaluation then form the beam.

Clearly, the quality of the solution BS obtains in general depending fundamentally on the heuristic function h. This function is typically developed in a manual, highly problem-specific way, frequently involving many computational experiments and comparisons of different options.

In a previous work [4], we presented a *Learning Beam Search* (LBS) framework to automate this task at least partially by using a machine learning (ML) model as heuristic function, which is trained offline on a large number of representative randomly generated problem instances in a reinforcement learning manner to approximate the expected length-to-go from a state to the target state. This approach was investigated on the well-known longest common subsequence (LCS) problem and a constrained variant thereof and yielded new state-of-the-art results for some benchmark instances.

The overall approach is inspired by the way Silver et al. [7] mastered chess, shogi, and Go with AlphaZero. In their approach, a neural network is trained to predict the outcome of a game state, called *value*, as well as to provide a *policy* for the next action to perform, and this network is used within a Monte Carlo Tree Search as guidance. Training samples are obtained by means of self-play. Regarding literature related to the guidance of BS by a ML model, besides our work, we are only aware of the work by Negrinho et al. [6], who examined this topic purely from a theoretical point of view.

Despite the success of our former LBS, we also recognized some weaknesses: (1) For instances with different numbers of input strings m and input string lengths n, individual ML models need to be trained. (2) Absolute values of the lengths-to-go of the candidate states in one level are actually not that relevant, but rather the differences among them as they already determine an ordering and therefore the beam selection. Note that absolute values may be relatively large in comparison to the differences, and a ML model trained to predict the absolute values may therefore make stronger errors in respect to small differences.

In this work, we address these weaknesses of the former approach regarding the LCS problem by proposing the *Relative Value Function Based Learning Beam Search* (RV-LBS). In it, a MLP is trained to predict a relative value indicating the difference of the expected solution length from a given state represented by a feature vector to the expected average solution length from all nodes at the current level. To support the training of the MLP, we also provide different features as input, among which is a compact fixed-size encoding of the distribution of differences of remaining string lengths to the average string length at the current level, making the approach in principle independent of the number of strings m.

2   Longest Common Subsequence Problem

We define a string s as a finite sequence of symbols from a finite alphabet Σ. Each string that can be obtained from s by deleting zero or more symbols from that string without changing the order of the remaining symbols is called subsequence. A *common subsequence* of a set of m non-empty strings $S = \{s_1, \ldots, s_m\}$ is a subsequence that occurs in all of these strings. The longest common subsequence (LCS) problem aims at finding a common subsequence of maximum length for S. For example, the LCS of strings AGACT, GTAAC, and GTACT is GAC. The problem is well-studied and has several applications, for example, in computational biology, where it is used to detect similarities between DNA, RNA, or protein sequences in order to derive relationships. For a fixed number m of input strings the LCS problem is polynomially solvable by dynamic programming in time $O(n^m)$ [3], where n denotes the length of the longest input string, while for general m it is NP-hard [5]. Dynamic programming becomes rapidly impractical when m grows. Therefore, many approaches have been proposed to heuristically solve the general LCS problem. The current state-of-the-art heuristic approaches for large m and n are based on BS with a theoretically derived function EX that approximates the expected length of the result of random strings from a partial solution by Djukanovic et al. [2] and also on our LBS [4].

Notations. We denote the length of a string s by $|s|$, and the maximum input string length of a set of m non-empty strings S by n. The j-th letter of a string s is $s[j]$, where $j = 1, \ldots, |s|$. We use $s[j, j']$ to denote the substring of s starting with $s[j]$ and ending with $s[j']$ if $j \leq j'$ or the empty string ε otherwise. The number of occurrences of letter $a \in \Sigma$ in string s is $|s|_a$. To ensure an efficient "forward stepping" in the strings, we use the following data structure prepared in preprocessing. For each $i = 1, \ldots, m$, $j = 1, \ldots, |s_i|$, and $a \in \Sigma$, $succ[i, j, a]$ stores the minimal position j' such that $j' \geq j \wedge s_i[j'] = a$ or 0 if a does not occur in s_i from position j onward.

3   State Graph

In the context of the LCS problem, the state graph is a directed acyclic graph $G = (V, A)$ with nodes V and arcs A. Each state (node) $v \in V$ is represented by a *position vector* $p^v = (p_i^v)_{i=1,\ldots,m}$ with $p_i^v \in 1, \ldots, |s_i| + 1$, indicating the remaining relevant substrings $s_i[p_i^v, |s_i|]$, $i = 1, \ldots, m$ of the input strings. These substrings form a LCS subproblem instance $I(v)$ induced by state v. The root node $r \in V$ has position vector $p^r = (1, \ldots, 1)$, and thus, strings $s_i[p^r, |s_i|] = s_i$, $i = 1, \ldots, m$. An arc $(u, v) \in A$ refers to transitioning from state u to state v by appending a valid letter $a \in \Sigma$ to a partial solution, and thus, arc (u, v) is labeled by this letter, i.e., $\ell(u, v) = a$. Appending letter $a \in \Sigma$ to a partial solution at state u is only feasible if $succ[i, p_i^v, a] > 0$ for $i = 1, \ldots, m$, and yields in this case state v with $p_i^v = succ[i, p_i^v, a] + 1$, $i = 1, \ldots, m$. As with each arc always exactly one letter is appended to a partial solution, the length (cost) of each arc $(u, v) \in A$ is one. States for which no feasible letter exist that can be appended to a partial solution are jointly represented by the single terminal state $t \in V$ with $p^t = (|s_i| + 1)_{i=1,\ldots,m}$. As the objective of the LCS problem is to find a maximum length string, $g(v)$ corresponds to the number of arcs of the longest identified r–v path. Filtering and dominance checks are applied in our BS exactly as explained in [2].

4   Relative Value Function Based Learning Beam Search

As RV-LBS is build upon LBS and the main LBS procedure is similar, we first describe the LBS.

The main LBS procedure starts with a randomly initialized MLP (for structure details see [4]), and an initially empty replay buffer R, which is realized as a first-in first-out (FIFO) queue of maximum size ρ and will contain the training data. The input provided to the MLP is a *feature vector* composed of the *remaining string lengths* $q_i^v = |s_i| - p_i^v + 1$, $i = 1,\ldots,m$, sorted according to non-decreasing values to reduce symmetries, and the *minimum letter appearances* $o_a^v = \min_{i=1,\ldots,m} |s_i[p_i^v, |s_i|]|_a$, $a \in \Sigma$ derived from a given node v. After initialization, a certain number z of iterations is performed. In each iteration, a new independent random problem instance is created and a BS with training data generation is applied. If the buffer R contains at least γ samples, the heuristic function h represented by the MLP is (re-)trained with random mini-batches from R.

The BS framework with training data generation receives as input parameters a problem instance I, heuristic function h, beam width β, and the replay buffer R to which new samples will be added. Initially, the beam B contains just the root state r created for the problem instance I. An outer while-loop performs the BS level by level until the beam B becomes empty. In each iteration, each node in the beam B is expanded by considering all feasible letters for the states the nodes represent and the set of successor nodes V_{ext} is created. Dominance checks and filtering are applied to reduce V_{ext} to only meaningful nodes. From each node in $v \in V_{\text{ext}}$ a training sample is produced with a certain small probability. To obtain a training sample, the subproblem instance $I(v)$ to which state v corresponds is determined, and an independent *Nested Beam Search* (NBS) call is performed for this subproblem with beam width β. This NBS returns the target node t' of a longest identified path from node v onward, and thus $g(t')$ will typically be a better approximation to the real maximum path length than $h(v)$. State v and value $g(t')$ are therefore together added as training sample and respective label (target value) to the replay buffer.

Although the MLP in the above-mentioned LBS approach approximates the expected LCS length from some nodes relatively well, it may also make stronger errors with respect to small differences among the nodes in V_{ext} to be evaluated, as the absolute values may be relatively large in comparison to the differences. We address this issue with our RV-LBS by re-defining the approximation goal of the heuristic function $h(v)$ as the difference of the expected solution length from a given node represented by a feature vector to the expected average solution length from all successor nodes of the current beam. Formally:

$$h(v) \approx \text{LCS}_{\text{exp}}(v) - \frac{1}{|V_{\text{ext}}|} \sum_{v' \in V_{\text{ext}}} \text{LCS}_{\text{exp}}(v'), \tag{1}$$

where $\text{LCS}_{\text{exp}}(v)$ denotes the expected solution length from node v represented by its feature vector. By evaluating solutions in relation to other states at a current BS level we expect to obtain a more precise differentiation ranking of the states.

For obtaining training samples, we utilize NBS again to get a reasonable approximation of $\text{LCS}_{\text{exp}}(v)$ and therefore target values

$$t'_v = \text{NBS}_g(v) - \frac{1}{|V_{\text{ext}}|} \sum_{v' \in V_{\text{ext}}} \text{NBS}_g(v'), \tag{2}$$

where $\text{NBS}_g(v)$ corresponds to the length-to-go approximation obtained from NBS for the subproblem instance induced by node v. To reduce the computational effort, we select only one level of each BS run uniformly at random, from which training samples are created for all nodes in V_{ext}.

To remain consistentce to the approximation goal as well as to get rid of the absolute remaining string lengths we perform an input *feature encoding* at each BS level by exploiting the following observation:

If all remaining string lengths q_i^v, $i = 1, \ldots, m$ of the nodes $v \in V_{\text{ext}}$ are large, the reduction of all q_i^v by the same cut-off value $b \geq 0$ does usually not make a significant difference for the choice of which nodes should be further pursued in the BS and consequently also our approximation goal.

For small string lengths, however, it may still be important to consider absolute lengths. We therefore calculate this cut-off value in dependence of $\overline{q_{\text{ext}}}$ and a parameter λ as $b^{\text{sl}} = \max(0, \overline{q_{\text{ext}}} - \lambda |\Sigma|)$, where

$$\overline{q_{\text{ext}}} = \frac{1}{m |V_{\text{ext}}|} \sum_{i=1}^{m} \sum_{v \in V_{\text{ext}}} q_i^v \tag{3}$$

is the average length of all remaining input strings for all nodes in V_{ext}.

Similar to the way for determining the cut-off value for the remaining string lengths, we calculate a cut-off value for the minimum numbers of letter occurrences. Let

$$\overline{o_{\text{ext}}} = \frac{1}{|\Sigma| |V_{\text{ext}}|} \sum_{a \in \Sigma} \sum_{v \in V_{\text{ext}}} o_a^v \tag{4}$$

be the average number of minimum letter occurrences for all nodes in V_{ext} and all letters. The cut-off value in dependence of $\overline{o_{\text{ext}}}$ and the parameter λ is determined by $b^{\text{mlo}} = \max(0, \overline{o_{\text{ext}}} - \lambda)$. The ultimate input features we provide to the MLP model for calculating $h(v)$ are:

(i) $\hat{q}_i^v = q_i^v - b^{\text{sl}}$, $\quad \forall v \in V_{\text{ext}}$, $i = 1, \ldots, m$, $\quad$ (ii) b^{sl},

(iii) $\hat{o}_a^v = o_a^v - b^{\text{mlo}}$, $\quad \forall v \in V_{\text{ext}}$, $a \in \Sigma$, $\quad$ (iv) b^{mlo}, $\quad$ (v) m.

Note that each cut remaining string length vector $\hat{q}_i^v$ in (i) is sorted according to non-decreasing values to reduce symmetries.

Downsampling. In order to enable RV-LBS to deal with different numbers of input strings, we compress the information of a remaining string lengths vector $q = (q_1, \ldots, q_m)$ into a smaller vector of constant size $m' < m$. As the smallest and thus the first values have higher impact and q_1 in particular also represents an upper bound on the length of the LCS on its own we directly keep $q_1, \ldots, q_k$ as features $q_1', \ldots, q_k'$, for a small k. In our experiments, $k = 3$ turned out to be a reasonable choice. The remaining $q_{k+1}, \ldots, q_m$ are sampled down into $m' - k$ values $q_{k+1}', \ldots, m'$. For this purpose, the original values are binned into $m' - k$ bins, rounding to the respective bin is done by the nearest integer, and the arithmetic mean values of each bin is determined.

A pseudocode for the BS with training data generation for RV-LBS is shown in Algorithm 1. Remember that this BS is called by the main (RV-)LBS procedure for many random instances. As the framework structure for generating training samples is very similar to that of LBS, we only describe the differences. In line 8 each node $v \in V_{\text{ext}}$ is augmented with the set of features obtained by applying the feature encoding- and downsampling approach with parameters λ and m' to each node v in relation to V_{ext}. If the buffer is provided and the current level is determined to create training samples, then target values for each node $v \in V_{\text{ext}}$ are calculated by Equation (2) and added together with the corresponding nodes v as training samples to the replay buffer.

Algorithm 1. Beam Search with optional training data generation for RV-LBS

1: **Input:** problem inst. I, heuristic function h, beam width β
2: only for training data generation: replay buffer R
3: **Output:** best found target node t
4: $B \leftarrow \{r\}$ with r being a root node for problem instance I
5: $t \leftarrow$ none // so far best target node
6: **while** $B \neq \emptyset$ **do**
7:     $V_{\text{ext}} \leftarrow$ expand all nodes $v \in B$ by considering all valid letters
8:     augment each $v \in V_{\text{ext}}$ with set features determined from v in relation to V_{ext}
9:     update t if a terminal node v with a new largest $g(v)$ value is reached
10:    **if** R given $\wedge$ level selected **then** // generate training samples?
11:        **for** $v \in V_{\text{ext}}$ **do**
12:            $t_v' \leftarrow \text{NBS}_g(v)$ // NBS call
13:        **end for**
14:        $\bar{t}' \leftarrow \sum_{v \in V_{\text{ext}}} t_v'/|V_{\text{ext}}|$
15:        **for** $v \in V_{\text{ext}}$ **do**
16:            add training sample $(v, t_v' - \bar{t}')$ to R
17:        **end for**
18:    **end if**
19:    $B \leftarrow$ select (up to) β nodes with largest f-values from V_{exp}
20: **end while**
21: **return** t

5   Experimental Evaluation

The RV-LBS algorithm for the LCS problem was implemented in Julia 1.7 using the Flux package for the MLP. All tests were performed on a cluster of machines with AMD EPYC 7402 processor with 2.80 GHz in single-threaded mode with a memory limit of 32 GB per run. We applied the proposed algorithm on the benchmark set `virus`, which was already used in [2]. The set consists of single instances with number of input strings $m \in \{10, 15, 20, 25, 40, 60, 80, 100, 150, 200\}$ and the length of the input strings $n = 600$. The alphabet size $|\Sigma| = 4$ for all instances.

Preliminary tests of RV-LBS on randomly created problem instances of size $m \in \{10, 100\}$, $n = 100$, $|\Sigma| = 4$ led to the following configuration: no. of LBS iterations $z = 500000$, min. buffer size for learning $\gamma = 45000$, beam width $\beta = 50$, max. buffer size $\rho = 50000$, cut-off parameter $\lambda = 1$, downsampling parameter $m' = 7$. Figure 1 shows on the left-hand side the impact of the downsampling parameter m' on the LCS solution length and the right-hand side illustrates exemplary box plots for final LCS lengths obtained with different values for the cut-off parameter λ. LBS is used as baseline.

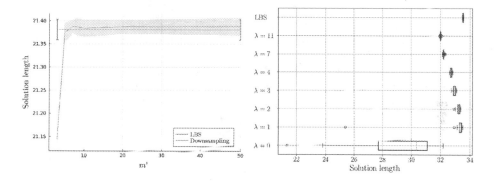

Fig. 1. Parameter calibration on randomly generated problem instances of size $n = 100$, $|\Sigma| = 4$, with $m = 100$ in the left and $m = 10$ in the right figure.

Finally, we trained 30 MLPs with RV-LBS, each on randomly generated problem instances of size $m = 10$, $n = 100$, $|\Sigma| = 4$, and used the best performing one thereafter in BS for solving the instances in the benchmark set `virus`. While all training with RV-LBS was done with $\beta = 50$, we followed [2] regarding test settings and applied BS on all benachmark instances with $\beta = 50$ to aim at low (computation) time and $\beta = 600$ to aim at high-quality solutions. Table 1 shows the obtained results. Column $|s_{RV-LBS}|$ and t_{RV-LBS} present the respective solution qualities and runtimes obtained by a BS with the trained MLP and column $|s_{lit-best}|$ and $t_{lit-best}$ those from the literature [2]. Although only small-size instances were used for the training of the MLP, a BS with the trained MLP yields competitive results on the benchmark instances to the state-of-the-art.

Table 1. LCS results on benchmark set `virus`.

Set	$|\Sigma|$	m	n	Low times ($\beta = 50$)				High-quality ($\beta = 600$)			
				$|s_{\text{RV−LBS}}|$	$t_{\text{RV−LBS}}$ [s]	$|s_{\text{lit-best}}|$	$t_{\text{lit−best}}$ [s]	$|s_{\text{RV−LBS}}|$	$t_{\text{RV−LBS}}$ [s]	$|s_{\text{lit-best}}|$	$t_{\text{lit−best}}$ [s]
Virus	4	10	600	222.0	0.19	225.0	0.04	222.0	3.60	227.0	2.88
Virus	4	15	600	194.0	0.33	201.0	0.23	200.0	3.58	205.0	2.24
Virus	4	20	600	184.0	0.20	188.0	0.18	189.0	3.50	192.0	2.69
Virus	4	25	600	191.0	0.25	191.0	0.06	194.0	4.08	194.0	2.20
Virus	4	40	600	167.0	0.26	167.0	0.17	169.0	4.08	170.0	2.24
Virus	4	60	600	161.0	0.30	163.0	0.04	163.0	4.15	166.0	2.38
Virus	4	80	600	156.0	0.32	158.0	0.19	160.0	4.59	163.0	2.70
Virus	4	100	600	153.0	0.39	156.0	0.19	156.0	5.48	158.0	0.90
Virus	4	150	600	152.0	0.50	154.0	0.06	155.0	6.90	156.0	0.66
Virus	4	200	600	151.0	0.63	153.0	0.09	153.0	7.90	155.0	1.22

6   Conclusions and Future Work

We presented a RV-LBS framework in which a MLP was trained to predict a relative value of a state and used this model thereafter in a BS. Moreover, we provided new features as input to the MLP to get rid of the absolute number of input strings and the string lengths. Training was done in a reinforcement learning manner by performing many BS runs on randomly created instances and calling a nested beam search to approximate the expected LCS length from a node. Although a MLP trained by RV-LBS on small-size instances was able to guide BS well on larger-size benchmark instances, we observed that the distribution of the encoded remaining string lengths at different BS levels obtained from larger-size instances has a larger standard deviation than smaller ones. Further normalization of features could be a promising direction.

References

1. Akeba, H., Hifib, M., Mhallah, R.: A beam search algorithm for the circular packing problem. Comput. Operat. Res. **36**(5), 1513–1528 (2009)
2. Djukanovic, M., Raidl, G.R., Blum, C.: A beam search for the longest common subsequence problem guided by a novel approximate expected length calculation. In: Nicosia, G., Pardalos, P., Umeton, R., Giuffrida, G., Sciacca, V. (eds.) LOD 2019. LNCS, vol. 11943, pp. 154–167. Springer, Cham (2019). https://doi.org/10.1007/978-3-030-37599-7_14
3. Gusfield, D.: Algorithms on Strings, Trees, and Sequences: Computer Science and Computational Biology. Cambridge University Press (1997)
4. Huber, M., Raidl, G.R.: Learning beam search: utilizing machine learning to guide beam search for solving combinatorial optimization problems. In: Nicosia, G., et al. (eds.) Machine Learning, Optimization, and Data Science. LNCS, vol. 13164, pp. 283–298. Springer International Publishing (2022). https://doi.org/10.1007/978-3-030-95470-3_22
5. Maier, D.: The complexity of some problems on subsequences and supersequences. J. ACM **25**(2), 322–336 (1978)

6. Negrinho, R., Gormley, M., Gordon, G.J.: Learning beam search policies via imitation learning. In: Bengio, S., et al. (eds.) Advances in Neural Information Processing Systems, vol. 31, pp. 10652–10661. Curran Associates, Inc. (2018)
7. Silver, D., et al.: A general reinforcement learning algorithm that masters chess, shogi, and Go through self-play. Science **362**(6419), 1140–1144 (2018)

Multi-day Container Drayage Problem with Active and Passive Vehicles

Ulrike Ritzinger$^{(\boxtimes)}$ ⓘ, Hannes Koller ⓘ, and Bin Hu ⓘ

AIT Austrian Institute of Technology GmbH Center for Energy,
Integrated Energy Systems, Giefinggasse 4, 1210 Vienna, Austria
{ulrike.ritzinger,hannes.koller,bin.hu}@ait.ac.at

Abstract. We consider a real-world container drayage problem, where containers are transported between an intermodal terminal, a container terminal and customer locations. Given a fleet of trucks and trailers, the goal is to efficiently utilize these resources to complete a number of customer orders. Orders consist of several tasks with time windows, such as picking up a container at the terminal, delivering it to a customer, and bringing the processed container back. While generating daily plans is already a complex task, this paper introduces novel approaches for generating solutions for a whole week. Hereby we exploit the possibility to re-arrange parts of the order within the week that are not time-critical. The results show that this approach is highly efficient to decrease the operational costs and to service more customer orders with the same amount of resources.

Keywords: Container drayage problem · Multi-day solution · Active and passive vehicles · Variable neighborhood search

1 Introduction

Road transportation is a popular mode for freight transportation. But considering the current transportation volume and the caused pollution due to emissions, the aim is to shift a part of it to rail freight and/or to cargo [2]. Intermodal freight transportation, where multiple modes of transport (truck, rail and ships) are used in combination is an attractive alternative for long distance trips (more than 700 km). The fact that the first and last mile of such long distance trips (so called *drayage operation* [7]) causes a substantial part of the total costs shows the importance of proper and efficient planning of the first and last mile. Furthermore, inefficient drayage operations can cause shipment delays, congestion at the terminals or customer locations, and an increase of carbon emission. These concerns further emphasize the importance of drayage operation optimization.

The container drayage problem (CDP) considers the transportation of containers between an intermodal terminal, a container terminal and customer locations. In this work, we investigate a real-world application considering a multi-day container drayage problem (MDCDP) in the area of Vienna. There

R. Moreno-Díaz et al. (Eds.): EUROCAST 2022, LNCS 13789, pp. 96–103, 2022.
https://doi.org/10.1007/978-3-031-25312-6_11

is a tri-modal transshipment center located at the port, where containers arrive and leave either by truck, train or ship and several carriers are responsible for the last-mile transport of the containers. The customer orders are distinguished into two categories: *import orders* and *export orders* as depicted in Fig. 1. Containers must be served at customer locations within a given time window and operational hours at the port and terminal must be met. The CDP belongs to the general class of pickup and delivery problems [11] which usually considers one resource. But in our case we have to deal with multiple resources such as trucks, drivers, trailers and containers. We model trucks and drivers as a single resource because each driver is assigned to his own truck. Trailers are a separate resource because at some customer locations it is allowed to uncouple the trailers while loading or unloading takes place. The containers are a separate resource as well and must meet the compatibility requirements between trailers and containers. Thus, we model our problem as an active-passive vehicle routing problem (VRP) [8,12], where passive vehicles refer to the trailers and active vehicles refer to the trucks, and these two must be synchronized. The given problem is static, thus all orders of one carrier are known in advance. Dynamic variants are considered in the literature as for example in [5,14], and a solution approach, which addresses the cooperation of multiple carriers is shown in [6]. Here, we consider the MDCDP and optimize the plan for several consecutive days (usually Monday to Friday). Existing literature on multi-day solution approaches consider only single resources problems [3,4].

In this work we deal with a rich set of constraints: the planning and synchronization of multiple resources, compatibility of trailers and containers, working time regulations, and the given time windows at the customer locations and the terminals. The aim is to improve the planning in order to reduce the operational costs of carriers and to increase the capacity of drayage operations within the planning horizon. The main contribution of this work is the extension of our previous CDP algorithm [10] to the MDCDP, so that several consecutive days are considered by solving the transitions between days efficiently.

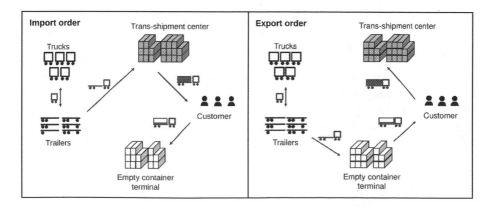

Fig. 1. Two categories of customer orders: *import orders* and *export orders*.

2   Problem Description

In the MDCDP a set of available trucks (together with their drivers) and a set of available trailers are given. The operating times of these two resources depend on the given driver regulations (daily and weekly regulations for working and driving times must be met). Each truck belongs to a given emission standard class and there exist several types of trailers with a different number of axes. All trucks and trailers are located at a single depot. Additionally, a set of orders is known before the start of the week. We consider two different order types: import order and export order as illustrated in Fig. 1. Each order consists of two parts, where each of them requests a container transport between two locations. An *import order* requires moving a full container from the port to the customer and later moving the emptied container from the customer to the container terminal. Whereas an *export order* initially moves an empty container from the container terminal to the customer where goods are loaded. The full container is then moved from the customer to the port. Another characteristic of an order is the given situation at the customer location. There are three possibilities for the (un-)loading process. The different pre- and post-conditions of tasks must be considered in the planning of truck routes, see Fig. 2:

- **Waiting:** The truck+trailer must wait at the customer location while the container is processed (e.g. space restrictions).
- **Uncoupling:** It is allowed to uncouple the trailer, which has the container loaded at the customer location. This allows leaving the truck to perform other tasks. After the (un-)loading process any truck is allowed to continue with the second task of the order.
- **Lifting:** Some customers have a crane which can lift the container from the trailer. Thus, the truck+trailer can leave the container at the customer's location and go on to perform other tasks. Another truck with a compatible trailer can be sent to pick up the container after (un-)loading has finished.

Each order has a given time window which defines when the service at the customer location must take place. Furthermore, the service time for all locations, the type of the loading process, the required time for (un-)loading, and the container type (important for trailer compatibility) is given.

Since the available resources are limited, not all orders of a week can be completed. However, maximizing the number of completed orders has top priority. Each truck has to execute a sequence of tasks, which is already challenging because of the given time windows, driver regulations, and different order types (arising pre- and post-conditions). But providing the sequence of tasks with feasible trailers is also a complex decision. This depends on the containers that have to be transported, the availability of trailers, and the toll costs on the highway. The latter depend on the emission class of the truck and the number of axes of the trailer. Finally, the overall goal is to optimize the routing of trucks and trailers such that all constraints are met, as many orders are completed as possible, and the total operational costs are minimized.

3   Solution Approaches

Here, we present our solution approaches for the given real-world MDCDP. First we describe the approach generating daily solutions and then we introduce the approach for solutions considering multiple consecutive days.

3.1   Solution Representation

In a feasible solution for the MDCDP, containers of the orders must be assigned to trailers respecting the compatibility and the availability of the trailer. Since trailers are passive vehicles, they must be assigned to available trucks. Thus, a solution consists of a set of truck routes and a set of trailer routes which must be synchronized. For an efficient solution representation we group the tasks of an order to so called *trailer nodes*. For example, in the case of *uncoupling* only the truck leaves and the trailer has to stay at the customer while the container is processed. Thus, the two tasks can be combined to one trailer node. For each trailer node we calculate the respecting time window, the service duration (including all service, loading and travel times), the trailer type, the start and end location. For the truck routes, we generate so called *truck nodes*, by splitting the nodes of the trailer routes whenever it is allowed for a truck to leave the trailer. Analogously, each truck node has a time window, a service duration, and a start and end location. Note, that required times to fulfill the pre- or post-conditions (e.g., time for decoupling) are included into the truck node as well.

3.2   Single Day Solution

A single-day solution of the CDP is generated by a combination of heuristics. First, the trailer routes are computed by a construction heuristic and all trailer nodes which cannot be feasibly inserted into a trailer route are stored on a so-called *dummy route*, i.e., the corresponding orders are unfulfilled. In order to obtain a complete solution, feasible truck routes are computed from the given trailer routes by the PILOT heuristic [13]. For further improvement of the solution we apply a variable neighborhood search algorithm (VNS) [9]. The key concept of our approach is the close interaction between the improving trailer

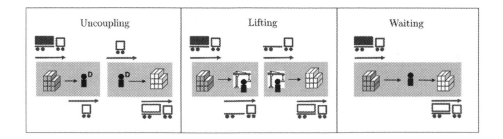

Fig. 2. Three possibilities of the (un-)loading process at the customer location.

routes and constructing the truck routes. All neighborhood structures operate on the trailer routes, whereas every move is evaluated by computing the corresponding truck routes using the PILOT heuristic. In the VNS, all neighborhood structures are traversed in a random order and with a *next improvement strategy*. Only better solutions are accepted, thus the move is only executed if the resulting truck solution has a better objective value than the current solution. The neighborhood structures, operators and settings for the VNS and PILOT heuristic are described in more detail in [10].

3.3   Multi-day Solution

Considering the problem over a multi-day horizon adds more flexibility and thus creates additional optimization potential. The most important new flexibility comes from the fact, that tasks at the transshipment center and at the empty container terminal are usually not as time-critical as tasks at customer locations. For example, returning an empty container to the container terminal does not strictly have to be accomplished on the same day as the corresponding import order. It can be postponed to the following day, where it can then be performed in combination with another task. This enables planning more efficient tours which either save operational costs or fulfill additional customer orders.

Figure 3 shows the two possibilities: If the first task of an order is allowed to process the day before the given customer's time window, it may be beneficial to already pick up the container on the previous day and place it at an intermediate facility (usually the depot) overnight. The remaining tasks are served on the next day. We call this a *pre-carriage* operation. The other possibility is named *post-carriage* operation. In this case, the last task of an order is allowed to process on the day after. In the solution, the according trailer nodes are added.

The **base algorithm (BA)** simply applies the VNS algorithm for every day of the week. To obtain a feasible weekly solution, the working and driving hours at the end of day are considered on the next day. But in order to exploit the advantage of combining tasks of orders between two consecutive days we introduce a **greedy algorithm (GA)**. The algorithm takes the solution of the BA and sequentially considers all transitions between two days. It iterates over all routes and examines for each route if *pre-carriage* or *post-carriage* opera-

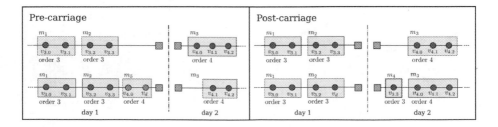

Fig. 3. Two possibilities how to combine trailer tasks of two consecutive days.

tions yield to an improvement of the objective value. If there is an improvement, the better one will be applied. Even tough the GA yields slightly better results, the disadvantage of this approach is its sequential/greedy nature and that it considers only tasks which are already inserted in the solution. Therefore we introduce a novel local search based algorithm, called **multi-day local search (MDLS)**. The MDLS also takes the BA as starting solution and selects a transition between two days randomly. Then it applies one of four defined operators (also selected randomly) in order to improve the solution. After a given number of non-improving iterations, the algorithm stops. The first two operators select two routes randomly (one of the current day and one of the next day) and apply either a *pre-carriage* or a *post-carriage* operation to the last and first task of the routes. Note, that in the case of two different trailer routes, the container compatibility of all tasks must be verified. The latter two operators insert unserved orders from the dummy route into the solution. They randomly select an order from the dummy route and try to insert it either as a *pre-carriage* or a *post-carriage* operation. Following a *next improvement strategy*, the accordingly generated trailer nodes are inserted into two randomly selected trailer routes.

4   Computational Experiments

We tested the algorithms (implemented in Java 8) on a set of instances based on real-world data. The fleet consists of 14 trucks of different emission classes (3, 4, 5, EEV), and 22 chassis of 8 different types with 1-3 axes. The costs per km of a truck is set to 1.2 € and the toll costs on Austrian highways depend on the emission class of the truck and the total number of axes [1]. While the resources are fixed, the instances vary in the number of orders (100–300 orders per week) and are generated randomly with the following parameters: The split of import and export orders is fifty-fifty. At 20% of the customer locations decoupling is not allowed and one-third of the customer locations have a crane for lifting the containers. Each order has a given time window of 30 min, a given container type which must meet the compatibility properties with the chassis, a loading time of 1, 2, or 3 h, and a given service time of 10 min at every location. Table 1 shows the average results of 15 instances per set of 10 runs per instance. For space reasons, the full results are in an external table[1].

The results show that our algorithms are able to find solutions with a high rate of served orders. Improvements are achieved when pre- or post-carriage operations are applied (GA and MDLS). The GA yields 1.3% improvement on average of total costs. Since the GA does not re-insert unfulfilled orders from the dummy route, no improvements w.r.t. served orders are possible. MDLS improves the results regarding the number of served orders, but the total costs may increase because of a higher mileage and longer working hours for the drivers. Given that the MDLS yields better results regarding the primary objective of maximizing the number of served requests, it clearly outperforms the other two approaches. Currently, a typical day of operation consists of 20-25 orders a day. Figure 4

---

[1] https://github.com/hkoller/ritzingeretal_mdcdp_2022.

Table 1. The average results for all approaches and instances: the percentage of served orders (ord^b), the truck costs per km ($cost^{km}$), the toll costs ($cost^t$), and the costs for drivers ($cost^d$) for the BA. Then, the improvements of costs (imp^{km}, imp^t, imp^d) and the improvement of total costs (imp^c) for the GA and the MDLS, and improvements for the percentage of served requests for the MDLS in (ord^m).

n	Base algorithm				Greedy algorithm				MDLS algorithm				
	ord^b	$cost^{km}$	$cost^t$	$cost^d$	imp^{km}	imp^t	imp^d	imp^c	ord^m	imp^{km}	imp^t	imp^d	imp^c
	[%]	[€]	[€]	[€]	[€]	[€]	[€]	[%]	[%]	[€]	[€]	[€]	[%]
100	100.0	10236.6	2553.7	4514.0	−150.3	−39.5	−12.1	1.2	100.0	−356.0	−99.6	−13.5	2.7
150	99.8	15371.9	3845.3	6620.5	−225.4	−63.2	−12.6	1.2	99.9	−580.7	−166.8	−15.4	3.0
200	95.7	17945.3	4505.7	8179.2	−316.6	−92.8	−20.6	1.4	96.8	−163.7	−50.3	140.3	0.2
250	86.4	18958.2	4710.4	9090.7	−312.0	−88.9	−21.7	1.3	87.1	−295.3	−113.4	126.3	0.8
300	78.1	19209.4	4789.5	9601.2	−324.7	−93.8	−32.5	1.3	78.7	−113.3	−74.2	165.8	0.0

shows an example plan: colored bars are the tasks performed by the trucks, light gray are the driving times between the locations and dark grey are waiting times. This output can be used for the planner either as a decision support or a quick estimation of resource utilization.

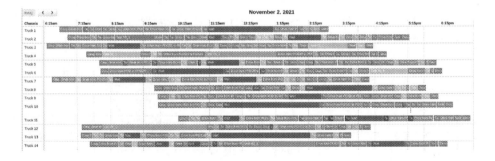

Fig. 4. Example for a daily plan with 14 trucks, 22 trailers, and 40 customer orders.

5 Conclusion

In this work, we investigated the MDCDP and presented three approaches for providing an efficient weekly solution for trucks and trailers. The primary goal was to serve as many customer orders as possible while efficiently utilizing the resources to minimize operational costs. We modeled our problem as an active-passive VRP and implemented a VNS algorithm for computing truck and trailer routes. Additionally, we presented novel approaches for generating solution for a whole week, resulting in larger instances with additional constraints on driver regulations. The results show that starting with the basic approach of considering the weekdays independently, the greedy algorithm is able to decrease the operational costs. This is achieved by incorporating *pre-carriage* and *post-carriage* operations that forwards or delays parts of the order that are not time-critical.

In addition, the MDLS algorithm is a powerful approach to increase the number of served orders with the same resources. In the future, we want to integrate the MDLS directly into the VNS algorithms to further improve the results.

Acknowledgements. This work has been partially funded by the BMK in the "Mobilität der Zukunft" program under grant number 867197 ("SmartCT").

References

1. ASFINAG Maut Service GmbH: Go-maut-tarife 2022 (2022). https://www.go-maut.at/wir-uber-uns/impressum/. 28 Apr 2022
2. BMK: Austria's 2030 mobility master plan - the new climate action framework for the transport sector: sustainable - resilient - digital (2021). https://www.bmk.gv.at/. Accessed 14 Nov 2021
3. Bruglieri, M., Mancini, S., Peruzzini, R., Pisacane, O.: The multi-period multi-trip container drayage problem with release and due dates. Comput. Oper. Res. **125**, 105102 (2021)
4. Clemente, M., Fanti, M.P., Nolich, M., Stecco, G., Ukovich, W.: Modelling and solving the multi-day container drayage problem. In: 2017 13th IEEE Conference on Automation Science and Engineering (CASE), pp. 231–236 (2017)
5. Escudero, A., Muñuzuri, J., Guadix, J., Arango, C.: Dynamic approach to solve the daily drayage problem with transit time uncertainty. Comput. Ind. **64**(2), 165–175 (2013)
6. Koller, H., et al.: Cooperative container trucking - system, model and solution. In: 2018 7th Transport Research Arena TRA, April 16–19, Vienna AT (2018)
7. Macharis, C., Bontekoning, Y.: Opportunities for or in intermodal freight transport rescarch: a review. Eur. J. Oper. Res. **153**(2), 400–416 (2004). management of the Future MCDA: Dynamic and Ethical Contributions
8. Meisel, F., Kopfer, H.: Synchronized routing of active and passive means of transport. OR Spectr. **36**, 297–322 (2014)
9. Mladenović, N., Hansen, P.: Variable neighborhood search. Comput. Oper. Res. **24**(11), 1097–1100 (1997)
10. Ritzinger, U., Hu, B., Koller, H., Dragaschnig, M.: Synchronizing trucks and trailers in a multiresource problem with variable neighborhood search. Transp. Res. Record **2610**(1), 28–34 (2017)
11. Ropke, S., Cordeau, J.F.: Branch and cut and price for the pickup and delivery problem with time windows. Transp. Sci. **43**(3), 267–286 (2009)
12. Tilk, C., Bianchessi, N., Drexl, M., Irnich, S., Meisel, F.: Branch-and-price-and-cut for the active-passive vehicle-routing problem. Transp. Sci. **52**(2), 300–319 (2018)
13. Voss, S., Fink, A., Duin, C.: Looking ahead with the pilot method. Ann. Oper. Res. **136**, 285–302 (2005)
14. Zhang, G., Smilowitz, K., Erera, A.: Dynamic planning for urban drayage operations. Transp. Res. Part E: Logist. Transp. Rev. **47**(5), 764–777 (2011)

On Discovering Optimal Trade-Offs When Introducing New Routes in Existing Multi-modal Public Transport Systems

Kate Han[1,2], Lee A. Christie[1,2], Alexandru-Ciprian Zăvoianu[1,2(✉)], and John McCall[1,2]

[1] School of Computing, Robert Gordon University, Aberdeen, Scotland, UK
{k.han,l.a.christie,c.zavoianu,j.mccall}@rgu.ac.uk
[2] National Subsea Centre, Aberdeen, Scotland, UK

Abstract. While self-driving technology is still being perfected, public transport authorities are increasingly interested in the ability to model and optimise the benefits of adding connected and autonomous vehicles (CAVs) to existing multi-modal transport systems. We propose a strategy that combines multi-objective evolutionary algorithms with macro-level mobility simulations based on publicly available data (i.e., Open Street Maps data sets and transit timetables) to automatically discover optimal cost-benefit trade-offs of introducing a new CAV-centred PT service to an existing transport system. The insightful results we obtained on a real-life case study aimed at improving the average commuting time in a district of the Leeds Metropolitan Area are very promising and indicative of our strategy's great potential to support efficient data-driven public transport planning.

Keywords: Multi-modal public transport · Macro-level mobility simulations · Reachability isochrones · Multi-objective evolutionary algorithms

1 Introduction and Motivation

In light of the urgent need to balance environmental and economic development goals, the establishment of sustainable low-carbon mobility systems has been identified as a key target by numerous local and regional transport authorities across the globe [4,13]. In most cases, the envisioned backbone of such environmentally friendly mobility policies is an effective multi-modal public transport (PT) system that can promote a shift away from private car use. However, the costs associated with introducing/expanding and operating PT should not be underestimated as they are often the main constraint when (re-)designing a PT system [14,15].

Unsurprisingly, the possibility to improve existing PT systems using zero-emission connected and autonomous vehicles (CAVs) has attracted the interest of

R. Moreno-Díaz et al. (Eds.): EUROCAST 2022, LNCS 13789, pp. 104–111, 2022.
https://doi.org/10.1007/978-3-031-25312-6_12

transport authorities and early test pilots indicate a relatively high level of public acceptance [2,12]. This is because, apart from the positive environmental impact, fleets of autonomous buses and shuttles are expected to have lower deployment costs (when compared with light rail alternatives) and lower operational costs (when compared with classical buses). Therefore, CAVs could bring important social benefits to local communities [3] as they are suitable for a niche deployment on routes where expected passenger volumes are too low to be economically viable otherwise.

Building on our initial findings regarding CAV route optimisation [9] and subsequent feedback from transport policy officers, in the present study, we demonstrate an effective way of combining macro-level mobility simulations with multi-objective evolutionary algorithms (MOEAs) [6] to discover realistic optimal trade-offs related to CAV-serviced PT routes.

2   Proposed Approach

Several graph-based data-driven techniques for simulating (at a macro level) the reachability provided by multi-modal transport systems have been proposed over the years [5,10,11]. As we aim to use PT accessibility assessments to inform fitness computations within MOEAs, simulation speed is highly critical and we developed a bespoke lightweight spatial-temporal modelling solution that delivers substantial efficiency by enabling the independent modelling of the static (i.e., roads, pathways, existing PT routes) and transient (i.e., candidate CAV route) parts of the PT network graph. Furthermore, our macro-mobility simulation is based on a reversible graph structure that facilitates the computation of both inbound and outbound reachability (isochrones) using Dijkstra's shortest path algorithm [8].

The abstract PT network graph used by our macro-level simulation is constructed by combining Open Street Maps (OSM) data sets (for road layout information) and General Transit Feed Specification (GTFS) files (for PT timetables). In instances where GPS coordinates do not line up exactly between the different data sources, small artificial edges are added to facilitate connections between OSM-based vertices and their nearest GTFS-based vertices.

For computing the average commuting time over a geographic area, we rely on a grid G of equidistant points with a spacing of 50m. For any grid point $g \in G$, $t_g(x)$ denotes the shortest multi-modal (baseline PT system, walking, new CAV service deployed on the route encoded in x) travel time to the target destination and is obtained by computing an inbound isochrone centred on the destination. Based on this, the optimal planning scenarios for CAV-serviced routes that we aim to investigate can be formally defined as multi-objective optimisation problems (MOOPs) that seek to:

$$\text{minimize } F(x) = (f_1(x), f_2(x), f_3(x))^T, \tag{1}$$

where $x \in [0,1]^d$ is a real-valued encoding of the d possible stops that can be included on the route and:

- $f_1(x)$ is the **average commuting time** (in seconds) to the target destination across the entire geographic study area:

$$f_1(x) = \frac{1}{|G|} \sum_{g \in G} t_g(x) \qquad (2)$$

- $f_2(x)$ indicates the **number of CAVs** required to operate the CAV service associated with route x and can be seen as a proxy for capital expenditure:

$$f_2(x) = n(x) \qquad (3)$$

- $f_3(x)$ indicates the minimal road **route length** (in meters) required by the layout of route x and can be seen as a proxy for operating expenses:

$$f_3(x) = length(x) \qquad (4)$$

It is important to note that the computation of $f_1(x)$ and $f_2(x)$ is based on characteristics of the CAV service associated with the route encoded in x. In order to define this service, we follow a 3-step process. Firstly, we create a list of the PT stops that will be serviced – i.e., all stops i for which $x_i \geq 0.5$. Secondly, the list of PT stops is sorted in a clockwise order based on the GPS coordinates of each stop[1]. Finally, a GTFS timetable of the new service is constructed subject to scenario constraints and parameters (e.g., operating times, desired frequency, travel speeds) and the number of vehicles required to deliver the service (i.e., $n(x)$) can be computed.

3   Exprimental Setup

Our real-life application scenario aims to support the West Yorkshire Combined Authority (WYCA) identify optimal routes for a CAV-centred approach to improve urban mobility in the North-West region of the Leeds Metropolitan Area (UK) illustrated in Fig. 1. This region contains 10 districts, is serviced by 1,015 PT stops for local and regional busses, and includes three multi-modal PT hubs centred on key railway stations.

The left hand plot from Fig. 1 indicates that the North of the region lacks high-frequency PT services. This is largely explained by a low population density that directly translates to reduced passenger volumes which in turn make high-frequency services unprofitable. Nevertheless, the presence of infrastructure (i.e., physical bus stops) is a strong argument for focusing our CAV-centred PT service case study on the northernmost district (i.e., Adel and Wharfedale). Another argument for singling out this area is that the current PT system was not explicitly designed to improve accessibility to other train stations apart from Leeds (Central) Station. By also providing easy access to the closest PT hub (i.e., Horsforth Station), a well-planned CAV-centred service could further stimulate low-carbon rail travel.

---

[1] The resulting order in which selected PT stops will be visited influences $length(x)$.

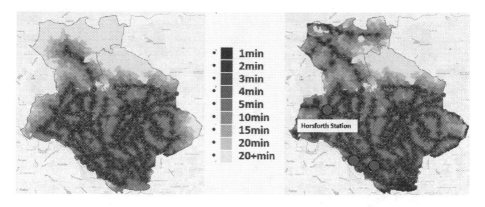

Fig. 1. Walking time to the 759 high-frequency PT stops (left) and to all 1,015 PT stops (right) in NW Leeds. Red marks indicate the 3 multi-modal PT hubs. (Color figure online)

Based on feedback from WYCA domain experts, the new CAV-centred service should: improve the average commuting time to Leeds Central Station by the 10 AM on a workday (i.e., this is the target destination for $f_1(x)$), be bi-directional and circular and have a minimal frequency of one bus every $10\,\text{min}^2$, include Horsforth Station, operate between 06:00 AM and 07:00 PM. When carrying out the macro-level simulations, we assume an average CAV speed of $32\,\text{km/h}$, a 30 s PT stop waiting time and an average walking speed of $5\,\text{km/h}$.

By fixing these macro-simulation constraints and parameters we obtained an instance of the the MOOP defined in Eqs. 1 to 4 that aims to find subsets of the $d = 121$ PT stops in Adel and Wharfedale that can be optimally serviced (by different CAV fleet sizes and along road routes of different lengths) in order to improve average area-wise commuting time[3]. We applied the well-known NSGA-II [7] multi-objective solver on this problem instance using literature recommended settings and a population size of 200. We set a budget of 50,000 fitness evaluation/optimisation and we carried out 10 independent runs. Initial populations were randomly generated, but we opted for a 95% chance of initialising PT stops as not selected – i.e., $0 \leq x_i < 0.5, \forall 1 \leq i \leq 121$.

4   Results and Interpretation

In Fig. 2a we present the Pareto front extracted from all the 500,000 candidate solutions explored during our experiments. While this result provides the most detailed view of existing trade-offs – e.g., the illustrated difference in average commuting time and route length between two solutions that require $n(x) = 6$

---

[2] During service hours, across any consecutive PT stops A, B, C along the service route, one should not wait more than 10 mins. in B for a CAV to either A or C.

[3] The baseline to improve is $f_1(x) = 3379s$ and its associated isochrone is presented in the top left subplot of Fig. 3.

CAVs –, the 2D Pareto projection from Fig. 2b focusing on $f_1(x)$ vs. $f_2(x)$ trade-offs highlights much better three important insights: the used constraints result in services that always require an even number of vehicles, using more than 8 CAVs only brings marginal improvements in terms of average commuting time, and services that require more than 14 CAVs can't improve average commuting time at all.

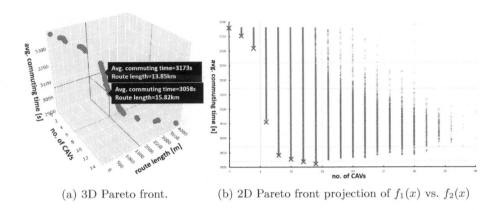

(a) 3D Pareto front.   (b) 2D Pareto front projection of $f_1(x)$ vs. $f_2(x)$

Fig. 2. Aggregated multi-objective optimisation results.

The isochrone plots from Fig. 3 focus on the 8 Pareto-optimal solutions from Fig. 2b as they provide details regarding the best improvements in average commuting time that can be achieved when introducing CAV-centred PT services requiring $n(x) = 2$ to 14 vehicles. The associate route shapes are also displayed and they indicate that: (i) at least 6 CAVs are needed to link the main poorly connected area, (ii) 8 CAVs can efficiently connect all problematic areas, (iii) the usage of 12 to 14 CAVs leads to the generation of a feeder service for the existing high-frequency PT route in the area (marked by dark green in the top left baseline isochrone plot from Fig. 3).

The subplots from Fig. 4 illustrate the best solutions requiring 8 vehicles that were discovered by the presently proposed approach and by human planners[4] (i.e., domain experts). While the expert solution has the advantage that it also improves accessibility in the adjacent district, with respect to the study area, it is Pareto-dominated by the automatically generated result which delivers an improvement in average commuting time of $\approx 13\%$ (compared to $\approx 5.5\%$) whilst also featuring a shorter route length.

---

[4] Best out of 3 attempts.

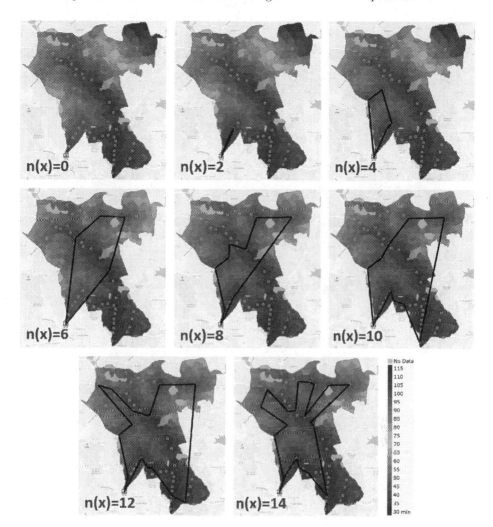

Fig. 3. Reachability isochrones of each $f_1(x)$ vs. $f_2(x)$ Pareto-optimal solution. The target of the commute is Leeds Central Station by 10 AM on a workday.

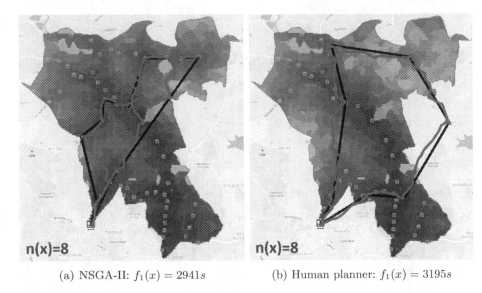

(a) NSGA-II: $f_1(x) = 2941s$ (b) Human planner: $f_1(x) = 3195s$

Fig. 4. Comparative routes (red = roads) and associated isochrones for the best solutions requiring $n(x) = 8$ CAVs. (Color figure online)

5   Conclusions and Future Work

In this paper, we have demonstrated an approach that combines multi-objective evolutionary algorithms and macro-level mobility simulations to support decision makers that wish to introduce a new route serviced by connected and autonomous vehicles (CAVs) to an existing public transport system (PT). Our approach facilitates the automatic discovery of optimal trade-offs related to improvements of the average commuting time across the analysed geographic area, investments required by the new route (i.e., capex), and cost associated with day-to-day route operation (i.e., opex).

As both the overall Pareto fronts and the individual routes we obtained have provided valuable insights to domain experts, we conclude that the proposed simulation↔optimisation strategy is a further step towards automating the production of realistic solutions that can tackle the increasingly complex challenges of public transport planning.

Moving forward, we plan to complement and refine our approach by investigating non-circular routes, experimenting with different route encodings and strategies for ordering selected PT stops, and improving our simulation assumptions using micro-mobility simulation results (e.g., obtained using the SUMO framework [1]).

Acknowledgments. The authors would like to acknowledge the support and constructive feedback provided by West Yorkshire Combined Authority transport policy officers.

This research was supported as part of ART-Forum, an Interreg project supported by the North Sea Programme of the European Regional Development Fund of the European Union.

References

1. Behrisch, M., Bieker, L., Erdmann, J., Krajzewicz, D.: SUMO-simulation of urban mobility: an overview. In: Proceedings of SIMUL 2011, The Third International Conference on Advances in System Simulation. ThinkMind (2011)
2. Bernhard, C., Oberfeld, D., Hoffmann, C., Weismüller, D., Hecht, H.: User acceptance of automated public transport: valence of an autonomous minibus experience. Transp. Res. Part F: Traffic Psychol. Behav. **70**, 109–123 (2020)
3. Borg, S.R., Lanng, D.B.: Automated busses to mobilize a suburb. In: The Royal Geographical Society (with IBG) Annual International Conference, Cardiff University (2018)
4. Brand, C., Anable, J., Tran, M.: Accelerating the transformation to a low carbon passenger transport system: the role of car purchase taxes, feebates, road taxes and scrappage incentives in the UK. Transp. Res. Part A: Policy Pract. **49**, 132–148 (2013)
5. Chondrogiannis, T., Nascimento, M.A., Bouros, P.: Relative reachability analysis as a tool for urban mobility planning: position paper. In: Proceedings of the 12th ACM SIGSPATIAL International Workshop on Computational Transportation Science, pp. 1–4 (2019)
6. Coello Coello, C., Lamont, G., Van Veldhuisen, D.: Evolutionary Algorithms for Solving Multi-Objective Problems. Genetic and Evolutionary Computation Series, Springer, New York (2007). https://doi.org/10.1007/978-0-387-36797-2
7. Deb, K., Pratap, A., Agarwal, S., Meyarivan, T.: A fast and elitist multiobjective genetic algorithm: NSGA-II. IEEE Trans. Evol. Comput. **6**(2), 182–197 (2002)
8. Dijkstra, E.W.: A note on two problems in connexion with graphs. Numerische mathematik **1**(1), 269–271 (1959)
9. Han, K., Christie, L.A., Zăvoianu, A.C., McCall, J.: Optimising the introduction of connected and autonomous vehicles in a public transport system using macro-level mobility simulations and evolutionary algorithms. In: Proceedings of the Genetic and Evolutionary Computation Conference Companion, pp. 315–316 (2021)
10. Innerebner, M., Böhlen, M., Gamper, J.: ISOGA: a system for geographical reachability analysis. In: Liang, S.H.L., Wang, X., Claramunt, C. (eds.) W2GIS 2013. LNCS, vol. 7820, pp. 180–189. Springer, Heidelberg (2013). https://doi.org/10.1007/978-3-642-37087-8_13
11. Kirchler, D.: Efficient routing on multi-modal transportation networks. Ph.D. thesis, Ecole Polytechnique X (2013)
12. Mouratidis, K., Serrano, V.C.: Autonomous buses: intentions to use, passenger experiences, and suggestions for improvement. Transp. Res. Part F: Traffic Psychol. Behav. **76**, 321–335 (2021)
13. Nakamura, K., Hayashi, Y.: Strategies and instruments for low-carbon urban transport: an international review on trends and effects. Transp. Policy **29**, 264–274 (2013)
14. Redman, L., Friman, M., Gärling, T., Hartig, T.: Quality attributes of public transport that attract car users: a research review. Transp. Policy **25**, 119–127 (2013)
15. Van Lierop, D., Badami, M.G., El-Geneidy, A.M.: What influences satisfaction and loyalty in public transport? a review of the literature. Transp. Rev. **38**(1), 52–72 (2018)

A Mathematical Model and GRASP for a Tourist Trip Design Problem

D. R. Santos-Peñate[1]([⊠]) [ID], J.A. Moreno-Pérez[2] [ID],
C.M. Campos Rodríguez[2] [ID], and R. Suárez-Vega[1] [ID]

[1] Dpto de Métodos Cuantitativos en Economía y Gestión/TIDES,
Universidad de Las Palmas de G.C., 35017 Las Palmas de Gran Canaria, Spain
{dr.santos,rafael.suarez}@ulpgc.es
[2] Instituto Universitario de Desarrollo Regional, Universidad de La Laguna,
San Cristóbal de La Laguna, Spain
{jamoreno,ccampos}@ull.edu.es

Abstract. We consider a tourist trip design problem with time windows and recommended occupancy levels at the points of interest. A 3-objective optimization model is formulated where the objectives are to maximize the total score and minimize total over occupancy and time gap. The multiobjective optimization problem is modeled as a mixed integer linear mathematical program. A GRASP is proposed to solve the problem.

Keywords: Tourist trip design problem · Occupancy · Mathematical programming · Multiobjective optimization · Heuristic

1 Introduction

In tourist routing problems and at certain points of interest (POIs) crowds of visitors can occur. The satisfaction experienced by the tourist and the image projected by the POI can be negatively impacted in such situations.

We study a problem of designing a tourist route with time windows where, in addition to maximizing tourist satisfaction and given recommended levels of occupancy at the POIs, the aim is to minimize both over occupancy and *lost time* in the route. Lost time occurs when the amount of time used to do the route is higher than the length of the route, defined as the minimum time required to do the route (travel time plus visit time in the best conditions). Lost time can be interpreted as waiting time. We formulate a mixed integer linear programming model to solve a TTDP with time windows and recommended occupancy levels for POIs.

The background to address the problem is the research that has been conducted on the Tourist Trip Design Problem (TTDP) found in the literature. Some surveys of the TTDP can be found in [4,6,7]. A review of algorithms proposed to solve the TTDP can be found in [3,6].

This research is partially financed by Gobierno de España, grant GOB-ESP2019-07, and Gobierno de Canarias, grant COVID-19-04.

R. Moreno-Díaz et al. (Eds.): EUROCAST 2022, LNCS 13789, pp. 112–120, 2022.
https://doi.org/10.1007/978-3-031-25312-6_13

The construction of algorithms that provide solutions in a very short time is especially relevant. Some articles in this respect include [1,2]. Proposals to balance the visits to the POIs and avoid congestion are presented in several works found in the literature [5,8] but, dislike our work, recommended occupancy levels for the POIs are not explicitly considered in the model.

2 Problem Statement and Mathematical Model

Consider a network $N(V,E)$ where $V = \{v_1, ..., v_n\}$ is the set of nodes and $E \subseteq V \times V$ is the set of edges. The travel time between nodes v_i and v_j is denoted $\bar{t}_{ij}$, it is the length of the shortest path (faster path) from v_i to v_j. A route is a sequence of nodes, $v_1, v_{i1}, ..., v_{ir}, v_n$, nodes v_1 and v_n are the initial and final points in the route. For a route, the initial and final points can be the same. Each node v_i, $1 < i < n$, is a point of interest (POI) and it has a score $s_i > 0$ which represents its attractiveness as a point to be visited. The POI v_i has opening and closing times L_i and U_i respectively, t_i is the duration of the visit and cap_i is the capacity of POI v_i. The recommended occupancy at POI v_i is c_i, it is desirable that at most c_i visitors enter point v_i at time τ ($c_i - \alpha_i \times cap_i$ where $0 \leq \alpha_i \leq 1$). And ρ_i is the contribution of a new visit to occupancy at POI v_i.

The length of a route, denoted T_r, is the summation of the total travel time and the total visit time. The time budget or available amount of time to do the route is T_{max}. Moreover, initial and final times, T_I and T_F, are given, so that the route should be done in the time interval $[T_I, T_F]$. We have that $T_{max} \leq T_F - T_I$, and τ_1, τ_n represent the starting route time and ending route time respectively. The lost time or gap is the difference between the duration of the route, given by T_r, and the time used to do it, $T_u - \tau_n - \tau_1$.

The function $\gamma_i(\tau)$ represents the occupancy level at instant τ. In order to define the occupancy function for a POI v_i in the interval $[L_i, U_i]$, we consider that the occupancy for a discrete set of instants $L = \bar{\tau}_1 < \bar{\tau}_2 <, ..., \bar{\tau}_q = U$ are known. The occupancy function is given by a piecewise linear function built from the known occupancy values.

We want to find the route from the initial point v_1 to the final point v_n which maximizes the total score, minimizes the total over occupancy, minimizes the lost time, and satisfies the time limitations constraints.

2.1 The Model

To state the model we use the following sets, and variables.

Index sets:

  $I = 1, ..., n$: index set corresponding to node set V.
  $I_1 = I \setminus \{1, n\}$: index set I excluding initial and final nodes in the route.
  $K = \{1, ..., q\}$: index set for time partition.

Variables:

$x_{ij} = 1$ if in the route we go from point v_i to point v_j, otherwise $x_{ij} = 0$.

τ_i: instant at which POI v_i is reached.

$\gamma_i(\tau)$: occupancy at v_i in time τ.

u_i: variables introduced in order to avoid subtours.

z_i: over occupancy at v_i.

a_{ik}: variable used to define the occupancy function, for v_i and $k \in K$.

y_{ik}: binary variable for the occupancy function, for v_i and $k = 1, ..., q - 1$.

Then the problem is stated as follows:

$$\min \left(- \sum_{(i,j) \in I_1 \times I} s_i x_{ij}, \sum_{i \in I_1} z_i, (\tau_n - \tau_1) - \sum_{i,j \in I} (t_i + t_{ij}) x_{ij} \right) \tag{1}$$

$$\sum_{j \neq 1} x_{1j} = 1 \qquad \sum_{i \neq n} x_{in} = 1 \tag{2}$$

$$\sum_{i \neq n} x_{ik} = \sum_{j \neq 1} x_{kj}, \qquad \forall k \neq 1, n \tag{3}$$

$$\sum_{i \neq n} x_{ik} \leq 1, \qquad \forall k \neq 1, n \tag{4}$$

$$\tau_n - \tau_1 \leq T_{max} \tag{5}$$

$$L_i \leq \tau_i \leq U_i, \qquad \forall i \neq 1, n \qquad T_I \leq \tau_i \leq T_F, \qquad \forall i \tag{6}$$

$$\tau_i + t_i + t_{ij} \leq \tau_j + M(1 - x_{ij}), \qquad \forall i, j \tag{7}$$

$$\tau_i = \sum_{k=1}^{q} a_{ik} \bar{\tau}_k, \forall i \tag{8}$$

$$a_{i1} \leq y_{i1}, \forall i \quad a_{ik} \leq y_{i,k-1} + y_{ik}, \forall i, k = 2, ..., q - 1 \quad a_{iq} \leq y_{i,q-1}, \forall i \tag{9}$$

$$\sum_{k=1}^{q} a_{ik} = 1, \forall i \quad \sum_{k=1}^{q-1} y_{ik} = 1; \forall i \quad \gamma_i = \sum_{k=1}^{q} a_{ik} \gamma_i(\bar{\tau}_k), \forall i \tag{10}$$

$$z_i \geq (-c_i + \gamma_i + \rho_i) - M\left(1 - \sum_{j \in I} x_{ij}\right), \forall i \neq 1, n \tag{11}$$

$$u_i - u_j \leq (n-1)(1 - x_{ij}) - 1, \qquad i, j \neq 1, i \neq j \tag{12}$$

$$2 \leq u_i \leq n, \qquad \forall i \neq 1 \tag{13}$$

$$\begin{aligned} &x_{ij} \in \{0, 1\}, \forall i, j; && 0 \leq z_i \leq cap_i - c_i, \forall i \neq 1, n, \\ &a_{ik} \geq 0, \forall i, k \in \{1, ..., q\}, && \gamma_i \geq 0, \forall i \\ &y_{ik} \in \{0, 1\}, \forall i, k \in \{1, ..., q - 1\}. && \end{aligned} \tag{14}$$

Algorithm 1. Construction phase

Set μ with $0 < \mu < 1$
$R = [1, n]$
$I_1(R) = \{1\}$
$\tau_1 = \tau_n = T_I$
$T_u = T_r = 0$
while *a new POI can be inserted* **do**
  $CL = \emptyset$
  for $i \in I_1 \setminus I_1(R)$ **do**
  | $CL = CL \cup \{(j(i), i)\}$
  end
  if $CL = \emptyset$ **then**
  | a new insertion is not possible. Break While
  end
  Set $p^* = \max\limits_{\{i : \exists (j, i) \in CL\}} p_i$
  Construct the Restricted Candidate List RCL as follows:
  $RCL = \left\{ (j, i) \in CL : p_i \geq \mu \times p^* \right\}$
  while *an insertion is not done and $RCL \neq \emptyset$* **do**
    Select at random an element (j, i) from RCL
    if *insertion of i is feasible* **then**
    | Update route R by insertion of i after node j, and
    | $I_1(R) = I_1(R) \cup \{i\}$
    else
    | $RCL = RCL \setminus \{(j, i)\}$
    end
  end
end
end

If the initial and final points coincide, in the formulation v_n represents node v_1 considered as the final point in the route. Expression (1) represents the objectives: maximizing the total score, minimizing over occupancy, and minimizing the lost time or gap. Constraints (2) indicate that v_1 and v_n are the initial and final points, respectively. Expression (3) represents the flow conservation conditions. Constraints (4) indicate that a POI is visited at most once. The time budget limitation is included in constraint (5) and the time windows restrictions are constraints (6). The conditions on the sequence of times are incorporated in expression (7). Constraints (8) to (10) define the occupancy function, and constraints (11) define z_i as the over occupancy at point v_i, with M representing a large number. Constraints (12) and (13) are included to avoid subtours. Expressions (14) are the domain constraints.

Algorithm 2. Insertion procedure

Insertion of node i between j and k in route R which includes arc (j, k)

$\tau_i' = \max\{\tau_j + t_j + \bar{t}_{ji}, L_i\}$, $\Delta T_u = (\tau_i' + t_i + \bar{t}_{ik}) - \tau_k$

$T_r' = T_r + t_i + \bar{t}_{ji} + \bar{t}_{ik} - \bar{t}_{jk}$, $T_u' = T_u + \Delta T_u$

if $T_r' > T_{max}$ **then**
| infeasible insertion. Stop Algorithm 2
end

for *k1 in route R* **do**
| **if** $\tau_{k1} \leq \tau_j$ **then**
| | $\tau_{k1}' = \tau_{k1}$
| **else**
| | $\tau_{k1}' = \tau_{k1} + \Delta T_u$
| | **if** $\tau_{k1}' > \min\{U_{k1}, T_F\}$ **then**
| | | infeasible insertion. Stop Algorithm 2
| | **end**
| **end**
end

Set R' the route R with insertion of i between j and k and times τ'

for *POI k1 from position(i) to position(n) in route R'* **do**
| Calculate $\gamma(\tau_{k1}') = \gamma_{k1}(\tau_{k1}') + \rho_{k1}$
| **if** $\gamma(\tau_{k1}') > c_{k1}$ **then**
| | calculate $\tau^* = \min\{\tau : \tau > \tau_{k1}' \text{ and } \gamma(\tau) = c_{k1}\}$
| | **if** $\tau^* > \min\{U_{k1}, T_F\}$ **then**
| | | infeasible insertion. Stop Algorithm 2
| | **end**
| | $\Delta T_u = \tau^* - \tau_{k1}'$
| | $\tau_{k1}' = \tau^*$
| | $T_u' = T_u' + \Delta T_u$
| | **for** *POI k2 from position(k1)+1 to position(n)* **do**
| | | $\tau_{k2}' = \tau_{k2}' + \Delta T_u$
| | | **if** $\tau_{k2}' > \min\{U_{k2}, T_F\}$ **then**
| | | | infeasible insertion. Stop Algorithm 2
| | | **end**
| | **end**
| **end**
end

insertion of i between j and k is feasible

$\tau_k = \tau_k', \forall k$, $T_r = T_r'$, $T_u = T_u'$

2.2 Problem Resolution

To solve the 3-objective optimization problem we apply a constraint method. We maximize the total score constrained to over occupancy and gap limitations and fix an upper bound for both over occupancy and the gap. The problem is

$$\max \sum_{(i,j) \in I_1 \times I} s_i x_{ij}$$
$$\text{subject to } (2) - (14), \ z_i \leq \zeta_i, \ (\tau_F - \tau_I) - \sum_{i,j}(t_i + t_{ij})x_{ij} \leq \beta \qquad (15)$$

where ζ_i is the highest over occupancy value admitted for POI i and β is the upper bound for the gap.

3   A Heuristic Algorithm to Solve the Problem

In this section we present a GRASP to solve the problem posed in Sect. 2. We consider that a solution to the problem can be represented by a list

$$R = [(v_1, \tau_1), (v_{i_1}, \tau_{i_1}), (v_{i_2}, \tau_{i_2}), ..., (v_{i_q}, \tau_{i_q}), (v_n, \tau_n)] \qquad (16)$$

where the nodes are pairwise different except perhaps the initial and final points which can be the same and $\tau_1 < \tau_{i_1} < \tau_{i_2} < ... < \tau_{i_q} < \tau_n$. We use notations (v_i, τ_i) and (i, τ_i) indistinctly. For simplicity, we can omit times in (16).

Algorithm 3. Pushing algorithm
Pushing operation for route
$R = [(v_1, \tau_1), (v_{i_1}, \tau_{i_1}), (v_{i_2}, \tau_{i_2}), ..., (v_{i_q}, \tau_{i_q}), (v_n, \tau_n)]$

---

for *position* $i = n - 1$ *to* $i = 2$ **do**
$\quad \delta = t_{i-1} + \bar{t}_{i-1,i}$
$\quad$ **if** $\tau_i - \tau_{i-1} > \delta$ **then**
$\quad\quad$ Calculate $\tau^* = \max\{\tau : \tau_{i-1} \leq \tau \leq \tau_i - \delta, \text{ and } \gamma_{i-1}(\tau) \leq c_{i-1}\}$
$\quad\quad \tau_{i-1} = \tau^*$
$\quad$ **end**
end

For the route R, we denote $I_1(R)$ the set made of the POIs in R and the initial node (v_1). That is, $I_1(R) = \{1, i_1, i_2, ..., i_q\}$. The score of the route is $S(R) = \sum_{i \in I_1(R)} s_i$ and the gap is $T_u - T_r = (\tau_n - \tau_1) - T_r$. For $i \in I_1 \setminus I_1(R)$ we define the unit profit of i for R as $p_i = \max_{j \in I_1(R)} \dfrac{s_i}{\Delta T_{ij}}$, where $\Delta T_{ij} = -\bar{t}_{jk} + \bar{t}_{ji} + \bar{t}_{ik} + t_i$ and j and k are consecutive points in the route R, that is, we go from node j to node k. Let $j(i) = \arg\{p_i\}$, which is equivalent to $j(i) = \arg\{\min_{j \in I_1(R)} \Delta T_{ij}\}$.

Fixed the parameter values, a route is built by application of a sequence of insertions. Once a route where no other POI can be inserted is built, an improvement procedure is applied. The construction phase is described in Algorithm 1. The insertion of a node in a route has to be done taking into account the occupancy limitations. If a node i is inserted between nodes j and k, times τ from node k to the final point of the route increase in at least ΔT_{ij} units. Due to occupancy limitations for some POIs, this increase could be bigger and the insertion could be unfeasible.

Algorithm 2 contains the insertion algorithm. For the initial and final points in the route, we consider $t_1 = 0$ and $U_n = T_F$. In order to avoid the algorithm stops too early giving very short routes, the gap time constraint in (15) is relaxed. The solution obtained is improved by application of several procedures such as the insertion of POIs at the end of the route, reduction of the gap with Algorithm 3, where a *pushing operation* is executed, and an exchange algorithm.

Table 1. Computational example

n	T_I (min)	T_F (min)	T_{max} (min)	Score	T_r (min)	T_u (min)	T_{visit} (min)	Gap (min)	$Time_1$ (s)	$Time_2$ (s)
25	600	900	240	130	234	234	150	0	0.01	0.05
				129	234	234	150	0	0.01	0.08
				96	218	218	150	0	0.01	0.05
50	600	900	240	167	212	212	150	0	0.02	0.14
				135	208	208	120	0	0.02	0.10
				185	214	214	120	0	0.02	0.10
75	600	900	240	166	204	204	150	0	0.03	0.19
				183	188	188	150	0	0.04	0.15
				177	196	196	120	0	0.04	0.16
100	600	900	240	161	208	208	120	0	0.06	0.21
				148	218	218	120	0	0.04	0.21
				164	224	224	180	0	0.05	0.24
25	600	1080	480	274	442	442	270	0	0.04	0.05
				276	468	468	300	0	0.04	0.04
				246	460	460	240	0	0.04	0.04
50	600	1080	480	312	432	432	300	0	0.08	0.11
				364	464	464	300	0	0.09	0.09
				370	452	452	300	0	0.12	0.08
75	600	1080	480	335	458	458	330	0	0.14	0.14
				334	396	437	300	41	0.13	0.14
				337	432	432	330	0	0.16	0.13
100	600	1080	480	352	392	433.33	300	41.33	0.21	0.19
				315	468	468	330	0	0.16	0.19
				378	466	466.82	390	0.82	0.21	0.19

4   Computational Example

We solve the TTDP for n POIs randomly generated in a $[0, 100] \times [0, 100]$ square, for $n = 25, 50, 75, 100$ and the metric L_1. For each n we generate three instances. The scores are randomly generated in $[1, 100]$. Times (in minutes) are $(T_I, T_F, T_{max}) = (600, 900, 240)$ and $(T_I, T_F, T_{max}) = (600, 1080, 420)$. The maximum capacity is 100 and $\alpha \in \{0.8, 0.9, 1\}$. The break instants in the occupancy function γ go from 540 to 1080 by steps of 60, and the values are integer numbers randomly generated between 30 and 100. The contribution value is $\rho = 1$ and $\beta = 45$. The initial and final points in the route are the same. The algorithm is executed 3 times for each of the 24 instances. Table 1 shows the best solution (route with maximum score) for each scenario $(n, T_I, T_F, T_{max}, instance)$. The last two columns contain the computational times (in seconds) required to find the solution, the time before the improvement and the time consumed by the improvement procedure, respectively. The rest of times presented in the table are given in minutes.

5   Conclusions

Tourist route design is an important issue in the tourist management field. The problem modelled in this paper is to find a tourist route taking into consideration time windows and occupancy constraints, and 3-objectives. We maximize the total score while the other two objectives are incorporated as constraints. We propose a GRASP to solve the problem heuristically and present some preliminary computational results. Although a deeper study of the problem and the proposed heuristic is required, with a more extensive computational analysis, the results obtained seem promising.

References

1. García, A., Vansteenwegen, P., Arbelaitz, O., Souffriau, W., Linaza, M.T.: Integrating public transportation in personalized electronic tourist guides. Comput. Oper. Res. **40**, 758–774 (2013)
2. Gavalas, D., Kasapakis, V., Konstantopoulos, C., Pantziou, G., Vathis, N., Zaroliagis, C.: The eCOMPASS multimodal tourist tour planner. Expert Syst. Appl. **42**(21), 7303–7316 (2015)
3. Gavalas, D., Konstantopoulos, C., Mastakas, K., Pantziou, G.: A survey of algorithmic approaches for solving tourist trip design problems. J. Heuristics **20**(3), 291–328 (2014)
4. Gunawan, A., Lau, H.C., Vansteenwegen, P.: Orienteering problem: a survey of recent variants, solution approaches and applications. EJOR **255**, 315–332 (2016)
5. Migliorini, S., Carra, D., Belusi, A.: Adaptative trip recommendation system: balancing travelers among POIs with MapReduce. In: 2018 IEEE International Congress on Big Data (BigData Congress), pp. 255–259. IEEE, (2018)
6. Ruiz-Meza, J., Montoya-Torres, J.R: A systematic literature review for the tourist trip design problem: Extensions, solution techniques and future research lines. Oper. Res. Perspect. **9**, 1–28 (2022)

7. Vansteenwegen, P., Souffriau, W., Van Oudheusden, D.: The orienteering problem: a survey. EJOR **209**, 1–10 (2011)
8. Wang, X., Leckie, C., Chan, J., Lim, K.H., Vaithianathan, T.: Improving Personalized Trip Recommendation by Avoiding Crowds. In: Proceedings ACM CIKM 2016, pp. 25–34. RMIT University, (2016)

A Large Neighborhood Search for Battery Swapping Station Location Planning for Electric Scooters

Thomas Jatschka[1(✉)], Matthias Rauscher[1], Bernhard Kreutzer[1],
Yusuke Okamoto[2], Hiroaki Kataoka[2], Tobias Rodemann[3],
and Günther R. Raidl[1]

[1] Institute of Logic and Computation, TU Wien, Vienna, Austria
{tjatschk,raidl}@ac.tuwien.ac.at,
{e1527543,e0927086}@student.tuwien.ac.at
[2] Honda R&D, Saitama, Japan
{yusuke_01_okamoto,hiroaki_kataoka}@jp.honda
[3] HRI Europe, Offenbach, Germany
tobias.rodemann@honda-ri.de

Abstract. We consider the Multi Objective Battery Swapping Station Location Problem (MOBSSLP) for planning the setup of new stations for exchanging depleted batteries of electric scooters with the aim of minimizing a three-part objective function while satisfying an expected amount of demand. Batteries returned at a station are charged and provided to customers again once they are full. We present a large neighborhood search (LNS) for solving MOBSSLP instances. The LNS makes use of a mixed integer linear program (MILP) to quickly find good solutions within a specified neighborhood. Multiple neighborhood structures given by pairs of destroy and repair operators are suggested. The proposed LNS is evaluated on instances generated by adapted approaches from the literature with up to 500 potential station locations and up to 1000 user trips. Solutions obtained from the LNS have on average ten to thirty percent better objective values on these instances than a state-of-the-art MILP solver.

Keywords: Facility location problem · Battery swapping stations · Mixed integer linear programming · Large neighborhood search

1 Introduction

A major hindrance for the large-scale adoption of electric vehicles (EVs) are the long battery recharging times. Especially for electric scooters, an attractive alternative to recharging depleted batteries is to replace them at dedicated stations.

This project was partially funded by Honda Research Institute Europe and Honda R&D Co., Ltd.

Once a depleted battery is returned to the station, the battery gets recharged and can then be made accessible to other customers again when fully charged.

In this work, we introduce the Multi Objective Battery Swapping Station Location Problem (MOBSSLP) and propose a large neighborhood search (LNS) [5] for solving it. In the MOBSSLP the task is to plan the setup of new stations for exchanging batteries of electric scooters or to extend existing stations with the aim of minimizing three different objectives combined in a linear fashion while satisfying an expected demand. The number of batteries a station can contain is decided by the number of battery modules assigned to the station. Battery swapping stations can be set up at dedicated locations which may differ in the maximum number of modules that can be added, opening times at which customers can exchange batteries, as well as setup and charging costs.

The MOBSSLP can be classified as a location-allocation problem [1] and is closely related to the capacitated multiple allocation fixed-charge facility location problem [2]. Moreover, the MOBSSLP is an adaption of the Multi-Period Battery Swapping Station Location Problem [3] in which customers are considered in an aggregated fashion, allowing better scalability to large numbers of customers and potential locations for stations.

For each of the three objectives of the MOBSSLP destroy and repair operators are presented. Additionally, we show how these operators can be effectively combined to consider all parts of the objective function together in the LNS. The LNS is implemented as a matheuristic [4] in which the repair operators make use of a mixed integer linear program (MILP).

We experimentally evaluate the proposed LNS on instances generated by adapted approaches from the literature. Results show that the LNS can outperform a general-purpose MILP solver, achieving solutions with objective values that are up to thirty percent smaller for instances with up to 500 potential station locations and up to 1000 user trips.

This work is based on parts on a master thesis [6], where more details and further results can be found.

2   Multi Objective Battery Swapping Station Location Problem

In the *Multi Objective Battery Swapping Station Location Problem* (MOBSSLP) the task is to plan the setup of stations for exchanging batteries of electric scooters or to extend already existing stations. We aim to minimize three different objectives combined in a linear fashion while satisfying a given demand in expectation. The three objectives are the setup cost for additional stations and extension modules, the cost for charging batteries, and the total duration of detours for users to exchange batteries. We consider a time horizon that is discretized into equally long consecutive time intervals represented by $\mathcal{T} = \{1, \ldots, t_{\max}\}$. Moreover, we assume the planning horizon to be cyclic, i.e., the predecessor of the first interval is the last one and the successor of the last one the first interval.

Battery swapping stations can be set up at any of n different locations $L = \{1, \ldots, n\}$. The costs for setting up a station at a location $l \in L$ with $s_l^{\mathrm{ini}} \in \mathbb{N}$

initial battery slots are given by $c_l \geq 0$. One can add up to $e_l^{\max} \in \mathbb{N}$ additional battery exchange (BEX) modules with capacity $s^{\mathrm{modul}} \in \mathbb{N}$ to the station at location l for a cost of $c_l^{\mathrm{modul}} \geq 0$ per module. Due to production limitations, the number of total BEX modules available is restricted, i.e., $z^{\mathrm{modules}} \in \mathbb{N}$ refers to the maximum number of available BEX modules. Customers can exchange batteries at l in the time intervals $T_l^{\mathrm{ex}} \subseteq T$. A battery that is returned to a station is recharged in the subsequent t^c time intervals. We distinguish between daytime and nighttime charging costs $c_l^{\mathrm{dch}} \geq 0$ and $c_l^{\mathrm{nch}} \geq 0$, respectively, per time interval with daytime referring to the set of time intervals $T^{\mathrm{dch}} \subseteq T$.

Customer travel demands are given for origin-destination (O/D) pairs Q; let $m = |Q|$ be the number of these O/D pairs and $w_q^l \geq 0$ be the expected detour time for the O/D pair $q \in Q$ when making a fastest possible detour to location $l \in L$ for exchanging batteries there. Let $\mathcal{I} \subset \mathbb{N}$ be the set of vehicle types we consider represented by the corresponding numbers of batteries. We assume that batteries are all of the same type. The expected number of users with vehicle type $i \in \mathcal{I}$ who need to change batteries on trip $q \in Q$ during a time interval $t \in T$ is denoted as d_{qi}^t.

A solution is primarily given by $x = (x_l)_{l \in L} \in \{0,1\}^n$ and $y = (y_l)_{l \in L}$ with $y_l \in \{0, \ldots, e_l^{\max}\}$, where $x_l = 1$ indicates that a swapping station is to be set up at location l and y_l is the corresponding number of additionally installed BEX modules. Additionally, let assignment variables a_{qli}^t denote the part of the expected demand of O/D pair $q \in Q$ w.r.t. vehicle type $i \in \mathcal{I}$ which we assign to a location $l \in L$ during time interval $t \in T_l^{\mathrm{ex}}$.

We express the MOBSSLP by the following MILP.

$$\min \alpha_{\mathrm{setup}} \sum_{l \in L} (c_l x_l + c_l^{\mathrm{modul}} y_l) +$$

$$\alpha_{\mathrm{charging}} \sum_{l \in L} \sum_{q \in Q} \sum_{i \in \mathcal{I}} \sum_{t \in T_l^{\mathrm{ex}}} c_{lt}^{\mathrm{ch}} \cdot i \cdot a_{qli}^t + \tag{1}$$

$$\alpha_{\mathrm{delay}} \sum_{l \in L} \sum_{q \in Q} w_q^l \cdot \sum_{t \in T_l^{\mathrm{ex}}} \sum_{i \in \mathcal{I}} a_{qli}^t$$

$$c_l^{\max} \cdot x_l \geq y_l \qquad\qquad \forall l \in L \quad (2)$$

$$\sum_{l \in L | t \in T_l^{\mathrm{ex}}} a_{qli}^t \leq d_{qi}^t \qquad\qquad \forall t \in T,\ i \in \mathcal{I},\ q \in Q \quad (3)$$

$$\sum_{t' \in T_l^{\mathrm{ch}}(t) \cup \{t\}} \sum_{q \in Q} \sum_{i \in \mathcal{I}} i \cdot a_{qli}^{t'} \leq s_l^{\mathrm{ini}} x_l + s^{\mathrm{modul}} y_l \qquad \forall l \in L,\ t \in T_l^{\mathrm{ex}} \quad (4)$$

$$\sum_{q \in Q} \sum_{l \in L} \sum_{t \in T_l^{\mathrm{ex}}} \sum_{i \in \mathcal{I}} i \cdot a_{qli}^t = \sum_{q \in Q} \sum_{t \in T_l^{\mathrm{ex}}} \sum_{i \in \mathcal{I}} d_{qi}^t \tag{5}$$

$$\sum_{l \in L | c_l > 0} x_l + \sum_{l \in L} y_l \leq z^{\mathrm{modules}} \tag{6}$$

$$x_l \in \{0,1\} \qquad\qquad \forall l \in L \quad (7)$$

$$y_l \in \{0, \ldots, e_l^{\max}\} \qquad\qquad \forall l \in L \quad (8)$$

$$0 \leq a_{qli}^t \leq \min\left(\frac{s_l^{\mathrm{ini}} + e_l^{\max} \cdot s^{\mathrm{modul}}}{i}, d_{qi}^t\right) \qquad \forall l \in L,\ t \in T_l^{\mathrm{ex}},\ i \in \mathcal{I},\ q \in Q \quad (9)$$

The objective function (1) is the linear combination of the different objectives with weights $\alpha_{\text{setup}} > 0$, $\alpha_{\text{charging}} > 0$ and $\alpha_{\text{delay}} > 0$. Inequalities (2) link variables x_l and y_l. Constraints (3) limit the amount of demand that can be assigned to the stations at each time interval. Inequalities (4) calculate the required capacity of a station at each location with $\mathcal{T}_l^{\text{ch}}(t)$ referring to the t^c subsequent time intervals succeeding $t \in \mathcal{T}$. Equality (5) ensures that all demand is satisfied. Constraint (6) restricts the total number of used BEX modules.

3   Large Neighborhood Search

In this section we present a large neighborhood search (LNS) based on the LNS presented in [3] for solving MBSSLP instances. Let (x, y, a) be a solution to the MOBSSLP. Moreover, let $L_0(x) \subseteq L$ be the set of locations with closed stations in x and $L_1(x) \subseteq L$ be the set of locations with open stations in x. In each iteration of the LNS, while the termination criterion has not yet been reached, a set of ν locations $L_{\text{destroy}} \subseteq L_1(x)$ is selected and destroyed by setting the number of modules to zero and un-allocating all associated demand. Afterwards, a repair procedure is applied to make the solution feasible again. For this purpose, first a set of ν' locations $L'_{\text{repair}} \subseteq L_0(x) \setminus L_{\text{destroy}}$ is selected. To generate the final repair set, we also add all locations in L_{destroy}, i.e. $L_{\text{repair}} = L'_{\text{repair}} \cup L_{\text{destroy}}$, to guarantee that we can always obtain a feasible solution. A solution is repaired w.r.t. a residual instance I of the original instance that only considers the demands of O/D pairs not assigned in the current partial solution. We first solve a relaxation of the MILP (1) to (9) in which we consider the y variables to be continuous. From the obtained solution which we denote with $(x, \tilde{y}, a)$ we then derive a feasible MOBSSLP solution as follows: First, all fractional $\tilde{y}$ values are rounded up, i.e., $y = (\lceil \tilde{y}_l \rceil)_{l \in L}$. Next, we greedily delete modules if the solution contains more than z_{modules} modules. Modules are deleted from locations $l \in L$ for which $\tilde{y}_l - \lfloor y_l \rfloor$ is the lowest. There may exist stations at locations $l \in L$ for which $s_l^{\text{ini}} < s^{\text{modul}}$. Removing such modules may result in an insufficient number of battery slots for satisfying the necessary demand. In such a case we iteratively close a random station and randomly add an equivalent number of modules to the remaining locations in the solution. This procedure is repeated until the total number of battery slots corresponds to the number of battery slots of the relaxed solution $(x, \tilde{y}, a)$. Finally, the demand is redistributed using the MILP (1)–(9) with the values of all x and y variables being fixed. For further details on how to repair a partial solution we refer to [6].

Next we present various selection operators for deciding which locations should be considered during the destroy and repair process. The operators are randomized greedy procedures that select locations according to their (potential) impact on the objective value w.r.t. to one or more objective goals. Moreover, locations are selected via tournament selection, i.e., to select one location a set of k (a strategy parameter) random candidate locations is first chosen randomly from $L_1(x)$ or $L_0(x)$, respectively. Then from this set the most promising candidate is chosen according to a criterion different for each selection operator and added to L_{destroy} or L'_{repair}, respectively. For the destroy selection schemes this procedure is repeated ν times and ν' times for repair selection schemes, where ν and ν' are further strategy parameters.

For each objective we define one destroy and one repair selection operator. For the *Construction-Based Destroy Operator* the most promising location l that is added to L_{destroy} in each iteration is the candidate for which $\delta_l^{\text{setup}} = \frac{c_l + c_l^{\text{modul}} y_l}{s_l^{\text{ini}} \mid s_l^{\text{modul}} y_l}$ is the highest. For the *Delay-Based Destroy Operator* the most promising candidate l is the location with highest δ_l^{delay} as specified by Eq. (10). Finally, for the *Delay-Based Charging Operator* the most promising candidate l is the location with highest δ_l^{ch} as specified by Eq. (11).

$$\delta_l^{\text{delay}} = \frac{\sum\limits_{q \in Q} \left(w_q^l \sum\limits_{i \in \mathcal{I}} \sum\limits_{t \in T_l^{\text{ex}}} a_{qli}^t \right)}{\sum\limits_{q \in Q} \sum\limits_{i \in \mathcal{I}} \sum\limits_{l \in T_l^{\text{ex}}} a_{qli}^t} \tag{10}$$

$$\delta_l^{\text{ch}} = \frac{\sum\limits_{q \in Q} \sum\limits_{i \in \mathcal{I}} \sum\limits_{t \in T_l^{\text{ex}}} c_{lt}^{\text{ch}} \cdot i \cdot a_{qli}^t}{\sum\limits_{q \in Q} \sum\limits_{i \in \mathcal{I}} \sum\limits_{l \in T_l^{\text{ex}}} i \cdot a_{qli}^t} \tag{11}$$

The repair selection operators select promising candidates in a similar way. More specifically, the *Construction-Based Repair Operator* chooses the location l for which ρ_l^{setup}, given by Eq. (12), is the lowest. The *Delay-Based Repair Operator* selects the candidate for which ρ_l^{delay}, given by Eq. (14), is the lowest. Finally, the *Charging-Based Repair Operator* selects the candidate for which ρ_l^{ch}, given by Eq. (15), is the lowest.

$$\rho_l^{\text{setup}} = \frac{c_l + c_l^{\text{modul}} \min(y_{\text{avg}}, e_l^{\text{max}})}{s_l^{\text{ini}} + s_l^{\text{modul}} \min(y_{\text{avg}}, e_l^{\text{max}})} \tag{12}$$

$$y_{\text{avg}} = \frac{\sum\limits_{l \in L_{\text{destroy}}} y_l}{\nu} \tag{13}$$

$$\rho_l^{\text{delay}} = \frac{\sum\limits_{q \in Q} \left(w_q^l \sum\limits_{i \in \mathcal{I}} \sum\limits_{t \in T_l^{\text{ex}}} d'^t_{qi} \right)}{\sum\limits_{q \in Q} \sum\limits_{i \in \mathcal{I}} \sum\limits_{t \in T_l^{\text{ex}}} d'^t_{qi}} \tag{14}$$

$$\rho_l^{\text{ch}} = \frac{\sum\limits_{q \in Q} \sum\limits_{i \in \mathcal{I}} \sum\limits_{t \in T_l^{\text{ex}}} c_{lt}^{\text{ch}} \cdot i \cdot d'^t_{qi}}{\sum\limits_{q \in Q} \sum\limits_{i \in \mathcal{I}} \sum\limits_{t \in T_l^{\text{ex}}} i \cdot d'^t_{qi}} \tag{15}$$

For the *Delay-Based Repair Operator* and the *Charging-Based Repair Operator* we also estimate which demands are potentially covered by a selected candidate l and do not consider these demands in the remaining steps of the selection procedure anymore. For further details we refer to [6].

The presented selection operators can also be combined to select locations according to multiple objective goals. In the most straight forward way, in each iteration of the LNS the repair and destroy operators are selected randomly, choosing from the above presented selection operators. We refer to these operators as *Mixed Destroy Operator* and *Mixed Repair Operator*, respectively.

In a more sophisticated way, the *Weighted Sum Destroy Operator* chooses the candidate l with the highest impact on the objective function, i.e., the largest value $\alpha_{\text{setup}} \cdot \delta_l^{\text{setup}} + \alpha_{\text{delay}} \cdot \delta_l^{\text{delay}} + \alpha_{\text{charging}} \cdot \delta_l^{\text{ch}}$.

Similarly, the *Weighted Sum Repair Operator* selects the candidate location l for which the estimated impact on the objective function is the lowest represented by the value $\alpha_{\text{setup}} \cdot \rho_l^{\text{setup}} + \alpha_{\text{delay}} \cdot \rho_l^{\text{delay}} + \alpha_{\text{charging}} \cdot \rho_l^{\text{ch}}$. Finally, the *Objective-Based Repair Operator* uses the same procedure as the delay- and charging-based repair operator to prevent already covered demand from being considered in future iterations of the selection procedure.

4   Computational Results

We test our LNS on artificial instances with properties chosen based on information provided by Honda R&D. We created six groups of instances identified by their number of station locations n and number of O/D pairs m as (n, m). For each subgroup we generate 30 instances. For more details on how the instances were generated, see [6]. On each instance, we test three different alpha configurations which differ in the α_{delay} parameter, i.e. $\alpha_{\text{charging}} = 0.01$, $\alpha_{\text{setup}} = 0.01$, and $\alpha_{\text{delay}} \in \{0.1, 1, 10\}$. Therefore, in the remainder of this section each configuration will be identified only by α_{delay}. For the parameters of the LNS we determined $\nu = \nu' = 5$ and $k = 5$ in preliminary experiments. For the procedure for constructing an initial solution for the LNS we refer to [6].

Table 1. Average optimality gaps, for different α_{delay} for each selection strategy.

	gap (%)								
	$\alpha_{\text{delay}} = 0.1$			$\alpha_{\text{delay}} = 1.0$			$\alpha_{\text{delay}} = 10.0$		
(n, m)	*constr*	*delay*	*charging*	*constr*	*delay*	*charging*	*constr*	*delay*	*charging*
(50, 100)	2.73	3.01	**2.61**	6.54	**5.60**	5.76	12.77	**10.94**	12.05
(100, 200)	2.77	**1.97**	2.80	6.69	**5.61**	6.81	22.41	**18.27**	25.82
(200, 400)	**4.49**	5.72	5.49	**17.43**	18.65	21.31	41.89	**36.78**	47.47
(300, 600)	**5.13**	6.88	6.31	**28.41**	29.13	32.32	62.37	**59.42**	67.99
(400, 800)	**6.50**	8.62	8.39	**33.75**	33.96	36.63	71.48	**70.21**	74.49
(500, 1000)	**7.98**	10.77	10.68	**36.16**	37.03	39.99	74.80	**74.25**	77.59

	gap (%)					
	$\alpha_{\text{delay}} = 0.1$		$\alpha_{\text{delay}} = 1.0$		$\alpha_{\text{delay}} = 10.0$	
(n, m)	*mixed*	*wsum*	*mixed*	*wsum*	*mixed*	*wsum*
(50, 100)	2.51	**2.42**	**5.84**	6.50	**8.87**	11.87
(100, 200)	2.72	**2.60**	**5.84**	6.06	**17.71**	20.15
(200, 400)	**3.34**	4.75	17.49	**17.30**	**38.52**	41.39
(300, 600)	5.07	**4.84**	**27.35**	28.35	**60.98**	62.21
(400, 800)	**6.59**	6.84	32.79	**32.78**	**70.15**	70.33
(500, 1000)	**8.16**	8.22	**36.30**	36.60	74 65	**74.06**

The proposed algorithms were implemented in Julia[1] 1.6.1 using the JuMP package[2] and Gurobi[3] 9.1 as underlying MILP solver. All test runs have been executed on an Intel Xeon E5-2640 v4 2.40 GHz machine in single-threaded mode with a global time limit of one hour per run.

We investigate five different strategies for selecting the locations considered in the destroy and repair procedures: *constr*, *delay* and *charging* use only the construction-, delay- and charging-based destroy and repair operators, respectively. Moreover, *mixed* and *wsum* use only the mixed selection operators and weighted sum selection operators, respectively. We evaluate the quality of solutions in terms of optimality gaps to the best lower bounds obtained by trying to solve the MILP given by Eqs (1)–(9) within the one hour time limit. Table 1 shows average optimality gaps, for all considered α_{delay} configurations. We can see that optimality gaps generally increase with growing instance size and growing α_{delay} value for all five strategies. As expected, we can observe that *delay* performs better, the higher α_{delay} is, i.e., as minimizing the delay becomes more important LNS operators destroying and repairing stations based on their

---

[1] https://julialang.org/.
[2] https://jump.dev/JuMP.jl/stable/.
[3] https://www.gurobi.com/.

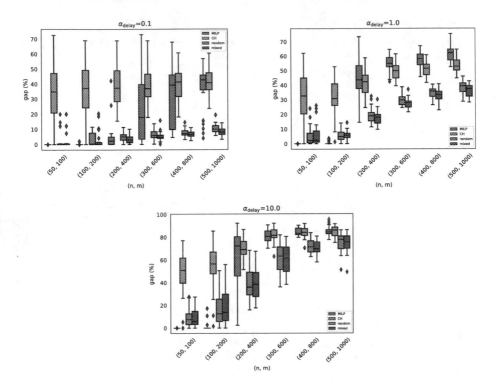

Fig. 1. Final optimality gaps when solving the MOBSSLP with different approaches.

induced delay produce better results. For lower values of α_{delay} *constr* shows the best performance. Regarding the multi-objective strategies, one can see that for $\alpha_{\text{delay}} = 0.1$ and $\alpha_{\text{delay}} = 1.0$ *mixed* is slightly more favorable. For $\alpha_{\text{delay}} = 10.0$ the difference becomes more evident, as *mixed* achieves up to 3% better results. In general the performance of the multi-objective strategies is comparable to the performance of the best single-objective strategy for each α_{delay}. Therefore, as expected, multi-objective strategies are more robust to changes of the weights of the objective function.

Finally, Fig. 1 compares the LNS with selection strategy *mixed* to other approaches. In particular, we compare the obtained results to those of an LNS using a uniform random selection strategy, denoted by *random*, to solutions generated by the initial construction heuristic, denoted by CH, as well as solutions obtained by Gurobi within one hour w.r.t. the MILP (1)–(9), denoted by MILP. Starting from (200, 400) our LNS approach is able to consistently achieve superior results with up to 29% lower objective values than those obtained by the MILP approach. Moreover, we can see that the LNS strongly improves the initial solution obtained by the construction heuristic. Finally, we performed one-sided Wilcoxon signed-rank tests between the solutions obtained by *mixed* and the solutions obtained by *random*. For almost all instance groups and values of α_{delay}, *mixed* achieved significantly better results than *random* within a 95% confidence interval.

5   Conclusion and Future Work

We considered the *Multi Objective Battery Swapping Station Location Problem* (MOBSSLP) and presented a large neighborhood search (LNS) using mixed integer linear programming (MILP) for repairing solutions. We proposed different strategies for selecting the locations for the destroy and repair procedure of the LNS. For larger instances our evaluation shows that our LNS far surpasses the performance of a state-of-the-art MILP solver in terms of solution quality. We have further seen that combining all single objective selection strategies results in a strategy more robust to changes in the weighting of the objective function.

For future work it seems promising to extend the approach to an Adaptive Large Neighborhood Search (ALNS) which then dynamically selects the most promising selection operator in each iteration. Moreover, it could also be interesting to research adapted variants of the MOBSSLP, considering aspects such as limited charging times or an overall budget for building stations and modules.

References

1. Boloori Arabani, A., Farahani, R.Z.: Facility location dynamics: an overview of classifications and applications. Comput. Ind. Eng. **62**(1), 408–420 (2012)
2. Farahani, R.Z., Hekmatfar, M.: Facility location: concepts, models, algorithms and case studies. Springer, Contributions to Management Science (2009)
3. Jatschka, T., Oberweger, F.F., Rodemann, T., Raidl, G.R.: Distributing battery swapping stations for electric scooters in an urban area. In: Olenev, N., Evtushenko, Y., Khachay, M., Malkova, V. (eds.) OPTIMA 2020. LNCS, vol. 12422, pp. 150–165. Springer, Cham (2020). https://doi.org/10.1007/978-3-030-62867-3_12
4. Maniezzo, V., Stützle, T., Voß, S.: Matheuristics, 1st edn. Annals of Information Systems, Springer Nature (2010)
5. Pisinger, D., Ropke, S.: Large neighborhood search. In: Gendreau, M., Potvin, J.Y. (eds.) Handbook of Metaheuristics, International Series in Operations Research, Management Science, vol. 146, pp. 399–419. Springer, Boston (2010). https://doi.org/10.1007/978-1-4419-1665-5_13
6. Rauscher, M.: A Matheuristic for Battery Exchange Station Location Planning for Electric Scooters. Master's thesis, TU Wien, Vienna, Austria (2022). https://catalogplus.tuwien.at/permalink/f/qknpf/UTW_alma71122610460003336

Shapley Value Based Variable Interaction Networks for Data Stream Analysis

Jan Zenisek[1,2(✉)], Sebastian Dorl[1], Dominik Falkner[3], Lukas Gaisberger[1], Stephan Winkler[1,2], and Michael Affenzeller[1,2]

[1] University of Applied Sciences Upper Austria, Softwarepark 11,
4232 Hagenberg, Austria
[2] Institute for Symbolic Artificial Intelligence Johannes Kepler University Linz,
Altenberger Straße 69, 4040 Linz, Austria
[3] RISC Software GmbH, Softwarepark 32a, 4232 Hagenberg, Austria
jan.zenisek@fh-hagenberg.at

Abstract. Due to the growing use of machine learning models in many critical domains, ambitions to make the models and their predictions explainable have increased recently significantly as new research interest. In this paper, we present an extension to the machine learning based data mining technique of *variable interaction networks*, to improve their structural stability, which enables more meaningful analysis. To verify the feasibility of our approach and it's capability to provide human-interpretable insights, we discuss the results of experiments with a set of challenging benchmark instances, as well as with real-world data from energy network monitoring.

Keywords: Interpretable machine learning · Shapley value · Data stream analysis · Energy network resilience · Photovoltaic systems

1 Background and Motivation

With the progressing digital transformation of all areas of life, more and more continuous data (i.e. data streams) is being recorded and subsequently evaluated with machine learned models in real-time. Prominent examples for this trend can be found in today's fast changing production industry (e.g. predictive maintenance), social media (e.g. opinion mining), the financial sector (e.g. real-time stock trading), or the energy sector (e.g. blackout prediction), to name just a few. In the research field of machine learning, speeding up training algorithms and improving the accuracy of resulting models represent ongoing and presumably infinite endeavors. However, especially when employed in critical domains, not just accurate, but interpretable models are necessary to enable trustworthy predictions. Making the models themselves, as well as their predictions explainable has been increasingly studied in the past few years [2]. However, recent efforts in producing interpretable machine learning models mostly consider *batch processed data*, whereas analyzing *real-time data streams* explicitly, has not gained

R. Moreno-Díaz et al. (Eds.): EUROCAST 2022, LNCS 13789, pp. 130–138, 2022.
https://doi.org/10.1007/978-3-031-25312-6_15

the same attention yet. Moreover, interpretable machine learning is mostly concerned with a set of dedicated input variables and one prediction target, which does not provide a comprehensive system insight.

In [6] these issues are addressed by using Variable Interaction Networks (VIN) [4] in order to analyze streaming data holistically and improve the understanding of system dynamics (e.g. potential concept drifts). While the results of this work show the applicability of VINs to detect changing system behavior quite accurately, they also depict structural instability of the continuously re-created networks, while analyzing the streaming data. Although this does not hamper the accuracy of change detection too much, as most network alterations are small, each alteration certainly impairs the networks' functionality for system interpretation by domain experts.

In the following Sect. 2, we describe the conventional approach to model and evaluate variable interaction networks on streaming data. After that, we present an extension to this, with the aim to decrease structural instability to support better interpretability. In Sect. 3 we show the feasibility of our extended approach by testing it on two data sets and we conclude briefly in Sect. 4.

2   Variable Interaction Networks

2.1   Modeling and Evaluation

Variable Interaction Networks (VIN) [4] are directed graphs, in which system variables are represented as nodes and their impact on each other as directed, weighted edges. The algorithm to create such models is as follows: For each independent system variable a model is trained, using the variable as target and all others as input. For this purpose, arbitrary machine learning methods may be employed. In a second step, for each model, the impact of each input variable for the respective target variable is calculated. This calculation is based on the *permutation feature importance* (PFI) [1], for example – the model error increase, which results from removing the information of a certain variable from the data set by shuffling its values. In a final step, the graph is constructed by adding a node for each variable and adding weighted, directed edges based on the calculated impacts. The resulting model structure provides a holistic system depiction as a *clear-box* since it is human-readable. It has proven to be successful, not only to model stable system states, but also to analyze system dynamics when evaluating data streams in a sliding window fashion (see [6] and Fig. 1). To this end, raw data is processed within a sliding window (Fig. 1a) by re-computing the VIN and comparing it to an initial version (Fig. 1b) using the *Normalized Discounted Cumulative Gain (NDCG)* or the *Spearman's rank correlation*, as proposed in [6]. This results in network similarity trend lines (Fig. 1c), which can be compared to the real system drift by using *Pearson's R* correlation coefficient, in case it is known. We define drift limits as *noDrift* = 1 and *fullDrift* = 0, to get a positive scale for correlation scores. Benchmark tests [6] show the effectiveness of VIN based drift detection, however, also report that these networks currently lack of structural stability. Reasons for this are that feature impact calculation using PFI is non-deterministic and heavily depends on the underlying models' estimation error. This instability compromises the interpretability of VINs and thus, motivated us to look for improvements.

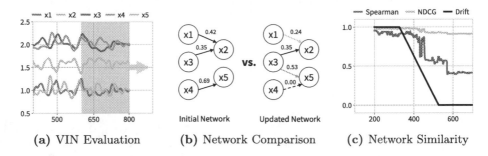

(a) VIN Evaluation   (b) Network Comparison   (c) Network Similarity

Fig. 1. Symbolic illustration of the VIN based data stream analysis approach on a set of time series data with manually introduced (i.e. known) drift. The edge design in 1b encodes the following states: black=unchanged, yellow=changed, green=new, dashed=vanished variable impact. (Color figure online)

2.2 Shapley Value Based Networks

To mitigate the issue of network instability, we extend the work in [6] and introduce a new variable impact calculation routine using the *Shapley Value* method [5], to replace the former Permutation Feature Importance (PFI) based one. The Shapley Value (SV) of a variable is the average gain to the mean model prediction, resulting from adding the variable, to all possible coalitions of the remaining variables. It is a solid mathematical concept from coalition game theory and enables local, i.e. observation-wise model interpretation: Variable impacts are evaluated for each data point individually, which has the potential to show effects of changing system behavior instantaneously. For comparability we adapted the calculation as follows: We scale the resulting absolute numbers to unit length within the interval $[0, 1]$, which was also performed for the PFI outcome. Measuring the effect of adding a variable was done in a reversed fashion: calculating the current impact, then removing the variable information by picking a random value from the variable's recordings and finally, re-calculating the impact. To reduce variance, we repeat this process 10 times and average the outcome, as we did for the shuffling routine of PFI. Eventually, we collect and average the observation-wise calculations to get a global mean for each variable impact.

3   Experiments

In the scope of this work and the focus of this section, we tested the effectiveness of the proposed Shapley Value (SV) extension to the variable interaction network approach compared to Permutation Feature Importance (PFI). Therein, we use different underlying learning algorithms, a varying sliding window size and two problem instances: a synthetically constructed benchmark problem describing dynamically changing communicating vessels over time and a real-world problem from the field of photovoltaic energy production.

3.1 Problem Instances

Benchmark Problem "Communicating Vessels (ComVes)": For this problem we designed a differential equation system to simulate data streams, which drift over time, first introduced and detailed in [6]. The system consists of two vessels, each continuously filled by an inlet, drained by an outlet and connected by a communication path. The system is designed to maintain a stable state, however, by manipulating the equation for the flow rate of the vessel connection, a concept drift can be introduced: a gradually clogging communication path, e.g. representing a maintenance problem.

Real-World Problem "Resilient Energy Networks (ResiNet)": The ResiNet-project is concerned with analyzing energy networks with regard to their resilience. As part of this, we developed prediction models for power production and consumption based on data from ca. 200 households from the region of Upper Austria, all equipped with roof-top mounted photovoltaic modules and battery packs. The measurements include data from 2016–2019 and were further linked to several geographic information and weather data from the Austrian weather forecasting system INCA [3]. To investigate network resilience and to test our extended VIN approach, we designed following what-if scenario: *What if... a small community of 3 systems is sharing its batteries by charging them together for higher network-independence? Can we detect a failing battery pack in such a scenario with our approach?* (cf. illustrated in Fig. 2a). For this purpose, we used the measured real-world system data, but re-calculated battery states and grid input/output differences, to simulate that the systems are connected and sharing their surplus energy produced. For instance, if the consumption of a system can be covered with the current energy production and the system's battery is already filled, surplus energy is shared equally amongst the other community members and only after that, left over energy is passed to the public grid. This way, a small virtual energy community is simulated, which should provide more grid independence. In order to enable more reasonable analysis, we used our domain knowledge and pre-selected input features for the modeling process in the case of this problem instance, instead of alternating all available features (cf. Figure 2b). For each of the experiment runs, we introduced rapid degradation of the charge/discharge rate of a random battery at a random point of time, using the data stream generation tool from [7]. By this means, we aim to simulate a probable, but not directly observable maintenance problem, which could impede the gained network independence, but potentially remains undetected due to the compensatory behavior of the interconnected energy community.

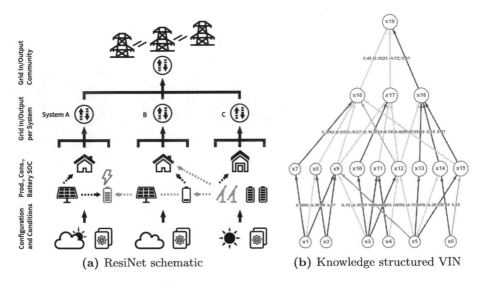

(a) ResiNet schematic   (b) Knowledge structured VIN

Fig. 2. Depiction of the ResiNet problem instance: In 2b the herein described *what-if-* scenario concerning a simulated, virtual energy community under changing conditions, is illustrated (cf. energy sharing in green, battery fault in red). In 2b the respectively modeled and subsequently evaluated VIN is displayed.

3.2   Results

To compile the foundation of the variable interaction networks (VIN), we trained regression models using multiple linear regression (LR), symbolic regression (SR) and random forest regression (RFR) with the configuration as in [6]. We defined a maximum normalized mean squared error (NMSE) of 0.5 for each model and a minimum variable impact of 0.1 as thresholds to take part within the network creation routine. Further on, we compare different sliding window sizes and both impact calculation methods – Permutation Feature Importance (PFI) and Shapley Values (SV) – for which we provide the calculated differences on each result plot. For the sake of brevity, we elaborate on results in the respective plot's caption and provide a brief discussion at the end of this subsection.

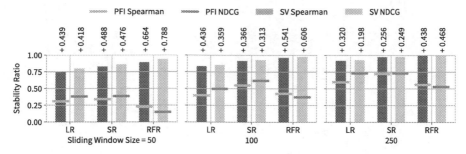

(a) ComVes: NDCG are slightly better than Spearman scores in most cases; best PFI scores with SR, worst with RFR; larger window sizes reveal more stability; SV scores are superior in all cases.

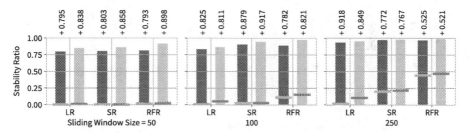

(b) ResiNet: NDCG are slightly better than the Spearman scores in most cases; RFR models work best, especially for PFI scores; SV are superior to PFI scores by far in any case.

Fig. 3. Standard Deviation (SD) of changes, representing the mean magnitude of network changes during sliding window evaluation. The lower the deviation, the better for model interpretability.

We set up two experiment types, each consisting of 10 runs with randomly sampled time series with a length of 1000 consecutive events originating from the described problem instances: one for testing network stability and one for drift detection. All models were trained on data partitions where systems were stable. To evaluate the stability of the created networks over time, we tested on time series data, which was again sampled from stable system states. In Fig. 4 the ratio of sliding window movements without resulting network change is illustrated. In Fig. 3 the magnitude of detected changes is given by reference to their standard deviation (SD) during the runs. To evaluate the drift detection capability of the approach, we tested on unseen data for which a concept drift has been introduced at a random point, after a fixed burn-in phase of 250 events – see details in Fig. 5.

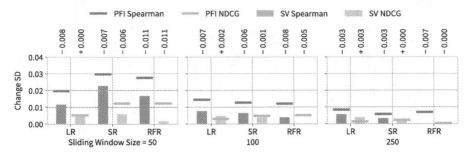

(a) ComVes: NDCG are better than the Spearman scores; larger window sizes reveal lower SDs; SV are better than PFI scores for most combinations of model and window size.

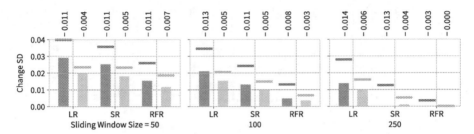

(b) ResiNet: RFR perform best, followed by SR and LR; NDCG are better than the Spearman scores; larger window sizes reveal lower SDs; SV scores are superior, no matter the model nor window size.

Fig. 4. Stability ratio test results, representing the ratio of sliding window movements without network change. Thus, a high ratio is desirable to increase model interpretability.

We want to highlight the superiority of the new SV over PFI based VINs in all test cases regarding network stability ratio when analyzing stable systems (Fig. 4). This also applies for the standard deviation of weight changes, as they are lower for SV based VINs in most cases (Fig. 3). Furthermore, in this analysis we see a pronounced improvement of using the NDCG over the Spearman scores. As shown in Fig. 5 both methods, SV and PFI, generate comparably good results in terms of drift detection performance. To this end, the SR based VINs for the benchmark data and the RFR based VINs for the real-world data perform best, as the high *Pearson R* correlation scores show. In summary, these results suggest that SV based VINs are superior to PFI based ones, since performance on stable systems is noticeably improved without losing the ability to detect system changes.

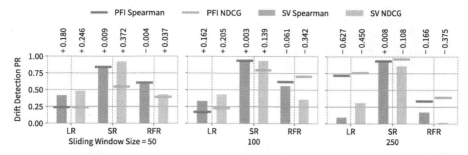

(a) ComVes: no clear winner between NDCG and Spearman scores; no clear winner between PFI and SV scores; SR models perform best by far at a high level with window sizes 100 and 250.

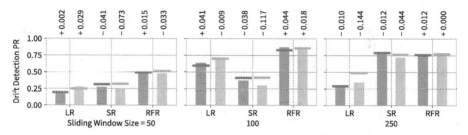

(b) ResiNet: NDCG/Spearman and PFI/SV with very similar scores; RFR performs best.

Fig. 5. Concept drift detection performance, represented by *Pearson's R* (PR) correlation coefficient of the network similarity and the known drift over time.

4   Conclusion and Outlook

With this work we presented an extension to the variable interaction network modeling and evaluation technique for data stream analysis, giving it more stability and thus, improving it's interpretation potential. Therefore, we propose a customized form of Shapley Values as alternative to the conventional permutation feature importance for computing network edge weights. The effectiveness of this extension has been shown for a benchmark and a real-world problem data set, both dealing with stable and changing system behavior.

Future work may consider other variable impact (i.e. feature importance) estimation measures to further improve the characteristics of variable interaction networks and broaden its application scope. Another promising lead is to investigate the potential of VINs for root-cause analysis, e.g. by analyzing those network paths with the highest change sum within a VIN, which is evaluated on data with concept drifts.

Acknowledgments. The work described in this paper was done within the projects "RESINET", funded by the European Fund for Regional Development (EFRE) and the country of Upper Austria as part of the program "Investing in Growth and Jobs 2014–2020" and "Secure Prescriptive Analytics", funded by the country of Upper of Austria as part of the program "#upperVISION2030".

References

1. Breiman, L.: Random forests. Mach. Learn. **45**(1), 5–32 (2001). https://doi.org/10.1023/A:1010933404324
2. Carvalho, D.V., Pereira, E.M., Cardoso, J.S.: Machine learning interpretability: a survey on methods and metrics. Electronics **8**(8), 832 (2019). https://doi.org/10.3390/electronics8080832
3. Haiden, T., Kann, A., Pistotnik, G., Stadlbacher, K., Wittmann, C.: Integrated nowcasting through comprehensive analysis (INCA)—system description. ZAMG Rep **61**, 1–60 (2010). https://www.zamg.ac.at/fix/INCA_system.pdf
4. Hooker, G.: Discovering additive structure in black box functions. In: Proceedings of the tenth ACM SIGKDD international conference on Knowledge Discovery and Data Mining, pp. 575–580 (2004). https://doi.org/10.1145/1014052.1014122
5. Shapley, L.S.: A value for n-person games. In: Kuhn, H., Tucker, A., (eds.), Contributions to the Theory of Games II vol. 2, no. 28, pp. 307–317 (1953). https://doi.org/10.1515/9781400881970-018
6. Zenisek, J., Kronberger, G., Wolfartsberger, J., Wild, N., Affenzeller, M.: Concept drift detection with variable interaction networks. In: Moreno-Díaz, R., Pichler, F., Quesada-Arencibia, A. (eds.) EUROCAST 2019. LNCS, vol. 12013, pp. 296–303. Springer, Cham (2020). https://doi.org/10.1007/978-3-030-45093-9_36
7. Zenisek, J., Wolfartsberger, J., Sievi, C., Affenzeller, M.: Streaming synthetic time series for simulated condition monitoring. IFAC-PapersOnLine **51**(11), 643–648 (2018). https://doi.org/10.1016/j.ifacol.2018.08.391

Symbolic Regression with Fast Function Extraction and Nonlinear Least Squares Optimization

Lukas Kammerer[1,2](✉) [ID], Gabriel Kronberger[1] [ID], and Michael Kommenda[1] [ID]

[1] Josef Ressel Center for Symbolic Regression Heuristic and Evolutionary Algorithms Laboratory, University of Applied Sciences Upper Austria, Hagenberg, Austria
lukas.kammerer@fh-hagenberg.at

[2] Department of Computer Science, Johannes Kepler University, Linz, Austria

Abstract. Fast Function Extraction (FFX) is a deterministic algorithm for solving symbolic regression problems. We improve the accuracy of FFX by adding parameters to the arguments of nonlinear functions. Instead of only optimizing linear parameters, we optimize these additional nonlinear parameters with separable nonlinear least squared optimization using a variable projection algorithm. Both FFX and our new algorithm is applied on the PennML benchmark suite. We show that the proposed extensions of FFX leads to higher accuracy while providing models of similar length and with only a small increase in runtime on the given data. Our results are compared to a large set of regression methods that were already published for the given benchmark suite.

Keywords: Symbolic regression · Machine learning

1 Symbolic Regression and FFX

Symbolic regression is a machine learning task in which we try to identify mathematical formulas that cover linear and nonlinear relations within given data. The most common algorithm for solving symbolic regression is genetic programming (GP), which optimizes a population of mathematical models using crossover and mutation. GP is in theory capable of finding models of any syntactical structure and complexity. However, disadvantages of GP are its stochasticity, its long algorithm runtime for nontrivial problems and its complex hyperparameter settings. These characteristics led to the development of non-evolutionary algorithms which produce more restricted models but have advantages in determinism, runtime or complexity of hyperparameters [3, 6, 9].

One of the first algorithms that was developed to tackle the shortages of GP is Fast Function Extraction (FFX) [9]. FFX generates a large set of *base functions* first, then it learns a regularized linear model using these base functions as terms. The set of base functions is a combination of the original features with several nonlinear functions such as $\exp(\dots)$ or $\log(\dots)$ and a predefined set of real-valued exponent values. Examples of base functions for problems with features $\{x_1, x_2\}$ are x_1, x_2, x_1^2, $\exp(x_1)$, $\exp(x_1^2)$, $\log(x_1)$ or $\log(x_2^{0.5})$.

The structure of FFX models with n features $\{x_1 \dots x_n\}$ is outlined in Eq. 1. Parameters $\{c_0, c_1, \dots, c_m\}$ are linear parameters of a model with m base functions. They are learned with ElasticNet regression [4]. ElasticNet regression identifies only the most relevant base functions due to its regularization by setting linear parameters c_i of irrelevant base functions to zero (sparsification). Therefore, learned models contain only a subset of the original base functions.

$$\hat{f}(\mathbf{x}) = c_0 + c_1 \, \text{func}_1(x_1^{e_1}) + \cdots + c_m \, \text{func}_m(x_n^{e_m})$$
$$\text{with func}_1, \dots, \text{func}_m \in \{\text{abs}(), \log(), \dots\} \text{ and } e_1, \dots, e_m \in \{0.5, 1, 2\} \tag{1}$$

1.1 Motivation and Objectives

A disadvantage of FFX is that only linear parameters are optimized. Parameters within nonlinear functions are not present. For example functions with feature x and nonlinear parameters k_i such as $\log(x + k_i)$ or $\exp(k_i x)$ have to be approximated by FFX with a linear model of several base functions. In this work, we extend the capabilities of FFX by adding such a real-valued parameter k to each generated base functions. Adding several nonlinear parameters to the possible model structure should allow to fit additive models with fewer base functions, as we have more degrees of freedom per base function.

The introduced nonlinear parameters are optimized in combination with the linear parameters by separable nonlinear least squares optmization (NLS) using a variable projection algorithm [2]. We call this new algorithm *FFX with Nonlinear Least Squares Optimization* (FFX NLS). We test whether FFX NLS leads to higher accuracy than the original implementation on the *PennML* benchmark suite [10] and compare the complexity of the generated models. Given, that we have more degrees of freedom to fit data with a single base function, we expect to find that it produces models with a lower number of base functions and therefore simpler models than the original FFX algorithm.

2 Algorithm Description

Similar to FFX, FFX NLS runs in several steps. First, base functions are generated. Then the most relevant base functions and the model's parameters are determined. In difference to FFX, the selection of relevant base function and the optimization of parameters are separate steps. FFX NLS performs the following four steps that are described in detail in the next sections:

1. Generate a list of all univariate base functions $\boldsymbol{f}$ (cf. Sect. 2.1).
2. Optimize all parameters $\boldsymbol{k}$ and $\boldsymbol{l}$ of a nonlinear model $l_0 + \sum_i l_i f_i(\boldsymbol{k}, \boldsymbol{x})$ that consists of the base functions as terms. $\boldsymbol{k}$ is a vector of all nonlinear parameters. $\boldsymbol{l}$ are linear parameters, $\boldsymbol{x}$ are features (cf. Sect. 2.2).

3. Select most important base functions of f with a regularized linear model and the nonlinear parameters k from the previous step (cf. Sect. 2.3).
4. The final model is created by optimizing all parameters again with nonlinear least squares optimization but only using the most important base function (cf. Sect. 2.4).

2.1   Base Functions

In step 1, we generate all univariate base functions f with placeholders for nonlinear parameters. For each feature x_i we create base functions of structure $func(ax_i^p + b)$ with $func \in \{id, log, exp, sqrt\}$, $p \in \{1, 2\}$ and two scaling values a and b with $id(x) = x$. The scaling values a and b are placeholder for nonlinear parameters that will be optimized later on. We also include bivariate base functions, which are described in Sect. 2.4.

We utilize the linear structure in the final model as well as mathematical identities of the used nonlinear functions to reduce the number of nonlinear parameters. Due to mathematical identities such as $log(ax_i) = log(a) + log(x_i)$ with a being a parameter that is trained later on, we can skip certain scaling values. In the case of logarithm, we can just use $log(x_i + b)$ instead of $log(ax_i + b)$ as base function as we can rewrite it to $log(c) log(x_i + d)$. Then we can skip $log(a)$ as it is constant in the final model and therefore summed up by the final model's intercept. The same applies to the exp-function, in which we can skip the multiplicative scaling value in the argument as we can rewrite $exp(x + a) = exp(x) exp(a)$ and skip $exp(a)$ in the final model.

2.2   Parameter Optimization with Variable Projection

The generated base functions f are combined to one large linear model $\hat{\Theta}(x) = l_0 + \sum_i l_i f_i(k, x)$ with l as vector of linear parameters and intercept and k as vector of nonlinear parameters. We use NLS to find the values in l and k that minimize the mean squared error (MSE) for given training data.

Since nonlinear least squares optimization is computationally expensive, we use a variable projection (VP) algorithm initially developed by Golub and Pereya [5] for optimizing all parameters l and k. The advantage of VP over plain NLS optimization is that VP utilizes the generated model's structure – a nonlinear model with several linear parameters l. Golub and Pereya call the given model structure a *separable least squares problem*. This setting is common in engineering domains. VP optimizes nonlinear parameters in k iteratively, while optimal linear parameters are solved exactly via ordinary least squares. Given the high number of linear parameters in the model (due to the large number of base functions), the use of VP is an important performance aspect of FFX NLS. We use the efficient VP algorithm by Krogh [8].

2.3   Base Function Selection

As we generate a very large number of base functions, we need to select the most relevant ones in order to create a both interpretable and well-generalizing model.

The number of selected base functions is thereby a hyperparameter of FFX NLS. In plain FFX, the selection of relevant base functions and the optimization of parameters is done in one step with a ElasticNet regression [4], as only linear parameters need to be optimized.

Since we also need to optimize nonlinear parameters, no simple way to combine NLS optimization and regularization of linear parameters is available. The VP algorithm by Chen et al. [2] uses Tikhonov regularization [4]. However, in initial experiments this algorithm was not beneficial for FFX NLS to identify relevant terms. Tikhonov regularization shrinks linear parameters, however, it did not provide the necessary sparsification of linear parameters and the algorithm in [2] is computationally more expensive. Alternatively, we use the already computed vector of nonlinear parameters k of the previous step as fixed constants and optimize the linear parameters l with a lasso regression [4]. Terms with a linear parameter $\neq 0$ are selected as most important base functions. We get the desired number of base functions by iteratively increasing the lasso regression's λ value in order to shrink more parameters to zero. Although this method ignores dependencies between linear and nonlinear parameters, it is still effective for selecting base functions both regarding runtime and further modelling accuracy.

2.4 Training of Final Model and Bivariate Base Functions

Similar to the parameter optimization in Sect. 2.2, we combine base functions to one single model and optimize all parameters again. In difference to the previous NLS optimization step, we take in this step only the most relevant base functions from Sect. 2.3. As parameters are not independent from each other, we repeat this step to get optimal parameters for a subset of base functions.

To cover interactions between features, we also include bivariate base functions. For this we take pairwise combinations of the previously generated univariate base function and multiply them to get one new base function for each pair. To prevent a combinatorial explosion of base functions and nonlinear parameters in highly multidimensional problems, we only consider the ten most important univariate base functions from Sect. 2.3 for to create bivariate base functions. We take the resulting $\binom{10}{2} = 45$ bivariate functions and append them to our existing list of univariate base functions. Then we repeat the steps described in Sect. 2.2 and 2.3 to determine the most important base functions across both univariate and bivariate base function for the final model. We consider only ten univariate base functions as a larger number did not provide any benefit in achieving our objectives.

3 Experimental Setup

We use *PennML* benchmark suite [10] for all experiments. This benchmark consist of over 90 regression problem and provides a performance overview of several common regression algorithms. We apply both FFX and FFX NLS on these problems to compare the algorithms' accuracies with each other and with other common regression algorithms. Thereby we take the experimental results from [7] for a comprehensive comparison as this work shows the results of the currently most accurate regression algorithms like GP CoOp as implemented in [1] for the PennML data.

We apply the same modelling workflow as in [10] in our experiments. For every regression problem in the benchmark suite, we repeat the modelling ten times. We shuffle the dataset in every repetition and take the first 75% of observations as training set and the remaining ones as test set. We perform a grid search with a 5-fold cross validation for each shuffled dataset for hyperparameter tuning and train one final model with these best hyperparameters. Eventually, we get ten different models for each original regression problem. Hyperparameters for all other algorithms are described in [7]. We use the following hyperparameter sets for both FFX and FFX NLS:

- Max. number of base function in final model $\in \{3, 5, 10, 20, 30, 50\}$
- Use bivariate base functions $\in \{\text{true}, \text{false}\}$
- Use nonlinear functions $\in \{\text{true}, \text{false}\}$
- FFX only: L1 ratio $\in \{0, 0.5, 1\}$

4   Results

As in the original experiments for this benchmark suite [10], we first calculate the median (mean squared) error of the ten models of each regression problem. Then

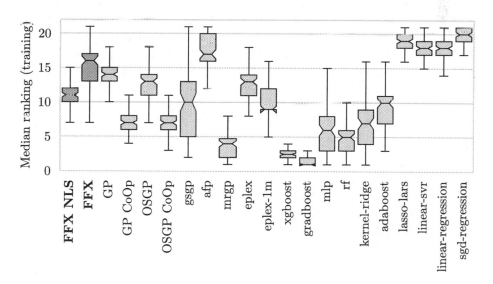

Fig. 1. Distribution of median rankings of the mean squared error on the training set.

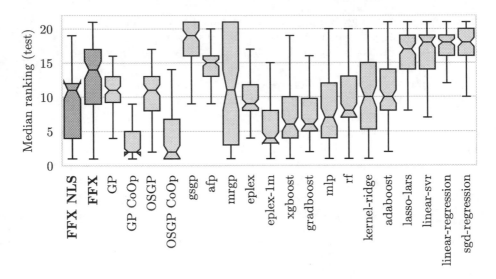

Fig. 2. Distribution of median rankings of the mean squared error on the test set.

we rank all regression methods by their median error for each problem. Figure 1 and 2 show the distribution of ranks for each algorithm for training and test across all regression problems in the benchmark suite. E.g. in Figure 1, gradient boosting was for most problems the most accurate algorithm in training.

Figure 1 and 2 show the distribution of rankings of each algorithm's median rank on the training set and test set. The optimization of nonlinear parameters in FFX NLS provided to more accurate models than FFX both in training and test. In comparison to other algorithms, FFX as well as FFX NLS perform better than linear models, which are on the right of Figure 1 (like linear regression or lasso regression). This is expected given both FFX methods can cover nonlinear dependencies and interactions in the data in contrast to purely linear methods. However, both algorithms perform worse than boosting methods or GP with NLS (GP CoOp) by Kommenda et al. [7]. Also this is plausible, as both methods have a more powerful search algorithm and a larger hypothesis space than FFX methods with their restricted model structures.

To analyze the size of models, we count the number of syntactical symbols in a model. E.g. the model $c_0 + \log x_1 + c_2$ has a complexity of six. We use this measure because it takes the added scaling terms within function arguments in FFX NLS into account. Figure 3a shows that both the size of models and the number of base function within models produced by FFX NLS and FFX are similar. FFX NLS models are just slightly shorter.

Figure 4 shows the median runtime across all pro per algorithm. While one FFX run takes less than a second for most problems, the runtime of FFX NLS ranges between one and a few seconds. Although the runtime increase is relatively large, it is still feasible to perform large grid searches in reasonable amount of time with FFX NLS. Both algorithms beat some GP-based algorithms and are on a similar level as boosting algorithms.

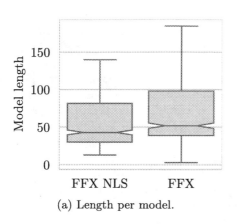

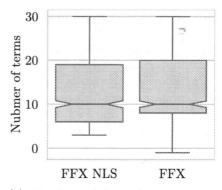

(a) Length per model.

(b) Number of base functions per model.

Fig. 3. Distribution complexity of all models from FFX and FFX NLS.

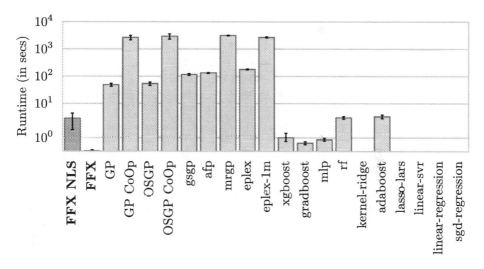

Fig. 4. Median runtime of all algorithms.

5   Conclusion

We proposed an extension of the model structure of the FFX algorithm. We added nonlinear scaling parameter which were optimized using the variable projection algorithm by Krogh [8] and separate base function selection, which we called FFX NLS. We achieved a large improvement in test accuracy in comparison to plain FFX on the PennML benchmark suite while providing models of similar complexity. Although the runtime of FFX NLS is higher than the one of FFX, it still finishes training within seconds.

However, FFX and FFX NLS still perform worse than many symbolic regression algorithms. Big advantages of FFX NLS towards GP-based algorithms are its short runtime, the low number of hyperparameters and the simple, comprehensible model structure. Compared to boosting algorithms, FFX NLS performs worse in accuracy but similar in runtime. However, boosting algorithms are considered black box methods and allow no readability of its models.

To sum it up, FFX is a promising tool for quick data exploration. It identifies interactions as well as nonlinear relations with simple hyperparameter configuration and quick execution. However, further improvements regarding accuracy are needed. Potential improvements are the combination of regularization and parameter optimization, as this are separate steps right now that deliberately ignore dependencies between linear and nonlinear parameters.

Acknowledgements. The authors gratefully acknowledge support by the Christian Doppler Research Association and the Federal Ministry for Digital and Economic Affairs within the *Josef Ressel Center for Symbolic Regression*.

References

1. Burlacu, B., Kronberger, G., Kommenda, M.: Operon C++ an efficient genetic programming framework for symbolic regression. In: Proceedings of the 2020 Genetic and Evolutionary Computation Conference Companion, pp. 1562–1570 (2020)
2. Chen, G.Y., Gan, M., Chen, C.P., Li, H.X.: A regularized variable projection algorithm for separable nonlinear least-squares problems. IEEE Trans. Autom. Control **64**(2), 526–537 (2018)
3. de França, F.O.: A greedy search tree heuristic for symbolic regression. Inf. Sci. **442**, 18–32 (2018)
4. Hastie, T., Tibshirani, R., Friedman, J.: The Elements of Statistical Learning. SSS, Springer, New York (2009). https://doi.org/10.1007/978-0-387-84858-7
5. Golub, G.H., Pereyra, V.: The differentiation of pseudo-inverses and nonlinear least squares problems whose variables separate. SIAM J. Numer. Anal. **10**(2), 413–432 (1973)
6. Kammerer, L., Kronberger, G., Burlacu, B., Winkler, S.M., Kommenda, M., Affenzeller, M.: Symbolic regression by exhaustive search: reducing the search space using syntactical constraints and efficient semantic structure deduplication. Genet. program. Theory Pract. **17**, 79–99 (2020)
7. Kommenda, M., Burlacu, B., Kronberger, G., Affenzeller, M.: Parameter identification for symbolic regression using nonlinear least squares. Genet. Program Evolvable Mach. **21**(3), 471–501 (2020)
8. Krogh, F.T.: Efficient implementation of a variable projection algorithm for nonlinear least squares problems. Commun. ACM **17**(3), 167–169 (1974)
9. McConaghy, T.: FFX: fast, scalable, deterministic symbolic regression technology. In: Riolo, R., Vladislavleva, E., Moore, J. (eds.) Genetic Programming Theory and Practice, vol. IX, pp. 235–260. Springer, New York (2011). https://doi.org/10.1007/978-1-4614-1770-5_13
10. Orzechowski, P., La Cava, W., Moore, J.H.: Where are we now? a large benchmark study of recent symbolic regression methods. In: Proceedings of the Genetic and Evolutionary Computation Conference, pp. 1183–1190 (2018)

Comparing Shape-Constrained Regression Algorithms for Data Validation

Florian Bachinger[1,2(✉)] [ID] and Gabriel Kronberger[1] [ID]

[1] Josef Ressel Center for Symbolic Regression Heuristic and Evolutionary Algorithms Laboratory, University of Applied Sciences Upper Austria, Hagenberg, Austria
`florian.bachinger@fh-hagenberg.at`
[2] Institute for Application-oriented Knowledge Processing (FAW), Johannes Kepler University, Linz, Austria

Abstract. Industrial and scientific applications handle large volumes of data that render manual validation by humans infeasible. Therefore, we require automated data validation approaches that are able to consider the prior knowledge of domain experts to produce dependable, trustworthy assessments of data quality. Prior knowledge is often available as rules that describe interactions of inputs with regard to the target e.g. the target must be monotonically decreasing and convex over increasing input values. Domain experts are able to validate multiple such interactions at a glance. However, existing rule-based data validation approaches are unable to consider these constraints. In this work, we compare different shape-constrained regression algorithms for the purpose of data validation based on their classification accuracy and runtime performance.

Keywords: Data quality · Data validation · Shape-constrained regression

1 Introduction

Modern applications record a staggering amount of data through the application of sensor platforms. These masses of data render manual validation infeasible and require automated data validation approaches. Existing rule-based approaches [5] can detect issues like missing values, outliers, or changes in the distribution of individual observables. However, they are unable to assess the data quality based on interactions of multiple observables with regard to a target. For example, they might falsely classify an outlier as invalid, even though it can be explained by changes in another variable. Alternatively, an observable might exhibit valid value ranges and distributions, whilst the error is only detectable in the unexpected interaction with other observables, e.g. one dependent variable remains of constant value while another changes.

For this purpose, we propose the use of shape constraints (SC) for data validation. We detail the general idea of SC-based data validation and provide a comparison of three algorithms: (1) shape-constrained polynomial regression

© The Author(s), under exclusive license to Springer Nature Switzerland AG 2022
R. Moreno-Díaz et al. (Eds.): EUROCAST 2022, LNCS 13789, pp. 147–154, 2022.
https://doi.org/10.1007/978-3-031-25312-6_17

(SCPR) [8], (2) shape-constrained symbolic regression (SCSR) [2,9] and (3) eXtreme gradient boosting (XGBoost) [3]. We compare classification accuracy, supported constraint types, and runtime performance based on data stemming from a use-case in the automotive industry.

2   SC-Based Data Validation

ML algorithms have long been applied for the purpose of data validation. Concept drift detection [6] applies e.g. ML models and analyzes the prediction error to detect changes in system behavior. These models are either trained on data from a manually validated baseline and detect subsequent deviations from this established baseline, or are trained continuously to detect deviations from previous states [7]. SC-based data validation, however, is able to assess the quality of unseen data without established baselines by using domain knowledge.

Quality of data is often assessed by analysis of the interaction of inputs values in regard to the target. The measured target must exhibit certain shape properties that we associate with *valid* data and *valid* interactions. SCR allows us to train prediction models on the potentially erroneous dataset, whilst enforcing a set of shape constraints. Therefore, the trained prediction model exhibits a higher error if the data contains outliers or erroneous segments that *violate* the provided constraints, as SCR is restricting the model from fitting to these values.

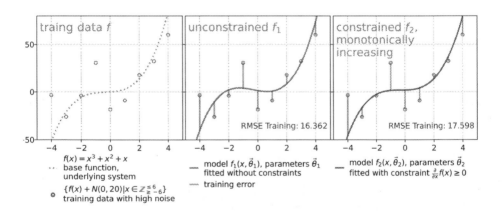

Fig. 1. Over-simplified showcase of SC-based data validation. The constrained model f_2 exhibits a higher error as it is restricted from fitting to certain data points, but it exhibits the monotonicity of the generating base function.

Figure 1 shows a simplified example where we sample training data from a third degree polynomial base function f, with added normally distributed noise. Subsequently, we train the linear factors $\vec{\theta}$ of two third degree polynomials, with and without constraints. The constrained model f_2 exhibits a higher training error as it includes no decreasing area $x \in [-1, 1]$ visible in f_1, but exhibits the monotonicity of the generating function as enforced by the constraints.

SC-based data validation requires two prerequisites: (1) precise constraints that describe *valid* system behavior and (2) a small set of manually validated data. These manually validated datasets are required to perform a one-time grid search to determine the best algorithm parameters for each application scenario. Later, for all arriving unseen datasets, a constrained model is trained on the full data. Similar to Fig. 1, datasets are labeled as *invalid* when the model exhibits a high training error and exceeds a threshold t.

3   Shape-Constrained Regression (SCR)

Shape-constrained regression (SCR) allows the enforcement of shape-properties of the regression models. Shape-properties can be expressed as restrictions on the partial derivatives of the prediction model that are defined for a range of the input space. This side information is especially useful when training data is limited. The combination of data with prior knowledge can increase trust in model predictions [4], which is an equally important property in data validation. Table 1 lists common examples of shape constraints together with the mathematical expression and compares the capabilities of the different algorithms.

3.1   Shape-Constrained Polynomial Regression (SCPR)

For regular polynomial regression (PR), a parametric (multi-variate) polynomial is fit to data. This is achieved by fitting the linear coefficients of each term using ordinary least squares (OLS). For SCPR, we include sum-of-squares constraints (a relaxation of the shape constraints) to the OLS objective function, which leads to a semidefinite programming problem (SDP) [10]. We use the commercial solver Mosek[1] to solve the second-order cone problem (SOCP) without shape constraints and the SDP with shape constraints. The algorithm parameters of PR and SCPR are: d the (total) degree of the polynomial, λ the strength of regularization, and α used to balance between 1-norm (lasso regression) and 2-norm (ridge regression) penalties. SCPR is able to incorporate all constraints of Table 1, is deterministic and produces reliable results in relatively short runtime.

3.2   Shape-Constrained Symbolic Regression (SCSR)

SCSR [9] uses a single objective genetic algorithm (GA) to train a symbolic regression model. After evaluation, in an additional model selection step, the constraints are asserted by calculating the prediction intervals on partial derivatives of the model. Any prediction model that violates a constraint is assigned the error of the worst performing individual, thereby preserving genetic material. Due to the probabilistic nature of the GA the achievement of constraints is not guaranteed.

---

[1] https://www.mosek.com.

3.3   XGBoost - eXtreme Gradient Boosting

XGBoost [3] builds an ensemble of decision trees with constant valued leaf nodes. It is able to consider monotonic constraints, however, these constraints can only be enforced on the whole input space of one input vector $\overrightarrow{x_i}$. It provides no support for larger intervals (extrapolation guidance), or multiple (overlapping) constraint intervals, like SCPR or SCSR. This results in fewer, less specific constraints available for XGBoost as summarized Table 1. XGBoost uses the parameters λ, α to determine the 1-norm (lasso regression) and 2-norm (ridge regression) penalties respectively.

Table 1. Examples of shape constraints. All constraints marked with • are enforced for a domain $[l_i, u_i] \subseteq \overrightarrow{x_i}$ of the full $\overrightarrow{x_i}$ input space. Multiple constraints can be defined over several partitions. Constraints for algorithms marked with ∗, however, can only be asserted on the full input space of $\overrightarrow{x_i}$. Constraints marked with ∘ are not available.

Property	Mathematical formulation	SCPR	SCSR	XGBoost
Positivity	$f(X) \geq 0$	•	•	∘
Negativity	$f(X) \leq 0$	•	•	∘
Monotonically increasing	$\frac{\partial}{\partial x_i} f(X) \geq 0$	•	•	∗
Monotonically decreasing	$\frac{\partial}{\partial x_i} f(X) \leq 0$	•	•	∗
Convexity	$\frac{\partial^2}{\partial x_i^2} f(X) \geq 0$	•	•	∘
Concavity	$\frac{\partial^2}{\partial x_i^2} f(X) \leq 0$	•	•	∘

4   Experiment and Setup

This section provides a short description of the data from our real-world use-case and discusses the experiment setup used to compare the investigated SCR algorithms based on this use-case. We follow the general description of SC-based data validation as described in Sect. 2.

4.1   Problem Definition - Data from Friction Experiments

Miba Frictec GmbH[2] develops friction systems such as breaks or clutches for the automotive industry. The exact friction characteristics of novel material compositions are unknown during development, and can only be determined by time- and resource-intense experiments. For this purpose, a friction disc prototype is installed in room filling test-rigs that rotate the discs at different velocities v, and repeatedly engage the discs at a varying pressure p to simulate the actuation of a clutch during shifting. Based on these measurements, the friction characteristics of new discs are determined. The friction coefficient μ denotes the ratio of friction force and normal load. It describes the force required to initiate and

---

[2] https://www.miba.com.

to maintain relative motion (denoted static friction μ_{stat} and dynamic friction μ_{dyn}) [1]. The value of μ is not constant for one friction disc, instead, it is dependent on the parameters: p, v and temperature T. Experts determine the quality of data by analyzing the interactions of p, v, T with regard to μ_{dyn}.

In friction experiments we encounter several known issues that render whole datasets or segments erroneous and that are only detectable when we investigate the interaction of inputs with regard to the target μ_{dyn}. Examples for such errors include: wrong calibration or malfunction of sensors, loosened or destroyed friction pads, or contaminated test benches from previous failed experiments. We were provided a total of 53 datasets consisting of 18 manually validated and 35 known invalid datasets that were annotated with a description of the error type.

$$\forall_{v,p,T} \ v \in [0,1] \land p \in [0,1] \land T \in [0,1] \implies$$

$$\left(0 \leq \mu_{dyn} \leq 1 \land \frac{\partial \mu_{dyn}}{\partial v} \in [-0.01, 0.01] \right.$$

$$\left. \land \frac{\partial \mu_{dyn}}{\partial p} \leq 0 \land \frac{\partial^2 \mu_{dyn}}{\partial p^2} \geq 0 \land \frac{\partial \mu_{dyn}}{\partial T} \leq 0 \land \frac{\partial^2 \mu_{dyn}}{\partial T^2} \geq 0 \right) \qquad (1)$$

$$\forall_{p,T} \ p \in [0,1] \land T \in [0,1] \implies \left(\frac{\partial \mu_{dyn}}{\partial p} \leq 0 \land \frac{\partial \mu_{dyn}}{\partial T} \leq 0 \right) \qquad (2)$$

4.2 Experiment Setup

We performed a hyper-parameter search using a two-fold cross validation over all valid datasets, repeated for each algorithm. As the constraints define expected behavior, each algorithm should be able to train models with low test error on valid data, whilst adhering to the constraints. Equation 1 lists the constraints for μ_{dyn}, which were provided by domain experts. Inputs p, v, T are individually scaled to a range of $[0, 1]$ and all constraints are defined for this full input space. Equation 2 lists the reduced constraints that are compatible with XGBoost's capabilities.

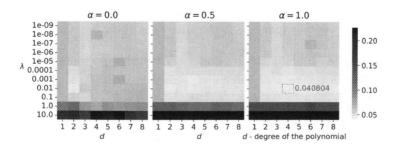

Fig. 2. Grid search results for SCPR over all validated datasets. Lower values signify better results.

Figure 2 visualizes the search space and best configuration for SCPR in a heatmap showing the sum of test RMSE over all valid datasets. Similar experiments and analysis were conducted for PR and XGBoost. For SCSR, we compared training and test error over increasing generation count. To prevent overfitting we select the generation with the lowest test error as a stopping criterion. In all subsequent training on unseen data, during the validation phase, the GA is stopped at this generation.

The resulting best SCR algorithm parameters were applied in the SC-based data validation phase for all available datasets. In this use-case, we divide the dataset into a new segment when one of the controlled input parameters p or v changed (cf. Fig. 3). We calculate the RMSE values per segment and mark the whole experiment as invalid if one segment exceeds the varied threshold t.

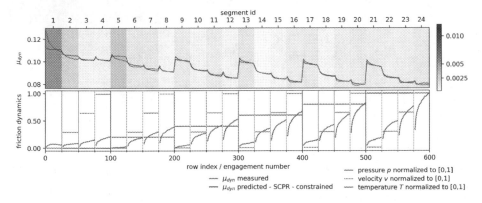

Fig. 3. Validation result for data of one friction experiment. SC-based data validation was able to detect the subtle deviations from expected behavior in the segments one and five with row IDs 0–25, 100–125. The drops in μ_{dyn}-measured are not motivated by the friction dynamics. This dataset was correctly labeled *invalid*.

5   Results

A comparison of the investigated SCR algorithms is visualized in Fig. 4. XGBoost supports fewer, less complex shape constraints and achieves only minimally better classification capabilities than the unrestricted PR baseline. The comparison with PR shows how many erroneous datasets are simply detectable due to the statistical properties of ML models. The objective function of minimized training error leads to models being fit to the behavior represented in the majority of the data, resulting in the detection of less represented behavior or outliers. SCPR and SCSR on the other hand exhibit significantly improved classification capabilities, which can be attributed to the increased restrictions added by the constraints and domain knowledge about expected *valid* behavior.

We subsequently varied the threshold value t to analyze the change in false-positive- and true-positive-rate as visualized Fig. 4. Higher values of t result in the detection of only severe errors and a lower false positives rate. Lower values of t cause a more sensitive detection and higher false positive rates.

The sharp vertical incline in the ROC-curve of Fig. 4 is caused by the numerous *invalid* datasets that exhibit severe errors like e.g. massive outliers. Such errors cause high training error regardless if constraints are applied and how restrictive they are. Eventually, for increasingly smaller values of t, even noise present in the data will result in a training error that exceeds t.

Figure 4 also compares the test RMSE values achieved by the best algorithm parameters on the 18 valid datasets. All three algorithms are similarly well suited for modeling friction data. Consequently, all conclusions about the data validation capabilities of individual algorithms are not biased by the training accuracy. With an average training time of 0.32 s per dataset and great classification capabilities, SCPR is best suited for SC-based data validation. In practical applications, the data quality assessment is implemented in automated data ingestion pipelines that require low latencies. SCPR adds only little in terms of computational effort but provides significant improvement in data quality.

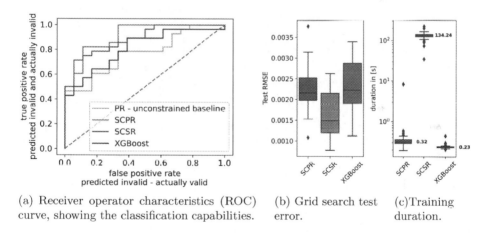

(a) Receiver operator characteristics (ROC) curve, showing the classification capabilities.   (b) Grid search test error.   (c) Training duration.

Fig. 4. Performance comparison of the three SCR algorithms and unconstrained PR.

6   Conclusions

SC-based data validation is a novel approach that allows the inclusion of prior knowledge in the quality assessment of previously unseen datasets. It can detect faults in the data that are only identifiable in the interaction of observables. With its low average runtime, SC-based data validation using SCPR is suitable for integration into data import pipelines to improve data quality. Moreover, trust in the validation results is facilitated by readable constraint definitions that can be provided by domain experts, or derived from expert knowledge. This trust is further increased through interpretable models created by the white- or gray-box ML algorithms SCPR and SCSR.

Based on our experiments, we recommend the application of SCPR for SC-based data validation. SCPR is easy to configure and excels in runtime time performance, as well as classification accuracy. For cases with larger number of variables or categorical data, XGBoost might be better equipped.

Acknowledgement. The financial support by the Christian Doppler Research Association, the Austrian Federal Ministry for Digital and Economic Affairs and the National Foundation for Research, Technology and Development is gratefully acknowledged.

References

1. Bhushan, B.: Introduction to Tribology, chap. Friction, pp. 199–271. Wiley (2013). https://onlinelibrary.wiley.com/doi/abs/10.1002/9781118403259.ch5
2. Bladek, I., Krawiec, K.: Solving symbolic regression problems with formal constraints. In: Proceedings of the Genetic and Evolutionary Computation Conference, GECCO 2019, pp. 977–984. Association for Computing Machinery, New York (2019). https://doi.org/10.1145/3321707.3321743
3. Chen, T., Guestrin, C.: XGBoost: a scalable tree boosting system. In: Proceedings of the 22nd ACM SIGKDD International Conference on Knowledge Discovery and Data Mining, KDD 2016, pp. 785–794. Association for Computing Machinery, New York (2016). https://doi.org/10.1145/2939672.2939785
4. Cozad, A., Sahinidis, N.V., Miller, D.C.: A combined first-principles and data-driven approach to model building. Comput. Chem. Eng. **73**, 116–127 (2015)
5. Ehrlinger, L., Wöß, W.: A survey of data quality measurement and monitoring tools. Front. Big Data, 28 (2022). https://doi.org/10.3389/fdata.2022.850611
6. Gama, J., Medas, P., Castillo, G., Rodrigues, P.: Learning with drift detection. In: Bazzan, A.L.C., Labidi, S. (eds.) SBIA 2004. LNCS (LNAI), vol. 3171, pp. 286–295. Springer, Heidelberg (2004). https://doi.org/10.1007/978-3-540-28645-5_29
7. Gama, J., Žliobaitė, I., Bifet, A., Pechenizkiy, M., Bouchachia, A.: A survey on concept drift adaptation. ACM Comput. Surv. **46**(4) (2014). https://doi.org/10.1145/2523813
8. Hall, G.: Optimization over nonnegative and convex polynomials with and without semidefinite programming. Ph.D. thesis, Princeton University (2018)
9. Kronberger, G., de Franca, F.O., Burlacu, B., Haider, C., Kommenda, M.: Shape-constrained symbolic regression-improving extrapolation with prior knowledge. Evol. Comput. **30**(1), 75–98 (2022). https://doi.org/10.1162/evco_a_00294
10. Parrilo, P.A.: Structured semidefinite programs and semialgebraic geometry methods in robustness and optimization. Ph.D. thesis, California Institute of Technology (2000)

Improving the Flexibility
of Shape-Constrained Symbolic
Regression with Extended Constraints

David Piringer[1(✉)], Stefan Wagner[1], Christian Haider[1], Armin Fohler[2],
Siegfried Silber[2], and Michael Affenzeller[1]

[1] Heuristic and Evolutionary Algorithms Laboratory, University of Applied Sciences
Upper Austria, Campus Hagenberg Softwarepark 11, 4232 Hagenberg, Austria
`david.piringer@fh-hagenberg.at`
[2] Linz Center of Mechatronics GmbH, Altenberger Straße 69, 4040 Linz, Austria

Abstract. We describe an approach to utilize a broader spectrum of
domain knowledge to model magnetization curves for high magnetic field
strengths $0 \leq H \leq 10^6$ with access to data points far below the saturation polarization. Thereby, we extend the implementation of Shape-
Constrained Symbolic Regression. The extension allows the modification of model estimates by a given expression to apply additional sets of
constraints. We apply the given expression of an Extended Constraint
row-by-row and compare the minimum and maximum outputs with the
target interval. Furthermore, we introduce regions and thresholds as
additional tools for constraint description and soft constraint evaluation.
Our achieved results demonstrate the positive impact of such additional
knowledge. The logical downside is the dependence on that knowledge to
describe applicable constraints. Nevertheless, the approach is a promising
way to reduce the human calculation effort for extrapolating magnetization curves. For future work, we plan to combine soft and hard constraint
evaluation as well as the utilization of structure template GP.

Keywords: Genetic programming · Symbolic regression · Shape
constraints · Extended constraints · Magnetization curves

1 Introduction and Related Work

The fundamental concept of data-based modeling is the discovery of a relationship $f(I) = y$ by using a suitable data set, which contains a feature set I and
a corresponding target y. Therefore, the data set is a core component of every
data-based modeling method and according to that, the acquisition of a satisfying data set is the logical first step. Nonetheless, this acquisition can be restricted
due to a variety of reasons, e.g. financial or physical limits. Despite that impairment, in some use cases the domain experts possess higher level knowledge about
the system. It is desirable to utilize exactly this type of knowledge in the modeling process.

© The Author(s), under exclusive license to Springer Nature Switzerland AG 2022
R. Moreno-Díaz et al. (Eds.): EUROCAST 2022, LNCS 13789, pp. 155–163, 2022.
https://doi.org/10.1007/978-3-031-25312-6_18

Various machine learning approaches bother with the introduction of higher level domain knowledge. This paper focuses on Genetic Programming (GP), established by John R. Koza [8]. The inspiration of GP is based on genetic algorithms [5], which refers to the principles of Darwinian natural selection. Originally, the population in GP consists of computer programs, which undergo an evolutionary process by crossover, mutation and selection. The field of applications for GP is diverse [2], one of them is Symbolic Regression (SR). In comparison to other machine learning methods such as random forests or neural networks, the advantage of SR is that the results represent closed mathematical formulas, which can be read and interpreted by humans.

In the past, there were multiple approaches to introduce additional domain knowledge into the evaluation mechanism of SR [3,4,9]. One of these approaches introduces Shape Constraints (SC) and is called Shape-Constrained Symbolic Regression. The approach utilizes Interval Arithmetic (IA) for the calculation and evaluation of that additional domain knowledge. The description of an SC for a target function which allows only positive output could look like the following: $f(I) \in [0, \infty]$ where I is a set of inputs. Besides the output, it is also possible to constrain the shape of the function using partial derivatives of any order. The effect of SC is the improved extrapolation behavior of the generated models, shown in [9]. Figure 1 shows a comparison between an SR model trained with and without SC. The effect of SC is clearly visible, because the model fits the test data and performs much better in extrapolation.

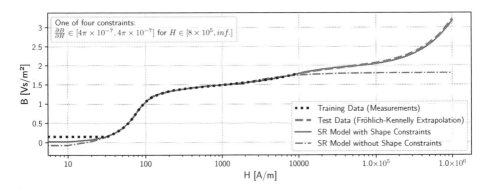

Fig. 1. Exemplary comparison of an SR model trained with and without SC.

On the contrary, it is only possible to evaluate SC against the defined target variable y, as the example with the positive output already shows. In some scenarios, it is helpful to evaluate against additional data columns, which do not represent the inputs or the target. For this case, it is necessary to support conversions of the evaluated target function, e.g. $\frac{f(I)}{h} \in [0, 1]$ where h is such an additional data column and not included in the input set I. In this paper we call that approach Extended Constraints (EC) and use them in combination with the original SC.

1.1 Motivation

Our motivation for this extended approach is to utilize a broader knowledge spectrum to fit magnetization curves (MC) of ferromagnetic materials. The main challenge for this modeling task is the sparse data set, which consists of a few data points far below the saturation polarization. Figure 1 illustrates that situation.

An MC describes the relation between magnetic flux density B and magnetic field strength H, which is also called B-H curve. Starting at the saturation point S of the material, the magnetic flux density B is growing linearly with a slope equal to the permeability of vacuum μ_0. Besides the B-H curve, there exists information about the magnetic polarization J and relative permeability μ_r in relation to H, whereby $0 \leq J \leq S$ and $1 \leq \mu_r \leq \infty$. There already exist some techniques to extrapolate MCs, which approximate quite well but cannot describe specific effects [10–13]. We want to model MC with B as target and H as input. The physical knowledge about B-H curves should be utilized as SC and the information about J and μ_r should be defined as EC.

2 Extended Constraints

An EC is a data structure containing a set of constraints and an expression, which fulfills the constraints. The expression can access all data columns provided by the data set, including the target column. But the actual values of the target column are swapped with the calculated model estimations. This approach can be seen as a type of post-processing for the estimations.

EC use the same syntax and semantics as SC for defining a constraint. Therefore, it is possible to constrain the output as well as the shape of the defined EC expression using partial derivatives of any order. However, the evaluation of EC does not use IA. Instead, we use the existing data points of the data set and apply the expression row-by-row. Afterwards, we initialize an interval with the minimum and maximum values of the calculated outputs. The interval is generated and evaluated for each constraint contained in the EC.

For this paper, we use soft constraint evaluation. Consequently, a value is calculated based on the severity of the constraint violation. Algorithm 1 shows the calculation of the violation for a constraint. When all constraints are evaluated, the average of all violations is added to the normalized mean squared error (NMSE), which is computed by comparing the estimations with the actual values. This is done to create a fitness landscape with hill-like increases for a better steering of the algorithmic search.

To prevent tremendously high violation values and/or unfair weighting when working with broad and narrow intervals simultaneously, we introduce thresholds. A threshold is part of a constraint and can limit each bound to a maximum. If the violation exceeds the threshold, it is set to 1. This results in normalized violation values. On the other hand, a manual configuration for each threshold is necessary.

Another extension for EC as well as SC are regions. Usually, SC are applied over the whole input range of a certain input. A region can redefine that interval

---

Algorithm 1. Calculation of constraint violations

1: $[e_l, e_u] \leftarrow$ *Estimation Interval e*
2: $[ta_l, ta_u] \leftarrow$ *Target Interval ta*
3: $[th_l, th_u] \leftarrow$ *Threshold Interval th*
4: $Error \leftarrow 0$
5: **if** $\neg(ta_l \leq e_l \leq ta_u)$ **then**
6:     $Error \leftarrow Error +$ CALCBOUNDVIOLATION($|e_l - ta_l|, th_l$)
7: **end if**
8: **if** $\neg(ta_l \leq e_u \leq ta_u)$ **then**
9:     $Error \leftarrow Error +$ CALCBOUNDVIOLATION($|e_u - ta_u|, th_u$)
10: **end if**
11: **return** $Error/2$

1: **function** CALCBOUNDVIOLATION(err, t)
2:     $t_{abs} \leftarrow |t|$
3:     **if** ISNAN(err) **then**
4:         **return** 1
5:     **else if** ISINFINITY(err) **and** $\neg$ISINFINITY(t_{abs}) **then**
6:         **return** 1
7:     **else if** ISINFINITY(t_{abs}) **then**
8:         **return** 0
9:     **else if** $err \leq 0$ **then**
10:         **return** 0
11:     **else if** $err > t_{abs}$ **then**
12:         **return** 1
13:     **else if** $t_{abs} > 0$ **then**
14:         **return** MIN($1, err/t_{abs}$)
15:     **else**
16:         **return** 1
17:     **end if**
18: **end function**

---

for an input. It is possible to narrow down or broaden up the interval. The usage of multiple regions per constraint is possible, however each input value is related to one region. When one or multiple regions are given, the calculation of EC cannot be performed row-by-row as mentioned earlier, because the data set can be insufficient for the defined region. Therefore, we decided to generate an n-dimensional vector with uniformly distributed random numbers between the lower and upper bound of a region. The vector also includes the lower and upper bound and the size n is equal to the row size of the data set.

3   Experiment Setup

To observe the effect of EC, we conducted 30 independent runs per experiment with and without EC (SC only) for four different materials in combination with three algorithms. Each material represents a data set with data points far below the saturation point, but with different measurements points for H.

The following algorithms were used to test the extended approach: Genetic Algorithm [5], Genetic Algorithm with Offspring Selection [1] and Age-Layered Population Structure Algorithm [6]. These algorithms are already implemented in HeuristicLab [2,7,14]. Because our objective is to observe the effects of EC and not to search for the best possible results, we did not conduct any parameter tuning methods, but we tried some different settings by hand. The final algorithm and parameter configurations are listed in Table 1.

Table 1. Parameter configuration for all algorithms.

Parameter	Value
Algorithm independent	
Crossover	Multi Symbolic Data Analysis Expression Crossover[a]
Crossover probability	100%
Mutator	Multi Symbolic Expression Tree Manipulator[b]
Mutation Probability	10%
Elites	1
Selector	Tournament Selection (Group Size = 2)
Max. Generations	500
Terminal Set	State variables and real-valued parameters
Function Set	+, -, *, /, tanh
Genetic Algorithm	
Population Size	2000
Offspring Selection Genetic Algorithm	
Population Size	2000
Selected Parents	2000
Max. Selection Pressure	100
Success Ratio	100%
Age-Layered Population Structure Genetic Algorithm	
Population Size (per Layer)	100
Mating Pool Range	1 (Current + Underlying)
Age Gap	10
Aging Scheme	Fibonacci
Age Layers	9

[a] Combination of: Depth Constrained, Diversity, Probabilistic Functional, Semantic Similarity and Subtree Swapping Crossovers.
[b] [2] Combination of: Change Node Type, Full Tree Shaker, One Point Shaker, Remove Branch and Replace Branch Manipulators.

The defined SC and EC are the same for every material but with slightly adjusted values for some material specific properties. Tables 2, 3 and 4 list the used SC and EC for the first material (M1). Notable is the strong focus of the defined EC on the test area, which should support the algorithm to find a better test approximation.

Table 2. Defined SC for all materials.

Constraint	Regions	Threshold	Weight
$\frac{\partial B}{\partial H} \in [4\pi \cdot 10^{-7}, 4\pi \cdot 10^{-7}]$	$H \in [8 \cdot 10^5, 10^6]$	$[-4\pi \cdot 10^{-7}, 4\pi \cdot 10^{-7}]$	3
$\frac{\partial B}{\partial H} \in [0, \infty]$	$H \in [0, 10^6]$	$[0, \infty]$	1
$\frac{\partial^2 B}{\partial^2 H} \in [-10, 0]$	$H \in [15000, 10^6]$	$[-10, 0.1]$	2

Table 3. EC for magnetic polarization J with $J = B - 4\pi \cdot 10^{-7} * H$.

Constraint	Regions	Threshold	Weight
$J \in [0, 1.96]$	$H \in [0, 10^6]$	$[0, 0.1]$	1
$J \in [1.956, 1.96]$	$H \in [5 \cdot 10^5, 10^6]$	$[-1, 0.1]$	2

Table 4. EC for relative permeability μ_r with $\mu_r = \frac{(B_n - B_{n-1})/(H_n - H_{n-1})}{4\pi \cdot 10^{-7}}$.

Constraint	Regions	Threshold	Weight
$\mu_r \in [1, 13500]$	$H \in [0, 10^6]$	$[-1, 500]$	1
$\mu_r \in [1, 1.005]$	$H \in [9 \cdot 10^5, 10^6]$	$[-1, 50]$	2

4   Results

Tables 5 and 6 present the training and test results containing the median and average root mean squared error (RMSE) for each algorithm and material (M1, M2, M3, M4) combination. The tables are split into columns without and with EC to show the difference. The highlighted numbers represent the best RMSE in the according row. As seen in the training results, the RMSE is slightly worse, which implies an increased difficulty for the algorithm to fit the given data points, caused by the additional constraints. Nevertheless, the differences are negligible. The test results show the impact of EC, because the RMSE with EC is significantly lower than the RMSE without EC. Accordingly, the algorithm could clearly utilize the additional information about the test data provided by the EC to find better solution candidates. Still, the strong focus of EC on the test data is noteworthy. All results show little to no difference between the used algorithms. Additionally, there is no obvious outlier between the materials regarding the RMSE. The increased computation time is also worth mentioning for EC, since more than twice as many constraints have to be calculated and evaluated.

Table 5. The table shows a slightly worse RMSE for the training set.

		Without			With EC		
		ALPS	GA	OSGA	ALPS	GA	OSGA
M1	Median	0.043	**0.017**	0.032	0.079	0.034	0.068
	Average	0.051	**0.017**	0.038	0.070	0.043	0.060
M2	Median	0.065	0.041	**0.032**	0.074	0.069	0.068
	Average	0.064	0.045	**0.038**	0.075	0.073	0.063
M3	Median	0.079	0.052	**0.049**	0.079	0.078	0.078
	Average	0.077	0.051	**0.046**	0.080	0.076	0.071
M4	Median	0.068	0.049	**0.036**	0.071	0.069	0.073
	Average	0.065	0.050	**0.041**	0.075	0.070	0.070

Table 6. This table shows the impact of EC for the test set, which leads to a significant decrease of the RMSE.

		Without			With EC		
		ALPS	GA	OSGA	ALPS	GA	OSGA
M1	Median	6.369	0.149	2.660	0.231	**0.071**	0.129
	Average	5.468	1.589	3.843	2.1	**0.118**	0.154
M2	Median	2.264	1.373	3.589	0.174	0.159	**0.142**
	Average	4.386	2.135	5.084	0.185	0.311	**0.159**
M3	Median	0.235	0.985	0.810	0.117	**0.105**	0.109
	Average	0.748	2.080	2.673	0.112	**0.109**	0.129
M4	Median	0.282	1.802	1.033	**0.126**	0.138	0.134
	Average	1.347	3.042	2.660	**0.134**	0.162	0.167

5 Conclusion and Outlook

Despite the challenging modeling task, the results look promising and indicate a relevance for future SR problems. The implemented approach achieved a significant boost in terms of test quality through the utilization of a broader spectrum of domain knowledge. Perhaps it is possible to reach even better qualities after fine-tuning the algorithm configurations. In relation to MC modeling, the shown approach has the potential to help domain experts in identifying the magnetization flux density B of ferromagnetic materials by reducing the human calculation effort for extrapolating MC.

Nevertheless, the approach has some downsides as well. It is only applicable when there is existing domain knowledge, which can be described with the shown methods. Additionally, the configuration of constraints can consume a lot of time, because it is difficult to identify the important constraints for the search process. Also, the amount of constraints has a direct, noticeable impact on the computation time, because the calculations are done for every evaluation of a solution.

In the future, we plan to merge the SC and EC implementations, as well as the utilization of IA for EC. Furthermore, we think that a combination of soft and hard constraints could have a positive effect on the search performance. Moreover, it is planned to combine EC with structure template GP, which enables a way to fixate parts of the syntax tree and therefore allows the definition of additional domain knowledge.

Acknowledgments. This work has been supported by the LCM - K2 Center within the framework of the Austrian COMET-K2 program.

References

1. Affenzeller, M., Wagner, S.: Offspring selection: a new self-adaptive selection scheme for genetic algorithms. In: Ribeiro, B., Albrecht, R.F., Dobnikar, A., Pearson, D.W., Steele, N.C. (eds.) Adaptive and Natural Computing Algorithms, pp. 218–221. Springer, Vienna (2005). https://doi.org/10.1007/3-211-27389-1_52
2. Affenzeller, M., Wagner, S., Winkler, S., Beham, A.: Genetic Algorithms and Genetic Programming: Modern Concepts and Practical Applications. CRC Press (2009)
3. Bladek, I., Krawiec, K.: Solving symbolic regression problems with formal constraints. In: Proceedings of the Genetic and Evolutionary Computation Conference, GECCO 2019, pp. 977–984. Association for Computing Machinery, New York (2019)
4. Haider, C., de França, F.O., Burlacu, B., Kronberger, G.: Using shape constraints for improving symbolic regression models. arXiv preprint arXiv:2107.09458 (2021)
5. Holland, J.H.: Adaptation in Natural and Artificial Systems: An Introductory Analysis with Applications to Biology, Control, and Artificial Intelligence. MIT Press (1992)
6. Hornby, G.S.: ALPS: the age-layered population structure for reducing the problem of premature convergence, GECCO 2006, pp. 815–822. Association for Computing Machinery, New York (2006)
7. Kommenda, M., Kronberger, G., Wagner, S., Winkler, S., Affenzeller, M.: On the architecture and implementation of tree-based genetic programming in heuristicLab, GECCO 2012, pp. 101–108. Association for Computing Machinery, New York (2012)
8. Koza, J.R.: Genetic Programming: On the Programming of Computers by Means of Natural Selection, vol. 1. MIT Press (1992)
9. Kronberger, G., de França, F.O., Burlacu, B., Haider, C., Kommenda, M.: Shape-constrained symbolic regression-improving extrapolation with prior knowledge. Evol. Comput. **30**(1), 75–98 (2022)
10. Labridis, D., Dokopoulos, P.: Calculation of eddy current losses in nonlinear ferromagnetic materials. IEEE Trans. Magn. **25**(3), 2665–2669 (1989)
11. Pechstein, C., Jüttler, B.: Monotonicity-preserving interproximation of B-H-curves. J. Comput. Appl. Math. **196**(1), 45–57 (2006)
12. Skarlatos, A., Theodoulidis, T.: A modal approach for the solution of the nonlinear induction problem in ferromagnetic media. IEEE Trans. Magn. **52**(2), 1–11 (2016)

13. Szewczyk, R.: Technical BH saturation magnetization curve models for spice, fem and mom simulations. J. Autom. Mob. Rob. Intell. Syst. **10**(2), 3–7 (2016)
14. Wagner, S., Affenzeller, M.: HeuristicLab: a generic and extensible optimization environment. In: Ribeiro, B., Albrecht, R.F., Dobnikar, A., Pearson, D.W., Steele, N.C. (eds.) Adaptive and Natural Computing Algorithms, pp. 538–541. Springer Vienna, Vienna (2005). https://doi.org/10.1007/3-211-27389-1_130

Shape-Constrained Symbolic Regression with NSGA-III

Christian Haider$^{(\boxtimes)}$ and Gabriel Kronberger

Josef Ressel Center for Symbolic Regression Heuristic and Evolutionary Algorithms
Laboratory, University of Applied Sciences Upper Austria, Hagenberg, Austria
christian.haider@fh-hagenberg.at

Abstract. Shape-constrained symbolic regression (SCSR) allows to
include prior knowledge into data-based modeling. This inclusion allows
to ensure that certain expected behavior is reflected by the resulting
models. This specific behavior is defined by constraints which restrict the
functional form e.g. monotonicity, concavity or model image boundaries.
That allows finding more robust and reliable models in the specific case
of highly noisy data or in extrapolation domains. This paper presents
a multi-objective approach to minimize the approximation error as well
as the constraint violations. Explicitly the two algorithms NSGA-II and
NSGA-III are implemented and compared against each other in terms of
model quality and runtime. Both algorithms are executed on a selected
set of benchmark instances from physics textbooks. The results indicate
that both algorithms are able to generate mostly feasible solutions and
NSGA-III provides slight improvements in terms of model quality. Moreover, an improvement in runtime can be observed when using NSGA-III.

Keywords: Symbolic regression · Shape-constraints · Many-objective
optimization

1 Introduction

Due to their high complexity, the behavior and certain phenomena of systems and
processes cannot be feasibly modeled from first principles alone. Thus, to handle
the permanently increasing demand of high efficiency and accuracy as well as
scale of experiments, data-based modeling or purely empirical approaches have
become a standard.

Traditionally, machine learning (ML) algorithms are designed to train models purely from data. These often leads to models represented as highly complex
functions forms (e.g. neural networks) whose inner structure and working cannot be easily understood. Such models are called black-box models. However,
it must be ensured that models found by data-driven algorithms conform to
the functional principles of the modeled system, to ensure correct functionality after deployment. This is a topic especially relevant for scientific ML when
side information is frequently available [3]. For example, physical laws such as

© The Author(s), under exclusive license to Springer Nature Switzerland AG 2022
R. Moreno-Díaz et al. (Eds.): EUROCAST 2022, LNCS 13789, pp. 164–172, 2022.
https://doi.org/10.1007/978-3-031-25312-6_19

conservation of energy, thermodynamics, or laws of gravity have to be enforced. This can be accomplished through *shape-constraints* [6,7,15].

One potential approach is shape-constrained symbolic regression (SCSR) [7,9]. Symbolic regression allows to find models represented as short closed-form functions [1,8,16]. This increases the interpretability and transparency of the models. SR finds the functional form as well as suitable parameters, which distinguishes this approach from conventional regression methods, where the functional form is already predefined and only the numerical coefficients have to be adjusted and optimized (e.g. neural networks).

In [9] the authors proposed shape-constrained symbolic regression (SCSR) a supervised machine learning approach that aims at both fitting training data and compliance with the given shape-constraints. It was shown that the resulting models, fit the training data well and even achieve slightly better training errors than standard genetic programming (GP) models in some cases, and that the models conform to the specified constraints.

In [7] the authors present a multi-objective approach to handle each shape-constraint separately. This leads very often to a high number of objectives which gets hard to solve for traditionally multi-objective algorithms, therefore an algorithm which can handle many objectives (more than three) is needed. For this reason we test the many-objective algorithm NSGA-III which is an extension of the traditional multi-objective approach NSGA-II to improve the evaluation of multiple constraints.

The paper is structured as follows: In Sect. 2, shape-constrained regression is presented in detail as well as the use of a many-objective approach. In Sect. 3, similar work in this area is highlighted and presented. Section 4 and 5 present the experiments performed and results obtained, and conclude with a summary of the findings.

2   Shape-Constrained Regression

Shape-constrained regression (SCR) allows to enforce desired properties and behavior by specifying constraints which refer to the shape of the function, whereby the model is a function mapping real-valued inputs to real-valued outputs. These constraints are formulated based on prior knowledge stemming from empirical observations, domain experts knowledge, or physical principles. Mathematically these constraints can either be defined over the model's output or its partial derivatives. Figure 1 shows the exemplary use of shape constraints. While the model on the right has no additional information defined by shape constraints and thus cannot represent the expected behavior (monotonically increasing over x), the constraint $\frac{\partial}{\partial x_1} f(x) > 0$ was specified for the model on the left and the model can better reflect the underlying behavior.

Table 1 highlights all mathematical definition of constraints considered in this work.

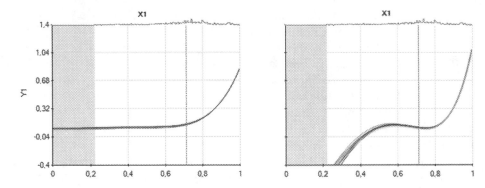

Fig. 1. Exemplary showcase of using additional information in form of shape constraints. Left we can see the model using shape-constraints and conforming to the known behavior. On the right side we see the model without any additional information.

Table 1. Mathematical formulation of constraints used in this work.

Property	Mathematical definition
Positivity	$f(x) > 0$
Negativity	$f(x) < 0$
Model bounds	$l \leq f(x) \leq u$
Monotonic-increasing	$\frac{\partial}{\partial x_1} f(x) > 0$
Monotonic-decreasing	$\frac{\partial}{\partial x_1} f(x) < 0$

To verify whether a model fulfills a given constraint or not, the minimum value of the partial derivative in the given domain has to be found. If the model is non-linear, this results in a non-linear optimization problem, which is often NP-hard to solve and therefore, approximation methods are needed. We can distinguish between two types of approximation methods for shape-constrained regression, pessimistic and optimistic approaches [5]. In this work interval arithmetic (IA) is used as approximation method for constraint evaluation in the same way as in [7].

2.1 Many-Objective Optimization for SCSR

Due to the resolution problem of using IA, multiple different conflicting objectives can occur. To handle this multiple objectives an approach which handles multiple objectives is needed. In [7] a multi-objective approach for dealing with multiple constraints is presented, but the number of constraints very often exceeds the maximum number foreseen for multi-objective approaches, which makes the use for a many-objective approach interesting.

The problem is modeled using a $1+n$ objective approach – one main objective and one objective for each constraint specified. The main objective (data-based loss function) is minimizing the approximation error, calculated using the normalized mean squared error (NMSE) in percent. The calculation of the NMSE is shown in Eq. 1, where y represents the target vector and $\hat{y}$ the prediction vector.

$$\text{NMSE}(y, \hat{y}) = \frac{100}{var(y)N} \sum_{i=1}^{N}(y_i - \hat{y}_i)^2 \tag{1}$$

The following objectives (physics-loss functions) are minimizing the constraint violations, whereas each constraint is treated as a separate objective. The violations are given by the sum of the superior and inferior bound violations:

$$P_i = P_i^{\text{inf}} + P_i^{\text{sup}} \tag{2}$$

where

$$
\begin{aligned}
P_i^{\text{inf}} &= |\min(\inf(f_i(x)) - \inf(c_i), 0)| \\
P_i^{\text{sup}} &= |\max(\sup(f_i(x)) - \sup(c_i), 0)|
\end{aligned} \tag{3}
$$

where $\sup(x)$ and $\inf(x)$ are functions returning the superior and inferior bounds of the intervals, $f_i(.)$ being the evaluation of the interval according to the i-th constraint and c_i is the feasibility interval for the i-th constraint.

3   Related Work

Currently, the inclusion of additional domain knowledge in data-based modelling gets more and more attention in literature and there are some recent papers targeting this topic [3,12,17]. Auguste et al. presented two new methods to include monotonic constraints in regression and classification trees [2].

The inclusion of prior knowledge in data-based modeling also plays an increasingly important role in modeling with neural networks as some recent articles show [11–13,18,19].

In [9] the authors introduce SCSR. The authors presented a single-objective approach, which uses a feasible/infeasible population split. The proposed method was tested on a set of instances taken from physics textbooks [20]. The results showed that using a-priori knowledge helps with finding useful solutions even on highly noise data and on extrapolation.

In [10] the authors present a multi-objective symbolic regression approach to minimize the approximation error on the training data as well as the constraint violations on the constraint dataset. Therefore, they extended the NSGA-II algorithm and used sampling to evaluate the constraints.

4   Experiments and Results

The solution quality as well as the runtime of both algorithms are used for comparison. The experiments are executed on a set of different test instances.

4.1   Algorithm Configuration

In this work two multi/many-objective evolutionary algorithms are used and compared to each other. Both presented algorithm start with a random initialized population, represented as expression trees. Followed by a repeating main-loop containing: fitness evaluation, parental selection, recombination, and mutation. Both algorithms are configured equally: max number of evaluation 500000, tournament selection with a crowded group size of 5, single-subtree crossover, and a mutator that either changes a single node or an entire subtree with a randomly initialized subtree. Further and more detailed parameter settings can be taken from [7].

4.2   Problem Instances

The problem instances from the *Feynman Symbolic Regression Database* [20] are used. However, we use only a subset of all instances are used, selected by the reported difficulty in [20] and only instances where shape-constraints could be derived. To generate training data, 300 points are sampled uniformly at random out of the expressions from Table 2. Afterwards we split the points so that the first 10% and last 10% are used as test set and the rest is used for training, this represents a test set outside the hull of the training data. In Table 3 and Eq. 6 all derived constraints for each instance are shown. The constraint's column shows in the first tuple the desired domain constraint the following values define the constraints for the partial derivatives of the model, where 0 means no constraint, 1 defines a monotonic increasing constraint, and -1 a monotonic decreasing function. The constraint definition for the *Pagie-1* instance follows the same principle, with the additional restriction that the defined constraints are valid only in a certain range of the input variables, which is shown in Eq. 6.

Table 2. Problem instances taken from [20]

Instance	Expression
I.6.20	$\exp\left(\frac{-\left(\frac{\theta}{\sigma}\right)^2}{2}\right)\frac{1}{\sqrt{2\pi}\sigma}$
I.9.18	$\frac{G\,m1\,m2}{(x2-x1)^2+(y2-y1)^2+(z2-z1)^2}$
I.30.5	$\mathrm{asin}\left(\frac{lambd}{nd}\right)$
I.32.17	$\frac{1}{2}\epsilon c\,Ef^2\frac{8\pi r^2}{3}\frac{\omega^4}{\left(\omega^2-\omega_0{}^2\right)^2}$
I.41.16	$\frac{h\,\omega^3}{\pi^2\,c^2\left(\exp\left(\frac{h\omega}{kbT}\right)-1\right)}$
I.48.20	$\frac{m\,c^2}{\sqrt{1-\frac{v^2}{c^2}}}$
II.35.21	$n_{rho}\,mom\,\tanh\left(\frac{mom\,B}{kbT}\right)$
III.9.52	$\frac{p_d\,Ef\,t}{h}\sin\left(\frac{(\omega-\omega_0)t}{2}\right)^2$
III.10.19	$mom\,\sqrt{Bx^2+By^2+Bz^2}$

Additionally, a regression problem from [14] is added, it is called Pagie-1 in the following. It is a problem instance with two variables as follows:

$$f(x, y) = \frac{1}{(1 + x^{-4})} + \frac{1}{(1 + y^{-4})} \tag{4}$$

It is evaluated over the range of:

$$-5 \le x \le 5 \quad \text{and} \quad -5 \le y \le 5 \quad (x, y \ne 0) \tag{5}$$

The training set for Pagie-1 consists of data points spaced 0.4 apart between the limits, which results in a set of 676 distinct x, y data points.

Table 3. Shape constraints used for each problem instance. *Input space* column refers to the variable domains. *Constraints* column represents the defined constraints over each variable.

Instance	Input space	Constraints
I.6.20	$(\sigma, \theta) \in [1..3]^2$	$([0..\infty], 0, -1)$
I.9.18	$(x1, y1, z1, m1, m2, G, x2, y2, z2)$	$([0..\infty], -1, -1, -1, 1, 1, 1, 1, 1, 1)$
	$\in [3..4]^3 \times [1..2]^6$	
I.30.5	$(lambd, n, d) \in [1..5]^2 \times [2..5]$	$([0..\infty], 1, -1, -1)$
I.32.17	$(\epsilon, c, Ef, r, \omega, \omega_0) \in [1..2]^5 \times [3..5]$	$([0..\infty], 1, 1, 1, 1, 1, -1)$
I.41.16	$(\omega, T, h, kb, c) \in [1..5]^5$	$([0..\infty], 0, 1, -1, 1, -1)$
I.48.20	$(m, v, c) \in [1..5] \times [1..2] \times [3..20]$	$([0..\infty], 1, 1, 1)$
II.35.21	$(n_{rho}, mom, B, kb, T) \in [1..5]^5$	$([0..\infty], 1, 1, 1, -1, -1)$
III.9.52	$(p_d, Ef, t, h, \omega, \omega_0) \in [1..3]^4 \times [1..5]^2$	$([0..\infty], 1, 1, 0, -1, 0, 0)$
III.10.19	$(mom, Bx, By, Bz) \in [1..5]^4$	$([0..\infty], 1, 1, 1, 1)$

$$f(x, y) \in [0..2]$$
$$\frac{\partial}{\partial x} f(x, y) \le 0, x < 0$$
$$\frac{\partial}{\partial x} f(x, y) \ge 0, x > 0$$
$$\frac{\partial}{\partial y} f(x, y) \le 0, y < 0 \tag{6}$$
$$\frac{\partial}{\partial y} f(x, y) \ge 0, y > 0$$

4.3 Results

Table 4 shows the result of 10 independent runs over all test instances. The error is represented as NMSE in percent. It can be observed that both algorithms give similar results, but NSGA-III gives slightly better results for each instance, but without being statistically significant. To test the significance, a two sample t-test was performed with the result of a p-value of 0.89259. In Table 5 the runtime performance of both algorithms is compared. It can be observed that the NSGA-III has a better runtime for each of the instances.

Table 4. Median test error (NMSE in %)

	NSGA-II	NSGA-III
I.6.20	20.88	**19.14**
I.30.5	7.32	**6.24**
I.32.17	7.17	**6.38**
I.41.16	18.50	**15.21**
I.48.20	24.19	**22.58**
II.35.21	14.60	**14.54**
III.9.52	89.03	**89.00**
III.10.19	11.30	**10.62**
Pagie-1	46.41	**40.71**

Table 5. Median runtime in seconds

	NSGA-II	NSGA-III
I.6.20	1798.02	**1407.67**
I.30.5	3621.99	**3604.91**
I.32.17	5812.10	**4504.23**
I.41.16	3858.61	**2879.05**
I.48.20	2825.38	**1647.43**
II.35.21	3217.67	**3045.41**
III.9.52	3009.62	**2064.16**
III.10.19	3939.14	**2254.29**
Pagie-1	4800.77	**4105.86**

5   Summary

NSGA-II and NSGA-III were compared for shape-constrained symbolic regression. The comparison of both methods was mainly motivated by the article [4] in which the advantages of NSGA-III over NSGA-II, when having more than three objectives is shown.

The two algorithms have been implemented in HeuristicLab and are benchmarked on a set of equation from physics textbooks *Feynman Symbolic Regression Database.*

The results showed that using NSGA-III over NSGA-II has slightly advantages for all instances. It is also shown that using NSGA-III can help with runtime. Although no statistical significant differences were achieved (t-test with p-value of 0.89259), it is shown that many-objective algorithms can help with performance increases on instances with more than three objectives. A more detailed comparison on instances with more than ten objectives will be investigated in further research.

Acknowledgement. The financial support by the Christian Doppler Research Association, the Austrian Federal Ministry for Digital and Economic Affairs and the National Foundation for Research, Technology and Development is gratefully acknowledged.

References

1. Affenzeller, M., Wagner, S., Winkler, S., Beham, A.: Genetic Algorithms and Genetic Programming: Modern Concepts and Practical Applications. Chapman and Hall/CRC (2009)
2. Auguste, C., Malory, S., Smirnov, I.: A better method to enforce monotonic constraints in regression and classification trees (2020)
3. Baker, N., et al.: Workshop report on basic research needs for scientific machine learning: Core technologies for artificial intelligence. Technical report, USDOE Office of Science (SC), Washington, DC (United States) (2019)
4. Deb, K., Jain, H.: An evolutionary many-objective optimization algorithm using reference-point-based nondominated sorting approach, part I: solving problems with box constraints. IEEE Trans. Evol. Comput. **18**(4), 577–601 (2014)
5. Gupta, M., et al.: Monotonic calibrated interpolated look-up tables. J. Mach. Learn. Res. **17**(109), 1–47 (2016)
6. Gupta, M., Louidor, E., Mangylov, O., Morioka, N., Narayan, T., Zhao, S.: Multidimensional shape constraints. In: International Conference on Machine Learning (ICML 2020), pp. 3918–3928. PMLR (2020)
7. Haider, C., de Franca, F.O., Burlacu, B., Kronberger, G.: Shape-constrained multiobjective genetic programming for symbolic regression. Appl. Soft Comput. **132**, 109855 (2023). https://doi.org/10.1016/j.asoc.2022.109855. ISSN 1568-4946
8. Koza, J.R.: Genetic Programming: On the Programming of Computers by Means of Natural Selection, vol. 1. MIT Press (1992)
9. Kronberger, G., de Franca, F.O., Burlacu, B., Haider, C., Kommenda, M.: Shape-constrained symbolic regression-improving extrapolation with prior knowledge. Evol. Comput. **30**(1), 75–98 (2022)
10. Kubalík, J., Derner, E., Babuška, R.: Symbolic regression driven by training data and prior knowledge. In: Proceedings of the 2020 Genetic and Evolutionary Computation Conference, pp. 958–966 (2020)
11. Li, L., Fan, M., Singh, R., Riley, P.: Neural-guided symbolic regression with asymptotic constraints (2019)
12. Liu, X., Han, X., Zhang, N., Liu, Q.: Certified monotonic neural networks. In: Advances in Neural Information Processing Systems, vol. 33, pp. 15427–15438. Curran Associates, Inc. (2020)
13. Muralidhar, N., Islam, M.R., Marwah, M., Karpatne, A., Ramakrishnan, N.: Incorporating prior domain knowledge into deep neural networks. In: 2018 IEEE International Conference on Big Data (Big Data), pp. 36–45 (2018)
14. Pagie, L., Hogeweg, P.: Evolutionary consequences of coevolving targets. Evol. Comput. **5**, 401–418 (1997)
15. Papp, D., Alizadeh, F.: Shape-constrained estimation using nonnegative splines. J. Comput. Graph. Stat. **23**(1), 211–231 (2014)
16. Poli, R., Langdon, W.B., McPhee, N.F., Koza, J.R.: A field guide to genetic programming. Lulu.com (2008)
17. Rai, A.: Explainable AI: from black box to glass box. J. Acad. Mark. Sci. **48**(1), 137–141 (2020)
18. Raissi, M., Perdikaris, P., Karniadakis, G.: Physics-informed neural networks: a deep learning framework for solving forward and inverse problems involving nonlinear partial differential equations. J. Comput. Phys. **378**, 686–707 (2019)

19. Stewart, R., Ermon, S.: Label-free supervision of neural networks with physics and domain knowledge. In: Proceedings of the Thirty-First AAAI Conference on Artificial Intelligence, AAAI 2017, pp. 2576–2582. AAAI Press (2017)
20. Udrescu, S.M., Tegmark, M.: AI Feynman: a physics-inspired method for symbolic regression. Sci. Adv. **6**(16), eaay2631 (2020)

Using Explainable Artificial Intelligence for Data Based Detection of Complications in Records of Patient Treatments

Marina Strobl[1], Julia Vetter[1], Gerhard Halmerbauer[2], Tilman Königswieser[3], and Stephan M. Winkler[1,4(✉)]

[1] School of Informatics, Communications and Media, University of Applied Sciences Upper Austria, Hagenberg, Austria
[2] School of Business and Management, University of Applied Sciences Upper Austria, Steyr, Austria
[3] Salzkammergut-Klinikum, Oberösterreichische Gesundheitsholding GmbH, Vöcklabruck, Austria
[4] Department of Computer Science, Johannes Kepler University, Linz, Austria
stephan.winkler@fh-ooe.at

Abstract. We analyze data of 18,000 patients for identifying models that are able to detect complications in the data of surgeries and other medical treatments. High quality detection models are found using data available for those patients, for whom general data as well as risk factors are available. For identifying these detection models we use explainable artificial intelligence, namely symbolic regression by genetic programming with three different levels of model complexity with respect to model size and complexity of functions used as building blocks for the identified models.

1 Introduction

Since 2015, FH Upper Austria and Oberösterreichische Gesundheitsholding (OÖG) have joined forces and develop the platform *Leistungsvergleich Medizin (LeiVMed)* for the monitoring and analysis of data from patient treatments. In the current research context, our main goal is to identify models that are able to detect complications (a posteriori) in the data of treatments; complications can be minor complications such as hematoma as well as major complications such as heart attacks or pneumonia, e.g. Our data base consists of approximately 18,000 samples storing information about the surgeries and treatments of seven different medical case classes.

Our main goal is to identify models that are able to detect complications in patient records. We use explainable artificial intelligence (AI), namely symbolic regression by genetic programming, to identify models with different degrees of complexity and varying subsets of data that are used.

© The Author(s), under exclusive license to Springer Nature Switzerland AG 2022
R. Moreno-Díaz et al. (Eds.): EUROCAST 2022, LNCS 13789, pp. 173–180, 2022.
https://doi.org/10.1007/978-3-031-25312-6_20

In Sect. 2 we describe the data basis used in this research, in Sect. 3 we describe the machine learning methods used for explainable artificial intelligence, and in Sect. 4 we summarize the modeling results; Sect. 5 concludes this paper.

2   Data Basis

Data Recorded for Primary and Secondary Patients. The data base we use here consists of 17,956 samples storing information about the surgeries and treatments of patients from seven different medical case classes: hernia, gallbladder, prostatectomy, hip arthroplasty, thyroid, colon, and rectum. All cases have been revised by study nurses and the respective data samples are collected within the LeiVMed system called data of "primary patients". In addition, we also use data of "secondary" patients; for these samples, the set of available features is significantly smaller.

In total, 123 features including demographic information (age, sex, body mass index (BMI), etc.), treatment and surgical information, and risk factors are stored in the LeiVMed data base. 66 of these features are available for *primary patients* and give information about the treatment and status before surgery. For *secondary patients*, no risk factors are recorded, which results in only 24 available pre-surgery features in those samples. Post-surgery features include the length of stay, complications, and services (laboratory, radiology, etc.). 57 features are available for primary patients after surgery, and 46 features are available for secondary patients. For secondary patients, no information about complications is recorded.

The average values of some exemplary crucial features such as age, ASA score (a score describing the fitness of patients before treatment, as defined by the American Society of Anesthesiologists (ASA) in 1963), the number of laboratory services before surgery, and risk factors are displayed in Table 1. We see that patients who undergo surgeries are on average older than 55 years with an average BMI of 27.23. The average ASA shows that most patients are normal healthy patients (ASA 1) or patients with mild systemic disease(s) (ASA 2). On average, 19.07% of the patients are smokers and 0.62% of all patients are receiving chemotherapy. However, rectum surgery is performed on 3.31% of the patients undergoing chemotherapy; the main reason for rectum surgery is carcinoma [1], which explains the high rate of patients with this risk factor.

Information About Patients with Complications. Information about complications occurring during or after surgery is only available for primary patients. These complications can be divided into minor and major complications; major complications are more severe complications such as myocardial infarction, pneumonia, or sepsis. When comparing non-complicated cases with those affected by complications we see statistically significant differences ($p < 0.0001$) regarding age, ASA score, the number of laboratory services before surgery, and emergency admission. Among patients with complications, there is a higher ratio of alcoholism as well as previous cancer diagnoses. However, the ratio of smokers is

Table 1. Average values of exemplary features recorded for patients of different medical cases: Age, ASA score, the number of laboratory services before surgery, and the information about diabetes, and the BMI are available for all patients, whereas information about risk factors (smoking, chemo therapies) are available only for primary patients.

Medical	General features available for all patients					Risk factors	
Case	Age	ASA sc	Lab. pre OP	Diabetes	BMI	Smoker	Chemo th
Gallbladder	57.427	1.878	52.571	10.47%	28.530	22.21%	0.31%
Hernia	59.301	1.742	15.401	6.11%	25.532	20.88%	0.16%
Hip arthr	67.030	2.011	33.229	11.57%	27.912	13.17%	0.09%
Colon	65.703	2.200	74.962	15.21%	26.733	17.33%	0.45%
Prostatect	64.353	1.863	22.209	9.67%	27.798	16.51%	0.00%
Rectum	65.125	2.157	62.913	13.21%	26.273	18.77%	3.31%
Thyroid	56.510	1.873	30.284	10.42%	27.849	24.59%	0.00%

not significantly higher in patients with complications compared to non-smoking patients. Average values for selected features for patients without complications as well as patients with complications are given in Table 2.

Table 2. Average values of patients without complications, with minor complications, and with major complications after surgeries: Differences in age and BMI do not show statistical significance, whereas the patients' ASA scores, the numbers of laboratory tests before surgery, the emergency admission rates, and risk factors alcoholism and cancer show significant differences.

Complications	General features available for all patients					Risk factors	
	Age	ASA sc	Lab. pre OP	Emergency	BMI	Alc	Cancer
None	59.976	1.820	33.547	5.94%	25.801	0.61%	1.18%
Minor	65.908	2.169	52.658	8.28%	25.945	1.56%	4.12%
Major	69.382	2.384	78.976	13.26%	25.774	3.24%	7.52%

3 Explainable AI: Machine Learning by Symbolic Regression Using Genetic Programming

In general, machine learning (ML) is understood as that branch of computer science that is dedicated to the development of methods for learning knowledge and models from given data.

In fact, ML is an essential step within the overall system identification process [2]. The system, which is investigated, might be of technical nature, a biological system, a finance system, or any other system - the essential point is that there are variables/features, which can be measured (here denoted as $x_1, x_2, \ldots, x_n$).

Machine learning algorithms are then used to identify models on the basis of data collections. These models are then often used to predict the investigated systems' behavior, to identify relevant relationships between variables, and in general to gain further insight into the investigated systems. Obviously, the collection of data is a very important step, as we will only be able to understand the system and its internal functionality correctly if its characteristic behavior is actually represented in the data.

Black box machine learning techniques are methods that produce models which are functions of the inputs and calculate outputs, where the internal functioning of the model is either hidden or too complicated to be analyzed (random forests or artificial neural networks, e.g.). *White box* modeling, on the contrary, produces models whose structure is not hidden, but can be analyzed in detail.

In this research we analyze the performance of white box modeling by genetic programming, which implements explainable artificial intelligence.

We use *symbolic regression*, a method for inducing mathematical expressions on data. The key feature of this technique is that the object of search is a symbolic description of a model, whose structure is not pre-defined. This is in sharp contrast with other methods of nonlinear regression, where a specific model is assumed and the parameters/coefficients are optimized during the training process. Using a set of basic functions we apply *genetic programming* (GP, [3]) as search technique that evolves symbolic regression models as combinations of basic functions through an evolutionary process. As the complexity of these models is limited, the process is forced to include only relevant variables in the models.

We use GP with offspring selection (OS) [3]. Applying offspring selection has the effect that new individuals are compared to their parents; in the strict version, children are passed on to the next generation only if their quality is better than the quality of both parents. Figure 1 shows GP with OS as used in the research discussed here. The functions set described in [4] (including arithmetic as well as logical ones) was used for building composite function expressions.

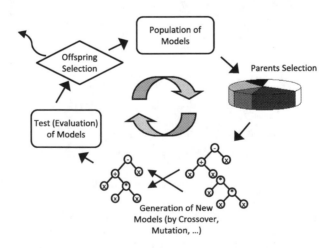

Fig. 1. Genetic programming with offspring selection [5].

4   Results: Identification Models for Complications

4.1   Model Identification Scenarios

As already described previously, our main goal is to identify models that are able to detect complications based on patient records. We pursued the following modeling scenarios that differ regarding the considered feature sets:

- On the one hand we want to identify models that use features available only for primary patients, on the other hand we want to identify models that use features that are available for all patients (primary as well as secondary).
- Additionally, on the one hand we want to identify models that use features available after surgery, on the other hand we want to identify models that only use features that are available before surgery.

These four feature sets are in the following denoted as the following scenarios:

- Scenario A: All available features
- Scenario B: All features available before surgery
- Scenario C: Features available for secondary patients
- Scenario D: Features available for secondary patients before surgery.

4.2   Modeling Configuration Setups

We used genetic programming implemented in HeuristicLab [6] using the following algorithmic configuration:

- Population size: 100
- Selection schemes: Proportional/random parent selection; strict offspring selection, maximum selection pressure 100
- Mutation rate: 15%

  Regarding model complexity we tested the following three configurations:

- *High complexity*: The maximum model size is set to 150 nodes, all arithmetic and logical functions available for GP in HeuristicLab are used.
- *Medium complexity*: The maximum model size is set to 50 nodes, all arithmetic and logical functions available for GP in HeuristicLab are used.
- *Low complexity*: The maximum model size is set to 50 nodes, only basic functions (+, −, ∗, /, and conditionals) are used.

4.3   Results

Using all four feature sets we tested the three previously mentioned modeling configurations applying 5-fold cross validation [7]. We here report test results analyzing the resulting receiver operating characteristic (ROC) curves [8] that illustrate the performance (true positive rate vs. false positive rate) of the identified classifiers for varying discrimination thresholds.

Scenario A: All Available Features. As shown in Fig. 2, using all available features we are able to train classifiers with a maximum AUC of approximately 80%. The best results are achieved using models of medium complexity.

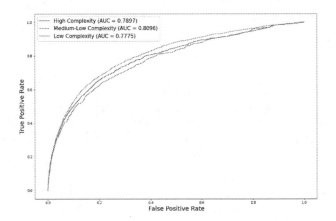

Fig. 2. Results for modeling scenario A (using all available features).

Scenario B: All Features Available Before Surgery. As shown in Fig. 3, using only those features that are available before surgery we get significantly worse results, namely classifiers with a maximum AUC of approximately 65% - 70%. There is no clear difference in modeling quality for different complexities of the models.

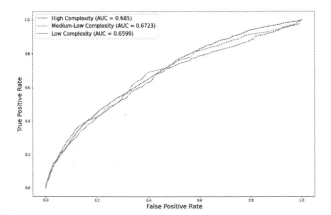

Fig. 3. Results for modeling scenario B (using all features available before surgery).

Scenario C: Features Available for Secondary Patients. As shown in Fig. 4, using all features that are available also for secondary patients we are again able to train classifiers with a maximum AUC of approximately 80%.

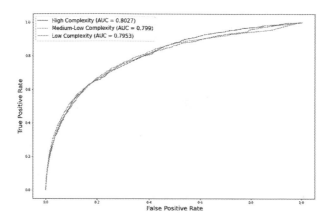

Fig. 4. Results for modeling scenario C (using all features available for secondary patients).

Scenario D: Features Available for Secondary Patients Before Surgery Finally, as shown in Fig. 5, using only those features that are available before surgery also for secondary patients, we get classifiers with a maximum area under the curve (AUC) of approximately 65% - 70%.

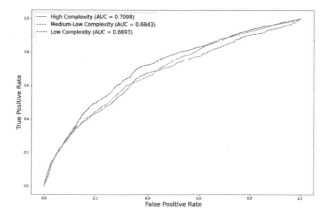

Fig. 5. Results for modeling scenario D (using features available for secondary patients before surgery).

5   Discussion and Conclusion

Our results clearly indicate that we are able to identify classification models that are able to identify complicative cases based on patient data. We see that the results using only data before surgery are significantly worse than the results achieved by also considering data after surgery. The most surprising fact is that the results achieved using all features (including risk factors) are not significantly better than the results using only the data available for secondary patients (for whom risk factors are not available).

Future work will concentrate on the identification of heterogeneous model ensembles as well as specific models for specific medical case classes.

Acknowledgements. The work described in this paper was supported by LeiVMed, a joint research project of FH OÖ and OÖG, as well as *TIMED*, FH OÖ's Center of Excellence for Technical Innovation in Medicine. The authors thank their colleague Louise Buur for careful proofreading of this paper.

References

1. Benson, A.B., et al.: Rectal cancer, version 2.2018, nccn clinical practice guidelines in oncology. J. National Comprehensive Cancer Netw. **16**, 874–901 (2018)
2. Ljung, L., (ed): System Identification, 2nd ed.: Theory for the User. Prentice Hall PTR, Upper Saddle Rive (1999)
3. Affenzeller, M., Winkler, S., Wagner, S., Beham, A.: Genetic Algorithms and Genetic Programming - Modern Concepts and Practical Applications, vol. 6 of Numerical Insights. CRC Press, Chapman & Hall (2009)
4. Winkler, S.M.: Evolution. Syst. Identifi. Mod. Concepts Practical Appli. Schriften der Johannes Kepler Universität Linz, Universitätsverlag Rudolf Trauner (2009)
5. Winkler, S.M.: Evolutionary Computation and Symbolic Regression in Scientific Modeling. Schriften der Johannes Kepler Universität Linz (2018)
6. Wagner, S., et al.: Architecture and design of the heuristiclab optimization environment. In: Advanced Methods and Applications in Computational Intelligence, Topics in Intelligent Engineering and Informatics, vol. 6. 197–261. Springer (2014). https://doi.org/10.1007/978-3-319-01436-4_10
7. Kohavi, R.: A study of cross-validation and bootstrap for accuracy estimation and model selection. In: Proceedings of the 14th international Joint Conference on Artificial Intelligence, vol. 2, pp. 1137–1143. Morgan Kaufmann (1995)
8. Bradley, A.: The use of the area under the ROC curve in the evaluation of machine learning algorithms. Pattern Recogn. **30**, 1145–1159 (1997)

Identifying Differential Equations for the Prediction of Blood Glucose using Sparse Identification of Nonlinear Systems

David Joedicke[1]([✉]) [iD], Daniel Parra[2] [iD], Gabriel Kronberger[1] [iD],
and Stephan M. Winkler[1] [iD]

[1] Josef Ressel Centre for Symbolic Regression Heuristic and Evolutionary Algorithms Laboratory, University of Applied Sciences Upper Austria, Hagenberg, Austria
david.joedicke@fh-ooe.at
[2] Universidad Complutense de Madrid, Madrid, Spain
dparra@ucm.es

Abstract. Describing dynamic medical systems using machine learning is a challenging topic with a wide range of applications. In this work, the possibility of modeling the blood glucose level of diabetic patients purely on the basis of measured data is described. A combination of the influencing variables insulin and calories are used to find an interpretable model. The absorption speed of external substances in the human body depends strongly on external influences, which is why time shifts are added for the influencing variables. The focus is put on identifying the best time-shifts that provide robust models with good prediction accuracy that are independent of other unknown external influences. The modeling is based purely on the measured data using Sparse Identification of Nonlinear Dynamics. A differential equation is determined which, starting from an initial value, simulates blood glucose dynamics. By applying the best model to test data, we can show that it is possible to simulate the long-term blood glucose dynamics using differential equations and few, influencing variables.

Keywords: Machine learning · Differential equations · Symbolic regression

1 Background and Motivation

Approximately 422 million people worldwide are diagnosed with diabetes and it accounts for an estimated 1.5 million deaths per year. Diabetes is a group of metabolic diseases with high blood sugar levels, which produces the symptoms of frequent urination, increased thirst, and increased hunger. Untreated, diabetes can cause many complications like ketoacidosis and nonketotic hyperosmolar coma. Serious long-term complications include heart disease, stroke, kidney failure, foot ulcers and damage to the eyes. Diabetes is due to either the pancreas

© The Author(s), under exclusive license to Springer Nature Switzerland AG 2022
R. Moreno-Díaz et al. (Eds.): EUROCAST 2022, LNCS 13789, pp. 181–188, 2022.
https://doi.org/10.1007/978-3-031-25312-6_21

not producing enough insulin, or the cells of the body not responding properly to the insulin produced. There are three main types of diabetes, which are different in its cause and symptoms. In this paper we use data of patients suffering from Type 1 diabetes, which results from the body's failure to produce enough insulin [1] [5].

1.1   Dynamical Systems and Differential Equations

Numerous systems and processes can be represented by dynamic models. Whenever there is change over time, we speak of dynamic systems. Dynamic systems are often difficult to model, since the underlying dependencies between the parameters of a system are not known. Due to this discrepancy between diverse applications and complexity in the mapping, the modeling of dynamic systems is a research area with various approaches [6].

In most applications, the differential equations of dynamic systems are not known. Instead, there are measurements of the individual variables. Our goal is to extract the differential equation system from the measurement data. Measurement errors, noise or unknown influences play a significant role here. In the case of modeling the blood glucose level, the course can be controlled by the supply of carbohydrates and insulin, unknown influences such as activity level, sleep quality or heart rate must be eliminated in the modeling step.

2   Prior Work

The evolution of blood glucose levels of diabetic patients has already been modelled using different machine learning methods such as support vector machines, gradient-boosting, or different types of neural networks. To better represent and analyse the dynamic behaviour of blood glucose, methods that provide less complex and more interpretable models are preferable [3].

Additionally to those static models the advantage of the usage of differential equations to predict the blood glucose dynamics is part of various research approaches. Gatewood et al. already introduced an idea to predict these dynamics using a fixed structure within a set of differential equations in 1970. They proposed to describe the change of the glucose value as $\frac{dg}{dt} = -m_1 g - m_2 h + J(t)$ and the net hypoglycemic promoting hormone as $\frac{dh}{dt} = -m_2 g + m_4 h + K(t)$, where m_1 to m_4 are positive constants, J and K represent the entry rate of glucose and insulin and t is time. They showed that it is possible to estimate the values for the m-parameters to describe the blood glucose level in the human body [10].

Additionaly to this very simple approach multiple papers adapted the idea to improve the results. Chervoneva et al. proposed an approach to estimate the parameters of a mathematical model based on a small number of noisy observations using generalized smoothing [9]. Shiang et al. performed those parameter estimation by minimizing the sum of squared residuals [8]. The described approaches fit parameters of pre-defined structures to measured data, while this paper introduces a possibility to create accurate models without further specification of the structure of the differential equations. Those models are still interpretable since only few, important terms are used to describe the underlying dynamic. Additionally we particularly predict the long-term blood glucose dynamics for an entire day. The known approaches mainly focus on the short-term behaviour, predicting values up to two hours.

3   Methodolgy

3.1   Data

We use the *Ohio T1DM Dataset* [2], which includes the health and wellbeing over 8 weeks for 12 anonymized patients with type 1 diabetes. For each of the patients multiple health data and live events are measured. The following variables are used to predict the glucose value:

- **Basal:** Long acting insulin, continuously infused
- **Bolus:** Short acting insulin, delivered to the patient at irregular time intervals
- **Meal:** Meals including the carbohydrate estimate for each meal

Combining all of the measured variables together creates a dataset with continuously measured data points every five minutes. There are two types of measurements: Influencing variables (basal, bolus and meals) can be influenced by the patients by taking insuline or eating something. Those impacts can be used to influence the blood glucose level directly. The glucose level itself can't be influenced directly, only indirect by the influencing variables. In this paper we describe the blood glucose level specifically for each patient, which is why we have used the specific dataset of a single test person, in which the data were recorded most completely. This dataset contains 17 days full of data. We are using 11 days for training and validation, the other 6 days are for testing the model.

3.2   Feature Engineering

Absorption of the Substances by the Body: Since the dissolution of substances in the body occurs with a time delay and not abruptly, we preprocessed both bolus and carbohydrate values using the Berger function: [7]

$$\frac{dA}{dt} = \frac{s \cdot t^s \cdot T_{50}{}^s \cdot D}{t \cdot (T_{50}{}^s + t^s)^2} - A \tag{1}$$

$$T_{50} = a \cdot D \cdot b \tag{2}$$

where A is the plasma insulin, D the insuline dose, t the time after the injection, s the time course of absorption and a and b are parameters to characterize dependency of T_{50} on D. In our preprocessing we calculated the Berger function with $s = 1.6$, $a = 5.2$ and $b = 41$

The Berger function converts a one-time recorded input such as the ingestion of insulin as well as carbs to such an extent that the uptake of the substance into the body does not take place abruptly but distributed over a longer period of time. The parameters from Eq. (1) determine exactly how the substance dissolves in the body.

Time-Shifts: Additionally to the specified dissolution of the carbohydrates and the bolus in the body we implemented a time-shift to both the carbohydrates and the bolus value. Introducing these time-shifts allows us to dampen the impact of different activity levels across different days. For example, if a person exercises, the ingested carbohydrates dissolve more quickly in the body than if the person went a day without exercise. We implemented time-shifts for thirty minutes in the past, having a data-point every five minutes. This leads to six shifts for both the bolus and the carbohydrates. Our goal is to find an optimal time-shift for both the carbohydrates and the bolus value during the training phase and use those time-shifts for the test data.

3.3   Algorithm

Sparse Identification of Nonlinear Dynamical Systems (SINDy) uses sparsity techniques and machine learning to discover differential equations underlying a dynamical system. SINDy takes advantage of the fact, that most dynamical systems have only a few relevant terms, making them sparse in the space of possible functions. The numerical difference at each time step t for each parameter is used to create a matrix X. For each parameter of X a so called library $\Phi(X)$ with nonlinear functions of the column of X, such as constants, polynomials and trigonometric functions is created. Each column of $\Phi(X)$ represents a term for the right hand side of a differential equation. Using sparse regression only those terms with relevance to the system are kept [4].

3.4   Grid Search

To detect the best model several steps were performed:

- Step 1: Find the best time-shift
- Step 2: Select best model with the detected time-shifts
- Step 3: Evaluate model with test data

The model for predicting the dynamics of glucose levels in blood should be as robust as possible to external influences, this is done as explained in Sect. 3.2 by introducing time-shifts for the supply of carbohydrates as well as insulin. We define a model as robust that achieves the lowest error of the glucose value across all training days. We use the average absolute error per prediction as the error value for the measurement of the quality of a model.

Step 1: Find Most Robust Time-Shift: In the first step, the best combination of the two defined time-shifts is to be found, i.e. for which shift of the two variables the most stable results are delivered. For this purpose, a model is created for each combination of carbohydrate shift and bolus shift for each of the training days. These models are then applied to all other combinations of time-shifts for all other training days. To find the best time-shift we used the following procedure: (1) Simulate blood glucose levels for all training days and time-shifts for each of the models. (2) Sort the results by the median error for each model and take the 10% best results per time-shift. (3) Define the best time-shift as the one with the lowest mean absolute error across those 10% of the best results.

Step 2: Select Best Model: After determining which of the time-shifts are the most robust ones, one of the models from all the training days has to be selected as the final model. We choose the model which has the lowest average error among the other training days, including all of the time-shifts for this validation step. This leads to a model, which is robust against different time-shifts which might occur due to different behaviours of the body on different days.

Step 3: Evaluate Model with Test Data: In the last step, the selected model is used to predict the blood glucose level of the days that were not used in the training. We took the first value of blood glucose level as the start value and predict the rest of the day integrating the differential equation selected in step 2. The quality of the predicted results is determined by the root mean squared error, the mean absolute error and the correlation. Each of the quality measurements has its advantages, using multiple of them allows a better comparison of the accuracy of the results. For a better interpretation of the results, we compare the determined glucose values with a simple, constant model (CM) in which we use the starting value as a constant value over the entire test range.

4   Results

The result of each step is the input for the next step: The optimal time-shifts are used to select the best model, this differential equation is then applied to calculate the prediction for the test data.

4.1   Best Time-Shift

The left part of Fig. 1 shows the mean absolute error of the 10% best results for the combination of each time-shifts across all days. The best time-shifts evaluated across all training days are the following:

- **Bolus:** 30 min
- **Carbohydrates:** 5 min

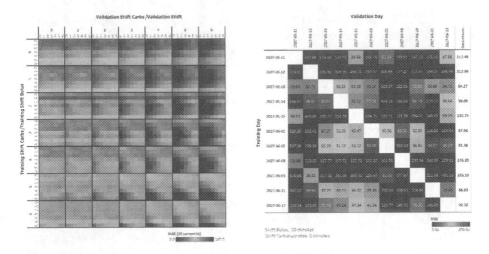

Fig. 1. Quality of models

4.2   Best Model

Using the time-shifts from the previous step the best model is selected. The right part of Fig. 1 shows the error of all the models for each days using the specified time-shifts. The best model is the model trained on the data of 13th of May 2027 which has the lowest validation error with an average mean absolute error of 64.27 $\frac{mg}{dL}$. The differential equation of this model is:

$$\frac{dG}{dT} = p_0 + p_1 \cdot b + p_2 \cdot C + p_3 \cdot G + p_4 \cdot B \cdot b + p_5 \cdot b^2 + p_6 \cdot b \cdot C + p_7 \cdot b \cdot G + p_8 \cdot C \cdot G + p_9 \cdot G^2 \tag{3}$$

$p_0 = \quad -1.14$	$G = $ Glucose
$p_1 = \quad 102.39$	$C = $ Carbohydrates (bergerized, time-shift: 5 minutes)
$p_2 = \quad -0.14$	$B = $ Bolus (bergerized, time-shift: 30 minutes)
$p_3 = \quad -7.69$	$b = $ Basal
$p_4 = \quad -0.21$	
$p_5 = \quad 648.80$	
$p_6 = \quad 12.80$	
$p_7 = -185.42$	
$p_8 = \quad -0.96$	
$p_9 = \quad 11.39$	

4.3   Predicted Values

Equation (3) is used to predict the blood glucose level with only the start value of the blood glucose level and the influencing variables. Figure 2 shows these results for all of the test days.

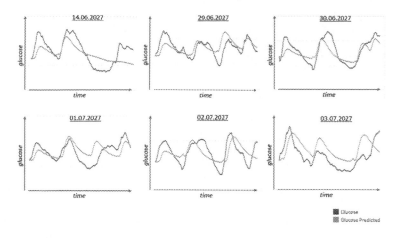

Fig. 2. Exemplary results

4.4 Quality of Results

Table 1 shows the quality of the different test days compared to the baseline results of a constant model (CM). It is clear that by using SINDy, the prediction of blood glucose levels works much better than with a simple constant model.

Table 1. Overview results

	RMSE [mg/dL]		MAE [mg/dL]		R^2
Interval	SINDy	CM	SINDy	CM	SINDy
14.06.2027	40.55	59.23	34.15	50.30	0.67
29.06.2027	28.41	46.30	20.92	28.41	0.50
30.06.2027	29.13	55.74	23.59	29.13	0.84
01.07.2027	35.01	48.42	28.16	40.59	0.39
02.07.2027	36.37	58.45	31.40	49.60	0.55
03.07.2027	49.17	50.41	45.68	37.89	0.56
Average	36.44	53.09	30.65	39.32	0.59

5 Summary and Outlook

Modeling blood glucose levels with SINDy makes it possible to predict the long-term course of blood glucose levels in a diabetic patient. The model found is robust to possible external unknown influences and therefore allows to give a valid prediction about the future development of the blood glucose level. Although the overall prediction during an entire day is close to the actual values, the longer the prediction horizon is the higher the deviation is. Modeling of shorter time periods was not addressed in this paper; based on the good results over a longer observation horizon, the knowledge gained will be applied to other time intervals in future experiments.

References

1. World Health Organization. Diabetes (2021). https://www.who.int/news-room/fact-sheets/detail/diabetes
2. Marling, C., Bunescu, R.: The OhioT1DM dataset for blood glucose level prediction: update 2020. CEUR Workshop Proc. **2675**, 71–74 (2020)
3. van Doorn, W.P.T.M., Foreman, Y.D., Schaper, N.C., et al.: Machine learning-based glucose prediction with use of continuous glucose and physical activity monitoring data: the maastricht study. PLoS One (2021)
4. Kaiser, E., Kutz, J.N., Brunton, S.L.: Sparse identification of nonlinear dynamics for model predictive control in the low-data limit. Proc. R. Soc. A. **474**, 20180335 (2018)
5. American Diabetes Association; Diagnosis and classification of diabetes mellitus. Diab. Care **32**(Suppl 1), S62–S67 (2009)
6. Raol, J.R., Girija, G., Singh, J.: Modelling and parameter estimation of dynamic systems. In: Control, Robotics & Sensors (2004)
7. Berger, M., Rodbard, D., et al.: Computer simulation of plasma insulin and glucose dynamics after subcutaneous insulin injection. Diab. Care **12**, 10 (1989)
8. Shiang, K.-D., Kandeel, F., et al.: A computational model of the human glucose-insulin regulatory system. J. Biomed. Res. **24**, 5 (2010)
9. Chervoneva, I., Freydin, B., Hipszer, B., Apanasovich, T.V., Joseph, J.I.: Estimation of nonlinear differential equation model for glucose-insulin dynamics in type I diabetic patients using generalized smoothing. Ann. Appl. Stat. **8**(2), 886–904 (2014)
10. Gatewood, L.C., Ackerman, E., Rosevear, J.W., Molnar, G.D.: Modeling blood glucose dynamics. Behav. Sci. **15**, 72–87 (1970)

Obtaining Difference Equations for Glucose Prediction by Structured Grammatical Evolution and Sparse Identification

Daniel Parra[1]([✉])📵, David Joedicke[2]📵, Alberto Gutiérrez[1,4]📵,
J. Manuel Velasco[1]📵, Oscar Garnica[1]📵, J. Manuel Colmenar[3]📵,
and J. Ignacio Hidalgo[1]📵

[1] Universidad Complutense de Madrid, Madrid, Spain
{dparra02,albegu02,mvelascc,ogarnica,hidalgo}@ucm.es
[2] University of Applied Sciences of Upper Austria, Hagenberg, Austria
David.Joedicke@fh-hagenberg.at
[3] Universidad Rey Juan Carlos, Madrid, Spain
josemanuel.colmenar@urjc.es
[4] Biztools S.L, Madrid, Spain
alberto.gutierrez@biztools.es

Abstract. Diabetes is one of the most common and difficult non-communicable diseases to deal with in our days. People with diabetes need to keep their glucose levels within a certain range to avoid health complications. Some patients must inject insulin to regulate their glucose levels, and estimating the necessary dose is not an easy task. In this paper, we investigate how to obtain expressions that predict glucose levels using variables such as previous glucose values, food ingestion (in carbohydrates), basal insulin dosing, and dosing of bolus of insulin. This paper proposes the combination of structured grammatical evolution and sparse identification to obtain difference equations governing the dynamics of the glucose levels over time. Glucose prediction serves as a tool for deciding the most convenient insulin dosing. Our technique produces promising results that provide explainable equations and use information usually managed by people with diabetes.

1 Introduction

Two main types of diabetes can be distinguished. Type 1 diabetes appears when the pancreas is unable to generate insulin. On the other hand, Type 2 diabetes is considered when the insulin does not correctly act in the organism, due to a poor response or insulin resistance of the cells [1]. People with diabetes should control their glucose levels to avoid possible health complications. Meals are one of the moments that may involve a large variation in glucose. For this reason, and in order to keep their levels within a healthy range, it may be necessary to inject the correct dose of insulin. To help people with diabetes to make decisions when calculating insulin dosage, we investigate how to develop explainable expressions that match glucose levels.

Symbolic Regression (SR) techniques were widely used in the past for obtaining those expressions [4,5]. Applying Genetic Programming (GP), or some of its variants, is one of the best ways to solve SR problems. Gaucel et al. [6] went a step forward and proposed the use of symbolic regression to obtain first-order Eulerian approximations of differential equations and then reconstruct the original differential equations using the mathematical properties of the approximation. In this paper, we investigate some ideas inspired by the cited papers. We propose to apply Structured Grammatical Evolution (SGE) [7] to learn difference equations that fit the glucose dynamics of a person with diabetes. The difference equations will be derived by SGE from the historical data of the patient. Thus data includes; interstitial glucose values, $G(t)$, basal rate of insulin administration, $B_I(t)$, bolus insulin injections, $I_B(t)$, and food intakes measured carbohydrates units, $F_{ch}(t)$. In addition, we apply sparse identification methods, [2], where second order non-linear variables are generated from the historical data mentioned above .

The obtained results are promising, as they can represent glucose dynamics, capturing the principal rises and falls in glucose levels. However, the values of the root mean squared error of the predicted values are still high, with remaining values around 50, for most cases, in the training and test phase. On the positive side, expressions are explainable, and execution times are low.

The rest of the paper is organized as follows. Section 2 gives a brief review of related work. Section 3 describes the methodology proposed in this paper. Section 4 presents the experimental results, and finally, Sect. 5 contains the conclusions and future work.

2   State of the Art

Continuous glucose monitoring devices have made it possible to improve some aspects of daily life for people with diabetes. This technology makes it possible to identify cases of hypoglycemia and hyperglycemia, detecting glucose values that exceed certain thresholds or even preventing them using predictive algorithms. In [12] the authors have developed a new short-term glucose prediction algorithm with a neural network that uses data from the monitoring system and information of carbohydrate intakes. Their database has simulated data (five virtual patients) and real data (a volunteer with type 1 diabetes).

In computer science, several works use neural networks focused on the problem of diabetes. In [13] the authors present a model for predicting glucose levels using a convolutional neural network. The model is a modification of a recently published model that has proven useful in acoustic signal processing (WaveNet). A common element between our paper and [13] is that both take their data from the OhioT1DM dataset.

Another example is [11], this paper compares four glucose prediction models. The data used are obtained from blood glucose and physical activity monitoring sensors of 10 patients over a period of 6 days. The group of models compared is: a feed-forward neural network (FNN), a self-organizing map (SOM), a neurofuzzy network with wavelets as activation functions (WFNN), and a linear regression model (LRM). The tests were performed using three different time horizons, 30, 60, and 120 min.

SGE focused on this problem has proven to be particularly effective. Lourenço et al. [8] analyze the performance of SGE to generate models for glucose prediction in patients with diabetes, using past glucose values, insulin injections, and carbohydrate intakes. According to the results of the study, SGE is able to develop glucose prediction models with higher accuracy compared to other grammar-based approaches. In [8] the robustness of the models is also claimed.

Following all the research in this field, we investigate here with a new proposal that combines SGE, sparse identification of non-linear systems, and difference equations identification.

3 Methodology

3.1 SGE

In this work, we apply SGE, a variant of conventional Grammatical Evolution (GE), whose main feature is the one-to-one mapping between genes and non-terminals. SGE aims to deal with some of the most criticized aspects of the classical GE version. One of these problematic aspects is low locality. The level of locality allows us to relate the impact of a genotype change on the phenotype. Having a high locality, a small change in genotype also implies a small change in genotype, allowing us to sample the search space efficiently. However, in the case of having a low locality of the representation, we could be approaching a random search. SGE provides higher locality as it ensures that changes in one position do not affect the derivation options of the other non-terminals. Another aspect that can be considered a problem in some cases is the redundancy, a representation is if different phenotypes produce the same genotype.

3.2 Sparse Identification

In some physical systems, it has observed that only a few terms are relevant and can define the entire dynamics of the system, making governing equations sparse in a high-dimensional non-linear function space. Here we consider a dynamic system, Eq. 1, that governs the future values of glucose based primarily on the current glucose value, the basal rate of insulin administration, carbohydrate intake, and bolus insulin injections. Particularizing $\vec{x}$ for our problem we obtain Eq. 2.

$$\frac{\mathrm{d}}{\mathrm{d}t}\vec{x}(t) = \vec{f}(\vec{x}(t)) \tag{1}$$

$$\vec{x}(t) = [(G(t), B_I(t), I_B(t), F_{ch}(t)], \vec{x}(t) \in R^n \tag{2}$$

To determine the function whose combination of terms has a real impact on the system, we will generate a new dataset using a library Θ (X) consisting of candidate non-linear functions. In this case, $\Theta(X)$ will be composed of polynomial and trigonometric terms.

$$\Theta(X) = \begin{bmatrix} \vdots & \vdots & \vdots & \vdots & \vdots & \vdots & \vdots & & \vdots \\ 1 & X & X^{P_2} & X^{P_3} & X^{P_4} & \vdots & sin(X) & cos(X) \\ \vdots & \vdots & \vdots & \vdots & \vdots & \vdots & \vdots & & \vdots \end{bmatrix} \tag{3}$$

where X^{P_2} are the quadratic non-linearities of X, as X^{P_3} represents the cubic non-linearities and so on. In this paper we use only X^{P_2}, applied to the variables of the problem we obtain:

$$X^{P_2} = \begin{bmatrix} G(t_0) \cdot B_I(t_0) & G(t_0) \cdot I_B(t_0) & G(t_0) \cdot F_C H(t_0) & \cdots & F_C H^2(t_0) \\ G(t_1) \cdot B_I(t_1) & G(t_1) \cdot I_B(t_1) & G(t_1) \cdot F_C H(t_1) & \cdots & F_C H^2(t_1) \\ \vdots & \vdots & \vdots & \vdots & \vdots \\ G(t_n) \cdot B_I(t_n) & G(t_n) \cdot I_B(t_n) & G(t_n) \cdot F_C H(t_n) & \cdots & F_C H^2(t_n) \end{bmatrix} \tag{4}$$

where t_0 represents the first time step, t_1 the subsequent time step, and so on.

3.3 Difference Equations

Difference equations, [10], are especially useful for understanding non-linear phenomena and processes occurring in different systems. An outstanding feature of difference equations is their simplicity. When studying the behavior of solutions of difference equations, simple computational tools, and graphical representations are used, although it is possible to observe the complex and diverse dynamics of difference equations.

SGE generates difference equations $\hat{G}(t)$, and in order to evaluate them, we solve the expressions numerically. Figure 1 shows this process. Starting from the values of all the variables in the dataset at the initial time (t_0), we calculate the glucose value for the next time step (t_1), $\hat{G}(t_1)$. In the following iterations, the next value, $\hat{G}(t_2)$ is computed using the obtained value of $\hat{G}(t_1)$, and the other variables of the dataset for t_1, over the expression in evaluation. Through this iterative process, we will obtain the prediction of G from the initial value up to the target time instant. The time step in the dataset is five minutes.

4 Experimental Results

To carry out our experiments we used the OhioT1DM dataset [9], which includes eight weeks of data related to the health and daily events of twelve patients with type 1 diabetes. From this dataset we select patients identified as 540 (*Dataset 1*), and 544 (*Dataset 2*). In order to work with this datasets, it was

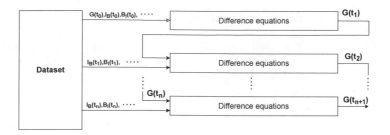

Fig. 1. Numerical resolution diagram.

necessary a preprocessing stage with several procedures, such as establish a common time stamp every five minutes, remove NaN values, interpolate values, and include Berger filtering of insulin records. *Dataset 1* includes glucose values, basal insulin, and insulin records. *Dataset 2* contains the variables of *Dataset 1* and incorporates the information about the meals. Some results obtained are shown below.

4.1   Results with Dataset 1

Data of approximately 8.5 h for training and 11.5 for the test from *Dataset 1*. The difference equation obtained as a solution by SGE is expressed by Eq. 5. Figures 2 and 3 show the glucose values for each time step obtained with Eq. 5, for the training and the test sets, respectively. In both cases, the blue line represents predicted values and the green line actual values. Equation 5 is able to capture some of the ups and downs of glucose even though, in the case of the test set, there is a gap of data in the section between approximately time steps t_{110} and t_{130}. Therefore, a local increase in error is observed in this area.

$$G(t+1) = B_I(t)^2 + I_B(t) + G(t) - G(t) \cdot I_B(t) + 4.45 \tag{5}$$

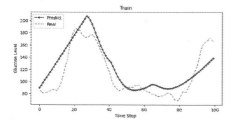

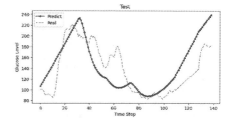

Fig. 2. Plot of Train prediction, Dataset 1

Fig. 3. Plot of Test prediction, Dataset 1

4.2   Results with Dataset 2 with Insulin Records

First we use Dataset 2 including insulin records, $I_B(t)$ but no meal information, $F_{ch}(t)$. For training and test, we have taken information of one day, obtaining through SGE the Eq. 6. Figures 4 and 5 show the glucose values for train and test using the equation obtained. Again, blue lines represent predicted values and green lines actual values. In the case of testing, the equation can capture the ups and downs of glucose, although, in the final part of the graph, it moves away from the actual values. This result is expected since difference equations loose precision for higher prediction horizons.

$$G(t + 1) = G(t) - G(t) \cdot B_I(t) + 0.3 \cdot G(t) \cdot I_B(t) + 15 \qquad (6)$$

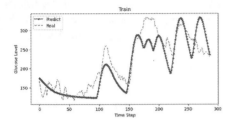
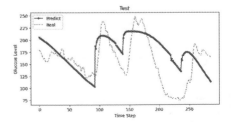

Fig. 4. Plot of Train prediction, Dataset 2, with $I_B(t)$ and no $F_{ch}(t)$

Fig. 5. Plot of Test prediction, Dataset 2, with $I_B(t)$ and no $F_{ch}(t)$

4.3   Results with Dataset 2 with Meal Information

After performing the tests with $I_B(t)$, we changed it to $F_{ch}(t)$ and started a new stage of experiments. After running our SGE engine we obtain Eq. 7 as the best solution. Figures 6 and 7 show the plot obtained from the Eq. 7. In this case, data from two days have been used for training and one day for test.

$$G(t + 1) = 89 \cdot B_I(t) \cdot G(t) \cdot 10^{-2} - 20 \cdot G(t)^2 \cdot 10^{-5} \cdot F_{ch}^{-2} - F_{ch}^2 + 20 \cdot 10 \quad (7)$$

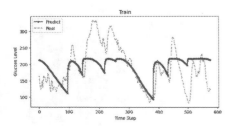
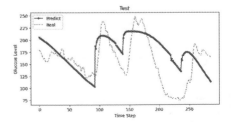

Fig. 6. Plot of Train prediction, Dataset 2, without $I_B(t)$ and with $F_{ch}(t)$

Fig. 7. Plot of Test prediction, Dataset 2, without $I_B(t)$ and with $F_{ch}(t)$

4.4   Discussion

The results obtained reveal some potential for glucose prediction, allowing the detection of glucose ups and downs, although it is still necessary to improve the accuracy of the expressions generated by SGE. In a field such as medicine, it is essential to keep the error of the results within safe values, as these can have a direct impact on the health of an individual. In the case of the SGE, we observe a limit value, that the function is unable to overcome, shortening the accuracy of the method. This limit can be caused by a poor generation of constants in the process of SGE, it would be interesting to carry out a more detailed analysis in the future.

Regarding the explainability of the expressions, Eq. 5 and 6 use the same variables and non lineal terms, which indicates some robustness in absence of information of the insulin injected. However, Eq. 7 shows a great impact of the information of the variable $F_{ch}(t)$ that includes the meal information. A deeper study will be necessary to understand the signs of those variables in the equations.

5   Conclusion and Future Work

In this work, we propose SGE combined with difference equations to generate models for glucose prediction. In addition, we apply sparse identification methods, generating second order non-linear variables. During the experiments, different combinations of variables were tested by adding and subtracting $I_B(t)$ and with $F_{ch}(t)$. The most important conclusions of this work are:

- SGE can generate expressions that correctly identify the ups and downs of glucose.
- Sparse Identification makes it easy to incorporate non-linear terms in the expressions generated by the grammar.
- Grammars, in particular the generation of constants, have a major impact on the solutions of grammatical evolution.
- Expressions generated with SGE are explainable, and execution times are low.

The results are promising, even though the prediction error is still high in comparison with other state of the art algorithms. A limitation we faced during this project was the grammar, specifically with the generation of constants. An improvement in this area could be interesting, as it is a critical component of the SGE. A new dataset is now available, allowing us to start a new batch of tests.

Acknowledgments. Work financed by the regional government of Madrid and co-financed by the EU Structural Funds through the Community of Madrid project B2017/BMD3773 (GenObIA-CM). Also financed by the PhD project IND2020/TIC-17435 and Spanish Ministry of Economy and Competitiveness with number RTI2018-095180-B-I00 and PID2021-125549OB-I00.

References

1. Atlas, D., et al.: International diabetes federation. IDF Diabetes Atlas, 7th edn. International Diabetes Federation, Brussels, Belgium (2015)
2. Brunton, S.L., Proctor, J.L., Kutz, J.N.: Discovering governing equations from data by sparse identification of nonlinear dynamical systems. Proc. Natl. Acad. Sci. **113**(15), 3932–3937 (2016)
3. Chen, C.-L., Tsai, H.-W., Wong, S.-S.: Modeling the physiological glucose-insulin dynamic system on diabetics. J. Theor. Biol. **265**(3), 314–322, 2010. ISSN 0022-5193. https://doi.org/10.1016/j.jtbi.2010.05.002, https://www.sciencedirect.com/science/article/pii/S0022519310002316
4. Contador, S., Velasco, J.M., Garnica, O., Hidalgo, J.I.: Glucose forecasting using genetic programming and latent glucose variability features. Appl. Soft Comput. **110**, 107609 (2021)
5. Contador, S., Colmenar, J.M., Garnica, O., Velasco, J.M., Hidalgo, J.I.: Blood glucose prediction using multi-objective grammatical evolution: analysis of the "agnostic" and "what-if" scenarios. Genetic Program. Evol. Mach. **23**(2), 161–192 (2022)
6. Gaucel, S., Keijzer, M., Lutton, E., Tonda, A.: Learning dynamical systems using standard symbolic regression. In: Nicolau, M., et al. (eds.) EuroGP 2014. LNCS, vol. 8599, pp. 25–36. Springer, Heidelberg (2014). https://doi.org/10.1007/978-3-662-44303-3_3
7. Lourenço, N., Assunção, F., Pereira, F.B., Costa, E., Machado, P.: Structured grammatical evolution: a dynamic approach. In: Ryan, C., O'Neill, M., Collins, J.J. (eds.) Handbook of Grammatical Evolution, pp. 137–161. Springer, Cham (2018). https://doi.org/10.1007/978-3-319-78717-6_6
8. Lourenço, N., Colmenar, J.M., Hidalgo, J.I., Garnica, Ó.: Structured grammatical evolution for glucose prediction in diabetic patients. In: Proceedings of the Genetic and Evolutionary Computation Conference, pp. 1250–1257 (2019)
9. Marling, C., Bunescu, R.: The ohio1dm dataset for blood glucose level prediction: update 2020. In: CEUR Workshop Proceedings, vol. 2675, pp. 71. NIH Public Access (2020)
10. Sharkovsky, A., Maistrenko, Y.L.T., Romanenko, E.Y.: Difference Equations and their Applications, vol. 250. Springer, Heidelberg (2012). https://doi.org/10.1007/978-94-011-1763-0
11. Zarkogianni, K., et al.: Comparative assessment of glucose prediction models for patients with type 1 diabetes mellitus applying sensors for glucose and physical activity monitoring. Med. Biol. Eng. Comput. **53**(12), 1333–1343 (2015). https://doi.org/10.1007/s11517-015-1320-9
12. Zecchin, C., Facchinetti, A., Sparacino, G., De Nicolao, G., Cobelli, C.: A new neural network approach for short-term glucose prediction using continuous glucose monitoring time-series and meal information. In: 2011 Annual International Conference of the IEEE Engineering in Medicine and Biology Society, pp. 5653–5656 (2011). https://doi.org/10.1109/IEMBS.2011.6091368
13. Zhu, T., Li, K., Herrero, P., Chen, J., Georgiou, P.: A deep learning algorithm for personalized blood glucose prediction. In: KHD@ IJCAI, pp. 64–78 (2018)

Model-Based System Design, Verification and Simulation

Modeling Approaches for Cyber Attacks on Energy Infrastructure

Andreas Attenberger[(✉)] [ID]

Research Unit Digital Forensics, Central Office for Information
Technology in the Security Sector (ZITiS), 81677 München, Germany
Andreas.Attenberger@zitis.bund.de
https://www.zitis.bund.de

Abstract. The widespread utilization of communication technology in modern energy production facilities and increasing connectivity of the associated devices with links to the internet can result in broad cyber attack surfaces. As a consequence, cyber security incidents in energy need to be studied closely in order to devise appropriate mitigation techniques. In this paper we discuss models for the analysis of threats focusing on energy infrastructure. While classic IT threat modeling approaches can be applied within this scope, there are certain limitations to these models. We demonstrate the shortcomings of existing methodologies by applying both the STRIDE model as well as the AVD model, which is more suited to energy security threats. By studying 40 security incidents in energy infrastructure, we demonstrate limitations of the aforementioned models and suggest extensions in order to more accurately describe cyber attacks on energy infrastructure. Future modeling approaches should consider the threat actors' motivations and allow analysis of complex multi-stage or multi-phase attacks.

1 Introduction

The increasing interconnectivity of devices does not only extend to the private domain with examples like connected car or smart home systems but is a development that is equally present in critical infrastructure including the energy supply domain. While offering various services to allow remote control and surveillance of for example power plants or other production facilities, these online services increase the attack surface and introduce novel vulnerabilities into critical infrastructure systems [4]. Furthermore, energy supply is one of the most critical and vulnerable elements in infrastructure both in civilian and military environments [11].

In computer science, several modeling approaches exist for defining assets and threats in the scope of system security. For example, the confidentiality, integrity and availability (CIA) model defines three basic attack surfaces for IT systems [12]. Confidentiality refers to the protection of data from access by unauthorized third parties with data integrity assuring that information is not being changed or tampered with during transfer or storage. Finally, availability

R. Moreno-Díaz et al. (Eds.): EUROCAST 2022, LNCS 13789, pp. 199–206, 2022.
https://doi.org/10.1007/978-3-031-25312-6_23

of system access needs to be guaranteed according to specifications. While the CIA model is a useful tool in assessing basic assets and threats in systems, it is limited by the broad and general nature of its elements.

A more specific approach to threat modeling is the STRIDE model to identify attacks involving Spoofing, Tampering, Repudiation, Information Disclosure, Denial of Service and Elevation of Privilege [13]. Spoofing refers to for example the falsification of identities for accessing data or services on a system. When data is manipulated or changed maliciously, it is referred to by tampering. The misattribution of system actions, for example reading and writing files, to different users or change of records regarding user activity is called repudiation. Information disclosure is describing issues regarding confidentiality of information as equally referred to in the CIA model. In terms of system availability, denial of service is characterized by deliberate actions towards restricting users' access by overwhelming and rendering the system unable to respond to user requests. Finally, elevation of privilege threats could allow attackers to attain stored information they are not authorized to process as well as the actuation of system processes beyond their allocated user rights.

While these models can be applied in general IT security scenarios, another model more suited to attacks on energy supply networks is the AVD (attack, vulnerability, damage) model [9]. This approach considers the type of attacks on systems, vulnerabilities exploited for the actions as well as the potential damage caused by the threat actors. Consequentially, the model allows a more fine-grained approach for looking at individual cyber attack features. For an attack, the AVD model considers a holistic approach taking into consideration the origin (local or remote), type of attack (ranging from spoofing to file execution or system probing) to the potential targets (e.g. networks, systems, users, etc.). Furthermore, details of vulnerabilities exploited during the malicious activities can be specified, for example within system configuration or implementation. The resulting impact of attacks is described by indicating the severity of the incident ranging from none to low, medium and high. Severity is additionally specified with respect to state effects regarding the CIA assets as well as performance effects like timeliness and precision.

Other models like TAVI exist for specific modeling of attacks on industrial control protocols [7]. The goal of this approach is for example to conduct risk evaluation for these control systems and utilizing this information for integrating appropriate protective measures already during system development. However, while these methods can only be applied to the specific technology in question, incidents in this field can typically span wide areas and diverse control system elements. Other approaches focus on security assets [3], attack methodologies or graph-based modeling [1]. As the STRIDE model is widely utilized and offers the flexibility for a wide range of applications, we chose to compare it to the AVD model as an example for an approach to energy infrastructure in particular.

2 Modeling Attacks with the STRIDE and AVD Models

We applied the aforementioned models, both the STRIDE as well as the AVD methods, to 40 cyber attacks on energy infrastructure collected during an internet search of publicly available information on these past incidents. While the bulk of the recorded incidents were centered in Europe, our list extends to events located for example in East Asia and North America. We excluded mere mentions of incidents as modeling is not feasible when there is no further information available on the system technology that has been compromised. During our preliminary search we first utilized basic categories to characterize the cyber threats by attributing them to the method employed, attack source (internal or external) and the goal of the attack. These elements are also present in the specific modeling approaches we subsequently applied to the documented cyber security breaches.

2.1 Energy Supply Company Example

Considering an example for the analysis of a specific incident [14], we show the individual application of the STRIDE and AVD models. In this attack, the threat actors attempted to blackmail a German energy supply company by utilizing ransomware in the internal company network. Parts of the network including data storage and communication services were out of service during several days. Preliminary classification was that this incident constituted a ransomware attack by an external attacker for blackmail. Table 1 shows an example classification of a cyber hack of a German energy supply company. With the STRIDE model, tampering and denial of service were identified as the attacks present in this security threat. AVD modeling identified the origin as a remote attacker with the execution and deletion of target data. The severity was considered high due to the several day outage of services. The damage was subsequently attributed to state effects regarding integrity and availability.

Table 1. a) STRIDE and b) AVD Models for a Cyber Attack on a German Energy Supply Company.

a)

Tampering	Denial of service

b)

Origin	Action	Target	Damage	Severity
Remote	Execute, Delete	Data	State Effect: Integrity, Availability	High

2.2 Overall Modeling Results

Applying the STRIDE model systematically to the aforementioned collection of 40 incidents reported in various media, most cyber attacks involve tampering, i.e.

altering the integrity of data on the systems under attack. Equally numerous are security breaches causing unauthorized access to data (information disclosure). Reason being that system sabotage typically involves both types of incidents. Slightly less often an elevation of privileges as well as threats to system availability (denial of service) have been observed. Spoofing has been reported in only 8 cases while repudiation did not occur. For 11 of the documented cyber incidents, the attacks can be classified in a single category while most cases fit at least two or more categories (16). In summary, most attacks center on tampering of data, information disclosure, denial of service and elevation of privileges. Table 3 gives an summary of the results as analyzed with the STRIDE model.

While the STRIDE model can quickly be applied, the AVD approach necessitates more detailed analysis of cyber attacks including a specific technological consideration. The same list of cyber attacks was considered with the AVD model, with an overview given in Table 2. It was found that most attack sources naturally are of remote origin with only 5 threats present internally in the targeted system. This corresponds to the fact that most attackers are located outside of the country whose networks are being targeted [5] with increasing interconnectivity allowing operation from locations worldwide. Typically, cyber hacks involve reading, copying and deleting data as well as executing malware. While read/copy incidents may not result in significant damage, most attacks are more severe and guided towards harming data integrity. Execute and delete Actions can additionally impair system availability. This means that within the AVD framework, system data is the most common target with 23 occurrences. It is of note that in 22 cases performance of the targeted system was not impaired. This is in line with the fact that many attacks are persistent with perpetrators active in systems for a significant amount of time before discovery [2].

Generally, the AVD model allows the identification of several aspects of cyber threats including an attacker's approach. A more fine-grained analysis is possible, for example allowing the distinction of espionage and ransomware attacks not possible with STRIDE. In turn, this allows a prioritized analysis of threats, which can be of advantage when dealing with a broad attack surface in commercial and critical infrastructure applications. Furthermore, the increased number of categories as well as sub-categories permits detailed consideration of several elements of cyber attacks at the same time. While the STRIDE model offers a quick overview about information security objectives threatened by an attack, the AVD model includes more information about an attacker's mode of operation. By introducing the severity measures, it is possible to compare individual incidents and discuss necessary action in accordance with the estimated risks. This is especially useful for organizations in order to prioritize threat handling within the scope of restricted resources regarding trained staff as well as security budget.

During application of the AVD model, one challenge was the attribution of specific vulnerabilities in the systems under attack. These are typically not disclosed in associated publications, most likely with the motivation of safeguarding from future threats by keeping system details confidential. As detailed

Table 2. Results of the AVD model as applied to 40 energy infrastructure cyber attacks.

Attack	Origin	Local (5), Remote (35)
	Action	Authenticate (5), Bypass (3), Delete (6), Eavesdrop (3), Execute (21), Flood (4), Misdirect (1), Modify (9), Probe (7), Scan (5), Spoof (4), Read/Copy (10), Terminate (2)
	Target	Data (23), Network (5), Process (10), System (11), User (10)
Vulnerability		Configuration (11), Implementation (5), Specification (3), Unknown (21)
Damage	State effect	Availability (18), Confidentiality (23), Integrity (17)
	Performance effect	Accuracy (12), Precision (5), Timeliness (4), Unknown (22)
	Severity	High (20), Low (3), None (4), Medium (13)

Table 3. List of STRIDE model threat elements present in previous energy infrastructure security incidents.

STRIDE model element	Occurences
Spoofing	8
Tampering	21
Repudiation	0
Information disclosure	20
Denial of service	18
Elevation of privileges	18

in the next section, certain attacks of higher complexity cannot or only partially be characterized with AVD and STRIDE.

3   Limits of AVD and STRIDE Modeling

We identified several aspects not covered widely enough by the aforementioned approaches. This includes the expressiveness of the approaches for complex attacks, lack of modeling elements regarding attack motivation and threat actor knowledge level.

Our results in threat model application show that the STRIDE model can offer basic evaluation of threats. However most previous cyber attack incidents display a complexity which is not sufficiently captured by this modeling approach. For example, the distinction between espionage and ransom ware threats cannot be accurately expressed with STRIDE. Generally, both models exhibit weaknesses when analyzing complex attacks threatening system functionality. These can often not be attributed correctly to the model structures. As an example, multi-stage attacks, which often occur in the area of critical infrastructure and associated security measures are beyond the scope of AVD and STRIDE. Often, these cyber incidents are characterized by multiple STRIDE categories that can be attributed simultaneously, especially with three or four aspects applicable. Consequentially, the same attacks are also attributed higher levels of severity when utilizing the AVD model. This is typically the case with multi-phase approaches or attacks that combine several strategies. These can involve, for example, denial of service attacks on client services in combination with wiping action in highly specialized infrastructure communication systems [8]. Additionally, many attacks are only preliminary intrusions for reconnaissance actions in order to gain in-depth information about the compromised system for preparing and conducting further, more complex and potentially more damaging actions. A possible remedy would be to seperate attacks in individual phases and then apply the AVD model individually to each phase. This approach is also taken for example by the Kill Chain methodology [1].

A second important limitation by the models at hand is that attack motivation is currently not sufficiently considered in the existing methods. For example, commercial or political motivations can contribute to risks a system would otherwise not be exposed to depending on the circumstances at the time in question. While it is possible to determine target systems and devices on a technical level, this technical categorization does not reveal an attacker's main motive. The target category within the AVD model does not suffice to express the importance of motivational objectives leading to the attack in the first place, which can be essential for attack mitigation. Depending on the nature of these basic motivations for threat actors, different types of threat techniques as well as targets might be chosen. Political motivation for example in light of political crises and tensions can play a significantly more pronounced role in energy infrastructure as opposed to motivations of attackers targeting companies in other domains like entertainment or consumer goods trading. Previously suggested extension options for the avd principle also mention regarding the financial impact of a cyber attack [9]. This can especially be of value to companies for gauging possible financial impact of incidents. Subsequently, it is possible to define the necessary budget for each threat mitigation action in relation to possible monetary harm. Furthermore, if an attacker's motivation is financial damage to an organization, possible targets can be identified accordingly.

Consequentially, we advocate for including non-technical motivational aspects, especially relating to the political climate on a national or international scale which is essential for adequate cyber threat modeling in energy infrastructue [6]. Additionally, this can extend to physical protection of technical devices, which are currently not or only implicitly included in the modeling approaches.

Finally, extending the AVD model to account for the complexity of likely threats including the know how necessary by the threat actors could introduce additional information to help identify and gauge threat risks.

4   Conclusion and Future Work

The results discussed above show that modeling cyber threats to energy infrastructure can be realized through common IT security models like STRIDE. Additional information and insight however can be gained by applying more specific models like AVD as demonstrated by analyzing past incidents. While the STRIDE model offers a basic, functional approach, the AVD model offers a modular structure with possibilities for future extension. Various other models exist regarding cyber threat models [1], partly with a focus on energy control infrastructure [7]. However, some focus only on narrow applications like protocol analysis for specific technology solutions. Future work should analyze the individual advantages and shortcomings of these approaches to yield a more aptly suited model taking into account the limitations as discussed in this work. Among the most important aspects to be integrated are the possibility for modeling complex, multi-phase incidents as well as including the attacker's motivations to allow appropriate risk evaluation. Such balanced modeling approaches can then be applied to develop early warning systems for helping safeguard critical infrastructure against the growing threat of cyber attacks. These capabilities will gain further significance due to the complexity and ensuing vulnerability of new energy supply solutions like smart grids [10].

Acknowledgement. We thank B.Sc. Moritz Schwab for compiling and analyzing the list of cyber incidents.

References

1. Al-Mohannadi, H., Mirza, Q., Namanya, A., Awan, I., Cullen, A., Disso, J.: Cyber-attack modeling analysis techniques: an overview. In: 2016 IEEE 4th International Conference on Future Internet of Things and Cloud Workshops (FiCloudW), pp. 69–76. IEEE (2016)

2. Alshamrani, A., Myneni, S., Chowdhary, A., Huang, D.: A survey on advanced persistent threats: techniques, solutions, challenges, and research opportunities. IEEE Commun. Surv. Tutor. **21**(2), 1851–1877 (2019)
3. Aufner, P.: The IoT security gap: a look down into the valley between threat models and their implementation. Int. J. Inf. Secur. **19**(1), 3–14 (2020)
4. Brown, A.S.: Scada vs. the hackers. Mech. Eng. **124**(12), 37–40 (2002)
5. Bundesamt für Sicherheit in der Informationstechnik: Bericht zur Lage der IT-Sicherheit in Deutschland 2020 (2020)
6. Desarnaud, G.: Cyber attacks and energy infrastructures: anticipating risks (2017)
7. Drias, Z., Serhrouchni, A., Vogel, O.: Taxonomy of attacks on industrial control protocols. In: 2015 International Conference on Protocol Engineering (ICPE) and International Conference on New Technologies of Distributed Systems (NTDS), pp. 1–6. IEEE (2015)
8. Case, D.U.: Analysis of the cyber attack on the Ukrainian power grid. Electr. Inf. Shar. Anal. Center (E-ISAC) **388**, 1–29 (2016)
9. Fleury, T., Khurana, H., Welch, V.: Towards a taxonomy of attacks against energy control systems. In: Papa, M., Shenoi, S. (eds.) ICCIP 2008. TIFIP, vol. 290, pp. 71–85. Springer, Boston, MA (2008). https://doi.org/10.1007/978-0-387-88523-0_6
10. He, H., Yan, J.: Cyber-physical attacks and defences in the smart grid: a survey. IET Cyber-Phys. Syst.: Theory Appl. **1**(1), 13–27 (2016)
11. Nussbaum, D., Dupuy, A.: The cyber-energy nexus: the military operational perspective. In: European Conference on Cyber Warfare and Security, pp. 713–718. Academic Conferences International Limited (2017)
12. Samonas, S., Coss, D.: The cia strikes back: redefining confidentiality, integrity and availability in security. J. Inf. Syst. Secur. **10**(3) (2014)
13. Shostack, A.: Experiences threat modeling at microsoft. In: MODSEC@ MoDELS 2008 (2008)
14. Zeitung für kommunale Wirtschaft: Cyberangriff legt Stadtwerke Langenfeld lahm (2019)

Simulation Setup for a Closed-Loop Regulation of Neuro-Muscular Blockade

Martin Hrubý[1]([✉]), Antonio Gonzalez[2], Ricardo Ruiz Nolasco[2], and Peter Biro[3]

[1] Brno University of Technology, Brno, Czech Republic
hrubym@fit.vutbr.cz
[2] RGB Medical Devices, Madrid, Spain
{agonzalez,rruiznolasco}@rgb-medical.com
[3] Medical Faculty, University of Zurich, Zürich, Switzerland

Abstract. We describe a simulation infrastructure for a comprehensive testing of safety, security and performance in a specific medical device (Relaxometry Controller) being developed by RGB Medical. The apparatus is designed to monitor and regulate patient's blood pressure and muscle relaxation during surgery and anesthesia. The controller is at the laboratory testing level under ongoing development and before practical deployment it needs full accreditation by national healthcare agencies. By having a simulation infrastructure, we investigated the controller's übehaviour in various pre-defined clinical test scenarios.

Keywords: Simulation in closed loop feedback control system ·
Medical device · Anesthesia · Neuro-muscular transmission

1 Introduction

We developed the infrastructure for a simulation setup designed to support the development of an infusion pump controller based on the NMTcuff™ (RGB Medical Devices, Alfonso Gomez 42, 28037 Madrid, Spain) technology for the purpose of relaxometric measurement of pharmacologically induced neuro-muscular transmission. Its first version was the popular TOFcuff™ device, which recently has evolved into the more advanced VISION DUO and VISION AIR/NMT multiparameter monitors. They incorporate the ability for objective surveillance of neuro-muscular transmission (NMT) during the infusion of neuro-muscular blocking agents (NBA) such as rocuronium or cisatracurium. These drugs are administered during general anesthesia for various types of surgery with the intention to inhibit inadvertent movement of the patient. Various states of neuro-muscular blockade may be necessary for different stages of surgery and anesthesia.

Our mission described herein is to develop a safe, reliable, and efficient control algorithm for an automated intravenous infusion of NBA. The objective of the infusion algorithm is to administer the right amount of the NBA that ensures the required level of neuro-muscular blockade over time. The latter is measured

R. Moreno-Díaz et al. (Eds.): EUROCAST 2022, LNCS 13789, pp. 207–214, 2022.
https://doi.org/10.1007/978-3-031-25312-6_24

in the traditional units of standard relaxometry: train of four ratio (TOFr), train of four count (TOFc), and post-tetanic count (PTC) [3]. The two corresponding goals are: 1) to maintain the necessary level of NMB during surgery, and 2) to enable the fastest possible recovery from NMB as soon as the surgery is finished, and the patient should emerge from anesthesia.

The algorithm takes into account the patient's response to drug doses (patient model) based on pharmacokinetic data from the literature that has been obtained in clinical practice [4,5]. The mentioned algorithm has at its core a 3-compartment pharmacokinetic model, which reflects reasonably well the dynamic changes of the drug concentration in the plasma. The calculated concentrations give an estimated pharmacodynamic effect on blocking the neuromuscular transmission on a simplified surrogate relaxometric scale encompassing 10 TOFr, 4 TOFc and 16 PTC levels. The validity of the patient model is essential for the overall performance of the algorithm. Due to lack of relevant clinical studies, we substituted the missing clinical data with experimental data.

2 Pharmacokinetic/Pharmacodynamic Model of Rocuronium

Pharmacokinetic (PK) and *Pharmacodynamic* (PD) models play a very important role in our simulation infrastructure. Based on clinical studies, these models describe the pharmacological effects caused by the drug on the human body (PD) as well as the metabolism and elimination of the drug (PK). In the herein reported case, we deal with rocuronium and its blocking effects on the neuromuscular transmission.

Pharmacokinetics describes the dynamic distribution of the intravenously administered drug within patient's body and the changes in its concentration over time. According to the employed model, the patient's body is divided into 3 compartments, which represent the blood volume (central compartment) and the perfused organs (a fast as well as a slow distribution compartment). Intercompartmental flows are described by differential Eqs. (1–3), with an input flow $I(t)$ modeling the intravenously administered drug. The state variable C_i defines an absolute current amount of the drug into the compartment i. Drug concentration C_{inp} in the central compartment represents the resulting effect on neuromuscular blockade (NMB).

$$\frac{dC_1}{dt} = I(t) - (k_{13} + k_{12})C_1 + k_{21}C_2 + k_{31}C_3 \tag{1}$$

$$\frac{dC_2}{dt} = k_{12}C_1 - k_{21}C_2 \tag{2}$$

$$\frac{dC_3}{dt} = k_{13}C_1 - k_{31}C_3 \tag{3}$$

Numerical simulation of Eqs. (1–3) is implemented using Euler integration method with $\Delta = 1\,\text{s}$ time step. The intercompartmental rate constants were obtained from a clinical study [1]. Their mean values for normal patients are $k_{12} = 0.259$, $k_{21} = 0.163$, $k_{13} = 0.060$, $k_{31} = 0.012$, $k_{10} = 0.119$ (min^{-1}).

The intravenous infusion $I(t) = B(t) + F(t)$ represents the input to this PK/PD system. $B(t)$ denotes a discrete input (a bolus in (ml)) administered at the time t. Similarly, $F(t)$ denotes a continual flow defined in $(ml\,hour^{-1})$. Rocuronium is being administered in a diluted solution at $10\,mg\,ml^{-1}$, while both eventual inputs need to be numerically transformed into appropriate weight (μg) and time units $(\mu g\,s^{-1})$.

The current amount $C_1(t)$ (μg) of rocuronium is distributed within so called volume of distribution V_d (ml), resulting in the current concentration $C_{inp}(t) = C_1(t)/V_d$ of rocuronium in the blood plasma. The volume of distribution is an uncertain attribute of PK/PD modeling and differs significantly among patients. For this reason, V_d is variable in our experiments with a default value $38\,ml\,kg^{-1}$ of patient's total body weight [1,2].

2.1   Pharmacodynamic Effect of Rocuronium

The neuro-muscular blocking effect of rocuronium is determined from the current C_{inp} concentration and is mapped into the proprietary TOF and PTC scales. Pharmacologic literature refers widely to the so called Hill function (4) computing the effect from C_{inp}, EC_{50} and γ, where EC_{50} denotes the concentration leading to half effect and γ is a shape coefficient.

$$E_i(C_{inp}) = \frac{C_{inp}^{\gamma}}{EC_{50}^{\gamma} + C_{inp}^{\gamma}} \cdot 100 \tag{4}$$

We assume that E_i denotes the NMB effect in four twitches $i = 1, 2, 3, 4$ of TOF method. Then we obtain TOF amplitudes $TOF_i = 100 - E_i$ in the TOF defined range $\langle 0, 100 \rangle$. See Table 1 for particular coefficients. Finally, we have TOF ratio $TOFr = TOF_4/TOF_1$ and TOF count $TOFc$ as the number of twitches with nonzero amplitude $TOF_i > 0$.

Table 1. Coefficients of effect function for four TOF twitches.

TOF twitch	EC_{50} $(\mu g\,ml^{-1})$	γ
1	0.823	4.79
2	0.823/1.1	4.79/1.1
3	0.823/1.3	4.79/1.25
4	0.823/1.5	4.79/1.33

Post-tetanic count (PTC) is the other measurement method, giving NMT on a 16-step integer scale from 0 to 15. PTC measurement becomes essential for NMT monitoring when $TOFC = 0$. In this case the TOF measurement cannot sense any deeper relaxation. When $TOFc = 0$, PTC has already arrived at approximately 8 counts. For this reason, we set the corresponding C_{inp} as the half effect concentration EC_{50} in the PTC's Hill function. This value can be obtained analytically from the inverse function $E_1^{-1}(100)$ in its maximum effect.

3   Architecture of the Simulation Infrastructure

Our simulation infrastructure consists of two separate tools *NMT-Simulator* and *Test Case Manager*. Both are interconnected using the REDIS database system. The whole distributed system is depicted in Fig. 1.

The internal NMT-Simulator is made of these four components:

– The medical device monitor incorporate the enhanced NMTCuff^{TM} monitoring functionality plus the controller (CNT) feature for the automated regulation of the patient's NMT. The controller implements various strategies of automated anesthesia.
– The infusion pump (PUMP) is a medical device that is remotely controlled by the monitor and provides the intravenous infusion of the drug. The infusion pump can administer discrete boluses (indicated in ml) or manage a continuous drug flow (indicated in $ml\,hour^{-1}$).
– The patient model (PM) is a mathematical model of patient's response to rocuronium. The model integrates PK/PD as they were described in Sect. 2. This component outputs the essential state variables such as C_{inp}, TOF and PTC effects, and the estimated time for total recovery.
– The NMT sensor (SENSOR) is measuring patient's NMT using TOF and PTC methods. Intervals between measurements samples are determined by the controller.

The Test Case Manager (TCM) is a computer program designed to manage all simulation experiments and to perform statistical postprocessing.

This distributed infrastructure has a star topology with REDIS in its core. All involved components are connected solely to REDIS, which simplifies the necessary communication among the interfaces. Apart from data storage capability, REDIS also grants a message brokering feature. The simulation process is based on sequential passing of activity between the components in a pre-defined communication protocol. Since all components need to implement just one technical interface (to REDIS) and to apply a simple protocol, the overall concept is very flexible and robust. Moreover, this concept allows for abstractions above the components, so that the technical implementation of each component may differ depending on the employed experiment. Every component can be plugged in as a real hardware or as its simulation model.

We consider currently the patient model in the form of mathematical construct only, however, real humans might participate in case of approved clinical experiments.

Every experiment is assigned a unique string identifier denoted as $expID$ (for example "vm.tc.fwsim.1"). This $expID$ identifies a corresponding data record (hash type) and message channel within REDIS. Data hash keys are accessed via

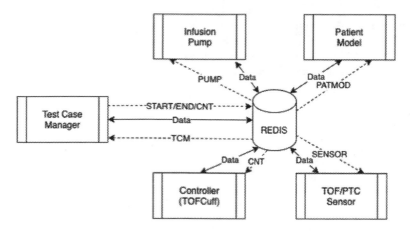

Fig. 1. Scheme of the simulation infrastructure. Dotted lines – control commands. Solid lines – data transfers.

hset expID key and hget expID key commands. The messaging follows the Publish/Subscribe paradigm, and therefore $expID$ defines a temporary channel for the $expID$ experiment, to which all components may send messages. All messages are broadcasted to all components. For more details, see the REDIS technical documentation [6].

4 The Simulation Protocol

All participants must subscribe for receiving messages at REDIS and implement correctly the following protocol. We may denote a REDIS message (sent or received) as tuple $(expID, msg)$ where $expID$ identifies the experiment, and msg holds the message body (with values START, END, CNT, PUMP, PM, SENSOR, TCM).

As it is stated above, TCM generates and executes simulation experiments under various conditions. For every experiment, TCM runs a procedure depicted in Algorithm 1. The procedure begins with generating a unique $expID$. Then TCM uploads a set of internal attributes describing the experiment into a corresponding REDIS data record that is shared among the distributed components. The simulation itself begins with $(expID, START)$ message. Upon this signal, all components download the experiment's data record, reset their internal state and get ready for a new experiment.

Finally, TCM repeats several simulation cycles with an increasing model time. The components are activated sequentially in the order TCM, CNT, PUMP, PM, SENSOR and then back to TCM. Every activated component executes its own procedure and then calls the successive component.

Algorithm 1. Managing a single experiment from TCM.

```
// experiment ID must match the vm.* pattern
expID := generate an unique experiment identifier
// start with initial model time
mtime := 0
// upload all experiment attributes to REDIS into expID data record
hset(expID, key, value) for all key
// initiate the experiment. All components get ready.
publish(expID, "START")
// run the simulation until the end of model time
while mtime <= MAXTIME {
    hset(expID, "mtime", mtime)
    // activate the first component in the loop
    publish(expID, "CNT")
    // wait until the loop ends when SENSOR calls TCM
    waitUntilMessage(expID, "TCM")
    // download the entire experiment data record and store it
    dict := hget(expID, key, value) for all keys
    save "dict" locally
    // shift the model time
    mtime := mtime + timeStep
}
// terminate the experiment
publish(expID, "END")
```

4.1 Controller Component (CNT)

On receiving $(expID, CNT)$, the controller decides about the next configuration of the infusion pump at $mtime$ in the context of the current $expID$ experiment. CNT outputs $bolus$ and $infusion$ attributes to the experiment's data record in REDIS. The course of anesthesia in the sense of NMT regulation has basically two phases. In the first one, the so called *initial bolus* is administered in order to achieve a NMB to the level suitable for tracheal intubation. In the second phase, the system is supposed to keep the NMT at a predefined target level on the surrogate TOF/PTC scale. This automated regulation is implemented in various strategies that are parts of our experimenting.

The controller outputs the initial bolus $iBolus$ at $mtime = 0$. The amount is set to 0.7 mg kg^{-1} of patient's body weight (this dosage may differ according to particular patient's muscle-to-fat ratio or particular goals of the surgical procedure). In the further simulation cycles ($mtime > 0$), the controller may execute the following simulation strategies.

Basic Strategy. CNT adminsters repeatedly *repeBolus* (ml) boluses in regular time intervals *repeStep* (s). This methods implements a trivial approach in anesthesia when the controller is not supplied with NMT measurements feedback.

Forward Simulation Strategy. This strategy is based on CNT's ability to predict future evolution of PK/PD aspects in patient's body. Technically, CNT contains an integrated patient model that follows the steps of infusion and can simulate the future evolution of patient's NMT. This method computes a minimal bolus dosage that ensures patient's target NMT from *mtime* till *mtime* + *fwRange*. This method is incorporated for experimental purposes only. Its numerical complexity disqualifies that from practical deployment in the medical device.

Analytic Strategy. This strategy comes from clinical experience. In a simplified version, we assume regular PTC measurements every three minutes. With each fresh sample *current* (PTC) of NMT measurement, if *current* $\leq$ *target* then NMB is higher than required, this cycle ends with no further dose administered. Otherwise, CNT instructs the pump to deliver another bolus (5) based on the amount of *iBolus*.

$$nBolus = (current - target) \cdot 0.04 \cdot iBolus \tag{5}$$

4.2 Patient Model Component (PM)

The patient model resets its internal state on every $(expID, START)$ command and loads experiment's attributes from REDIS, such as patient's weight (V_d) and sensitivity to rocuronium (EC_{50}, γ).

In every simulation cycle, on receiving $(expID, PM)$ message, PM computes its internal PK/PD numerical simulation from the previous *mtime* to the current *mtime* in Δ time steps. PM exports C_{inp}, TOF amplitudes, TOFr, TOFc, PTC value and cumulative consumption of rocuronium. Moreover, PM invokes a nested simulation that steps further in model time until $TOFr \geq 0.95$ appears, and presents it as the so called *total recovery*.

5 Experimenting

The goal of this testing is to investigate the robustness of the implemented anesthesiological strategies across a wide range of configurations of patients and their metabolic capacities. The experimenting is managed by TCM that randomly samples all configurations and submits the results through the simulation infrastructure. The space of all configurations is given by a Cartesian product of range of weight, patient's sensitivity to rocuronium, and of V_d, which represents various anesthesiological scenarios, which in turn are tailored according to specific surgical procedures

The Test Case Manager statistically evaluates the time series of state variables outcoming from the patient model. Special care is taken for scenarios when NMB is permitted to be less intense. Inadvertant moves by the patients may cause harm and must therefore be suppressed by providing an adequate level of

NMB. A secondary goal is to minimize the total drug consumption of rocuronium, which beyond its economical relevance, also may shorten the time needed for total recovery. The desired level of total recovery from NMB is generally viewed as $TOFr \geq 0.95$, that in our practice has to be confirmed three times in a row. Before that level is achieved, anesthesia must be maintained.

6   Conclusion

We presented our simulation infrastructure that allows to extensively test various anestesiological strategies with an automated regulation of neuro-muscular blockade. Since in this area of medical research, real clinical data is scarce, simulation based on models is a feasible way to obtain experience with control algorithms and in order to optimize the underlying algorithm. Moreover, the presented architecture can inspire also other drug dosing/clinical effect projects.

Acknowledgements. This project has received funding from the ECSEL Joint Undertaking (JU) under grant agreement No 876852. The JU receives support from the European Union's Horizon 2020 research and innovation programme and Austria, Czech Republic, Germany, Ireland, Italy, Portugal, Spain, Sweden, Turkey.

References

1. Cooper, R.A., Maddineni, V.R., Mirakhur, R.K., Wierda, J.M., Brady, M., Fitzpatrick, K.T.: Time course of neuromuscular effects and pharmacokinetics of rocuronium bromide (Org 9426) during isoflurane anaesthesia in patients with and without renal failure. Brit. J. Anaesth. **71**, 222–226 (1993)
2. Vermeyen, K., Hoffmann, V., Saldien, V.: Target controlled infusion of rocuronium: analysis of effect data to select a pharmacokinetic model. Brit. J. Anaesth. **90**, 183–188 (2003)
3. Hakim, D., Drolet, P., Donati, F., Fortier, L.P.: Performing post-tetanic count during rocuronium blockade has limited impact on subsequent twitch height or train-of-four responses. Can. J. Anaesth. **63**, 828–833 (2016)
4. Sunnen, M., Schläpfer, M., Biro, P.: Automated quantitative relaxometry for deep neuromuscular blockade in robot-assisted prostatectomy. Rom. J. Anaesth. Intensive Care **27**, 29–34 (2020)
5. Schultz, P., Ibsen, M., Østergaard, D., Skovgaard, L.T.: Onset and duration of action of rocuronium-from tracheal intubation, through intense block to complete recovery. Acta Anaesthesiol. Scand. **45**, 612–617 (2001)
6. REDIS. https://redis.io

Textile in the Loop as Automated Verification Tool for Smart Textile Applications

Phillip Petz(✉), Josef Langer, and Florian Eibensteiner

Univeristy of Applied Sciences Upper Austria, Hagenberg, Austria
{phillip.petz,josef.langer}@fh-hagenberg.at,
florian.eibensteiner@fh.hagenberg.at

Abstract. In this paper, we present a new approach for an automated test tool to characterize the behaviour of Smart Textiles. Smart Textiles are a combination of textile fabrics and conductive elements which change their electrical properties as a result of applied pressure, tension or temperature. The used materials as well as the manufacturing method result in a complex response caused by thread rearrangements, abrasions or tensions in the fabric and is reflected in overshooting and undershooting, drifts and offsets during the measurements. In order to test and characterize the textiles, we have developed an automated test environment that can generate mechanical stress as well as temperature changes and drive the textile with dedicated waveforms that are then measured and analysed. The response is used to iteratively refine the models of the textiles and provide more reliable measurement results under various mechanical and thermal loads.

Keywords: Conductive textiles · System design · Verification and simulation

1 Introduction

Textile sensors are well suited for the detection of movements and vital parameters due to their natural proximity to the human body. In the field of motion detection, different sensor concepts have been presented in prototype series in conjunction with conventional clothing [1,4]. It was noticeable that despite the use of similar sensor material, a separate investigation of the textile and its electronic and mechanical characteristics was necessary in each individual application [5]. A reuse of existing textile sensor strips for future projects is therefore only possible with reduced accuracy or increased effort in the design phase.

As a reference to the established test and development standard of Hardware in the Loop, this paper discusses the possibility of automated characterization and evaluation of conductive textiles. Similar to Hardware in the Loop, testsignals from simulations are applied to a textile under test and the material's response to these signals is recorded. By looping the response back, a behaviour model of the textile can be created and improved through iterative simulations.

© The Author(s), under exclusive license to Springer Nature Switzerland AG 2022
R. Moreno-Díaz et al. (Eds.): EUROCAST 2022, LNCS 13789, pp. 215–222, 2022.
https://doi.org/10.1007/978-3-031-25312-6_25

2   Concept

MATLAB is used for the automatic generation of SPICE models and netlists. These models can be used and tested in simulations with the new sensor front end. The simulated test signals are transferred to a server. A supervisor notifies the corresponding microcontroller of a new test run. The measurement and test devices can be addressed via the standard SCPI. The environmental parameters are controlled and measured via various test rigs. The system response of the textile is transmitted from the microcontroller back to the server and to MATLAB or Python. By matching the textile response from the test bench and the simulation results, the accuracy of the model is improved iteratively. An overview of the whole system can be seen in Fig. 1.

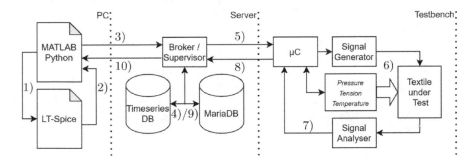

Fig. 1. Concept visualisation of a Textile in the Loop system. The sequence of operations between the programs, databases and the testbench is marked by the numbers.

3   Workflow

MATLAB (version R2021a) is used for simulation creation, LTspice (version XVII, 17.0.24.0) for calculation and Python (version 3.10) for communication with the server. The web server provides a TICK-Stack (Telegraf (1.21.2), InfluxDB (v1.8.10), Chronograf (1.9.1) and Kapacitor (OSS 1.6.2)) with an additional installation of Grafana (v8.3.4) for plotting data in real-time. A custom Broker/Supervisor with access to a MariaDB (8.0.29), a Java based User-Interface with React and custom REST-API is used for coordination of simulations and measurements. The requirements for the microcontroller of the test stand are the communication with the web server via Ethernet or WiFi as well as the connection with the measuring devices and test stands for configuration and measurement. Microcontrollers of the ESP32 series from Espressif are used for this purpose. The ESP32-PoE controller can be further operated via the Ethernet cable, which further simplifies the installation. The following chapter describes the initialisation of the programs, how they are started and how information can be exchanged between the programs.

3.1   Initialisation

The paths to the programs, a simulation folder and other supporting scripts are defined and loaded. The parameters of the simulation (simulation type, duration, ...) are defined in a structure in the corresponding folder. The specific parameters can be loaded by defining the project path while the general functions to create the simulation can be shared between simulations. A possible example for a simple RC transient circuit is shown in Listing 1.1.

Listing 1.1. Example configuration for a simple RC circuit.

```
1  clear  Circuit
2  Circuit.fileName  =  'RCexample';
3  Circuit.Res  =  10e3;
4  Circuit.Cap  =  155e-6;
5  Circuit.Vmax  =  5;
6  Circuit.f  =  2;
7  Circuit.endtime  =  5.00;
8  Circuit.analysistype  =  'tran';
```

3.2   Information Exchange

The *makeComponent* function can be used to link components in the simulation with nets via defined net names. The components are added to a circuit structure as a structure with name, start and end nodes and their type. Afterwards all structures are converted into the text format for nets in LTspice and the resulting file is moved into the simulation folder. The path to the LTspice executable, the simulation folder and the name of the netlist are passed.

The results of the simulation are stored in a raw file by LTspice. This file can then be opened and interpreted by MATLAB. In addition to the data, this format contains a lot of meta information such as title, date or the number of variables. The relevant information can be read out via the matrices or vectors. Alternatively, LTspice can handle *.wav* files well. By generating *.wav* files in MATLAB and importing them into LTspice as source or exporting LTspice of signals in *.wav* files, simulation stimuli or results can be easily transferred between the programs.

The data transfer to the web server is done via Python, where the Python program is called again by MATLAB after the simulation. Since the results of the simulation are already available in structures like *time* and *signals* in the MATLAB workspace, the results can easily be transferred and stored in *.mat* files. At this point it should be mentioned that in Python the format of LTspice could be used as well. Storage in *.mat* files was chosen for faster comparison of measurements, since in subsequent steps the *.mat* files can be easily loaded from the simulation folders and plotted or used with each other in calculations.

The Python packages Numpy and SciPy as well as a custom module for communication with InfluxDB via a websocket and the InfluxDB line protocol are used. Using the supervisor on the server, the simulation data is stored in its own time series. The entire meta information of the simulation, like excitation voltage, frequency, date or time is stored in the provided MariaDB. The supervisor uses a MariaDB connector, HTTP-Requests for communication with the InfluxDB, MQTT for requests to a broker and a REST API.

The same web interface with API calls can be used by the microcontroller, notifying it of the new measurements via MQTT. The controller can load the metadata of the simulation, time series, as well as the SCPI, G-code and custom commands and output them via its dedicated communication ports. At the same time there is the possibility to perform measurements without previous simulation via the web interface. For this purpose, a microcontroller and its connected devices can be selected in the webinterface and the commands for measurements can be generated via a react mask. The transmission of the control and measurement commands at the test stand is done via UART or Ethernet.

Upon start of the measurement, a new dashboard with the respective databases and measurement labels is created by the broker via the Grafana API. This dashboard is stored in MariaDB and can be accessed via the web interface. During the measurement, measurement data is continuously read out by the microcontroller from the laboratory measuring devices and test benches and transferred to InfluxDB via the API. The microcontroller is in constant contact with the server and the supervisor during the measurement and can be reconfigured, stopped or restarted by MQTT messages during the measurement. On the web interface, the data is displayed in real time during the measurement.

After the measurement, the broker is notified of completion via MQTT and data such as the end time and duration is added to the database. MATLAB can now call a Python script again, which downloads the measurement data via the REST interface and saves it to a *.mat* file. In MATLAB, the results of the simulation as well as the results from the measurement are now available for further processing in *.mat* files.

4   Simulation and Measurements

The description of the electrical behavior of conductive textiles in the presence of acting and environmental factors can come from physical, textile models [2,3] or from data-based models (Textile Sensor Calibration, Sensor Models). When a model is created, based on physical rules, it is referred to as whitebox modeling because the underlying relationships of the system are well understood and can be modeled. In data-based models, a transformation of the influencing parameters to measurable output variables is created. With more data, a better approximation of the system can be created, which is why it is also referred to as Big Data. Through both types of modeling, in addition to the simulation and prediction of the behavior, a calibration and compensation can be performed with the created models.

Figure 2 shows a circuit simulation with simple electrical components and a textile model with two terminals. Its resistance and thus the current and voltage change in the network can be modeled as a function of conductance, shape and temperature. Alternatively, the LTspice directive TEMP can be used to model the temperature dependence.

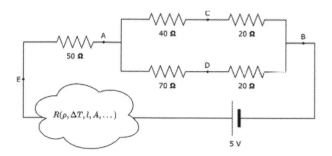

Fig. 2. Circuit simulation with textile model in lower left corner. The resistance R is dependent on ρ, ΔT, and it's geometry, defined by l and A. More parameters are possible, but are neglected for this example. The rest of the circuit can be changed as desired and represents here a simplified analog front end with signal generation and filtering elements.

4.1   Temperature Model

The complexity of modeling and simulation of conductive textiles depends on the level at which the simulation is to be performed. The simplest is the simulation of a conductive thread, which has a defined electrical resistance due to its coating and geometry. A physical model that determines the resistance as a function of temperature, conductance and geometric shape is given in Eq. 1.

$$U(t)[V] = \frac{\rho(x,y)[\Omega] \cdot l(x,y)[m]}{A(x,y)[m^2]} \cdot (1 + \alpha(x,y) \cdot \Delta T[C^\circ]) \cdot I(t)[A] \qquad (1)$$

In this model, it is assumed that the change in length due to an acting tensile force leads to a uniform shrinkage of the material. Inhomogeneities due to elastic moduli are neglected. Furthermore, the voltage and current are shown as a function of time, since deviations can occur between current and voltage due to parasitic capacitances and inductances. This resistance model can now be modeled according to the quantities of conductivity, shape and temperature in and included in simulations.

4.2   Temperature Test Stand

For the simplest case of temperature dependence, an experimental setup is set up for targeted temperature specification and measurement. A high precision Negative Temperature Coefficient Thermistor (NTC) with a setup height of 0.1 [mm] and an absolute accuracy of 0.1 ppm and a relative accuracy of 0.01 [°C] is used for the measurement. The resistance of the NTC is used with a Source Measurement Unit (SMU) from Keithley. The SMU can be used to measure resistances in the range of 1 [mΩ] to 10 [GΩ] with an error less than 1 [%] of the measurement range. The SMU has several terminals that can be switched between. The front terminals are used for the measurement of the NTC. The conversion of the resistance values to temperature were taken from the data sheet.

The back of the SMU was connected to textile samples. These fabrics were placed between two Peltier elements with the NTC. The voltage and current for the Peltier elements were provided by a Siglent SPD 3303C programmable laboratory power supply. The laboratory power supply has two independent outputs, therefore each of the two Peltier elements can be supplied independently of each other. Cooling fans on a mounted radiator were used with a fixed voltage to increase the heat transfer with the room. A schematic picture for the overview of the experimental setup is shown in Fig. 3.

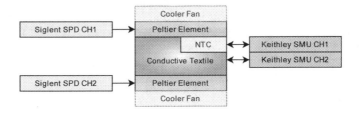

Fig. 3. Setup with SMU, power supply, NTC, Peltier and textile element.

4.3   Measurements

Temperature and test curves were created in MATLAB to explain the relationship between the temperature and the measured resistance. Following the workflow described in Sect. 3, the change in resistance as a function of temperature was measured in the experimental setup. The recorded values of NTC and conductive textile were stored in the database and MATLAB. The model presented in Sect. 4.1 was then used to determine the temperature coefficient α. In Fig. 4, the measured values of the NTC can be seen in the upper part of the graph. The second plot shows the resistance curve measured at the textile. Since the two resistance curves show the same course with a change in temperature, it was shown that the textile also has a negative temperature coefficient.

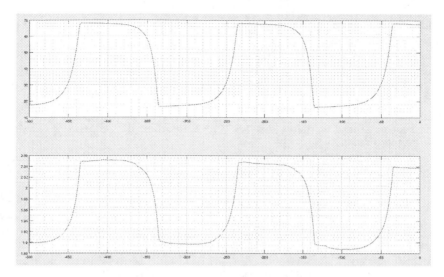

Fig. 4. Measured temperature from the NTC and corresponding measured resistance from the textile.

By referring to the reference temperature of 23 [°], the corresponding temperature was calculated for the measured resistance. The initial condition in MATLAB can now be revised and improved via this connection, which automatically adjusts the simulation results in LTspice in accordance with the properties of the textile at the testbench.

5   Results

As a result, reproducible tests can now be carried out and the unknown, complex piezoresistive nonlinear behavior of the textiles like overshooting and undershooting, drifts and gain errors can be comprehensibly characterized. The separation of measurement devices at the textile manufacturer and the developer of the measurement circuits allows faster iteration cycles and better integration in the developed prototype or product.

Using the example of temperature, the potential of the Textile in the Loop concept was demonstrated. Simulations in Matlab can be transferred to circuit simulations in LTspice. The simulated results can be analyzed in MATLAB. Furthermore, automated measurements can be transferred to a server and documented and exchanged with project and research partners. By transferring and storing the configuration, reproducible measurements can be carried out independent of location in order to investigate the complex behavior of the textiles.

References

1. Langer, J., Eibensteiner, F., Peterka, J., Knaack, P.: Pressure sensitive shoe insoles and socks for rehabilitation applications. In: 2018 IEEE 12th International Conference on Application of Information and Communication Technologies (AICT), pp. 1–6. IEEE (2018). https://doi.org/10.1109/ICAICT.2018.8747024
2. Li, L., Au, W.M., Hua, T., Wong, K.S.: Design of a conductive fabric network by the sheet resistance method. Text. Res. J. **81**(15), 1568–1577 (2011). https://doi.org/10.1177/0040517511410105
3. Li, L., Au, W.M., Wan, K.M., Wan, S.H., Chung, W.Y., Wong, K.S.: A resistive network model for conductive knitting stitches. Text. Res. J. **80**(10), 935–947 (2010). https://doi.org/10.1177/0040517509349789
4. Petz, P., Eibensteiner, F., Langer, J.: Sensor shirt as universal platform for real-time monitoring of posture and movements for occupational health and ergonomics. Procedia Comput. Sci. **180**, 200–207 (2021). https://doi.org/10.1016/j.procs.2021.01.157
5. Wohlrab, S., Petz, P., Eibensteiner, F., Langer, J.: Influences of coating and spandex compositions of conductive textiles used as strain sensors (2021)

Orchestrating Digital Twins for Distributed Manufacturing Execution Systems

Tomáš Fiedor, Martin Hruška[✉], and Aleš Smrčka

Faculty of Information Technology, Brno University of Technology, Brno, Czech Republic
{ifiedortom,ihruska,smrcka}@fit.vutbr.cz

Abstract. We propose a generic framework for generating scenarios for orchestrating digital twins of distributed manufacturing execution systems (MES). The orchestration is a typical technique for configuring, managing and coordinating the communication in various types of system. We focus on its particular application for testing of distributed systems: e.g., when a new version of MES is about to be released one may create the testing scenario observing the behaviour of the older version already deployed in the production and then use the scenario to orchestrate the digital twin to test the new version. Specifically, we build on communication logs captured from a manufactory with deployed MES and create an abstract model of communication inside the distributed system and abstract models of messages passed in the communication. Based on these models we then generate a scenario which is further used to orchestrate the digital twin. Moreover, our approach can also automatically extrapolate the new testing scenarios from the derived models allowing efficient automated testing.

1 Introduction

One of the main challenges of the Industry 4.0 is to develop secure and bug-free components, especially in distributed, manufacturing execution systems. These systems usually include manufacturing machines paired with controlling terminals, industrial control systems (ICS), and/or system that controls the whole manufactory process (manufactory execution system). Development and testing of such systems is quite complex because their components (1) work in distributed environment, (2) use different communication protocols, (3) use different software ranging from low-level embedded software to complex information systems, (4) require interaction between humans and machines, and (5) often cannot be tested in a real-world environment during the common traffic.

Moreover, any bug or security issue may be quite costly which can be substantiated by the expected grow of the market of ICS security up to \$22.2 billions by 2025 [1]. Quality assurance teams usually utilize some form of test automation while keeping effort spent on the testing itself. Unfortunately, test automation of distributed manufacturing systems is hard for two main reasons.

First, testing in a real-world environment (so called out-of-the-lab testing) is expensive. Hence, we usually construct the so called digital twin: a virtual environment where components (such as production machines) are emulated or simulated to replicate the digital copy of manufacturing process. Such a copy can then be used for testing in an environment as close as possible to a real system.

R. Moreno-Díaz et al. (Eds.): EUROCAST 2022, LNCS 13789, pp. 223–231, 2022.
https://doi.org/10.1007/978-3-031-25312-6_26

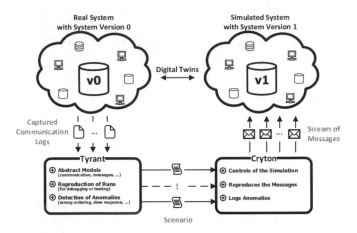

Fig. 1. Scheme of our solution.

The other problem is how to model the communication among number of quite different components common in manufacturing process. The communication within the system is often purpose-specific and requires strong domain knowledge. Hence, creating the automated test suite is complicated as it requires effort spent on precise test environment setup and deterministic test case description.

In this work, we propose a generic framework for creating automated test suites for digital twins of manufacturing execution systems (MES). The framework analyses the communication captured from a run of the real system, learns a model of the communication protocol and models of data sent. Based on these models, we generate test scenarios that are used for orchestration of corresponding digital twin. In particular, we suggest to use such scenarios for automated testing of systems, e.g., when a new version of MES is being developed.

2   Framework for Generating Orchestration Scenarios

We propose a generic framework that can be applied to various settings of distributed MES systems. In this paper, however, we will demonstrate it on a particular use case consisting of various types of nodes communicating using various protocols. We assume the following infrastructure: the distributed system consists of an Enterprise Resource Planning (ERP) system, the MES system that controls the actual production, manufacturing machines and their corresponding terminals used by human operators. We expect that the communication between particular components uses different protocols and data structures, e.g.: (1) MES and ERP communicate using REST protocol with XML data, (2) MES and Terminal communicate using REST protocol with JSON data, and (3) MES communicates with machines using OPC-UA protocol, although some minor manual tweaks for understanding specific-purpose data might be necessary.

An overview of our framework is shown in Fig. 1. Our framework requires logs of communication collected from a real-world system, e.g., with an older version of MES system under testing: the collected log usually represents either expected communication in the system, or a log of communication that led to some incident. The log is in form of a sequence of messages between pairs of communicating components logged with the timestamps of the communication and the data that were transferred. We derive two kinds of model based on this log: (1) model of the data transmitted in the messages, and (2) the model of the whole communication in the system. To model communication, we convert the log to a so called event calendar which provides efficient and direct manipulation with seen messages. Then, we eventually convert event the calendar to a finite automaton (where every event is a symbol) which is more abstract representation but provides options for postprocessing (e.g., by applying length abstraction to generate new test cases) or analyses (e.g., by searching for particular string representing an error behaviour). From the derived (abstract) models, we generate a so called scenario: a sequence of concrete messages that will be sent in a real-world or simulated environment. A scenario is later used by a digital twin orchestrator to perform simulation of real system in digital twin. In our case, we use the Cryton tool [2] to orchestrate simulated environment. Other orchestrators that conform to our format of scenarios can be naturally used as well. Finally, based on the result of orchestration developers can observe whether the new version in a digital twin behaves as expected.

The framework can also be quite easily extended to support the performance testing of the digital twins. In particular, we propose to mine selected performance metrics (e.g., among others, the duration of communications) from the captured logs. The metrics are then used for comparison of runs from different environments or from different versions to detect, e.g., anomalies in the performance.

Related work. There has been several different approaches for modelling communication in manufactory and deriving new test cases. [5] uses Finite Automata to model the communication in systems, however, their approach is limited to learning only fixed number of components. Another approach is the process mining [10], a mature technique for modelling event based system. We see the technique as not suited well for MES systems as it analyses one-to-one communications and is restricted to a single thread per node [8]. Modelling of communication for anomaly detection [9] implements an approach based on probabilistic automata. The usual communication in manufactory is, however, mostly deterministic, hence, no probabilistic transitions are created in derived automaton. Finally, we can mention approaches of [4,6,7] which are research prototypes only and possible not mature enough for use case in real-world distributed systems.

3   Modelling Messages

In distributed system, components usually communicate through messages. We assume, that each message that was captured in the log has the following parts: (1) a timestamp (when the message was sent), (2) data (what was sent), and, (3) a type (what kind of message was sent). A suitable data representation of such messages can be a challenging task, especially, when modelling the communication among different components. The representation should be unified for different kinds of data formats (such as JSON, XML or YAML), should preserve the original semantics, and should allow generating new test cases from the observed data (e.g., extrapolating extreme values from the underlying domains).

Communication logs usually contain lots of subsets of messages that are structurally similar to each other and differ only in a certain aspects (mainly in the data that were sent and the type of the message). Thus, we propose classification of the messages into a groups of similar messages before creating abstract models. In particular, we classify the seen messages based on the so called fingerprint of the message (i.e., the spanning tree of the nested structure with respect to the fields of the data) and based on the type of the message. The idea is that messages having similar structure (but that differ in, e.g., number of items in a list, or values in leaves) should have the same abstract model. For each such class, we construct an abstract model that represents all seen messages of the given class. Such a model can then be used not just to reproduce the communication but also to create new (potentially unseen) messages, e.g., by generating syntactically-similar messages.

We propose to model the messages using the following representation (simplified for the sake of presentation). We assume two types of nodes: (1) a leaf node is a quadruple $n = \langle k, l, u, V \rangle$, where k is a key associated with the node (e.g., as in JSON key-value pairs), l (resp. u) is the minimum (resp. maximum) number of occurrences of the node in the given part of message, and V is the set of all seen values for the node; and (2) a composite node is a quadruple $n = \langle k, l, u, N \rangle$, where k, l, and u are defined the same as previously and N is a set of child nodes (either leaves or composite). We assume that the root of every message is represented by the $root$ key. Note that we support also other types of nodes, e.g., the attribute node, used in XML format, but due to the space constrains we omit their description.

To create abstract models, we process input log message by message (which are in XML or JSON format). Atomic values correspond to leaf nodes and composite values (lists, dictionaries, nested tags) correspond to composite nodes. Further, we will work with predicate c over node n written as $c(n)$ (e.g., representing that node n has a specific key). We denote set of all possible predicates as C.

We define the function $reduce$ over a set of leaves $\{n_1, \ldots, n_m\}$ with the same key k as $reduce(\{\langle k, l_1, u_1, V_1 \rangle, \ldots, \langle k, l_n, u_n, V_n \rangle\}) = \langle k, \sum_1^n l_i, \sum_1^n u_i, \bigcup_1^n V_i \rangle$; similarly, we define the $reduce$ of a set of composite nodes $\{n_1, \ldots, n_m\}$ corresponding to a key k as $reduce(\{\langle k, l_1, u_1, N_1 \rangle, \ldots, \langle k, l_n, u_n, N_n \rangle\}) = \langle k, \sum_1^n l_i, \sum_1^n u_i, \bigcup_1^n N_i \rangle$. Then, for composite nodes, we define the $group$ and $reduce$ function as $grpreduce(\langle k, l, u, N \rangle, \langle c_1, \ldots, c_m \rangle) = \langle k, l, u, N' \rangle$, where $\langle c_1, \ldots, c_m \rangle$ are predicates and $N' = \bigcup_1^m \{reduce(\{n \in N \mid c_i(n)\})\}$. Basically, the operation groups the children nodes according to a given predicate (e.g., it groups children named with the same key), merges their values and aggregates their occurrences.

Finally, we define the $merge$ of two nodes ($n \circ n'$) with the same key k as follows: (1) $\langle k, l_1, u_1, V_1 \rangle \circ \langle k, l_2, u_2, V_2 \rangle = \langle k, min(l_1, l_2), max(u_1, u_2), V_1 \cup V_2 \rangle$, and (2) $\langle k, l_1, u_1, N_1 \rangle \circ \langle k, l_2, u_2, N_2 \rangle = \langle k, min(l_1, l_2), max(u_1, u_2), Merged(N_1, N_2) \cup Copy(N_1, N_2) \cup Copy(N_2, N_1) \rangle$, where $Merged(N, N') = \{n \circ n' \mid \exists c \in C \, \exists n \in N \, \exists n' \in N' : c(n) \land c(n')\}$ and $Copied(N, N') = \{n \mid \exists c \in C \, \exists n \in N \, \forall n' \in N' : c(n) \land \neg c(n')\}$. We choose values of minimal and maximal number of occurrences to cover both nodes. In the composite nodes, we group the children satisfying the same criteria and recursively merge them. If there is a child node from N_1 (resp.

N_2) with no node from N_2 (resp. N_1) that matches the same criterion the first node is simply copied to the result. For simplicity, we assume that a criterion c is satisfied by maximally one node in one subtree. Finally, for each class and its messages with the root nodes $r_1, \ldots, r_n$, we compute the final abstract node n representing the class as $n = grpreduce(r_1, \langle c_1, \ldots, c_m \rangle) \circ \ldots \circ grpreduce(r_n, \langle c_1, \ldots, c_m \rangle)$.

4   Modelling Communication of Monitored System

Once we derived the models of messages communicated in a system, we further learn the communication protocol used in the environment. We first use an intermediate data structure called the *event calendar* to represent messages in the monitored system where each event corresponds to one message. The messages are ordered chronologically in the calendar by their timestamps. This way we can represent the communication using different protocols and data formats in a unified and regular manner and we are not limited to a fixed number of components. That would not be possible with other representations which need predefined topology of a represented system. The calendar is later used to generate scenario precisely reproducing the learnt communication by transforming each event to a single step in a scenario for orchestrating digital twin.

Moreover, we want to generate new test cases allowing to experiment on scenarios which have not yet been seen but are similar to a real-world situations. Such scenarios bring sometimes more testing value since they are relatively easy to generate in contrast to the time demanding process of writing tests manually. Hence, we propose to transform the event calendar to *finite automaton* and apply, e.g., length abstraction which over-approximates language of the automaton. In the following paragraphs, we define our method in a formal way.

An event is a tuple $e = (t, s, r, time, m)$ where t is the type of communication protocol (i.e., OPC-UA or REST), s is the identification of the sender, r is the identification of the receiver, *time* is a timestamp, and m is an abstract representation of the sent message described in the previous section. Event calendar c is a list of events $c = (e_1, \ldots, e_n)$. A finite automaton is tuple $\mathcal{A} = (Q, \Sigma, \delta, I, F)$ where Q is a finite set of states, Σ is a finite alphabet, $\delta \subset Q \times \Sigma \times 2^Q$ is a transition relation, $I \subseteq Q$ is a set of initial states, $F \subseteq Q$ is a set of final states. A language $\mathcal{L}$ of automaton $\mathcal{A}$, denoted by $\mathcal{L}(\mathcal{A})$, is a subset of Σ^*. A run ρ of automaton $\mathcal{A}$ is a sequence of states $(q_1, \ldots, q_n)$ such that $\forall 1 \leq i \leq n - 1 : \exists a \in \Sigma : q_{i+1} \in \delta(q_i, a)$. A word $w = a_1, \ldots, a_n$ is accepted by the automaton $\mathcal{A}$ iff there is a run $\rho = (q_1, \ldots, q_{n+1})$ of $\mathcal{A}$ such that $\forall 1 \leq i \leq n : q_{i+1} \in \delta(q_i, a_i)$ and $q_{n+1} \in F$. A language $\mathcal{L}_q$ of a state $q \in Q$ is a set $\{w = a_1, \ldots, a_n \mid w$ *is accepted by a run* $\rho = q_1, \ldots, q_{n+1}$ *such that* $q_1 \in I \wedge q_{n+1} \in F\}$.

Event calendar $c = (e_1, \ldots, e_n)$ is transformed to a finite automaton $\mathcal{A}_c = (Q^c, \Sigma, \delta^c, I^c, F^c)$ as follows: the set of states is $Q^c = \{q_1, \ldots, q_{n+1}\}$, the alphabet Σ is obtained by transforming each event $e = (t, s, r, time, m)$ to an unique symbol a^e by applying a hashing function over $(t, s, r, time)$, i.e., giving away m, the set of initial states is $I^c = \{q_1\}$ and the set of final states is $F^c = \{q_{n+1}\}$. Finally, $\forall 2 \leq i \leq n + 1 : (q_{i-1}, a^{e_i}, \{q_i\})$ is added to δ^c.

In order to create the new scenarios, we need to overapproximate the models. In particular, we propose to use the length abstraction transforming the automaton $\mathcal{A}$ to an abstracted automaton $\mathcal{A}^k$ by merging all states with the same language with respect to a given length. Formally, a length abstraction over an automaton $\mathcal{A} = (Q, \Sigma, \delta, I, F)$ is an equivalence relation $\alpha^k \subseteq Q \times Q$ such that $(p, p') \in \alpha^k$ iff $\mathcal{L}_p^n = \mathcal{L}_{p'}^n$ where $\mathcal{L}_q^n = \{w' \mid \exists w \in \mathcal{L}_q : w' \text{ is a prefix of } w \wedge \text{length of } w' \text{ is up to } n\}$. We denote an equivalence class of $q \in Q$ by $[\![q]\!]$. An abstracted automaton $\alpha^k(\mathcal{A}) = (Q_\alpha, \Sigma, \delta_\alpha, I_\alpha, F_\alpha)$ is obtained using α^k in the following way: $Q_\alpha = \{[\![q]\!] \mid q \in Q\}$, for each $q \in \delta(p, a)$ there is $([\![p]\!], a, X) \in \delta_\alpha$ such that $[\![q]\!] \in X$, and finally, $I_\alpha = \{[\![q]\!] \mid q \in I\}$ and $F_\alpha = \{[\![q]\!] \mid q \in F\}$.

The length abstraction overapproximates language of the original automata, i.e., $\mathcal{L}(\mathcal{A}) \subseteq \mathcal{L}(\mathcal{A}_\alpha)$ meaning that there may exist a word $w = a_1, \ldots, a_n$ such that $w \in \mathcal{L}(\mathcal{A}_\alpha) \wedge w \notin \mathcal{L}(\mathcal{A})$. Both automata have the same alphabet which was originally derived from a set of events. Therefore, it is possible to convert the word w to series of actual messages. Supposing that w is not in the language of the original automaton, we thus obtain a series of events not present in the original system that can be used as a new test case for testing MES system in a digital twin.

5   Generating Scenario

Finally, we generate a scenario that will be used for orchestration of the digital twin of the tested system. We iterate over the event calendar and, for each event, we generate one step in the scenario. Each step consists of sending messages in the digital twin. The concrete messages sent during the orchestration are generated from the abstract representation. By default, we support exact replication of the seen communication, however, we provide also an experimental support for, e.g., generating syntactically or semantically similar messages.

We implemented our framework in our tool *Tyrant* [3] which generates scenarios for the orchestrating tool *Cryton*. Cryton uses as an input a configuration for creating the digital twin (i.e., a description of digital twin components) and a scenario generated by Tyrant in the YAML format.

In the following, we will illustrate the transformation of communication logs from real system to YAML scenario. We remark, we consider a system consisting of ERP system, MES system, and manufacturing machines and their corresponding terminals used by human operators. Listing 1.1 shows a message between ERP and MES. The message is stored in the file 20211207-125952.xml which has a timestamp encoded in its name. The message is in XML format and its semantics is that there are 42 items of Material 1 in stocks. Listing 1.2 shows a message between a machine and MES. The message was sent one second after the previous one. The message semantics is that the value of the node 0 should be set to 99 in Machine 001. Finally, Listing 1.3 shows a generated scenario consisting of two steps. The first step is executed in (logical) time 0 h, 0 min, 0 s: the orchestrator will send a message from ERP to MES using the REST protocol. The message has the XML data attached. The second steps are executed one second after the first step: the orchestrator will send another message from MES to Machine 001 using OPC-UA protocol. The message says that a value of the node with path 0 should be set to 99.

We implemented the proposed framework in the tool called the *Tyrant*. We tested our approach on the captured communication provided by a partner company that offers

Listing 1.1. 20211207-125952.xml

```xml
<DataSource>
 <Data>
   <Name>Material1</Name>
   <Value>42</Value>
 </Data>
</DataSource>
```

Listing 1.2. MES and Machine message

```
SampleDataTime              ; Value ; Name       ; Path
2021-12-07 12:59:53.617 ;   99   ; Machine 001 ; 0
```

Listing 1.3. Generated scenario

```yaml
---
timestamps:
- delta:
    seconds: 0
    minutes: 0
    hours: 0
  steps:
  - type: ERP
    host: ERP
    target: MES
    args:
      xml: |-
        <DataSource>
          <Data>
            <Name>Data1</Name>
            <Value>42</Value>
          </Data>
        </DataSource>
- delta:
    seconds: 1
    minutes: 0
    hours: 0
  steps:
  - type: OPC-UA
    host: MES
    target: Machine 001
    args:
     value: 99
     node: 0
```

a MES as their product. We were able to successfully generate valid scenarios for the Cryton tool which then subsequently orchestrated a digital twin using our scenarios. However, our Tyrant is still prototype and it would need extensive collaboration with the company to deploy it to production.

6   Conclusion

In this work, we proposed a generic framework for orchestrating the digital twins of distributed systems in manufacturing environments. The main challenges of generating scenarios suitable for orchestrating digital twins is finding suitable models for (1) the communication in the systems, and (2) the actual sent messages during the communications. We proposed to use the simple approach: finite automata for communication and simple abstract representation for messages.

However, in our experience applying the framework in practice requires much more effort. Lots of testing scenarios and components require specific preparation before the orchestration: e.g., setting of the initial database or sending specific sequence of (hard-coded) messages to prepare the system that are usually not being captured in the communication log. Currently, our tool supports a concrete use case in a concrete manufacturing environment. Hence, extending our solution to a more broader class of manufacturing environments is our future work.

Acknowledgement. The work was supported by the project No. 20-07487S of the Czech Science Foundation, by the ECSEL JU under grant agreement No 876852., and by the FIT BUT internal project FIT-S-20-6427.

References

1. MarketsandMarkets Research Pvt. Ltd.: Industrial Control Systems (ICS) Security Market worth $22.2 billion by 2025. https://www.marketsandmarkets.com/PressReleases/industrial-control-systems-security-ics.asp, Last accessed 11 Nov 2021
2. Repository of Cryton. https://gitlabdev.ics.muni.cz/beast-public/cryton, Last Accessed 11 Nov 2021
3. Repository of Tyrant. https://pajda.fit.vutbr.cz/tacr-unis/tyrant, Last Accessed 11 Nov 2021
4. Christopher Ackermann. Recovering views of inter-system interaction behaviors. In: Working Conference on Reverse Engineering 2009, Lille, France, pp. 53–61, vol. 10 (2009)
5. Beschastnikh, I., Brun, Y., Ernst, M.D., Krishnamurthy, A.: Inferring models of concurrent systems from logs of their behavior with csight. In: ICSE '14, Hyderabad, India, pp. 468–479. ACM (2014)
6. Comparetti, P.M., Wondracek, G., Krügel, C., Kirda, E.: Prospex: Protocol specification extraction. In S&P 2009, Oakland, California, USA, pp. 110–125. IEEE Computer Society (2009)
7. Hsu, Y., Shu, G., Lee, D.: A model-based approach to security flaw detection of network protocol implementations. In: ICNP 2008, Orlando, Florida, USA, pp. 114–123. IEEE Computer Society (2008)
8. Leemans, M., van der Aalst, M.P.: Process mining in software systems: Discovering real-life business transactions and process models from distributed systems. In: MODELS, Ottawa, Canada, pp. 44–53. IEEE (2015)

9. Matousek, P., Havlena, V., Holík, L.: Efficient modelling of ICS communication for anomaly detection using probabilistic automata. In: IM 2021, Bordeaux, France, pp. 81–89. IEEE (2021)
10. van der Aalst, W.M.P.: Process Mining - Data Science in Action, Second Edition. Springer (2016). https://doi.org/10.1007/978-3-662-49851-4

Automata with Bounded Repetition in RE2

Michal Horký, Juraj Síč, and Lenka Turoňová(✉)

Faculty of Information Technology, Brno University of Technology,
Brno, Czech Republic
{xhorky23,sicjuraj,ituronova}@fit.vutbr.cz

Abstract. *Regular expression* (*regex*) matching has an irreplaceable role in software development. It is a computationally intensive process often applied on large texts. Predictability of its efficiency has a significant impact on the overall usability of software applications in practice. A problem is that standard approaches for regex matching suffer from high worst case complexity. An unlucky combination of a regex and text may increase the matching time by orders of magnitude. This can be a doorway for the so-called *Regular Expression Denial of Service* (ReDoS) attack in which the attacker causes a denial of service by providing a specially crafted regex or text. We focus on one of the sources of these attacks, which are regex with bounded repetition (e.g., '(ab)100'). Succinct representation and fast matching of such regexes can be archived by using a novel counting-set automaton. We present a C++ implementation of a matching algorithm based on the counting-set automaton. The implementation is done within RE2, which is a fast state-of-the-art regex matcher. We perform experiments on real-life regexes. The experiments show that implementation within the RE2 is faster than the original C# implementation.

1 Introduction

Regular expression (*regex*) matching plays a significant role in software development. They are powerful means of automatically manipulating text, e.g., searching, finding and replacing, data validation, or syntax highlighting [18]. As stated in [2–4], about $30 - 40\%$ of the Python, Java, and JavaScript software uses regex matching.

Regexes are only a small part of big projects so they often lack testing and analysis. However, a single poorly-written regex may lead to catastrophic consequences, such as failed input validation, leaky firewalls and even events such as the recent catastrophic outage of Cloudflare services [8] or Stack Overflow [1]. The problems are caused by the so-called *Regex Denial of Service* (ReDoS), a denial of service attack based on a high-complexity evaluation of matching regex against a malign text, where an attacker provides a crafted text that forces the worst-case time complexity of the matching engine.

This work has been supported by the FIT BUT internal project FIT-S-20-6427 and the Czech Science Foundation (project No. 19-24397S).

This may severely impact the performance especially of the *backtracking-based* regular matchers (such as regex matching engines of wide-spread programming languages .NET, Java, JavaScript, Perl, Python, etc.) since the evaluation of vulnerable regexes against the malign input takes polynomial or exponential time in the length of the input. *A backtracking regex engine* constructs a *non-deterministic finite automaton* (NFA) from the regex and then simulates the NFA on the input text [4].

An alternative approach is to use so-called *offline DFA simulation* [15] that uses a precomputed *deterministic finite automaton* (DFA) with much lower worst-case complexity (wrt the length of input text). The major drawback of offline DFA simulation is the state explosion of the DFA construction, which can cause significant performance issues when using this method in practice [18].

To prevent the state space explosion, some matching engines (such as RE2 [7], grep [9], or Rust [6]) use a variant of *Thompson's algorithm* [17] (an on-the-fly subset construction). However, they work with highly non-deterministic automata which can cause a slowdown due to the computation of large DFA states. This problem can be partially solved by caching already visited parts of the DFA (a technique used by modern matchers). A step within a cached part is then a constant time operation, the same as for the offline DFA simulation. However, regexes that cause exploding determinization are problematic for all variants, explicit determinization, as well as cached or non-cached NFA simulation [18].

A frequent cause of the DFA explosion are regexes with *the bounded repetition*. Repeated patterns, such as '(ab){1,100}', can be succinctly expressed by a novel succinct and fast deterministic machine called the *counting-set automaton* (CsA) proposed in a recent paper by Turoňová et al. [18]. This machine is an automaton with so-called *counting sets*, a special type of registers that can hold bounded integer values. It also supports a limited selection of simple set operations that can be implemented in constant time.

The main contribution of this paper is an efficient implementation of regexes matching using this novel CsA within the state-of-the-art matcher RE2 and its evaluation against the original CsA-based matcher of [18] implemented in C# and other state-of-the-art matchers. We show that RE2 extended with CsA is faster compared to the original C# matcher from [18] and for regexes with bounded repetition it can beat existing state-of-the-art matchers.

2 Preliminaries

We consider a fixed finite *alphabet* of *characters/symbols* Σ (presumably a large one such as Unicode). *Words* are sequences of characters from Σ, with the empty sequence denoted by ε. *Languages* are sets of words. The operators of *concatenation* $\cdot$ and *iteration* $*$ applied on words or languages have the usual meaning. We consider the usual basic syntax of *regexes* generated by the grammar

$$R ::= \alpha \mid (R) \mid R\,R \mid R \mid R \mid R* \mid R\{n,m\}$$

where $n, m \in \mathbb{N}$, $0 \leq n$, $0 < m$, $n \leq m$, and α is a *character class*, i.e., a set of characters from Σ. A character class is most often of the form a, .,

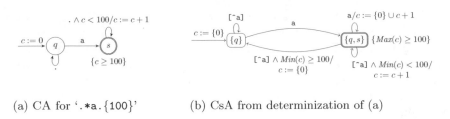

(a) CA for '.*a.{100}'   (b) CsA from determinization of (a)

Fig. 1. CA and CsA. The transitions are labeled by their *guard*, which specifies the input character class and possibly restricts counter (or counting set) values, separated by '/' from the counter *update*. In (b), the notation $\{0\}\cup c+1$ stands for the set of values obtained by *incrementing* each value in c, *adding* 0, and *removing* values larger than the upper bound of the counter, 100 for (b). The edges denoting initial states are labelled with *initial values* of the counters. Final states are in (a) and (b) labelled with an *acceptance condition* on counters, e.g. $\{c \geq 100\}$ in (a).

$[a_1-b_1a_2-b_2 \dots a_n-b_n]$, or $[\hat{}a_1-b_1a_2-b_2 \dots a_n-b_n]$, denoting a singleton containing the character $a \in \Sigma$, the entire set Σ, a union of n intervals of characters, or the complement of the same, respectively.

The *language* of a regex R, denoted $L(R)$, is constructed inductively to the structure of R, from its atomic sub-expressions, character classes, using the language operations denoted by the regex combinators. They are understood as usual: two regexes in a sequence stand for the *concatenation* of their languages, '|' is the *choice* or *union*, '*' is the *iteration*, and '{n,m}', is the *bounded iteration*, equivalent to the union of i-fold concatenations of its operand for $n \leq i \leq m$.

Automata-Based Regex Matching. Matching engines that are based on automata theory usually work by constructing a NFA for a given regex and then simulating it on a given text by using on-the-fly subset construction, i.e. creating parts of the DFA needed for matching. This method can be very efficient for regexes without bounded iteration, as there are constructions such that the size of created NFA is linear to the size of the regex. However, to transform bounded iteration $R\{n,m\}$ to NFA, we have to unfold it, i.e. concatenate m copies of the NFA for R. The constructed automata would be then too big for larger values of m. Therefore, we use approach introduced in [18] where such regexes are transformed into succinct *counting automata* and their simulation is achieved by using deterministic *counting-set automata*.

Counting Automata. Regexes with bounded iteration can be succinctly represented by using *counting automata* (CA) [18]. As an example, in Fig. 1a there is a CA for the regex '.*a.{100}'. As seen in the figure, a transition of the CA can reset a counter to 0, keep it unchanged, increment it, and test whether its value belongs to a specified constant interval. The values of every counter c can only reach values in between 0 and some $\max_c \in \mathbb{N}$ (the maximum number which c is compared against). A run of a CA over a word goes through a sequence of configurations, pairs of the form (q, ν) where q is a control state and ν is a counter valuation, a mapping of counters to their integer values. For instance, one of the CA runs from Fig. 1a on the word a^{100} generates configurations $(q, c = 0), (s, c = 0), (s, c = 1), \ldots, (s, c = 99)$, but the CA can postpone the transition into s arbitrarily, leading to different values of c. It is easy to see that one can construct an NFA whose set of states is the set of reachable configurations of a CA; the runs of such an NFA would go precisely through the same configurations as the runs of the CA over the same word.

Counting-Set Automata. Matching with CA can be accomplished by determinizing them to DFA, however, that would still result in the blow-up that we are trying to evade. We therefore determinize CA into the so-called *counting-set automata* (CsAs) [18]. The CsA is a deterministic machine that simulates the DFA but achieves succinctness by computing the counter values only at runtime, as values of a certain kind of registers. Since a single DFA state contains many counter values paired with CA control states, these registers must be capable of holding a *set* of integer values. We call these registers, which store sets of integers, *counting sets*. A transition may then update a counting set c by incrementing all its elements, resetting it to the singleton $\{0\}$, adding the element 0 or 1 to it, and test whether the minimal or the maximal value in the set belongs to some constant interval.[1] A counting set for a counter c is also restricted to only contain values between 0 and $\max_c$ (the set-increment operation removes values greater than $\max_c$). An example of a CsA is the automaton obtained by determinizing the CA from Fig. 1a, shown in Fig. 1b. The authors of [18] show how a CA can be determinised into a CsA of a size independent of the counter bounds (unlike DFA, which may be exponentially large).

3   Implementation

We have implemented[2] CA and CsA-based matching in RE2 [7]. RE2 is an automata-based C++ regex matching library that implements Thompson's algorithm. It starts by simplifying the input regex and then compiling it into NFA. The compilation compiles multi-byte UTF-8 characters down to an automaton that reads the input one byte at a time, so the UTF-8 decoding is built into the automaton [14]. To keep the amount of generated transitions small, it does not generate a new transition for each character (byte), but it labels transitions with character (byte) classes for which the automaton always behaves the same. The matching itself then uses an optimized version of Thompson's on-the-fly determinization algorithm. RE2 treats the states of the DFA as a cache. When the cache fills, it frees all the states and starts over again, thus it is able to work in a fixed amount of memory [14].

---

[1] These operations can be implemented to work in constant time (see [18]), hence simulation of CsA gives a fast matching algorithm for bounded repetition.

[2] The implementation can be found at https://gitlab.com/MichalHorky/DP-re2-repository.

Table 1. Experimental evaluation of CsA-based RE2 and CA (times are given in milliseconds). CA denotes the time from the loading of input regex to the counting automaton being created. CsA denotes the time of the determinization of the counting automaton. CsA without timeouts denotes the time of the determinization, which was run only on regexes on which CA implementation did not suffer from timeout. The timeout was set to 1–800 s.

	CA		RE2 (CsA)		
	CA	CsA	CA	CsA	CsA (no CA timeouts)
Mean	10 966	73 433	8	62 709	11 136
Median	254	11 338	4	1 990	1 050
Timeouts	0	14	0	5	0

For bounded iteration operator $R\{n,m\}$, RE2 uses unfolding during parsing which can cause a significant blow-up during determinization, especially for higher bounds. In fact, RE2 does not support bounds larger than 1000. We therefore implemented support for CsA-based matching of these regexes where we can divide implementation into three main steps:

1. parsing the regex using the original RE2 implementation,
2. translation of the regex to CA by using generalization (as defined in [18]) of the Antimirov's partial derivative construction (keeping the byte classes approach of original RE2), and
3. the CsA-based matching itself using CA obtained in the previous step.

There are two kinds of matching implemented. The first is the so-called *full matching*, which matches only the whole input string, and *the partial matching*, which matches the string anywhere on the line. Similarly to original RE2, the matching is done on the fly, i.e. we create only those parts of CsA which are needed for given input text.

4   Experiments

We experimentally evaluated our implementation by

- comparing the efficiency of creating CA from regexes and determinizing them into CsA with the original C# implementation called CA, and
- comparing the regex matching of our solution with the matcher used in grep, original RE2 and the matcher CA.

We used the benchmark from [18] which contains regexes with non-trivial bounded repetition selected (1) from the database coming from an Internet-wide analysis of regexes collected from over 190,000 software projects [5]; (2) from databases of regexes used by *network intrusion detection systems* (NIDSes), in particular, Snort [11], Bro [13], Sagan [16], and the academic papers [19,20]; (4) the RegExLib database of regexes [12]; and (5) industrial regexes from [10], used for security purposes.

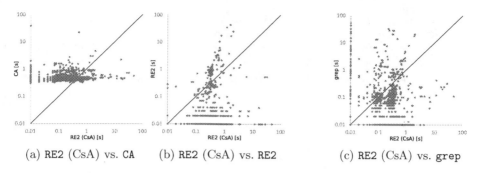

(a) RE2 (CsA) vs. CA   (b) RE2 (CsA) vs. RE2   (c) RE2 (CsA) vs. grep

Fig. 2. Comparison of CsA-based matching implemented in RE2 with CA, original RE2, and grep.

4.1 Comparison with the Matcher CA

We took 37 regexes which were difficult for the original CA-based C# matcher CA and compared the runtime of creating CA from the regexes and determinizing them into CsA.

The results in Table 1 show that CsA-based RE2 is faster for both translations of the regex into CA and their determinization. The determinization part of the RE2 implementation takes a long time on some regexes on which CA suffers from timeout, therefore we also give the results of the RE2 implementation for those regexes on which CA does not suffer from timeout to show that CsA-based RE2 is much faster.

4.2 Regex Matching Comparison

We compared our CsA-based regex matching implemented in RE2 with original RE2 and the matchers CA and grep. We used 2320 regexes from the benchmark set of [18] and we run them within the benchmark tool of [18]. The actual comparison of matching times was based on 2148 benchmarks, where CsA-based RE2 algorithm found the correct number of matches. The results of the original RE2 implementation were considered as a reference for the number of matches. Also, each of the individual comparisons was made based only on those regexes, for which both of the compared tools get the correct number of matches. Note that the comparison with grep and also the overall statistics are done on a smaller set of regexes. It is because grep uses different semantics of regexes, causing it to quit after reading only several characters and reporting zero matches on such regexes. Therefore, regexes for which the time and the number of matches of grep were zero, and the other tools find a match or their matching time was larger than zero (i.e. grep quit after reading just several characters while the other tools try to find a match in the whole input text), were not considered.

Table 2. The benchmarks statistic of the individual tools. Times are given in seconds, and the timeout was set to 60 s. The supplied times are based on 1625 benchmarks on which none of the tools suffers from error or timeout, and the regex suits the `grep`'s semantics. For the timeout statistics, the regexes for which the tools suffer from timeout were also added, resulting in a set of 1640 regexes being used for the timeout statistics.

	RE2	grep	CA	RE2 (CsA)
Mean	0.153	0.537	0.480	0.399
Median	0	0.06	0.43	0.28
Std. deviation	1.614	3.175	0.207	1.739
Timeouts	1	10	2	2

The result of the comparison between CsA-based `RE2` implementation and other tools in the form of scatter plots is in Fig. 2. Comparing the `C#` and `C++` implementations of CsA-based matching, the `C++` implementation was faster for 1908 out of 2145 benchmarks. For original `RE2`, CsA-based `RE2` was faster for 139 benchmarks, while for `grep`, CsA-based `RE2` was faster for 269 benchmarks. For `grep`, the total number of benchmarks was 1629 caused by the different semantics of regexes. Even though original `RE2` and `grep` win more often, there are clearly regexes, for which CsA-based `RE2` implementation is faster than these two. Those are often the regexes with the counting loops with larger bounds.

Table 2 contains the statistic of matching times of individual tools. Comparing the two CsA-based algorithms, the one implemented within `RE2` is faster. Even though `grep` wins most of the time compared with CsA-based `RE2` (as shown in Fig. 2c), there are regexes on which CsA-based `RE2` is significantly faster, making the overall mean better for CsA-based `RE2`. `grep` also suffers from the most timeouts compared with other tools.

Original `RE2` is the fastest among all the tools. It also suffers from timeout the least. Considering the plot in Fig. 2b, the speed of original `RE2` still drops on regexes with counting loops with higher bounds on which CsA-based `RE2` is faster. The usage of the CsA-based algorithm in `RE2` is determined by a constructor parameter. This allows the developer to choose the CsA-based algorithms or the original algorithms. If the developer has control over the regexes (i.e., the regexes are not supplied by the user), the developer can use the CsA-based algorithm for the counting-heavy regexes and the original algorithms for the rest of the regexes, where the numerous `RE2` optimizations are faster. This could be also done automatically, where CsA-based matching would be chosen for example by some limit on the counter bounds.

References

1. Outage postmortem. https://stackstatus.net/post/147710624694/outage-postmortem-july-20-2016, Accessed 14 Mar 2022

2. Chapman, C., Stolee, K.T.: Exploring regular expression usage and context in python. In: Proceedings of ISSTA 2016. Association for Computing Machinery (2016)
3. Davis, J.C.: Rethinking regex engines to address redos. In: Proceedings of ESEC/FSE 2019. Association for Computing Machinery (2019)
4. Davis, J.C., Coghlan, C.A., Servant, F., Lee, D.: The impact of regular expression denial of service (redos) in practice: an empirical study at the ecosystem scale. In: Proceedings of ESEC/FSE 2018. Association for Computing Machinery (2018)
5. Davis, J.C., Michael IV, L.G., Coghlan, C.A., Servant, F., Lee, D.: Why aren't regular expressions a lingua franca? an empirical study on the re-use and portability of regular expressions. In: Proceedings of ESEC/FSE 2019. Association for Computing Machinery (2019)
6. docs.rs: regex - rust. https://docs.rs/regex/1.5.4/regex/
7. Google: Re2. https://github.com/google/re2
8. Graham-Cumming, J.: Details of the cloudflare outage on july 2, 2019. https://blog.cloudflare.com/details-of-the-cloudflare-outage-on-july-2-2019, Accessed 14 Mar 2022
9. Haertel, M., et al.: GNU grep. https://www.gnu.org/software/grep/
10. Holík, L., Lengál, O., Saarikivi, O., Turoňová, L., Veanes, M., Vojnar, T.: Succinct determinisation of counting automata via sphere construction. In: Lin, A.W. (ed.) APLAS 2019. LNCS, vol. 11893, pp. 468–489. Springer, Cham (2019). https://doi.org/10.1007/978-3-030-34175-6_24
11. Roesch, M., et al.: Snort: a network intrusion detection and prevention system. http://www.snort.org
12. RegExLib.com: The Internet's first Regular Expression Library. http://regexlib.com/
13. Sommer, R., et al.: The Bro Network Security Monitor. http://www.bro.org
14. Russ, C.: Regular expression matching in the wild (2010). https://swtch.com/rsc/regexp/regexp3.html, Accessed 18 May 2021
15. Sipser, M.: Introduction to the theory of computation. SIGACT News 27(1), 27–29 (1996)
16. The Sagan team: The Sagan Log Analysis Engine. https://quadrantsec.com/sagan_log_analysis_engine/
17. Thompson, K.: Programming techniques: regular expression search algorithm. Commun. ACM 11(6), 419–422 (1968)
18. Turoňová, L., Holík, L., Lengál, O., Saarikivi, O., Veanes, M., Vojnar, T.: Regex matching with counting-set automata. Proc. ACM Program. Lang. 4(OOPSLA) (2020)
19. Češka, M., Havlena, V., Holík, L., Lengál, O., Vojnar, T.: Approximate reduction of finite automata for high-speed network intrusion detection. In: Beyer, D., Huisman, M. (eds.) TACAS 2018. LNCS, vol. 10806, pp. 155–175. Springer, Cham (2018). https://doi.org/10.1007/978-3-319-89963-3_9
20. Yang, L., Karim, R., Ganapathy, V., Smith, R.: Improving NFA-based signature matching using ordered binary decision diagrams. In: Jha, S., Sommer, R., Kreibich, C. (eds.) RAID 2010. LNCS, vol. 6307, pp. 58–78. Springer, Heidelberg (2010). https://doi.org/10.1007/978-3-642-15512-3_4

Integrating OSLC Services into Eclipse

Jan Fiedor[1,2], Bohuslav Křena[1], Aleš Smrčka[1], Ondřej Vašíček[1,2(✉)],
and Tomáš Vojnar[1]

[1] Faculty of Information Technology, Brno University of Technology,
Brno, Czech Republic
ivasicek@fit.vutbr.cz
[2] Honeywell International s.r.o., Brno, Czech Republic

Abstract. Transforming analysis and verification tools to web services
can make them more easily accessible and easier to use, especially if the
services use standardized interfaces. One can use UNITE, an adapter, to
transform almost any analysis or verification tool with a command-line
interface to an OSLC-compliant web service. Open Services for Lifecycle Collaboration (OSLC) is a robust and extensible open standard for
integrating tools across the entire development lifecycle which offers support of data from a wide range of domains. In this paper, we propose
UNIC, a plug-in for the Eclipse IDE which serves as a universal client
for utilizing analysis or verification tools hosted as web services using
UNITE. UNIC allows such tools to be executed directly from the IDE
and allows their outputs to be visualized using its UI. UNIC is usable for
a very wide range of tools and use cases thanks to its highly extensible
and configurable architecture. It is in fact a universal OSLC client usable
with any OSLC-compliant service. We have tested UNIC with a number
of analysis and verification tools and also successfully deployed it in the
industry.

1 Introduction and Motivation

Due to the ever-growing software complexity, a wide variety of automated design,
analysis, and verification tools needs to be used as part of the software development process. Yet, many of such tools struggle to find their applications in
practice despite the functionality they offer being of high interest. From our
experience, the reasons for this are often of a quite practical nature: their installation and configuration is difficult even for experienced developers, they require
a lot of computational resources not available locally, the work they perform
runs for long periods of time, their integration with other software development
tools is not easy, etc.

A common way to deal with these issues is to provide a tool's functionality
as a web service which can be used remotely, allowing the tool to be offloaded to
a remote server where it has more resources available and can be maintained by
specialists. With more tools exposed in this way, standardized communication
and representation of data is important. OSLC [12] provides both and therefore

© The Author(s), under exclusive license to Springer Nature Switzerland AG 2022
R. Moreno-Díaz et al. (Eds.): EUROCAST 2022, LNCS 13789, pp. 240–249, 2022.
https://doi.org/10.1007/978-3-031-25312-6_28

is often the technology of choice. Moreover, there are tools, such as UNITE [14], which transform command-line tools into OSLC-compliant web services. Still, it is difficult for users to communicate with such services directly via their OSLC interface. It is expected that an OSLC-compliant client will perform these tasks on behalf of the users, yet many users do not have such client at their disposal.

To address this issue, we have developed UNIC, a Unite Client for Eclipse, which is also a universal OSLC client usable with any OSLC-compliant service. With UNIC, users can invoke remote tools directly from the Eclipse IDE with a single press of a button and get the results. Each tool may require different inputs and configuration, and produce different outputs. UNIC was thus designed to be highly extensible and configurable to meet the needs of any tool. In this paper, we will discuss the architecture of UNIC, describe how the developers can configure it for their tools, and show how it simplifies the invocation of remote tools for the users.

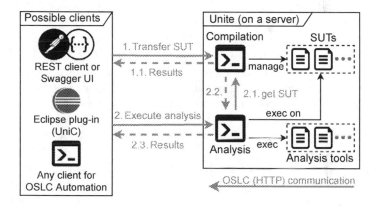

Fig. 1. An overview of UNITE's architecture.

2   Open Services for Lifecycle Collaboration (OSLC)

OSLC [12] is an open standard for integrating tools across the entire development lifecycle. It consists of a number of specifications each for a different integration domain, such as Quality Management, Requirements Management, or Automation. OSLC participants can be clients (consumers) and/or servers (producers) who interact with each other using RESTful API's, standard HTTP messages, and serialized resource representation (e.g., RDF or JSON). Their interfaces are modeled according to a selected domain specification which most importantly specifies the types and semantics of resources used for communication and functionality that should be supported for each resource. A core aspect of OSLC is its extensibility. Domain specifications aim to only specify a minimal amount of requirements for compliancy and allow new resources, resource properties, or capabilities to be added by OSLC participants to extend the domain according to their own specific needs.

OSLC's popularity is currently growing both in the academia and in the industry. For a list of OSLC-compliant products see [4].

3   Overview of Unite

UNITE [14] is a universal adapter which can be used to transform any non-interactive command-line analysis or verification tool to an OSLC-compliant web service. UNITE's interface is modeled based on the OSLC Automation domain [13] which consists of three main resources – Automation Plans, Automation Requests, and Automation Results. Automation Plans represent units of automation offered by a server. UNITE uses these to represent available analysis tools or their configurations. Automation Requests are what clients create when they want to request execution of one of the available analysis tools. Finally, Automation Results are produced by the server and can contain any outputs of the executed analysis tool (e.g., standard outputs or files) and information about the execution.

UNITE's architecture is shown in Fig. 1. It consists of two components – the Analysis sub-adapter and the Compilation sub-adapter. When a client wants to analyse their SUT they first need to transfer its files to the server and then they might need it to be compiled to make it executable. This can be achieved using the Compilation sub-adapter which manages SUT (system-under-test) resources and has an Automation Plan devoted to creating them. The Analysis sub-adapter can then be used to execute analysis tools on the previously created SUT. New analysis tools can be added by creating configuration files which most importantly specify an Automation Plan for the analysis tool. Such an Automation Plan needs to define its input parameters which essentially mimic the command-line arguments of the given tool. A simplified Automation Plan is often sufficient

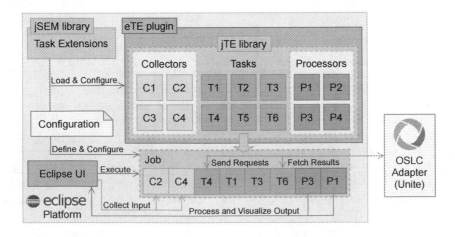

Fig. 2. An overview of the architecture of UNIC.

and/or most suitable which only contains a single input parameter representing all possible command-line arguments as a single string.

We have so far tested UNITE with a number of analysis and verification tools such as FACEBOOK INFER [3], ANACONDA [6], and VALGRIND [11]. UNITE is also being used in the Arrowhead Tools project and with in-house tools such as HiLiTE [2] in Honeywell.

4   Unite Client (UniC) for Eclipse

UNIC utilizes the JTE [9] (Java Task Executor) and JSEM [8] (Simple Extension Manager for Java) libraries to provide all of its functionality. It provides JTE tasks which handle collection of input data, communication with UNITE, and processing of output data (e.g. analysis results). The JTE library handles (parallel) execution of tasks (or sequences of task) and the JSEM library allows anyone to add their own tasks through extensions. UNIC for Eclipse then uses the ETE [7] (Eclipse Task Executor) plugin to integrate JTE's task execution functionality into the Eclipse IDE. Moreover, it also provides tasks for collecting input data and visualizing results in the Eclipse UI. Utilizing these libraries is crucial for providing flexibility to support any tool UNITE may be wrapping. Users can either write their own tasks handling the communication or configure and use the built-in tasks which are sufficient for most of the tools wrapped by UNITE.

4.1   Architecture

Figure 2 shows the architecture and basic principles behind UNIC. The ETE plugin uses the JSEM library to load all built-in and user-provided tasks and register them in JTE. Based on the configuration, ETE determines which tasks should be directly executable and thus exposed to the users via context menu entries in the Eclipse UI.

While one may use a single task to handle the interaction with a specific tool, a more common way is to define sequences of tasks called jobs. Jobs can chain simple tasks together to provide complex functionality while fostering modularity and reusability. This is important as interaction with most of the tools boils down to the same communication sequences which only differ in their input data and ways to process their output data. With this in mind, ETE categorizes tasks into generic tasks, input data collectors and output data processors.

Generic tasks mainly handle interactions with the tools wrapped by UNITE. They handle registration of required input data, remote execution of tools, polling for execution state, and fetching output data once it is available. Input data collectors are tasks that are able to provide input data required by the remotely executed tools. For example, a static analysis tool needs source code files to analyze as its input. For this purpose, the ETE plugin provides an input data collector that can collect files from an Eclipse project, which is usually what the users want to analyze. Output data processors are tasks that are able to transform output data produced by the remotely executed tools into a more user-friendly representation. For example, a static analysis tool may produce reports on issues found in the analyzed source code. These reports usually contain information such as the type of the issue and the line(s) of code where the issue was found. The ETE plugin provides an output data processor which can parse these reports and transform them into Eclipse markers, automatically associating the reported issues with specific lines in the source code which are visible in all Eclipse source code editors.

4.2   Configuration

In order to use UNIC with a specific tool wrapped by UNITE, it needs to be configured first. As mentioned in the previous section, configuration is done by defining sequences of tasks called jobs. The definition of tasks and jobs is done through Java Properties file(s). While a job (and all of its tasks) can be defined in a single file, it may also be split between multiple files. This is convenient when reusing previously defined tasks or jobs. Moreover, UNIC also supports global task configuration which can be used to define values of variables which can then be referenced in the definitions of tasks and jobs.

UNIC can load the configuration either from local directories or from Eclipse plugins. The local directories can be specified in Eclipse preferences, under the Task Executor section. Eclipse plugins can provide the configuration through the ETE Task Provider extension point. The developers may extend the `EclipsePluginTaskDirectoryProvider` to load the configuration from Java Properties file(s) stored in an Eclipse plugin, making it easy to move the configuration from a local directory to an Eclipse plugin.

While each tool is different, the task sequences to interact with them are often similar, especially when they handle input and output data in a similar fashion. Therefore, the best way to define a task sequence for a new tool is to modify an existing task sequence. One may refer to the `ete-verifit-infer` module in the `ete-verifit-tasks` project[1] for a task sequence for the FACEBOOK INFER static analyser [3]. This task sequence suffices with built-in tasks, which are part of UNIC and its libraries, and is loaded by an ETE Task Provider. Any tool developer using UNITE to transform their tool into an OSLC-compliant web service can adapt this task sequence to allow UNIC to execute their tool and provide this task sequence to the users through an update site.

Figure 3 shows the most important parts of a task sequence (job) definition. Both tasks and jobs are loaded through extensions. The `infer` prefix represents the name of the extension to use to load the task or job. The `ConfigurableJobExtension` is a generic extension able to load a wide variety of jobs and configure them with a sequence of preconfigured tasks. The tasks to be part of the job are specified under the `config.tasks` entry, which contains a list of tasks to be executed as part of the job. The `info` section contains additional information about the job. The `provides` entry specifies the concrete

---

[1] https://pajda.fit.vutbr.cz/verifit/ete-verifit-tasks.

```
1 infer.extension=c.v.f.g.v.jte.ConfigurableJobExtension
2 infer.info.provides=c.v.f.g.v.jte.Pipeline
3 infer.info.name=verifit.infer
4 infer.info.ete.label=Analyse with Facebook Infer (BUT server)
5 infer.info.ete.category=user-task
6 infer.config.tasks[]=collectFiles,collectSutProperties,\
7   registerSut,checkSutRegistration,performAnalysis,\
8   getAnalysisResult,extractInfoFromAnalysisResult,\
9   checkForAnalysisErrors,processInferOutput
```

Fig. 3. Excerpt of UNIC task sequence (job) definition for FACEBOOK INFER.

task implementation the extension is providing. In this case, the `Pipeline` class is a type of job which executes the tasks in the order they are listed under the `config.tasks` entry and also redirects output of each task to the input of the next task in the sequence. The `name` entry holds a unique name of the task, the `config.tasks` entry utilizes these names to reference concrete tasks to be used. The `ete.category` and `ete.label` entries are used by the ETE plugin to determine if the task or job should be available for the user in the menu and under which label.

The `config.tasks` entry defines the sequence of tasks to be executed in order to interact with a specific tool. Usually, the sequence starts with input data collectors. The `collectFiles` task collects all files in an Eclipse project and packs them into a ZIP archive. The `collectSutProperties` task collects project-specific information, such as the build command which is required by INFER in order to perform an analysis. The next five tasks handle interaction with UNITE. The `registerSut` task sends the ZIP archive to UNITE and the `checkSutRegistration` task waits until the files in the ZIP archive are finished registering. The `performAnalysis` task then starts the analysis of the files registered by the previous tasks. The `getAnalysisResult` task polls UNITE until the analysis is finished and fetches the analysis results. To streamline the processing of the results for the output data processors, the `extractInfoFromAnalysisResult` task extracts the analysis output from the analysis results in the OSLC format and passes it to the last two tasks. The `checkForAnalysisErrors` task checks if the analysis finished successfully and if not, it shows an error in the Problems view. Finally, if the analysis was successful, the `processInferOutput` task processes the issues found by INFER and transforms them into Eclipse markers to visualize them in the Problems view.

Naturally, tasks used in jobs need to be configured as well. For example, all OSLC request tasks realizing interaction with UNITE may contain parameters which may be different depending on the type of request and/or the tool they are interacting with. Figure 4 shows the definition of parameters for an OSLC request registering input files for the analysis. The `unite.request.params` entry lists the names of input parameters to add to the request and the entries under

```
1 unite.request.params[]=unpackZip,buildCommand,compile
2 unite.request.param.unpackZip=true
3 unite.request.param.buildCommand=${unite.sut.buildCommand}
4 unite.request.param.compile=false
```

Fig. 4. Excerpt of FACEBOOK INFER's `registerSut` task configuration.

the `unite.request.param` section define the values of these parameters. As the build command differs for each project, it must be specified by the user. Therefore, the value of the `buildCommand` entry is set to the value of the `unite.sut.buildCommand` variable which is set by the `collectSutProperties` task, based on what the user specified in the project properties, and propagated by the `Pipeline` job to the consecutive tasks in the task sequence. This way, any collector task can collect user-defined input and make it available in consecutive tasks.

4.3 Usage

The simplest way to start using UNIC is to install it from the VeriFIT update site[2]. One can also find UNIC configuration for the FACEBOOK INFER static analyser there (under the name *Infer on BUT server (eTE Task)*). This configuration executes the FACEBOOK INFER publicly available on one of the BUT servers and can be used to quickly test the functionality of UNIC. After this configuration is installed, the *Analyse with Facebook Infer (BUT server)* entry will show up in a popup menu under the *Tasks* category as shown in the bottom-left part of Fig. 5.

Some configurations may require additional input from the user. For example, INFER requires a build command in order to analyse a project. As the build command may differ from project to project, the user must specify it in the project's properties (UNITE section, SUT page). After that, the user can right-click on an Eclipse project, select the *Analyse with Facebook Infer (BUT server)* task under the *Tasks* category, and let UNIC handle everything. When the analysis is finished, UNIC will fetch the results and process them. In case of INFER, it transforms them into Eclipse markers, adding one marker for each error found by INFER as shown in the Problems view in the bottom-right part of Fig. 5. These markers are linked with specific lines in concrete source code files where the error was found, and the user can jump to these locations from the Problems view. The code editors also show these errors as editor markers with their description in a hover text as can be seen in the center of Fig. 5.

4.4 Industrial Use

UNIC has already been adopted by the industry thanks to its flexibility and ease of use. A number of teams in Honeywell are using UNIC as their OSLC client

---

[2] https://verifit1.fit.vutbr.cz/eclipse/.

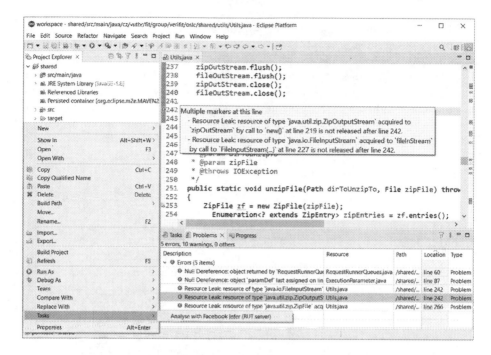

Fig. 5. Executing FACEBOOK INFER and visualizing its results in the Eclipse IDE.

of choice for integrating remote analysis tools into various Eclipse-based IDEs. They have three other OSLC clients available, however, those are not compatible with the Eclipse platform. Moreover, UNiC can be easily configured, making it the best option to quickly test interactions with new OSLC-compliant analysis tools. For example, it took less then an hour to configure UNiC for HILiTE [2], a proprietary test vector generation tool taking models as inputs and producing reports as outputs.

5   Related Work

To the best of our knowledge, there are no other projects targeting universal use of analysis tools using OSLC. There are, however, two similar ones which differ in key aspects.

The first one is the MagpieBridge LSP framework [10] which aims to provide means of executing static analysis tools from any IDE using the Language Server Protocol (LSP). The MagpieServer is a language server which runs analyses instead of providing features such as code completion. The main difference from our approach is that MagpieBridge focuses only on static analysis tools and IDEs, and that it does not use OSLC. LSP further assumes that servers and clients have access to a shared file system which limits its applicability for remote execution of tools. An interesting area to explore would be using UNiC's libraries to extend the MagpieServer to execute analysis tools through UNITE remotely.

The second project similar to our approach is EATA [5] developed by FBK ES. This project features adapters for analysis tools using the OSLC Automation domain and also a user interface plug-in for the Eclipse IDE. We were unable to find any publications about these adapters but were able to inspect their source code and documentation. These adapters seem to serve a similar role as UNITE and UNIC but only for FBK tools and not for universal use of a wide range of tools by others. According to their documentation, support for new tools can be added but requires modifications of the source code both on the server side and the client side. In comparison, UNITE and UNIC are universal and new tools can be added through configuration files.

6   Conclusion

We introduced UNIC, a Unite Client for Eclipse, which allows analysis and verification tools available as web services using UNITE to be executed directly from the Eclipse IDE and allows their outputs to be visualized using the Eclipse UI. UNIC is further usable as an universal OSLC client for a wide range of other use cases thanks to its highly extensible and configurable architecture.

UNIC has already been successfully deployed in the industry. Honeywell uses it as their fourth OSLC client which is best suited for integrating tools into Eclipse-based IDEs and for validating the interactions with new OSLC-compliant tools.

As for future work, we are currently integrating UNITE and UNIC with the Eclipse Arrowhead Framework [1] which will allow UNIC clients to automatically discover available UNITE servers and to automatically retrieve configuration for available analysis tools.

Acknowledgement. Research leading to these results has received funding from the EU ECSEL Joint Undertaking under grant agreement n° 826452 (project Arrowhead Tools) and from The Ministry of Education, Youth and Sports of the Czech Republic. The work was further supported by the project 20-07487S of the Czech Science Foundation and the FIT BUT internal project FIT-S-20-6427.

References

1. Eclipse arrowhead framework (2022). https://projects.eclipse.org/projects/iot. arrowhead
2. Bhatt, D., Madl, G., Oglesby, D., Schloegel, K.: Towards scalable verification of commercial avionics software. In: Proceedings of Infotech@Aerospace'10. AIAA (2010)
3. Calcagno, C., Distefano, D.: Infer: an automatic program verifier for memory safety of c programs. In: Bobaru, M., Havelund, K., Holzmann, G.J., Joshi, R. (eds.) NFM 2011. LNCS, vol. 6617, pp. 459–465. Springer, Heidelberg (2011). https://doi.org/10.1007/978-3-642-20398-5_33
4. El-khoury, J.: An analysis of the OASIS OSLC integration standard, for a cross-disciplinary integrated development environment: analysis of market penetration, performance and prospects. Technical Report, KTH, Mechatronics (2020)

5. EATA (2022). http://gitlab.fbk.eu/ESProjects/EATA
6. Fiedor, J., Mužikovská, M., Smrčka, A., et. al.: Advances in the ANaConDA framework for dynamic analysis and testing of concurrent C/C++ programs. In: Proceedings of ISSTA 2018, ACM (2018)
7. Fiedor, J.: eTE - eclipse task executor. https://pajda.fit.vutbr.cz/verifit/ete
8. Fiedor, J.: jSEM - Simple extension manager for Java. https://pajda.fit.vutbr.cz/verifit/jsem
9. Fiedor, J.: jTE - Java task executor. https://pajda.fit.vutbr.cz/verifit/jte
10. Luo, L., et. al.: MagpieBridge: a general approach to integrating static analyses into IDEs and editors. In: Proceedings of ECOOP 2019. LIPIcs, Schloss Dagstuhl - LZI (2019)
11. Nethercote, N., Seward, J.: Valgrind: a framework for heavyweight dynamic binary instrumentation. In: Proceedings of of PLDI 2007, ACM (2007)
12. OASIS: Open Services for Lifecycle Collaboration. https://open-services.net/ (2022)
13. Ribeiro, F. (eds.). OASIS working draft 1 OSLC automation version 2.1 Part 1: specification (2022). https://rawgit.com/oasis-tcs/oslc-domains/master/auto/automation-spec.html
14. Vašíček, O.: Unite - GitLab (2022). https://pajda.fit.vutbr.cz/verifit/unite

Developing an Application in the Forest for New Tourism Post COVID-19 -Experiments in Oku-Nikko National Park-

Yuko Hiramatsu[1], Atsushi Ito[1(✉)], and Akira Sasaki[2(✉)]

[1] Chuo University, 742-1Higashinakano, Hachioji, Tokyo 192-039, Japan
susana_y@tamacc.chuo-u.ac.jp, atc.00s@g.chuo-u.ac.jp
[2] GClue Inc., 134-3 Ikkicyo Tsuruga Aza Kamiiai, Aizu-Wakamatsu,
Fukushima 965-0006, Japan
akira@gclue.jp

Abstract. Tourism, which has developed in line with the development of transport, has had to undergo major changes. As the push for SDGs spreads across the world, and for safe travel post-COVID-16, environmentally friendly smallgroup tourism is being promoted. It would be beneficial if the smartphones, which is used daily lives, could be useful in the nature for small groups of novice walkers to walk safety and knowing some new information about the area. However, the signal conditions are not always perfect in forests. Therefore, we have developed a smartphone application using Bluetooth Low Energy (BLE) beacons equipped with solar panels in Nikko National Park in Japan. Japan has long had the concept of forest bathing. Walking in the forest is told to have positive effects on the body and in the mind. We tried to clarify one of effects of forest bathing by measuring brain waves. We measured the effects of walking in nature by conducting simple EEG measurements while walking and measuring the degree of relaxation in the forest in 2021.

Keywords: BLE Beacon · Tourism · Forest bathing · Simple EEG measurement device

1 Introduction

1.1 Current Status and Issues of Tourism - Impact of Promotion of SGDs and COVID-19 on Tourism-

Before COVID-19, over tourism became a big issue in many famous places in the world. According to the report of World Tourism Organization in 2020, there were 1.5 billion international tourist arrivals worldwide in 2019, 4% increasing from the previous year [1]. Increased tourists bring economic benefits to local

Supported by JSPS Kakenhi (17H02249,18K111849,2K12598).

shops. However, the phenomenon also brings many harmful effects. Environmental problems such as litters, traffic congestion, housing and rising prices of commodities are some of the negative effects on the people who live there. Under COVID-19, tourism became the new stage. The number of tourists abroad has decreased. In addition, safety has become a consideration. The new guidelines of the United Nations World Tourism Organization (UNWTO) (Global Guidelines to Restart Tourism, 2020.6 [2]) told to create personalized and small group tours for Post COVID-19. It is not practical for a tour guide to provide information on forests one by one when considering tourism for a small number of people, so we will use IT to supplement information and guide tourists. We are developing an application in order to realize this new trend in tourism. This is not only a necessary arrangement as a transitory measure after COVID-19 but is also beneficial for the future protection of the global environment, with a focus on the SDGs. It is useful to make tourists aware of the benefits of forests in order to take care of them. Local people also realize that forests are not only valuable when they are logged, but that the forests themselves are a source of material that can attract tourists.

1.2   Our Research

We provided cultural information for foreign tourists at the main street using beacon application at the first step near station of Nikko [3,4]. We have had a series of experiments to improve the beacon system and validated it. We used BLE Beacons to send tourists to messages from shops on the main street. Many foreign used to walk up the street directly to the shrine named Toshogu, one of the world heritage sites, without giving the shop a second glance. Doors are sliding and not very bright inside in old traditional Japanese shops. The fronts appearance is traditional Japanese way and we did not hope to change it. Using our application, tourists get signals and would look at Japanese-style shops and traditional Japanese information or some seasonal information. There are a lot of information on the Internet. However, most of them are written by tourists. On the other hand, old Japanese shop owners knew local history and culture deeply. The information would be attractive for foreign tourists. Then, at the 2nd step, we set BLE Beacons in Oku-Nikko, where is higher and colder than the area of the first step. It snows in winter. We had tests and experiments to use BLE Beacon in Nikko National Park, forest area named Senjogahara from 2017 with cooperation of Nikko National Park Management Office [5]. 21 Beacons are set on the boards on the wood path (See Fig. 1). If tourists see a bird and hat want to know more about, they can find its name and description in the bird book of our application. In addition, we are developing a tool for walking in the forest. Considering the global issue of forest protection, forest bathing will be attracting attention as a form of post COVID-19. The strong point of forest bathing is not only income for the local people, but also brings awareness to the people that forests are not an obstacle to cultivation, but a meaningful resource for tourism. In addition, tourists can cultivate attitudes for the importance of forests and the diversity of life that lives in nature. Forest bathing is also beneficial for tourists themselves. Forest bathing is effective in reducing stress and affirming the power of the forest. However, it tended to be something that tourists themselves felt somehow and not clear of the basis.

Fig. 1. Our application and BLE Beacon on the signboard

2   Related Works

2.1   Bluetooth Low Energy Beacon

Since the widespread use of smartphones, Bluetooth has been widely used and implemented in a variety of application. It is short-range and low-cost wireless tool. Practical developments such as commercial connected lighting and location-based services are expected to progress and LE Audio to be implemented in the future. More detailed studies are being carried out in Japan, for example, on location measurement. (K. Omura and T. ManabeT, 2021 [6]) On the other hand, a team has directly captured the activity of neurons in brain tissue by connecting lightweight, miniature Bluetooth devices to the rat brain (Shinnosuke Idogawa, Koji Yamashita et al., 2021 [7]) Now, we use it for tourism.

2.2   Forest Bathing

Forest bathing is now spreading from Japan to the world. The effects of forest bathing were introduced in general, such as featured in TIME (QING LI May 1, 2018 [8]). Studies of forest bathing in Japan have reported that, even for as little as 20 min, on the physical side, there is a decrease in blood pressure, pulse rate, stress hormones such as cortisol in saliva, an increase in parasympathetic nerve activity and a decrease in sympathetic nerve activity (Koyama, 2009 [9]). In addition, there is said to be an improvement in mood in psychological terms, with higher positive emotions and a sense of recovery, and there are reports of studies that have analyzed forest air and measured phytoncide components such as terpenes emanating from the trees (Takeda, 2009 [10]). However, these studies have not yet reached a scale where they can be used for general purposes, as they are often influenced by forest weather conditions and the individual factors of the subjects (Takayama, 2012 [11]), and the measurement methods are complicated, especially regarding physiological aspects. The number of subjects for each measurement method is often around 10. In other words, there are prolems in examining regional and individual differences in the number of subjects and the re-search environment, and there is a need for more research on a larger number of subjects and over a wider area. In addition, even if the benefits of forest bathing are to be linked to tourism development, it is necessary to position it as a sustainable form of tourism, and studies on this point are rare. The use of local tourism resources (i.e., forests) is always subject to an environmentally sensitive analytical framework. In many cases, the numbers of subjects are around 10. It is necessary for research on larger numbers of subjects and over wider areas.

3   Our Application in Oku-Nikko

We have developed an application using BLE Beacon at Oku-Nikko National Park in Japan for the purpose of small-group tours, considering the unstable signal conditions in the forest. According to our experiments, BLE beacons provided information with-in a range of 80m at the street on the town in Nikko. However, the waves reach about only 20 1 m in the forest of Oku-Nikko. We installed solar panels to secure a power source on the beacons. The contents are information on the location, map, distance to the bus stop, timetable of bus schedule, botanical book, and local weather forecast (See Fig. 2). However, there were several problems. One of the challenges was the impact of the forest environment on the beacons. Since it is in high place and the climate is changeable. The area is a wetland ratified by the Ramsar Convention. We sometimes find the box of beacon cause condensation. In addition, it snows in winter, and in the summer, the foliage can be overgrown, making it difficult for sun-light to reach the device. After several improvements, including the selection of solar panels and waterproofing, the system is now ready for stable use in 2021. We are now in the process of demonstrating it for walks that will allow tourists to feel the effects of forest bathing themselves in the National Park in Oku-Nikko.

4   An Experiment Using EEG Sensor at Nikko National Park

4.1   Summary of the Experiment

We had an experiment for beacon operation check and for contents' evaluation of the application in August 2021. We also performed brain waves measurement in order to know whether participants were relaxed or not. The lightweight EEG

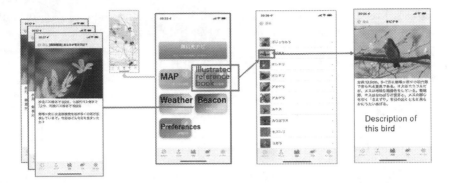

Fig. 2. Our application for national park

sensor attached to a bandana will be used to quantitatively measure the effects of forest bathing. We have a plan to show the relaxation level of the EEG sensor to tourists through an illustrated display on a smartphone application. This will be a system that tourists can directly see and feel on the spot. 10 Participants walks with the sensors along several routes on the experiment from July 31 to August 2 in 2021. (Average age 20.6) The participants answered they like to walk in the forest in the preliminary questionnaire. However, 6 of them answered that daily exercise time is 0–1 hour. All participants used the application at first. Then they parted and went on a forest walk wearing bandana in which EEG sensor (see Fig. 3).

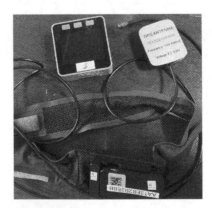

Fig. 3. Bandana with a simple electroencephalograph (EEG) and a GPS device

4.2   Results of the Research in Oku-Nikko National Park

(1) Evaluation of the application (n = 10)

The application is evaluated on a five-point Likert scale for each function. The results averaged 3.88/5.00. Two results are shown as Fig. 4 and Fig. 5. The

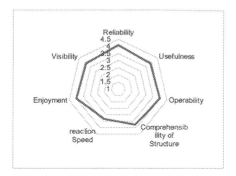

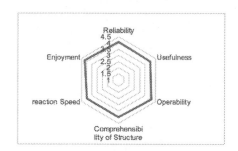

Fig. 4. Evaluation of beacon points

Fig. 5. Evaluation of weather page

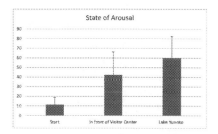

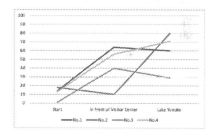

Fig. 6. State of arousal (average)

Fig. 7. State of arousal (personal data)

reaction speed of the beacon point was low because it reacted from almost 10m in front of the beacon or right in front of it depending on the location. This point is difficult to improve because of the nature of beacons. However, the information in the illustrated book and the distance to the bus stop are only a few meters apart and do not cause any problems for tourists.

(2) Effects of Forest Bathing at Senjogahara walking (n = 4).

Walking of one group Time: From 9:45 to 11:50 Weather: Sunny to cloudy Temperature: 27.3 °C–24.8 °C Humidity: around 60Participants answered the effects of Forest bathing by the Positive and Negative Affect Schedule (PANAS) as a subjective evaluation. Although the number of data is small (just 4 persons), the experiment showed that the level of arousal improved after forest bathing compared to beginning of the walking by Subjective evaluation (See Fig. 6). That arousal mean refresh. The result of t-test told that was significant. We found a significant difference be-tween the conditions t (3) = 0.007, p > 0.05).

When the group walked along a waterfall in the forest and stopped to enjoy the nature, their α waves simultaneously increased. (See Fig. 8). (Data of a participant was missing value) The blue line is α wave. The red one is β wave.

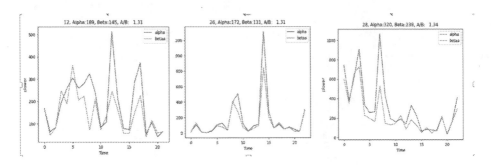

Fig. 8. Simple electroencephalograph data of the 3 participants

4.3   Results of the Research at Shibuya in Tokyo

We had another experiment at Shibuya on June 25th in June 2022 by the same members as Fig. 8. Shibuya is a crowded area in Tokyo. One sample of the data is shown as Fig. 9. (Temperature 34 °C, Humidity 62%, Sunny day) There were many buildings and cars. Various sounds were heard, such as cars and noises leaking from shops. B wave became higher than α wave at many points.

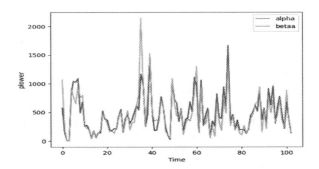

Fig. 9. EEG in Shibuya, Tokyo

5   Conclusion

Our research started to collect linguistic landscapes near Nikko Station and developed an application to know the information on shops. Then we have had research in Oku-Nikko. There are petitions for posting information in Senjoga-hara, which is in a Oku-Nikko National Park, so even if the number of foreign tourists increases, it is not easy to make new multilingual signboards. Emer-gency information cannot be easily increased beyond the existing notices, too. We developed applications that not only compensates for the lack of such infor-mation, but also actively started to demonstrate the benefits of forest bathing. The results of our experiments shew the effect of Forest bathing. However, Data is very small. In addition, these experiments were carried out in COVID-19, so the participants ware masks. One of the benefits of forest bathing is said to be the scent, but this data is lacking in this case. We should continue research. On the other hand, we got one step closer to our goal of measuring the effects of forest bathing by wearing a simple EEG measuring form and encouraging tourists to feel the effects of Forest bathing. It was possible to acquire data with the simple electroencephalograph in the natural area of Oku-Nikko and also in the crowded Shibuya area. In addition, the ease and the inconspicuous use of bandanas ensured that the device did not attract attention to people in the Shibuya. We concluded that would be used by tourists. In the future, the system will be developed to enable tourists to experience the benefits of walking in forests, and we would like to support forest walking tourism from a technical perspective.

References

1. "World Tourism Barometer." United Nations World Tourism Organization, vol. 18, no. 1 (2020)
2. The United Nations World Tourism Organization (UNWTO), "Global Guidelines to Restart Tourism", June 2020
3. Hiramatsu Y., Ito A., Sato F., et al.: A service model using bluetooth low energy beacons-to provide tourism information of traditional cultural sites-, IARIA In Conference on advanced Service Computing, p. 1519, March 2016
4. Ioannou, A., Antoniou, C.: Peacemaking affordances of shareable interfaces: a provocative essay on using technology for social change. In: Zaphiris, P., Ioannou, A. (eds.) LCT 2017. LNCS, vol. 10295, pp. 12–21. Springer, Cham (2017). https://doi.org/10.1007/978-3-319-58509-3_2
5. Sasaki, A., Fu, X., Hayashi, R., Hiramatsu, Y., et al.: A study on the development of tourist support system using ICT and psychological effects. Appl. Cogn. Inf. Commun. 1024 (2020)
6. Omura, K., Manabe, T.: Performance evaluation using plural smartphones in bluetooth low energy positioning system. EICE Trans. Fundam. **E104-A**(2), 371–374 (2021)
7. Idogawa, S., Yamashita, K., Sanda, R, Numano, R., et al.: A lightweight, wireless blue-tooth-low-energy neuronal recording system for mice. Sens. Actuators B, Chem. **331**, 129423 (2021)
8. Li, Q.: Forest Bathing Is Great for Your Health. Here's How to Do It, TIME, 1 May 2018. https://time.com/5259602/japanese-forest-bathing/. Accessed 28 June 2022
9. Koyama, Y., et al.: The relationship between changes in salivary cortisol and the subjective impression of Shinrinyoku (Taking in the atmosphere of the forest, or forest bathing). Physiol. Anthropol. **14**(1), 21–24 (2009)
10. Takeda, A., Kondo, T., Takeda, S., Okada, R., Kobayashi, O.: Good mind-healing and health keeping effects in the forest walking. Japan Heart Found. **41**(4), 405–412 (2009). Japanese
11. Takayama, N., Kagawa, T.: Study on a function of the environment as the restorative environment using the attention restoration theory. J. Japanese Inst. Landscape Archit. **76**(5) (2013)

GPU-Accelerated Synthesis
of Probabilistic Programs

Roman Andriushchenko🆔, Milan Češka$^{(\boxtimes)}$🆔, Vladimír Marcin,
and Tomáš Vojnar🆔

Faculty of Information Technology, Brno University of Technology,
Brno, Czech Republic
ceskam@fit.vutbr.cz

Abstract. We consider automated synthesis methods for finite-state
probabilistic programs satisfying a given temporal specification. Our goal
is to accelerate the synthesis process using massively parallel graphical
processing units (GPUs). The involved analysis of families of candidate
programs is the main computational bottleneck of the process. We thus
propose a state-level GPU-parallelisation of the model-checking algorithms for Markov chains and Markov decision processes that leverages
the related but distinct topology of the candidate programs. For structurally complex families, we achieve a speedup of the analysis over one
order of magnitude. This already leads to a considerable acceleration of
the overall synthesis process and paves the way for further improvements.

1 Introduction

Probabilistic programs are a powerful modelling language used to describe systems containing probabilistic uncertainty or employing randomisation. Their cor-
rectness and efficiency can be described using probabilistic temporal constraints.
Modern *probabilistic model checkers* such as STORM [10] or PRISM [11] can automatically verify that a given finite-state program meets the constraints.

The existing model checkers typically require a fixed program, which is often
not the case in practice. In the early stages of the system development, the
designers deal with an incomplete description containing some *holes*. A hole
represents some undefined component or a partially implemented controller.
The aim of the *program synthesis* is to complete these holes such that the resulting program meets the given specification. To automate this process, one usually
starts with the so-called *sketch* [1] – a system description with holes representing
a family of programs (realisations) – and lets the automatic *synthesizer* fill in
this description to obtain a program that satisfies a given specification. Figure 1
illustrates the synthesis process for probabilistic programs.

Automated synthesis of probabilistic programs represents a tremendous
challenge, particularly due to the state-space explosion problem that affects

This work has been supported by the Czech Science Foundation grant GJ20-02328Y
and the FIT BUT internal project FIT-S-20-6427.

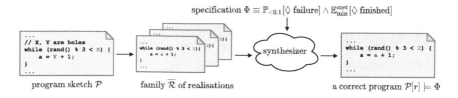

Fig. 1. The workflow of the synthesis process.

the synthesis in a twofold manner: not only the number of possible solutions is exponential wrt. the number of considered holes, but also the state space of each program usually grows exponentially wrt. the length of the program's description. Over the last years, there has been a significant improvement in analysing probabilistic program sketches. One of the most efficient state-of-the-art method is the approach of [2] combining *abstraction refinement* on families of realisations and *counterexample-guided inductive synthesis*.

Further, in the last decade, we have seen the emergence of many-core *single instruction, multiple threads* hardware, namely GPUs, as high-performance general-purpose processing devices utilised in various computationally-intensive scientific applications. The GPU computing also improved analysis of probabilistic programs. Several GPU-accelerated model-checking algorithms have been implemented [5,12] in order to increase the scalability of program verification. In this paper[1], we leverage modern GPUs to speed up the inductive synthesis method [2], which is crucial for designing complex programs.

Key contributions. We have extended GPU-accelerated model-checking algorithms [5,12] for Markov chains (MCs) and Markov decision processes (MDPs) to be effectively used in the synthesis of probabilistic programs. In the case of MC and MDP model checking of individual sketch realisations, we typically achieve an acceleration ranging from a factor 4 to 20 comparing to the best performing sequential baseline. The acceleration depends on the structural complexity of the realisations. For simple realisations, our parallelisation is not able to overcome the baseline using a topological solver [13]. Therefore, we design a metric that helps the synthesizer choose the most suitable model-checking algorithm.

To evaluate the GPU-acceleration of the synthesis process, we consider program sketches from several application domains. In the complicated cases, where the topological solver cannot be effectively used, we achieved the overall speedup up to the factor 4. This is close to the theoretical limit given by the Amdahl's law reflecting the amount of parallelisable parts of the synthesis loop. Our work is thus a first step towards effective GPU-acceleration of the synthesis process.

2   Background

The proposed GPU-parallelisation builds on the tool PAYNT [3] that enables the inductive synthesis of probabilistic programs. The starting point is a program

---

[1] Short version of https://www.fit.vut.cz/study/thesis-file/24076/24076.pdf.

sketch representing a family of programs and a *specification* expressed using a probabilistic logic formula. The goal of the synthesis is to find a program that satisfies the specification or prove that such a program does not exist within the family. We formalise below the main concepts.

Problem Formulation

We consider sketches in the PRISM [11] language. The sketch is a program description that contains some undefined parameters (holes) with associated options from finite domains. The sketch represents a finite family of finite-state Markov chains with related but distinct topologies. Let $\mathcal{P}$ be a sketch containing holes from the set $\mathcal{H} = \{H_k\}_k$ with R_k being the set of options available for the hole H_k. Let $\overline{\mathcal{R}} = \prod_k R_k$ denote the set of all hole assignments (realisations), $\mathcal{P}[r]$ denote the program induced by a substitution $r \in \overline{\mathcal{R}}$ and $\mathcal{D}_r$ denote the underlying Markov chain (MC). The size of the set $\overline{\mathcal{R}}$ is exponential in $|\mathcal{H}|$.

For simplicity, we consider (unbounded) *reachability* properties[2]. For a set T of *target states*, the MC D satisfies a reachability property $\phi \equiv \mathbb{P}_{\bowtie\lambda}[\Diamond T]$ (with $\lambda \in [0, 1]$ and $\bowtie \in \{\leq, \geq\}$) if the probability to reach T from the *initial* state s_0 meets $\bowtie \lambda$. The synthesis problem is then formalised as follows: Find a realisation $r \in \overline{\mathcal{R}}$ such that $\mathcal{D}_r$ satisfies ϕ or prove that such a realisation does not exist. We also support variants of maximal/minimal synthesis problems where the goal is to find a realisation maximising/minimising the reachability probability.

Existing Synthesis Methods

Synthesis methods can be classified into two orthogonal groups: i) *complete* methods allowing to prove optimality of the given solution or non-existence of such, and ii) *incomplete* methods leveraging various smart search strategies and evolutionary algorithms [8,9]. Our goal is to parallelise the oracle-guided inductive synthesis approach [2], representing a state-of-the-art complete synthesis method for probabilistic programs.

We consider two orthogonal oracles. An *inductive* counterexample-based oracle (CE) can examine a single realisation $r \in \overline{\mathcal{R}}$ to infer statements about other realisations [6]; in particular, the CE oracle constructs an MC D_r, model checks it against the specification Φ and, in the case of unsatisfiability, provides a *counterexample*. On the other hand, a *deductive* AR oracle based on *abstraction refinement* argues about sets of realisations $\mathcal{R} \subseteq \overline{\mathcal{R}}$ by considering (an aggregation of) these realisations at once [7]; the AR oracle uses Markov Decision Processes (MDPs) as a computationally feasible abstraction of such sets of realisations and performs MDP model checking to reason about their satisfiability. We also support a *hybrid* synthesis method [2] combining these two oracles.

---

[2] The extension to Probabilistic Computational Tree Logic is straightforward [4].

GPU Computational Model

Modern GPUs provide a massively parallel architecture where thousands of threads perform the same actions over their data. Since GPUs can perform parallel operations on multiple data sets, they are commonly used for non-graphical tasks such as scientific computation or machine learning. Each GPU program consists of a *host* part that runs on the CPU and a *device* part composed of so-called *kernels*. The kernels are parallel programs that are executed as sets of *threads* on the GPU. The threads are organised into groups called thread *blocks*.

GPUs employ the *Single Instruction Multiple Threads* (SIMT) model of execution, which means that each thread is executed independently with its own instruction and local state. Threads of a single block are split into *warps* and can synchronise through lightweight barriers. The execution of several warps may be interleaved to cover waiting times when accessing the slow global memory. Threads in a warp execute the same instructions (even memory loads) in a lockstep fashion and therefore it is desirable that the memory accesses for these threads are physically coalesced and that their code paths do not diverge.

3   Parallelisation Strategy

We performed a detailed profiling of the sequential implementation of the hybrid synthesis method over a representative set of benchmarks. We identified that on average about 68% of run-time is spent in procedures responsible for the MC model-checking (i.e. examining candidate realisations) and for the MDP model-checking (analysing the set of realisations). About 22% of run-time is spent by the CE construction, and the remaining 10% is distributed over the model construction, SAT solving and auxiliary functions. Although the CE construction takes a significant part of the run-time, its effective GPU parallelisation is problematic as it requires frequent synchronisation over very short computational blocks. Based on these observations, we focus on the parallelisation of the MC and MDP model-checking procedures. For this parallelisation goal, the Amdahl's law gives us a theoretical limit on the average acceleration of the overall synthesis process around a factor 3. In the rest of the paper, we show that this limit can be achieved and further improved by modifying the synthesis algorithm.

Parallel MC Model Checking

The MC model-checking procedure boils down to the solution of a system of linear equations   [4]. In order to scale to large MCs, modern tools [10,11] use iterative methods, in particular, the Gauss-Seidel method or the topological method [13] that decomposes the MC into strongly-connected components (SCCs) that are solved individually in the topological order. The topological method is very efficient for systems with a large number of small SCCs but otherwise causes a significant overhead. Moreover, it is not suitable for GPU-parallelisation due to the required synchronisation among the SCCs and slow memory access. In our approach, we parallelise the Jacobi method that simplifies the Gauss-Seidel approach and has no data dependencies within a single iteration. Its sequential implementation is typically slower, but it is very suitable for the parallelisation as it is given as a chain of matrix-vector multiplications.

The basic parallelisation scheme is similar as in [5], i.e., each thread calculates one entry of the resulting vector using a sparse representation of the transition matrix. We, however, employ a very optimised version of the parallel matrix-vector multiplication and *a pyramid-scheme reduction* provided by the Thrust library[3] for the parallel detection of the convergence.

Parallel MDP Model Checking

Similarly as above, the MDP model checking is implemented using iterative methods, in particular, using various variants of value and policy iteration [4] with the possibility to apply the topological ordering based on the SCC decomposition. As in [12], we parallelise the value iteration that boils down to a similar scheme as for the MC model checking. Additionally, we implement our own version of a *segmented reduction* that is responsible for selecting the optimal action in each state based on the value vectors. It is optimised for small segments typically appearing during the value iteration, thus providing better performance then standard solutions.

Family-Based Parallelisation

The proposed state-based parallelisation can accelerate synthesis for large models having enough states to map to individual threads and to hide the memory access latency. To accelerate analysis of large families of models having fewer states, we further propose an orthogonal parallelisation enabling parallel analysis of multiple MCs/MDPs, allowing for a better utilisation of the GPU architecture.

The scheme leverages the fact MCs in the analysed family have related topology. In particular, the MDP $\mathcal{M}^{\overline{\mathcal{R}}}$ abstracting a family $\overline{\mathcal{R}}$ of realisations can be described using a single rectangular matrix $\mathfrak{M}$. Then, every subfamily $\mathcal{R} \subseteq \overline{\mathcal{R}}$, abstracted using the MDP $\mathcal{M}^{\mathcal{R}}$, can be described as a row selection of the original matrix $\mathfrak{M}$. Similarly, every realisation $r \in \overline{\mathcal{R}}$ induces the MC $\mathcal{D}_r$ with its transition matrix being a row selection of $\mathfrak{M}$. Parallel analysis of multiple MCs/MDPs is then carried out using the same Jacobi/value iteration method on a shared matrix $\mathfrak{M}$, where each MC/MDP under consideration has its own solution vector.

4   Experimental Results

Setting. The proposed parallelisation was implemented on top of PAYNT [3]. All experiments are run on an Ubuntu 20.04 machine with Intel XeonE5-2620 at

---

[3] http://code.google.com/p/thrust/.

3.2 GHz and using up to 64 GB RAM; the GPU-acceleration is being run on the NVIDIA GPU GeForce GTX 1080 with 8 GB memory. We consider four benchmarks (*crowds, maze, dpm, wlan*) that have varying structural complexity in order to illustrate strengths and weaknesses of our approach. To showcase scalability, we investigated different variants of these benchmarks with an increasing number of transitions. For more details about the benchmarks, see[4].

MC/MDP Model Checking Parallelisation

We first investigate the efficiency of the proposed GPU parallelisation of the model checking methods. Figures 2, 3, 4 and 5 show the speedup gained by the proposed parallelisation of the Jacobi (MC) or value (MDP) iteration compared to the sequential iteration (left) and to the topological method (right).

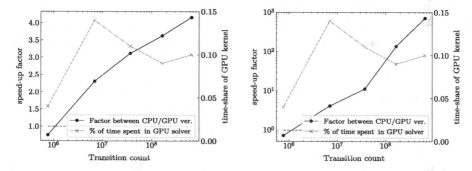

Fig. 2. Achieved speedup of the MC model checking on the *crowds* model comparing to the Jacobi method (left) and the topological method (right).

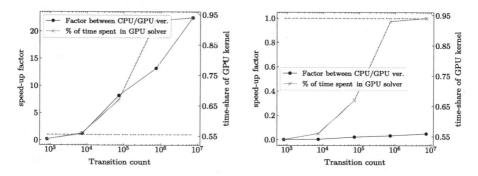

Fig. 3. Achieved speedup of the MC model checking on the *maze* model comparing to the Jacobi method (left) and the topological method (right).

We can see (the left part of the figures) that the GPU-parallelisation of the Jacobi/value iteration always outperforms the sequential variant. The achieved

---

[4] https://www.fit.vut.cz/study/thesis-file/24076/24076.pdf.

speedup largely depends on the number of iterations required to obtain the result. For instance, in the *crowds* model, the Jacobi method converges after only ≈300 iterations, implying that the matrix multiplications were not the crucial part of that computation. On the other hand, solving the *maze* model involves ≈20,000 iterations, leading to a 22-fold speedup.

When comparing the (parallel) Jacobi/value iteration against its topological-based modification (the left part of the figures), the structure of the underlying models plays a key role. In particular, having a large number of trivial SCCs in a model benefits the topological solver, but can drastically slow down convergence of the Jacobi/value iteration. In our benchmark suite, we present both types of models: the *crowds* and *dpm* models contain only a handful of trivial SCCs, while the *maze* and *wlan* models are characterised by overwhelming majority of SCCs that are trivial. This difference is directly reflected in the performance comparison of the (parallel) Jacobi/value iteration with respect to the topological method. For instance, when dealing with the *crowds* model containing few trivial SCCs, our proposed method achieves a 700x speedup compared to the topological method; on the other hand, when faced with the *maze* model, the topological method prevails. Nevertheless, the benefits of having a large number

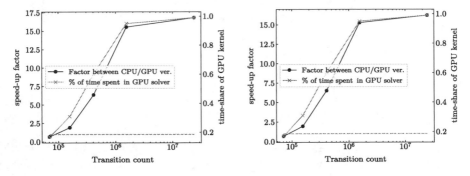

Fig. 4. Achieved speedup of the MDP model checking on the *dpm* model comparing to standard value iteration (left) and the topological-based value iteration (right).

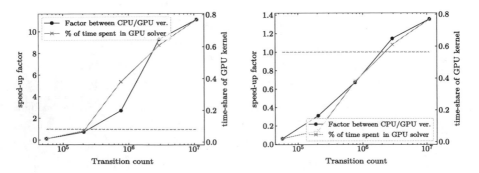

Fig. 5. Achieved speedup of the MDP model checking on the *wlan* model comparing to standard value iteration (left) and the topological-based value iteration (right).

of trivial SCCs diminish for the topological sort when dealing with MDPs where the inherent nondeterminism complicates the underlying structure of the models. In such a case, the GPU-parallelised value iteration can outperform the topological method given large enough models, as illustrated on the *wlan* model.

Finally, observe that in all eight cases the speedup of the GPU-parallelised model checking exhibits an increasing trend with respect to the number of transitions, indicating a strong degree of scalability of the proposed solution.

Family-Based Parallelisation

To investigate the proposed family-based parallelisation, we set up an experiment where the synthesizer processes a sketch for the *dpm* model using the abstraction refinement approach and processes the produced subfamilies of realisations simultaneously. We focus on *dpm* since this is the model that demonstrated the best speedup when model checking was considered.

In the following table, we report, for a varying number of families being analysed in parallel, the speedup of

Families	1	16	32	64	256	508
speedup	0.68	**3.21**	**1.81**	0.72	0.21	0.06

the synthesis compared to the sequential abstraction refinement. We can see that, while initially growing, the speedup starts to fall when considering large batches of families. This is attributed to the fact that different families induce different MDPs, and the value iteration method needs a varying number of iterations for their analysis. Therefore, when analysing a batch of such families in parallel, the length of the computation is dictated by the longest time needed to process each individual family.

Impact on Synthesis

The demonstrated speedup achieved by parallelising model-checking algorithms directly translates to the speedup of the overall synthesis process. For example, during the synthesis of the *dpm* benchmark, where model checking constitutes 74.5% of the total work, parallelising this part on the GPU allowed us to achieve a 3.82x speedup of the synthesis process, matching the theoretical speedup limit of 3.9 given by the Amhdahl's law. Overall, the success of the proposed solution can also depend on factors outside the scope of parallelisation, e.g. dynamics of the hybrid synthesis that works either in the inductive CE mode (and works with MCs) or in the deductive AR mode (and deals with MDPs), convergence of the applied iterative methods, as well as structural properties of the underlying models: the size of the quotient MDP, the number of SCCs, etc. Nevertheless, the presented work enables a significant speedup of the synthesis process and represents the first step towards efficient GPU-accelerated methods.

References

1. Alur, R., et al.: Syntax-guided synthesis. In: Formal Methods in Computer-Aided Design, vol. 1 (2013)
2. Andriushchenko, R., Češka, M., Junges, S., Katoen, J.: Inductive synthesis for probabilistic programs reaches new horizons. In: TACAS 2021 (2021)
3. Andriushchenko, R., Češka, M., Junges, S., Katoen, J., Stupinský, S.: PAYNT: a tool for inductive synthesis of probabilistic programs. In: CAV 2021 (2021)
4. Baier, C., Katoen, J.P.: Principles of model checking. MIT Press, Cambridge (2008)
5. Bosnacki, D., Edelkamp, S., Sulewski, D., Wijs, A.: Parallel probabilistic model checking on general purpose graphics processors. In: STTT 13 (2011)
6. Češka, M., Hensel, C., Junges, S., Katoen, J.-P.: Counterexample-guided inductive synthesis for probabilistic systems. Formal Aspects Comput. **33**(4), 637–667 (2021). https://doi.org/10.1007/s00165-021-00547-2
7. Češka, M., Jansen, N., Junges, S., Katoen, J.P.: Shepherding hordes of Markov chains. In: TACAS 2019 (2019)
8. Gerasimou, S., Calinescu, R., Tamburrelli, G.: Synthesis of probabilistic models for quality-of-service software engineering. Autom. Softw. Eng. **25**(4), 785–831 (2018)
9. Harman, M., Mansouri, S.A., Zhang, Y.: Search-based software engineering: trends, techniques and applications. ACM Comp. Surveys **45**(1), 11:1–11:61 (2012)
10. Hensel, C., Junges, S., Katoen, J.P., Quatmann, T., Volk, M.: The probabilistic model checker storm. In: CAV 2017 (2017)
11. Kwiatkowska, M., Norman, G., Parker, D.: Prism 4.0: verification of probabilistic real-time systems. In: CAV 2011 (2011)
12. Sapio, A., Bhattacharyya, S.S., Wolf, M.: Efficient model solving for markov decision processes. In: ISCC 2020 (2020)
13. Ábrahám, E., Jansen, N., Wimmer, R., Katoen, J.P., Becker, B.: DTMC model checking by SCC reduction. In: QEST 2010 (2010)

Static Deadlock Detection in Low-Level C Code

Dominik Harmim[(✉)], Vladimír Marcin, Lucie Svobodová, and Tomáš Vojnar

Faculty of Information Technology, Brno University of Technology, Brno, Czech Republic
iharmim@fit.vut.cz

Abstract. We present a novel scalable deadlock analyser L2D2 capable of handling C code with low-level unstructured lock manipulation. L2D2 runs along the call tree of a program, starting from its leaves, and analyses each function just once, without any knowledge of the call context. L2D2 builds function summaries recording information about locks that are assumed or known to be locked or unlocked at the entry, inside, and at the exit of functions, together with lock dependencies, and reports warnings about possible deadlocks when cycles in the lock dependencies are detected. We implemented L2D2 as a plugin of the Facebook/Meta INFER framework and report results of experiments on a large body of C as well as C++ code illustrating the effectiveness and efficiency of L2D2.

1 Introduction

Nowadays, programs often use *multi-threading* to utilise the many processors of current computers better. However, concurrency does bring not only speed-ups but also a much larger space for nasty errors easy to cause but difficult to find. The reason why finding errors in concurrent programs is particularly hard is that concurrently running threads may *interleave* in many different ways, with bugs hiding in just a few of them. Such interleavings are hard to discover by testing even if it is many times repeated.

Coverage of such rare behaviours can be improved using approaches such as *systematic testing* [22] and *noise-based testing* [7, 9, 10]. Another way is to use *extrapolating dynamic checkers*, such as [11, 12], which can report warnings about possible errors even if those are not seen in the testing runs, based on spotting some of their symptoms. Unfortunately, even though such checkers have proven quite useful in practice, they can, of course, still miss errors. Moreover, monitoring a run of large software through such checkers may also be quite expensive.

On the other hand, approaches based on *model checking*, i.e., exhaustive state-space exploration, can guarantee the discovery of all potentially present errors — either in general or at least up to some bound, which is usually given in the number of context switches. However, so far, the scalability of these techniques is not sufficient to handle truly large industrial code, even when combined with methods such as *sequentialisation* [17, 19], which represents one of the most scalable approaches in the area.

The work was supported by the project 20-07487S of the Czech Science Foundation and the Brno Ph.D. Talent Scholarship Programme.

R. Moreno-Díaz et al. (Eds.): EUROCAST 2022, LNCS 13789, pp. 267–276, 2022.
https://doi.org/10.1007/978-3-031-25312-6_31

An alternative to the above approaches, which can scale better than model checking and can find bugs not found dynamically (though for the price of potentially missing some errors and/or producing false alarms), is offered by approaches based on *static analysis*, e.g., in the form of *abstract interpretation* [5] or *data-flow analysis* [15]. The former approach is supported, e.g., in Facebook/Meta INFER— an open-source framework for creating highly scalable, compositional, incremental, and interprocedural static analysers based on abstract interpretation [4].

INFER provides several analysers that check for various types of bugs, such as buffer overflows, null-dereferencing, or memory leaks. However, most importantly, INFER is a *framework* for building new analysers quickly and easily. As for *concurrency-related bugs*, INFER provides support for finding some forms of *data races* and *deadlocks*, but it is limited to *high-level* Java and C++ programs only and fails for C programs, which use a *lower-level lock manipulation* [1,6].

In this paper, we propose a *deadlock checker* that fits the common principles of analyses used in INFER and is applicable even to *C code* with *lower-level lock manipulation*. Our checker is called L2D2 for "low-level deadlock detector".

As is common in INFER, L2D2 computes function summaries *upwards* along the call tree, starting from its leaves, and analyses every function just once, without knowing anything about its call contexts. The summaries contain various pieces of information about locks that are assumed to be locked/unlocked at the entry of a function, that may be locked/unlocked at the end of the function, that may be both locked and unlocked inside a function, as well as about lock dependencies (saying that some lock is locked while another is still held). If L2D2 detects a loop in the lock dependencies, it warns about possible deadlocks. L2D2 uses multiple heuristics to reduce the number of false alarms, such as detection of locks serving as gate locks.

To show the effectiveness and efficiency of L2D2, we present experiments in which we managed to apply it to 930 programs with 10.3 million lines of code (MLoC) in total, out of which 8 contained known deadlocks. L2D2 rediscovered all the deadlocks, and, out of the remaining 922 programs, it claimed 909 deadlock-free and reported false alarms for 13 of the programs only. The code included benchmarks coming from the CPROVER tool derived from the Debian GNU/Linux distribution, the code of the grep, sort, tgrep, and memcached utilities, and the EPROSIMA/FAST-DDS middleware.

Related Work. To the best of our knowledge, L2D2 is the only currently existing, publicly available, *compositional static deadlock analyser* for *low-level code*. Below, we briefly discuss approaches that we consider to be the closest to it.

RACERX [8] is a top-down, non-compositional, flow-sensitive and context-sensitive analysis for C programs based on computing so-called *lock sets*, i.e., sets of currently held locks, constructing a *static lock-order graph*, and reporting possible deadlocks in case of cycles in it. It employs various heuristics to reduce false-positive reports. Some of the ideas concerning the lock sets are similar to those used in L2D2, and some of the heuristics used in RACERX inspired those used in L2D2.

The deadlock analyser implemented within the CPROVER framework [16] targets C code with POSIX threads and uses a combination of multiple analyses to create a context-sensitive and sound analysis. It also builds a lock-order graph and searches for cycles to detect deadlocks. Its most costly phase is the pointer analysis used. An experimental comparison with this tool is given in Sect. 4.

STARVATION [2] is implemented in the INFER framework, and hence it is bottom-up, context-insensitive, and compositional. It detects deadlocks by deriving lock dependencies for each function and checking whether some other function uses the locks in an inverse order. It is thus similar to L2D2, but STARVATION is limited to *high-level* Java and C++ programs with *balanced locks* only. Moreover, it implements many heuristics explicitly tailored for Android Java applications.

GOODLOCK [13] is a well-known *dynamic analysis* for Java programs implemented in Java PathFinder (JPF) [14]. As a representative of dynamic analysers, it inherits their dependence on the concrete execution (or executions) of the given software seen for detecting possible deadlocks. It monitors the lock acquisition history by creating a *dynamic lock-order graph*, followed by checking the graph for the existence of deadlock candidates by searching for cycles in it. To increase chances of spotting even rarely occurring deadlocks, not directly seen in the given execution, it makes *deadlock predictions* based on an exponential number of permutations of a single execution. A drawback of this approach is that it may produce a high rate of false positives.

AIRLOCK [3] is one of the state-of-the-art dynamic deadlock analysers. It adopts and improves the basic approach from GOODLOCK by applying various optimisations to the extracted lock-order graph. Moreover, AIRLOCK, operating on-the-fly, runs a polynomial-time algorithm on the lock graph to eliminate parts without cycles, followed by running a higher-cost algorithm to detect actual lock cycles.

2 Static Deadlock Detection in Low-Level Concurrent C Code

This section presents the design of the L2D2 analyser. We first introduce the main ideas of the analysis, and then discuss it in more detail.

As already mentioned, L2D2 is designed to handle *C code* with *low-level, unstructured lock manipulation*. It does not start the analysis from the entry code location as done in classical inter-procedural analyses based, e.g., on [20]. Instead, it performs the analysis of a program function-by-function *along the call tree, starting from its leaves*. Therefore, each function is analysed just once without any knowledge of its possible call contexts. For each analysed function, L2D2 derives a *summary* that consists of a *pre-condition* and a *post-condition*. The summaries are then used when analysing functions higher up in the call hierarchy. The obtained analysis is *compositional* on the level of functions, and when used in conjunction with some version control system, it allows one to focus on *modified functions* and their dependants only with no need to re-analyse the unchanged functions (which is typically a vast majority of the code).

```
1   void f(Lock *L3') {
2       lock(&L4);
3       unlock(&L3');
4       lock(&L2);
5       ...
6       unlock(&L4); }
7   void *t1(...) {
8       lock(&L1);
9       lock(&L3);
10      ...
11      f(&L3);
12      unlock(&L1); }
13  void *t2(...) {
14      lock(&L2);
15      ...
16      lock(&L1); }
```

Listing 1. A sample low-level code causing a deadlock

L2D2 does not perform a classical *alias analysis*, i.e., a precise analysis for saying whether some pairs of accesses to locks may alias (such an analysis is considered too expensive — no such sufficiently precise analysis works compositionally and at scale). Instead, L2D2 uses *syntactic access paths* [18], computed by the INFER framework, to represent lock objects. Access paths represent heap locations via expressions used to access them. In particular, an access path consists of a base variable followed by a sequence of field selectors. According to [1], the access paths' syntactic equality is a reasonably efficient way to say (in an under-approximate fashion) that heap accesses touch the same address. The mechanism is indeed successfully used, e.g., in the production checker RACERD [1] to detect data races in real-world programs.

We will use Listing 1 to illustrate some ideas behind L2D2. It works in two phases. In the first phase, it computes a summary for each function by looking for lock and unlock events (lock/unlock calls in the listing) in the function. When a call of a user-defined function appears in the analysed function during the analysis (like on line 11 in the listing), L2D2 uses a summary of the function if available. Otherwise, the function is analysed on demand, effectively analysing the code bottom-up (when a recursive call is encountered, it is skipped). The summary is then applied to an *abstract state* at the call site. In the listing, the summary of f will be applied to the abstract state of t1.

In the second phase, L2D2 looks through all computed summaries of the analysed program and focuses on so-called *dependencies* that are a part of the summaries. These dependencies represent possible locking sequences of the analysed program. The obtained set of dependencies is interpreted as a relation. L2D2 computes the transitive closure of this relation and reports a deadlock if some lock depends on itself in the closure. If we run L2D2 on the code in Listing 1, it will report a potential deadlock due to the cyclic dependency between the locks L1 and L2 that arises when the thread t1 holds L1 and waits on L2 and the thread t2 holds L2 and waits on L1.

2.1 Computing Function Summaries

This section outlines the structure and computation of the summaries used by L2D2 when analysing some function f. Intuitively, the pre-condition expresses what states of locks f expects from its callers, and the post-condition reflects the effect of f on the locks. More precisely, the post-condition includes the lockset and unlockset sets, holding information about which locks *may be locked* and *unlocked*, resp., at the exit of f. The pre-condition consists of the locked and unlocked sets, stating which locks are *expected to be locked* and *unlocked*, resp., upon a call of f. Note that the locked/unlocked sets are maintained but not used in the basic algorithm introduced later in this section. They are used to detect possible *double-locking/unlocking*, see Sect. 3. Next, the summary's post-condition contains the so-called *lock dependencies* (deps) in the form of pairs of locks (L2, L1) where locking of L1 was observed while L2 was locked. This exact situation can be seen in Listing 1 on line 16.

```
f:  PRE-CONDITION
 locked={L3'}
 unlocked={L2, L4}
     POST-CONDITION
 lockset={L2}
 unlockset={L3', L4}
 wereLocked={L2, L4}
 deps={(L4, L2)}
 order={(L3', L2)}
t1:  PRE-CONDITION
 unlocked={L1, L2, L3, L4}
     POST-CONDITION
 lockset={L2}
 unlockset={L1, L3, L4}
 wereLocked={L1, L2, L3, L4}
 deps={(L1, L2), (L1, L3),
    (L1, L4), (L3, L4)}
t2:  PRE-CONDITION
 unlocked={L1, L2}
     POST-CONDITION
 lockset={L1, L2}
 wereLocked={L1, L2}
 deps={(L2, L1)}
```

Listing 2. Summaries for the functions from Listing 1

Two more sets are a part of the summary's post-condition. First, the wereLocked set contains information on which *locks may be locked and then again unlocked* within f. This is needed to detect lock dependencies with such locks in functions higher up in the call hierarchy. Such a situation can be seen in Listing 1. The lock L4 is locked and then unlocked again within the function f. In this case, the lock will not be in lockset, and we would have no information that it was locked there. Consequently, we would not create any lock dependencies w.r.t. this lock. However, this lock will appear in wereLocked, so we can create dependencies with it (like the dependency (L1, L4) in the function t1 when calling f on line 11, which could not be created otherwise).

The last sets that are a part of L2D2's post-conditions are denoted as the order sets. They comprise pairs of locks (L3', L2) where locking of L2 was seen when L3' was unlocked before within the same function. Such a pair is produced, e.g., on line 4 in Listing 1. These sets help L2D2 to better determine the order of operations in functions. Without it, we would create, e.g., the non-existent dependency (L3, L2) in the function t1 when calling f on line 11. It should not be created because L3 is unlocked in f on line 3 before L2 is locked on line 4. Note that the lock L3 from the function t1 is passed to f as L3'. We resolve such situations by replacing the function's formal parameters with the actual ones at the concrete call site.

Algorithm 1: Lock acquisition

Data: lock L being locked; abstract state S
1 **def** lock(L, S):
2   **if** $L \notin S.locked \cup S.unlocked$ **then**
3      $S.unlocked \leftarrow S.unlocked \cup \{L\}$;
4    $S.lockset \leftarrow S.lockset \cup \{L\}$;
5    $S.unlockset \leftarrow S.unlockset \setminus \{L\}$;
6    $S.wereLocked \leftarrow S.wereLocked \cup \{L\}$;
7    $S.deps \leftarrow S.deps \cup (S.lockset \times \{L\})$;
8    $S.order \leftarrow$
    $S.order \cup (S.unlockset \times \{L\})$;

Algorithm 2: Lock release

Data: lock L being unlocked; abstract state S
1 **def** unlock(L, S):
2   **if** $L \notin S.locked \cup S.unlocked$ **then**
3      $S.locked \leftarrow S.locked \cup \{L\}$;
4    $S.unlockset \leftarrow$
    $S.unlockset \cup \{L\}$;
5    $S.lockset \leftarrow S.lockset \setminus \{L\}$;

Algorithm 3: Integrating a summary of a callee

Data: summary χ of a callee; abstract state S

1 **def** apply_summary(χ, S):
2     $\chi \leftarrow$ replace_formals_with_actuals(χ);
3   **if** $\exists L : L \in \chi.unlocked \land L \notin S.unlockset$ **then** $S.unlocked \leftarrow S.unlocked \cup \{L\}$;
4   **if** $\exists L : L \in \chi.locked \land L \notin S.lockset$ **then** $S.locked \leftarrow S.locked \cup \{L\}$;
5     $S.lockset \leftarrow (S.lockset \cup \chi.lockset) \setminus \chi.unlockset$;
6     $S.unlockset \leftarrow (S.unlockset \setminus \chi.lockset) \cup \chi.unlockset$;
7     $S.wereLocked \leftarrow S.wereLocked \cup \chi.wereLocked$;
8     $S.deps \leftarrow S.deps \cup ((S.lockset \times \chi.wereLocked) \setminus \chi.order)$;

Listing 2 gives the summaries for the functions in Listing 1, omitting the empty sets.

The high-level algorithm for the summary's computation is given in Algorithms 1–3. Algorithm 1 shows how the abstract state is updated whenever locking occurs during the analysis. First, it updates the pre-condition by adding the lock to the unlocked set if this locking is the first operation with that lock in the given function f (lines 2–3). Intuitively, this reflects that the lock should be unlocked before calling f; otherwise, we would encounter double-locking. Next, the lock acquisition takes place, meaning that the lock is added to lockset and removed from unlockset (lines 4–5). Moreover, the lock is added to wereLocked (line 6). Finally, we derive new dependencies and order edges by considering all pairs (L', L) where L' is an element of lockset and unlockset, resp., and L is the acquired lock (lines 7–8). Algorithm 2 then updates the abstract state when some lock is released. It is analogical to the algorithm for locking, but it does not update the wereLocked, deps, and order sets.

Algorithm 3 integrates a callee's summary with the abstract state of an analysed function. Initially, the summary is updated by replacing the formal parameters with the actual ones (line 2). We also check that all the locks that should be locked/unlocked before calling the callee are present in lockset/unlockset, resp. If they are not, they must be locked/unlocked even before the currently analysed function. Hence, we update the pre-condition (lines 3–4). On lines 5–7, the lockset, unlockset, and wereLocked sets are appropriately modified. At last, new dependencies between the currently held locks and locks acquired in the callee are introduced (line 8). However, we exclude all the dependencies from the order set to avoid adding such (L', L) dependencies where L' was unlocked before locking L in the callee.

As L2D2 is based on abstract interpretation, we must further define the *join* operator for combining states along *confluent program paths* (e.g. in if statements), the *entailment* operator allowing the analysis to detect it has reached a fixpoint and stop, and the *widening* operator accelerating the analysis of loops. Since we are interested in locking patterns along any possible path, we define the join operator as the union of incoming states' values for all the sets in the summaries. The entailment operator is defined as testing for a subset on all the sets. The widening operator is made equal to the join operator as we are working with summaries on finite and not too large domains.

2.2 Reporting Deadlocks

Checking for deadlocks takes place after the summaries for all functions in the analysed program are computed. L2D2 then merges all of the derived lock dependencies into one set R. This set is interpreted as a relation, and its transitive closure R^+ is computed. If any lock L depends on itself in the closure, i.e., $(L, L) \in R^+$, a potential for a deadlock has been detected. For deadlocks using two locks, L2D2 then looks for dependencies that cause the deadlock. In particular, it looks for a lock L' s.t. $(L, L') \in R^+ \wedge (L', L) \in R^+$ and reports the dependencies (a generalisation to more locks is, of course, possible).

3 Increasing Analysis Accuracy

L2D2 further implements three heuristics intended to decrease the number of possible false alarms. We now introduce the two most important (with the third one being a simple support for recursive locks).

As *double-locking/unlocking* errors are quite rare in practice, the first heuristic uses their detection as an indication that the analysis is over-approximating too much. Instead of reporting such errors, L2D2 resets (some of) the working sets. Namely, if a lock acquisition leads to double-locking, it is assumed that L2D2 followed some non existent path, and `lockset` is no longer trustworthy. Therefore, it is erased, and the only lock left in it is the currently acquired one as this is the only one about which we can safely say it is locked. For that, the following statement is added to Algorithm 1: **if** $L \in S.lockset$ **then** $S.lockset \leftarrow \{L\};$. When releasing a lock, we then check whether it may already be unlocked. If so, `lockset` is erased, eliminating any dependencies that the locking error would cause. For that, we add the following to Algorithm 2: **if** $L \in S.unlockset$ **then** $S.lockset \leftarrow \emptyset;$. Finally, we check double-locking/unlocking when a function call is encountered. We ask whether some lock that should be locked/unlocked in the callee is currently released/held, resp. If such a lock is found, it is assumed that L2D2 used a non-existent path to reach the function call, and so `lockset` is discarded, and the `lockset` of the callee will be used instead. We implement this by adding the following to Algorithm 3: **if** $(S.lockset \cap \chi.unlocked \neq \emptyset) \vee (S.unlockset \cap \chi.locked \neq \emptyset)$ **then** $S.lockset \leftarrow \chi.lockset;$.

The second heuristic used in L2D2 is the detection of so-called *gate locks* [13], i.e., locks guarding other locks (upon which deadlocks on the nested locks are not reported). Whenever we detect a possible deadlock — represented by two reverse dependencies $d_1 = (L, L')$ and $d_2 = (L', L)$ — we check whether the same gate lock protects them. If so, we do not report a deadlock. We check this by computing the intersection of the `guards`, i.e., all locks locked before the program points where the dependencies d_1 and d_2 were captured. In particular, we do not report a deadlock for dependencies d_1 and d_2 if $\text{guards}(d_1) \cap \text{guards}(d_2) \neq \emptyset$.

4 Experimental Evaluation

L2D2 has been implemented in OCaml as a plugin of INFER, and it is publicly available[1]. We now report on various experiments we have performed with it. All of the

---

[1] https://github.com/svobodovaLucie/infer.

experiments were run on a machine with the AMD Ryzen 5 5500U CPU, 15 GiB of RAM, 64-bit Ubuntu 20.04.4 LTS, using INFER version v1.1.0-0e7270157.

In our first set of experiments, we have applied L2D2 on a set of 1,002 C programs with POSIX threads derived from a Debian GNU/Linux distribution, originally prepared for evaluating the static deadlock analyser based on the CPROVER framework proposed in [16]. The benchmark consists of 11.3 MLoC. Eight of the programs contain a known deadlock. Like

Table 1. Results of L2D2 and CPROVER on non-deadlocking programs of the CPROVER test-suite

Checker	**programs claimed safe**	Programs Raising alarms	Programs Failed to analyse
CPROVER	**292**	114	588
L2D2$_{mode\,1}$	**906**	11	77
L2D2$_{mode\,2}$	**896**	21	77

CPROVER, L2D2 was able to detect all the deadlocks. The results for the remaining 994 programs are shown in Table 1 (for L2D2, mode 1/mode 2 refer to using/not using the double-locking-based heuristic), with some more details also in Table 2 discussed below. We can see that, in mode 1, L2D2 produced 11 false alarms only (77 programs failed to compile since the INFER's front-end did not support some of the constructions used). We find this very encouraging, considering that the CPROVER's deadlock detector produced 114 false alarms. Moreover, L2D2 consumed 83 min only whereas CPROVER needed 4 h to handle the programs it correctly analysed, producing 453 timeouts (w.r.t. a 30-minute time limit), and ran out of the available 24 GB of RAM in 135 cases (according to [16], the results were obtained on Xeon X5667 at 3 GHz running Fedora 20 with 64-bit binaries).

Table 2 provides our further experimental results. Unlike Table 1, the table gives not only numbers of programs in which an alarm was raised, but it gives concrete numbers of the alarms (more alarms can be raised in a single program). Moreover, it shows how L2D2 behaved on multiple further real-life

Table 2. Detailed results on EPROSIMA/FAST-DDS, sort, grep, memcached, tgrep

	kLoC	alarms mode 1	alarms mode 2	dead-locks	runtime (mm:ss)
FAST-DDS	110	3	6	0	06:53
memcached	31	6	7	0	00:08
sort	7.2	0	0	0	00:02
grep	8.7	0	0	0	00:03
tgrep	2.4	0	0	0	00:01
CPROVER	10,164	23	80	8	83:23

programs. In particular, EPROSIMA/FAST-DDS 2.6.1 is a C++ implementation of the Data Distribution Service of the Object Management Group. For its analysis, we replaced the C++ guard lock used, which is so far not supported by L2D2, by a normal lock (exploiting the fact that INFER automatically adds all needed unlock calls). Next, we analysed memcached version 1.6.10, a distributed memory object caching system. The source code of this program was pre-processed by FRAMA-C [21], and we report on the size of the pre-processed code (likewise with all the further mentioned programs). Finally, we also analysed grep 3.7, tgrep (a multi-threaded version of find combined with grep by Ron Winacott), and GNU Coreutils sort 8.32. The alarms raised for FAST-DDS are false alarms caused by some intricacy of C++ locks for which L2D2 was not prepared. We were not able to check the status of the alarms raised for memcached, but we consider them likely false alarms. However, we find the results provided by L2D2 as quite encouraging since the numbers of false alarms are low w.r.t. the number of programs and their extent, and, moreover, we believe that there is space for further improvements (especially, but not only for C++ locks).

References

1. Blackshear, S., Gorogiannis, N., O'Hearn, P., Sergey, I.: RacerD: compositional static race detection. In: Proceedings of ACMPL (OOPSLA), vol. 2, pp. 144:1–144:28 (2018)
2. Brotherston, J., Brunet, P., Gorogiannis, N., Kanovich, M.: A Compositional Deadlock Detector for Android Java. In: Proceedings of ASE 2021. IEEE (2021)
3. Cai, Y., Meng, R., Palsberg, J.: Low-Overhead Deadlock Prediction. In: Proc. of ICSE 2020. ACM (2020)
4. Calcagno, C., et al.: Moving fast with software verification. In: Havelund, K., Holzmann, G., Joshi, R. (eds.) NFM 2015. LNCS, vol. 9058, pp. 3–11. Springer, Cham (2015). https://doi.org/10.1007/978-3-319-17524-9_1
5. Cousot, P., Cousot, R.: Abstract interpretation: a unified lattice model for static analysis of programs by construction or approx. of fixpoints. In Proceedings of POPL 1977. ACM (1977)
6. Distefano, D., Fähndrich, M., Logozzo, F., O'Hearn, P.: Scaling Static Analyses at Facebook. Commun. ACM **62**(8), 62–70 (2019)
7. Edelstein, O., Farchi, E., Goldin, E., Nir, Y., Ratsaby, G., Ur, S.: Framework for testing multi-threaded java programs. Concur. Computat. Pract. Exper. **15**(3–5), 485–499 2003
8. Engler, D., Ashcraft, K.: RacerX: Effective, static detection of race conditions and deadlocks. In: Proceedings of SOSP 2003. ACM (2003)
9. Fiedor, J., Hrubá, V., Křena, B., Letko, Z., Ur, S., Vojnar, T.: Advances in noise-based testing of concurrent software. Softw. Test. Verif. Reliab. **25**(3), 272–309 (2015)
10. Fiedor, J., Mužikovská, M., Smrčka, A., Vašíček, O., Vojnar, T.: Advances in the ANaConDA Framework for Dynamic Analysis. In: Proceedings of ISSTA 2018. ACM (2018)
11. Flanagan, C., Freund, S.: FastTrack: efficient and precise dynamic race detection. In: Proceedings of PLDI 2009. ACM (2009)
12. Flanagan, C., Freund, S., Yi, J.: Velodrome: a sound and complete dynamic atomicity checker for multithreaded programs. In: Proceedings of PLDI 2008. ACM (2008)
13. Havelund, K.: Using Runtime analysis to guide model checking of java programs. In: Havelund, K., Penix, J., Visser, W. (eds.) SPIN 2000. LNCS, vol. 1885, pp. 245–264. Springer, Heidelberg (2000). https://doi.org/10.1007/10722468_15
14. Havelund, K., Pressburger, T.: Model checking java programs using java pathfinder. Inter. Jour. on STTT **2**(4), 366–381 (2000)
15. Kildall, G.: A Unified Approach To Global Program Optimization. In: Proceedings of POPL1973. ACM (1973)
16. Kroening, D., Poetzl, D., Schrammel, P., Wachter, B.: Sound static deadlock analysis for c/pthreads. In Proc. of ASE 2016. ACM (2016)
17. Lal, A., Reps, T.: Reducing concurrent analysis under a context bound to sequential analysis. In: Gupta, A., Malik, S. (eds.) CAV 2008. LNCS, vol. 5123, pp. 37–51. Springer, Heidelberg (2008). https://doi.org/10.1007/978-3-540-70545-1_7
18. Lerch, J., Späth, J., Bodden, E., Mezini, M.: Access-path abstraction: scaling field-sensitive data-flow analysis with unbound. Access Paths. In: Proceedings of ASE 2015. IEEE (2015)

19. Nguyen, T.L., Fischer, B., La Torre, S., Parlato, G.: Lazy sequentialization for the safety verification of unbounded concurrent programs. In: Artho, C., Legay, A., Peled, D. (eds.) ATVA 2016. LNCS, vol. 9938, pp. 174–191. Springer, Cham (2016). https://doi.org/10.1007/978-3-319-46520-3_12
20. Reps, T., Horwitz, S., Sagiv, M.: Precise Interprocedural dataflow analysis via graph reachability. In Proceedings of POPL1995. ACM (1995)
21. Signoles, J., Cuoq, P., Kirchner, F., Kosmatov, N., Prevosto, V., Yakobowski, B.: FramaC A Software Analysis Perspective. Formal Asp. Comput. **27**, 22 (2012)
22. Wu, J., Tang, Y., Cui, H ., Yang, J.: Sound and precise analysis of parallel programs through schedule specialization. In: Proceedings of PLDI 2012. ACM (2012)

Applications of Signal Processing Technology

3D Ultrasound Fingertip Tracking

Eugen Pfann$^{(\boxtimes)}$ ⓘ and Mario Huemer ⓘ

Institute of Signal Processing, Johannes Kepler University Linz, Linz, Austria
eugen.pfann@jku.at

Abstract. This contribution describes a 3D fingertip tracking system based on a planar array of ultrasound (US) transducers. The echo paths between US transducer pairs are measured periodically in order to detect the distance to reflecting objects. Due to the signal bandwidth provided by the latest capacitive micromachined ultrasonic transducer technology it is possible to resolve the US echo paths with sufficient accuracy and speed.

Keywords: Motion tracking · Ultrasound · HMI · Gesture recognition

1 Introduction

In recent years many innovative gesture recognition products to augment the user experience for device and application control came to market. Depending on the application these devices are often based on inertial measurement unit sensors or accelerometers for wearables [10] or, for example, on the sensing of E-field variations [7] for desktop units. At the same time different technologies including ultrasound (US) sensor technology for gesture capturing are actively researched. A strong focus in this area is on US gesture recognition for interaction with smart devices using low US frequencies in the 18–24 kHz band which can be generated by available built-in speakers [2,3,6,11]. A system capable of 2D finger tracking using the same low US frequency range can be found in [8].

Extending the US frequency range to higher frequencies and exploiting increased bandwidth requires dedicated US transducers for US signal generation and recording. However, especially when US frequencies do not exceed 95 kHz relatively inexpensive signal processing hardware and the common 192 kHz audio sampling rate can be used. A US based hand gesture recognition system based on capacitive micromachined ultrasonic transducer (CMUT) technology [1] is reported in [9] where the frequency band above 20 kHz is used.

Whereas gesture recognition applications do not necessarily require high spatial resolution as long as there are sufficient distinguishing features between the gestures, this is different for the tracking of small target reflectors in the presence of interfering objects. In order to demonstrate the benefits of enhanced resolution due to increased signal bandwidth this work presents a system for the 3D tracking of a fingertip over an US transducer array. The system employs CMUT technology components [4,5] and uses a frequency range from about 65 kHz to 90 kHz.

R. Moreno-Díaz et al. (Eds.): EUROCAST 2022, LNCS 13789, pp. 279–286, 2022.
https://doi.org/10.1007/978-3-031-25312-6_32

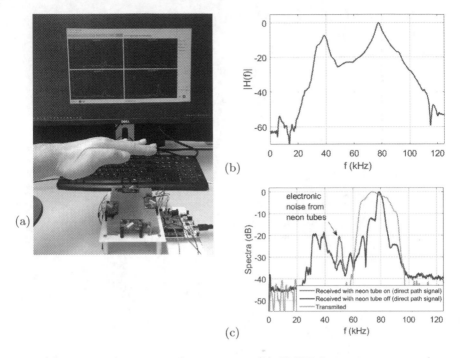

Fig. 1. (a) US transducer array demonstrator; (b) CMUT frequency response (transmitter to receiver including circuitry); (c) US transmit and receive spectra.

2   Ultrasound Gesture Tracking Demonstrator

A demonstrator for a planar array of four CMUTs [4] was built to perform US distance measurements to reflecting objects in the vicinity of the array (Fig. 1(a)). The transducers are mounted with the sound port facing upwards. For a single measurement one transducer transmits a short US pulse (duration $\approx 60\mu s$) while the echos are recorded on the 3 remaining transducers. To cover all possible echo paths the transmitting transducer is changed in a circular fashion for each consecutive measurement. The recorded signals are passed via a micro-controller to a host PC where the distances to the reflecting objects are extracted.

The transmit to receive frequency response of the used CMUT devices is shown in Fig. 1(b). For this demonstrator the higher frequency band from 65 kHz to 90 kHz was selected. This facilitates the design of analogue filters to suppress acoustic interference in the audio range. It also avoids a typical frequency region of electronic noise from neon-tubes. This is shown in Fig. 1(b) along with the spectra of the transmit pulse and receive signal. Although only the higher frequency band is targeted also frequencies in the lower band are excited. However, those frequencies are not used for receive processing.

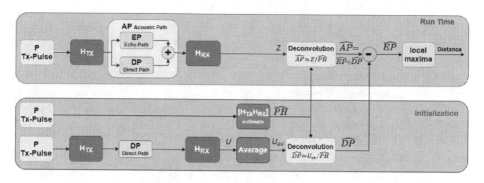

Fig. 2. Deconvolution based echo path identification.

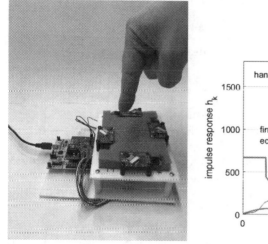

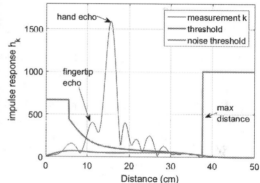

Fig. 3. Ultrasound fingertip track-   **Fig. 4.** Echo path impulse response measure-
ing.   ment.

3   Echo Path Length Estimate

The tracking of the target reflector is based on continuous measurements of the
echo path lengths between multiple pairs of transducers. A common method to
identify the delay of an acoustic pulse is based on the matched filter principle
where the receive signal is correlated with the transmit pulse [11]. This is the
SNR-optimal receiver for the isolated pulse case, but for multiple closely spaced
echos when receive pulses start overlapping the identification of the single echo
path is affected. In this case an enhanced resolution was obtained by direct
identification of the acoustic path as illustrated in Fig. 2.

The receive processing is performed in the frequency domain and the spectrum of the acoustic path $AP(\Omega)$ is estimated from the receive spectrum $Z(\Omega)$
via Wiener deconvolution according to

$$\widehat{AP}(\Omega) = \frac{Z(\Omega)}{\widehat{PH}(\Omega)} \cdot \frac{1}{1 + 1/\widehat{SNR}_{RX}(\Omega)} \cdot W(\Omega) \qquad (1)$$

where $\widehat{PH}(\Omega)$ is an estimate of the receive pulse without acoustic path influence (i.e. the transmit pulse processed by transmit and receive filters), $\widehat{SNR}_{RX}(\Omega)$ is an estimate of the receive SNR and $W(\Omega)$ is a window function. A subsequent IFFT operation provides the time domain impulse response of the acoustic path where local maxima are associated with individual echo paths. The window function $W(\Omega)$ is essential to sufficiently suppress the sidelobes of strong paths, which would otherwise be erroneously identified as separate echo paths.

Figure 2 shows that the acoustic path consists of the echo path EP and the direct path DP between transmitting and receiving transducer. Although the transducers are mounted with the sound port facing upwards a strong direct path signal will be recorded as the mounted US transducers have an approximate cardioid directivity [1]. The direct path is often much stronger than the echo signal except for large reflectors in close proximity of the array. To aid the echo path measurements it is thus necessary to pre-record the direct path signals in an initialization phase and subtract them from the measurements during run-time.

If the direct path DP is line of sight only without any reflections, which might be the case for a completely flat transducer array without reflections at its borders [5], it is possible to derive a sufficiently accurate estimate $\widehat{PH}(\Omega)$ from DP by eliminating the direct path delay. However, for the demonstrator array shown in Fig. 3 additional reflections are observed for example due to the transducer connectors and mounting screws which protrude over the transducer plane. In this case an estimate $\widehat{PH}(\Omega)$ can be obtained in a pre-initialization phase by averaging the responses over multiple transducer samples.

A typical echo path impulse response after subtraction of the direct path is shown in Fig. 4 for the scenario in Fig. 3 where the index finger is pointing towards the transducer array. It can be observed that due to the proximity of the fingertip to the transducer array this is the shortest echo path, but due to the small surface area of the fingertip it is not the strongest echo. The echo from the fist behind is significantly stronger. This emphasizes the need for an IFFT window function for sidelobe suppression and also the need of sufficient high bandwidth of the ultrasound signal which translates into narrow mainlobes of the echo path impulse response and provides high spatial resolution of the echo path.

The location of the closest reflection point to the transducer array is associated with the shortest echo path length and thus with the first local maxima in the echo path impulse response above a noise threshold. The threshold is scaled with $1/r$ as shown in Fig. 4 according to the spreading loss of soundwaves. This should also safeguard against erroneous detection of direct path residuals which could not be completely eliminated. The minimum possible distance is defined by the length of the direct path.

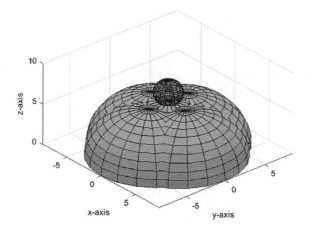

Fig. 5. Geometry for fingertip position estimate.

4   Fingertip Localization

Each echo path length measurement provides the distance from the transmitter via the reflector -i.e. the fingertip- to the receiving transducer. Assuming distinct reflections points this defines a rotational ellipsoid with the transducers at the focal points and the reflector at the surface. Measurements between alternating transducer pairs will be subject to different reflection points and hence depend on the geometry of the reflector. To this end the fingertip is modeled as a sphere with a diameter of 1.2 cm as shown in Fig. 5 along with the rotational ellipsoids associated with the four edge path and two diagonal path measurements.

To facilitate the fingertip position estimate the echo path measurements which define the major axes of the rotational ellipsoids are augmented by the sphere diameter. The center of sphere is then calculated as the intersection of these augmented rotational ellipsoids and the fingertip position is obtained as the closest point of the sphere to the transducer array.

Although three path measurements would be sufficient to calculate the 3D coordinates of the sphere centre, a maximum likelihood estimate is used in this work which applies the measurements of all six echo paths. Assuming uncorrelated measurement noise the sphere center coordinates $\xi = [\xi_x, \xi_y, \xi_z]^T$ are estimated as

$$\hat{\xi} = \operatorname*{argmin}_{\xi} \sum_{i=1}^{6} \left(L_{a_i} - \|\mathbf{x}_{R_i} - \xi\| - \|\xi - \mathbf{x}_{T_i}\| \right)^2 \tag{2}$$

with the coordinates of the transmitter ($\mathbf{x}_{T_i}$) and receiver ($\mathbf{x}_{R_i}$) and the augmented echo path length L_{a_i} of the ith measurement, respectively.

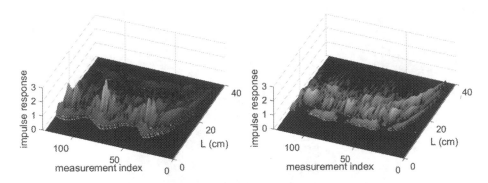

Fig. 6. Echo path impulse responses over time with the threshold applied, for (left) an edge path and (right) a diagonal path.

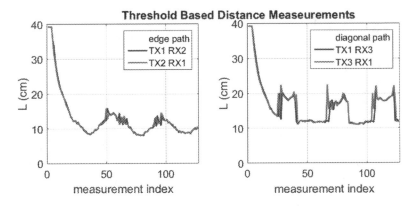

Fig. 7. Measured echo path distances for thresholding.

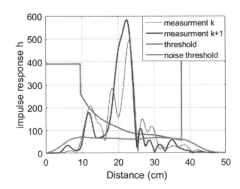

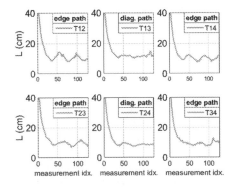

Fig. 8. Subsequent echo path impulse responses. The fingertip echo of the second measurement dropped below the threshold.

Fig. 9. Distance measurements with advanced peak search.

5   Fingertip Tracking Experiment

For the fingertip tracking experiment discussed in this section, the hand with the index finger pointing towards the transducer array is initially approaching the array from outside the maximum recording range of 15 cm (also see Fig. 3). Once the fingertip is approximately 4 cm above the array the index finger performs a clockwise circular motion.

Figure 6 shows the sequence of echo impulse responses after applying the threshold and Fig. 7 depicts the associated echo path length measurements. It can be observed that especially for the diagonal path where the geometry is less favourable the fingertip echo can drop below the threshold.

This scenario is also plotted in Fig. 8 which shows two consecutive echo path impulse responses. At time k the fingertip echo is above the threshold, but at time $k+1$ due to destructive interference from the strong hand echo the fingertip echo drops below the threshold. In these cases the algorithm returns the hand echo distance instead resulting in the discontinuous measurements shown on the right hand side of Fig. 7.

The performance can be improved when tracking the fingertip echo also below the threshold with a bias against too rapid distance changes, and combining consecutive measurements of the same echo path but with reversed transmitter and receiver. The resulting distance measurements are shown in Fig. 9. The associated 3D fingertip trajectory is calculated according to Sect. 4 and is plotted in Fig. 10.

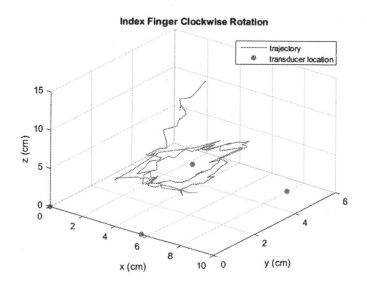

Fig. 10. Fingertip trajectory.

6   Conclusions

This contribution presented a 3D fingertip tracking system based on echo path measurements of a planar US transducer array. To isolate the small fingertip echo from the stronger hand echo a sufficient high spatial resolution of the echo path was required. This resolution was obtained by using the 65 kHz to 90 kHz US frequency band of the CMUT transducers.

References

1. Anzinger, S., et al.: Low power capacitive ultrasonic transceiver array for airborne object detection. In: 2020 IEEE 33rd International Conference on Micro Electro Mechanical Systems (MEMS), pp. 853–856 (2020)
2. Cheng, H., Lou, W.: PD-FMCW: push the limit of device-free acoustic sensing using phase difference in FMCW. IEEE Trans. Mob. Comput., 1 (2022). https://doi.org/10.1109/TMC.2022.3162631
3. Ibrahim, E.A., Geilen, M., Huisken, J., Li, M., de Gyvez, J.P.: Low complexity multi-directional in-air ultrasonic gesture recognition using a tcn. In: 2020 Design, Automation Test in Europe Conference Exhibition (DATE), pp. 1259–1264 (2020). https://doi.org/10.23919/DATE48585.2020.9116482
4. Infineon Technologies AG: Product brief ES - IM70A135UT; XENSIV^{TM} MEMS microphone with 70 dB(A) SNR and ultrasonic receiving/sending capabilities, December 2011. https://www.infineon.com/dgdl/Infineon-MEMS_IM70A135UT-ProductBrief-v01_00-EN.pdf?fileId=8ac78c8c7ddc01d7017e4d7af9084967
5. Infineon Technologies AG: XENSIV^{TM} MEMS microphones with ultrasonic capabilities, June 2022. https://www.infineon.com/cms/en/product/promopages/mems-microphones/
6. Ling, K., Dai, H., Liu, Y., Liu, A.X., Wang, W., Gu, Q.: Ultragesture: fine-grained gesture sensing and recognition. IEEE Trans. Mob. Comput. **21**(7), 2620–2636 (2022). https://doi.org/10.1109/TMC.2020.3037241
7. Microchip: XDM160225 - 3Dtouchpad, November 2021. https://www.microchip.com/en-us/development-tool/DM160225
8. Nandakumar, R., Iyer, V., Tan, D., Gollakota, S.: Fingerio: using active sonar for fine-grained finger tracking. In: Proceedings of the 2016 CHI Conference on Human Factors in Computing Systems, CHI 2016, pp. 1515–1525. Association for Computing Machinery, New York (2016). https://doi.org/10.1145/2858036.2858580, https://doi.org/10.1145/2858036.2858580
9. Saez, B., Mendez, J., Molina, M., Castillo, E., Pegalajar, M., Morales, D.P.: Gesture recognition with ultrasounds and edge computing. IEEE Access **9**, 38999–39008 (2021). https://doi.org/10.1109/ACCESS.2021.3064390
10. Tap Systems Inc: Tap, June 2022. https://www.tapwithus.com/
11. Van Dam, B., Murillo, Y., Li, M., Pollin, S.: In-air ultrasonic 3d-touchscreen with gesture recognition using existing hardware for smart devices. In: 2016 IEEE International Workshop on Signal Processing Systems (SiPS), pp. 74–79 (2016). https://doi.org/10.1109/SiPS.2016.21

An Artificial Skin from Conductive Rubber

Sabrina Affortunati$^{(\boxtimes)}$ and Bernhard Zagar

Johannes Kepler University, Linz 4040, Austria
sabrina.affortunati@jku.at

Abstract. Electrical impedance tomography (EIT) is a non-invasive technique that allows the detection and localization of impedance changes. By using impedance tomography to detect impedance changes in rubber with carbon nanotubes, an artificial skin for robots can be obtained. The goal of this work is a complex impedance tomography which allows at the same time to localize force and to detect objects in the proximity of the surface. For this purpose a rubber with carbon nanotubes was used, the necessary electronics for the excitation of the electrodes and for the measurement was developed and the evaluation of the inverse reconstruction problem was implemented on the computer. Results for a real-valued reconstruction are shown and a simulation is used to study the complex reconstruction.

Keywords: Complex electrical impedance tomography · Carbon nanotubes · Inverse problem

1 Introduction

Human-robot communication is an interesting field of research. To bring robot and human closer together not only visual and oral communication but also tactile communication are of great importance. Even with prostheses, tactile awareness would help the patient not only through better control but also through reduced phantom limb pain [4]. For these purpose it is necessary to create an artificial skin able to recognize caresses and strength at the same time. Many different techniques have been experimented to create an artificial skin: piezoresistive, optical, magnetic and electrical [1]. The use of impedance tomography is inexpensive and very versatile. For the development of an artificial skin rubber with carbon nanotubes was used. Carbon nanotubes enable conductivity of rubber and thus make the application of impedance tomography possible [7]. In impedance tomography, electrodes are placed around the perimeter of the region of interest (ROI). A current source is connected to one electrode and the resulting potential distribution is measured at the remaining electrodes. The whole operation is then performed for each electrode. A change in impedance in the ROI (Ω) causes a different potential distribution and can thus be measured at the electrodes. By derivation from Maxwell's equations, the problem of impedance tomography can be formulated mathematically as follows.

© The Author(s), under exclusive license to Springer Nature Switzerland AG 2022
R. Moreno-Díaz et al. (Eds.): EUROCAST 2022, LNCS 13789, pp. 287–294, 2022.
https://doi.org/10.1007/978-3-031-25312-6_33

$$\nabla \cdot (\gamma \nabla u) = 0 \tag{1}$$

$$\int_\Omega \frac{\partial u}{\partial \boldsymbol{n}} \gamma = \begin{cases} +i, & \text{for excitation electrode.} \\ -i, & \text{for ground electrode.} \\ 0, & \text{otherwise.} \end{cases} \quad u + z_l \frac{\partial u}{\partial \boldsymbol{n}} \gamma = V_l \quad \text{on electrode } l \tag{2}$$

where $\gamma = \sigma + \imath \omega \epsilon$ is the complex admittivity and u is the potential. Equation 1 is the mathematical formulation of the problem in Ω, while Eq. 2 are the boundary conditions. [2]

The electrodes for the measurement were selected by an Arduino through multiplexer. To transfer the measured values to the computer, the AC voltage was converted to a DC voltage with a lock-in amplifier and the values were transferred to the computer with the Arduino. The inverse ill-posed problem was solved in Matlab. For this, a sensitivity matrix was calculated by finite element (FEM) simulation and the inverse problem was solved with regularization.

2   Experimental Setup

The experimental setup consists of the hardware which is used for excitation and measurement, and the sensor made of conductive rubber. In this chapter, the hardware and the functionality of the sensor will be discussed in more detail.

2.1   Hardware

The basic structure of the hardware can be seen in Fig. 1. The six main components, which are described in more detail here, are controlled from the computer via an Arduino. The Arduino is also used to transmit the measured values to the computer, where the solution of the inverse problem and thus the reconstruction are done.

DDS Synthetizer. The AD9850 [5] was used as a signal generator. It provides the necessary input signal for the voltage controlled current source. It uses direct digital synthesis (DDS) to generate a sinusoidal signal whose frequency can be set between (0.0291 Hz and 125 MHz) via Arduino using 32 bits. The amplitude of the output signal can be adjusted by an external resistor. A benefit of the chip is its wide frequency range and easy programming.

BP Filter. Since the output signal of the AD9850 is a non-zero average signal, it is necessary to filter out the DC component, therefore a fourth-order Butterworth high-pass filter with a cut-off frequency of 1 kHz was designed. Since it is also necessary to suppress the effects of aliased images, which come from the discrete signal before the D/A converter, the signal is also filtered by a Butterworth low-pass filter with a cut-off frequency of 600 kHz.

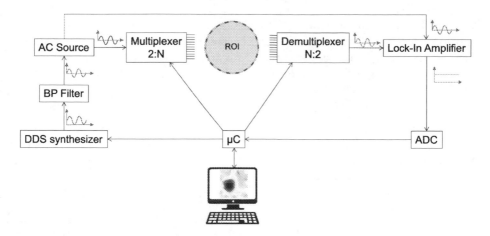

Fig. 1. Schematic representation of the used experimental setup. The arrows indicate the direction of the communication or the signal. The graphs next to the arrows sketch the waveform in the corresponding path.

AC Source. The current source is one of the most important components in the EIT hardware as it generates the signal used to excite the sensor. When designing the current source, care must be taken to obtain low DC error, good AC behaviour, high compliance voltage and high internal impedance. Especially the last requirement plays an important role in impedance tomography as it ensures that the current flowing through the sample is independent of the conductivity of the sample, and thus the boundary condition of Eq. 2 can be fulfilled.

The voltage controlled current source finally used is based on the current source presented in [6], which uses a composite amplifier consisting of the high precision amplifier ADA4870 and the high speed amplifier LT6275. Characteristic values obtained with a LTSpice simulation are given in Table 1. The current source is compared with a triple amplifier enhanced Howland current source (TOAEHCS) often mentioned in literature. As can be seen from the values, an improvement is achieved by the composite amplifier, but we have also a higher component cost. Even the output impedance at 100 kHz was improved by about one fifth.

Table 1. Simulated values for the current source.

	CAEHCS	TOAEHCS
Output current offset/nA	150	250
Bandwith/MHz	25.9	13.4
Output noise density @ 100 kHz/nV Hz$^{-0.5}$	11.7	15.2
Output impedance @ 100 kHz/MΩ	22.6	16.7

Multiplexer/Demultiplexer. The ADG1408 (8×1) and ADG1409 (4×1) were used as multiplexers. These are characterized by a very small and flat on-resistance. Since adjacent electrodes were always used for excitation in the application, it was possible to address them simultaneously by combining one ADG1409 and two ADG1408s.

Lock-In Amplifier. In order to measure the in-phase and quadrature component of the signals on the electrodes, the balanced modulator/demodulator AD630 was used as a lock-in amplifier. This gave a DC signal proportional to the amplitude to be measured. The input signal of the voltage-controlled current source served as the reference signal.

ADC. The output voltage of lock-in amplifier was digitized with a 4-Channel (2 used) 16-Bit ADC. The ADS1115 was used and the communication with the Arduino was done via I2C. The main feature of this ADC is the programmable comparator which allows measurements of large and small signals with high resolution (LSB size from 187.5 µV to 7.8125 µV).

2.2 Sensor

The sensor used consists of rubber and carbon particles. The conductivity of the material can be modulated by changing the amount of carbon particles [7]. The ratio of conductivity to the amount of filler is described by the percolation curve. This is characterized by a rapid increase in conductivity as the percolation threshold is passed, followed by a flattening out of the curve. Just as the conductivity changes with the quantity of particles, the admittivity also changes with pressure [3], as this leads to a local decrease in the distance between the filler particles. Since the rubber becomes conductive due to the carbon particles and its admittivity depends on the pressure, a local resolution of the force can be obtained by using impedance tomography.

For the measurement, 16 electrodes of copper were attached around a block of conductive rubber (4 on each side) with silver conductive epoxy adhesive, see Fig. 2. The top was isolated from the finger/object by an insulating foil, to prevent DC current from flowing through the finger.

3   Results

3.1   Solution of the Inverse Problem

The inverse problem to be solved represents a non-linear and ill-posed problem. In order to solve it, it is therefore necessary to incorporate a priori information through processes such as regularization or machine learning. In this case, Noser (Newton's One Step Error Reconstructor) was used for reconstruction. This is a method based on the least squares method. The recursive Newton's method

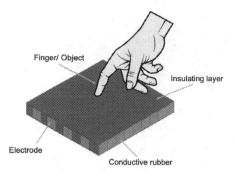

Fig. 2. Model of the sensor including electrodes, insulating tape and object to be detected.

$(\gamma^{new} = \gamma^{old} - [\mathbf{F}'(\gamma^{old})]^{-1}\mathbf{F}'(\gamma^{old}))$ is converted to a one step method using an initial guess of γ and substituting the ill-conditioned matrix $\mathbf{F}'(\gamma^{old})$, more detailed information can be found in [8]. Through the one step approximation the Noser algorithm results as a fast algorithm suitable for live monitoring, the disadvantage is the resulting loss of accuracy.

3.2   Measurement Results

To test the hardware and reconstruction procedures, measurements were made with a current of 1 mA amplitude and a frequency of 20 kH. However, only the real part was considered. For the complex reconstruction, please refer to the following subsection, where it was tested by simulation. Figure 3 shows the results obtained when pressure is applied by a finger at one point. The pressure causes the carbon particles in the polymer to rearrange and form new conductive paths, thereby locally increasing the conductivity. This can also be seen in the figure, where the two lower images show the reconstruction to the situations shown above. The results give an accurate determination of the point at which the force acts, but the Noser algorithm produces artefacts as e.g. that the point at which the force is applied is spread to a larger area.

3.3   Simulation Results

In order to detect and locally resolve not only pressure but also proximity, it is necessary to perform a complex reconstruction. Therefore, the quadrature component is also taken into account and thus also a capacitive coupling through the outside. The complex reconstruction was only carried out with simulated results. For this purpose, the finite element method (FEM) was used to simulate the approach of a finger to the sensor. The finger was simulated by nested cylinders, the assumed values of the admittivities of the different layers of the finger are shown in Fig. 4.

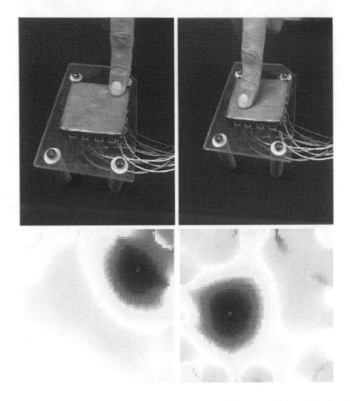

Fig. 3. Change in conductivity due to application of force as shown in the photos. Red pixels mark a positive change, blue a negative change. (Color figure online)

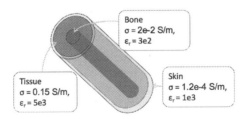

Fig. 4. Simulation model of the finger with assumed values of conductivity and permittivity for skin, tissue and bone

The results of the simulation and reconstruction are shown in Fig. 5. It can be observed that as the distance between the finger and the sensor diminishes, there is a negative change in the reconstructed permittivity, whereas the value of the conductivity does not really change. Only when force is applied by the finger, due to the local increase in conductivity, there is a change in both the real and imaginary parts.

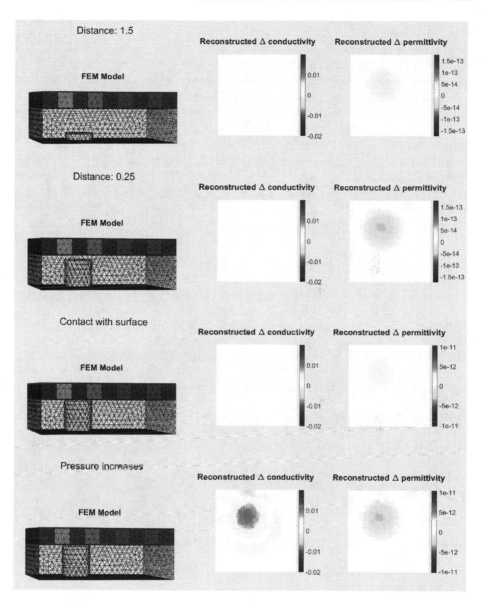

Fig. 5. Results of complex impedance tomography. The first column shows the FEM model, the second column shows the real part of the reconstruction and the rightmost column shows the imaginary part of the reconstruction. The distance between the finger and the sensor decreases from top to bottom. Blue marks a negative change, red a positive change. (Color figure online)

4 Conclusion

A prototype for an artificial skin based on impedance tomography was developed. This is capable of detecting and localizing applied force. The disadvantage of EIT is the poor spatial resolution, which is compensated by the cheapness and versatility of the method. By means of a simulation, it was shown how a possible complex-valued impedance tomography could detect not only force but also proximity, and could thus be used for robots to provide additional safety. The difficulty that emerges from the simulation is the relationship between the in phase and quadrature components: The quadrature component is much smaller and therefore difficult to measure in the actual setup. One idea to solve this problem would be to use a signal with a higher frequency to strengthen the capacitive coupling and consequently measure the approximation.

References

1. Silvera-Tawil, D., Rye, M., Soleimani, M., Velonaki, M.: Electrical Impedance Tomography for Artificial Sensitive Robotic Skin: a review. IEEE Sensors J. (2015). https://doi.org/10.1109/JSEN.2014.2375346
2. Mueller, J.E., Siltanen, S.: Linear and Nonlinear Inverse Problems with Practical Applications. (2012). https://doi.org/10.1137/1.9781611972344
3. Heng, Y., et al.: Strain-sensitive electrical conductivity of carbon nanotube-graphene-filled rubber composites under cyclic loading. Nanoscale **11**(2), 578–586 (2019)
4. Chortos, A., Liu, J., Bao, Z.: Pursuing prosthetic electronic skin. Nature Materials. **15**(9), 937–950 (2016). https://doi.org/10.1038/nmat4671
5. Analog Devices: CMOS, 125 MHz Complete DDS Synthesizer. AD9850 datasheet (2004)
6. Jiang, N.: A Large Current Source with High Accuracy and Fast Settling. In: Analog Dialogue, pp. 52–10 (2018)
7. Rahaman, M., Khastgir, D., Aldalbahi, A.K. (eds.): Carbon-Containing Polymer Composites. SSPCM, Springer, Singapore (2019). https://doi.org/10.1007/978-981-13-2688-2
8. Margaret, C., et al.: NOSER: An algorithm for solving the inverse conductivity problem. Int. Imag. Syst. Technol. **2**, 66–75 (1990)

Neural Network Based Single-Carrier Frequency Domain Equalization

Stefan Baumgartner[1,2]([📧]) [ID], Oliver Lang[1] [ID], and Mario Huemer[1,2] [ID]

[1] Institute of Signal Processing, Johannes Kepler University Linz, Linz, Austria
{stefan.baumgartner,oliver.lang,mario.huemer}@jku.at
[2] JKU LIT SAL eSPML Lab, Johannes Kepler University Linz, Linz, Austria

Abstract. The task of equalization on the receiver side of a wireless communication system is typically accomplished with model-based estimation methods. However, the utilization of data-driven approaches, e.g., neural networks (NNs), for equalization is in focus of current research. In this work, we investigate two different NNs for single-carrier frequency domain equalization. We elaborate on how existing model knowledge can be incorporated into NNs, we introduce a data normalization scheme required for the regarded NNs, and we compare these data-driven methods with model-based approaches concerning performance and complexity.

Keywords: Model-inspired neural networks · Single-carrier frequency domain equalization

1 Introduction

Equalization, also known as data estimation, has to be conducted on the receiver side of a wireless communication system to combat the effects of multipath propagation on transmitted data. This task is typically accomplished by using model-based estimation methods. However, methods yielding optimal performance are generally computationally infeasible, requiring the use of less complex, sub-optimal methods in practice. Additionally, modeling errors and wrong statistical assumptions may severely impair their performance. Since some of the aforementioned issues can be resolved with data-driven approaches like neural networks (NNs), data estimation with NNs has been investigated [7,9] recently. In most of the currently published works, NN-based equalization is regarded for multiple-input multiple-output (MIMO) communication systems over uncorrelated Rayleigh fading channels. In this work, we employ two different model-inspired NNs[1] for single-carrier frequency domain equalization (SC-FDE) systems. For SC-FDE, where assumptions typically made for the aforementioned MIMO systems do not hold, it turns out that without data normalization the regarded NNs perform poorly. We introduce required pre-processing steps of the data, and we compare the NN-based approaches concerning performance and complexity with model-based equalizers.

---

[1] We refer to an NN whose structure is deduced from model knowledge as "model-inspired".

R. Moreno-Díaz et al. (Eds.): EUROCAST 2022, LNCS 13789, pp. 295–302, 2022.
https://doi.org/10.1007/978-3-031-25312-6_34

2   System Model

In SC-FDE communication systems [4], data is transmitted via an SC modulation scheme in a block-wise manner. That is, blocks of N_d payload data symbols are separated by guard intervals of length N_g. In this work, we regard employing a deterministic sequence, the so-called unique word (UW), as a guard interval [11]. Assuming a sufficiently long guard interval, this transmission scheme allows processing each data block individually and independently of all other transmitted data blocks on receiver side. At the transmitter, the transmit sequence containing payload and guard intervals is upsampled and root-raised cosine (RRC) pulse shaped. The resulting signal is transmitted over a multipath channel and additionally disturbed by additive white Gaussian noise (AWGN). On receiver side, every received data block including its succeeding guard interval is transformed to frequency domain, followed by matched filtering (MF), downsampling, and equalization. The equivalent complex baseband model of SC-FDE data transmission with UW guard intervals can be formulated as [8]

$$\mathbf{y}_{\mathrm{r}}' = \tilde{\mathbf{H}}' \mathbf{F}_N \begin{bmatrix} \mathbf{d}' \\ \mathbf{u}' \end{bmatrix} + \mathbf{w}' , \tag{1}$$

where $\mathbf{y}_{\mathrm{r}}' \in \mathbb{C}^N$, $N = N_d + N_g$, is the received vector at the input of the equalizer, i.e., after applying discrete Fourier transform (DFT), MF, and downsampling on a received block of data including the guard interval. Since MF is conducted in frequency domain, the matched filter can be adapted optimally to the channel distorted transmit pulse. This leads to a real-valued diagonal matrix $\tilde{\mathbf{H}}' \in \mathbb{R}^{N \times N}$, where the main diagonal consists of the sampled frequency response of the cascade of upsampler, pulse shaping filter, multipath channel, matched filter, and downsampler. Furthermore, $\mathbf{F}_N \in \mathbb{C}^{N \times N}$ is the N-point DFT matrix, $\mathbf{d}' \in \mathbb{S}'^{N_d}$ is the transmitted data vector containing data symbols drawn from the symbol alphabet $\mathbb{S}' \subset \mathbb{C}$, $\mathbf{u}' \in \mathbb{C}^{N_g}$ is the UW, and $\mathbf{w}' \sim \mathcal{CN}(\mathbf{0}, N\sigma_n^2\tilde{\mathbf{H}}')$ is the matched filtered, circularly symmetric complex Gaussian noise vector in frequency domain, where σ_n^2 is the variance of the AWGN in time domain. Assuming perfect channel knowledge on receiver side, removing the influence of the known UW on the received vector $\mathbf{y}_{\mathrm{r}}'$ leads to the model

$$\mathbf{y}' = \mathbf{y}_{\mathrm{r}}' - \tilde{\mathbf{H}}'\mathbf{M}''\mathbf{u}' = \tilde{\mathbf{H}}'\mathbf{M}'\mathbf{d}' + \mathbf{w}' = \mathbf{H}'\mathbf{d}' + \mathbf{w}' , \tag{2}$$

with $\mathbf{M}' \in \mathbb{C}^{N \times N_d}$ and $\mathbf{M}'' \in \mathbb{C}^{N \times N_g}$ consisting of the first N_d columns of $\mathbf{F}_N$ and the remaining N_g columns of $\mathbf{F}_N$, respectively, and $\mathbf{H}' = \tilde{\mathbf{H}}'\mathbf{M}'$.

3   Model-Based Equalizers

Based on (2), several model-based approaches exist to estimate $\mathbf{d}'$. In the following, we present only two methods with which we compare the NN-based equalizers.

Applying the Bayesian Gauss-Markov theorem [5] on (2) yields the (comparatively low-complex) linear minimum mean square error (LMMSE) estimator

$$\hat{\mathbf{d}}' = \mathbf{M}'^H \left(\tilde{\mathbf{H}}' \mathbf{M}' \mathbf{M}'^H + \frac{N\sigma_n^2}{\sigma_d^2} \mathbf{I} \right)^{-1} \mathbf{y}', \tag{3}$$

where σ_d^2 is the variance of the symbol alphabet $\mathbb{S}'$.

A broadly known non-linear data estimation method is the decision feedback equalizer (DFE). In this iterative method, a symbol-wise LMMSE estimation of the data symbol d'_k, $k \in \{0, ..., N_d - 1\}$ with the smallest error variance is conducted in every iteration, followed by slicing to the nearest possible symbol. For a comprehensive description of the method, we refer to [1], where the implemented DFE is elaborated for a different communication system.

4 Neural Network Approaches

We investigate to replace a model-based equalizer by an NN, whereby all other processing steps on receiver side (transformation of the received data to frequency domain, matched filtering, and downsampling) remain the same. Since standard methods for, e.g., NN training, assume real-valued input data, we map the complex-valued model (2) to its corresponding real-valued model. The complex-to-real transformation is carried out by mapping all vectors $\mathbf{a}'$ and matrices $\mathbf{A}'$ to

$$\mathbf{a} = \begin{bmatrix} \mathrm{Re}\{\mathbf{a}'\} \\ \mathrm{Im}\{\mathbf{a}'\} \end{bmatrix} \quad \text{and} \quad \mathbf{A} = \begin{bmatrix} \mathrm{Re}\{\mathbf{A}'\} & -\mathrm{Im}\{\mathbf{A}'\} \\ \mathrm{Im}\{\mathbf{A}'\} & \mathrm{Re}\{\mathbf{A}'\} \end{bmatrix},$$

respectively. The real-valued system model follows to

$$\mathbf{y} = \tilde{\mathbf{H}}\mathbf{M}\mathbf{d} + \mathbf{w} = \mathbf{H}\mathbf{d} + \mathbf{w}, \tag{4}$$

with $\mathbf{w} \sim \mathcal{N}(\mathbf{0}, \frac{1}{2}N\sigma_n^2\tilde{\mathbf{H}})$ and a real-valued data vector $\mathbf{d} \in \mathbb{S}^{2N_d}$ containing symbols from the real-valued alphabet $\mathbb{S} = \mathrm{Re}\{\mathbb{S}'\} = \mathrm{Im}\{\mathbb{S}'\}$, since a symmetric alphabet $\mathbb{S}'$ is assumed.

The NNs are trained to estimate the one-hot representations $\mathbf{d}_{\mathrm{oh},k} \in \{0,1\}^{|\mathbb{S}|}$ of the data symbols d_k (for the definition of the one hot mapping $d_k \mapsto \mathbf{d}_{\mathrm{oh},k}$ we refer to [1]). That is, the output of a trained NN-based data estimator is an estimate $\hat{\mathbf{d}}_{\mathrm{oh}} \in \mathbb{R}^{2N_d|\mathbb{S}|}$ of $\mathbf{d}_{\mathrm{oh}} \in \{0,1\}^{2N_d|\mathbb{S}|}$ consisting of the stacked one-hot vectors $\mathbf{d}_{\mathrm{oh},k}$ instead of an estimate of the data vector $\mathbf{d} \in \mathbb{R}^{2N_d}$. Combined with a quadratic loss function for NN training, the outputs $\hat{\mathbf{d}}_{\mathrm{oh},k}$ of a trained NN-based data estimator contain approximations of the posterior probabilities $\Pr(d_k = s_j|\mathbf{y})$, where s_j is the jth symbol of $\mathbb{S}$, $j \in \{0, ..., |\mathbb{S}|-1\}$ (c.f., e.g., [9]).

4.1 Data Normalization

The investigations of NN-based data estimation for unique word (UW)-OFDM systems [1] highlighted the importance of data normalization for communication systems other than MIMO systems over uncorrelated Rayleigh fading channels. We have investigated several options for data normalization. In the following, we introduce the data normalization scheme that lead to the best performance of the regarded NN-based equalizers. After conducting this normalization, the resulting noise is white and its variance is independent of the channel realization.

Considering the real-valued model (4), the signal-to-noise ratio (SNR) at the input of the equalizer can be written as

$$\text{SNR} = \frac{E_{\mathbf{d}}[\|\tilde{\mathbf{H}}\mathbf{M}\mathbf{d}\|_2^2]}{E_{\mathbf{w}}[\|\mathbf{w}\|_2^2]} = \frac{E_{\mathbf{d}}[\mathbf{d}^T\mathbf{M}^T\tilde{\mathbf{H}}\tilde{\mathbf{H}}\mathbf{M}\mathbf{d}]}{E_{\mathbf{w}}[\mathbf{w}^T\mathbf{w}]} = \frac{\sigma_d^2}{N\sigma_n^2} \cdot \frac{\text{tr}\{\tilde{\mathbf{H}}\mathbf{M}\mathbf{M}^T\tilde{\mathbf{H}}\}}{\text{tr}\{\tilde{\mathbf{H}}\}}, \quad (5)$$

with the trace operator $\text{tr}\{.\}$, and with $E_{\mathbf{d}}[.]$ and $E_{\mathbf{w}}[.]$ denoting the expectation operators averaging over the probability mass function of $\mathbf{d}$ and the probability density function of $\mathbf{w}$, respectively. The variance of an element w_j of the noise vector $\mathbf{w}$, $j \in \{0, ..., 2N - 1\}$, is given by

$$\text{var}(w_j) = \frac{1}{2}N\sigma_n^2[\tilde{\mathbf{H}}]_{jj} = \frac{\sigma_d^2}{2\,\text{SNR}} \cdot \frac{\text{tr}\{\tilde{\mathbf{H}}\mathbf{M}\mathbf{M}^T\tilde{\mathbf{H}}\}}{\text{tr}\{\tilde{\mathbf{H}}\}}[\tilde{\mathbf{H}}]_{jj}, \quad (6)$$

where the relation between σ_n^2 and the SNR, given by Eq. (5), is inserted in the last step. In order to obtain a noise variance $\text{var}(w_j)$ which is independent of both the index j and the channel realization, the system model (4) is multiplied by $\mathbf{K} = \kappa\tilde{\mathbf{H}}^{-1/2}$, with $\kappa = \sqrt{\text{tr}\{\tilde{\mathbf{H}}\}/\text{tr}\{\tilde{\mathbf{H}}\mathbf{M}\mathbf{M}^T\tilde{\mathbf{H}}\}}$. The normalization is implemented as part of pre-processing by multiplying both $\mathbf{y}$ and $\tilde{\mathbf{H}}$ by $\mathbf{K}$.

4.2   Knowledge Aided Fully-Connected Neural Network

We term the first approach as knowledge-aided fully connected NN (KAFCNN), which consists of two sequential building blocks. In the second block it incorporates the knowledge that the transmitted data symbols are defined in time domain, but are estimated on basis of the received data in frequency domain. This should reduce the required number of learnable parameters leading to an easier trainable NN. Besides, the NN-based data estimator should output estimates for the one-hot data vectors. To this end, we reformulate the data vector $\mathbf{d}$ as $\mathbf{d} = \mathbf{D}_{\text{oh}}\mathbf{s}$, where $\mathbf{s} = [s_0, ..., s_{|\mathbb{S}|-1}]^T$ consists of the stacked symbols of the real-valued symbol alphabet $\mathbb{S}$ and

$$\mathbf{D}_{\text{oh}} = \begin{bmatrix} \mathbf{d}_{\text{oh},0}^T \\ \vdots \\ \mathbf{d}_{\text{oh},N_d-1}^T \end{bmatrix} =: \begin{bmatrix} \mathbf{c}_0 \cdots \mathbf{c}_{|\mathbb{S}|-1} \end{bmatrix}$$

contains the one-hot data symbol vectors. The columns of $\mathbf{D}_{\text{oh}}$ are defined as the vectors $\mathbf{c}_i \in \{0, 1\}^{N_d}$, $i \in \{0, ..., |\mathbb{S}| - 1\}$. Consequently, the normalized real-valued system model can be reformulated as

$$\kappa\tilde{\mathbf{H}}^{-1/2}\mathbf{y} = \kappa\tilde{\mathbf{H}}^{1/2} \begin{bmatrix} \mathbf{M}\mathbf{c}_0 & \mathbf{M}\mathbf{c}_1 & \cdots & \mathbf{M}\mathbf{c}_{|\mathbb{S}|-1} \end{bmatrix} \mathbf{s} + \kappa\tilde{\mathbf{H}}^{-1/2}\mathbf{w}. \quad (7)$$

Based on this reformulated model, the inputs of KAFCNN, as well as its structure are defined. Given the inputs $\kappa\tilde{\mathbf{H}}^{-1/2}\mathbf{y}$ and $\mathrm{diag}(\kappa\tilde{\mathbf{H}}^{-1/2})$, the first building block, a fully connected NN (FCNN), is employed to estimate $\mathbf{a}_i := \mathbf{M}\mathbf{c}_i s_i$. The FCNN is comprised of L hidden layers, n_h neurons per hidden layer, as well as weighted residual connections[2] and SELU activation functions [6] for a better training behavior. Its outputs, the estimates $\hat{\mathbf{a}}_i$, are further processed in the second block by exploiting the orthogonal columns of $\mathbf{M}$. That is, each $\hat{\mathbf{a}}_i$ is multiplied by $\frac{1}{N\,s_i}\mathbf{M}^T$ to obtain the estimates $\hat{\mathbf{c}}_i = \frac{1}{N\,s_i}\mathbf{M}^T\hat{\mathbf{a}}_i$, and thus $\hat{\mathbf{D}}_{\mathrm{oh}}$ and $\hat{\mathbf{d}}_{\mathrm{oh},k}$.

4.3   DetNet

Original Version. The layer structure of DetNet, which is proposed in [9] for MIMO systems, is inferred by deep unfolding [3] an iterative projected gradient descent method that is applied to the optimization problem of the model-based maximum likelihood estimator for the normalized system model

$$\hat{\mathbf{d}} = \arg\max_{\mathbf{d}\in\mathbb{S}^{2N_d}} p(\kappa\tilde{\mathbf{H}}^{-1/2}\mathbf{y}|\mathbf{d}) = \arg\min_{\mathbf{d}\in\mathbb{S}^{2N_d}} \underbrace{||\tilde{\mathbf{H}}^{-1/2}\mathbf{y} - \tilde{\mathbf{H}}^{1/2}\mathbf{M}\mathbf{d}||_2^2}_{f(\mathbf{d})}, \qquad (8)$$

where $p(\kappa\tilde{\mathbf{H}}^{-1/2}\mathbf{y}|\mathbf{d})$ is a conditional probability density function. The kth iteration step of a projected gradient descent optimization applied to (8) can be written as

$$\hat{\mathbf{d}}_k = \Pi\left[\hat{\mathbf{d}}_{k-1} - \delta_k \left.\frac{\partial f(\mathbf{d})}{\partial \mathbf{d}}\right|_{\hat{\mathbf{d}}_{k-1}}\right] = \Pi\left[\hat{\mathbf{d}}_{k-1} + 2\delta_k\mathbf{M}^T(\mathbf{y} - \tilde{\mathbf{H}}\mathbf{M}\hat{\mathbf{d}}_{k-1})\right], \quad (9)$$

where δ_k is the step size and $\Pi[.]$ describes a non-linear projection to a convex subspace $\mathcal{D}$ containing the set of possible data vectors $\mathbf{d}$, i.e. $\mathbb{S}^{2N_d} \subset \mathcal{D} \subset \mathbb{R}^{2N_d}$. The structure of the kth layer of the L DetNet layers, $k \in \{0, ..., L-1\}$, is deduced from Eq. (9). That is, the layer input $\hat{\mathbf{d}}_{k-1}$ is transformed to a temporal layer variable $\mathbf{q}_k$ following

$$\mathbf{q}_k = \hat{\mathbf{d}}_{k-1} + \delta_{1k}\mathbf{M}^T\mathbf{y} - \delta_{2k}\mathbf{M}^T\tilde{\mathbf{H}}\mathbf{M}\hat{\mathbf{d}}_{k-1}, \qquad (10)$$

where δ_{1k} and δ_{2k} are learnable parameters. This temporal variable is forwarded to an FCNN with a single hidden layer of dimension d_h, which replaces the projection $\Pi(.)$, followed by one-hot demapping to obtain the layer output $\hat{\mathbf{d}}_k$. To improve the training behavior and performance of DetNet, weighted residual connections (with weighing factor β, as already described for KAFCNN), a loss function similar to that of GoogLeNet [10], and d_v-dimensional auxiliary variables $\mathbf{v}_k$ to pass unconstrained information from layer to layer are employed additionally. We refer to [9] for further details. In the following, this original approach is termed "DetNet v1".

---

[2]   Let $\mathbf{v}_{\mathrm{in}}^{(q)}$ and $\mathbf{v}_{\mathrm{hid}}^{(q)}$ denote the input and the output of the qth hidden layer. When employing a weighted residual connection, the input $\mathbf{v}_{\mathrm{in}}^{(q+1)}$ of the follow-up hidden layer is $\mathbf{v}_{\mathrm{in}}^{(q+1)} = \beta\mathbf{v}_{\mathrm{in}}^{(q)} + (1-\beta)\mathbf{v}_{\mathrm{hid}}^{(q)}$, with $\beta \in [0,1[$.

Adjusted Version. Since DetNet is deduced by deep unfolding, the number of required layers corresponds to the number of iterations of the underlying iterative method. For iterative optimization methods, the condition number of the Hessian matrix of the optimization problem influences the number of iterations until convergence. Consequently, preconditioning is supposed to help in reducing the number of required layers of DetNet and in enhancing its performance. For UW-OFDM systems, we have already observed that Jacobi preconditioning boosts the performance of DetNet, particularly at higher signal-to-noise ratios (SNRs) [1]. It turns out that Jacobi preconditioning is not useful for SC-FDE systems, since the diagonal of $\mathbf{M}^T\tilde{\mathbf{H}}\mathbf{M}$ would be employed as a preconditioning matrix, which is a scaled identity matrix. Also, other approaches like, e.g., symmetric Gauss-Seidel preconditioning do not improve the performance of DetNet for SC-FDE systems. Consequently, we explored other approaches to adjust the cost function, from which the layer sturcture of DetNet is deduced, such that the condition number of its Hessian matrix decreases. The adjusted cost function $||\tilde{\mathbf{H}}^{-1/4}(\tilde{\mathbf{H}}^{-1/2}\mathbf{y} - \tilde{\mathbf{H}}^{1/2}\mathbf{M}\mathbf{d})||_2^2$ turns out to feature a Hessian matrix with a distinctly smaller condition number. Empirical investigations revealed, that inferring the layer structure from the adjusted cost function, leading to an adjusted computation of the temporal layer variable

$$\mathbf{q}_k = \hat{\mathbf{d}}_{k-1} + \delta_{1k}\mathbf{M}^T\tilde{\mathbf{H}}^{-1/2}\mathbf{y} - \delta_{2k}\mathbf{M}^T\tilde{\mathbf{H}}^{1/2}\mathbf{M}\hat{\mathbf{d}}_{k-1}\,, \tag{11}$$

turns out to be beneficial for the achieved bit error ratio (BER) performance at higher SNRs. However, the adjusted cost function corresponds to the cost function of the maximum likelihood estimator for a noise vector with a covariance matrix $\tilde{\mathbf{H}}^{-1/2}$, while the noise in the normalized system model is white. This leads to a degradation of the performance of the adjusted DetNet at lower SNRs, which is shown in Sect. 5. We refer to the adjusted version of DetNet as "DetNet v2".

5 Results

The regarded equalizers are evaluated in a simulation of an SC-FDE system with parameters $N = 32$, $N_d = 20$, $N_g = 12$, an RRC roll-off factor $\alpha = 0.3$, an oversampling factor $U = 2$, and a sampling frequency of $38.4\,\mathrm{MHz}$. The data symbols are drawn from a QPSK modulation alphabet. We compare the performance of the equalizers in terms of their achieved BER for uncoded data transmission in a specified E_b/N_0 range, where E_b/N_0 is a measure for the SNR, E_b is the mean energy per bit, and N_0 is the noise power spectral density on receiver side. The BER results are obtained by averaging over 7000 multipath channels following the channel model from [2], where the channel delay spread is specified to be $\tau_{\mathrm{RMS}} = 100\,\mathrm{ns}$. The transmission is conducted in form of data bursts containing 1000 blocks of payload data. The channel is assumed to be stationary for a single data burst, but to be changing independently of all other channel realizations from burst to burst. The BER results are obtained for perfect channel knowledge on receiver side.

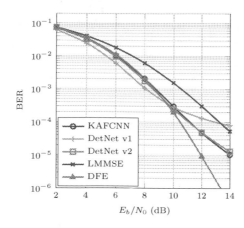

Fig. 1. BER performance comparison.

For NN training, the training set consisted of sample data transmissions over 25000 different channels, whereby every data burst in the training set was comprised of 500 blocks of payload data. The E_b/N_0 for a sample transmission is chosen randomly within the range $[5\,\mathrm{dB}, 15\,\mathrm{dB}]$.

For KAFCNN, $L = 12$, $n_h = 250$, $\beta = 0.8$, and a learning rate $\eta = 10^{-3}$ is the best hyperparameter combination found. DetNet v1 performs best with the hyperparameter setting $L = 22$, $d_h = 200$, $d_v = 20$, $\beta = 0.5$, and $\eta = 5 \cdot 10^{-4}$. For DetNet v2, $L = 15$ layers are required, which are distinctly fewer than for DetNet v1, confirming our expectation. The remaining hyperparameter configuration of DetNet v2 is $d_h = 200$, $d_v = 20$, $\beta = 0.5$, and $\eta = 6 \cdot 10^{-4}$. All NNs are trained with a batch size of 512 for 60 epochs.

As shown in Fig. 1, DetNet v1 is the best performing data estimator at low SNRs. Since DetNet v2 is inferred from the optimization function of the maximum likelihood estimator with different noise statistics, it is not surprising that it cannot achieve the same performance as DetNet v1. However, at higher SNRs the condition number of the Hessian matrix of the maximum likelihood estimator's cost function seems to be the dominating factor for the performance of both DetNets, leading to a distinctly better BER performance of DetNet v2. KAFCNN, in turn, exhibits a nearly equivalent performance as DetNet v2, and clearly outperforms the LMMSE estimator over the whole regarded E_b/N_0 range. As already observed for UW-OFDM [1], also for SC-FDE the BER curves of NN-based equalizers flatten out at higher SNRs and do not descend as steeply as the BER curve of the model-based DFE does.

Neglecting data normalization, DetNet v2 requires 562000 real-valued multiplications for the equalization of a block of payload data, while the nearly equally performing KAFCNN has a 33% higher inference complexity. This confirms that deducing the layer structure of an NN-based data estimator from model knowledge can highly reduce its inference complexity. In comparison, for the DFE[3], 30000 real-valued multiplications are needed once per data burst to determine all estimation vectors $\mathbf{e}_k$ required for estimating the data symbols d_k, and further 5100 real-valued multiplications are required for the equalization of a single payload block. That is, the equalization complexity of the DFE is distinctly lower than that of the NN-based approaches. A more detailed derivation of the complexity of the regarded equalizers is omitted due to space limitations.

6 Conclusion

In this paper, we have investigated the applicability of NN-based equalizers for SC-FDE systems. We have introduced a data normalization scheme for NN-based data estimators in SC-FDE systems, and we have compared their achieved BER performance and their computational complexity to model-based approaches. The BER performance of the regarded NNs is promising, however, their flattening out BER behavior at higher SNRs, as well as their comparably high inference complexity are still issues to be solved, motivating future research on this topic.

References

1. Baumgartner, S., Bognár, G., Lang, O., Huemer, M.: Neural network based data estimation for unique word OFDM. In: Proceedings of the 55th Asilomar Conference on Signals, Systems, and Computers, pp. 381–388 (2021)
2. Fakatselis, J.: Criteria for 2.4 GHz PHY Comparison of Modulation. IEEE Document (1997), IEEE P802.11-97/157r1
3. Hershey, J.R., Le Roux, J., Weninger, F.: Deep unfolding: model-based inspiration of novel deep architectures. arXiv preprint arXiv:1409.2574 (2014)
4. Huemer, M., Koppler, A., Weigel, R., Reindl, L.: A review of cyclically extended single carrier transmission with frequency domain equalization for broadband wireless transmission. Eur. Trans. Telecommun. 14(4), 329–341 (2003)
5. Kay, S.M.: Fundamentals of Statistical Signal Processing: Estimation Theory, vol. 1. Prentice Hall, Hoboken (1993)
6. Klambauer, G., Unterthiner, T., Mayr, A., Hochreiter, S.: Self-normalizing neural networks. In: Proceedings of the 31st International Conference on Neural Information Processing Systems (NIPS), pp. 972–981 (2017)
7. O'Shea, T., Hoydis, J.: An introduction to deep learning for the physical layer. IEEE Trans. Cogn. Commun. Netw. 3(4), 563–575 (2017)
8. Reinhardt, S., Buzid, T., Huemer, M.: Receiver structures for MIMO-SC/FDE systems. In: Proceedings of the 2006 IEEE 63rd Vehicular Technology Conference, pp. 1401–1405 (2006)
9. Samuel, N., Diskin, T., Wiesel, A.: Learning to detect. IEEE Trans. Sig. Process. 67(10), 2554–2564 (2019)
10. Szegedy, C., et al.: Going deeper with convolutions. In: Proceedings of the IEEE Conference on Computer Vision and Pattern Recognition, pp. 1–9 (2015)
11. Witschnig, H., Mayer, T., Springer, A., Maurer, L., Huemer, M., Weigel, R.: The advantages of a Known Sequence versus cyclic Prefix in a SC/FDE system. In: Proceedings of the 5th International Symposium on Wireless Personal Multimedia Communications, vol. 3, pp. 1328–1332 (2002)

---

[3] The complexity analysis is conducted in the same way as in [1].

Smooth Step Detection

Michael Lunglmayr[1]([⊠]) [iD], Yuneisy Garcia Guzman[1] [iD], Felipe Calliari[2] [iD],
and Gustavo Castro do Amaral[2] [iD]

[1] Institute of Signal Processing, Johannes Kepler University, 4040 Linz, Austria
{michael.lunglmayr,yuneisy.garcia_guzman}@jku.at
[2] Center for Telecommunication Studies of the Pontifical Catholic University of Rio
de Janeiro, 22451-090 Rio de Janeiro, Brazil
{felipe.calliari,gustavo}@opto.puc-rio.br

Abstract. We investigate the detection of smooth steps in a measured
signal using an algorithm based on linearized Bregman iterations (LBI).
Such smooth steps occur when a trend break does not occur abruptly but
gradually over multiple samples. We extend the detection algorithm by
an approximate deconvolution add-on that enables reliable step detection while even allowing reducing the number of iterations of the LBI
algorithm. We present simulation results in the context of fiber fault
detection demonstrating the detection performance that is achievable
with this combined approach, allowing reducing the required number of
iterations by approximately 40%.

Keywords: Step detection · Sparse estimation · Linearized bregman
iterations

1 Introduction

Trend break detection, or step filtering, is a prolific problem that manifests in
multiple areas of science, from econometrics [9] to fiber monitoring [8] (here,
e.g., to detect faults in fiber-optic cables), and from quantum computing [5] to
biochemistry [7].

In [2], an investigation of different methods for trend break detection is
described. There it was shown that by employing algorithms from sparse estimation, other methods could be outperformed. In [8], especially in the context of
fiber fault detection, it was shown that for sparse estimation, algorithms based
on linearized Bregman iterations (LBI) show an exceptionally good performance
while maintaining a structure that is especially beneficial for digital hardware
implementation.

The research reported in this paper has been partly funded by BMK, BMDW, and
the State of UpperAustria in the frame of SCCH, part of the COMET Programme
managed by FFG. This work is supported by: the COMET-K2 "Center for Symbiotic
Mechatronics" of the Linz Center of Mechatronics (LCM), funded by the Austrian
federal government and the federal state of Upper Austria. The authors would like to
acknowledge the support from Brazilian agencies CNPq, Capes, and FAPERJ.

R. Moreno-Díaz et al. (Eds.): EUROCAST 2022, LNCS 13789, pp. 303–310, 2022.
https://doi.org/10.1007/978-3-031-25312-6_35

Using sparse estimation for detecting steps is based on the following model

$$\mathbf{y} = \mathbf{A}\boldsymbol{\beta} + \mathbf{n}. \tag{1}$$

Here, the $m \times 1$ vector $\mathbf{y}$ is typically obtained by measurements containing steps at unknown locations. $\mathbf{n}$ is an unknown $m \times 1$ noise vector. $\boldsymbol{\beta}$ is a sparse vector of dimension $p \times 1$ where its non-zero elements represent the positions of steps in $\mathbf{y}$. An estimate of this vector is obtained by the sparse estimation process, e.g. by Algorithm 1 which is described below. For this estimation the known $m \times p$ matrix

$$\mathbf{A} = \begin{bmatrix} 1 & 1 \, 0 \, 0 \cdots 0 \, 0 \\ 2 & 1 \, 1 \, 0 \cdots 0 \, 0 \\ 3 & 1 \, 1 \, 1 \cdots 0 \, 0 \\ \vdots & \vdots \, \vdots \quad \ddots \, \vdots \, \vdots \\ p-2 & 1 \, 1 \, 1 \cdots 1 \, 0 \\ p-1 & 1 \, 1 \, 1 \cdots 1 \, 1 \end{bmatrix}, \tag{2}$$

is used. This model consists of a lower triangular matrix composed of ones representing all possible step positions in the measurement vector $\mathbf{y}$. Furthermore, an additional column is added (becoming the first column of $\mathbf{A}$) to model a slope that is typically present in measurements of optical fibers caused by distance-related damping of the measured signal.

In [8], the following algorithm for estimating $\boldsymbol{\beta}$ was proposed, as described in Algorithm 1. As one can see from the description of the algorithm, in its main loop (beginning from line 3) the main complexity is spent on additions as the algorithm is composed of simple vector operations with the rows of $\mathbf{A}$. The complexity is however spent in a large number of iterations N, where a typical value has been reported in [8] to be in the order of millions. Even when splitting a measured profile $\mathbf{y}$ into smaller sections, as investigated in [1], that significantly reduces the complexity while maintaining the estimation performance, there is still room for improvement in terms of complexity requirements. When analyzing the iteration results after the algorithm's main loop (line 16), one can observe, that the estimated $\boldsymbol{\beta}$ vector is not comprised of single non-zero values at step positions but of non-zero clusters around the step position. These clusters will vanish when using a very large number of iterations. Figure 1 shows example results around step positions for different iteration numbers N. These numbers are specified in the figure's legend as multiples of the number of measured samples m.

Following these observations, in Algorithm 1 we detected only the peak positions (line 18) in the estimated $\boldsymbol{\beta}$ (to estimate the step amplitudes we perform a least-squares estimation afterwards; line 20). This allows for avoiding running the algorithm with an excessive number of iterations. The recent work [3] represents a significant improvement of the approach. The characteristics of the clusters given a certain number of the algorithm's iterations were used in a compensation technique, called approximate deconvolution, ushering a performance increase even for a low number of iterations. This technique also prevents events

---

Algorithm 1. LBOTDR: Linearized Bregman Iteration for OTDR Fiber Profile Analysis from [8]

Input: Measurement vector y, λ, β_{start}, v_{start}, N
Output: Estimated $\hat{\beta}$, N_c

1:   $\beta^{(0)} \leftarrow \beta_{\text{start}}$
2:   $\mathbf{v}^{(0)} \leftarrow v_{\text{start}}$, $k \leftarrow 1$
3:   **while** $k < N$ **and** stopping criterion not fulfilled **do**
4:      **for** $j = 1..p$ **do**
5:         $\beta_j^{(k)} \leftarrow \text{shrink}\left(v_j^{(k)}, \lambda\right)$
6:      **end for**
7:      $i \leftarrow ((k-1) \bmod m) + 1$ $\triangleright$ cyclic re-use of rows of $\mathbf{A}$
8:      $\|\mathbf{a}_i\|_2^2 \leftarrow \sigma^2 i^2 + i$
9:      $e \leftarrow \left(y_i - \sigma i \beta_1^{(k)} - \sum_{s=2}^{i+1} \beta_s^{(k)}\right)$
                                           $\triangleright$ instantaneous error with inner product
10:    $d \leftarrow \frac{1}{\|\mathbf{a}_i\|_2^2} e$
11:    $\mathbf{v}_1^{(k+1)} \leftarrow \mathbf{v}_1^{(k)} + \sigma i d$
12:      **for** $j = 2..(i+1)$ **do**
13:         $v_j^{(k+1)} \leftarrow v_j^{(k)} + d$
14:      **end for**
15:      $k \leftarrow k + 1$
16:   **end while**
17:   $\beta_1^{(N)} \leftarrow \sigma \beta_1^{(N)}$
18:   $l \leftarrow \textsc{PeakLocations}(\beta^{(N)}, t_p)$
19:   $\mathbf{A}' \leftarrow \mathbf{A}(l, :)$
20:   $\beta' \leftarrow (\mathbf{A}'^T \mathbf{A}')^{-1} \mathbf{A}' \mathbf{y}$
21:   $\hat{\beta} \leftarrow \mathbf{0}$
22:   **for** $j = 1..$length of l **do**
23:      $\hat{\beta}_{l_j} \leftarrow \beta'_j$
24:   **end for**
25:   $N_c \leftarrow k$

---

of low magnitude from being overshadowed by nearby events of higher magnitude, which also positively impacts the algorithm's performance.

2   Approximate Deconvolution

When analyzing the estimation results for β, we observed that the shape of the cluster did not significantly change for a fixed number of iterations, except for scaling with the step size. Figure 2 shows examples of cluster shapes as well as their average in the presence of noise. This gave rise to modeling the clustering effect as a convolution of a vector with single non-zero elements per step with a pre-defined cluster shape. For our approach, we found the samples of the cluster by running multiple simulations, normalizing the cluster to height one, and averaging over it. The idea of the approximate deconvolution is to, after peak detection, scale up the cluster shape by the peak amplitude and subtract

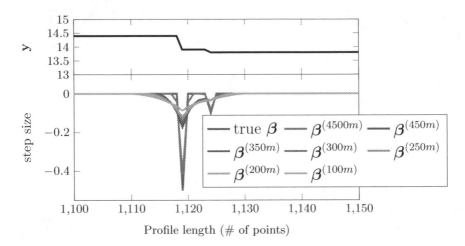

Fig. 1. Fiber profiles with abrupt and smooth steps with corresponding clusters in the LBI estimation results.

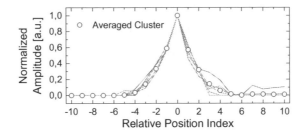

Fig. 2. Example cluster shapes in the presence of noise as well as their average. Taken from [3].

this scaled cluster shape from all points around the peak (except the peak itself) [3]. Compared to the rest of Algorithm 1, the complexity of such an approximate deconvolution can be considered negligible.

In this work, we extend this approach to steps that do not occur abruptly but follow a smooth transition, i.e., over the span of several points. Figure 3 shows the differences between abrupt and smooth steps[1]. As one can see in the middle plot on the right in this figure, a smooth step is reflected in the β-vector (the step amplitudes) as a cluster (as we deal with sampled signals, a smooth transition downwards can be represented as a decreasing sequence of negative amplitudes starting from zero, followed by an increasing sequence of negative amplitudes going back to zero again). For smooth steps, such clusters appear due to signal characteristics in contrast to the case of abrupt steps, where clusters only resulted from the algorithm itself, especially when using

---

[1] although the term *smooth step* may sound a little cumbersome at first, it is actually used across many disciplines from machine learning [4] to computer graphics [6].

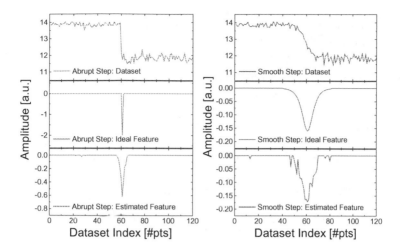

Fig. 3. Fiber profiles with abrupt and smooth steps with corresponding clusters in the LBI estimation results.

a low number of iterations. However, as we describe below, the approximate deconvolution method can also deal with a combination of these two clustering effects, caused by smooth transitions and by algorithmic non-idealities. Often the localization of a step occurs in a processing phase after data acquisition, such that the data is contaminated with the characteristics of the physical system causing such smooth transitions instead of abrupt ones. Following a simplistic system theory analysis, one could conjecture, thus, that the cluster shape of the whole measurement system (MS) is the combination of the cluster (i.e. the impulse response) of the data acquisition system (DAS) and data processing system (DAP) via a convolution operation, such that: $h_{MS} = h_{DAS} * h_{DAP}$, where h_{DAS} and h_{DAP} denote the cluster shapes (impulse responses) of the individual systems, respectively (although, the relationship is not exactly a convolution, due to the non-linearity of Algorithm 1).

3   Smooth Step Detection

We investigated the performance of the LBI algorithm with and without the approximate deconvolution in the presence of smooth steps. To generate a smooth transition, we obtained β by convoluting a vector, containing single pulses at step positions, with a hyperbolic secant (sech) that was stretched to a desired pulse width w and has been scaled such that the sum of the samples of the hyperbolic secant pulse was equal to one (this way the overall magnitude of the corresponding smooth step is the same as it would have been for an abrupt step). We obtained the combined cluster shape influenced by the LBI algorithm itself and the secant pulse together by noiseless test simulations. The normalized and averaged cluster shape was then used for approximate deconvolution in evaluation simulations with random step positions and random step sizes using the simulation environment that has been described in [8].

4   Simulation Results

In the following, we present the simulation results obtained by simulating 1000 profiles using hyperbolic secants of width $w = 21$ over different numbers of iterations. As performance metrics we use the true positive rate, the false positive rate, and the Matthew's Correlation Coefficient (MCC):

$$\text{MCC} = \frac{TP \cdot TN - FP \cdot FN}{\sqrt{(TP+FP)(TP+FN)(TN+FP)(TN+FN)}}, \tag{3}$$

Figure 4 shows the simulation results when using the most strict evaluation method, where a step is only counted to be truly detected when the detection occurred exactly at a non-zero position of the vector defining β *before* being convoluted with the hyperbolic secant. The figure shows the results when only using Algorithm 1 (LB), when using the Algorithm 1 on parts of a profile, and combining the detection results as described in [1] (marked as LBI split in the plots;

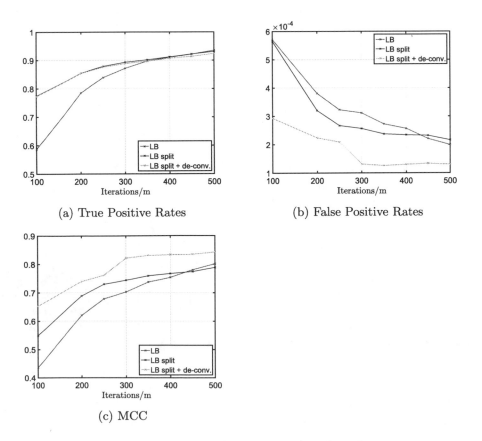

(a) True Positive Rates

(b) False Positive Rates

(c) MCC

Fig. 4. Detection results requiring exact detection.

as commented above this method allows significantly reducing the complexity of the algorithm while still maintaining a comparable detection performance to running the algorithm on the full profile). Furthermore, the results of the combination of the latter variant of the algorithm and the approximate deconvolution are also shown (LB split + de-conv.). Figure 5 describes the performance results using the abovementioned metrics but now counting a true detect if a smooth step was detected within the non-zero elements of β *after* convolution with the hyperbolic secant. This might be considered to be another legit way of measuring the detection of a smooth step as, there, a step does not occur at a single sample but is stretched over multiple samples (as it is naturally indicated when there are non-zero clusters in β). Although, there is obviously an offset between the results when requiring exact detection compared to when softening the requirements for correct detection as shown in Fig. 4, from both results it can be seen that when adding the approximate deconvolution method the results can be significantly improved while reducing the number of iterations. With the combination, the performance using $300 \cdot m$ iterations is better than when using $500 \cdot m$ iterations without using this add-on, resulting in an iteration reduction of 40%.

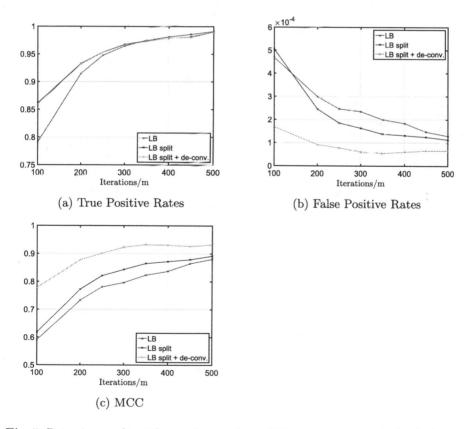

(a) True Positive Rates

(b) False Positive Rates

(c) MCC

Fig. 5. Detection results with true detect when within non-zero interval of sech cluster.

5   Conclusion

We investigated an approximate deconvolution method add-on for linearized Bregman-based step detection to reliably detect smooth steps that occur in real-world scenarios. We investigate the performance of this method in the context of fiber fault detection. The results show that, with this add-on, the detection performance is significantly better than without, while significantly allowing reducing the number of iterations of the linearized Bregman algorithm, which is a crucial complexity parameter of the algorithm.

References

1. Castro do Amaral, G., Calliari, F., Lunglmayr, M.: Profile-splitting linearized bregman iterations for trend break detection applications. Electronics **9**(3), 423 (2020)
2. Amaral, G.C., Garcia, J.D., Herrera, L.E., Temporao, G.P., Urban, P.J., von der Weid, J.P.: Automatic fault detection in WDM-PON with tunable photon counting OTDR. J. Lightwave Technol. **33**(24), 5025–5031 (2015)
3. Garcia Guzman, Y., Calliari, F., Castro do Amaral, G., Lunglmayr, M.: A fiber measurement system with approximate deconvolution based on the analysis of fault clusters in linearized bregman iterations. arXiv preprint (eess.SP) arXiv:2111.02798 (2021)
4. Hazimeh, H., Ponomareva, N., Mol, P., Tan, Z., Mazumder, R.: The tree ensemble layer: differentiability meets conditional computation. In: Proceedings of the 37th International Conference on Machine Learning, ICML'20, JMLR.org (2020)
5. Keith, D., Gorman, S.K., Kranz, L., He, Y., Keizer, J.G., Broome, M.A., Simmons, M.Y.: Benchmarking high fidelity single-shot readout of semiconductor qubits **21**(6), 063011 (2019). https://doi.org/10.1088/1367-2630/ab242c
6. Kessenich, J.: The opengl shading language, language version: 1.40, document revision, 08 November 2009. http://www.opengl.org/registry/doc/GLSLangSpec.Full. 1.40.05.pdf
7. Loeff, L., Kerssemakers, J.W., Joo, C., Dekker, C.: Autostepfinder: a fast and automated step detection method for single-molecule analysis. Patterns **2**(5), 100256 (2021)
8. Lunglmayr, M., Amaral, G.C.: Linearized bregman iterations for automatic optical fiber fault analysis. IEEE Trans. Instrum. Measur. **68**(10), 3699–3711 (2018)
9. Stock, J.H.: Unit roots, structural breaks and trends. Handbook Econ. **4**, 2739–2841 (1994)

Optical Preprocessing and Digital Signal Processing for the Measurement of Strain in Thin Specimen

Alexander Spaett[✉] and Bernhard G. Zagar

Institute for Measurement Technology, Johannes Kepler University Linz,
Altenberger Straße 69, 4040 Linz, Austria
alexander.spaett@jku.at

Abstract. Measuring the stress-strain curves of fibers is a challenging task. Due to their dimensions contacting methods for the measurement of the strain such as foil strain gauges are not applicable. Therefore, we propose using a laser-speckle extensometer with high dispaclement resolution in the range of 0.1 µm. This is achievable by using both, optical preprocessing and digital signal processing. Optical filtering prevents aliasing and lowers the systems sensitivity to unwanted shifts, perpendicular to the loading direction. With help of the cross power spectral density (CPSD) and the coherence small displacements can be estimated.

Keywords: Strain measurement · Subjective laser speckle patterns · Fibers

1 Measuring the Stress-Strain Curve of Thin Fibers

In order to characterize material properties, amongst other methods, stress-strain curves are utilized. Obtaining these from specimen which are small in at least one dimension requires contactless measurement of the strain. In this paper therefore, we present a system based on laser-speckle patterns for the characterization of thin fibers. Both, laser-speckle-imaging as well as video extensometers follow the same principle of tracking markers on the specimen's surface to estimate the strain. In case of laser-speckle-imaging, laser-speckle-patterns, such as the one depicted in Fig. 1(a), are used as fiducial markers. Even though these patterns are randomly looking, they are determinstic for each surface under invariant illumination and imaging conditions. Laser-speckle patterns can be observed when an optically rough surface is illuminated by sufficiently coherent light. They can be thought of as a fingerprint of the corresponding surface area. Laser-speckle patterns offer the benefit of having a contrast equal to unity as well as being applicable for a very wide temperature range.

2 Optical Preprocessing

For strain estimation, one has to estimate the displacements $a_{y,\mathrm{EA}}$ and $a_{y,\mathrm{EB}}$ of two, ideally infinitely small, surface elements A and B separated by the

R. Moreno-Díaz et al. (Eds.): EUROCAST 2022, LNCS 13789, pp. 311–317, 2022.
https://doi.org/10.1007/978-3-031-25312-6_36

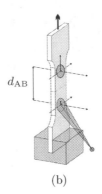

(a)   (b)

Fig. 1. (a) Image of a typical laser-speckle-pattern. (b) Dumbbell shaped specimen with two coherently illuminated spots on the surface.

baselength d_{AB}. Subsequently, the strain can be calculated using the expression $\varepsilon = (a_{y,EA} - a_{y,EB}) \cdot d_{AB}^{-1}$. In practice, it is not possible to estimate the displacement of an infinitely small surface area. Instead, the average shift of a larger area $a_{y,\text{Spot}}$ is to be estimated, which can be seen in Fig. 1(b). Since one cannot directly access the displacement of local elements, it is necessary to track the displacement of markers, in this case the laser speckle patterns, in the image plane.

One problem which arises when trying to estimate the average displacement of one of the two surface areas is that the laser-speckle-pattern, on which the estimate is based on, also gets displaced in $x-$direction [4]. Therefore, it is important to minimize the measurement system's sensitivity to such a transverse motion. This can be achieved by employing filtering in the Fourier plane of the 4f-optical setup [5]. The filtering also reduces the dimensionality of the estimation problem to one dimension and thus allowing for the use of a linescan camera instead of an areascan camera. Additionally, Fourier filtering allows controlling the speckle size in $y-$direction. This is important in order to minimize the occurrence of spatial aliasing.

Under the certain conditions [3], the displacement of the speckle pattern in $y-$direction $a_{K,y}$ in the image plane is related to the displacment $a_{P,y}$ in $y-$direction of the corresponding surface element A or B by

$$a_{K,y} = -a_{P,y} \cdot \frac{1}{M}. \tag{1}$$

The demagnification for the 4f-optical system in use is $M = 1.000$, and may therefore be ommited in the equation above.

3   Digital Signal Processing

In the context of strain measurement via laser-speckle-patterns digital signal processing is used for the estimation of the displacements $a_{y,\text{SpotA}}$ and $a_{y,\text{SpotB}}$.

This is done by estimating the shift of the speckle pattern observed by the linescan CCD camera. As outlined in Sect. 1 this then directly leads to an estimate for the strain. The goal is to reach a resolution and an accuracy of about 0.1 μm equating to 1/70 of the CCDs pixel pitch for the displacement measurement of each spot.

An evolution over time of a speckle pattern captured by the linescan camera is presented in Fig. 2(a). One can observe both speckle patterns, the two colored regions in the image, originating from the surface elements A and B. In Fig. 2(b) the windowed data used for the estimation of the discplament is shown. Here, it becomes evident that only a little amount of data containing information is available for each step in time. This not only limits the achievable frequency resolution of the spectra, but also leads to higher variance estimates which could be potentially biased.

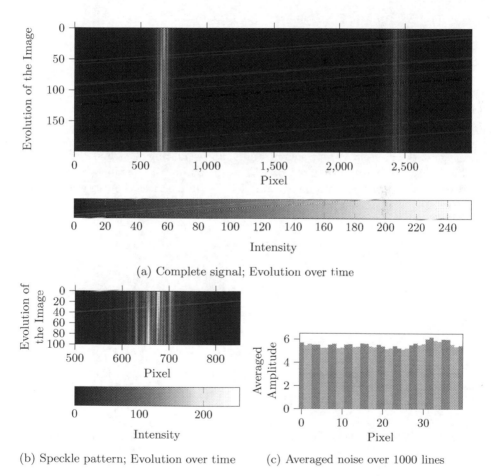

(a) Complete signal; Evolution over time

(b) Speckle pattern; Evolution over time   (c) Averaged noise over 1000 lines

Fig. 2. Visualization of different parts of the received data, recorded by a linescan CCD camera with 3000 pixel. Subfigure (a) includes the complete images, showing that two scattering spots on a surface have been observed over time. Subfigures (b) and (c) are used to visualize selected parts of the received signal.

In Fig. 2(c) the average noise of regions not containing any speckle pattern is depicted. A pattern of similar average noise values for pixel n and $n+1$, with n being an even number, can be observed. It is assumed that this pattern is due to the two different readout-channels of the camera and that it is also present in the pixel containing the speckle pattern. This correlated noise would then lead, independant of the signal shape, to a bias towards a phase of $\varphi = 0$ and therefore lowering the magnitude of the estimated displacement. Hence, it is important to try and correct for these artifacts in the signal processing routine applied, see Fig. 4 second step.

The estimation of the displacement revolves around the cross power spectral density (CPSD) and the Fourier shift theorem. The CPSD can be defined with help of the Fourier Transforms $B_i(f)$ and $B_m(f)$ of the images $b_i[n]$ and $b_m[n]$ as [1]

$$G_{im}(s) = \lim_{L \to \infty} \frac{1}{L} \mathcal{E}\left\{B_i^*(f, L) \cdot B_m(f, L)\right\}. \tag{2}$$

In the equation above f is a spatial frequency, L is the length of the data and $\mathcal{E}$ denotes the expecatation operation. If image b_m is simply a shifted version of image b_i then according to the Fourier shift theorem, the phase of CPSD is proportional to the shift applied. Ideally the phase would then look like the one depicted in Fig. 3(a). However, for real data the phase is distorted due to noise as can be seen in Fig. 3(b). Therefore, further improvements taking the non-ideal phase into account are necessary. This is done by calculating the weighted average of the phase over all frequency bins. For weighting the squared coherence value of each bin is utilized. As can be seen in Fig. 4, showing the complete routine, we then get an estimated value for the shift. After the estimation for a pair of images is finished, the next pair of linescan images will be analysed.

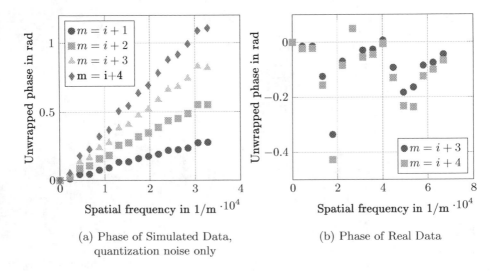

(a) Phase of Simulated Data, quantization noise only

(b) Phase of Real Data

Fig. 3. Phases of the CPSD calculated for lines m and i, for simulated and real data.

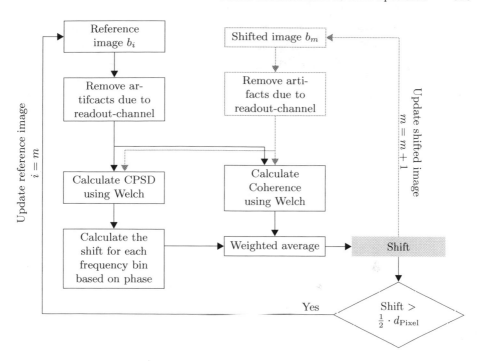

Fig. 4. Digital signal processing routine for the estimation of laser speckle pattern shifts over time.

4   Measurement Results

A result achieved by using the aforementioned methods is presented in Fig. 5. A hair has been mounted on a translation stage and displaced in steps of $\Delta a_{P,y} = 0.1$ µm for a total displacement of $\Delta a_{P,y,total} = 100$ µm. The expected reference displacement matches the estimated displacement especially well for the first 200 steps. After 1000 steps the total error is only about 1.22 µm, which is roughly $\frac{1}{6} d_{Pixel}$ of the cameras pixel pitch. While we consider this a satisfying result, one can observe that the estimated displacement is almost exclusively smaller than the reference displacement. Therefore, the estimate has to be considered to be biased. Possible sources of the bias have been identified to be:

- Sample has not been placed in the optics focal plane
- Rotation of the samples y_P−axis compared to the corresponding camera axis y_K
- Correlated noise sources [1]
- Short datalength can lead to a bias in the estimate of the CPSD, comparable to spectral leakage [2].

Further investigation and reduction of these factors are necessary in order to improve the shift estimate.

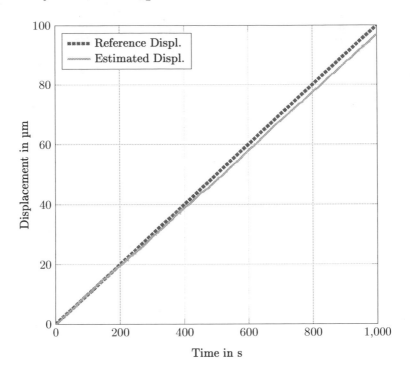

Fig. 5. Measurement result of a hair mounted on a translation stage. The displacement increments between two images have been set to 0.1 μm.

5   Summary and Outlook

In this short paper we have shown, that it is possible to measure small displacements in the range of 0.1 μm with the help of laser-speckle patterns and optical preprocessing followed by digital signal processing. This then allows for the estimations of strains within thin specimen like fibers. The measurement results presented are already within the range of our goals, however improvements can be made by correcting for a small bias which is observable in Fig. 5. Further investigation on the bias as well as its correction will be carried out.

References

1. Bendat, J.S., Piersol, A.G.: Engineering applications of correlation and spectral analysis. Wiley, New York 2nd ed., [rev. and expanded] edn. (op 1993)
2. Schmidt, H.: Resolution bias errors in spectral density, frequency response and coherence function measurements, i: general theory. J. Sound Vib. **101**(3), 347–362 (1985). https://doi.org/10.1016/S0022-460X(85)80135-8, https://www.sciencedirect.com/science/article/pii/S0022460X85801358
3. Spaett, A., Zagar B. (eds.): Strain measurement within thin fibers based on subjective laser speckle patterns. In: 7th International Conference on Sensors Engineering and Electronics Instrumentation Advances (2021)

4. Yamaguchi, I.: Speckle displacement and decorrelation in the diffraction and image fields for small object deformation. Optica Acta: In. J. Optics **28**(10), 1359–1376 (1981). https://doi.org/10.1080/713820454
5. Zagar, B.G., Kargel, C.: A laser-based strain sensor with optical preprocessing. IEEE Trans. Instrum. Measur. **48**(1), 97–101 (1999)

Lower Limbs Gesture Recognition Approach to Control a Medical Treatment Bed

Christina Tischler[1], Klaus Pendl[1], Erwin Schimbäck[1], Veronika Putz[1], Christian Kastl[1], Thomas Schlechter[2(✉)], and Frederick Runte[3]

[1] Linz Center of Mechatronics GmbH, 4040 Linz, Austria
christina.tischler@lcm.at
[2] University of Applied Sciences Upper Austria, 4600 Wels, Austria
thomas.schlechter@ieee.org
[3] HANNING ELEKTRO-WERKE GmbH & Co. KG,
33813 Oerlinghausen, Germany
frederick.runte@hanning-hew.com
https://www.lcm.at/ , https://www.fh-ooe.at/ , https://www.hanning-hew.com/

Abstract. Human machine interaction is showing increasing importance in various areas. In this context a gesture control using machine learning algorithms for a contactless control of a therapy table has been identified as interesting application. Predefined lower limb gestures are performed by an operator, classified by a pocket worn tag, and the results are transferred wirelessly to a remote controller. Two algorithms were compared using a k-nearest neighbor (KNN) and a convolutional neural network (CNN), which are responsible for the classification of the gestures. By using the KNN an accuracy in the range of 75%–82% was achieved. Compared to KNN, CNN achieves 89.1% by applying the categorical classifier and 93.7% by applying the binary classifier. Simplification of work and convenience in using the therapy table can be achieved by high accuracy and fast response of the control system.

Keywords: Machine learning · Neural network · Gesture recognition

1 Introduction

Motion control is gaining in popularity since it has the potential to simplify everyday tasks for users. Depending on the application, certain gestures are preferred and are used accordingly. To implement selected applications, the choice of gestures strongly influences performance. Not all movements are suitable for all applications, whereby a pre-selection must happen. The most common applications are related to upper limb gestures, such as gesture control in the automotive sector [1], the interpretation of sign language [2] or in the smart home sector [3,4]. Different implementations have already proven that the recognition of upper limb gestures with the help of camera systems or in applications with

R. Moreno-Díaz et al. (Eds.): EUROCAST 2022, LNCS 13789, pp. 318–326, 2022.
https://doi.org/10.1007/978-3-031-25312-6_37

3 degrees of freedom (DOF) motion sensors provide promising results, since a variety of easy-to-learn gestures with the involving hand/arm movements are possible [5]. Recently, also the interest in using lower limb gestures for human machine interaction has gained increasing interest, as it allows for the hands-free control of a device. Recent work successfully documents human activity recognition (HAR) using lower limb gestures, e.g. by using smartphones or dedicated inertial measurement units (IMU) as sensor, see e.g. [6,7]. This contribution introduces an approach for using lower limb gestures as input to control a medical treatment bed. The document is structured as follows. Section 2 describes the problem statement. Section 3 points out how the preprocessing and the data acquisition was implemented. A brief description of the compared machine learning approaches follows in Sect. 4. Results and conclusion are described in Sect. 5 and 6.

2   Problem Statement

A major drawback of current medical treatment beds is the non-hands-free operation, which lacks convenience for the operator. To facilitate hands–free operation of a medical treatment bed, this contribution presents a solution for adjusting the height of the treatment bed using predefined lower limb gestures. This leads to the advantage of avoiding the operation of a switch or button as well as the use of force when controlling the height of the bed. The usage of a wirelessly connected battery-driven pocket-worn tag, which recognizes the performed gesture using motion data and forwards the related command to the control of the treatment bed, enables the contact-less control (Fig. 1). To enable a stable and correct recognition of the movements, a library of at least three input gestures needs to be defined, and an algorithm for recognizing these gestures has to be implemented. Since lower limb gestures are very restricted in terms of execution, unlike upper limb movements, the selected gestures must be judiciously selected, which are described briefly in Sect. 3. The wireless edge device (Fig. 2) experiences constant unintended movement when performing gestures, since it is loosely carried in the pocket. Consequently, an orientation filter should be implemented to compensate any altered orientation of the tag in a user's pocket to avoid possible misinterpretations. To guarantee fast performance, the delay time between performed gesture and actuation has to be minimized in order to control the medical treatment bed within a defined time-frame. Due to the applied up and down control of the treatment bed, fast stop conditions have to be implemented for safety regulations to prevent injuries. The required implementation of a gesture recognition algorithm on an edge device as well as the carrying position of the tag are essential challenges of this work.

3   Data Acquisition and Preprocessing

Various gestures were evaluated; eight lower limb gestures were chosen for further development (Table 1). The selection contains gestures representing typical movements performed by a therapist (G1 to G5) and potential gestures for controlling

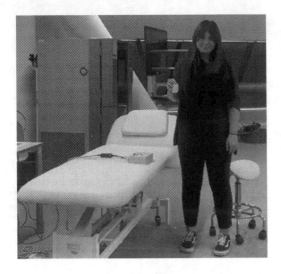

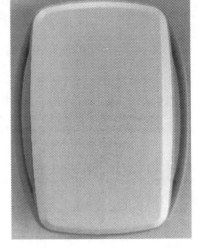

Fig. 1. Application test setup   **Fig. 2.** Edge device with house

the table (G7 to G8). Prior to the recording of the gestures, eight participants were selected and instructed to place a wireless tag in their pocket (The tag was positioned in the pocket on the side of the leg used for the performance of the gesture). After an initial review, the acquired data was grouped into 4 Classes (see Table 1): Class 0 contains gestures that represent everyday movements (G1 to G3) and must not affect the control, and gestures (G4, G5), that proved to be less intuitive to be performed during the measurement campaign. Class 1 reflects the gesture tapping, making a possibility for a start and stop condition. Due to its low execution time, in future applications tapping can be used as an indicator, informing the system to start a gesture that is responsible for controlling the table, or to stop this gesture in order to achieve a standstill mode. Class 2 and Class 3 represent the control gestures, in that G7 ("Pumping up/down", i.e. an upward motion of the leg with bent knee) is equivalent to moving the treatment bed up and G8 ("Pumping sideways", i.e. moving the leg with bent knee from the left to the right) indicates moving the treatment bed down. The gestures were demonstrated to the test participants, and the participant was instructed to perform each gesture ten times for 30 s. All predefined lower limb gestures (Table 1) were performed by test subjects as well as recorded. They carried the edge device in the trouser pocket of the executing leg. During the measurement campaign, data was recorded and stored for further processing. Prior to classification, all recorded raw data was processed by applying a stationary filter and an orientation filter, which are described in the following.

3.1   Stationary Filter

During recording of various gestures, every movement was performed for 30 s. A short pause was kept during the performance of the tapping (G6), which can

Table 1. Predefined gestures and classes used for classification

Gesture number	Gesture description	Retakes	Duration	Class
G1	Walking	10	30 s	Class 0
G2	Standing still	10	30 s	Class 0
G3	Massage	10	30 s	Class 0
G4	Foot circle left	10	30 s	Class 0
G5	Foot circle right	10	30 s	Class 0
G6	Tapping 2x	10	30 s	Class 1
G7	Pumping up/down	10	30 s	Class 2
G8	Pumping sideways	10	30 s	Class 3

be seen in Fig. 3. For processing these data and teaching a neural network using temporal segments (blocks) of input data, these pauses could generate errors when evaluating gestures. Thus, a stationary filter was developed for recognizing and extracting the elementary pauses. The stationary part was removed from the data, while the non-stationary parts were defined as taps and kept for further analysis. A median absolute deviation has been used for this filter, defining an upper and lower bound in which the stationary range must be located. All recorded signals were considered and used for the evaluation. A pre/post comparison of the signals can be seen in Fig. 3 and 4.

3.2 Orientation Filter

The orientation of the tag in the pocket is a crucial point for the recognition of the gestures using 3D motion data: its initial orientation is unknown, and — depending on size and shape of the pocket — it may repeatedly change its orientation during usage. To compensate for this, an adaptive orientation filter is used. From the acquired motion data, it estimates the direction of gravity w.r.t. to the coordinate frame of the tag. Intended motion is segmented from unintended shifts of tag orientation by assuming, that the position of the tag only slowly changes, compared to orientation changes caused by the executed movements. Consequently, only low frequency components of the recorded acceleration data are used to calculate a rotation matrix, which aligns the z-axis of the coordinate frame of the tag with the direction of gravity. To achieve the filtering step with minimum time delay, the required low–pass filter is implemented as adaptive Kalman Filter, which enables sufficient filtering while only delaying the signal by one sample. With the adaptive orientation filter, the unknown orientation of the motion pattern is compensated, and the processed data can be used for further processing.

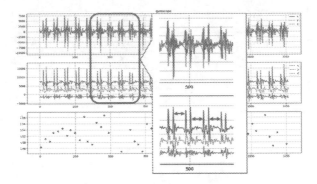

Fig. 3. Tapping movement with pauses

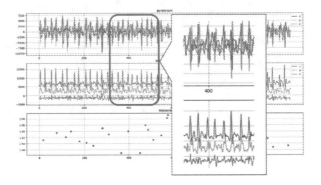

Fig. 4. Tapping movement with extracted pauses

4   Machine Learning Approaches

Convolutional neural networks and k-nearest neighbour are subareas of artificial neural networks. Both methods are commonly used for different applications especially in science, since it has to reach all potential areas and which made major developments possible. The process of the two machine learning methods beginning at raw data up to gesture recognition is almost identical, as shown in Fig. 5. After applying the implemented orientation and stationary filters the filtered data was divided into test and training data for the purpose of training the models, and cross-validation was applied. For training the classifiers, a window size (length of a (sliding) cut-out of a time sequence of data) of 128 and an overlap size of 103 were selected. All algorithms and functions were implemented in python. The difference between the two methods is explained in the next subsections.

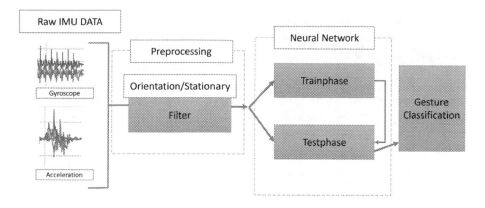

Fig. 5. Full sequence from preprocessing to gesture classification

4.1 KNN

The most common algorithms for classification of data, is the KNN, since it learns more often quicker than CNN due to its simple training. KNN is a feature-based approach, where N features are calculated from the training data to train a classifier. The classification is based on the Euclidean distance in the N-dimensional feature space [8]. A new data set is recalculated by features, whereby the KNN searches for the nearest k = 10 "neighbors" and assigns the data set to the most frequently occurring neighbors. Before the filtered data set was used to train the classifier, features were calculated first with the length of the defined window size. In each case eight different features were calculated for the data with the length of the window size. For instance, the mean, variance, kurtosis and min/max values were calculated for the signals.

4.2 CNN

CNNs are already used in many applications, like facial recognition, investigation of climate change or advertisements [9]. Such a network can be used above all also in the purely technical branches like the control of a motor for the operation of a medical treatment bed. Using the CNN approach, information is extracted along the time dimension, used for classification. Compared to KNN, no feature selection has to be done in advance. Frequently, CNNs learn in the two dimensional domain, while in the case of human activity recognition, the one dimensional domain is considered [10]. For this purpose, the model can learn an internal representation of the data along the time dimension and achieve very good performance.

5 Results

After implementation of the two machine learning methods, the first models were generated and evaluated. Figure 6 illustrates a complete recorded sequence of all gestures (G1-G8), performed by a single participant. The first observation of the recorded raw data gives the impression of an excellent distinction between the eight lower limb gestures. This perception is deceptive, as possible influencing factors, such as the rotation of the tag or the execution speed of the gestures, are not considered. Figure 7 shows two illustrations with three subplots corresponding to the raw data in the first two images and the result of the binary model in the third subplot. KNN model delivers mainly an inactive status, although an active gesture (G7, G8) was executed after 800 samples. KNN binary classifier achieves an overall accuracy of 75%. Compared to the KNN model, the data set was applied to the trained CNN model where a distinction has been made between active and inactive regions as shown in Fig. 8, resulting in an overall accuracy of 93.7%.

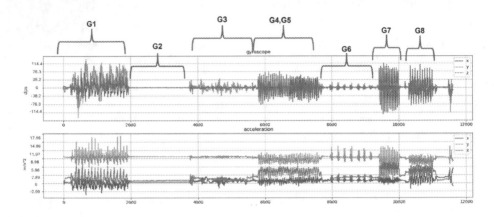

Fig. 6. Sequence of all gestures executed by one participant

Due to the importance of distinguishing the active gestures (G7, G8), the test data set was processed by the categorical algorithms of the KNN and CNN models. In Fig. 9 and 10, the subplots of the KNN and CNN methods are shown. As in Fig. 10, the first two subplots are the raw signals of the recordings. The KNN model provides an overall accuracy of 82.7%. In the first line, class 0 was detected, which again does not correspond to the accuracy, because as in the binary case, an active gesture should be detected. For some samples, class 1 was detected, although at the time of execution this gesture was not executed. The categorical CNN approach, on the other hand, achieved an overall accuracy of 89.1%. The gesture tapping was often confused with the gesture pumping up and down, since the model did not provide the correct prediction. Class 1 was correctly recognized on average over 92%.

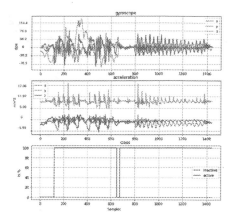

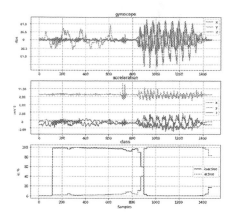

Fig. 7. KNN model using binary classifier

Fig. 8. CNN model using binary classifier

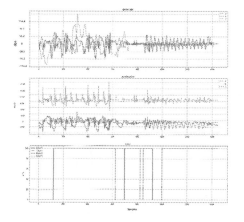

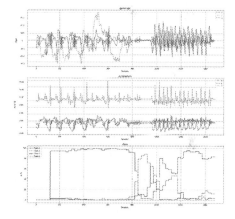

Fig. 9. KNN model using categorical classifier

Fig. 10. CNN model using categorical classifier

6   Conclusion and Future Work

For this purpose, we implemented two different machine learning algorithms to correctly detect gestures for controlling a medical treatment bed. Data was collected of eight different test subjects, which were used for training of the models. Binary and categorical approaches of a KNN and CNN were considered to measure the robustness of the detection accuracy of the developed models. By comparing the models, the CNN model approach performed significantly higher in both cases of binary and categorical analysis. Additional analysis will be performed using the CNN, primarily to adjust the model parameters in order to achieve better results. Important is to increase the accuracy and to minimize the delay time. Currently the delay time is about 1–2 s. In order to train a

CNN model, it is advantageous to use a larger data set, where additional participants need to be recorded. Including multiple gestures in class 0 can also help to avoid false detection. Furthermore, the tapping gesture may be eliminated, as it often is mistaken with pumping up/down motion and is too slow to be detected. To use this gesture as a termination condition for an emergency stop is consequently impossible, since the detection is too slow. The achieved results are already promising when applied in reality. Currently, this system is still under development, so some areas can still be optimized to become even more accurate.

Acknowledgements. This work has been supported by the COMET-K2 Center of the Linz Center of Mechatronics (LCM) funded by the Austrian federal government and the federal state of Upper Austria.

References

1. Shaotran, E., Cruz, J.J., Reddi, V.J.: GLADAS: gesture learning for advanced driver assistance systems. vol. 1, no. 1, pp. 9 (2019). arXiv: 1910.04695
2. Jayaprakash, R., Majumder, S.: Hand gesture recognition for sign language: a new hybrid approach. In: Proceedings of the Int'l Conference IP, Comuter Vision and Pattern Recognition (2011)
3. Chen, F., et al.: Finger angle-based hand gesture recognition for smart infrastructure using wearable wrist-worn camera. Appl. Sci. **8**, 369 (2018)
4. Dinh, D.-L., Kim, T.-S.: Smart home appliance control via hand gesture recognition using a depth camera. In: Littlewood, J., Spataru, C., Howlett, R.J., Jain, L.C. (eds.) Smart Energy Control Systems for Sustainable Buildings. SIST, vol. 67, pp. 159–172. Springer, Cham (2017). https://doi.org/10.1007/978-3-319-52076-6_7
5. Putz, V., Mayer, J., Fenzl, H., Schmidt, R., Pichler-Scheder, M., Kastl, C.: Cyber-physical mobile arm gesture recognition using ultrasound and motion data. In: IEEE Conference on Industrial Cyberphysical Systems (ICPS), pp. 203–208 (2020). https://doi.org/10.1109/ICPS48405.2020.9274795
6. Bloomfield, R.A., Teeter, M.G., McIsaac, K.A.: A convolutional neural network approach to classifying activities using knee instrumented wearable sensors. IEEE Sens. J. **20**(24), 14975–14983 (2020). https://doi.org/10.1109/JSEN.2020.3011417
7. San Buenaventura, C.V., Tiglao, N.M.C.: Basic human activity recognition based on sensor fusion in smartphones. In: IFIP/IEEE Symposium on Integrated Network and Service Management (IM), pp. 1182–1185 (2017)
8. Bustoni, I.A., Hidayatulloh, I., Ningtyas, A., Purwaningsih, A., Azhari, S.: Classification methods performance on human activity recognition. J. Phys. Conf. Ser. **1456** 012027 (2020). https://doi.org/10.1088/1742-6596/1456/1/012027
9. Albawi, S., Mohammed, T.A., Al-Zawi, S.: Understanding of a convolutional neural network. In: International Conference on Engineering and Technology (ICET), pp. 1–6 (2017). https://doi.org/10.1109/ICEngTechnol.2017.8308186
10. O'shea, K., Nash, R.: An introduction to convolutional neural networks (2015). arXiv preprint arXiv:1511.08458

Artificial Intelligence and Data Mining for Intelligent Transportation Systems and Smart Mobility

JKU-ITS Automobile for Research on Autonomous Vehicles

Novel Certad[1]([✉]) [ID], Walter Morales-Alvarez[1] [ID], Georg Novotny[1,2] [ID],
and Cristina Olaverri-Monreal[1] [ID]

[1] Chair for Sustainable Transport Logistics 4.0, Johannes Kepler University Linz,
Linz, Austria
{novel.certad_hernandez,walter.morales_alvarez,
cristina.olaverri-monreal}@jku.at
[2] UAS Technikum Wien, Höchstaedtplatz 6, 1200 Vienna, Austria
georg.novotny@technikum-wien.at
https://www.jku.at/its

Abstract. In this paper, we present our brand-new platform for Automated Driving research. The chosen vehicle is a RAV4 hybrid SUV from TOYOTA provided with exteroceptive sensors such as a multilayer LIDAR, a monocular camera, Radar and GPS; and proprioceptive sensors such as encoders and a 9-DOF IMU. These sensors are integrated in the vehicle via a main computer running ROS1 under Linux 20.04. Additionally, we installed an open-source ADAS called Comma Two, that runs Openpilot to control the vehicle. The platform is currently being used to research in the field of autonomous vehicles, human and autonomous vehicles interaction, human factors and energy consumption.

Keywords: ADS-equipped vehicle · Autonomous vehicle ·
drive-by-wire · ADAS · ROS

1 Introduction

Developing an automated vehicle for research is a difficult task that requires effort, knowledge, and most of the time a big budget. The first milestone to achieve this automation is to provide the vehicle with drive-by-wire capabilities that allow the developers to control its actuators with digital signals. Most of the research platforms that can be found in the literature relied on complex adaptations of expensive and sometimes unreliable electro-mechanical structures to steer the vehicle and actuate over the throttle and brake pedals. Nowadays, a lot of commercial vehicles, with Society of Automotive Engineers (SAE), level

This work was partially supported by the Austrian Ministry for Climate Action, Environment, Energy, Mobility, Innovation and Technology (BMK) Endowed Professorship for Sustainable Transport Logistics 4.0., IAV France S.A.S.U., IAV GmbH, Austrian Post AG and the UAS Technikum Wien. It was additionally supported by the Austrian Science Fund (FWF), project number P 34485-N.

2 functionalities, interact with the actuators using on-board computers that communicate through a CAN bus. Although it is technically possible to access the CAN through an available port like the On-board Diagnostics II (OBDII), the encoding and decoding process of the CAN frames relies on the availability of a proprietary database owned by the automotive company that developed the car. As a result, there is a growing community of automotive enthusiasts, constantly reverse-engineering CAN databases, allowing users to gain partial control of some vehicles. In this paper, different possibilities to achieve drive-by-wire capabilities in a TOYOTA RAV4 hybrid SUV were considered. The final decision was taken under the following premises:

- The vehicle has to maintain all the original functionalities and driving capabilities.
- Low or no intervention at all in the original structure of the vehicle.
- It has to be possible for a human driver to take over the control of the vehicle instantly at any moment.
- Fast development and integration (less than six months).
- Low cost (less than twenty thousand Euros).

While lots of papers focus on perception, control, planning, mapping, decision-making, and other autonomous vehicle software-related technologies, the hardware and physical architecture design are rarely discussed [4]. In this paper, we will present the placement of the sensors, power management system, and data management implemented in the vehicle along with the software architecture of the vehicle.

The remainder of this paper is organized as follows: the Sect. 2 describes the sensors and physical architecture design; Sect. 3 details all the software implemented; Sect. 4 presents some experiments already carried out using the vehicle. Finally Sect. 5 concludes the present study outlining future research.

2   Hardware Setup

As stated above, the vehicle used is a RAV4 hybrid SUV from TOYOTA. The additional hardware is divided into three modules according to their main functionalities:

- **Processing and communication:** it contains the processing unit and storage along with all the necessary network infrastructure for communication between sensors and the processing unit, synchronization of the acquisition, and reading the car's data. The components of the module are colored green in Fig. 1.
- **Sensors:** it consists of the Light Detection And Ranging (LIDAR) sensors, cameras, Inertial Measurement Unit (IMU) and Global Navigation Satellite System (GNSS) as can be seen in Fig. 1 colored yellow.
- **Power management:** This module is in charge of providing power to the other two modules. These components are colored red in Fig. 1.

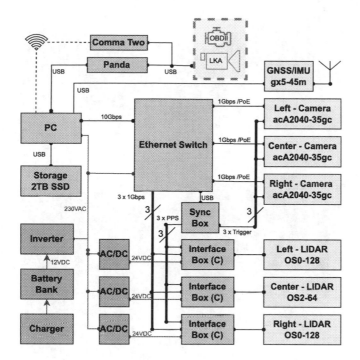

Fig. 1. This diagram depicts the connection between all the modules and sensors available in the vehicle. Sensors are shown in yellow, green is used to depict the processing & communication components, and the power management module can be seen in red. (Color figure online)

2.1 Sensors

The JKU-ITS Automobile is equipped with different sensors to perceive the surrounding environment and locate the vehicle within it.

LIDAR Sensors: The vehicle is equipped with three different LIDARs. An OS2 (range from 1 to 240 m, 22.5° of vertical Field of View (FoV), and 64 layers) is in the center of the roof. This sensor has a long range of view, covering objects far away from the car (Fig. 2a). Two OS0 (range from 0.3 m to 50 m, 90.0° of Vertical FoV, and 128 layers) cover the objects in the direct vicinity of the vehicle. One is in the front-left part of the roof, and the other is in the rear-right part. As seen in Fig. 2a, both OS0 sensors are inclined 22.5° towards the plane to cover the sides of the vehicle. This configuration with three LIDAR sensors allows us to cover the whole area surrounding the car without noticeable dead zones (Fig. 2b).

Cameras: Three acA2040-35gc Basler GigE cameras (3.2MP, Angle of View: 79.0° horizontal, 59.4° vertical) are located on the roof, covering a horizontal field of view of approximately 200°, as seen in Fig. 2c. The cameras are configured to

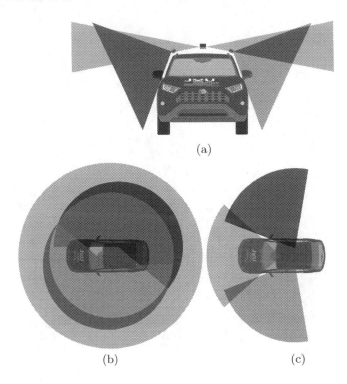

(a)

(b)   (c)

Fig. 2. (a) depicts the location of the three LIDAR sensors and the vertical FoV associated with each one of them. (b) shows the horizontal FoV of the LIDAR sensors. Lastly, (c) depicts the horizontal FoV covered by the three cameras.

acquire 10 frames per second according to an 10 Hz signal (trigger) generated by the synchronization box.

GNSS INS: The GNSS receiver (3DMGX5-45) is located underneath the center-LIDAR. It has a maximum refreshing rate 4 Hz, and provides the raw Global Positioning System (GPS) data, raw IMU data, and Kalman filtered odometry data. The GNSS receiver is also connected to an external antenna. The device is connected directly to the processing unit via USB.

2.2   Processing and Communication

This module is in charge of connecting every sensor to the processing unit.

Processing Unit: The processing unit varies according to the configuration of the vehicle. Most of the time, it is only utilized for data acquisition, and the processing is done afterwards. The base setup uses a Mini PC (Intel Core i3, 8 GB RAM) and a high-speed (up to 1050 MB/s) external Solid State Drive (SSD) for data storage.

Network Switch: The core of the communication module is the network switch (GS728TXP - Netgear, 28×1Gbit, 4×10Gbit ports, Power over Ethernet (PoE)). The three cameras and the three LIDARs are connected to the same network using six 1Gigabits per second (Gbps) ports. The Processing unit is connected using a 10Gbps port. The required bandwidth was calculated to ensure the system works without losing packages. The required bandwidth to acquire images 10 Hz was 30 MB/s per camera ($BW_{cameras}$). Similarly, to acquire point-clouds 10 Hz using the OS2 LIDAR, 30 MB/s bandwidth is required (BW_{OS0}). The OS0 LIDARs have twice the number of layers compared to the OS2, thus the required bandwidth is 60MB/s (BW_{OS2}). Considering only the LIDARs and cameras, the total bandwidth (BW_{Total}) was calculated by applying the following formulas:

$$BW_{Total} = 3 \times BW_{cameras} + 2 \times BW_{OS0} + BW_{OS2} \tag{1}$$

$$BW_{Total} = 3 \times 30MB/s + 2 \times 60MB/s + 30MB/s = 240MB/s \tag{2}$$

$$BW_{Total} = 1.92Gbps \tag{3}$$

The data streams produced by the GNSS/IMU, the car's state read from the Black Panda, and the overhead created by the Robot Operating System (ROS) headers are negligible compared to the LIDARs and cameras. The real total bandwidth (BW_{Total}) is expected to be a little bigger considering these three small data streams. However, using a 10Gbps link between the network switch and the processing unit provides about 4 times the required bandwidth.

Sync Box: The Synchronization Box is a microcontroller unit that generates 10 Hz signals to trigger each one of the cameras, and three PPS signals 1 Hz to synchronize the LIDAR frames acquisition.

Black Panda and Comma Two: Both devices were developed by *comma.ai* [2]. Black Panda is a universal car interface that provides access to the communication buses of the car through the OBDII port. Comma Two is an embedded system designed to run *Openpilot* (see Sect. 3). It has a front camera to perceive the road and a back camera for driver monitoring, including infrared LEDs for night. A Black Panda is integrated within the Comma Two, allowing the connection to the OBDII port and the stock Lane Keeping Assist (LKA)'s camera of the vehicle.

Only one of the devices can be connected (to the OBDII port) at the same time. When acquiring data without the need for Advanced Driving Assistant Systems Advanced Driving Assistant Systems (ADAS), we use the Panda device. Otherwise, we operate the *Openpilot* software with Comma Two. The connection between the Black Panda and the processing unit is established via USB-C, while Comma Two uses a WIFI network to connect to the processing unit.

Drive-by-wire is enabled by sending commands to the vehicle through either device.

2.3   Power Management

Since the vehicle is hybrid, it was originally equipped with an auxiliary battery used to power the vehicle's electrical system (as in a conventional vehicle) and a battery pack (244.8 V) for powering the electrical motors. To avoid damage to the original vehicle equipment, we designed an independent power system for the sensors. The system is powered by five 12VDC–120Ah batteries connected to a pure sine-wave inverter able to produce 230 VAC. A power outlet is connected to the inverter to distribute the voltage between the LIDARs, the network switch, and the computers. The cameras are powered via PoE fed by the network switch. There is also a battery charger connected to the batteries. It relies on a conventional 230 VAC input.

3   Software Architecture

The software is almost completely based on ROS [7]. We developed a custom package to launch the ROS-driver for each sensor and the associated transformations. The drivers used by the sensors were:

- *microstrain_mips*: is the ROS driver for microstrain IMU. The *microstrain.launch* file is used to start the GNSS/IMU stream.
- *pylon-ROS-camera*: is the ROS driver supplied by Basler to be used with the Ethernet cameras.
- *ouster-lidar/ouster_example*: is the ROS driver to start the sensor-stream of the three LIDARs.

Sensor Calibration. The intrinsic calibration of the cameras was achieved using the standard ROS package *camera_calibration*. The extrinsic calibration was made following the automatic procedure described in [1] with the available ROS package. The three cameras and the two side-LIDARs were calibrated using the center-LIDAR location as the reference frame.

Automated Driving Systems (ADS). The JKU-ITS automobile achieved SAE level 3 under certain conditions, that enabled the vehicle to drive in automated mode until a take over request was triggered. To this end, the vehicle relies on an open-source ADS developed to run on the Comma Two device, called Openpilot [3]. Openpilot runs several ADAS within the same embedded hardware including: LKA, Adaptive Light Control (ALC), Forward Collision Warning (FCW), Adaptive Cruise Control (ACC), and Lane departure warning (LDW).

We also developed a custom bridge that allowed us to connect ROS with the Openpilot's message manager (cereal). The bridge was written in python. When the Black Panda is connected, the car's state can be read from the OBDII port. Drive-by-wire is also possible using this bridge. When the Comma Two is connected, the bridge also allows us to send and receive messages to or from Openpilot (e.g. engage or disengage the ADAS).

4 Results

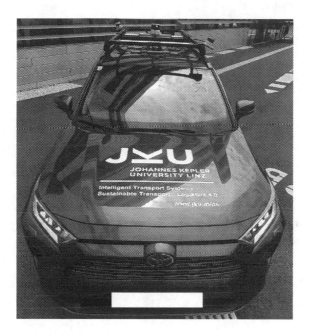

Fig. 3. JKU-ITS Automobile picture showing the LIDAR sensors and cameras mounted over the roof rack

The resulting platform with the sensors is shown in Fig. 3. It has been used in several demonstrations and also has been central to two already published projects. In [8], the battery energy estimation model in SUMO (Simulation of Urban Mobility) was compared with the battery energy consumption of the vehicle. It was found that there exist big differences between the estimated model and the real data. Then in [6], the response of drivers to a take-over request at different driving speeds while being engaged in non-driving-related tasks, was studied. In addition, further experiments are been conducted with a haptic guidance system to avoid sudden obstacles on the road [5].

5 Conclusion and Future Work

The JKU-ITS Automobile is a modular platform that was developed to perform research on autonomous vehicles at the ITS-Chair Sustainable Transport Logistics 4.0. at the Johannes Kepler University Linz in Austria.

The vehicle is fully functional and geared with the required sensors, and further implementations are being conducted. Three more cameras will soon cover 360° FoV around the vehicle. We also plan to assemble a custom connector to extract the Pulse per Second (PPS) signal from the GNSS and feed it to the Synchronization Box. The migration of the software from ROS1 to ROS2 is already been implemented.

References

1. Beltrán, J., Guindel, C., de la Escalera, A., García, F.: Automatic extrinsic calibration method for lidar and camera sensor setups. IEEE Trans. Intell. Transp. Syst. (2022). https://doi.org/10.1109/TITS.2022.3155228
2. Comma.ai, I: Comma three - make driving chill with our beautiful new hardware (2022). https://comma.ai/. (Accessed 29 June 2022]
3. Comma.ai I: openpilot (2022). https://github.com/commaai/openpilot
4. de Miguel, M.Á., Moreno, F.M., García, F., Armingol, J.M., Martin, R.E.: autonomous vehicle architecture for high automation. In: Moreno-Díaz, R., Pichler, F., Quesada-Arencibia, A. (eds.) EUROCAST 2019. LNCS, vol. 12014, pp. 145–152. Springer, Cham (2020). https://doi.org/10.1007/978-3-030-45096-0_18
5. Morales-Alvarez, W., Certad, N., Tadjine, H.H., Olaverri-Monreal, C.: Automated driving systems: Impact of haptic guidance on driving performance after a take over request. In: 2022 IEEE Intelligent Vehicles Symposium (IV) (2022)
6. Morales-Alvarez, W., Marouf, M., Tadjine, H.H., Olaverri-Monreal, C.: Real-world evaluation of the impact of automated driving system technology on driver gaze behavior, reaction time and trust. In: 2021 IEEE Intelligent Vehicles Symposium Workshops (IV Workshops), pp. 57–64 (2021). https://doi.org/10.1109/IVWorkshops54471.2021.9669230
7. Quigley, M., et al.: Ros: an open-source robot operating system. In: Proceedings of the IEEE International Conference on Robotics and Automation (ICRA) Workshop on Open Source Robotics, Kobe, Japan (May 2009)
8. Validi, A., Morales-Alvarez, W., Olaverri-Monreal, C.: Analysis of the battery energy estimation model in sumo compared with actual analysis of battery energy consumption. In: 2021 16th Iberian Conference on Information Systems and Technologies (CISTI), pp. 1–6 (2021). https://doi.org/10.23919/CISTI52073.2021.9476579

Development of a ROS-Based Architecture for Intelligent Autonomous on Demand Last Mile Delivery

Georg Novotny[1,2][✉][iD], Walter Morales-Alvarez[1][iD], Nikita Smirnov[1][iD], and Cristina Olaverri-Monreal[1][iD]

[1] Chair for Sustainable Transport Logistics 4.0, Johannes Kepler University Linz, Linz, Austria
{georg.novotny,walter.morales_alvarez,nikita.smirnov_vladimirovich, cristina.olaverri-monreal}@jku.at
[2] UAS Technikum Wien, Höchstaedtplatz 6, 1200 Vienna, Austria
georg.novotny@technikum-wien.at
https://www.jku.at/its

Abstract. This paper presents the development of the JKU-ITS Last Mile Delivery Robot. The proposed approach utilizes a combination of one 3D LIDAR, RGB-D camera, IMU and GPS sensor on top of a mobile robot slope mower. An embedded computer, running ROS1, is utilized to process the sensor data streams to enable 2D and 3D Simultaneous Localization and Mapping, 2D localization and object detection using a convolutional neural network.

Keywords: Last mile delivery · Mobile robot · Sensors · Sensor-fusion · ROS1

1 Introduction

The use of mobile robots as delivery aids for postal delivery has seen an upswing in recent years. In addition to Amazon, there are several other manufacturers specializing in "last mile delivery" [16]. The ITS-Chair Sustainable Transport Logistics 4 0. has developed several concepts and solutions to contribute to a more sustainable delivery of goods that requires less traffic [6,8]. On one hand, this is because the last mile of the delivery accounts for up to 75% of the total supply chain costs [14] and, on the other hand, customer needs and consumer behavior have changed significantly in times of e-commerce and mobile shopping.

Two global megatrends in particular, urbanization and e-commerce, are strong drivers of ever-increasing demand for last-mile delivery services. Urbanization refers to the trend of more and more people moving to urban areas in general and to "megacities" with 10 million inhabitants and more in particular. It is estimated that between 82 and 90% of the world's population, depending on the region, will live in major cities by 2050 [14]. In addition, e-commerce is

R. Moreno-Díaz et al. (Eds.): EUROCAST 2022, LNCS 13789, pp. 337–344, 2022.
https://doi.org/10.1007/978-3-031-25312-6_39

steadily increasing, and more and more retail goods are being ordered online. In 2021, the revenue of B2C eCommerce in Germany alone grew by 16% and is expected to reach $7.385 billion by 2025 [12]. Thus, greater geographic concentration and increasing online orders per person trigger a rapid increase in the amount of packages that need to be handled. For Germany, for example, it is predicted that 5.68 billion shipments will need to be handled annually by 2025 compared to 2.167 billion in 2012 [4].

The increasing demand for parcels in cities leads to a much higher number of delivery trucks in city centers, which puts additional strain on the existing infrastructure, causes congestion, and negatively impacts on health, environment, and safety. As a result, growing customer awareness and new government regulations force courier services to increase their efforts to operate in a sustainable and environmentally friendly manner. To overcome these challenges, we present an autonomous delivery robot that can navigate in an urban environment. To this end, we developed a software and hardware architecture for a mobile robot for the delivery of packages and letters within the campus of the Johannes Kepler University in Linz Upper Austria (JKU).

The remainder of this paper is structured as follows: In Sects. 2 and 3 we describe the system concepts, including the hardware, sensor, and software setup. In Sect. 4 we present the results, finally Sect. 5 concludes the paper outlining future research.

2 Hardware Setup

Figure 1 gives an overview of the implemented hardware components which are described in detail in the next section. Although the mobile robot has autonomous capabilities, an operator station is needed to provide a safety fallback and a teleoperation system. In addition, the mobile robot itself needs to be equipped with numerous sensors ranging from 3D LIDAR for obstacle avoidance and mapping, and a front facing camera for obstacle classification as well as for teleoperation.

The LMDBot was built upon a prototype of the "Spider ILD01" slope lawn mower [1] as a base platform which was equipped with a wooden parcel station, to store the packages to be delivered. The original holonomic lawn mower has been transformed into a quasi Ackermann robot in which the chain drive responsible for steering the four wheels has been placed on only two wheels.

2.1 Sensor Suit

To allow the LMDBot to perceive the environment and move throught it, we provided the robot with the common sensor suit that can be found in autonomous driving. This configuration included several types of sensors whose data guarantee a secure driving through an urban environment (Fig. 1). Specifically the sensors are:

Fig. 1. Last Mile Delivery Robot (LMDBot) hardware setup (1) Ouster OS1, (2) Ublox C94-M8P, (3) Phidgets Spatial 3/3/3 Inertial Measurement Unit, (4) Intel Realsense D435, (5) 2 × 12V Lead-Acid Batteries, (6) Steering Encoder, (7) Propulsion Encoder

LIDAR Sensor: The robot is provided with a Light Detection And Ranging (LIDAR) on the roof that serves to obtain 3D distance information of the environment that is used to localize the robot and detect pedestrians. The selected sensor is the 128 layer LIDAR OS-1 manufactured by Ouster. This sensor has uniform distribution of lights, an effective range of 120 m, a vertical field of view of 45° and a horizontal field of view of 360°. We placed the LIDAR on a Fused Filament Fabrication (FFF) printed platform of 0.3 m over the roof of the robot to minimize the points that are detected due to light ray colliding with the roof of the robot.

Depth Camera: We equipped the LMDBot with the depth camera Intel Realsense D435 RGB-D to detect pedestrians and extract dense depth information of the near objects in front of the vehicle. This sensor extracts depth information using two IR cameras for stereo-vision that are overlayed with an IR projector to aid the stereo vision in low light and low feature scenes. Additionally, the sensor possesses a RGB camera that we used to implement an object detection algorithm.

GNSS INS: To localize the LMDBot in the environment and track its movements, we provided the robot with the combination of one u-blox GPS [15], one

Phidgets Spatial IMU [10]. With this system we can obtain the position of the robot in local and global coordinates.

Encoders: Finally, we also equipped the LMDBot with two FOTEK rotary encoders, one for the propulsion and one for the steering motor. These rotary encoders connect to a low level controller to track the speed and steering of the robot.

2.2   Processing

We had to minimize the size and weight of the processing units because the LMDBot main cargo is supposed to be the deliveries that will be placed inside the vehicle. We also had to ensure that the processing units could operate without interruption, given the large volume of data collected by the sensors. For these reasons, we selected two embedded processors, one with a dedicated GPU to ensure quick image data processing and one that requires low energy. The processing units are as follows:

Main Computer. We chose the Nvidia Jetson AGX Xavier Developer Kit [9] to perform the mapping, localization and, path planning. It additionally provided us CUDA capabilites that also allowed us to deploy the deep learning models to perform pedestrian detection.

Low Level Control Computer. We chose the Raspberry Pi 3B+ for the low level control due to its simplicity. It communicated with the main computer via ethernet and received the speed and steering commands from the main computer. The low level controller used these commands to calculate the amount of voltage that was needed by the motor actuators of the robot to achieve the desired speed and steering commands.

2.3   Network Communication

To transfer data between the LIDAR the main computer and the low level control computer we used an router of 1 Gbps per channel. The router allows the different components of the system to communicate using the TCP/IP protocol. On the other hand, the GPS INSS and the camera interface with the main computer through USB 3.2 which provides rapid data transmission.

2.4   Power Management

We equipped the robot with two batteries of 95 AH and 850 A peak current each, since the actuators of the robot require 24V DC to operate, and require high current due to the robot's weight. To segregate the power channels, we linked the robot's components via a fuse box for safety. We also attached a switch to

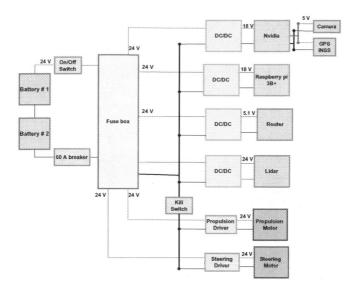

Fig. 2. Power management diagram of the robot.

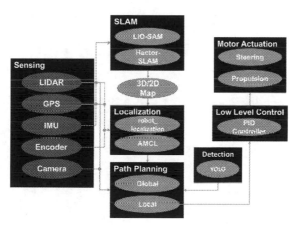

Fig. 3. Overview of software components and interaction between them

turn the robot on and off, as well as a secondary switch to the DC motors to stop the robot without turning it off. Finally, a circuit breaker safeguards the systems from current spikes that might damage the hardware. The connection diagram can be seen in Fig. 2.

3   Software Architecture

The following section will provide information about the various software components utilized on the LMDBot.

3.1 ROS Architecture

The Robot Operating System (ROS) [11] is used as high-level API to evaluate sensor data and control actuators via our developed low-level control either via keyboard or joystick inputs. The Fig. 3 visualizes an overview of the implemented software components.

Sensor Calibration: The Intel Realsense D435 RGB-D is a camera whose intrinsic parameters are already provided by the manufacturer. As a result, there was no need to use any intrinsic calibrator package. The extrinsic calibration, providing translation in x, y, and z as well as roll, pitch and yaw between the camera and the LIDAR, was created following the algorithm described in [1]. To ease the extrinsic calibration of the IMU we mounted it exactly below the origin of the LIDAR using the aforementioned FFF printed structure.

Detection: To detect objects that lie along the path of the robot, we applied the Convolutional Neural Network (CNN) *YOLOV4* [2] to the image stream from the RGB-D camera. To improve the adaptability of the CNN to our use case, we re-configured it to detect only people, dogs, cats, ducks, scooters, and bicyclists, as these are the main dynamic objects on the campus of the JKU.

Mapping: The mapping process of the campus was performed using two different methods. On the one hand, we performed classical 2D mapping with *Hector-SLAM* [5], on the other hand, we created a 3D map using *LIO-SAM* [13]. To create the mandatory 2D LIDAR for *Hector-SLAM* we cut the 3D information of the Ouster OS1 to a 2D plane utilizing the *pointcloud_to_laserscan* ROS package.

Localization: The localization was done based on the *Adaptive Monte Carlo localization (AMCL)* [3] as well as the *robot_localization* package. *AMCL* takes over the global localization in the 2D map and the *robot_localization* package fuses the sensor data of the wheel encoders, IMU and the GPS signal by means of Extended Kalman Filter (EKF) and then feeds them into *AMCL*.

Low Level Control: To control our robot, we implemented a PID controller for the drive motor and a PID controller for the control motor, where the controlled distance was the linear and angular velocity in x and around the z axis, respectively. For initial tuning of the PID parameters we relied on Visual Odometry from RTAB-Map [7]. Furthermore, for low-level control, we simplified our vehicle model to that of a bicycle with the origin lying in the middle of the rear axis.

4   Results

A 2D map was generated by relying on the Hector-SLAM [5]. The corresponding 3D map was produced using LIO-SAM [13]. Finally, the objects in the vicinity were detected relying on the YOLO CNN V4 [2]. The results are visualized in Fig. 4.

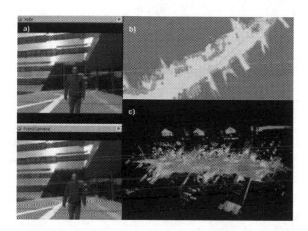

Fig. 4. a) Object detection, b) Generated 2D map of the JKU campus, c) Dense 3D map of the JKU campus

As visible in Fig. 4 b) the 2D map is quite noisy, we believe the high number of glass fronts in combination with dynamic objects (pedestrians) played a significant role here. As Fig. 4 c) depicts the generated 3D map extends far beyond the actual campus of JKU, which can result in better localization as the buildings in the background can be used as landmarks.

5   Conclusion and Outlook

In this paper a prototype of a last mile delivery robot has been presented. We introduced our hardware as well as software stack and presented results in terms of generated 3D and 2D maps.

Further work will deal with creating more precise maps, to ease the path planning, and evaluating the performance of autonomous delivery between two or more positions in the geographic coordinate system available at the JKU campus. Further, we will investigate route optimization methods for the parcel delivery framework.

Acknowledgements. This work was supported by the Austrian Ministry for Climate Action, Environment, Energy, Mobility, Innovation and Technology (BMK) Endowed Professorship for Sustainable Transport Logistics 4.0., IAV France S.A.S.U., IAV GmbH, Austrian Post AG and the UAS Technikum Wien.

References

1. Beltrán, J., Guindel, C., de la Escalera, A., García, F.: Automatic extrinsic calibration method for lidar and camera sensor setups. IEEE Trans. Intell. Transp. Syst. (2022). https://doi.org/10.1109/TITS.2022.3155228
2. Bochkovskiy, A., Wang, C., Liao, H.M.: Yolov4: Optimal speed and accuracy of object detection. CoRR abs/2004.10934 (2020). https://arxiv.org/abs/2004.10934
3. Dellaert, F., Fox, D., Burgard, W., Thrun, S.: Monte carlo localization for mobile robots. In: Proceedings 1999 IEEE International Conference on Robotics and Automation (Cat. No.99CH36288C), vol. 2, pp. 1322–1328 (1999). https://doi.org/10.1109/ROBOT.1999.772544
4. Keller, S.: Prognose: Sendungsmenge der Kurier-, Express- und Paketdienste (Jun 2021). https://de.statista.com/statistik/daten/studie/1126464/umfrage/prognostizierte-sendungsmenge-von-kurier-express-und-paketdiensten-in-deutschland/. (Accessed 4 May 2022)
5. Kohlbrecher, S., Von Stryk, O., Meyer, J., Klingauf, U.: A flexible and scalable slam system with full 3d motion estimation. In: 2011 IEEE International Symposium on Safety, Security, and Rescue Robotics, pp. 155–160. IEEE (2011)
6. Kopica, F., Morales, W., Olaverri-Monreal, C.: Automated delivery of shipments in urban areas. In: 6th International Physical Internet Conference (2019)
7. Labbé, M., Michaud, F.: Rtab-map as an open-source lidar and visual simultaneous localization and mapping library for large-scale and long-term online operation. J. Field Robot. **36**(2), 416–446 (2019)
8. Liu, Y., Novotny, G., Smirnov, N., Morales-Alvarez, W., Olaverri-Monreal, C.: Mobile delivery robots: mixed reality-based simulation relying on ros and unity 3d. In: 2020 IEEE Intelligent Vehicles Symposium (IV), pp. 15–20. IEEE (2020)
9. Nvidia: Jetson agx xavier developer kit | nvidia developer (2022). https://developer.nvidia.com/embedded/jetson-agx-xavier-developer-kit. (Accessed 14 June 2022)
10. Phidgets: Phidgetspatial precision 333 high resolution - 1044_0 at phidgets (2022). https://www.phidgets.com/?&prodid=32. (Accessed 4 May 2022)
11. Quigley, M., et al.: Ros: an open-source robot operating system. In: ICRA workshop on open source software, vol. 3, p. 5, Kobe, Japan (2009)
12. Rabe, L.: E-Commerce-Einzelhandel - Umsatz weltweit 2025 (Jul 2021). https://de.statista.com/statistik/daten/studie/244110/umfrage/globaler-umsatz-von-e-commerce/#statisticContainer, (Accessed 4 May 2022)
13. Shan, T., Englot, B., Meyers, D., Wang, W., Ratti, C., Daniela, R.: Lio-sam: Tightly-coupled lidar inertial odometry via smoothing and mapping. In: IEEE/RSJ International Conference on Intelligent Robots and Systems (IROS), pp. 5135–5142. IEEE (2020)
14. Slabinac, M.: Innovative solutions for a "Last-Mile" delivery-a European experience. Business Logistics in Modern Management (2015)
15. u-blox: C94–m8p | u-blox (2022). https://www.u-blox.com/en/product/c94-m8p. (Accessed 4 May 2022)
16. Ueland, S.: 10 Autonomous Robots for Last-mile Deliveries (Jun 2021). https://www.practicalecommerce.com/10-autonomous-robots-for-last-mile-deliveries. (Accessed 4 May 2022)

Contrastive Learning for Simulation-to-Real Domain Adaptation of LiDAR Data

Alejandro Barrera$^{(\boxtimes)}$, Fernando García , and Jose Antonio Iglesias

Universidad Carlos III de Madrid, Madrid, Spain
alebarre@pa.uc3m.es, fegarcia@ing.uc3m.es, jiglesia@inf.uc3m.es

Abstract. The accuracy of supervised deep learning algorithms is heavily dependent on the availability of annotated data and, in many cases, labeling this data accurately involves a very large outlay. Consequently, simulated data becomes an enticing option, since this data can be parameterized to resemble a real environment. However, the domain shift cannot be disregarded. To tackle this problem, we present a method which formulates an cloud-to-cloud translation as an image-to-image task from simulated to real scenarios. Our approach is capable of learning to extract the best features from the geometry of the environment, encode the information into a voxelized representation and generate a version similar to the one captured by a real sensor for complete scenarios. Our results on the CARLA to SemanticKITTI translation demonstrate that our method is able to provide adequate samples that help improve the accuracy, for selected categories of the SemanticKITTI validation set, of a semantic segmentation network trained only on real data.

Keywords: Domain adaptation · LiDAR · Semantic segmentation · Deep learning · Computer vision

1 Introduction

Perception systems play a crucial role in Advanced Driver Assistance Systems guaranteeing a better understanding of the environment. In particular, with the increase of available computational resources and the implementation of supervised learning algorithms in this field, the necessity for large amounts of training data with a wide range of urban scenarios is emerging. However, the volume of data and accuracy required for each annotation makes the task non-trivial, resulting in a burdensome and extremely expensive task.

To address this fundamental problem, some papers [1,11] rely on synthetic data which can be modeled according to the requirements of real systems and Domain Adaptation (DA) techniques [7,12] that help to bridge the drop in network performance due to the disparity between the features of the two domains. However, only a few methods study the translation of three-dimensional representations [1,8,11].

Inspired by the aforementioned papers, we propose an approach that performs Simulation-to-Real domain adaptation between point clouds from the CARLA simulator [4] and the public dataset SemanticKITTI [2]. The method relies on a technique for image-to-image translation called Contrastive Unpaired Translation (CUT) [7] and a network designed for 3D semantic segmentation, namely PolarNet [10], to harness the characteristics of LiDAR (Light Detection And Ranging) sensors. Unlike other LiDAR-based methods, our representation mitigates information loss while improving the efficiency by encoding the raw point cloud features through a minimized version of a PointNet network to obtain a voxelized representation [10]. Then, it generates new samples that, thanks to our contrastive and context consistency modules, retain the simulated content, albeit now similar to those captured by a real sensor, to provide a larger catalog of scenes that can be processed by our semantic segmentation network [10] or any algorithm that accepts this representation.

To the best of our knowledge, we are the first to propose the integration of a two-dimensional domain adaptation method to create realistic voxelized representations of point clouds for general scenarios.

2   Related Works

By delving into DA methods, we observe that the well-established architectures focus on conditional image-to-image translation, where the input image takes the resemblance of the output [12]. On the other hand, the task of three-dimensional translation remains almost uncharted today due to the breach between the two domains.

The most straightforward alternative to preserve all the information is to perform point-wise DA as in PointDAN [8], where local and global alignment of object point clouds is applied through self-adaptive attention nodes. However, the processing of LiDAR point clouds is highly inefficient due to their high density of information, which forces many to focus only on the translation of individual objects.

Since the distribution shift of LiDAR point clouds is mostly caused by appearance and spatial distribution changes, some strategies formulate this task as image-to-image translation. In [1], they rely into a Bird's Eye View (BEV) representation of simulated point clouds and use the CycleGAN [12] to mimic the appearance in BEV. Likewise, EPointDA [11] uses Range View (RV) representations and the CycleGAN to adapt the sparsity of the real domain.

To decrease the density of point clouds without relying on hand-crafted representations, some approaches such as PolarNet [10] encode the features for the complete scene into a pseudo-image by using a dedicated network.

Another essential aspect is the alignment of features for multi-modal scenarios. In [1] a semantic segmentation consistency is integrated to preserve the identity and aspect of each label. Similarly, [6] uses contrastive learning to compare patch-wise the structural disparity of two semantic segmentation representations and align their features.

3   Method Description

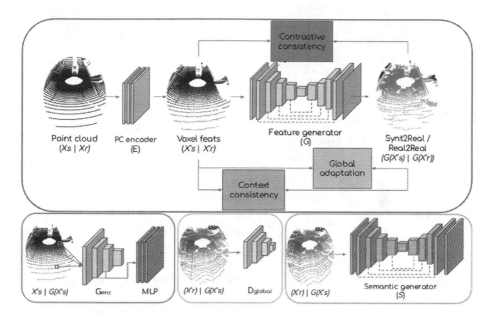

Fig. 1. Overview of our method. In the orange box we portray the overall description of the method. In the red, green and purple box we show the networks and inputs for the modules Contrastive consistency, Global adaptation and Context consistency. (Color figure online)

This section provides a detailed description of the proposed framework which is depicted in the Fig. 1. As explained before, we create a synthetic dataset which is voxelized and finally, transformed into a realistic representation of features.

3.1   Dataset Generation

Our synthetic LiDAR gathered from the CARLA simulator is endowed with point semantic information of its environment and designed to mimic the specifications of SemanticKITTI LiDAR, such as the number of planes and channels and pose that minimizes domain shift. However, there are several aspects that are not possible to simulate with the semantic LiDAR sensor like real noise or point dropout. This further underlines the importance of DA algorithms.

As we need to translate the synthetic domain to the real domain to subsequently perform semantic segmentation, it is important to keep the same categories available in both datasets, leaving the rest unlabeled. The details of the comparison of both datasets are shown in the Table 1, where the range is limited to $51.2 \times 51.2 \times 4$ m with a resolution of 0.2 m on each axis.

Table 1. Comparison of the per-class frequency, number of samples and total points, between the training splits of the generated dataset in CARLA vs the SemanticKITTI.

	Unlabeled	Car	Person	Bicyclist	Motorcyc.	Road	Sidewalk	Ot. ground
SemKITTI	0.043	0.043	0.0003	0.0001	0.00004	0.206	0.151	0.004
CARLA	0.05	0.06	0.001	0.003	0.003	0.46	0.11	0.013
	Building	Fence	Vegetation	Terrain	Pole	Tr. sign	Samples	Npoints
SemKITTI	0.13	0.075	0.263	0.08	0.003	0.0005	$19,130$	$2,195M$
CARLA	0.045	0.017	0.073	0.155	0.005	0.0005	$22,518$	$4,264M$

3.2 Point Cloud Adaptation

As in [10], we let the network learn the best features from the synthetic (Xs) and real (Xr) point clouds. In brief, the PC encoder module (E), based on a small PointNet-like architecture, decompose the geometry components of the point cloud and the distance of each coordinate to the center of the voxel into a group of features that are learned in each forward pass. As point clouds are inherently unordered and should be invariant to input permutation, we apply a MaxPool operation for each pillar and then rearrange it into a grid-like representation, suitable for exploiting image-to-image translation techniques, with different vertical slices as channels.

On the other hand, our pipeline uses generative adversarial networks (GANs), where the feature generator (G) must be able to create samples that mimic the style (e.g. noise, rings distribution) of the target representation using our voxel features ($X's$ and $X'r$). After some experiments detailed in Sect. 4, we integrated the U-Net-shaped network presented in [10], which can exploit the cited representation and preserves better the global context of our datta. We replace the activation functions by the ones in the CUT model, the dropout function by a normal dropout and added a final activation function to the output as in CUT.

At the same time, our global adaptation block is instructed to determine the realism of different groups of voxels from the generated samples ($G(X's)$). It is built upon a PatchGAN discriminator, however, we modify the output channels so our generator gets feedback at each height level.

The distinctive aspect of the CUT method, which we use in the present work, is the contrastive or PatchNCE loss that stabilizes the training by penalizing the generator when a patch in the final representation ($G(X's)$) has changed to the extent that it is impossible to discern its location in the original sample ($X's$). Features are taken at different levels of the generator's encoder and a few small Multilayer Perceptron (MLP) classifiers (H) are trained to select the positive patch between a list of locations. Our loss can be represented as follows:

$$\mathcal{L} = \mathcal{L}_{GAN}(G, D_{global}, X's, X'r) + \mathcal{L}_{NCE}(G, H, X's, X'r) \tag{1}$$

here, D_{global} is the discriminator in the global adaptation block, $X's$ and $X'r$ are the voxelized synthetic and real point clouds, $\mathcal{L}_{GAN}$ describes the generator's adversarial loss and $\mathcal{L}_{NCE}$ represents the PatchNCE loss [7].

3.3   Semantic Segmentation Guidance

Patch selection in CUT is performed randomly, which is very efficient. However, in the case of scenarios with a wide catalog of classes, it may be insufficient to ensure the preservation of the context of our scene. To address this, we propose to double the number of patches and use a semantically guided contrastive learning that leverages pillar-wise labels to emphasize the consistency of road agents and underrepresented categories such as cars, pedestrians, bicycles and poles.

As was introduced in Sect. 1, in order to preserve the identity of each voxel and guide our generator towards a representation that performs better in the real domain, we include a semantic generator (S), which is a twin of our feature generator (G) and is pre-trained on a few samples of the real domain. Including these modifications, the generator's multi-task training loss follows the equation:

$$
\begin{aligned}
\mathcal{L} =& \mathcal{L}_{GAN}(G, D_{global}, X's, X'r) \\
&+ \mathcal{L}_{NCE_{sem}}(G, H, X's, X'r, Y's) + \mathcal{L}_{semIdt}(G, S, X's, Y's)
\end{aligned}
\tag{2}
$$

where $Y's$ and $Y'r$ are the labels of synthetic and real voxelized representations and $\mathcal{L}_{semIdt}$ involves a Cross Entropy loss combined with a Lovász-Softmax loss to preserve each voxel ID [10].

4   Experiments and Results

In this section we detail the experiments that validate the effectiveness of the proposed method that bridges the gap between the datasets in Sect. 3.1.

4.1   Evaluation Metrics and Implementation Details

We follow two different metrics to evaluate our method:
Frechet Inception Distance (FID) [3] assesses the similarity between generated and real samples. However, since it uses a network already trained on a 3-channel representation, we propose an encoding in which each height level takes the value of a power of 2 and the addition in three different groups will result in an RGB value.
Intersection Over Union (IOU) [2] provides an estimation of the points correctly classified. Our evaluation takes as reference the validation set of the SemanticKITTI dataset over all classes in Table 1.

Unless otherwise specified, we first pre-train the PC encoder and semantic generator networks until we find there is no improvement. Then, we freeze the PC encoder and the semantic generator and train the whole pipeline for 20 epochs, when the discriminator loss is nearly 0. Finally, if we assess the quality of our samples on the semantic segmentation task, we keep our PC encoder as well as the feature generator frozen, and train a semantic generator from scratch on the real samples and (depending on the training) on the generated samples until we reach the results of the pre-training. To avoid training on artifacts, we only use voxels that were correctly predicted. In our training we follow the curriculum suggested in [7] and [10], but remove all data augmentation to create realistic representations with the same occlusions and patterns, and modify some parameters to improve the stability of our training. To this end, we normalize the PC encoder output for the range $[0, 1]$ to be accepted by our feature generator. In addition, we include the RaLSGAN (relativistic average least squares) loss [5] as well as soft domain labels [9] and noise at the input of each network.

4.2   Method Assessment

First, we analyze, using the FID metric, the contribution of the proposed feature generator to the realism of our representation replacing the encoder with a hand-crafted binary representation. We also examine the feasibility of our generator for the exploitation of features obtained by our encoding network.

Table 2. FID metrics (lower is better) comparing synthetic and the generated images with the SemanticKITTI images of the validation split. On the left we train our generator on a binary representation, while on the right it is given by our encoder.

Source	Synth$_{binary}$	Baseline$_{binary}$	Ours$_{binary}$	Synth$_{PCenc.}$	Baseline$_{PCenc.}$	Ours$_{PCenc.}$
FID	172.85	60.63	44.91	100.03	> 500	49.30

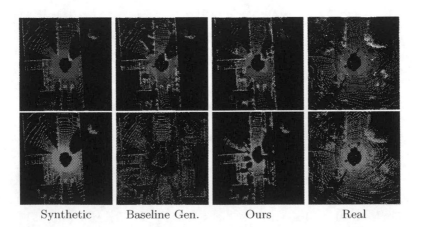

Synthetic   Baseline Gen.   Ours   Real

Fig. 2. Comparison between the inputs mentioned in the Table 2 vs real representation.

As shown in Table 2, the distance between our proposal and the real domain is smaller than that obtained by the baseline generator in [7] and the synthetic domain. Figure 2 depicts BEV-encoded point clouds as explained in Sect. 4.1. For the first experiment (first row) both generators mimic the specific representation of LiDAR rings and adjust the height of some areas to the real representation (in the binary representation, they turn from green to red). We also noticed that the pre-training of the PC encoder (second row) leads to a reduced distance from the synthetic domain, since some voxels share a common feature space, and the baseline generator fails to create a representation without entering collapse mode. Thus, it is proven our generator is able to adapt to this representation.

As far as both metrics are concerned, we report the results of the previous experiment and a new test where we added the context consistency module. In these experiments we obtain FID 49.30 vs 78.13, and the mIoU on their own labels is 18.16 vs 50.31, respectively. Therefore, we conclude that not always the shortest distance performs better in semantic segmentation task, since the creation of artifacts may lead to the modification of some voxels' ID, but at the same time, it could benefit the similarity. In general, synthetic samples are often used in datasets with reduced availability of labels. Therefore, in the Table 3, we compare two sets of real samples on a training that only use real samples, a training that adds all synthetic samples (R+S) and adding all the generated samples from our method (R+G). The encoder and our generative model will learn from each set to design realistic representations and then assist in the semantic segmentation task. Our results prove that only training for a few epochs R+G deliver results (early mIoU) comparable to those of the real training and also demonstrate a small improvement over all experiments that increases the fewer real samples available. Figure 3 illustrates the results of our representation for the different sets mentioned where the categories Person and Bicyclist excel over the others.

Table 3. Intersection over union on SemanticKITTI validation set over the 13 common classes for the different sets of real samples.

Labeled	Source	early mIoU	mIoU	Car	Person	Bicyclist	Motorcyc.	Road	Sidewalk	Ot. ground	Building	Fence	Vegetation	Terrain	Pole	Tr. sign
	Real	50.93	51.52	93.10	26.76	35.22	0.00	90.98	72.39	0.08	86.28	32.52	81.45	67.37	57.83	25.79
19130	R+S	49.23	51.86	92.89	33.46	56.01	0.00	90.59	70.49	0.42	86.49	27.21	77.87	64.07	56.56	18.13
	R+G	**52.26**	**52.61**	93.68	36.57	46.22	0.00	91.47	73.29	0.46	88.66	28.26	78.57	66.83	57.45	22.54
	Real	42.07	47.92	89.02	14.06	26.62	0.00	88.35	70.12	0.58	86.78	31.28	78.67	64.93	52.61	19.93
1000	R+S	42.23	48.65	87.73	21.21	35.61	0.00	89.50	70.65	1.65	85.67	26.90	78.68	65.35	49.54	20.03
	R+G	**46.67**	**50.55**	89.71	25.68	39.27	0.00	89.73	71.91	0.63	86.77	28.86	80.10	70.54	53.90	20.08

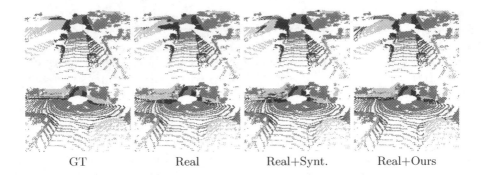

GT   Real   Real+Synt.   Real+Ours

Fig. 3. Qualitative results. Ground-truth is compared against the trainings using only real, real and synthetic samples and real plus our generated samples. Each row corresponds to one set of labeled images as in the Table 3.

5   Conclusions

We introduced a domain adaptation algorithm to bridge the gap between simulation and real voxelized representations. Compared to other algorithms, our method leverages a three-dimensional representation as well as CUT-based consistency and adversarial strategies to create realistic representations of features for 3D semantic segmentation for entire scenes. As future work, we will create an end-to-end architecture by integrating a decoder network to transform back our representation into a point cloud.

Acknowledgements. Research conducted within the project PEAVAUTO-CM-UC3M. The research project PEAVAUTO-CM-UC3M has been funded by the call "Programa de apoyo a la realización de proyectos interdisciplinares de I+D para jóvenes investigadores de la Universidad Carlos III de Madrid 2019-2020 under the frame of the Convenio Plurianual Comunidad de Madrid-Universidad Carlos III de Madrid.

References

1. Barrera, A., Beltrán, J., Guindel, C., Iglesias, J.A., García, F.: Cycle and semantic consistent adversarial domain adaptation for reducing simulation-to-real domain shift in lidar bird's eye view. In: 2021 IEEE International Intelligent Transportation Systems Conference (ITSC), pp. 3081–3086. IEEE (2021)
2. Behley, J., et al.: Semantickitti: A dataset for semantic scene understanding of lidar sequences. In: Proceedings of the IEEE/CVF International Conference on Computer Vision, pp. 9297–9307 (2019)
3. Borji, A.: Pros and cons of gan evaluation measures. Comput. Vis. Image Underst. **179**, 41–65 (2019)
4. Dosovitskiy, A., Ros, G., Codevilla, F., Lopez, A., Koltun, V.: Carla: An open urban driving simulator. In: Conference on Robot Learning, pp. 1–16. PMLR (2017)
5. Jolicoeur-Martineau, A.: The relativistic discriminator: a key element missing from standard gan. arXiv preprint arXiv:1807.00734 (2018)

6. Liu, W., Ferstl, D., Schulter, S., Zebedin, L., Fua, P., Leistner, C.: Domain adaptation for semantic segmentation via patch-wise contrastive learning. arXiv preprint arXiv:2104.11056 (2021)
7. Park, T., Efros, A.A., Zhang, R., Zhu, J.-Y.: Contrastive learning for unpaired image-to-image translation. In: Vedaldi, A., Bischof, H., Brox, T., Frahm, J.-M. (eds.) ECCV 2020. LNCS, vol. 12354, pp. 319–345. Springer, Cham (2020). https://doi.org/10.1007/978-3-030-58545-7_19
8. Qin, C., You, H., Wang, L., Kuo, C.C.J., Fu, Y.: Pointdan: A multi-scale 3d domain adaption network for point cloud representation. In: Advances in Neural Information Processing Systems 32 (2019)
9. Salimans, T., Goodfellow, I., Zaremba, W., Cheung, V., Radford, A., Chen, X.: Improved techniques for training gans. In: Advances in Neural Information Processing Systems 29 (2016)
10. Zhang, Y., et al.: Polarnet: An improved grid representation for online lidar point clouds semantic segmentation. In: Proceedings of the IEEE/CVF Conference on Computer Vision and Pattern Recognition, pp. 9601–9610 (2020)
11. Zhao, S., et al.: ePointDA: An end-to-end simulation-to-real domain adaptation framework for LiDAR point cloud segmentation. arXiv preprint arXiv:2009.03456 (2020)
12. Zhu, J.Y., Park, T., Isola, P., Efros, A.A.: Unpaired image-to-image translation using cycle-consistent adversarial networks. In: Proceedings of the IEEE International Conference On Computer Vision, pp. 2223–2232 (2017)

Deep Learning Data Association Applied to Multi-object Tracking Systems

J. Urdiales(✉) ⓘ, D. Martín ⓘ, and J. M. Armingol ⓘ

Intelligent System Lab, Universidad Carlos III de Madrid, Av. de la Universidad 30, Leganés, Spain
jurdiale@ing.uc3m.es

Abstract. In this work, a robust and reliable multi-object tracking (MOT) system for autonomous vehicles is presented. In crowded urban road scenes accurate data association between tracked objects and incoming new detections is crucial. To achieve that, a combination of deep learning techniques and a square-root unscented Kalman filter is used. The system follows a tracking-by-detection paradigm and the new deep learning architecture presented is based on Siamese and convolutional LSTM networks. The effectiveness of the proposed system has been tested using the Argoverse dataset.

Keywords: Autonomous driving · Deep learning · Multi-object tracking

1 Introduction

Autonomous driving needs robust and reliable 3D multi-object tracking (MOT) systems to complete its deployment. The biggest challenge these systems face is in urban environments, where multiple dynamic objects appear in close proximity to each other and where occlusions frequently occur. Current state-of-the-art online 3D multi-object tracking studies approach this problem by following the tracking-by-detection paradigm [4,7,12,26]. These methods first apply a kind of object detector to estimate object-tracked features such as location, rotation and size on a given scene using available sensors input. Next, in the data association step, newly detected objects are associated with previous tracks, which is commonly solved via NN (nearest neighbor) algorithms, like the Hungarian algorithm [22,30]. In the last stage of the process, the status of the objects being tracked is updated based on the detection associated with them.

For Kalman filter [15] based algorithms [1], like the one presented in this work, the key challenge is to achieve a robust and reliable data association between detected objects and existing tracks. We approach this problem by designing a neural network architecture based on Siamese CNN and convolutional LSTM networks [29] for the association task. By applying deep learning techniques, the performance of tracking systems based on the Kalman filter is improved, as

---

Supported by organization Universidad Carlos III de Madrid.

R. Moreno-Díaz et al. (Eds.): EUROCAST 2022, LNCS 13789, pp. 354–361, 2022.
https://doi.org/10.1007/978-3-031-25312-6_41

those systems are able to re-identify tracking objects from one frame to the next more accurately, which allows them to assign more stable IDs to those objects. More stable IDs mean more stable and accurate trajectories, which improves the performance of the Kalman filter.

We have chosen the Argoverse dataset [3] to test the proposed MOT system, which requires both 2D (image) and 3D (position, size and orientation) information. During training and for each frame, the dataset provides seven ring images and the required 3D information. From these images, the 2D bounding box belonging to each labeled object in the scene is extracted and fed to the re-identification network. With this network output, the re-identification problem is solved, which allows matching each new detection with its corresponding tracked object from previous frames. Then, the Kalman filter receives the new 3D object information to update tracked objects state and trajectory through successive frames.

The major contribution of the proposed algorithm consists in the use of LSTM convolutional neural networks. As a result, the association stage can take advantage of the past history of each track instead of using only the last available detection. This allows for the extraction of more robust spatiotemporal features. In addition, by taking this approach the system performs properly even in cases where erroneous past detections appear in the history of each tracked object. By introducing false positives detections of the same track during the training stage, the system is able to learn to detect these false positives.

2   Background

MOT systems have been continuously developed during the last years [7,10]. In the state of the art, deep learning techniques have been applied to numerous tasks related to MOT systems. Some authors use convolutional neural networks (CNN) and Siamese networks for re-identification and visual tracking [9,18,23, 24]. Other works use deep learning techniques for prediction and update tasks of the state of the objects being tracked, for example, to predict the position of one object in successive frames [6]. Recurrent neural networks have also been used during the re-identification stage to solve the association problem [21]. In most of these works, neural networks are used for each task to be performed, giving MOT algorithms entirely based on deep learning techniques.

2.1   Siamese Networks

A Siamese neural network is a neural network architecture that contains two or more identical subnetworks. Here the word identical means that they have the same layers, with the same configuration, parameters and weights. All weights are shared across all subnetworks. The objective is to learn a similarity function to compare the similarity between the template image and the candidate image. A Siamese network architecture is a Y-shaped network that takes two images as inputs and returns similarity as output.

The concept of Siamese networks was initially introduced for signature verification and fingerprint recognition [2,5]. The concept was later adapted to person re-identification [17,34] and face recognition and verification [28]. In that paper, the Siamese network called FaceNet learns a mapping from face images to a compact Euclidean space where distances directly correspond to a measure of similarity.

In the field of MOT systems, Taixé et al. [16] presented one of the first Siamese CNN network (SiameseCNN) for pedestrian tracking. The proposed network requires as input a stack of two target images and their optical flow. Then a gradient boosting classifier is used to generate the final matching probability. The inputs of the gradient boosting classifier are the output of the CNN and a set of contextual features derived from the position and size of the compared input patches. Fiaz et al. [8] proposed the CNN with structural input (CNNSI) network. It is a system in which end-to-end learning is used to train the network to learn the similarity between the target and the candidate patches.

2.2   Convolutional LSTM Networks

A convolutional LSTM network or convLSTM is a type of recurrent neural network for spatiotemporal prediction that has convolutional structures in both the input-to-state and state-to-state transitions. Initially, convLSTM networks were designed for the precipitation nowcasting problem [29], but by stacking multiple convLSTM layers we are able to build a network model for general spatiotemporal sequence problems.

Recently, it is common to find works where a combination of CNN and LSTM networks are used in the field of computer vision [13,32], image segmentation [33], MOT [9,27,31], or even time series prediction [19]. In the case of MOT, the general idea is to use a CNN network to extract visual features and an LSTM or RNN network to extract motion features. Next, these features are combined to make the final statistic or score to match new detections with previously tracked objects. However, CNN and LSTM networks work separately and few MOT related studies are using convLSTM networks.

3   Deep Learning Re-identification

A new deep learning approach based on two different architectures has been used for the association stage. In the proposed architecture, for each track and frame, first, an LSTM convolutional network (convLSTM) [29] extracts the spatiotemporal features from the input sequence. This sequence is formed by the $N = 8$ previous detections of the current track. Next, a Siamese convolutional neural network [16] have been used to compute the similarity distance between the output of the convLSTM network and all the new detections coming from current frame. This architecture, called AppNet, is shown in Fig. 1.

Once all the similarity distances have been computed for the current frame, a cost matrix is made. This cost matrix is solved using the Hungarian algorithm, whose output is the final result of the association step.

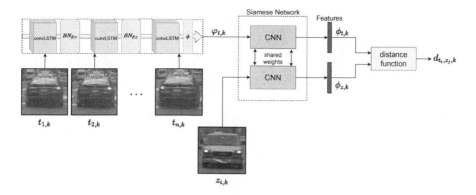

Fig. 1. AppNet network architecture.

The two networks that compose AppNet are trained together as a single one using an end-to-end learning approach along with the Normalised Double-Margin-Based Contrastive Loss [11].

3.1 Convolutional LSTM Network

The appearance of the same object in different frames may vary due to the lighting conditions, occlusions and the movement of the object itself, among others. In order to develop a system more robust to such changes, a convolutional LSTM neural network has been chosen. These networks are able to extract spatiotemporal features from the input data. Thanks to this, a more robust representation of existing tracked objects can be obtained. By feeding the Siamese network with the output of the convLSTM network we obtain better results than those from feeding the Siamese network only with a single detection.

The developed convLSTM network architecture is made up of several layers, which can be seen in Fig. 2. There are four convolutional LSTM layers followed by a CNN decoder made up of two convolutional layers. The numbers bellow the layers represent the number of channels of each layer output. Batch normalization layers are represented in red.

3.2 Kalman Filter Tracking

In this work, the square-root unscented version of the Kalman filter (SR-UKF) [20] is used. The unscented version of the Kalman filter allows modeling nonlinear motions for the objects being tracked without resorting to linearizations of the equations of motion. This is why this version is superior to the extended Kalman filter (EKF) [14] when dealing with nonlinear motions and trajectories. On the other hand, the square root version of the UKF offers improved numerical stability by operating directly with the square root of the state covariance matrix [20].

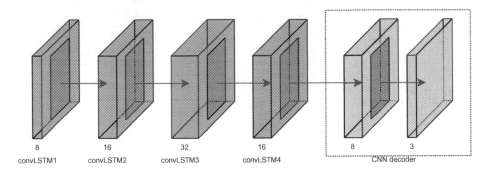

Fig. 2. ConvLSTM layer architecture. (Color figure online)

The algorithm works in a two-step process. First, in the prediction step, a new frame arrives and the Kalman filter produces estimates of the current state variables and their uncertainties. State vector variables can be seen in Eq. 1. In this step, the position of the tracked objects is estimated for the new frame and the association step takes place. Secondly, with the matching between tracked objects and new detections already done, in the correction step, previous estimates are updated using the new noisy detections. The system model used is a constant velocity model with the state vector denoted by

$$x_k = [x, y, z, \sigma, l, w, h, v_x, v_y, v_z]^T, \tag{1}$$

where (x, y, z) is the current object position. σ is object orientation. (l, w, h) represents the length, width and height of the object respectively. Finally, (v_x, v_y, v_z) is the current object velocity.

Measurement vector is described by

$$z_k = [x, y, z, \sigma, l, w, h]^T, \tag{2}$$

where it can be seen that the velocity is not part of the measurement vector, since the velocity is not measured but is an estimate of the Kalman filter.

In addition to the prediction and update stages, we use the SR-UKF [20] to implement a fault-detection system based on the filter innovation vector and the χ^2 distribution calculated from it. This fault-detection system is applied before the AppNet cost matrix calculation to reduce the computational cost of the association stage.

4   Results and Conclusions

We evaluate our method on the Argoverse open dataset. This dataset consist of 113 scenes of 15–30 s each divided into three sets: 65 scenes for training, 24 scenes for validation and 24 segments for test. Note that ground truth labels are only available for training and validation sets.

The tests conducted focus on cars on the validation set. The detection of objects in images and point clouds is outside the scope of this work, so we have chosen to use the public detections offered by the Argoverse dataset. The results are shown in Table 1.

Table 1. Evaluation results on Argoverse dataset.

Method	Class	MOTA (%) ↑	MOTP ↓	#FP ↓	#Misses ↓	#IDS ↓	#FRAG ↓
Baseline [3]	Vehicle	63.15	0.37	17385	19811	122	323
PMBM [25]	Vehicle	68.70	0.375	10644	20782	271	1116
AppNet	Vehicle	64.58	0.37	5944	4866	712	832

As shown in the above table, our method performs similar to other state-of-the-art MOT trackers based on more classical approaches. Also note that the algorithm developed outperforms the baseline proposed by the Argoverse dataset, which is based on the use of a Kalman filter. This shows that the inclusion of deep learning techniques in the tracker pipeline improves the results obtained by more classical methods.

In the future, the proposed algorithm could be improved by replacing the Kalman filter with deep learning techniques based on recurrent neural networks, leading to a proposal based entirely on advanced deep learning networks.

Acknowledgments. Grant PID2019-104793RB-C31 and RTI2018-096036-B-C21 funded by MCIN/AEI/10.13039/501100011033 and SEGVAUTO-4.0-CM (P2018/EMT-4362) funded by the Comunidad de Madrid.

References

1. Bewley, A., Ge, Z., Ott, L., Ramos, F., Upcroft, B.: Simple online and realtime tracking. In: 2016 IEEE International Conference on Image Processing (ICIP), pp. 3464–3468 (2016). https://doi.org/10.1109/ICIP.2016.7533003
2. Bromley, J., Guyon, I., LeCun, Y., Säckinger, E., Shah, R.: Signature verification using a "siamese" time delay neural network. In: Proceedings of the 6th International Conference on Neural Information Processing Systems, NIPS 1993, pp. 737–744. , Morgan Kaufmann Publishers Inc., San Francisco (1993)
3. Chang, M.F., et alJ.: Argoverse: 3d tracking and forecasting with rich maps. In: 2019 IEEE/CVF Conference on Computer Vision and Pattern Recognition (CVPR), pp. 8740–8749 (2019). https://doi.org/10.1109/CVPR.2019.00895
4. Choi, W.: Near-online multi-target tracking with aggregated local flow descriptor. In: 2015 IEEE International Conference on Computer Vision (ICCV), pp. 3029–3037 (2015). https://doi.org/10.1109/ICCV.2015.347
5. Dey, S., Dutta, A., Toledo, J.I., Ghosh, S.K., Lladós, J., Pal, U.: Signet: Convolutional siamese network for writer independent offline signature verification. CoRR abs/ arXiv: 1707.02131 (2017)

6. Fang, K., Xiang, Y., Li, X., Savarese, S.: Recurrent autoregressive networks for online multi-object tracking. In: 2018 IEEE Winter Conference on Applications of Computer Vision (WACV), pp. 466–475 (2018). https://doi.org/10.1109/WACV.2018.00057

7. Fiaz, M., Mahmood, A., Jung, S.K.: Tracking noisy targets: A review of recent object tracking approaches (2018)

8. Fiaz, M., Mahmood, A., Jung, S.K.: Convolutional neural network with structural input for visual object tracking. In: Proceedings of the 34th ACM/SIGAPP Symposium on Applied Computing, SAC 2019, pp. 1345–1352. Association for Computing Machinery, New York (2019). https://doi.org/10.1145/3297280.3297416

9. Gómez-Silva, M.J.: Deep multi-shot network for modelling appearance similarity in multi-person tracking applications. Multimedia Tools Appli. **80**(15), 23701–23721 (2021). https://doi.org/10.1007/s11042-020-10256-2

10. Gómez-Silva, M.J., de la Escalera, A., Armingol, J.M.: Deep learning of appearance affinity for multi-object tracking and re-identification: A comparative view. Electronics **9**(11) (2020)

11. Gómez-Silva, M.J., Armingol, J.M., de la Escalera, A.: Deep part features learning by a normalised double-margin-based contrastive loss function for person re-identification. In: Proceedings of the 12th International Joint Conference on Computer Vision, Imaging and Computer Graphics Theory and Applications (VISIGRAPP 2017) (6: VISAPP), pp. 277–285 (2017)

12. Yang, H., Qu, S., Zheng, Z.: Visual tracking via online discriminative multiple instance metric learning. Multimedia Tools Appli. **77**(4), 4113–4131 (2017). https://doi.org/10.1007/s11042-017-4498-z

13. Islam, M.Z., Islam, M.M., Asraf, A.: A combined deep cnn-lstm network for the detection of novel coronavirus (covid-19) using x-ray images. Inf. Med. Unlocked **20**, 100412 (2020). https://doi.org/10.1016/j.imu.2020.100412, https://www.sciencedirect.com/science/article/pii/S2352914820305621

14. Julier, S.J., Uhlmann, J.K.: New extension of the Kalman filter to nonlinear systems. In: Kadar, I. (ed.) Signal Processing, Sensor Fusion, and Target Recognition VI, vol. 3068, pp. 182–193. International Society for Optics and Photonics, SPIE (1997). https://doi.org/10.1117/12.280797

15. Kalman, R.E.: A New Approach to Linear Filtering and Prediction Problems. J. Basic Eng. **82**(1), 35–45 (1960). https://doi.org/10.1115/1.3662552

16. Leal-Taixé, L., Canton-Ferrer, C., Schindler, K.: Learning by tracking: Siamese cnn for robust target association. In: 2016 IEEE Conference on Computer Vision and Pattern Recognition Workshops (CVPRW), pp. 418–425 (2016)

17. Li, W., Zhao, R., Xiao, T., Wang, X.: Deepreid: Deep filter pairing neural network for person re-identification. In: 2014 IEEE Conference on Computer Vision and Pattern Recognition, pp. 152–159 (2014). https://doi.org/10.1109/CVPR.2014.27

18. Ma, C., Huang, J.B., Yang, X., Yang, M.H.: Robust visual tracking via hierarchical convolutional features. IEEE Trans. Pattern Anal. Mach. Intell. **41**(11), 2709–2723 (2019). https://doi.org/10.1109/TPAMI.2018.2865311

19. Maggiolo, M., Spanakis, G.: Autoregressive convolutional recurrent neural network for univariate and multivariate time series prediction. ArXiv abs/ arXiv: 1903.02540 (2019)

20. Van der Merwe, R., Wan, E.: The square-root unscented kalman filter for state and parameter-estimation. In: 2001 IEEE International Conference on Acoustics, Speech, and Signal Processing, vol. 6, pp. 3461–3464 (2001)

21. Milan, A., Rezatofighi, S.H., Dick, A., Reid, I., Schindler, K.: Online multi-target tracking using recurrent neural networks. In: Proceedings of the Thirty-First AAAI Conference on Artificial Intelligence, AAAI 2017, pp. 4225–4232. AAAI Press (2017)
22. Munkres, J.: Algorithms for the assignment and transportation problems. J. Society Indust. Appli. Math. **5**(1), 32–38 (1957). http://www.jstor.org/stable/2098689
23. Nam, H., Baek, M., Han, B.: Modeling and propagating cnns in a tree structure for visual tracking (2016)
24. Nam, H., Han, B.: Learning multi-domain convolutional neural networks for visual tracking. In: 2016 IEEE Conference on Computer Vision and Pattern Recognition (CVPR), pp. 4293–4302 (2016). https://doi.org/10.1109/CVPR.2016.465
25. Pang, S., Radha, H.: Multi-object tracking using poisson multi-bernoulli mixture filtering for autonomous vehicles. In: ICASSP, IEEE International Conference on Acoustics, Speech and Signal Processing - Proceedings, vol. 2021, pp. 7963–7967 (2021)
26. Possegger, H., Mauthner, T., Roth, P.M., Bischof, H.: Occlusion geodesics for online multi-object tracking. In: 2014 IEEE Conference on Computer Vision and Pattern Recognition, pp. 1306–1313 (2014). https://doi.org/10.1109/CVPR.2014.170
27. Sadeghian, A., Alahi, A., Savarese, S.: Tracking the untrackable: Learning to track multiple cues with long-term dependencies. In: Proceedings of the IEEE International Conference on Computer Vision (ICCV) (October 2017)
28. Schroff, F., Kalenichenko, D., Philbin, J.: Facenet: A unified embedding for face recognition and clustering. In: 2015 IEEE Conference on Computer Vision and Pattern Recognition (CVPR), pp. 815–823 (2015). https://doi.org/10.1109/CVPR.2015.7298682
29. Shi, X., Chen, Z., Wang, H., Yeung, D.Y., Wong, W.k., Woo, W.c.: Convolutional lstm network: A machine learning approach for precipitation nowcasting. In: Cortes, C., Lawrence, N., Lee, D., Sugiyama, M., Garnett, R. (eds.) Advances in Neural Information Processing Systems, vol. 28 (2015)
30. Wojke, N., Bewley, A., Paulus, D.: Simple online and realtime tracking with a deep association metric. In: 2017 IEEE International Conference on Image Processing (ICIP), pp. 3645–3649 (2017). https://doi.org/10.1109/ICIP.2017.8296962
31. Xiang, J., Zhang, G., Hou, J.: Online multi-object tracking based on feature representation and bayesian filtering within a deep learning architecture. IEEE Access **7**, 27923–27935 (2019). https://doi.org/10.1109/ACCESS.2019.2901520
32. Yang, R., et al.: Cnn-lstm deep learning architecture for computer vision-based modal frequency detection. Mech. Syst. Signal Process. **144**, 106885 (2020). https://doi.org/10.1016/j.ymssp.2020.106885, https://www.sciencedirect.com/science/article/pii/S0888327020302715
33. Ye, L., Liu, Z., Wang, Y.: Dual convolutional lstm network for referring image segmentation. IEEE Trans. Multimedia **22**(12), 3224–3235 (2020). https://doi.org/10.1109/TMM.2020.2971171
34. Yi, D., Lei, Z., Liao, S., Li, S.Z.: Deep metric learning for person re-identification. In: 2014 22nd International Conference on Pattern Recognition, pp. 34–39 (2014). https://doi.org/10.1109/ICPR.2014.16

A Methodology to Consider Explicitly Emissions in Dynamic User Equilibrium Assignment

Mehmet Ali Silgu[1,3(✉)], Ismet Goksad Erdagi[1,5], Selin Hulagu[1], Sercan Akti[1],
Hazal Akova[1], Gorkem Akyol[1], Sadullah Goncu[1,4], Gokhan Goksu[1],
and Hilmi Berk Celikoglu[1,2]

[1] ITU ITS Research Lab, Technical University of Istanbul (ITU), 34469 Istanbul, Turkey
msilgu@itu.edu.tr, masilgu@bartin.edu.tr
[2] Department of Civil Engineering, Technical University of Istanbul, 34469 Istanbul, Turkey
[3] Department of Civil Engineering, Bartın University, 74100 Bartın, Turkey
[4] Department of Civil Engineering, Fatih Sultan Mehmet University, 34445 Istanbul, Turkey
[5] Department of Civil and Environmental Engineering, University of Pittsburgh, Pittsburgh, PA, USA

Abstract. This work presents a methodology to obtain Dynamic User Equilibrium (DUE) over a road network considering the exhausted gas effect of motorized traffic. On purpose, three emission models are integrated to the traffic simulator AIMSUN, and an entire modeling structure is proposed. The proposed methodology is tested on both a hypothetical test network and a real-world network in Istanbul, Turkey. With the use of dynamic traffic assignment components of AIMSUN, emissions are incorporated into dynamic cost functions. Furthermore, link travel times are considered in the dynamic cost functions in conjunction with emissions. The DUE condition is converged according to dynamic cost functions. Results with the employment of different emission models on a real road network are compared and discussed.

Keywords: Dynamic traffic assignment · Vehicular emissions · Traffic simulation · Optimization

1 Introduction

The environmental aspects of transportation problems have been gaining significant focus in recent years. According to the United States Environmental Protection Agency (USEPA) [1], road transportation has become the greatest source of carbon monoxide (CO), nitrogen dioxide (NO_x), and sulfur dioxide (SO_x) emissions, and the vast majority of deaths are due to air pollution [2]. Furthermore, greenhouse emissions also have a major contribution to climate change as well. With the objective of reducing transportation-related emissions, researchers have proposed various methodologies. In this regard, this study pays special attention to environmentally friend transportation planning approaches.

From a planning perspective, one of the ways of addressing environmental issues in transportation engineering requires the consideration of environmental perspectives

© The Author(s), under exclusive license to Springer Nature Switzerland AG 2022
R. Moreno-Díaz et al. (Eds.): EUROCAST 2022, LNCS 13789, pp. 362–369, 2022.
https://doi.org/10.1007/978-3-031-25312-6_42

for transportation network flow modeling. Integrating such environmental perspectives into modeling methodologies (i.e., Dynamic Traffic Assignment) is an active topic in the literature [3]. The ultimate objective of a traffic assignment is to mimic the movement of vehicular traffic under some simplifications and finally to use the outputs as a means for planning purposes, such as estimating the emission volumes caused by vehicular traffic and proposing necessary policies to reduce the emissions. With regards to the time dimension of traffic assignment, assignment approaches can be categorized into three; dynamic traffic assignment (DTA), semi-dynamic traffic assignment, and static traffic assignment (STA) [3]. Compared to the STA or semi-STA approaches, a DTA model conducts network loading and routing dynamically through time-varying O-D matrices. Furthermore, DTA models can capture some properties of traffic flow dynamics (i.e., queue spillback, speed variations) more accurately than the STA. Consequently, the integration of emission models to DTA models and investigating strategies to reduce vehicular emissions is an important research objective in this regard.

In the work we have summarized in this paper, a methodology is developed, considering the dynamic variation of emissions explicitly throughout the modeling horizon. To this end, various vehicular emission models have been integrated into the proposed model structure to observe the emission effects on traffic. Later, the proposed methodology is tested on two different networks through simulations. Two scenarios are designed to observe the effects of emissions on network loading procedures. In the first scenario, the dynamic cost functions are written considering only the link travel times. For the second scenario, emissions and travel times are considered together in dynamic cost functions. Prior to case study modeling, the proposed methodology is tested on the Nguyen-Dupuis test network with hypothetical traffic demand data. Following trials at the test network, the proposed modeling structure is used to simulate flows over a medium-large scale road network of the main campus of Istanbul Technical University (ITU) using real-world measurements.

Furthermore, using the ITU campus network, this paper also aims to contribute to the green campus project vision of the university [4]. The rest of the paper is organized as follows; in the next section, a brief literature review on environmentally friend DTA studies is presented. In Sect. 3, the experimental design is given. In Sect. 4, the evaluation of results is explained. The paper is concluded in Sect. 5 with final remarks.

2   Literature Review

The literature review is given in two folds; first, a review of environmentally-friend network flow modeling is presented, and second, a review of the utilized emission models is given.

2.1   Review on Environmentally-Friend Network Flow Modeling

One of the first integration of environmental measures into the network flow modeling studies dates back to the 1990s. Tzeng and Chen (1993) [5] proposed a methodology to obtain optimal flow patterns with regard to three measures; total travel time for road users, air pollution for nonusers, and travel distance variations. Through a multiobjective problem formulation, an optimization procedure is proposed. The proposed framework is tested on one test network and one real-world network, namely the Taipei traffic network. This framework is one of the first attempts to integrate emissions into the planning frameworks, making it a novel contribution at that time. Ahn and Rakha [6] developed a route choice approach combined with emission estimation tools using the macroscopic traffic flow models. Using the proposed methodology, the authors present a microsimulation-based case-study to investigate the relationship between route choice and emissions with the additional incorporation of energy consumption of vehicles into the modeling structure. The main research question in this paper is "Is faster highway route choice always the best from an environmental perspective?". A microsimulation model is formed using the field measurements from Northern Virginia, USA. A route choice approach is presented and tested using the MOBILE6 emission estimation tool developed by EPA [7]. The results show that lower emissions in the arterial corridor can be achieved; however, a faster route does not always yield the lowest exhausted emission. Comprehensively utilizing the arterials is required for the network-wide minimization of emissions. Aziz and Ukkusuri [8] present a framework for DTA models with the ultimate objective of signal control for urban traffic using emission-based measures. The representation of traffic flow for the signal control is conducted through Cell Transmission Model (CTM), and the proposed framework is formulated as a mixed-integer program to obtain a system-optimal solution. The framework is tested on a hypothetical network through analytical methods. According to the results, congestion in signalized intersections can be relieved using the proposed framework, and lower emissions are obtained. The study in [9] investigates the network-wide effects of environmentally friendly routing strategies through a microsimulation-based case-study, conducted in Ohio, USA. Based on the results, 3.3% to 9.3% fuel savings have been obtained using eco-routing strategies. Finally, the authors strongly emphasize network configuration's importance on the degree of fuel savings and emission reductions. The study in [10] presents an optimization-based traffic assignment framework for the environmentally sustainable management of networks. With the use of toll pricing and traffic management policies, the proposed framework aims to determine an optimal policy to reduce exhausted vehicular emissions through a set of emission functions based on traffic flow and speed measurements. The proposed framework is tested on the Sioux-Falls network through a simulation study. According to the results, accumulated emissions on congested network links are more accurately represented compared to the other methodologies. Patil [11] presents an eco-friendly static traffic assignment (E-STA) strategy through user equilibrium (UE) and system optimal (SO) assignment approaches. The emission models, MOBILE and EMFAC [12] are integrated into the E-STA strategy, and the proposed methodology is tested on two-link and multi-link hypothetical networks. One of the distinguishing aspects of this study is that study provides experimental results for using only environmental assignment strategies is not feasible, which is an important outcome at that time. Khiyami et al. [13] developed an environmental traffic assignment framework to allocate the traffic flows on a road network to minimize energy consumption and emission. The proposed framework is formulated as a convex optimization problem and solved for user equilibrium and system-optimal cases.

2.2 Overview of Emission Models

The emission models provide estimations by using emission factors defined as the pollutants emitted per unit distance, time, or mass fuel burnt by vehicles [14]. The existing emission models in the literature can be classified as static or dynamic. There are three model types defined for static and dynamic emission models each; aggregated, average-speed, traffic situation, and regression, modal, and instantaneous models, respectively. Within this context, only the utilized models are explained in this review. Interested readers can refer to the study in [15] for a more detailed review of emission modeling literature.

In this work, we have made use of three different emission models integrated to the proposed model structure, namely, Barth and Boriboonsonsim [16], MOVESTAR [17], and QUARTET [18]. By selecting these three different emission models, the proposed framework includes both static and dynamic emission models, allowing for a comprehensive evaluation.

3 Experimental Design

In this section, scenario definitions, test networks, simulation environment, and simulation settings are presented.

3.1 Scenario Definition

In the work we have summarized, our ultimate objective has been to propose a methodology to obtain dynamic user equilibrium (DUE) over a road network considering the exhausted emissions explicitly. To this end, two separate scenarios are generated: a DUE solution based on delays and a DUE solution based on delays and emissions. In the first scenario, only the delays are minimized; in the second scenario, both delays and emissions are minimized over a network. According to Friesz et al. [19], an objective function based on effective delay has the following equilibrium properties.

Theorem 1. *Assume that a vector of departures* $h^* \in \Lambda$ *is a dynamic user equilibrium with simultaneous route and departure time choices if,*

$$h_p^*(t) > 0, \quad p \in \mathcal{P}_{ij} \Rightarrow \underbrace{\psi_p(t, h^*)}_{\substack{\text{effective delay} \\ \text{operator}}} \quad \underset{\substack{\text{almost} \\ \text{every}}}{a.e.} \quad t \in [t_0, t_f] \tag{1}$$

where, Λ *is defined as the following.*

$$\Lambda = \underbrace{\left\{ h \geq 0 : \sum_{p \in \mathcal{P}_{ij}} \int_{t_0}^{t_f} h_p(t)dt = Q_{ij} \qquad \forall (i,j) \in \mathcal{W} \right\}}_{\text{Set of feasible path departure vector}} \subset \left(^2[t_0, t_f]\right)^{|\mathcal{P}|} \tag{2}$$

In this formulation, $\mathcal{P}$ is the set of paths in the network, $\mathcal{W}$ is the set of O-D pairs in the network, Q_{ij} is the O-D demand between $(i, j) \in \mathcal{W}$, $\mathcal{P}_{ij}$ is the subset of paths that connect O-D pair (i, j), t is the time parameter in a time horizon $[t_0, t_f]$, $h(t)$ is the complete vector of departure rates $h(t) = (h_p(t) : p \in \mathcal{P})$, $h_p(t)$ is the departure rate along path p at time t, $\psi_p(t, h)$ is the travel cost along path p with the departure time t under the departure profile h, and $v_{ij}(h)$ is the minimum travel cost between O-D pair (i, j) for all paths and departure profiles. Based on Theorem 1, we can define a travel time operator such as $T_p(\cdot) : \mathfrak{R}_+ \mapsto \mathfrak{R}_+$, $\forall p \in \mathcal{P}$, where the operator calculates the travel times on all paths. Then, the following objective function can be minimized over a network, which will yield a DUE solution based on the effective delay given in Eq. (3). Albeit, such an objective function is consequently constrained by network attributes and conservation of flows as well.

$$\min_{h \in \Lambda} \sum_{p \in \mathcal{P}} T_p(h_p)h_p, \tag{3}$$

Using the Theorem 1 and objective function in Eq. (3), we can explicitly introduce the vehicular emissions into the objective function. By denoting the $E_p^m(\cdot)$ as the emission operator where the operator calculates the amount of m pollutants emissions on path p. The modified dynamic objective has the following form.

$$\min_{h^* \in \Lambda} \quad \alpha \sum_{p \in \mathcal{P}} \Delta t \sum_{k=1}^{n} T_p^k(h^*)h_p^k + \sum_{m \in M} \beta_m \sum_{p \in \mathcal{P}} \Delta t \sum_{k=1}^{n} E_p^{m,k}(h^*)h_p^k$$

$$s.t. \quad h \in \Lambda_d = \left\{ h \geq 0 : \sum_{p \in \mathcal{P}_{ij}} \Delta t \sum_{k=1}^{n} h_p^k = Q_{ij}, \forall (i,j) \in \mathcal{W} \right\} \tag{4}$$

3.2   Test Networks, Simulation Environment, and Simulation Settings

The proposed methodology is tested on two networks. The first network is the Nguyen-Dupuis [20] test network, and the second is the ITU campus network. Schematics for both networks are given in Fig. 1a and Fig. 1b, respectively.

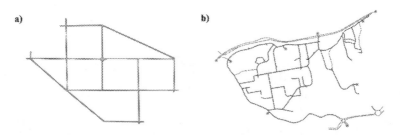

Fig. 1. a) Nguyen-Dupuis test network, b) Istanbul Technical University Campus.

Nguyen-Dupuis test network consists of 13 nodes, 19 links, and 4 O-D pairs. The demand data used for this test network is synthetic. On the other hand, the ITU network consists of 78 nodes, 178 links, and 344 O-D pairs. The demand data is collected through real-world measurements (i.e., observed speeds on links, turning ratios at intersections), which are used to obtain demand profiles (for morning peak hours) and calibration for the simulation model. Simulations are conducted on AIMSUN simulation software [21], where both networks are modeled using the AIMSUN network editor. Furthermore, dynamic objective functions and emission models have been integrated to the simulator.

4   Results

Before diving into the results, we should note that AIMSUN uses the mesoscopic simulation tools to obtain a DUE for scenarios, except for intersections on the network, which are solved through microscopic simulation. For all scenarios, the convergence measure used is the relative gap (Rgap) [22]. Table 1 presents the emission results for Nguyen-Dupuis test network with respect to utilized emission models.

Table 1. The results of emitted pollutants for the Nguyen-Dupuis network with respect to emission models.

Scenario/Pollutant		HC (gr)	NO_X (gr)	CO (gr)	CO_2 (gr)
Barth's Model	DUE delay	4.70E+04	8.27E+05	3.85E+05	1.10E+09
	DUE emissions + Delay	3.92E+04	6.88E+05	3.21E+05	9.13E+08
QUARTET	DUE delay	2.59E+04	9.65E+03	6.31E+04	–
	DUE emissions + Delay	2.16E+04	8.04E+03	5.26E+04	–
MOVESTAR	DUE delay	4.84E+04	9.95E+05	5.83E+05	1.77E+09
	DUE emissions + Delay	3.58E+04	5.35E+05	4.67E+05	1.45E+09

As observed, the proposed framework can reduce the emitted pollutants, verified through three different emission models. Although the Nguyen-Dupuis network is only used for testing purposes, the amount of reduction in pollutants is evident, which ranges between 40%–15%, depending on the used emission model. Table 2 presents the results for the ITU network with respect to scenarios and utilized emission models. The same pattern in Table 1 can also be observed in Table 2. The testing of the proposed framework on a real-world network with field measurements resulted in reduced emitted pollutants between 12%–28%, which is a significant improvement.

Table 2. The results of emitted pollutants for the ITU network with respect to emission models.

Scenario/Pollutant		HC (gr)	NO_X (gr)	CO (gr)	CO_2 (gr)
Barth's Model	DUE delay	1.18E+05	4.38E+05	8.39E+05	2.80E+09
	DUE emissions + Delay	9.16E+04	3.53E+05	6.60E+05	2.18E+09
QUARTET	DUE delay	6.35E+04	1.44E+04	1.04E+05	–
	DUE emissions + Delay	5.66E+04	1.16E+04	8.68E+04	–
MOVESTAR	DUE delay	1.26E+05	5.09E+05	8.33E+05	2.57E+09
	DUE emissions + Delay	1.06E+05	4.45E+05	7.32E+05	1.83E+09

5   Conclusion

In this study, we have proposed a methodology to obtain DUE over a road network considering vehicular traffic emissions. The proposed methodology is tested on two networks by integrating three different emission models to the AIMSUN traffic simulator. The initial testing of the proposed model structure is conducted on a test network and, further testing is conducted on a real-world network piece using field measurements. Using the AIMSUN simulator, designed DUE scenarios are tested. Although the results differ between the utilized emission models, the proposed methodology can provide fairly significant improvements in terms of emitted pollutants for all emission models. The difference between emission models can be attributed to their own frameworks. For example, the selection of vehicle type is an important factor in this regard, and some models do not possess such a distinction in their model structure. As future extensions, the authors plan on expanding the scope of this framework through more complex networks and traffic facilities.

Acknowledgments.   This work is supported by the Scientific and Technological Research Council of Turkey (TUBITAK) under Project 218M307.

References

1. United States Environmental Protection Agency, Sources of greenhouse gas emissions. https://www.epa.gov/ghgemissions/sources-greenhouse-gas-emissions. Accessed 06 Aug 2020
2. WHO: Reducing Global Health Risks through Mitigation of shortlived climate pollutants - scoping report for policy makers. World Health Organization (2015)
3. Wang, Y., Szeto, W.Y., Han, K., Friesz, T.L.: Dynamic traffic assignment: a review of the methodological advances for environmentally sustainable road transportation applications. Transp. Res. Part B **111**, 370–394 (2018)

4. Istanbul Technical University, ITU Climate Action Plan, 2021–2026. https://urldefense.com/
v3/__https://sustainability.itu.edu.tr/docs/librariesprovider76/itu-files/istanbul-technical-uni
versity-2021-2026-climate-action-plan-cap.pdf__;!!NLFGqXoFfo8MMQ!tE4_WBBfjdnkR
qCHRVZZN612fCZWmIcU2PH2EmJ56SawY8HSFV2OJScRvKyn8PaImh_CiaW9SzP2
sF3mwCT4k8woj9Q$. Accessed 26 June 2022

5. Tzeng, G.H., Chen, C.H.: Multiobjective decision making for traffic assignment. IEEE Trans.
Eng. Manag. **40**(2), 180–187 (1993)

6. Ahn, K., Rakha, H.: The effects of route choice decisions on vehicle energy consumption and
emissions. Transp. Res. Part D Environ. **13**(3), 151–167 (2008)

7. EPA: User's Guide to Mobile6, Mobile Source Emission Factor Model. EPA420-R-02-001,
Ann Arbor, Michigan (2002)

8. Aziz, H.M.A., Ukkusuri, S.V.: Unified framework for dynamic traffic assignment and signal
control with cell transmission model. Transp. Res. Rec. **2311**, 73–84 (2012)

9. Ahn, K., Rakha, H.: Network-wide impacts of eco-routing strategies: a large-scale case study.
Transp. Res. Part D Environ. **25**, 119–130 (2013)

10. Kolak, O.I., Feyzioglu, O., Birbil, ŞI., Noyan, N., Yalcindag, S.: Using emission functions
in modeling environmentally sustainable traffic assignment policies. J. Ind. Manag. Optim.
9(2), 341–363 (2013)

11. Patil, G.R.: Emission-based static traffic assignment models. Environ. Model. Assess. **21**(5),
629–642 (2015). https://doi.org/10.1007/s10666-015-9498-7

12. California Air Resource Board: EMFAC2007 version 2.3 User's guide: calculating emission
inventories for vehicles in California (2007)

13. Khiyami, A., Keimer, A., Alexandre, B.: Structural analysis of specific environmental traffic assignment problems. In: Proceedings of 21st International Conference on Intelligent
Transportation Systems, Hawaii, USA (2018)

14. Smit, R., Ntziachristos, L., Boulter, P.: Validation of road vehicle and traffic emission models–a
review and meta-analysis. Atmos. Environ. **44**(25), 2943–2953 (2010)

15. Wang, Y., Szeto, W.Y., Han, K., Friesz, T.L.: Dynamic traffic assignment: a review of methodological advances for environmentally sustainable road transportation applications. Transp.
Res. Part B Methodol. **111**, 370–394 (2018)

16. Barth, M., Boriboonsomsin, K.: Real-world carbon dioxide impacts of traffic congestion.
Transp. Res. Rec. **2058**(1), 163–171 (2008)

17. Wang, Z., Wu, G., Scora, G.: MOVESTAR: an open-source vehicle fuel and emission
model based on USEPA MOVES. https://github.com/ziranw/MOVESTAR-Fuel-and-Emi
ssion-Model. Accessed 26 June 2022

18. QuARTET: Assessment of current tools for environment assessment in QUARTET. DRIVE
II Project V2018: QUARTET (1992)

19. Friesz, T.L., Bernstein, D., Smith, T., Tobin, R., Wie, B.: A variational inequality formulation
of the dynamic network user equilibrium problem. Oper. Res. Int. J. **41**(1), 80–91 (1993)

20. Han, K., Eve, G., Friesz, T.L.: Computing dynamic user equilibria on large-scale networks
with software implementation. Netw. Spat. Econ. **19**(3), 869–902 (2019)

21. AIMSUN: Aimsun Next Version 20 User's Manual TSS—transport simulation systems,
Barcelona, Spain (2020). www.aimsun.com

22. Chiu, Y.C., et al.: Dynamic Traffic Assignment: A Primer. Transportation Research Board:
Transportation Network Modeling Committee, Washington, DC (2011)

Sensitivity Analysis for a Cooperative Adaptive Cruise Control Car Following Model: Preliminary Findings

Sadullah Goncu[1,3]([✉]), Mehmet Ali Silgu[3,4], Ismet Goksad Erdagı[3,5], and Hilmi Berk Celikoglu[2,3]

[1] Department of Civil Engineering, Fatih Sultan Mehmet University, 34445 Istanbul, Turkey
sadullahgoncu@gmail.com, sgoncu@fsm.edu.tr
[2] Department of Civil Engineering, Technical University of Istanbul, 34469 Istanbul, Turkey
[3] Technical University of Istanbul (ITU), ITU ITS Research Lab, 34469 Istanbul, Turkey
[4] Department of Civil Engineering, Bartın University, 74100 Bartın, Turkey
[5] Department of Civil and Environmental Engineering, University of Pittsburgh, Pittsburgh, PA, USA

Abstract. Microscopic traffic simulations are powerful tools to evaluate transportation systems. For a simulation model to represent reality at a satisfactory level, models require calibration. Calibration implies that inputs to the model (e.g., driving behavior), must be set correctly so that modeled traffic conditions can mimic reality properly. However, calibration is a cumbersome process. As the complexity of the model increases, even running the simulation alone can be time-consuming. Sensitivity Analysis (SA) can be used in this regard. SA can be defined as the study of model parameters to determine which input parameter (or combination of them) influences the model output more than the rest of the parameters. This study provides a preliminary SA for the Cooperative Adaptive Cruise Controlled vehicle car-following model with the use of microscopic simulation environment SUMO (Simulation of Urban Mobility).

Keywords: Sensitivity · Cooperative adaptive cruise control · $H\infty$ controller · Traffic simulation

1 Introduction

Microscopic traffic simulations are one of the most preferred tools in traffic engineering for modeling, optimizing, and evaluating small to medium-sized real-world transportation systems. Like any real system, the presence of variance, the errors caused by the data collection procedure, and the approximations in the modeling processes are some of the leading causes of uncertainties in the modeling of real-world systems, and microscopic traffic simulations suffer from these systematic uncertainties as well. One of the main attributes of microscopic traffic simulations is to mimic driving behavior on an individual level through car-following and lane-change models. Although the lane-change models are relatively young in terms of research history, car-following models are a well-established subject, with studies dating back to the 1950s. The investigation of the uncertainty and means to tackle these modeling challenges is an interesting topic in the context of microscopic traffic simulations. As models are the abstractions of reality, a real-world system is investigated by managing the uncertainties in the modeling procedure. Hence, a model that aims to represent the longitudinal driving behavior (i.e., car-following behavior) undoubtedly will suffer from many uncertainty sources such as the variance of driver characteristics, errors in traffic data capture, and modeling inaccuracies [1, 2]. Some recent studies even share interesting results regarding driving behavior variance in the real world. For example, in [3], a naturalistic driving study is presented where it is revealed that the Wiedemann [4] car-following model fails to mimic Chinese drivers' behavior. From a modeling perspective, reducing and managing these uncertainties requires robust, tailored approaches to represent the real system (i.e., driver profile). Calibration methods are presented in the literature to address this issue. Calibration implies that the models' inputs must be set correctly to represent reality properly. However, this is easier said than done. Due to uncertainty sources mentioned before, indirect estimation (direct calibration) of model parameters is a daunting task. As the complexity of models increases, even running the simulations alone can be incredibly time consuming. Due to the limitations on time availability and computational power, a reasonable approach is to calibrate only the influential parameters (i.e., parameters whose variations significantly impact the model output) of the model. At this point the Sensitivity Analysis (SA) enters the modeling canvas. Sensitivity Analysis (SA) can be defined as the study of model parameters to determine which input parameter(s) influences the model output more than the rest of the parameters. SA can give qualitative and quantitative insights to the modeler about the effect of parameters which can be crucial for modeling [5]. Through proper SA, a modeler can determine which parameters to calibrate and ease the computational complexity of the calibration process.

In this work we have summarized, we present a preliminary SA for a car-following model proposed for Cooperative Adaptive Cruise Controlled (CACC) vehicles with [6] with the use of microscopic simulation environment SUMO (Simulation of Urban Mobility) [7]. This work is an extension of the study from [8], which has proposed a novel H_∞ controller for the combined control of freeway traffic by adopting coordinated Ramp Metering (RM) and Variable Speed Limiting (VSL) strategies. The rest of the paper is organized as follows; in the next section, an overview of commonly used SA methods is briefly explained, followed by a literature review of the SA studies on microscopic traffic simulations. In Sect. 3, experimental design is presented. In Sect. 4, the results of the conducted SA are given. The paper concludes with Sect. 5 with final remarks.

2   Overview of Sensitivity Analysis Methods

The literature about SA is very extensive in the modeling community. However, few examples exist in the traffic modeling literature. Based on these few examples, we can categorize the used methodologies in two; one at a time (OAT) and analysis of variance (ANOVA).

In OAT, model parameters are evaluated individually, one by one, concerning their effect on the model outputs. Although this approach provides a simplistic perspective, it has some drawbacks, such as ignoring the correlations between the parameters because they are not evaluated simultaneously. The ANOVA approach on the other hand is a local methodology that investigates the neighborhood of a specific point in the input space. Examples of both approaches that have been utilized in traffic modeling can be found in the literature. For example, the study in [5] utilizes the OAT approach through the Elementary Effects (EE) method [9] for a microscopic traffic simulation. The mentioned EE method is the most well-known methodology of OAT approaches. The EE method is a stochastic and qualitative method that aims to make a local change in the parameters one by one and observe the global effect on the model output. Based on the output change, an index is generated for each parameter to identify the influential ones. Ge and Menendez [10] also utilized the EE method with some modifications, which involves a different sampling method to improve the computational efficiency of the EE. Another prominent approach, ANOVA is also utilized for microscopic traffic simulations. Ciuffo et al. [11] used the ANOVA approach to present a global sensitivity analysis for the IDM [12] car-following model, which is quite unique considering that, as the model complexity increases, obtaining a global sensitivity index is quite challenging. The proposed study in [11] provides a robust approach to conducting SA on complex simulation models with reasonable computational time through variational methods. Siddharth and Ramadurai [13] present a SA for a VISSIM [14] simulation model to calibrate the model specifically for India's motorway traffic conditions. For the interested readers, a survey about this subject can be found in [15].

3   Experimental Design

In this study we have summarized, we present a preliminary SA for a car-following model proposed for CACC vehicles through the SUMO microscopic traffic simulation environment. Through this work, in conjunction with our previous work [8], we aim to explore the sensitivity of the CACC car-following model on the desired time headway parameter (t_{hw}). In order to achieve this particular research objective, a comparative study on a real network piece in Istanbul, Turkey, has been presented using real demand data. Using the demand data, IDM car-following model has been calibrated, which is the selected car-following model for the human drivers. Regarding the car-following models utilized for human-driven vehicles, the subject of SA is already somewhat existing in the literature. However, for CACC vehicles, literature is still evolving. In order to contribute to this topic, the presented study aims to provide some preliminary findings.

3.1   Network Characteristics

The used network is a freeway section in Istanbul, Turkey, on the E-80 freeway. A schematic representation of this freeway stretch is given in Fig. 1. This freeway stretch, previously used in [8], has one off-ramp and four on-ramps with varying distances between them. Additionally, the number of lanes also varies throughout the stretch as well. In this study, the throughput at the end of the Segment 6 (see Fig. 1.) is selected as the model output. Selecting throughput as the model output allows us to make an assessment of sensitivity based on the utilized capacity of this particular freeway stretch.

Furthermore, the applied freeway traffic control strategies under different simulation scenarios allow us to observe the best possible outcome in terms of capacity and make a definitive assessment of the models' sensitivity. The freeway traffic control strategies applied are explained in the following section.

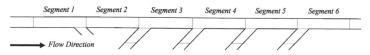

Fig. 1. A schematic representation of the E-80 freeway stretch in Istanbul, Turkey

3.2   Control Scenarios and Simulation Settings

As mentioned, freeway traffic control strategies are incorporated into the simulation to comprehensively assess models' sensitivity based on utilized freeway capacity. As the base case scenario, no control strategies are adopted, serving as our reference scenario. The first control strategy we have utilized is the H_∞ State Feedback Controller (SFC), proposed in our previous studies [8, 16]. We have adopted H_∞ SFC as a ramp metering (RM) algorithm to regulate vehicle inflow towards mainstream traffic. Furthermore, H_∞ SFC is also adopted as an integrated controller of ramp metering and variable speed limit (VSL). As a comparison scenario, we also utilized the ALINEA [17] RM algorithm as an additional control scenario. All control strategies are integrated into the SUMO simulation environment using the TRACI (Traffic Control Interface) module. Combined with our no-control scenario, four different control scenarios have been used.

As for the number of CACC vehicles in traffic composition, we have used 42 different penetration rates for our simulation study. Penetration ratios start from 0% to 20% with 1% percent increments, from 22% to 40% with 2% increments, from 44% to 60% with %4 increments, from 65% to 80% with 5% increments, 90% and 100% have been used. Furthermore, our time headway parameter, which is the main investigated model input, is changed to the following values; 0.6 s, 0.8 s, 1.0 s, and 1.2 s. Together with the control scenarios, parameter values, and penetration ratios, a total of 672 simulation runs are conducted. For all of the simulation trials, the simulation duration is 10800 s (3 h), and the simulation time step is 0.1 s. Each simulation took 5–10 min, depending on the control strategy. A general overview of simulation scenarios is presented in Fig. 2., where Only RM represents the H_∞ SFC as an RM algorithm and RM + VSL represents the integrated control of freeway traffic with the use of H_∞ SFC through RM and VSL applications.

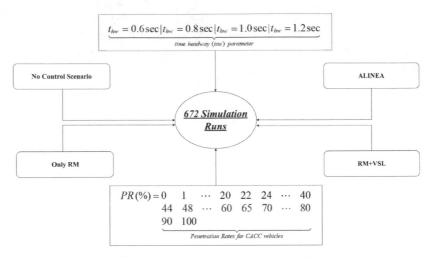

Fig. 2. An overview of simulation trials.

4   Results

Results of simulation runs are presented in two folds; firstly, a direct comparison of the control scenario with respect to the no control scenario is presented. Secondly, an overall comparison of all control scenarios with respect to the time headway parameter is given. The graph in Fig. 3. Visualizes SA results between no control scenario and control scenarios individually. As can be observed from Fig. 3. For $t_{hw} = 1.0$ s, control scenarios of ALINEA, Only RM, and RM + VSL outperform the no control scenario by 1.5%, 2%, and 2.2%, respectively, at the full penetration rate (i.e., 100%). Furthermore, in all cases, we observe the change in throughput with respect to t_{hw} is existent, indicating sensitivity to the time headway parameter. Additionally, the sensitivity of the CACC car-following model to the time headway parameter also has the transferability attribute since we can observe a similar pattern in the controlled scenarios as well.

After the individual comparisons between control scenarios, another comparison with respect to time headway parameter values is also presented in Fig. 4. According to the results in Fig. 4., the highest throughput value for each control case is achieved for $t_{hw} = 1.0$ seconds. There is a recurring pattern of decrease in utilized capacity in all of the controlled scenarios. After the 60% penetration rate, the throughput of the system outperforms the initial throughput values for all controlled cases. Furthermore, we can observe an increasing throughput gap if we compare the controlled and no control scenarios for the time headway values of 0.6s, 0.8s, and 1.0 s. However, this gap declines after the time headway value of 1.2 s. This decrease can be attributed to the loss of utilized capacity due to the relationship between time headway and traffic flow capacity. As the vehicle headways increase, the system's total flow decreases, and lower throughput is observed for no control scenario.

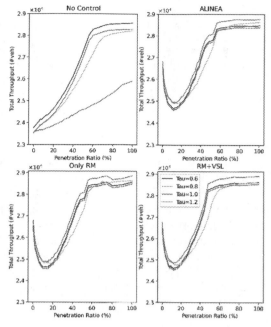

Fig. 3. SA results of CACC car-following model with respect to control scenarios

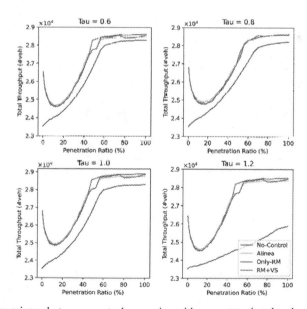

Fig. 4. Comparisons between control scenarios with respect to time headway parameter.

5   Conclusions

In this work we have summarized, we present a preliminary SA for the CACC car-following model, considering a single model input, time headway, and as the model output, the throughput of the simulation model is considered. Presented SA is conducted through a case-study using real network piece with field measurements. With the use of real demand data and several freeway traffic control strategies, we assessed the results based on utilized freeway capacity in this segment. The used SA approach in this presented study falls into the category of OAT methods. Although the results indicate that CACC car-following model is sensitive to the time headway parameter, the degree of sensitivity is still unknown. In order to obtain the degree of sensitivity, other parameters of the model must be investigated in a similar manner. Only after that sensitivity indexes of all parameters can be identified, and a strategy for the calibration process can be drawn. In the future, the authors of this study plan to expand upon this work with the ultimate goal of developing a robust strategy to calibrate the CACC car-following model utilized in this study.

Acknowledgments. This work is supported by the Scientific and Technological Research Council of Turkey (TUBITAK) under Project 120M576.

References

1. Ossen, S., Hoogendoorn, S.P., Gorte, B.G.H.: Interdriver differences in car-following: a vehicle trajectory-based study. Transp. Res. Rec. 2(1), 121–129 (2006)
2. Kesting, A., Treiber, M.: Calibrating car-following models by using trajectory data. Transp. Res. Rec. **2088**(1), 148–156 (2008)
3. Zhu, M., Wang, X., Tarko, A., Famg, S.: Modeling car-following behavior on urban expressways in shanghai: a naturalistic driving study. Transp. Res. Part C: Emerg. Technol. **93**, 425–445 (2018)
4. Wiedemann, R., Reiter, U.: Microscopic traffic simulation, the simulation system—mission, Background and Actual State. CEC Project ICARUS, Project No V1052, Final Report (1992)
5. Ciuffo, B., Punzo, V., Qualietta, E.: Kriging meta-modelling to verify traffic micro-simulation calibration methods. In Proceedings of the 90th Transportation Research Board Annual Meeting, Washington DC., USA, 22–26 January 2011 (2011)
6. Milanés, V., Shladover, S.E.: Modeling cooperative and autonomous adaptive cruise control dynamic responses using experimental data. Transp. Res. Part C: Emerg. Technol. **48**, 285–300 (2014)
7. Krajzewicz, D.: Traffic simulation with SUMO – simulation of urban mobility. In: Barceló, J. (ed.) Fundamentals of Traffic Simulation International Series in Operations Research & Management Science, vol. 145, pp. 269–293. Springer, New York (2010). https://doi.org/10. 1007/978-1-4419-6142-6_7
8. Silgu, M.A., Erdagi, I.G., Goksu, G., Celikoglu, H.B.: Combined control of freeway traffic involving cooperative adaptive cruise controlled and human driven vehicles using feedback control through SUMO. IEEE Trans. Intell. Transp. Syst. **23**, 11011–11025 (2021)
9. Morris, M.D.: Factorial sampling plans for preliminary computational experiments. Technometrics **33**(2), 161–174 (1991)

10. Ge, Q., Menéndez, M.: An efficient sensitivity analysis approach for computationally expensive microscopic traffic simulation models. Int. J. Transp. **2**(2), 49–64 (2014)
11. Ciuffo, B., Punzo, V., Montanino, M.: Global sensitivity analysis techniques to simplify the calibration of traffic simulation models: methodology and application to the IDM car-following model. IET Intell. Transp. Syst. **8**, 479–489 (2014)
12. Treiber, M., Hennecke, A., Helbing, D.: Congested traffic states in empirical observations and microscopic simulations. Phys. Rev. E **62**(2), 1805–1824 (2000)
13. Siddharth, S., Ramadurai, G.: Calibration of VISSIM for Indian heterogeneous traffic conditions. Procedia. Soc. Behav. Sci. **104**, 380–389 (2013)
14. PTV Planning Transport Verkehr AG.: User's Manual, VISSIM 7.0. Karlsruhe, Germany (2015)
15. Rrecaj, A.A., Bombol, K.: Calibration and validation of the VISSIM parameters-state of the art. TEM J. **4**(3), 255–269 (2015)
16. Silgu, M.A., Erdagi, I.G., Goksu, G., Celikoglu, H.B.: H_∞ state feedback controller for ODE model of traffic flow. IFAC-PapersOnLine. **54**(2), 19–24 (2021)
17. Hadj-Salem, H., Blosseville, J.M., Papageorgiou, M.: ALINEA: a local feedback control law for on-ramp metering; a real-life study. In: Proceedings of Third International Conference on Road Traffic Control, pp. 194–198 (1990)

On Smart Mobility and Data Stream Mining

Javier J. Sanchez-Medina[1]([🔒])(iD), Juan Antonio Guerra-Montenegro[1](iD),
Agustin J. Sanchez-Medina[2](iD), Itzíar G. Alonso-González[3](iD),
and David Sánchez-Rodríguez[3](iD)

[1] Innovation Center for Information Society – CICEI. ULPGC, Las Palmas, Spain
{javier.sanchez,juanantonio.montenegro}@ulpgc.es
[2] University Institute for Cybernetics – IUCTC, ULPGC, Las Palmas, Spain
agustin.sanchez@ulpgc.es
[3] Institute for Technological Development and Innovation in Communications –
IDeTIC, ULPGC, Las Palmas, Spain
{itziar.alonso,david.sanchez}@ulpgc.es

Keywords: Smart mobility · Data stream mining · On-line learning

1 Introduction

Smart Mobility is a concept within Smart Cities, which are "cities in which ICT is merged with traditional infrastructures, coordinated and integrated using new digital technologies" [9]. According to the United Nations 2/3 of world population is expected to live in cities by 2050. Therefore, mobility is a keystone for providing citizens access to services. In this context, Smart Mobility allows to make the most from a multi-modal transportation planning [10], while providing urban managers and planners data intensive decision making support tools.

In this context, two important elements nowadays are on one side the availability of data and on the other the need of online machine learning methodologies. First, many elements in smart mobility are Data-Driven, such as Connected Vehicles, the Internet of Things, Sensor Networks [5] or Indoor Localization.

However, it is obvious that with the accelerating rate of growth of the data constantly springing from mobility systems, it becomes harder and harder to apply traditional Machine Learning methodologies, in order to extract knowledge from it. It becomes too big and obsolete too fast. A smarter approach is to extract such knowledge – to build the models – while data is being produced. That strategy is sometimes called *Data Stream Mining*, which can process and apply preprocessing, machine learning techniques, etc. on the fly, without any need for storing all the coming data. Two key characteristic of Data Stream Mining based strategies is that they can be adaptive and incremental.

In this communication, our intention is to share a few paradigmatic examples of the application of that kind of machine learning to smart mobility projects, in order to motivate practitioners to consider the pros and cons of such approach. Two examples worth mentioning follow. First, the work in [12], where they share

R. Moreno-Díaz et al. (Eds.): EUROCAST 2022, LNCS 13789, pp. 378–383, 2022.
https://doi.org/10.1007/978-3-031-25312-6_44

a "smart traffic management platform", (STMP). Their goal is to integrate online data streams coming from heterogeneous sources, such as Internet of Things (IoT) networks, smart networks or social media. A very important element to this platform is their argued capability of detecting concept drift, which is a useful feature in order to trigger adaptation or model commutation strategies.

In [16] a traffic sign detection, tracking and recognition methodology is shared including an incremental framework with three components, an off-line detector, an online detector, and motion model predictor, to achieve simultaneous detection and tracking. The sensor used as an input to the system is merely a mono-camera on a moving vehicle under non-stationary environments.

These and some other State of the Art works will be discussed in order to present the topic an its current penetration in the Smart Mobility arena.

2 Data Stream Mining

Data Stream Mining (DSM) is know by some other names, such as Adaptive ML, Online Machine Learning or Continual Learning. In essence, it is about the extraction of knowledge from databases, in an incremental, adaptive way. Traditional Machine Learning (ML) is developed over the following assumptions:

- *Data Ingestion and Preparation Finalized a priori.* All the needed data to train the planned models is available before the training phase. That means a data compilation campaign, and all the needed data cleaning and consolidation has to be ended before even starting to apply ML.
- *Infinite time/computing power available.* Tipically, it is assumed that there is no limit on either storage capacity or computing power or time.
- *Stochastic Stability of the Phenomenon.* The phenomenon to be modelled is assumed to have stable statistic characteristic across the sampling time, such as mean, autocorrelation and variance.

That assumptions are easily proved insufficient for many real-world applications. Real-world applications need to be trained with limited amounts of data, need to be trained in equipment with limited resources, and the phenomena to be modelled is, in the majority of cases, stochastically unstable with time.

That is the so called concept drift [7], and can be detected directly, by monitoring change in the mean, standard deviation, or covariance of the observed variable. It can also be detected indirectly, by monitoring the performance of the trained model, with time, which is worsen in the event of concept drift.

These are the main reasons explaining why there is a call for total new revision of Machine learning methodologies, devising methods where incremental and adaptive learning are possible. Methods need to be able to be trained incrementally, as new data is arriving, and to be able to adapt, by modifying or discarding the learned models when there is concept drift in the event modeled.

3 Current Penetration of DSM in Smart Mobility

Some exemplary topics in Smart Mobility where Data Stream Mining is making a difference are presented in this section:

3.1 Mobility on Demand

Mobility on demand (MOD) is, as defined by the US Department of Transportation, a new approach to mobility in which transportation is conceived as a commodity and transportation modes have defining features like cost, journey time, wait time, number of connections, convenience, and other attributes.

There is no Smart Mobility planning where Shared mobility and Micromobility are not in the center ring. A common and very important element of this leg of Smart Mobility is that they are intensively data driven. That is why Machine Learning approximations come very naturally. In [1] they place decisions as the inputs for a central managing a fleet ride-hailing system. Their methodology is about applying approximate dynamic programming to get high-quality operational dispatch strategies, in an attempt of answering three key questions: what car is best for each demanded trip, when to recharge each car, when should a vehicle be re-positioned to a different area to address an expected demand. Even if this is not exactly approached from AI and Machine Learning, they do apply adaptation to determine ride pricing.

In [2] we have another example of DSM application. They implement an incremental methodology for the prediction of bike counts for a bike sharing system fleet. That is an essential need of such services to spread the vehicles availability with respect to the potential demand for any shared mobility architecture.

In this case, the incremental learning aspect is implemented by updating the regression coefficient β after received every mini-batch of observations.

There is yet another interesting application which was proposed in [8], where a reinforcement learning-based technique is applied to create a distributed autonomous vehicle relocation system and an allocation ride request system for a shared mobility-on-demand agent (SAMoD), allowing each vehicle to autonomously learn how to balance and select requests based on a current and historical per-demand record. This model was tested using real NYC Taxi data [8], where they evaluate the impact of ride-sharing previously learnt assignment, re-balancing behavior developed by serving single vehicle requests. Q-learning was used in this application, due to its independence against a predefined model of the environment, and its ability to capture agent's experiences learnt from the interaction with the environment. The case study environment was previously divided by geographical areas and requests where classified based on their origin and their destination, allowing each agent to consider the neighboring zones of its actual location to make its "decision". This architecture runs online, with real-time data. Hence, it supports dynamic ride sharing and gathers historical data throughout the agent's lifetime in order to learn request patterns.

3.2 Traffic Predictive Modeling

A very important branch of Intelligent Transportation Systems as a whole, also of Smart Mobility, is Traffic Modeling. It is a key feature that Traffic engineers, planners and managers do value and need. There is that relatively new branch of reinforcement learning, *deep reinforcement learning* [11], which can be found in many works to solve different problems related to traffic management and ITS.

The development of big data-driven smart management solutions presents a challenge because of various problems, namely the volatility of traffic conditions, the dynamism of big data streams, and the high-frequency of unlabeled data generation originated from different data sources.

Smart Mobility, when it is big-data driven, poses great development challenges. The variability of traffic conditions, the dynamism of big-data streams and the problem of unlabeled data coming from different sensors, with different characteristics, are just some of them.

To cope with these difficulties, an expansive smart traffic management platform was developed in [12] was proposed, based on deep reinforcement learning and incremental machine learning. This approach integrates heterogeneous big data stream sources, such as social media, smart sensor networks and the Internet of Things, to deliver different tasks, like traffic flow forecasting, optimized traffic control decisions, commuter sentiment analysis and concept drift detection.

Traffic congestion is a pandemic issue in many urban traffic networks, due to an insufficient infrastructure capacity, and it unchains many complications such as accidents or severe traffic jams. An interesting approach to solve this undesired situation is ramp metering, which aims to control traffic density by keeping it near its critical value threshold. There is a very well known methodology to do this in [14].

In [4] authors proposed an on-the-fly traffic congestion predictive modeling also based on a Deep Learning. The incremental learning aspect is addressed based on different context temporal data segments, from short-term to long-term, that are added as features to the model. Furthermore, these temporal data segments are dynamically selected for prediction, varying the weighting of each segment.

Finally, another good example of the application of DSM to Traffic Modeling is in [15], where a real-time crash prediction modelling architecture based on Support Vector Machine is shared. The training of the model has an off-line phase, where the model is learned using the existing historical data, and an on-line phase where the model is updated as new data is coming. They call this a "warm start" strategy.

3.3 Social Network Event Detection

Smartphones and other personal devices are commonly found in current ITS developments together with inputting social network interchanges as information sources. There is a keen interest on urban managers on grasping what is happening on the Internet about their area.

In [6] and Indonesian project is shared, where social networks play a central role in order to sampling the current traffic state. They do real time sentiment analysis in order to extract users' opinions on mobility services. But since the sentiment analysis methodology is not on English language, that poses additional challenges. For example, cultural challenges like speakers using negation instead of strong negative words. That makes it a bit harder for training good sentiment detection models. The incremental and adaptability element in this work is in their proposed architecture ability of learning new keywords and elements around transportation services.

In a similar way to collaborative filtering models for recommendation systems are being used in ITS for detecting real time traffic events, traffic or road status. For instance, in [13] they detect related tweets while incrementally learning the causes of traffic events and updating a cause-ontology set. The base language is Arabic for this application.

3.4   Multimodality

Multimodality is one of the greatest challenges for urban mobility planning nowadays. It is crucial to find ways of harmonizing citizen needs and all of the mobility possibilities, both private and public.

In [3], a Bayesian-probabilistic method is proposed to incorporate learning of users' travel preferences in a multi-modal routing system. The proposed architecture learns preference parameters incrementally, based on travel choices made by travellers. For each user a preference model is created, which is demonstrated to be learnt quickly this way.

Acknowledgements. This work was partially funded in part by the Consejería de Economía, Conocimiento y Empleo del Gobierno de Canarias (ProID2020010009), Spain; and by Agencia Canaria de Investigación, Innovación y Sociedad de la Información (ACIISI) de la Consejería de Economía, Industria, Comercio y Conocimiento and by Fondo Social Europeo (FSE) Programa Operativo Integrado de Canarias 2014-2020, Eje 3 Tema Prioritario 74 (85%).

References

1. Al-Kanj, L., Nascimento, J., Powell, W.B.: Approximate dynamic programming for planning a ride-hailing system using autonomous fleets of electric vehicles. Eur. J. Oper. Res. **284**(3), 1088–1106 (2020)
2. Almannaa, M.H., Elhenawy, M., Guo, F., Rakha, H.A.: Incremental learning models of bike counts at bike sharing systems. In: 2018 21st International Conference on Intelligent Transportation Systems (ITSC), pp. 3712–3717. IEEE (2018)
3. Arentze, T.A.: Adaptive personalized travel information systems: a Bayesian method to learn users' personal preferences in multimodal transport networks. IEEE Trans. Intell. Transp. Syst. **14**(4), 1957–1966 (2013)
4. Bartlett, Z., Han, L., Nguyen, T.T., Johnson, P.: A novel online dynamic temporal context neural network framework for the prediction of road traffic flow. IEEE Access **7**, 153533–153541 (2019)
5. Del Ser, J., Sanchez-Medina, J.J., Vlahogianni, E.I.: Introduction to the special issue on online learning for big-data driven transportation and mobility. IEEE Trans. Intell. Transp. Syst. **20**(12), 4621–4623 (2019). https://doi.org/10.1109/TITS.2019.2955548

6. Fiarni, C., Maharani, H., Irawan, E.: Implementing rule-based and Naive Bayes algorithm on incremental sentiment analysis system for Indonesian online transportation services review. In: 2018 10th International Conference on Information Technology and Electrical Engineering (ICITEE), pp. 597–602. IEEE (2018)
7. Gama, J., Žliobaitė, I., Bifet, A., Pechenizkiy, M., Bouchachia, A.: A survey on concept drift adaptation. ACM Comput. Surv. (CSUR) **46**(4), 1–37 (2014)
8. Guériau, M., Dusparic, I.: SAMoD: shared autonomous mobility-on-demand using decentralized reinforcement learning. In: 2018 21st International Conference on Intelligent Transportation Systems (ITSC), pp. 1558–1563. IEEE (2018)
9. Klimczuk, A., Tomczyk, Ł.: Inteligentne miasta przyjazne starzeniu-przykłady z krajów grupy wyszehradzkiej (smart, age-friendly cities: Examples in the countries of the visegrad group (v4)). Rozwój Regionalny i Polityka Regionalna **34**(2016), 79–97 (2016)
10. Lenz, B., Heinrichs, D.: What can we learn from smart urban mobility technologies? IEEE Pervasive Comput. **16**(2), 84–86 (2017). https://doi.org/10.1109/MPRV.2017.27
11. Mnih, V., et al.: Human-level control through deep reinforcement learning. Nature **518**(7540), 529–533 (2015)
12. Nallaperuma, D., et al.: Online incremental machine learning platform for big data-driven smart traffic management. IEEE Trans. Intell. Transp. Syst. **20**(12), 4679–4690 (2019). https://doi.org/10.1109/TITS.2019.2924883
13. Nsouli, A., Mourad, A., Azar, D.: Towards proactive social learning approach for traffic event detection based on Arabic tweets. In: 2018 14th International Wireless Communications & Mobile Computing Conference (IWCMC), pp. 1501–1506. IEEE (2018)
14. Papageorgiou, M., Hadj-Salem, H., Blosseville, J.M., et al.: ALINEA: a local feedback control law for on-ramp metering. Transp. Res. Rec. **1320**(1), 58–67 (1991)
15. Sun, P., Guo, G., Yu, R.: Traffic crash prediction based on incremental learning algorithm. In: 2017 IEEE 2nd International Conference on Big Data Analysis (ICBDA), pp. 182–185. IEEE (2017)
16. Yuan, Y., Xiong, Z., Wang, Q.: An incremental framework for video-based traffic sign detection, tracking, and recognition. IEEE Trans. Intell. Transp. Syst. **18**(7), 1918–1929 (2017). https://doi.org/10.1109/TITS.2016.2614548

Smart Vehicle Inspection

Peter Tapak[1]([✉]), Michal Kocur[1], Matej Rabek[1], and Juraj Matej[2]

[1] Institute of Automotive Mechatronics, Faculty of Electrical Engineering
and Information Technology, Slovak University of Technology in Bratislava,
Ilkovičova 3, 812 19 Bratislava, Slovakia
peter.tapak@stuba.sk
[2] TESTEK, a.s., Authorized Technical Service for Technical Inspections of Vehicles,
P.O.Box 84, Placheho 14, 841 02 Bratislava, Slovakia

Abstract. Periodical vehicle inspection is a common practice amongst
European countries. The paper describes the smart phone application
utilisation in the inspection process and presents the outcomes of the
first years of using this app at Slovak technical inspection stations.

Keywords: Vehicle inspection · Smart phone application · On board
diagnostics · Vehicle safety · Brake testing

1 Introduction

Periodical vehicle safety inspection (PTI) is a technical service provided by vehicle inspection service stations to prevent traffic accidents caused by vehicle malfunction. The importance of PTI is summarized in [7]. Usually, the vehicles are checked if they comply with national safety regulations. In many countries these inspections are performed together with the emission inspection, which objective is to check the vehicles' emission regulations compliance. The importance of road-worthiness checks is not only that it verifies if the vehicle is working properly, however it is also important for environmental reasons. In the European Union, there are two types of assessment: on-the-spot roadside inspections and periodic checks, where owners have to take the vehicle to an inspection service station.

The periodical technical vehicle inspection is carried out in the European Union, former the European Community, European Economic Community, since late 70's by directive 77/143/EEC [1]. Since April 2014, all European Union member states have to carry out periodic safety and emission inspections for most types of motor vehicles by the EU directive 2014/45 [2]. The PTI process varies across EU countries, nevertheless usually following checks are performed during inspection:

Technical inspections relate to the condition and maintenance of the vehicle, and in particular to:

– axles, brakes, wheels, tyres, wheel alignment,

R. Moreno-Díaz et al. (Eds.): EUROCAST 2022, LNCS 13789, pp. 384–391, 2022.
https://doi.org/10.1007/978-3-031-25312-6_45

- frame/body, including vehicle identification (chassis number, licence plates),
- exhaust system, environmental nuisances such as noise and exhaust emissions,
- steering,
- lighting/electrical systems, electrical equipment,
- windows, mirrors, visibility,
- accessories,
- pedals, seats, seat belts,
- electronic safety systems,

The paper focuses on passenger cars which have to be inspected in Slovakia within four years after their first registration and then every two years thereafter. It is the same schedule as Germany's which is the EU country with the largest number of passenger cars in EU.

In Slovak Republic many changes have been applied to PTI policies and supervising, due to fraudulent behaviour at the PTI service stations.

It is not the point of this paper to analyse the reasons of these frauds. However, the malfunctions can lead to very dangerous situations on road, therefore actions to prevent cheating at PTI stations have been taken in Slovakia. Since 2019 there is mandatory to have surveillance cameras to prevent cheating at every PTI station in Slovak Republic. Intensified supervision increased PTI failure rate in 2019 from 6.2% to 13.1% in other words the failure rate was more than doubled in march 2019 as can be seen from statistics in Fig. 1.

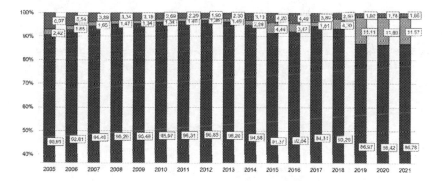

Fig. 1. PTI pass rate. (green - passed, yellow - major defect, red - dangerous defect) (Color figure online)

Presented mobile application, mSTK can be found at [5]. Since 1st of January 2020 it has been mandatory to use this smartphone app during the PTI tests in Slovakia to perform the following tasks:

- taking and uploading photograph of odometer to national server,
- taking and uploading photograph of vehicle identification number (VIN) to national server,

– reading diagnostic trouble codes from car's on board diagnostics port (OBD) and uploading them to national server,

– measuring acceleration of the vehicle during brake test, calculating the results and uploading measurement and the results to the national server.

The smart app utilization in PTI process contributes to fraud prevention at PTI service stations in the following way:

1. The internet connection is necessary to perform any task using the app,
2. the technician has to enter his credentials to be able to perform any task,
3. the VIN photograph prevents using different vehicle for tests,
4. the odometer photograph prevents from faking the odometer values in the national system,
5. the app sends location of the taken photographs to prevent performing the test outside the PTI service station (the photograph can not be taken without localization services enabled),
6. it double checks VIN by reading it from OBD as well,
7. it reads diagnostics trouble codes via OBD, these can not be ignored by the technician,
8. the location of the device is stored and uploaded to national server during the brake driving test, to make certain that it was performed at declared location under the declared conditions.

2   Mobile App

The app starts at the main activity screen shown in Fig. 2. It shows inspetor's name on top and the list of assigned inspections is below. The inspections are identified by car registration number and the car make and model.

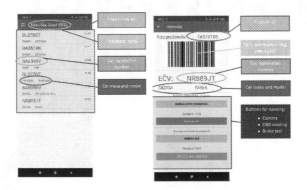

Fig. 2. Main activity screen (left), Inspection detail (right)

The pictures are taken using any camera present on the mobile device. After taking the picture it is resized to 640 by 480 pixels resolution and compressed into JPEG format the compression level is adjusted to yield size lower than 100 kilo bytes. It is not possible to use a file as a photograph to prevent cheating. Fig. 3 shows screenshot of photograph of odometer. It shows ABS and power steering malfunction, however it could have been be ignored by the inspector before the app with OBD reading became mandatory at PTI service stations.

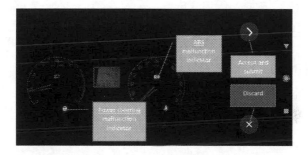

Fig. 3. Odometer photograph with malfunction indicators.

2.1 Diagnostics Reading

Despite the fact that it is possible to read much more information from the vehicle using proprietary HW and SW, the presented solution aims to work independently on vehicle make or manufacturer, because it uses open OBD II standards. It is possible to design and develop special OBD reader like in [9]. It does not put any additional expenses on equipment and software licences on the PTI service stations since it uses cheap and widely available wireless OBD reader, ELM327 (see e.g. [3]). The goal is to read diagnostics trouble codes available via open OBD service. There is many smartphone apps available to read the DTCs via ELM327 OBD reader, however this application integrates more PTI tasks and processes and focuses also on fraud protection by providing following information:

- ELM327 voltage - it is the voltage measured by the ELM 327 reader on the OBD port pins,
- VIN - vehicle identification umber - it is compared with the number in the information system,
- DTCs - diagnostics trouble codes

There is more communication going on between the phone and ELM327 such as reset to defaults, vehicle OBD protocol detection, supported services list etc. These are not important to be described in detail in this paper. All the responses of the car are stored and submitted to national server to allow further analysis of these data in the cases of wrong or suspicious inspections. These data also serve to help with debugging and research activities, since 2020 is the first year of employing these devices in such large scale. Fig. 4 shows OBD reading activity. The results are shown in the upper part. If the car does not provide VIN via standard OBD service, it shows XXXXXXXXXXXXXXXX instead. below VIN the DTCs are displayed. The rest of the screen shows overall progress in % and it also puts check marks to the successfully finished tasks to give technician better feedback of what is going on, because there can be delays if some reading fails and it is started over few times. There can be cars which are not readable by ELM327 reader, therefore it is possible to finish the measurement without obtaining the data. However, the inspector has to at least try, in other words the app has to connect to ELM327 via bluetooth, it has to read the voltage and it has to try to send requests to the car several times. All this communication is stored and submitted to server. It indicates the unsuccessful reading by orange colour of the OBD read button in the app in this case (Fig. 2 on right).

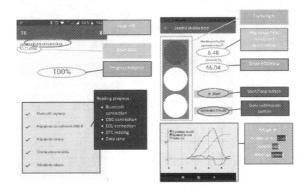

Fig. 4. OBD reading activity/brake testing activity

2.2   Brake Testing

Drive brake testing became a very important feature of this application. It is a common practice to test the vehicle brakes at a roller bench device (for further information on brake testing see e.g. [8]). There are vehicles or situations in which a different brake test should be used. Not all roller benches are suitable for 4 wheel driven vehicles or for agricultural vehicles. In Slovak republic there is possible to make PTI of agricultural vehicles on site, to prevent transportation of these vehicles to PTI service stations. In these cases the drive brake test is an alternative to roller brake test in Slovak republic legislation based on United Nations Economic Commission for Europe Agreement [4]. Decelerometers, such as MAHA VZM300 [6], where utilized in this tests until 2020 in Slovakia. It gave a large space for fraudulent behaviour because no data for verification of the test results were available and there was no guarantee that the test was performed at all.

Following the regulations, function of brake shall be determined by measuring the stopping distance in relation to the initial speed of the vehicle and/or by measuring the mean fully developed deceleration during the test. It would be possible to measure the stopping distance by phones positioning sensors such as GNSS and inertial measurement unit (IMU) using dead reckoning. Fully developed deceleration is obtained by the phone's IMU in this application. The fully developed deceleration (d_m) shall be calculated as the average deceleration over the interval v_b to v_e according the following formula:

$$d_m = \frac{v_b^2 - v_e^2}{25.92(s_e - s_b)} \tag{1}$$

where

- v_0 = initial vehicle speed in km/h: it a vehicle speed at the moment when the driver starts to break,
- v_b = vehicle speed at $0.8v_0$ in km/h,
- v_e = vehicle speed at $0.1v_0$ in km/h,
- s_b = distance traveled between v_0 and v_b in meters,
- s_e = distance traveled between v_0 and v_e in meters.

The initial results were similar to devices used for this purpose before and the data were consistent. However, it would not be possible to use any device for measurement of such crucial safety system as the brakes are without any former calibration or testing. Each phone has to be tested for accuracy of its accelerometers at steady states every 2 years. This process however does not put any significant cost increase, because the price and frequency of calibration is similar to those of previously used devices.

The GUI is simple since it is intended to be used while driving.

The screenshot from drive brake test activity is in Fig. 4.

3   First Years of Usage Results

There have been more than 10000 diagnostics trouble codes detected until the end of year 2020 which is the first year the app became mandatory. Most of these were emission inspection related which is performed as a separate service in Slovakia. Table 1 shows monthly summary of DTC readinegs. It presents PTI related DTCs in separate lines. The bottom line shows the summary of all, PTI and emission related trouble codes.

Since January 1st 2021 the only way how to perform brake drive test has been the mobile app measurement. More than 100000 test have been made in 2021. It has very small failure ratio, however it brings more than increased supervision. For vehicles which are road legal, but hard to bring to PTI station or which are too big to fit to PTI station, it is possible to make the inspection on site. This applies mostly to agricultural vehicles or heavy vehicles such cranes etc. Since the

Table 1. Diagnostic Trouble Codes Monthly Count. DTC: Diagnostics trouble code; Part: affected part of the vehicle; Class: Classification of vehicle defects - B: Major Defect - with influence on road safety and environment, but no imminent danger (car is still roadworthy for next 60 days to allow necessary repairs) (abbreviations: ABS anti-lock braking system, EBS - electronic braking system, EPS - electronic power steering)

DTC/Month	1	2	3	4	5	6	7	8	9	10	11	12	Total	Part	Class
P0504	5	2			3	2	3	1	0	2	1	1	20	EBS	B
P0552	1												1	EPS	B
P0553				1									1	EPS	B
P0555				1									1	EBS	B
P0557						1							1	EBS	B
P2299	1			1					1		2	1	6	EBS	B
U0121		1		2	1	2	3	1	2	1	1		14	ABS	B
U0415	1	2	2	1	1	2		1			1		11	ABS	B
U0418				2					1	1			4	EBS	B
C0041											1		1	EBS	B
P0556												1	1	EBS	B
P0573									1			1	2	EBS	B
...	...	...	...	...	...	...	...	...	...	...	...	...	...		
Total	...	...	...	...	...	...	...	...	...	...	...	...	10183		

price of suitable smartphones is less than a tenth of the cheapest decelerometer used before, the PTI station can have more of them and can inspect more vehicles on site (Table 2).

Table 2. Number of brake drive test performed by mobile app in 2021 in Slovak Republic

Number of drive tests	Major defects	Dangerous defects
135913	195	36

4 Conclusion

The introduction of mobile app into inspection process in 2020 made the process more transparent and strengthened the supervision. It helped to maintain pass rates at the level which was obtained by implementing video surveillance. The number of brake driving test performed by the presented app shows the importance of designing such tool. Despite the low test pass rate, the app helped to find more than 200 vehicles with defects in braking systems, which definitely presented risk for road safety. Further development of the app focuses on the fuel and electrical energy consumption, e-call and advanced driver assistance systems.

Acknowledgment. This work has been partially supported by the Slovak Grant Agency VEGA project 1/0745/19 and partially granted by the grant KEGA 030STU-4/2021.

References

1. 77/143/eec (1976). http://data.europa.eu/eli/dir/1977/143/oj. Accessed 1 Jan 2020
2. Directive 2014/45/eu (2014). http://data.europa.eu/eli/dir/2014/45/oj. Accessed 18 Nov 2019
3. Elm 327 (2017). https://www.elmelectronics.com/wp-content/uploads/2017/01/ELM327DS.pdf. Accessed 15 July 2021
4. Agreement concerning the adoption of harmonized technical united nations regulations for wheeled vehicles, equipment and parts which can be fitted and/or be used on wheeled vehicles and the conditions for reciprocal recognition of approvals granted on the basis of these united nations regulations (2019). http://www.unece.org/trans/main/wp29/wp29wgs/wp29gen/wp29fdocstts.html. Accessed 17 Jan 2019
5. mstk (2020). https://play.google.com/store/apps/details?id=sk.deletech.uitk&authuser=0. Accessed 1 Jan 2020
6. Maha vzm 300 (2021). https://www.maha.de/en/products/brake-testing-technology/decelerometer/vzm-300~p1111. Accessed 15 July 2021
7. Martín-delosReyes, L.M., et al.: Effect of periodic vehicle inspection on road crashes and injuries: a systematic review. Int. J. Environ. Res. Public Health **18**(12) (2021). https://www.mdpi.com/1660-4601/18/12/6476
8. Olmeda, E., Garrosa, M., Sánchez, S.S., Díaz, V.: Development and characterization of a compact device for measuring the braking torque of a vehicle. Sensors **20**(15), 4278 (2020). https://doi.org/10.3390/s20154278
9. Yen, M.H., Tian, S.L., Lin, Y.T., Yang, C.W., Chen, C.C.: Combining a universal OBD-II module with deep learning to develop an eco driving analysis system. Appl. Sci. **11**(10) (2021). https://www.mdpi.com/2076-3417/11/10/4481

Computer Vision, Machine Learning for Image Analysis and Applications

Impact of the Region of Analysis on the Performance of the Automatic Epiretinal Membrane Segmentation in OCT Images

Mateo Gende[1,2] (ID), Daniel Iglesias Morís[1,2] (ID), Joaquim de Moura[1,2(✉)] (ID), Jorge Novo[1,2] (ID), and Marcos Ortega[1,2] (ID)

[1] Grupo VARPA, Instituto de Investigación Biomédica de A Coruña (INIBIC), Universidade da Coruña, A Coruña, Spain
{m.gende,daniel.iglesias.moris,joaquim.demoura,jnovo,mortega}@udc.es
[2] Centro de investigación CITIC, Universidade da Coruña, A Coruña, Spain

Abstract. The Epiretinal Membrane (ERM) is an ocular pathology that can cause permanent visual loss if left untreated for long. Despite its transparency, it is possible to visualise the ERM in Optical Coherence Tomography (OCT) images. In this work, we present a study on the impact of the analysis region on the performance of an automatic ERM segmentation methodology using OCT images. For this purpose, we tested 5 different sliding windows sizes ranging from 14×14 to 224×224 pixels to calibrate the impact of the field of view under analysis. Furthermore, 3 different approaches are proposed to enable the analysis of the regions close to the edges of the images. The proposed approaches provided satisfactory results, with each of them interacting differently with the variations in window size.

Keywords: Computer-aided diagnosis · Optical coherence tomography · Epiretinal membrane · Segmentation · Deep learning

1 Introduction

The Epiretinal Membrane (ERM) is an ocular pathology consisting of a thin fibrocellular layer of tissue that may appear over the retina. Although this film is mainly transparent, its development over the photosensitive tissue of the eye can lead to complications. Once it reaches a certain stage, the ERM may start to contract over itself. Since it is adhered to the tissue of the retina, it may exert a traction. This traction deforms the underlying tissue, producing wrinkles or puckers. If the ERM is present over the macula, the part of the eye that is responsible for sharp vision, the deformations it might induce can lead to visual distortion, a loss of vision and, eventually, may cause a macular hole. If treated on time, the ERM may be removed while preserving patient vision. Conversely, a late diagnosis may lead to irreversible deformations of the tissue and the consequent vision loss [12].

R. Moreno-Díaz et al. (Eds.): EUROCAST 2022, LNCS 13789, pp. 395–402, 2022.
https://doi.org/10.1007/978-3-031-25312-6_46

Optical Coherence Tomography (OCT) is an ocular imaging technique that uses low coherence light to sweep the tissue and obtain three-dimensional visualisations of the underlying histological structure [8,10]. Despite being mostly transparent, the ERM can be visualised in OCT imaging. Its appearance is that of a bright film located in the boundary between the vitreous body and the retinal tissue, an area that is known as the Inner Limiting Membrane, or ILM. Due to the high visibility and the advantages that this imaging technique supposes in terms of cross-sectional visualisation, OCT is a standard imaging modality used for the detection and assessment of the ERM [5].

Typically, the ERM is diagnosed by an ophthalmologist visually inspecting each OCT slice. This process can become tiresome and repetitive, due to the great volume of images to analyse and may lead to subjectivity in the detection. Because of this, various works have approached the automatisation of this screening process. Wilkins et al. [14] first proposed a semi-automatic approach, involving an initial manual annotation made by an expert and a progressive automatic refinement of the affected area. More recently, some works have introduced fully automatic methods for ERM presence classification in OCT images. Sonobe et al. [13] trained a Convolutional Neural Network (CNN) to determine the pathology that each image presented, and compared the results with those obtained with Support Vector Machines (SVMs). In this comparison, the deep learning methods achieved much better results than the SVMs. Parra-Mora et al. [11] used four convolutional neural network architectures for the classification of OCT slices. These models achieved high performance in discriminating ERM cases.

On the other hand, few studies have addressed the segmentation of the ERM in OCT slices. As reference, Baamonde et al. proposed different ways to characterise the ERM in OCT images using conventional hand-crafted features [1,3,4]. Additionally, the authors present a multi-stage methodology for the conversion of a segmentation problem into a classification one by extracting a series of vertical image patches from the OCT slices [2]. This classification is performed by extracting and selecting a subset of relevant features and using classical machine learning techniques. In the work of Gende et al. [6], the authors presented a complete methodology in which a series of square windows is extracted around the ILM. These windows are then classified by a CNN, automatising the feature extraction and selection process by allowing the deep learning models to be trained directly from the image patches. This methodology was able to outperform the previous methods while also considerably simplifying the inference process. However, the effects of different window sizes that calibrate the field of view under analysis on this methodology has not been assessed. Furthermore, this methodology is limited in the amount of tissue it can analyse close to the image edges, since windows cannot be extracted outside of the image bounds, as illustrated in Fig. 1.

In this work, we present a study on the impact that the size of the extracted windows has on the performance of the classification models for the segmentation of the ERM. In this study, we compare the results obtained using five window

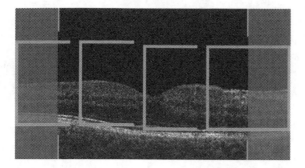

Fig. 1. Illustration of the limitations of the existing methodology concerning image boundaries. Those spots lying on the highlighted areas cannot be directly analysed.

sizes ranging from 14 × 14 to 224 × 224. Furthermore, we analyse 3 different approaches to overcome the limitations posed by the existing methodologies in terms of analysing the areas that are close to the image bounds: A basic, Zero Padding approach in which the part of the windows lying outside of the image bounds is filled with zeros; a Border Extension approach in which the final column is extended outwards and a Border Reflection approach in which the image is reflected along the vertical axis around the image border.

2   Methodology

2.1   ERM Segmentation Methodology

In order to segment the ERM in each OCT slice, we followed the three-step methodology proposed by Gende *et al.* [6]. The first step is to obtain the location of the ILM, the area that is susceptible to ERM proliferation. Next, a series of windows is extracted from the OCT image. Each of these windows is centred on an ILM pixel, and contains the visual information surrounding the point of interest. Finally, each window is classified by using a DenseNet-121 [9] classifier, returning a label for each ILM pixel indicating if the spot is healthy or diseased. This architecture has been used in similar medical image segmentation tasks with encouraging results [6,7]. By accumulating all of these labels and assigning them to the original ILM pixels, a segmentation of the ERM can be produced, as illustrated in Fig. 2.

2.2   Impact of the Region of Analysis

The size of the extracted windows has an impact on the amount of visual information that is incorporated into the classification process, that is, the field of view that is particularly under analysis to determine each potentially pathological case. This in turn translates into an impact on the ability of the system to discriminate between healthy and diseased spots. Additionally, in the window

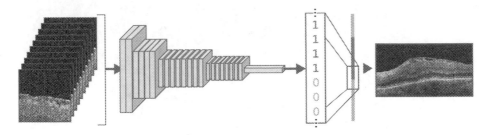

Fig. 2. Summary of the ERM segmentation methodology. Windows are extracted from the original OCT slice. These windows are classified by a CNN, and the resulting class labels are used to reconstruct a segmentation of the ERM.

extraction process, pixels close to the edges of the image cannot be directly analysed, since the area surrounding each of these pixels would lie out of bounds. This constraint becomes more restrictive the more the window width is increased.

In order to study the impact that the field of view has on the performance of the ERM segmentation methodology, different configurations were tested and analysed. On the one hand, a series of DenseNet-121 models were trained using five different window sizes: 14×14, 28×28, 56×56, 112×112, and 224×224 pixels. Furthermore, 3 different approaches aimed at overcoming the limitations related to image boundaries were tested. A schematic representation of the proposed approaches can be seen in Fig. 3.

- **Zero Padding**: This baseline approach consists of filling the area of the window lying out of bounds with zeros. This way, no additional information is incorporated into the classification process. This approach creates a synthetic border at the point where the original image ends.
- **Border Extension**: The second approach consists of replicating the final row or column of original image pixels outwards until the edge of the window. This avoids generating a synthetic border at the edge of the image, but in turn may incorporate more noise in the window.
- **Border Reflection**: The final approach reflects the original image along the axis located at its edge. This way, the original look of the image is preserved, providing a more seamless transition where the original image border would be located and replicating the information already contained in the window.

3   Results and Discussion

The five window sizes that determine the fields of view under analysis were combined with the three approaches for a total of 15 different configurations. For each of these configurations, a series of CNNs were trained and evaluated. To train and validate these models, a dataset consisting of 2,427 OCT slices belonging to 20 patients was used. Out of these 20 patients, 8 presented ERM signs while 12 were healthy. In each OCT image, ERM presence or absence

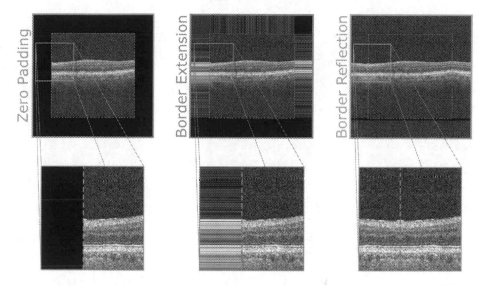

Fig. 3. Detailed viewts of each of the three proposed approaches that allow the analysis of pixcls close to the image boundary.

was marked as a height value for each column. In total, 251,994 columns were annotated as pathological, out of a total of 1,308,160 image columns. The models were trained using a 4-fold cross-validation at the eye level, cnsuring each eye appears in a test set once. Online augmentation was uscd in the form of random shear transformations, rotations, intensity variations and horizontal flipping. The loss employed was Cross-entropy, and Adam was used for optimisation. Training was allowed to run for a maximum of 75 epochs for each configuration, saving the model that performed best in validation for testing.

The results that were obtained by testing each of the proposed configurations can be found on Table 1. As for the proposed approaches that enable analysis close to the image edges, the Zero Padding approach is the most affected by window size, achieving Dice scores of 0.573 and 0.517 with the more extreme window sizes, comparatively worse than the 0.675 obtained with windows of the size 112 × 112. While the Border Extension approach decays in performance with larger windows, as is expected from the approach that has the biggest impact on the look of the patches, it outperforms the other two for the smaller window sizes of 14 × 14 and 28 × 28. The Border Reflection approach gives the overall best result out of the three proposed when combined with windows of size 56 × 56, with a Dice Coefficient of up to 0.699.

Complementarily, Fig. 4 shows an example of the segmentation results produced by models trained with the Border Reflection approach for different window sizes. As we can see, the obtained results show that intermediate window sizes tend to give better results than either of the extreme sizes. In addition, a smaller field of view tends to leave out relevant information for the classification,

Table 1. Test results for each of the proposed configurations. Bold indicates best results for each of the metrics.

	14×14	28×28	56×56	112×112	224×224
	Zero padding approach				
Accuracy	0.821 ± 0.039	0.863 ± 0.019	0.869 ± 0.016	$\mathbf{0.879 \pm 0.015}$	0.859 ± 0.050
Precision	0.526 ± 0.131	0.633 ± 0.135	0.621 ± 0.122	$\mathbf{0.657 \pm 0.126}$	0.647 ± 0.156
Recall	0.660 ± 0.243	0.692 ± 0.201	$\mathbf{0.726 \pm 0.165}$	0.709 ± 0.075	0.565 ± 0.324
Specificity	0.860 ± 0.037	0.906 ± 0.029	0.899 ± 0.019	$\mathbf{0.920 \pm 0.011}$	0.905 ± 0.081
Jaccard	0.414 ± 0.152	0.486 ± 0.141	0.506 ± 0.145	$\mathbf{0.513 \pm 0.088}$	0.373 ± 0.197
Dice	0.573 ± 0.152	0.645 ± 0.122	0.663 ± 0.125	$\mathbf{0.675 \pm 0.075}$	0.517 ± 0.245
	Border extension approach				
Accuracy	0.832 ± 0.042	0.859 ± 0.020	0.858 ± 0.042	$\mathbf{0.870 \pm 0.022}$	0.861 ± 0.032
Precision	0.559 ± 0.135	0.625 ± 0.111	0.604 ± 0.141	$\mathbf{0.682 \pm 0.098}$	0.649 ± 0.140
Recall	0.678 ± 0.203	0.701 ± 0.150	$\mathbf{0.703 \pm 0.186}$	0.652 ± 0.219	0.604 ± 0.212
Specificity	0.871 ± 0.033	0.898 ± 0.024	0.891 ± 0.023	$\mathbf{0.920 \pm 0.045}$	0.915 ± 0.051
Jaccard	0.440 ± 0.148	0.490 ± 0.111	$\mathbf{0.493 \pm 0.168}$	0.481 ± 0.130	0.434 ± 0.145
Dice	0.601 ± 0.137	$\mathbf{0.652 \pm 0.096}$	0.647 ± 0.153	0.641 ± 0.122	0.594 ± 0.142
	Border reflection approach				
Accuracy	0.827 ± 0.036	0.859 ± 0.031	$\mathbf{0.882 \pm 0.017}$	0.871 ± 0.025	0.840 ± 0.039
Precision	0.549 ± 0.123	0.635 ± 0.171	$\mathbf{0.697 \pm 0.142}$	0.656 ± 0.142	0.618 ± 0.111
Recall	0.665 ± 0.179	0.687 ± 0.177	$\mathbf{0.744 \pm 0.172}$	0.684 ± 0.157	0.649 ± 0.188
Specificity	0.869 ± 0.019	0.906 ± 0.032	$\mathbf{0.917 \pm 0.041}$	0.917 ± 0.008	0.888 ± 0.067
Jaccard	0.429 ± 0.131	0.485 ± 0.148	$\mathbf{0.544 \pm 0.118}$	0.505 ± 0.144	0.440 ± 0.079
Dice	0.592 ± 0.123	0.644 ± 0.128	$\mathbf{0.699 \pm 0.094}$	0.662 ± 0.128	0.608 ± 0.077

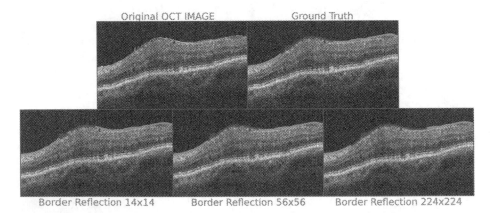

Fig. 4. Examples of the results obtained for different window sizes combined with the Border Reflection approach.

while a wider one may include visual features of regions unrelated to the patch on which the window is centred.

4 Conclusions

The early detection of the ERM in OCT images is paramount in order to preserve patient vision. In this work, we propose a series of improvements for the automatic segmentation of this relevant pathology in OCT slices. These consist in three different approaches that enable the analysis of the slices close to the image borders. Furthermore, we study the impact that five different window sizes have on the performance of the detection of the ERM and its combination with the three proposed approaches. These combinations were trained and validated on a representative dataset consisting of 2,427 OCT scans. The satisfactory results that were obtained show that intermediate window sizes provide the best performance, with the Zero Padding approach being most affected by either very small or very large windows. For the two smaller window sizes, the Border Extension approach performed better than the other two. Out of all the tested configurations, the Border Reflection approach combined with windows of size 56×56 provides the best results, achieving a Dice Coefficient of 0.699 ± 0.094, this way providing a robust and accurate segmentation of the ERM, contributing to the early diagnosis of this pathology.

Acknowledgements. This research was funded by Instituto de Salud Carlos III, Government of Spain, [DTS18/00136]; Ministerio de Ciencia e Innovación y Universidades, Government of Spain, [RTI2018-095894-B-I00]; Ministerio de Ciencia e Innovación, Government of Spain through the research project [PID2019-108435RB-I00]; Consellería de Cultura, Educación e Universidade, Xunta de Galicia, Grupos de Referencia Competitiva, [ED431C 2020/24] and predoctoral grants [ED481A 2021/161] and [ED481A 2021/196]; Axencia Galega de Innovación (GAIN), Xunta de Galicia, grant ref. [IN845D 2020/38]; CITIC, Centro de Investigación de Galicia ref. [ED431G 2019/01] receives financial support from Consellería de Educación, Universidade e Formación Profesional, Xunta de Galicia through the ERDF (80%) and Secretaría Xeral de Universidades (20%).

References

1. Baamonde, S., de Moura, J., Novo, J., Charlón, P., Ortega, M.: Automatic identification and characterization of the epiretinal membrane in OCT images. Biomed. Opt. Express **10**(8), 4018 (2019). https://doi.org/10.1364/boe.10.004018
2. Baamonde, S., de Moura, J., Novo, J., Charlón, P., Ortega, M.: Automatic identification and intuitive map representation of the epiretinal membrane presence in 3D OCT volumes. Sensors **19**(23), 5269 (2019). https://doi.org/10.3390/s19235269
3. Baamonde, S., de Moura, J., Novo, J., Ortega, M.: Automatic detection of epiretinal membrane in OCT images by means of local luminosity patterns. In: Rojas, I., Joya, G., Catala, A. (eds.) IWANN 2017. LNCS, vol. 10305, pp. 222–235. Springer, Cham (2017). https://doi.org/10.1007/978-3-319-59153-7_20

4. Baamonde, S., de Moura, J., Novo, J., Rouco, J., Ortega, M.: Feature definition and selection for epiretinal membrane characterization in optical coherence tomography images. In: Battiato, S., Gallo, G., Schettini, R., Stanco, F. (eds.) ICIAP 2017. LNCS, vol. 10485, pp. 456–466. Springer, Cham (2017). https://doi.org/10.1007/978-3-319-68548-9_42

5. Chua, P.Y., Sandinha, M.T., Steel, D.H.: Idiopathic epiretinal membrane: progression and timing of surgery. EYE **36**(3), 495–503 (2022). https://doi.org/10.1038/s41433-021-01681-0

6. Gende, M., De Moura, J., Novo, J., Charlón, P., Ortega, M.: Automatic segmentation and intuitive visualisation of the epiretinal membrane in 3D OCT images using deep convolutional approaches. IEEE Access **9**, 75993–76004 (2021). https://doi.org/10.1109/ACCESS.2021.3082638

7. Gende, M., de Moura, J., Novo, J., Ortega, M.: End-to-end multi-task learning approaches for the joint epiretinal membrane segmentation and screening in OCT images. Comput. Med. Imaging Graph. **98**, 102068 (2022). https://doi.org/10.1016/j.compmedimag.2022.102068

8. Huang, D., et al.: Optical coherence tomography. Science **254**(5035), 1178–1181 (1991). https://doi.org/10.1126/science.1957169. https://www.science.org/doi/abs/10.1126/science.1957169

9. Huang, G., Liu, Z., Van Der Maaten, L., Weinberger, K.Q.: Densely connected convolutional networks. In: 2017 IEEE Conference on Computer Vision and Pattern Recognition (CVPR), pp. 2261–2269 (2017). https://doi.org/10.1109/CVPR.2017.243

10. de Moura, J., Novo, J., Charlón, P., Barreira, N., Ortega, M.: Enhanced visualization of the retinal vasculature using depth information in OCT. Med. Biol. Eng. Comput. **55**(12), 2209–2225 (2017). https://doi.org/10.1007/s11517-017-1660-8

11. Parra-Mora, E., Cazañas-Gordon, A., Proença, R., da Silva Cruz, L.A.: Epiretinal membrane detection in optical coherence tomography retinal images using deep learning. IEEE Access **9**, 99201–99219 (2021). https://doi.org/10.1109/ACCESS.2021.3095655

12. Rahman, R., Stephenson, J.: Early surgery for epiretinal membrane preserves more vision for patients. Eye **28**(4), 410–414 (2014). https://doi.org/10.1038/eye.2013.305

13. Sonobe, T., et al.: Comparison between support vector machine and deep learning, machine-learning technologies for detecting epiretinal membrane using 3D-OCT. Int. Ophthalmol. **39**(8), 1871–1877 (2018). https://doi.org/10.1007/s10792-018-1016-x

14. Wilkins, J.R., et al.: Characterization of epiretinal membranes using optical coherence tomography. Ophthalmology **103**(12), 2142–2151 (1996). https://doi.org/10.1016/s0161-6420(96)30377-1

Performance Analysis of GAN Approaches in the Portable Chest X-Ray Synthetic Image Generation for COVID-19 Screening

Daniel Iglesias Morís[1,2] , Mateo Gende[1,2] , Joaquim de Moura[1,2(✉)] ,
Jorge Novo[1,2] , and Marcos Ortega[1,2]

[1] Centro de Investigación CITIC, Universidade da Coruña,
Campus de Elviña, s/n, 15071 A Coruña, Spain
{daniel.iglesias.moris,m.gende,joaquim.demoura,jnovo,mortega}@udc.es
[2] Grupo VARPA, Instituto de Investigación Biomédica de A Coruña (INIBIC),
Universidade da Coruña, Xubias de Arriba, 84, 15006 A Coruña, Spain

Abstract. COVID-19 mainly affects lung tissues, aspect that makes chest X-ray imaging useful to visualize this damage. In the context of the global pandemic, portable devices are advantageous for the daily practice. Furthermore, Computer-aided Diagnosis systems developed with Deep Learning algorithms can support the clinicians while making decisions. However, data scarcity is an issue that hinders this process. Thus, in this work, we propose the performance analysis of 3 different state-of-the-art Generative Adversarial Networks (GAN) approaches that are used for synthetic image generation to improve the task of automatic COVID-19 screening using chest X-ray images provided by portable devices. Particularly, the results demonstrate a significant improvement in terms of accuracy, that raises 5.28% using the images generated by the best image translation model.

Keywords: Computer-aided diagnosis · Portable chest X-ray ·
COVID-19 · Deep learning · Synthetic image generation

This research was funded by Instituto de Salud Carlos III, Government of Spain, DTS18/00136 research project; Ministerio de Ciencia e Innovación y Universidades, Government of Spain, RTI2018-095894-B-I00 research project; Ministerio de Ciencia e Innovación, Government of Spain through the research project with reference PID2019-108435RB-I00; Consellería de Cultura, Educación e Universidade, Xunta de Galicia through the predoctoral grant contracts ref. ED481A 2021/196 and ED481A 2021/161, respectively; and Grupos de Referencia Competitiva, grant ref. ED431C 2020/24; Axencia Galega de Innovación (GAIN), Xunta de Galicia, grant ref. IN845D 2020/38; CITIC, Centro de Investigación de Galicia ref. ED431G 2019/01, receives financial support from Consellería de Educación, Universidade e Formación Profesional, Xunta de Galicia, through the ERDF (80%) and Secretaría Xeral de Universidades (20%).

R. Moreno-Díaz et al. (Eds.): EUROCAST 2022, LNCS 13789, pp. 403–410, 2022.
https://doi.org/10.1007/978-3-031-25312-6_47

1   Introduction

The COVID-19 represents a challenge for the healthcare services since its emergence at the end of the year 2019 in Wuhan, Hubei, China [1]. This disease is caused by the coronavirus SARS-CoV-2, an extremely contagious pathogen, that was rapidly spread worldwide, aspect that forced the World Health Organization to declare this pathology as a global pandemic in March 2020. The main diagnostic tool to confirm the infection of COVID-19 is the RT-PCR test, which is considered as the gold-standard [2]. However, this tool is limited to provide a binary diagnosis and, therefore, it is unable to quantify some important aspects as the disease severity on each patient. As the COVID-19 mainly affects the respiratory tissues, the chest X-ray imaging modality is useful to visualize the extent of the pathology [3]. To perform the chest X-ray captures, there are 2 main types of radiological devices: fixed and portable. In the current situation of global pandemic, the American College of Radiology (ACR) recommends the use of portable devices as they are easier to decontaminate and more versatile [4]. However, despite this recommendation, they provide a lower quality and level of detail in their captures. As chest X-ray visualization is a complex, tedious and subjective task that must be performed by expert clinicians, the lower quality of the provided images makes this process even more challenging. Additionally, given the situation that the healthcare services are suffering due to the pandemic, health workers are experiencing a great amount of workload, context where the Computer-Aided Diagnosis (CAD) systems can be very useful to help them to take decisions [5]. In the last years, the medical imaging analysis domain has been supported by the computer vision and machine learning techniques. Particularly, the deep learning, a subarea of machine learning, has demonstrated its great performance dealing with this kind of problems [6].

In the context of COVID-19 diagnosis using chest X-ray imaging, some works have addressed the problem of the automatic COVID-19 screening with the support of deep learning strategies. As this is a relevant issue, given the current critical health situation, many efforts have been done to tackle it, both using datasets composed of captures provided by fixed devices (as reference, [7–9]) as well as by portable devices (as reference, [10–14]). However, despite these works provide robust and relevant results, deep models need a great amount of labelled data to be trained even though it exists a data scarcity problem in domains such as biomedical imaging. More precisely, in the scope of COVID-19, its recent emergence makes the information gathering even more challenging, aspect that implies an accused data scarcity.

To mitigate data scarcity, synthetic image generation has emerged during the last years as a powerful data augmentation strategy [15], which is often performed using a Generative Adversarial Network (GAN) architecture [16]. Moreover, there are several implementations of GANs that aim at performing the task of image translation, such as the Conditional GANs (Pix2Pix), the Cycle-Consistent Adversarial Networks (CycleGAN) or the Contrastive Unpaired Translation (CUT) models. This kind of models are able to convert images from a certain scenario to another different scenario and vice versa. Particularly, in the

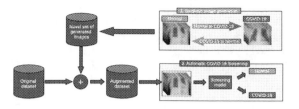

Fig. 1. Schematic description of the proposed methodology, that can be divided in 2 parts: synthetic image generation and automatic COVID-19 screening.

field of the COVID-19 chest X-ray image generation, the work from Morís *et al.* [13] addressed the problem of generating synthetic images using a CycleGAN and a dataset of portable chest X-ray images in the field of the COVID-19 screening. Lately, a work from the same authors [14] demonstrated that adding the novel set of generated images to the original dataset to increase its dimensionality can improve the performance of the automatic COVID-19 screening model. Nevertheless, even though the obtained satisfactory results, the reference works only addressed part of the problem, as they only use the CycleGAN, without analyzing the performance of other alternative image translation architectures.

In this work, we propose the performance analysis of 3 different state-of-the-art GAN approaches for portable chest X-ray synthetic image generation, one of them specifically tailored to work with paired datasets (Pix2Pix) and 2 designed to work with unpaired datasets (CycleGAN and CUT). On the second part of the work, the novel set of generated image is used to improve the performance of an automatic COVID-19 screening task, evaluating the synthetic image generation with a finalist scenario. For these purposes, we use a dataset divided in 2 different classes, Normal and COVID-19. Overall, this proposal can be seen as a relevant contribution to the clinical community, as it solves a critical problem given the current situation of world health crisis.

2   Materials and Methods

An schematic representation of the methodological process is depicted in Fig. 1. There, it can be seen that, first of all, the synthetic image generation process is performed in order to obtain a novel set of images. Then, this set of images is added to the original dataset in order to increase its dimensionality. Finally, the automatic COVID-19 screening model is trained using this augmented dataset. However, it is important to note that the training set is composed of both original and generated images but the test set is only composed of original images, in order to perform a comparison with the baseline on equal conditions.

2.1   Dataset

The portable chest X-ray imaging dataset was provided by the Complexo Hospitalario Universitario de A Coruña (CHUAC) and specifically designed for the purposes of this work, having 797 Normal control cases (without evidences of pulmonary affectation that could present abnormalities in other parts of the visualized region) and 2,071 genuine COVID-19 cases. The captures were performed using 2 portable chest X-ray devices: Agfa dr100E and Optima Rx200.

2.2 Synthetic Image Generation

For the synthetic image generation, 2 different pathways are followed: the one that converts from Normal to COVID-19 and the one that converts from COVID-19 to Normal. In the same way, both pathways are followed by the 3 considered image translation models, Pix2Pix [17], CycleGAN [18] and CUT [19], as this kind of image translation architectures have demonstrated satisfactory results for similar tasks of image generation [13]. For these 3 architectures, the same training details apply. First of all, for the training process, all the images of the dataset are used. With regards to the generator models, the selected configuration uses a ResNet with 6 residual blocks as it demonstrated to obtain robust and relevant results in similar problems [13,14]. On the other hand, all the input images are resized to 512×512 pixels. Moreover, all the models are trained during 200 epochs using the Adam optimizer algorithm with a constant learning rate of $\alpha = 0.0002$ and a mini-batch size of 1.

2.3 Automatic COVID-19 Screening

To understand the impact of the novel set of synthetic images on the model effectiveness, we performed an automatic COVID-19 screening. For these purposes, we used a DenseNet-161 as the deep network architecture due to its demonstrated capability dealing with a similar context [7]. The training process is set to 200 epochs and all the images are resized to a resolution of 512×512 pixels. In terms of dataset splitting, the 60% of the samples were used for training, the 20% for validation and the remaining 20% for test. Furthermore, the cross-entropy was used as loss function. In this case, the Stochastic Gradient Descent (SGD) [20] was selected to optimize the weights of the network, using a constant learning rate of $\alpha = 0.01$, a first-order momentum of 0.9 and a mini-batch size of 4. Finally, other relevant detail is that, to have a better understanding of the network behaviour, the training process is repeated 5 times, performing a different random dataset splitting for each repetition.

3 Results and Discussion

The results of the test set for the automatic COVID-19 screening are depicted in Table 1 where the baseline approach refers to the case of training with only original images, the approach 1 refers to the data augmentation approach that uses the images generated by the Pix2Pix model, the approach 2 refers to the case of using the images generated by the CycleGAN model and the approach 3 refers to the case of using the images generated by the CUT model. Overall,

Table 1. Results from the test set for the baseline approach and the 3 approaches of data augmentation.

	Baseline	Approach 1 (Pix2Pix)	Approach 2 (CycleGAN)	Approach 3 (CUT)
Accuracy	93.33% ± 4.68%	90.69% ± 5.00%	97.43% ± 2.41%	98.61% ± 1.24
Precision	92.64% ± 5.30%	94.52% ± 4.67%	98.55% ± 1.18%	98.47% ± 1.03%
Recall	94.30% ± 4.76%	86.94% ± 11.47%	96.25% ± 3.79%	98.75% ± 1.48%
Specificity	92.36% ± 5.74%	94.44% ± 4.99%	98.61% ± 1.08%	98.47% ± 1.02%
F1-Score	93.41% ± 4.60%	89.96% ± 5.96%	97.63% ± 2.52%	98.61% ± 1.24%
AUC	0.9748 ± 0.0230	0.9626 ± 0.0247	0.9891 ± 0.0109	0.9962 ± 0.0040

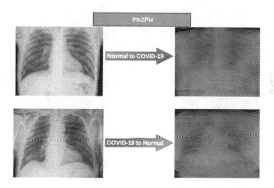

Fig. 2. Examples of synthetic images generated by Pix2Pix for both pathways.

as expected, the approach 1 has a performance drop in comparison with the baseline due to the bad quality of the images generated by Pix2Pix. However, it is remarkable that this drop is smaller that could be expected. In fact, the mean accuracy drops from 93.33% to 90.69% and the standard deviation remains very similar and both the recall and F1-Score experience an important drop, being the mean value lower than 90%. On its way, the mean AUC value drops from 0.9748 to 0.9626. The most remarkable performance drop can be seen in the case of recall, where the standard deviation rises from 4.76% to 11.47%. However, it is also remarkable that there is an improvement in terms of precision and specificity. With regards to the other 2 approaches of data augmentation, there is an improvement for all the metrics in comparison with the baseline. Furthermore, the approach 3 obtains a greater performance in comparison with the approach 2, thus concluding that the CUT model generates more useful synthetic images than CycleGAN. Particularly, in the case of the CycleGAN, the mean accuracy improves from 93.33% to 97.43% and to 98.61% in the case of the CUT. Something similar happens with the value of AUC, with an improvement from 0.9748 to 0.9891 in the case of the CycleGAN and to 0.9962 in the case of the CUT. Other point that must be noticed is that not only the mean values improve globally, but also the standard deviation values. In fact, the standard deviation of the accuracy lowers from 4.68% to 2.41% in the case of the CycleGAN and to

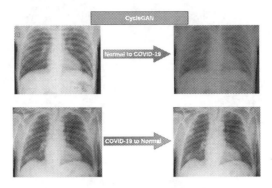

Fig. 3. Examples of images generated by the CycleGAN model for both scenarios.

1.24% in the case of the CUT. Moreover, for the AUC, this improvement means a standard deviation drop from 0.0230 to 0.0109 with the CycleGAN and to 0.0040 with the CUT.

On the other hand, some examples of synthetic images generated by the Pix2Pix model are depicted in Fig. 2. There, it can be seen that the model generates images with a low quality whose appearance is far from a real chest X-ray image. This can be explained because Pix2Pix is designed to work with paired datasets, while in this work it is necessary to use a method able to deal with unpaired datasets. On the other hand, both the CycleGAN and the CUT are designed to work with this kind of datasets, aspect that is reflected on the quality of the generated images. Some representative examples of both approaches of image generation can be seen in Fig. 3 and Fig. 4 in the case of the CycleGAN and the CUT, respectively. There, it can be clearly seen a notable difference in contrast with those images generated by Pix2Pix. In this case, the obtained images have a realistic appearance, coherent with a real chest X-ray capture, that show well-synthesized differences in pulmonary regions.

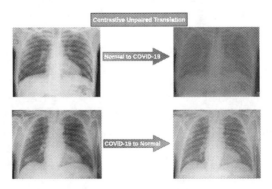

Fig. 4. Examples of synthetic images generated by the CUT models in both pathways.

4   Conclusion

In this work, we propose the analysis of 3 different state-of-the-art GAN architectures for synthetic image generation (Pix2Pix, CycleGAN and CUT) in the context of an automatic COVID-19 screening using portable chest X-ray images. Results demonstrate that the Pix2Pix is inadequate for the problem, as it is only capable of dealing with paired datasets, while the dataset used for the purposes of this work contains unpaired data. This leads to a poor performance of the model, generating considerably different images in comparison with a real chest X-ray image. The opposite results can be seen in the case of the Cycle-GAN and the CUT. In fact, the generated synthetic images have a good quality and a realistic appearance. In the same way, the models are able to generate well-synthesized differences in the pulmonary regions, aspect that is clinically relevant. These conclusions apply in the same way for the automatic COVID-19 screening performance. As expected, the data augmentation using the images generated by Pix2Pix implies a performance drop, while both the images generated by the CycleGAN and the CUT are able to improve the evaluation metrics values. Overall, the best performance is achieved using the images generated by the CUT model, obtaining a $98.61\% \pm 1.24\%$ of accuracy and a 0.9962 ± 0.0040 of AUC.

References

1. Ciotti, M., Ciccozzi, M., Terrinoni, A., Jiang, W.-C., Wang, C.-B., Bernardini, S.: The COVID-19 pandemic. Crit. Rev. Clin. Lab. Sci. **57**(6), 365–388 (2020)
2. Waller, J.V., et al.: Diagnostic tools for coronavirus disease (COVID-19): comparing CT and RT-PCR viral nucleic acid testing. Am. J. Roentgenol. **215**(4), 834–838 (2020)
3. Jacobi, A., Chung, M., Bernheim, A., Eber, C.: Portable chest X-ray in coronavirus disease-19 (COVID-19): a pictorial review. Clin. Imaging **64**, 35–42 (2020)
4. Kooraki, S., Hosseiny, M., Myers, L., Gholamrezanezhad, A.: Coronavirus (COVID-19) outbreak: what the department of radiology should know. J. Am. Coll. Radiol. **17**(4), 447–451 (2020)
5. Halalli, B., Makandar, A.: Computer aided diagnosis-medical image analysis techniques. Breast Imaging **85** (2018)
6. Suzuki, K.: Overview of deep learning in medical imaging. Radiol. Phys. Technol. **10**(3), 257–273 (2017). https://doi.org/10.1007/s12194-017-0406-5
7. de Moura, J., Novo, J., Ortega, M.: Fully automatic deep convolutional approaches for the analysis of COVID-19 using chest X-ray images. Appl. Soft Comput. **115**, 108190 (2022)
8. Narin, A., Kaya, C., Pamuk, Z.: Automatic detection of coronavirus disease (COVID-19) using X-ray images and deep convolutional neural networks. Pattern Anal. Appl. **24**(3), 1207–1220 (2021)
9. Alvarez-Rodríguez, L., de Moura, J., Novo, J., Ortega, M.: Does imbalance in chest X-ray datasets produce biased deep learning approaches for COVID-19 screening? (2021)

10. Vidal, P.L., de Moura, J., Novo, J., Ortega, M.: Pulmonary-restricted COVID-19 informative visual screening using chest X-ray images from portable devices. In: Sclaroff, S., Distante, C., Leo, M., Farinella, G.M., Tombari, F. (eds.) ICIAP 2022. LNCS, vol. 13231, pp. 65–76. Springer, Cham (2022).https://doi.org/10.1007/978-3-031-06427-2_6

11. De Moura, J., et al.: Deep convolutional approaches for the analysis of COVID-19 using chest X-ray images from portable devices. IEEE Access **8**, 195594–195607 (2020)

12. Morıs, D.I., de Moura, J., Novo, J., Ortega, M.: Comprehensive analysis of the screening of COVID-19 approaches in chest X-ray images from portable devices. In: European Symposium on Artificial Neural Networks, ESANN 2021, pp. 1–6 (2021)

13. Morís, D.I., de Moura, J., Novo, J., Ortega, M.: Cycle generative adversarial network approaches to produce novel portable chest X-rays images for COVID-19 diagnosis. In: ICASSP 2021–2021 IEEE International Conference on Acoustics, Speech and Signal Processing (ICASSP), pp. 1060–1064 (2021)

14. Morís, D.I., de Moura Ramos, J.J., Buján, J.N., Hortas, M.O.: Data augmentation approaches using cycle-consistent adversarial networks for improving COVID-19 screening in portable chest X-ray images. Expert Syst. Appl. **185**, 115681 (2021)

15. Tanaka, F.H.K.d.S., Aranha, C.: Data augmentation using GANs (2019). arXiv preprint arXiv:1904.09135

16. Creswell, A., White, T., Dumoulin, V., Arulkumaran, K., Sengupta, B., Bharath, A.A.: Generative adversarial networks: an overview. IEEE Signal Process. Mag. **35**(1), 53–65 (2018)

17. Isola, P., Zhu, J.-Y., Zhou, T., Efros, A.A.: Image-to-image translation with conditional adversarial networks. In: Proceedings of the IEEE Conference on Computer Vision and Pattern Recognition, pp. 1125–1134 (2017)

18. Zhu, J.-Y., Park, T., Isola, P., Efros, A.A.: Unpaired image-to-image translation using cycle-consistent adversarial networks. In: Proceedings of the IEEE International Conference on Computer Vision, pp. 2223–2232 (2017)

19. Park, T., Efros, A.A., Zhang, R., Zhu, J.-Y.: Contrastive learning for unpaired image-to-image translation. In: Vedaldi, A., Bischof, H., Brox, T., Frahm, J.-M. (eds.) ECCV 2020. LNCS, vol. 12354, pp. 319–345. Springer, Cham (2020). https://doi.org/10.1007/978-3-030-58545-7_19

20. Ketkar, N.: Stochastic gradient descent, pp. 113–132 (2017)

Clinical Decision Support Tool for the Identification of Pathological Structures Associated with Age-Related Macular Degeneration

Iván Barrientos[1,2], Joaquim de Moura[1,2](✉), Jorge Novo[1,2],
Marcos Ortega[1,2], and Manuel G. Penedo[1,2]

[1] Grupo VARPA, Instituto de Investigación Biomédica de A Coruña (INIBIC),
Universidade da Coruña, A Coruña, Spain
{ivan.barrientos.lema,joaquim.demoura,jnovo,mortega,mgpenedo}@udc.es
[2] Centro de Investigación CITIC, Universidade da Coruña, A Coruña, Spain

Abstract. In the field of ophthalmology, different imaging modalities are commonly used to carry out different clinical diagnostic procedures. Currently, both optical coherence tomography (OCT) and optical coherence tomography angiography (OCT-A) have made great advances in the study of the posterior pole of the eye and are essential for the diagnosis and monitoring of the treatment of different ocular and systemic diseases. On the other hand, the development of clinical decision support systems is an emerging field, in which clinical and technological advances are allowing clinical specialists to diagnose various pathologies with greater precision, which translates into more appropriate treatment and, consequently, an improvement in the quality of life of patients. This paper presents a clinical decision support tool for the identification of different pathological structures associated with age-related macular degeneration using OCT and OCT-A images. The system provides a useful tool that facilitates clinical decision-making in the diagnosis and treatment of this relevant disease.

Keywords: CAD system · Deep learning · OCT · OCT-A · AMD

1 Introduction

Age-related macular degeneration (AMD) represents one of the leading causes of vision loss in older adults. This relevant eye disease is an age-related condition that results from a gradual deterioration of light-sensitive cells in the tissue at the back of the eye. Specifically, AMD mainly affects peripheral blood vessels, causing different signs of systemic and retinal vascular deterioration. New emerging ophthalmic imaging technologies, such as optical coherence tomography (OCT) and optical coherence tomography angiography (OCT-A), have great potential to support early diagnosis of this relevant eye disease. On the one hand, OCT is a non-invasive imaging technique that uses low-coherence light

R. Moreno-Díaz et al. (Eds.): EUROCAST 2022, LNCS 13789, pp. 411–418, 2022.
https://doi.org/10.1007/978-3-031-25312-6_48

to capture two-dimensional and three-dimensional micro-resolution scans of the retina, allowing a more precise evaluation of its main morphological structures. On the other hand, OCT-A is a more recent technique for the capture of high-resolution images of the choroidal and retinal circulations without the need for dye injections. In particular, OCT-A detects the blood movement using intrinsic signals to capture the precise location of the blood vessels. Consequently, this ophthalmological test has great potential to improve the understanding of the pathophysiology of the eye fundus, providing relevant information for the diagnosis and monitoring of the AMD treatment.

Given the great relevance of this topic, several authors have addressed the development of intelligent systems for the identification, segmentation and characterisation of different regions of clinical interest using OCT and OCT-A images. As reference, in the field of OCT imaging, we can find different proposals for the precise identification of different morphological structures, such as retinal layers [5,6] or retinal vessels [10,11]. We can also find different proposals for the segmentation of regions with the presence of pathological fluid or the presence of the epiretinal membrane [1,2]. On the other hand, in the field of OCT-A imaging, different methodologies have been proposed for the identification of structures of clinical interest [3,9] or the calculation of different computational biomarkers [4,12]. Despite the considerable efforts that were made to develop automated methods to support clinical diagnosis, there is still no platform that integrates OCT and OCT-A images for the diagnosis of AMD, so this problem is only partially addressed.

Taking this into account, in this work, we present a clinical decision support tool for the identification of different pathological structures associated with AMD using OCT and OCT-A, two widely used imaging modalities with great diagnostic potential. For this purpose, we have designed a fully automatic solution based on deep learning strategies, which is initially composed of three complementary modules. A first module that automatically distinguishes between OCT and OCT-A images; it is useful to differentiate the type of image for a more accurate and efficient diagnosis. The second module is able to differentiate healthy patients from those with the following pathologies on OCT images: choroidal neovascularization (CNV), diabetic macular edema (DME) and drusen. The third module is able to automatically classify the OCT-A images as retinal vein occlusion (RVO) or healthy. Finally, these modules were integrated into a web platform, offering different functionalities, such as patient management or the intuitive visualisation of results through clinical reports, facilitating the work of ophthalmologists.

2   Materials and Methods

2.1   Dataset

OCT Dataset. This dataset consists of 84,484 OCT images, corresponding to 26,315 healthy patients, 37,205 patients diagnosed with CNV, 11,348 patients diagnosed with DME and 8,616 patients with the presence of drusen deposits. Therefore, this dataset contains 4 classes (NORMAL, CNV, DME and DRUSEN). All OCT images were selected from retrospective cohorts of adult patients from the Shiley Eye Institute at the University of California San Diego, the California Retinal Research Foundation, Medical Center Ophthalmology Associates, and the Beijing Tongren Eye Center. This dataset is publicly available to the scientific community [8].

OCT-A Dataset. This dataset consists of 1,551 images obtained by an OCT-A capture device (Topcon DRI OCT Triton Plus swept source), where 870 are images of patients diagnosed with RVO and 681 are images without the presence of RVO. Therefore, two classes (RVO and NON-RVO) are analysed in this work. Specifically, these images were obtained at the Complejo Hospitalario Universitario de Santiago (CHUS) from different patients in accordance with the Declaration of Helsinki.

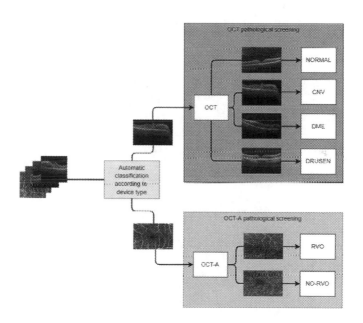

Fig. 1. Schematic representation of 3 computational modules to support the diagnosis of different ocular diseases.

2.2 Methodology

Figure 1 shows a schematic representation of the different computational modules that were developed for pathological screening. Each of these modules is explained in more detail below.

Module of Classification According to Device Type. For the design of a clinical decision support tool based on the integration of different smart modules, it is very useful to differentiate the type of image we are working with. As a consequence, we can obtain more accurate, reliable and repeatable results. With this in mind, we have designed a fully automatic module for image classification between OCT and OCT-A classes.

Module of OCT Pathological Screening. This smart module is able to differentiate automatically healthy patients from those diagnosed with the pathologies present in the OCT dataset. Specifically, OCT images will be classified into CNV for patients with choroidal neovascularisation, DME for patients with diabetic macular edema, DRUSEN for patients with presence of drusen deposits and NORMAL for healthy patients.

Module of OCT-A Pathological Screening. In this smart module, the system is able to automatically classify the OCT-A images between patients diagnosed with retinal vein occlusion (RVO) or healthy patients (NON-RVO).

2.3   Training Details

In this work, we exploit the potential of the DenseNet-161 [7] architecture pretrained on the ImageNet dataset. For the training process, we have divided the datasets into mutually exclusive subsets for training (60%), validation (20%) and testing (20%). In addition, a cross-entropy loss function was used to adjust the weights of the models during the training stage. Regarding the optimisation of the model, Stochastic Gradient Descent was used with a learning ratio constant of 0.01, a mini-batch size of 16 and a first order momentum of 0.9. Finally, in order to achieve consistent results, the training step was repeated 5 times with random samples, which allows to calculate the averages of the results obtained and thus to evaluate the overall performance of all the proposed smart modules.

2.4   Clinical Decision Support Tool

All the smart modules, developed in this work, were integrated into a clinical decision support tool, facilitating clinical decision making in the diagnosis and treatment of AMD using OCT and OCT-A images. In addition, this web-based platform offers different functionalities, such as patient management or the intuitive visualization of results through different clinical reports that can be exported to PDF format or sent automatically by e-mail. This tool is fully scalable, allowing easy integration of new smart modules to support the diagnosis of new diseases or other types of medical imaging.

3   Results and Discussion

In this section, we present the experimental results of the proposed computational modules for the automatic identification of different pathological structures related to AMD using OCT and OCT-A images. For the validation of each smart module, the following metrics are calculated: Accuracy, Precision, Recall and F1-score.

1st Analysis: Classification According to Device Type. In this first analysis, we studied the performance of the proposed system to classify the input images according to 2 types of devices: (OCT and OCT-A). As expected, the system was able to adequately classify all images contained in the analyzed dataset, since it is a simple classification problem. In this sense, the obtained results demonstrate the powerful learning capability of deep neural networks to extract discriminative features for medical image analysis.

2nd Analysis: OCT Pathological Screening. In this second analysis, we studied the performance of the proposed system to classify OCT images according to 4 classes: (NORMAL, CNV, DME and DRUSEN). Figure 2a shows the progression of the accuracy and Fig. 2b the progression of the loss, both for the training and for the validation stages, considering 5 independent repetitions. As we can see, the training process has been completed after model stabilization before 40 epochs, obtaining accuracy values close to 1 for training and 0.975 for validation.

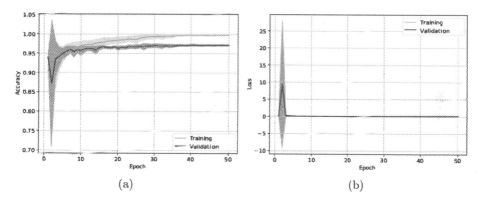

(a)   (b)

Fig. 2. Results of the second analysis after 5 independent repetitions, in terms of mean ± standard deviation. (a) Representation of the evolution of accuracy in training and validation. (b) Representation of the evolution of loss in training and validation.

Complementarily, Table 1 shows the performance measures obtained in the test stage. As we can see, satisfactory results were obtained for each category, reaching a mean accuracy value of 0.9718 ± 0.0011. In particular, we can observe that the highest value obtained for the F-score is 0,9826 ± 0,0018 for the NORMAL class. On the contrary, the lowest value obtained for the F-score is 0,9103 ± 0,0041 for the DRUSEN class.

Table 1. Recall, Precision and F1-score for each class of the module of OCT pathological screening using the test dataset.

Class	Recall	Precision	F1-score
NORMAL	0,9838 ± 0,0013	0,9814 ± 0,0037	0,9826 ± 0,0018
CNV	0,9807 ± 0,0020	0,9808 ± 0,0024	0,9808 ± 0,0019
DME	0,9598 ± 0,0059	0,9680 ± 0,0029	0,9639 ± 0,0034
DRUSEN	0,9122 ± 0,0059	0,9085 ± 0,0069	0,9103 ± 0,0041

3rd Analysis: OCT-A Pathological Screening. In this third analysis, we studied the performance of the proposed system to classify OCT-A images according to 4 classes: (RVO and NON-RVO). Once again, Fig. 2a illustrates the progression of the accuracy, as well as Fig. 2b the progression of the loss, for both training and validation stages, considering 5 independent repetitions. As we can see, in this case, the training process has been completed after the stabilization of the model before 75 epochs, both for training and validation stages. As for the loss, we can see a very large variation in the initial epochs, but as accuracy stabilises, the loss decreases considerably, reaching values close to 0 (Fig. 3).

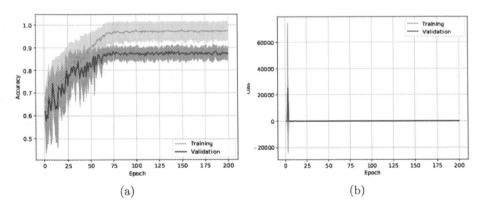

(a)   (b)

Fig. 3. Results of the third analysis after 5 independent repetitions, in terms of mean ± standard deviation. (a) Representation of the evolution of accuracy in training and validation. (b) Representation of the evolution of loss in training and validation.

Additionally, we present the Table 2 with the values obtained for each class and represented by the Recall, Precision and F1-score metrics. In general, the results that were obtained by the proposed system with the test dataset are satisfactory, since it achieves a mean accuracy value of 0.8695 ± 0.0414. As we can see, the obtained results demonstrate the suitability of the model for the identification of different pathological structures related to AMD using OCT-A imaging.

Table 2. Recall, Precision and F1-score for each class of the module of OCT-A pathological screening using the test dataset.

Class	Recall	Precision	F1-score
RVO	$0,8757 \pm 0,0239$	$0,8890 \pm 0,0519$	$0,8823 \pm 0,0360$
NON-RVO	$0,8615 \pm 0,0681$	$0,8455 \pm 0,0323$	$0,8534 \pm 0,0486$

4 Conclusions

In this work, we propose a clinical decision support tool for the identification of different pathological structures associated with AMD using OCT and OCT-A images. For this purpose, we have designed a fully automatic solution based on deep learning, which is initially composed of 3 smart modules. A first module that automatically distinguishes between OCT and OCT-A images. The second module is able to differentiate healthy patients from those with the following pathologies on OCT images: CNV, DME and drusen deposits. The third module is able to automatically classify the OCT-A images as RVO or healthy patients. Finally, these modules were integrated into a web platform, offering different functionalities, such as patient management or the intuitive visualisation of results through clinical reports, facilitating the work of the ophthalmologists. Two representative datasets have been used for the validation of this work. The first dataset is composed of 84,484 OCT images differentiated into four classes: (NORMAL, CNV, DME and DRUSEN). The second dataset is composed of 1,551 OCTA images differentiated into two classes: (RVO and NON-RVO). The proposed system provided accurate results in all the designed smart modules, demonstrating a significant potential in the early diagnosis, treatment and monitoring of AMD.

Acknowledgements. This research was funded by Instituto de Salud Carlos III, Government of Spain, DTS18/00136 and PI17/00940 research projects; Ministerio de Ciencia e Innovación y Universidades, Government of Spain, RTI2018-095894-B-I00 research project; Ministerio de Ciencia e Innovación, Government of Spain through the research project with reference PID2019-108435RB-I00; Consellería de Cultura, Educación e Universidade, Xunta de Galicia, Grupos de Referencia Competitiva, grant ref. ED431C 2020/24 and postdoctoral grant ref. ED481B 2021/059; Axencia Galega de Innovación (GAIN), Xunta de Galicia, grant ref. IN845D 2020/38; CITIC, Centro de Investigación de Galicia ref. ED431G 2019/01, receives financial support from Consellería de Educación, Universidade e Formación Profesional, Xunta de Galicia, through the ERDF (80%) and Secretaría Xeral de Universidades (20%).

References

1. Baamonde, S., de Moura, J., Novo, J., Rouco, J., Ortega, M.: Feature definition and selection for epiretinal membrane characterization in optical coherence tomography images. In: Battiato, S., Gallo, G., Schettini, R., Stanco, F. (eds.) ICIAP 2017. LNCS, vol. 10485, pp. 456–466. Springer, Cham (2017). https://doi.org/10.1007/978-3-319-68548-9_42
2. de Moura, J., Vidal, P.L., Novo, J., Rouco, J., Ortega, M.: Feature definition, analysis and selection for cystoid region characterization in Optical Coherence Tomography. Procedia Comput. Sci. **112**, 1369–1377 (2017)
3. Díaz, M., de Moura, J., Novo, J., Ortega, M.: Automatic wide field registration and mosaicking of OCTA images using vascularity information. Procedia Comput. Sci. **159**, 505–513 (2019)
4. Díaz, M., Novo, J., Cutrín, P., Gómez-Ulla, F., Penedo, M.G., Ortega, M.: Automatic segmentation of the foveal avascular zone in ophthalmological OCT-A images. PLoS One **14**(2), e0212364 (2019)
5. Fang, L., Cunefare, D., Wang, C., Guymer, R.H., Li, S., Farsiu, S.: Automatic segmentation of nine retinal layer boundaries in OCT images of non-exudative AMD patients using deep learning and graph search. Biomed. Opt. Express **8**(5), 2732–2744 (2017)
6. González-López, A., de Moura, J., Novo, J., Ortega, M., Penedo, M.G.: Robust segmentation of retinal layers in optical coherence tomography images based on a multistage active contour model. Heliyon **5**(2), e01271 (2019)
7. Huang, G., Liu, Z., Van Der Maaten, L., Weinberger, K.Q.: Densely connected convolutional networks. In: Proceedings of the IEEE Conference on Computer Vision and Pattern Recognition, pp. 4700–4708 (2017)
8. Kermany, D.S., et al.: Identifying medical diagnoses and treatable diseases by image-based deep learning. Cell **172**(5), 1122–1131 (2018)
9. Linderman, R., Salmon, A.E., Strampe, M., Russillo, M., Khan, J., Carroll, J.: Assessing the accuracy of foveal avascular zone measurements using optical coherence tomography angiography: segmentation and scaling. Transl. Vis. Sci. Technol. **6**(3), 16 (2017)
10. de Moura, J., Novo, J., Rouco, J., Penedo, M.G., Ortega, M.: Automatic detection of blood vessels in retinal OCT images. In: Ferrández Vicente, J.M., Álvarez-Sánchez, J.R., de la Paz López, F., Toledo Moreo, J., Adeli, H. (eds.) IWINAC 2017. LNCS, vol. 10338, pp. 3–10. Springer, Cham (2017). https://doi.org/10.1007/978-3-319-59773-7_1
11. Niemeijer, M., Garvin, M.K., van Ginneken, B., Sonka, M., Abramoff, M.D.: Vessel segmentation in 3D spectral OCT scans of the retina. In: Medical Imaging 2008: Image Processing, vol. 6914, pp. 597–604. SPIE (2008)
12. Sandhu, H.S., et al.: Automated diagnosis of diabetic retinopathy using clinical biomarkers, optical coherence tomography, and optical coherence tomography angiography. Am. J. Ophthalmol. **216**, 201–206 (2020)

Deep Features-Based Approaches for Phytoplankton Classification in Microscopy Images

David Rivas-Villar[1,2]([✉]) [ID], José Morano[1,2] [ID], José Rouco[1,2] [ID],
M. G. Penedo[1,2] [ID], and Jorge Novo[1,2] [ID]

[1] Centro de investigación CITIC, Universidade da Coruña, A Coruña 15071, Spain
{david.rivas.villar,j.morano,jrouco,mgpenedo,jnovo}@udc.es
[2] Grupo VARPA, Instituto de Investigación Biomédica de A Coruña (INIBIC),
Universidade da Coruña, A Coruña 15006, Spain

Abstract. Certain phytoplankton species can produce potent toxins that can raise health concerns, especially if these species proliferate in water sources. Furthermore, phytoplankton can drastically and rapidly multiply their population in water, increasing the possibility of dangerous contamination. Nowadays, preventive water analyses related to phytoplankton are routinely and manually performed by the experts. These methods have major limitations in terms of reliability and repeatability as well as throughput due to their complexity and length. Therefore, the automatization of these tasks is particularly desirable to lower the workload of the experts and ease the whole process of potability analysis. Previous state of the art works can segment and classify phytoplankton from conventional microscopy images of multiple specimens. However, they require classical image features, which need ad-hoc feature engineering, a complex and lengthy process. Thus, employing novel deep learning-based deep features is highly desirable as it would improve the flexibility of the methods. In this manuscript, we present a study regarding the performance of different pre-trained deep neural networks for the extraction of deep features in order to identify and classify phytoplankton. The experimental results are satisfactory as we improve the performance of the state of the art approaches. Furthermore, as we eliminate the need for classical image features, we improve the adaptability of the methods.

Keywords: Microscope images · Phytoplankton classification · Deep features · Deep learning

This research was funded by Consellería de Cultura, Educación e Universidade, Xunta de Galicia through the predoctoral grants contract ref. ED481A 2021/147 and ref. ED481A 2021/140 and Grupos de Referencia Competitiva, grant ref. ED431C 2020/24; CITIC, Centro de Investigación de Galicia ref. ED431G 2019/01, receives financial support from Consellería de Educación, Universidade e Formación Profesional, Xunta de Galicia, through the ERDF (80%) and Secretaría Xeral de Universidades (20%).

R. Moreno-Díaz et al. (Eds.): EUROCAST 2022, LNCS 13789, pp. 419–426, 2022.
https://doi.org/10.1007/978-3-031-25312-6_49

1   Introduction

Phytoplankton is relevant due to its unique properties, like producing oxygen or being the basis of the aquatic food chain. Moreover, phytoplankton species can increment their numbers exponentially, given the right conditions, a process called blooming. Additionally, some species can produce toxins that are harmful to humans. The main issue regarding these toxins is that they cannot be effectively removed using common purification techniques [9]. Consequently, the blooming of toxin-producing species in freshwater reservoirs must be continuously monitored in order to avoid public health concerns. Furthermore, blooming processes are difficult to predict, so the quality of the water must be checked periodically.

The monitoring of freshwater sources is, currently, a completely manual task done by highly trained experts. Due to its complexity, this process exhibits reliability and repeatability issues. These limitations can be mitigated using objective protocols and criteria, established among experts. Despite this, the manual nature and the amount of work involved in this process have motivated the creation of various methods that automate some of the phases of this task. The different developed approaches are classified in two main groups: sample gathering and specimen detection and classification approaches.

Sample gathering methods automatically collect water samples. These approaches usually employ a submersible contraption capable of capturing images of phytoplankton. Thus, these methods greatly reduce the amount of work that is done by the experts, but the trade-off is that the produced images tend to be of less quality than those produced by a conventional microscope. Therefore, although capturing images with a microscope is a manual process, the higher quality of the images as well as the general availability and cost-effectiveness of regular microscopes equipped with digital cameras make their use desirable.

Classification approaches mainly use images with a single phytoplankton specimen, captured using automatic samplers [2,4,7]. These methods are highly dependent on the particular acquisition features of each particular device. On the other hand, some methods employ microscopy images [1,11–13] containing multiple specimens per image (multi-specimen images), thus requiring to locate each specimen, separating them from each other and from the background (specimen detection). Several of these methods [1,12,13] employ ad-hoc image capture approaches which require an expert taxonomist to manually adjust the microscope's magnification and focal point on a per-image or even per-specimen basis. This makes these methods unsuitable for automating potability analyses as they do not decrease the expert's workload since they do not release them from the imaging, detection and identification tasks. However, these methods are suitable for automating the cell counting processes. Recently, Rivas-Villar et al. [10,11] proposed an automatic approach that uses a systematic imaging procedure, fixing the microscope's magnification and focal point. This procedure can release experts from the imaging tasks, as they do not need to identify the specimens in order to adjust the microscope settings for each one.

In terms of methods, detection and classification approaches are usually based on classical image features [7,10] or, more recently, novel deep learning methods [2]. Deep learning methods are based on creating complex networks composed of multiple specialized layers that are trained using examples [8]. These layers discover many low-level representations of the input data, which are useful in subsequent, deeper, layers to provide high-level features representing the original data [8]. Deep features leverage these characteristics by directly extracting the internal representations of the data from the neural networks. Once the deep features are extracted, they can be treated like classical features. Furthermore, deep features obtained from pretrained networks are desirable as the models do not need to be trained from scratch, a time and data intensive task. In this regard, Deep feature approaches have also been successfully used for phytoplankton classification, alone [4] or in conjunction with classical feature extraction approaches [11]. However, to the best of our knowledge, no work in the state of the art has performed an in depth study on their performance for phytoplankton-related potability analysis.

Currently, the best state of the art methods [11] use classical features in combination with deep features. Classical features, despite their good performance, need feature engineering, which is a time-consuming process. Therefore, maintaining the existing pipelines while eliminating this feature requirement is desirable as it would allow for more flexibility in the methods.

In this work, we propose to conduct a detailed study of the performance of deep features for the classification of phytoplankton specimens. We propose to analyze the performance of different networks for deep feature extraction, particularly from ResNet [5] and DenseNet [6], testing different configurations for each one. Following the state of the art, we study the performance of deep features for phytoplankton classification, firstly differentiating genuine phytoplankton from spurious elements and then classifying the indicated phytoplankton specimens into a set of relevant species.

2   Materials and Methods

In order to test the performance of deep features in this domain, we propose a phytoplankton detection and segmentation pipeline. From a dataset of systematically captured multi-specimen images [11], we firstly detect a set of candidate specimens. Next, these candidates are filtered in two subsequent classification steps. The first step of the pipeline, candidate detection, produces bounding boxes containing a single specimen each, as well as segmentation masks. Next, these boxes are classified, firstly separating true phytoplankton from spurious elements (phytoplankton detection), and later, dividing the genuine phytoplankton in a set of species (species classification).

For these steps, we use the dataset proposed in [11]. This dataset contains multi-specimen images of phytoplankton captured with a fixed focal point and at a fixed magnification of 10×. The dataset contains 293 images that include phytoplankton specimens from a varied set of species. Additionally, images also contain a notable number of spurious elements such as zooplankton, minerals, or garbage. The ground truth for this dataset are bounding boxes enclosing the phytoplankton specimens, manually marked by an expert.

For the species classification step, we select two representative toxic species, *Woronichinia naegeliana* and *Anabaena spiroides*. Additionally, we also select *Dinobryon sociale*, a non-toxic species whose complicated characteristics (transparent capsule, small individual size, etc.) allow it to be a good system benchmark. Finally, a generic "others" is also included. It contains the rest of the species that also appear in this dataset but are not considered for classification.

In the first step, to detect the candidate specimens, we use the approach proposed in the reference work [11]. Particularly, this method thresholds the images and selects all the potential candidates. These candidates are then filtered, according to size, as detections smaller than $5\mu m$ cannot be phytoplankton. Next, a novel colony merging algorithm is proposed to fuse sparse specimens into single detections, resulting in the appropriate single specimen bounding boxes.

For both classification steps, the same methodology is used. Specifically, we propose to test deep features. Deep features are generally extracted from pre-trained convolutional neural networks, bypassing their classification layers. These features can then be used, like classical features, with a classifier to produce the desired output. One of their main advantages is the use of pre-trained networks, avoiding the data and time intensive task of training the models from scratch.

Deep features are extracted for each candidate in two different ways: masked and unmasked. Unmasked features use the whole bounding box to compute the features. On the other hand, the masked approach uses the segmentation masks to mask the bounding box images, focusing the information on the specimen itself. This approach is also used in the reference work [11]. The masked approach only includes the relevant information for the classification, that is, the specimen itself. However, as it discards the background data, this could erase potentially important information.

The extracted features are used with Support Vector Machines (SVM) and Random Forest (RF) as classifiers for the extracted deep features, as these methods provided the best results in previous works [10,11]. The best hyperparameters for these methods are found from the set established in the reference work [11], ensuring fair comparisons.

In this work, we propose to test the state of the art networks ResNet [5] and DenseNet [6]. Both networks are tested in different configurations of depth, and consequently parameters and number of features extracted. In particular, we test ResNet going from 18 layers up to 152 and DenseNet from 121 to 201 layers. Both of these networks are pre-trained in the ImageNet [3] dataset and are not fine-tuned in any way.

To evaluate the performance of deep features in the classification tasks, different metrics are needed as the targets of each step are different. Specifically, for the phytoplankton detection step, we use precision at 90% of recall. In this classification, the main concern is keeping most of the genuine phytoplankton

Table 1. Results for phytoplankton detection, measured in precision at 90% of recall. Best result highlighted in bold.

Model	SVM		Random forest	
	Unmasked	Masked	Unmasked	Masked
ResNet-18	78.39%	65.55%	79.41%	58.61%
ResNet-34	80.56%	69.48%	81.13%	67.07%
ResNet-50	84.06%	69.06%	73.44%	67.46%
ResNet-101	78.39%	72.51%	78.92%	69.06%
ResNet-152	84.06%	64.11%	73.44%	69.06%
DenseNet-121	79.46%	70.32%	79.46%	72.06%
DenseNet-169	80.56%	67.07%	**88.55%**	75.34%
DenseNet-201	84.68%	69.47%	81.70%	73.90%

specimens so that they can be later separated into species. Thus, a high recall is needed to ensure correct results. The species classification step is proposed as a multi-class problem, with three species and the fourth "others" class. The metric to evaluate the performance of this step is the global classification accuracy. The evaluation metrics for both steps are the same as in the reference work [11] which enables direct result comparison.

The dataset is split 80–20, with 80% of the multi-specimen images dedicated to training and validation. We use a 10-fold cross validation with grid search to obtain the best parameters with which the system is then retrained. The remaining 20% of the images were used to test the proposed approach. This approach is also used in the reference work [11], ensuring direct comparisons.

3   Results and Discussion

The experimental results corresponding to the two classification steps using the deep features that were extracted from ResNet and DenseNet are presented in Tables 1 and 2. In particular, Table 1 details the results of the phytoplankton detection while Table 2 provides the results of the species classification.

Firstly, the results for the phytoplankton detection step represented in Table 1 are satisfactory. Particularly, the best result in terms of precision at 90% of recall is obtained by the DenseNet-169 using Random Forest and unmasked features. Generally, the unmasked features outperform the masked features in this task, both with RF and SVM. Thus, this indicates that the contextual information contained in the background which outlines the specimen, such as the shape, or regularity of the specimens is key in differentiating between phytoplankton and spurious elements. This is specifically relevant in the cases of detritus, which can present similar colors, sizes, or textures to phytoplankton. However, their shape can be remarkably distinct from that of genuine phytoplankton. Furthermore, since neither phytoplankton nor the spurious elements are homogeneous groups,

Table 2. Results for the species classification, measured in global accuracy. Best result highlighted in bold.

Model	SVM		Random forest	
	Unmasked	Masked	Unmasked	Masked
ResNet-18	86.72%	86.72%	78.91%	80.47%
ResNet-34	82.81%	82.81%	80.47%	78.91%
ResNet-50	81.25%	85.95%	80.47%	83.59%
ResNet-101	79.69%	**89.06%**	77.34%	85.16%
ResNet-152	84.38%	83.56%	81.25%	82.03%
DenseNet-121	87.50%	85.94%	85.94%	86.72%
DenseNet-169	83.59%	83.59%	82.81%	83.59%
DenseNet-201	82.81%	85.16%	84.38%	76.56%

the extra information provided by not masking the images can help classifying complex elements. Therefore, while masking the features results in the information being focused on the specimen, in this classification step it deteriorates the results. In terms of the classifiers, both methods are similar with some instances producing better results than others, depending on the particular network configuration tested.

The performance for the species classification, shown in Table 2, is also satisfactory. In this step, the best result in terms of overall accuracy is obtained by ResNet-101 using SVM and masked features, producing an 89.06% of global accuracy. In this step, the results of masked and unmasked features are closer than in the previous phase, often interchanging the top result position for each network and classifier. Contrary to the previous step, the best result is produced using masked features. All the elements in this classification step are phytoplankton, therefore, the shape and regularity features provided by the unmasked features are less relevant. Thus, masking the bounding boxes improves the results for this step since the background information is not as relevant and masking it highlights the finer details contained within the specimens themselves.

Overall, comparing the results for both steps to one another, we can see that both classifications are remarkably different. These steps have to deal with similar issues regarding inter-class similarity and intra-class differences. Particularly, in the case of the phytoplankton detection due to the very inclusive nature of both groups (phytoplankton and non-phytoplankton), these limitations are more notable. The differences between both classifications are evidenced by the contrast in the tested configurations that offer the best results in each one. The first step produces its top result using a DenseNet in conjunction with unmasked features and RF. On the other hand, the best result for the species classification step uses a ResNet using SVM and masked features. This, coupled with the complexity of each of the classification tasks separately, confirms that creating specific network and classifier configurations for each one is beneficial.

3.1   State of the Art Comparison

The best results for the proposed method and its variations are compared to the reference work in Table 3. As the same dataset and metrics are used, the comparison between both works is direct.

Table 3. Results for the reference work and our proposal.

Method	Phytoplankton detection (Precision at 90% recall)	Species classification (Overall accuracy)
Rivas-Villar et al. [11]	84.07%	87.50%
Ours	88.55%	89.06%

When comparing our current approach to the reference work, we can see that we improve the results in both classification approaches. Particularly, in phytoplankton detection, our method improves by almost 5% while in species classification the performance gain is less than 2%. In the phytoplankton detection step, the reference work obtained its best result using only deep features. However, even in this case, exploring deep features in-depth is beneficial as our approach improves the reference work results. Importantly, our approach also eliminates the need for classical features which were used in combination with deep features in the reference work to obtain the species classification result. Therefore, in this step, we improve the results and increase the flexibility of the method while reducing the workload derived from feature tuning.

4   Conclusions

In this work, we propose to study in-depth the performance of deep features to classify phytoplankton specimens. Deep features eliminate the need to train models from scratch, a data and time intensive process. Thus, using deep features for these tasks is very convenient. Consequently, we test deep features from ResNet and DenseNet in several depth configurations for two phytoplankton classification steps. From a dataset of systematically captured microscopy multi-specimen images, we obtain images containing a single candidate specimen. Firstly, these images are classified, separating true phytoplankton from spurious elements (phytoplankton detection). Then the genuine phytoplankton is separated into a relevant set of species (species classification).

The experimental results obtained by the proposed method are satisfactory as they provide accurate classifications. Moreover, they improve the performance of the state of the art while avoiding the costly feature tuning of classical approaches. Particularly, in phytoplankton detection we improve the results around 5% and approximately 2% in species classification.

References

1. Baek, S., et al.: Identification and enumeration of cyanobacteria species using a deep neural network. Ecolog. Indicat. **115**, 106395 (2020). https://doi.org/10.1016/j.ecolind.2020.106395
2. Correa, I., Drews, P., Botelho, S., Souza, M.S.D., Tavano, V.M.: Deep learning for microalgae classification. In: 2017 16th IEEE International Conference on Machine Learning and Applications (ICMLA), pp. 20–25 (2017). https://doi.org/10.1109/ICMLA.2017.0-183
3. Deng, J., Dong, W., Socher, R., Li, L., Li, K., Li, F.-F.: Imagenet: a large-scale hierarchical image database. In: 2009 IEEE Conference on Computer Vision and Pattern Recognition (CVPR), pp. 248–255 (2009). https://doi.org/10.1109/CVPR.2009.5206848
4. González, P., Castaño, A., Peacock, E.E., Díez, J., Del Coz, J.J., Sosik, H.M.: Automatic plankton quantification using deep features. J. Plankton Res. **41**(4), 449–463 (2019)
5. He, K., Zhang, X., Ren, S., Sun, J.: Deep residual learning for image recognition. In: 2016 IEEE Conference on Computer Vision and Pattern Recognition (CVPR), pp. 770–778 (2016)
6. Huang, G., Liu, Z., van der Maaten, L., Weinberger, K.Q.: Densely connected convolutional networks. In: Proceedings of the IEEE Conference on Computer Vision and Pattern Recognition (CVPR), pp. 4700–4708 (2017)
7. Nagashima, Y., Matsumoto, Y., Kondo, H., Yamazaki, H., Gallager, S.: Development of a realtime plankton image archiver for AUVs. In: 2014 IEEE/OES Autonomous Underwater Vehicles (AUV), pp. 1–6 (2014). https://doi.org/10.1109/AUV.2014.7054424
8. Nanni, L., Ghidoni, S., Brahnam, S.: Deep features for training support vector machines. J. Imaging **7**(9) (2021). https://doi.org/10.3390/jimaging7090177, https://www.mdpi.com/2313-433X/7/9/177
9. Paerl, H.W., Paul, V.J.: Climate change: links to global expansion of harmful cyanobacteria. Water Res. **46**(5), 1349–1363 (2012). https://doi.org/10.1016/j.watres.2011.08.002
10. Rivas-Villar, D., Rouco, J., Penedo, M.G., Carballeira, R., Novo, J.: Automatic detection of freshwater phytoplankton specimens in conventional microscopy images. Sensors **20**(22), 6704 (2020)
11. Rivas-Villar, D., Rouco, J., Carballeira, R., Penedo, M.G., Novo, J.: Fully automatic detection and classification of phytoplankton specimens in digital microscopy images. Comput. Meth. Prog. Biomed. **200**, 105923 (2021). https://doi.org/10.1016/j.cmpb.2020.105923
12. Rodenacker, K., Hense, B., Jütting, U., Gais, P.: Automatic analysis of aqueous specimens for phytoplankton structure recognition and population estimation. Microsc. Res. Tech. **69**, 708–20 (2006). https://doi.org/10.1002/jemt.20338
13. Schulze, K., Tillich, U.M., Dandekar, T., Frohme, M.: PlanktoVision - an automated analysis system for the identification of phytoplankton. BMC Bioinform. **14**(1), 115 (2013). https://doi.org/10.1186/1471-2105-14-115

Robust Deep Learning-Based Approach for Retinal Layer Segmentation in Optical Coherence Tomography Images

Alejandro Budiño[1,2], Lucía Ramos[1,2]([✉]), Joaquim de Moura[1,2], Jorge Novo[1,2], Manuel G. Penedo[1,2], and Marcos Ortega[1,2]

[1] Centro de Investigación CITIC, Universidade da Coruña,
Campus de Elviña, s/n, 15071 A Coruña, Spain
[2] Grupo VARPA, Instituto de Investigación Biomédica de A Coruña (INIBIC),
Universidade da Coruña, Xubias de Arriba, 84, 15006 A Coruña, Spain
l.ramos@udc.es

Abstract. In recent years, the medical image analysis field has experienced remarkable growth. Advances in computational power have made it possible to create increasingly complex diagnostic support systems based on deep learning. In ophthalmology, optical coherence tomography (OCT) enables the capture of highly detailed images of the retinal morphology, being the reference technology for the analysis of relevant ocular structures. This paper proposes a new methodology for the automatic segmentation of the main retinal layers using OCT images. The system provides a useful tool that facilitates the clinical evaluation of key ocular structures, such as the choroid, vitreous humour or inner retinal layers, as potential computational biomarkers for the analysis of different neurodegenerative disorders, including multiple sclerosis and Alzheimer's disease.

Keywords: Computer-aided diagnosis · Optical coherence tomography · Computational retinal biomarkers · Neurodegenerative disorders

1 Introduction

The human retina can be affected by multiple age-related diseases or as a consequence of an underlying ocular disorder. The progressive ageing of the world's population is leading to a steady increase in the incidence of different ocular and systemic diseases [4]. Neurodegenerative diseases represent a major concern for countries with ageing populations, as their prevalence tends to increase dramatically, partly due to the rise of the elderly population in recent years. In particular, multiple sclerosis and Alzheimer's disease, two of the most important neurodegenerative diseases, cause neuronal damage that, according to recent studies, can be early detected by morphological changes in the main structures of the retina, such as thinning of the nerve fibre layer. As there are currently

R. Moreno-Díaz et al. (Eds.): EUROCAST 2022, LNCS 13789, pp. 427–434, 2022.
https://doi.org/10.1007/978-3-031-25312-6_50

no effective therapies, early diagnosis with appropriate treatment is essential to ensure a good quality of life for patients affected by these relevant neurodegenerative diseases. On the other hand, diabetic macular edema is the most common cause of blindness among diabetic patients [2,8]. This relevant eye disorder is mainly caused by the accumulation of intraretinal fluid, especially between the plexiform layers of the retina [7,9]. In this regard, morphological assessment of the integrity of the retinal layers is essential for the diagnosis, treatment and monitoring of these retinal disorders and the most convenient technology available for this purpose is the Optical Coherence Tomography (OCT) [11]. Figure 1 shows a representative example of an OCT image with different retinal layers and regions of clinical interest manually labelled by a clinical expert.

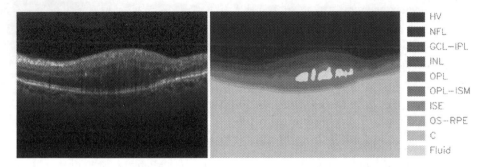

Fig. 1. Representative example of an OCT image with different retinal layers and regions of clinical interest that were manually labelled by a clinical expert: vitreous humour (HV), nerve fiber layer (NFL), ganglion cell layer to inner plexiform layer (GCL-IPL), inner nuclear layer (INL), outer plexiform layer (OPL), outer plexiform layer to inner segment myeloid (OPL-ISM), inner segment layer (ISE), outer segment layer to retinal pigment epithelium (OS-RPE), choroid (C) and pathological fluid regions (Fluid).

OCT is an emerging optical imaging modality that allows the capture of highly detailed images of the morphology of the retina and choroid, noninvasively and in real time. Once captured, these images must be visually inspected by clinical experts to detect possible morphological alterations, which is a subjective, tedious, and time-consuming task. In this sense, diagnostic support systems allow the automatic extraction of objective and valuable data to provide support for decision-making in clinical practice. In addition, the automatic extraction of reliable retinal biomarkers is a cost-effective way to screen large populations at high risk for these relevant diseases, enabling faster diagnosis and quicker treatment for a better quality of life.

Given the great relevance of this topic, several authors have addressed the development of computer-aided diagnosis (CAD) systems for retinal layer segmentation using OCT images. As a reference, Qiaoliang et al. [6] developed a method called DeepRetina that employs an improved version of the encoder Xception65, which extracts the features map and is passed to an ASPP (Atrous

Spatial Pyramid Pooling), which obtains multiscale information of the features. Then, an encoder-decoder module is used to obtain the boundary lines between the layers. The obtained results show an IoU between 90% and 95% for each layer. Kugelman et al. [5] proposes an architecture based on Recurrent Neuronal Networks (RNN), a kind of net in which the outputs can be used as inputs. The system is composed of four RNNs that analyze the image in different directions and two fully connected layers at the output. The results obtained by this system are between 95% and 99% IoU. In the work of González-López et al. [3], the authors proposed an active contour-based model to segment different retinal boundaries. Specifically, this proposal uses the horizontal placement of retinal layers and their relative location in the analysed images to constrain the search space and restrict the possible movements of the model to reach the different desired layers. Ben-Cohen et al. [1] proposed a fully convolutional network to obtain the segmentation. This work introduces a method to counter the uncertainty of the net to determine the class of the pixels near a boundary. For this, Dijkstra algorithm is used to draw the boundary by selecting the pixels that minimize a cost function. In this case, only four layers are segmented, showing that the boundaries are predicted with a precision of between 1 and 1.8px of the ground truth. Despite the effort of the scientific community to develop automated segmentation methodologies, the problem has only been partially researched from the point of view of computational biomarkers extraction and its clinical relevance for ocular pathologies.

Therefore, in this work, we propose a fully automatic solution for the segmentation and representation of the different retinal layers using OCT images. For this purpose, the designed pipeline consists of two main steps. First, the main retinal layers and the choroidal region are segmented using a deep learning-based strategy. Then, the system computes a set of clinically relevant computational biomarkers based on the morphological features extracted from the OCT images with great potential for early diagnosis, treatment and monitoring of relevant diseases.

2 Methodology

The proposed methodology receives, as input, an OCT image centred on the macular region of the retina. As illustrated in Fig. 2, the designed pipeline is composed by two main stages. First, the system segments the main retinal regions of clinical interest (retinal layers, vitreous humour, choroid, and pathological fluid) and then, the results are post-processed to improve the quality of the target regions. Finally, the segmented structures are analysed to extract a set of relevant computational biomarkers. All the steps of this process are described in more detail in the following subsections.

2.1 Segmentation of Retinal Layers and Fluid Regions

The first step of the proposed methodology consists of the design and implementation of a fully automatic method for the segmentation of the main retinal

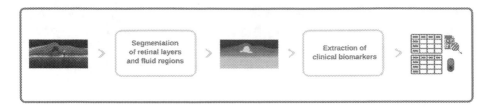

Fig. 2. Main scheme of the proposed methodology.

layers, the vitreous humour, the choroidal region and the regions of pathological fluid. For this purpose, we exploit the potential of the U-Net [10] architecture. This fully convolutional encoder-decoder network was originally conceived for use in medical image segmentation tasks. Specifically, in this work, the behaviour of two different encoders (ResNet-34 and DenseNet-169) combined with a transfer learning strategy (models pre-trained on the ImageNet dataset) is analysed. In this way, we can test the consistency and coherence of the proposed methodology more robustly. These encoders were chosen for their simplicity and adequate results for many similar tasks.

Training Details. For the training process, the OCT dataset was divided into mutually exclusive subsets for training (60%), validation (20%) and test (20%). All the CNN models were trained using a 10-fold cross-validation strategy, being calculated the binary cross-entropy loss. Thus, all the partitions were independent of each other and all the images of a patient belonged to a single partition. In addition, a batch size of 10 was used, as it gave the best results in previous tests. A Stochastic Gradient Descent (SGD) algorithm with a constant learning rate of 0.00001 and a first-order momentum of 0.9 was applied. Finally, a data augmentation process in the form of random shear transformations, rotations (between –5 and 5°C) and horizontal flips was also applied to make the model more robust and avoid over-fitting.

Post-processing. In this phase, we designed a strategy to reduce the segmentation errors in two regions of interest: the vitreous humour (region above the NFL layer) and the choroid (region below the OS-RPE layer). This strategy is possible because we know a priori (from domain knowledge) that the pathological fluid regions never appear inside of these regions of interest. Furthermore, we also know that the NFL and OS-RPE layers delimit the retina. Therefore, we can assign all the pixels of these regions of interest to their respective classes, correcting possible misclassified regions.

2.2   Extraction of Clinical Biomarkers

The last step of the proposed methodology consists of the design and implementation of a method for the extraction of a set of relevant biomarkers with great potential for the diagnosis of different eye diseases. For this purpose, the proposed method calculates different biomarkers based on the information obtained from the different retinal layers and regions with the presence of pathological fluid. On the one hand, the method provides information on the thickness of each retinal layer and the whole retina, including the mean, the standard deviation, the maximum, and the minimum. On the other hand, the method also provides the measurements of each detected cyst, such as the area, height and width measurements, and the shape factor. Figure 3 shows a representative example of the different biomarkers that were extracted by the proposed methodology.

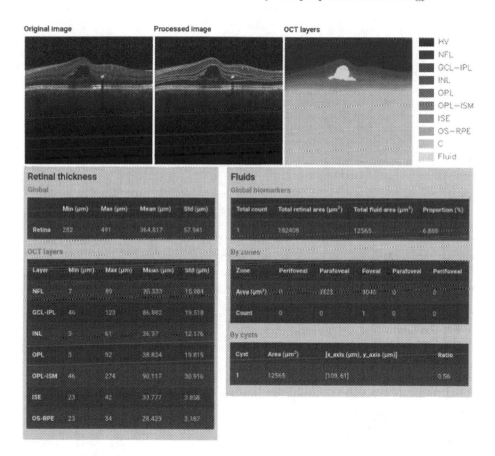

Fig. 3. Representative example of the extraction of different clinical biomarkers.

3   Results and Discussion

We conducted different experiments to validate the suitability of the proposed methodology using the public dataset provided by the *Vision and Image Processing (VIP) Laboratory* of Duke University[1]. This dataset contains OCT images

---

[1] https://people.duke.edu/~sf59/Chiu_BOE_2014_dataset.htm.

from 6 patients diagnosed with DME and 4 healthy. For each patient, there are 11 scans labelled at the pixel level. The acquisition device is an OCT Spectralis by Heidelberg Engineering. These images have an axial resolution of $3.87\,\mu m/px$; lateral of $11.07 - 11.57\,\mu m/px$, and azimuthal of $118 - 128\,\mu m/px$.

Figure 4 shows the behaviour obtained in the training stage using the U-Net architecture with the encoders (ResNet-34 and DenseNet-169). In particular, the results are presented in terms of the mean $\pm$ standard deviation after a 10-fold cross-validation at the eye level. As we can see, the models converge quickly in both configurations, demonstrating in all cases an adequate behaviour.

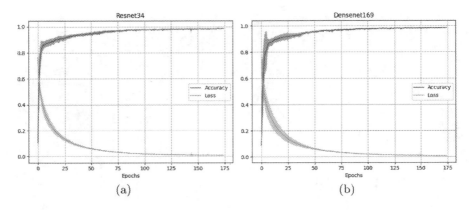

Fig. 4. Results of the training stage after a 10-fold cross-validation. (a) Mean $\pm$ standard deviation of the accuracy and loss for U-Net architecture with ResNet-34 encoder. (b)Mean $\pm$ standard deviation of the accuracy and loss for U-Net architecture with DenseNet-169 encoder.

Figure 5 (a) presents the confusion matrix at the test stage for the proposed method using the U-Net architecture with the ResNet-34 encoder. For this configuration, the system achieves the worst accuracy of 63.7% for the fluid class and the best accuracy of 99.7% for the choroid class. In general, it is observed that in regions where the boundaries tend to be clearer, the results that were obtained are better. In addition, Fig. 5 (b) shows the confusion matrix for the other configuration (U-Net with DenseNet-169 encoder). Similarly, the worst reported accuracy is 64.5% for the fluid class while the best reported accuracy is 99.6% for the humor vitreo and choroid classes. Therefore, both configurations achieved satisfactory results, demonstrating the potential of the proposed system to obtain relevant biomarkers for the diagnosis of different diseases.

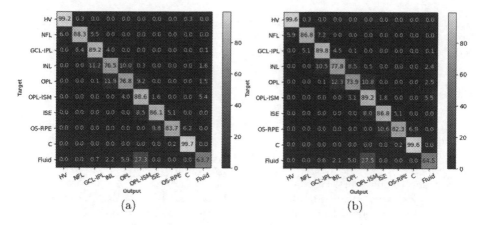

Fig. 5. Confusion matrices of the test stage. (a) Confusion matrix for the proposed method using U-Net architecture with ResNet-34 encoder. (b) Confusion matrix for the proposed method using U-Net architecture with DenseNet-169 encoder.

4 Conclusions

The analysis of the main retinal layers in OCT images is a relevant topic for the diagnosis and treatment of relevant pathologies such as multiple sclerosis, Alzheimer's disease or DME, one of the main causes of blindness in developed countries. In this work, we propose a novel methodology for the segmentation and representation of the different regions of clinical interest. These regions include the main layers of the retina, the vitreous humour, the choroid, and the pathological fluid. To this end, we exploit the potential of the U-Net architecture with a transfer learning approach. For this purpose, we consider 2 representative encoders that were pre-trained on the ImageNet dataset. Then, the system computes a set of clinically relevant computational biomarkers based on the morphological features extracted from the OCT images with great potential for early diagnosis, treatment and monitoring of relevant diseases. For validation, a study has been performed to evaluate the effect of the application of different encoders. In general, the results were satisfactory for all the configurations, demonstrating the capability of providing relevant biomarkers for the diagnosis of different diseases and, therefore, its great potential to be applied in healthcare, both for decision-making and automatic batch data processing in a centralized system.

Acknowledgements. This research was funded by Instituto de Salud Carlos III, Government of Spain, DTS18/00136 research project; Ministerio de Ciencia e Innovación y Universidades, Government of Spain, RTI2018-095894-B-I00 research project; Ministerio de Ciencia e Innovación, Government of Spain through the research project with reference PID2019-108435RB-I00; Consellería de Cultura, Educación e Universidade, Xunta de Galicia, Grupos de Referencia Competitiva, grant ref. ED431C 2020/24 and postdoctoral grant ref. ED481B 2021/059; Axencia Galega de Innovación (GAIN), Xunta de Galicia, grant ref. IN845D 2020/38; CITIC, Centro de Investigación de

Galicia ref. ED431G 2019/01, receives financial support from Consellería de Educación, Universidade e Formación Profesional, Xunta de Galicia, through the ERDF (80%) and Secretaría Xeral de Universidades (20%).

References

1. Ben-Cohen, A., et al.: Retinal layers segmentation using fully convolutional network in oct images (2017). https://www.rsipvision.com/wp-content/uploads/2017/06/Retinal-Layers-Segmentation.pdf
2. Ding, J., Wong, T.Y.: Current epidemiology of diabetic retinopathy and diabetic macular edema. Curr. Diab. Rep. **12**(4), 346–354 (2012)
3. González-López, A., de Moura, J., Novo, J., Ortega, M., Penedo, M.: Robust segmentation of retinal layers in optical coherence tomography images based on a multistage active contour model. Heliyon **5**(2), e01271 (2019)
4. Klein, R., Klein, B.E.: The prevalence of age-related eye diseases and visual impairment in aging: current estimates. Investigat. Ophthalmol. Vis. Sci. **54**(14), ORSF5-ORSF13 (2013)
5. Kugelman, J., Alonso-Caneiro, D., Read, S.A., Vincent, S.J., Collins, M.J.: Automatic segmentation of OCT retinal boundaries using recurrent neural networks and graph search. Biomed. Opt. Expr. **9**(11), 5759 (2018). https://doi.org/10.1364/boe.9.005759, https://doi.org/10.1364/boe.9.005759
6. Li, Q., et al.: DeepRetina: layer segmentation of retina in OCT images using deep learning. Transl. Vis. Sci. Technol. **9**(2), 61 (2020). https://doi.org/10.1167/tvst.9.2.61
7. de Moura, J., Novo, J., Penas, S., Ortega, M., Silva, J., Mendonça, A.M.: Automatic characterization of the serous retinal detachment associated with the subretinal fluid presence in optical coherence tomography images. Proc. Comput. Sci. **126**, 244–253 (2018)
8. de Moura, J., Samagaio, G., Novo, J., Almuina, P., Fernández, M.I., Ortega, M.: Joint diabetic macular edema segmentation and characterization in OCT images. J. Digit. Imaging **33**(5), 1335–1351 (2020)
9. de Moura, J., Novo, J., Rouco, J., Penedo, M.G., Ortega, M.: Automatic identification of intraretinal cystoid regions in optical coherence tomography. In: ten Teije, A., Popow, C., Holmes, J.H., Sacchi, L. (eds.) AIME 2017. LNCS (LNAI), vol. 10259, pp. 305–315. Springer, Cham (2017). https://doi.org/10.1007/978-3-319-59758-4_35
10. Ronneberger, O., Fischer, P., Brox, T.: U-Net: convolutional networks for biomedical image segmentation. In: Navab, N., Hornegger, J., Wells, W.M., Frangi, A.F. (eds.) MICCAI 2015. LNCS, vol. 9351, pp. 234–241. Springer, Cham (2015). https://doi.org/10.1007/978-3-319-24574-4_28
11. Samagaio, G., Estévez, A., de Moura, J., Novo, J., Fernández, M.I., Ortega, M.: Automatic macular edema identification and characterization using OCT images. Comput. Meth. Prog. Biomed. **163**, 47–63 (2018)

Impact of Increased Centerline Weight on the Joint Segmentation and Classification of Arteries and Veins in Color Fundus Images

José Morano[1,2(✉)] ⓘ, David Rivas-Villar[1,2] ⓘ, Álvaro S. Hervella[1,2] ⓘ,
José Rouco[1,2] ⓘ, and Jorge Novo[1,2] ⓘ

[1] Centro de Investigación CITIC, Universidade da Coruña, A Coruña, Spain
{j.morano,david.rivas.villar,a.suarezh,jrouco,jnovo}@udc.es
[2] VARPA Research Group, Instituto de Investigación Biomédica de A Coruña
(INIBIC), Universidade Da Coruña, A Coruña, Spain

Abstract. The analysis of the retinal vasculature represents a fundamental step in the diagnosis of multiple diseases, both ophthalmic and systemic. A comprehensive analysis includes the segmentation of vessels as well as their classification into arteries and veins. So far, multiple deep learning-based approaches have emerged that perform both tasks jointly. Currently, the state-of-the-art works are based on fully convolutional neural networks. In these works, the joint problem is approached either as a semantic segmentation task (SST) or as a set of multiple segmentation subtasks (MSS). These subtasks usually target arteries, veins and vessels. Unlike the SST approach, the MSS approach gives raise to complete segmentation maps. To address the low performance in the segmentation of small vessels, a state-of-the-art work proposes a SST approach that uses custom weight masks to increase the importance of vessel centerline pixels. In this work, we study the impact of increasing the importance of the central pixels of the blood vessels in training deep neural networks following the MSS approach. The experiments conducted in a public dataset demonstrate that increasing the weight of vessel centerlines improves the segmentation of small vessels, but worsens the overall segmentation. Thus, increasing the centerline weight is actually a relevant trade-off to be taken into account.

This work was funded by Instituto de Salud Carlos III, Government of Spain, and the European Regional Development Fund (ERDF) of the European Union (EU) through DTS18/00136 research project; Ministerio de Ciencia e Innovación, Government of Spain, through RTI2018-095894-B-I00 and PID2019-108435RB-I00 research projects; Axencia Galega de Innovación (GAIN), Xunta de Galicia, ref. IN845D 2020/38; Xunta de Galicia and the European Social Fund (ESF) of the EU through the predoctoral grant contracts refs. ED481A 2021/140, ED481A 2021/147, and ED481A-2017/328. Consellería de Cultura, Educación e Universidade, Xunta de Galicia, through Grupos de Referencia Competitiva, grant ref. ED431C 2020/24; CITIC, Centro de Investigación de Galicia ref. ED431G 2019/01, is funded by Xunta de Galicia and the EU (ERDF Galicia 2014-2020 Program).

R. Moreno-Díaz et al. (Eds.): EUROCAST 2022, LNCS 13789, pp. 435–443, 2022.
https://doi.org/10.1007/978-3-031-25312-6_51

Keywords: Retina · Artery/vein classification · Deep learning

1   Introduction

The analysis of the retinal blood vessels represents an essential step in the diagnosis of several diseases, both ophthalmic and systemic—e.g., glaucoma and diabetes, respectively [7]. This is because these and other diseases produce significant changes in the retinal vasculature, particularly in small vessels. A complete retinal vasculature analysis requires to segment and classify the vessels into arteries and veins (A/V). The segmentation of vessels allows the measurement of various features of these structures with proven relevance in the diagnostic process. Furthermore, their classification enables the measurement of features separately for arteries and veins. This is particularly useful, as there are multiple diseases that affect A/V differently. Despite their convenience, performing these tasks in the clinical practice is problematic. Mainly for two reasons. First, they are highly challenging—so they must be performed by expert clinicians—and laborious. And second, they are partially subjective, so the results of different experts may present significant differences. All these issues motivate the research on automatic methods.

To date, several methods have been proposed to address the segmentation and classification of retinal vessels [1,3,5,9]. Early works approached the joint segmentation and classification problem as a 2-stage process [2,11]. In the first stage, all the vessel pixels were identified, and then, in the second, all the identified pixels where classified into arteries and veins. The first methods following this approach were mostly based on ad hoc and traditional supervised learning methods [2]. Later, other works applied convolutional neural networks (CNNs) [11]. Nevertheless, the 2-stage approach followed by these works has one important problem: the propagation of errors from the first stage to the second stage. To avoid this issue, several works proposed to approach the joint segmentation-classification problem as a single multiclass semantic segmentation task (SST) using fully convolutional neural networks (FCNN) [3,5]. Commonly, approaches of this type consider 4 classes: *background*, *artery*, *vein* and *uncertain*. *Uncertain* class comprises all the pixels whose classification is not unique or cannot be determined by experts. Vessel crossings—areas where a vein overlaps an artery or vice versa—are the most common example of the first type. One of the main issues of the SST approach is that it gives raise to incomplete segmentation maps in vessel crossings, since the network is forced to classify each pixel into a single class. To resolve this issue, some works proposed to approach the joint problem as a set of multiple segmentation subtasks (MSS) [1,9]. The standard MSS approach comprises the following subtasks: the segmentation of arteries, veins and the whole vascular tree (i.e., all vessels).

Beyond the continuity of vessel segmentation maps, almost all state-of-the-art works face another problem: although they achieve highly positive results on wide vessels, the results on small vessels (arterioles and venules) are comparatively negative. This is mainly due to the unequal contribution to the loss of smaller and bigger vessels. To improve the segmentation of small vessels, Hemelings et al.

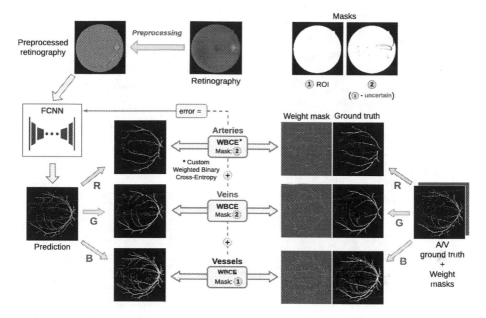

Fig. 1. MSS approach with custom weighting. Weighted binary cross-entropy (WBCE) function is applied only to the pixels within the region of interest (ROI) of each class. The ROI of the vessels includes all the background and vessel pixels. The ROI for arteries and veins (ROI_{AV}) excludes uncertain pixels.

[5] proposed training an FCNN using a loss function that weights more heavily the vessel centerline pixels. Although the proposal is well justified, the article [5] lacks an in-depth analysis of the real impact that the weight factor has on the segmentation of small arteries and veins (often called arterioles and venules). Additionally, to the best of our knowledge, this mechanism has not been applied in any of the works following the MSS approach, which conveniently addresses the discontinuity issue present in the SST approach. In this work, we perform a comprehensive study of the impact of applying the weighting strategy from [5] in training deep neural networks following the MSS approach [1,9]. For this end, we perform several experiments with different weighting factors of the vessel centerlines in a public reference dataset, and evaluate the models in full arteries and veins segmentation as well as arterioles and venules segmentation.

2   Methodology

To jointly classify and segment A/V with a particular weighting of vessel center-lines, we follow a MSS approach based on [9]. The proposed approach is depicted in Fig. 1. As it is done in [9], the problem of simultaneously segment and classify veins and arteries is decomposed into 3 related subtasks: the segmentation of arteries, veins and vessels (i.e., both arteries and veins). Thus, the network output consists of 3 channels, each containing the probability map of one of the aforementioned structures. The total loss is computed as the sum of the errors of segmenting each structure. Each individual error is computed as the weighted binary cross-entropy between the predicted probability map and the ground truth segmentation. To increase the weight of the central pixels of the vessels by a certain factor in the loss computation, we use custom weight masks with the same spatial resolution as the original image (see Fig. 1). To compute the error, we only include the pixels within the region of interest (ROI). The ROI comprises all pixels that contain some information. This excludes all the black pixels at the edges of the image. Furthermore, in the segmentation of arteries and veins, we also exclude the uncertain pixels, since its classification is unknown. We will refer to the ROI without the uncertain pixels as ROI_{AV}.

Formally, the multi-segmentation loss with custom weighting is defined as:

$$\mathcal{L}\left(\mathbf{f}(\mathbf{r}), \mathbf{s}\right) = -\sum_{c=1}^{3} \sum_{ROI_c} w_c \cdot BCE(\mathbf{f}(\mathbf{r})_c, \mathbf{s}_c) \ ,$$

where $\mathbf{r}$ is the input retinography; $\mathbf{f}(\mathbf{r})$, the network output; $\mathbf{s}$, the ground truth; ROI_c, the set of all the pixels within the specific ROI mask of class c (i.e., ROI or ROI_{AV}, depending on the case); w_c, $\mathbf{f}(\mathbf{r})_c$ and $\mathbf{s}_c$, the weight mask, the network prediction and the ground truth, respectively, of the given pixel for class c; and BCE, the Binary Cross-Entropy function.

2.1 Preprocessing

To correct the inter- and intra-image illumination and contrast variability, we performed an image preprocessing consisting in a channel-wise global contrast enhancement and a local intensity normalization [3,9]. Formally, the preprocessing method is defined as follows:

$$I_{norm}^{C} = \sigma_0 \frac{I^C - I_l^C}{\sigma_{I^C - I_l^C}} \ , \tag{1}$$

where I_{norm}^C is the resulting normalized channel C, I^C is the channel C of the input retinography, I_l^C is I^C after applying a low-pass filter and $\sigma_{I^C - I_l^C}$ is the global standard deviation of the channel resulting from the subtraction of the low-pass filtered channel I_l^C to the input channel I^C.

As in [9], we use $\sigma_0 = 1$. Also, we use a Gaussian filter with zero mean and standard deviation $\sigma = 10$ as the low-pass filter.

2.2 Network Architecture

In line with previous works [3,5,9], we use U-Net [10] as the network architecture. U-Net is an FCNN composed of two main paths nearly symmetrical: a contracting path (encoder), and an expansive path (decoder). In addition, the network features skip connections via concatenation between both paths. The only differences in our architecture from the original are as follows. In our case, the number of input channels is 3, since we use RGB images. Similarly, the number of output channels is 3—one per structure (arteries, veins and vessels). Lastly, we apply a sigmoid activation function at the last convolutional layer.

2.3 Data

For the experiments in this work, we used the public dataset Retinal Images vessel Tree Extraction (RITE) [6]. This dataset is a reference standard for A/V segmentation. It is composed of 40 color fundus images and their corresponding manual segmentation maps. Each pixel of a manual segmentation map is assigned to one of the following classes: *artery, vein, uncertain* or *crossing*. The *uncertain* class comprises the vessel pixels which clinical experts cannot determine whether they are veins or arteries. The *crossing* class is assigned to pixels from regions where a vein overlaps an artery or vice versa.

Ir order to train the networks following the proposed approach, we adapted the ground truth images from RITE, and obtained, a priori, their skeleton masks—necessary for the online building of the weight masks. Since the proposed approach aims to simultaneously segment arteries, veins and vessels, we converted the original manual annotations to RGB images containing, in each channel, the complete segmentation map of one structure. Thus, artery and vein segmentation maps also include vessel crossings. This adaptation is the same as the one performed in [9]. The skeleton masks are obtained from the adapted ground truth using the Zhang-Suen thinning algorithm [12]. The weight masks are computed online from the pre-computed skeleton masks of each structure.

2.4 Quantitative Evaluation

Quantitative evaluation of the models is performed by comparing the predicted segmentation masks with those manually annotated by the experts. In particular, we compute the area under Precision-Recall curve (AUC-PR) in the segmentation of arteries and veins. Also, in addition to the traditional evaluation, which considers the full ROI, we compute the AUC-PR values only for the areas where arterioles and venules (arteries and veins narrower than 5 pixels) are located.

2.5 Experimental Details

The selection of methods and hyperparameters was based on previous works [5, 9]. To train the models, we use the Adam optimization algorithm [8] with the following parameter values: initial learning rate $\alpha = 1 \times 10^{-4}$, and decay rates $\beta_1 = 0.9$ and $\beta_2 = 0.999$. The learning rate is constant during the whole training. The training is stopped when the validation loss does not improve for 200 epochs. To initialize the parameters of the networks, we use the random method of He et al. with Uniform distribution [4]. To artificially increase the number of training samples, we use data augmentation consisting of slight affine transformations (shearing, rotation and scaling), intensity and color variations, and horizontal and vertical flipping. These transformations are applied online on each sample— at random—during the training.

Table 1. AUC-PR (%) in A/V segmentation for different weighting factors and areas. The best results for each area and structure are highlighted in bold.

Structure	Area	Weighting factors			
		1	2	5	10
Arteries	Full ROI	**81.97 ± 0.22**	81.25 ± 0.31	80.97 ± 0.29	79.88 ± 1.71
	Small vessels	78.67 ± 0.41	78.23 ± 0.39	79.52 ± 0.59	**80.00 ± 0.33**
Veins	Full ROI	**87.16 ± 0.24**	86.77 ± 0.08	86.28 ± 0.26	85.10 ± 1.39
	Small vessels	80.03 ± 0.57	80.28 ± 1.07	81.33 ± 0.20	**81.39 ± 1.12**

In order to measure the impact of the weighting factor of the vessel center-lines, we performed experiments with 4 different values of this hyperparameter: 1, 2, 5 and 10. In addition, to consider the stochasticity of the networks training, we performed 4 training repetitions with random initialization. This is done for all the alternatives. The quantitative evaluation detailed in Sect. 2.4 is then performed for each trained model. The reported results represent the mean of the different training repetitions. In all the tables, the mean values are always shown with the corresponding standard deviation.

3   Results and Discussion

Table 1 shows the mean AUC-PR values in A/V segmentation for the models trained with different weighting factors. Also, we include the AUC-PR both for the entire ROI and for the areas where small vessels are located. Since we performed 4 training repetitions, each AUC-PR value is presented with the corresponding standard deviation. Complementarily, Fig. 2 shows representative examples of the predicted probability maps that were obtained by the models trained using different weighting factors. As can be seen in Table 1, increasing the weight of vessel centerlines improves the segmentation and classification of small vessels, but worsens the overall segmentation. These results are in line with the predicted segmentation maps shown in Fig. 2. The models trained with high weighting factors segment arterioles and venules more precisely, but they also segment vessels that are not actually present in the ground truth; i.e., they tend to over-segment.

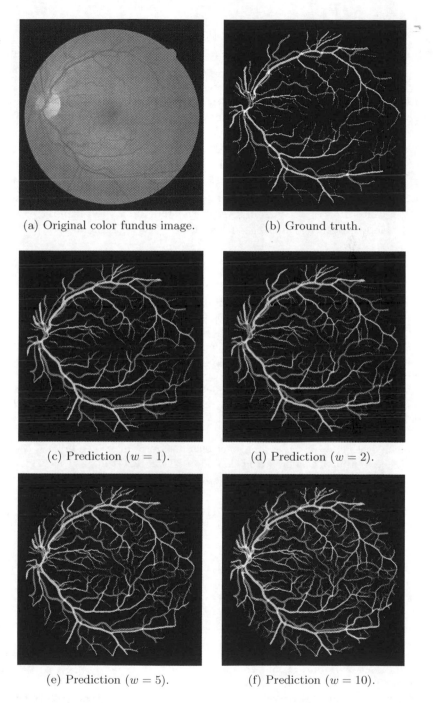

(a) Original color fundus image.   (b) Ground truth.

(c) Prediction ($w = 1$).   (d) Prediction ($w = 2$).

(e) Prediction ($w = 5$).   (f) Prediction ($w = 10$).

Fig. 2. Examples of the probability maps obtained by the models trained with different weighting factors.

4   Conclusions

In this work, we comprehensively studied the impact of increasing the importance of the centerlines of the blood vessels in training deep neural networks for the simultaneous segmentation and classification of arteries and veins in color fundus images. To this end, we adapted a common state-of-the art approach, and compared the segmentation performance for arteries and veins for different weighting factors of the vessel centerlines. All the experiments were performed using the RITE reference dataset. The quantitative and qualitative results in this dataset clearly demonstrate that increasing the weight of the centerlines of the vessels improves the segmentation of small vessels, but worsens the overall segmentation, as the models tend to over-segment. Thus, increasing the weight of the vessel centerlines represents an interesting trade-off to be taken into account when developing deep learning-based methods for A/V segmentation.

References

1. Chen, W., et al.: TW-GAN: topology and width aware GAN for retinal artery/vein classification. Med. Image Anal. 102340 (2021). https://doi.org/10.1016/j.media. 2021.102340
2. Dashtbozorg, B., Mendonça, A.M., Campilho, A.: An automatic graph-based approach for artery/vein classification in retinal images. IEEE Trans. Image Process. **23**(3), 1073–1083 (2014). https://doi.org/10.1109/TIP.2013.2263809
3. Girard, F., Kavalec, C., Cheriet, F.: Joint segmentation and classification of retinal arteries/veins from fundus images. Artif. Intell. Med. **94**, 96–109 (2019). https:// doi.org/10.1016/j.artmed.2019.02.004
4. He, K., Zhang, X., Ren, S., Sun, J.: Delving deep into rectifiers: surpassing human-level performance on imagenet classification. In: Proceedings of the 2015 IEEE International Conference on Computer Vision (ICCV),pp. 1026–1034. ICCV, Washington, DC, USA (2015). https://doi.org/10.1109/ICCV.2015.123
5. Hemelings, R., Elen, B., Stalmans, I., Van Keer, K., De Boever, P., Blaschko, M.B.: Artery-vein segmentation in fundus images using a fully convolutional network. Computer. Med. Imaging Graph. **76**, 101636 (2019). https://doi.org/10.1016/j. compmedimag.2019.05.004
6. Hu, Q., Abràmoff, M.D., Garvin, M.K.: Automated separation of binary overlapping trees in low-contrast color retinal images. In: Mori, K., Sakuma, I., Sato, Y., Barillot, C., Navab, N. (eds.) Medical Image Computing and Computer-Assisted Intervention - MICCAI 2013, pp. 436–443. Springer, Berlin Heidelberg, Berlin, Heidelberg (2013). https://doi.org/10.1007/978-3-642-40763-5_54
7. Kanski, J.J., Bowling, B.: Clinical Ophthalmology: A Systematic Approach. Elsevier Health Sciences, seventh edn. (2011)
8. Kingma, D.P., Ba, J.: Adam: a method for stochastic optimization. In: 3rd International Conference on Learning Representations, ICLR, San Diego, CA, USA, 7–9 May 2015, Conference Track Proceedings (2015)
9. Morano, J., Álvaro S. Hervella, Novo, J., Rouco, J.: Simultaneous segmentation and classification of the retinal arteries and veins from color fundus images. Artif. Intell. Med. **118**, 102116 (2021). https://doi.org/10.1016/j.artmed.2021.102116

10. Ronneberger, O., Fischer, P., Brox, T.: U-net: convolutional networks for biomedical image segmentation. In: Navab, N., Hornegger, J., Wells, W.M., Frangi, A.F. (eds.) Medical Image Computing and Computer-Assisted Intervention - MICCAI 2015, pp. 234–241. Springer International Publishing, Cham (2015). https://doi.org/10.1007/978-3-319-24574-4_28
11. Welikala, R., et al.: Automated arteriole and venule classification using deep learning for retinal images from the UK biobank cohort. Comput. Biol. Med. **90**, 23–32 (2017). https://doi.org/10.1016/j.compbiomed.2017.09.005
12. Zhang, T.Y., Suen, C.Y.: A fast parallel algorithm for thinning digital patterns. Commun. ACM **27**(3), 236–239 (1984). https://doi.org/10.1145/357994.358023

Rating the Severity of Diabetic Retinopathy on a Highly Imbalanced Dataset

Ángela Casado-García[1], Manuel García-Domínguez[1],
Jónathan Heras[1](✉), Adrián Inés[1], Didac Royo[2],
and Miguel Ángel Zapata[2,3]

[1] Departamento de Matemáticas y Computación, Universidad de La Rioja,
Logrono, Spain
{angela.casado,manuel.garciad,jonathan.heras,adrian.ines}@unirioja.es
[2] UPRetina, Barcelona, Spain
{didac,mazapata}@upretina.com
[3] Hospital Vall Hebron, Passeig Roser 126, Sant Cugat del Vallès,
08195 Barcelona, Spain

Abstract. Diabetic Retinopathy (DR) is an ocular complication of diabetes that leads to a significant loss of vision. Screening retinal fundus images allows ophthalmologists to early detect and diagnose this disease; however, the manual interpretation of images is a time-consuming task. Deep image classification models deal with this drawback and provide an efficient method to diagnose DR, but they are mainly trained with balanced dataset were all stages of DR are equally represented—a scenario that does not reflect the reality during screening. In this work, we have conducted a study of Deep Learning models to rate the severity of Diabetic Retinopathy from digital fundus images when working with a highly imbalanced dataset. Our approach, that is based on the ensemble of several ResNetRS models, achieves an agreement rate with the specialists above that of primary care physicians (κ of 0.81 vs. 0.75). In addition, our method can also be applied in a binary fashion to determine whether a case is derivable or non-derivable; achieving again an agreement with the specialists above that of primary care physicians (κ of 0.76 vs. 0.64).

Keywords: Diabetic retinopathy · Fundus · Imbalanced data · Deep learning · Ensemble

1 Introduction

Diabetic Retinopathy is an ocular complication of diabetes that is caused by the deterioration of the blood vessels that supply the retina [14]. As this disease

This work was partially supported by Ministerio de Ciencia e Innovación [PID2020-115225RB-I00/AEI/10.13039/501100011033]. Ángela Casado-García has a FPI grant from Community of La Rioja 2020. Manuel García-Domínguez has a FPI grant from Community of La Rioja 2018. Adrián Inés has a FPU Grant [16/06903] of the Spanish Ministerio de Educación y Ciencia.

R. Moreno-Díaz et al. (Eds.): EUROCAST 2022, LNCS 13789, pp. 444–451, 2022.
https://doi.org/10.1007/978-3-031-25312-6_52

progresses, there is a very significant loss of vision; and, therefore, screening eyes, together with a timely consultation and treatment, is instrumental for early detection and diagnosis of this pathology. Unfortunately, the manual interpretation of retinal fundus images is a time-consuming task for ophthalmologists, and this has led to the development of computer-aided diagnosis systems based on computer vision techniques and, currently, Deep Learning methods [1].

Deep Learning models have become the de-facto approach to deal with image classification problems in biomedicine [8] and this is also the case for diagnosing Diabetic Retinopathy [1]. The effectiveness of Deep Learning models lies in the quantity and quality of the data that is fed to train them; therefore, for those models to be useful, the datasets employed to train them should reflect the reality that the models will found when deployed in the real world [4]. However, most models for detecting the different stages of Diabetic Retinopathy are small (the largest dataset is available at Kaggle with 88702 images, but it contains many images with poor quality and incorrect labeling [7]) and do not reflect the reality found during screening (where the majority of images belong to healthy patients, and there are few images of patients with Diabetic Retinopathy, specially for the late stages of this disease) [9].

In this work, we present a study conducted to construct a Deep Learning model to rate the severity of Diabetic Retinopathy using the data provided by the CatSalut (Servei Català de la Salut)—a highly imbalanced dataset that reflects the reality of screening where healthy images are found more frequently than unhealthy images. In addition, we have compared the level of agreement of primary care physicians and our approach against a ground truth set by retina specialists. The developed approach has been designed to rate the severity of Diabetic Retinopathy from digital fundus images, but it can be also applied in a binary fashion to determine whether a case is derivable or non-derivable. Again, the level of agreement of this binary approach, and primary care physicians have been compared against a ground truth set by three retina specialists.

2   Dataset

The CatSalut dataset employed in this work was created from retinal images of a private database, a nationwide database that collected retinal information from patients attending to the healthcare centre for a diabetic retinopathy screening process. Images of the database were acquired using different non-mydriatic fundus cameras, all of them approved by the National Health Service for Diabetic Screening in the UK [2]. Technicians were instructed to perform posterior pole retinal photography, centred on the macula and including the optic disc and vascular arcades [16]. The patients' information from the images was anonymised before sending them to the reading centre where three retina specialists characterised the images for changes in the macula, retina, and optic disc. In addition, we combined this private dataset with the public Kaggle Diabetic Retinopathy dataset[1].

---

[1] https://www.kaggle.com/c/diabetic-retinopathy-detection/overview/evaluation.

The dataset consists of 148027 images that are split into three groups: 139816 images for training, 95% (these images are further split into 125834 images for training, 90%; and 13982 for validation, 10%) and 8211 for testing, 5%. The test set only contains images from the CatSalut dataset; whereas, both the training and validation sets contain images from both the CatSalut and Kaggle dataset (the training set contains 82027 images from CatSalut, a 65%, and 43807 from Kaggle, a 35%; and the validation set contains 9114, a 65%, and 4868 from kaggle, a 35%). All the images of the dataset were pre-processed by cropping them centred on the retina, equalised, and resized to size 512 × 512.

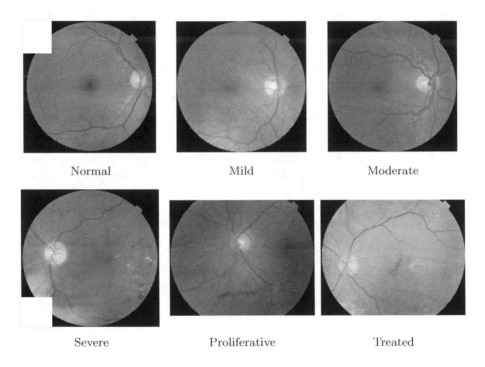

Normal   Mild   Moderate

Severe   Proliferative   Treated

Fig. 1. Stages of diabetic retinopathy included in the CatSalut dataset.

The dataset contains images from 5 stages of Diabetic Retinopathy (normal, mild, moderate, severe, and proliferative) and one additional category that accounts for retinas with Diabetic Retinopathy that have already received treatment, see Fig. 1. For the binary case, retinas labelled as normal or mild are deemed as non-derivable; whereas moderate, severe, proliferative and treated are all classified as derivable. The distribution of the classes in each dataset is provided in Table 1.

In this study, we used the weighted Kappa coefficient (κ) with quadratic weights as our rating strategy for inter variability rating. The interpretation of Cohen's Kappa coefficient is 1 for perfect agreement, while pure chance would be rated as 0. Values are often interpreted as follows: below 0.20 is regarded as

Table 1. Dataset composition. We have included the binary labels and how that relates to the full diabetic retinopathy staged labelling.

Class	Training	Validation	Testing
Normal	104026 (82.6%)	11509 (82.5%)	7092 (86.4%)
Mild	8891 (7.0%)	1014 (7.3%)	361 (4.4%)
Moderate	10809 (8.6%)	1218 (8.5%)	639 (7.8%)
Severe	1002 (0.8%)	122 (0.7%)	24 (0.3%)
Proliferative	420 (0.3%)	56 (0.4%)	7 (0.9%)
Treated	686 (0.5%)	63 (0.5%)	88 (1.1%)

poor, 0.21–0.40 as fair, 0.41–0.60 as moderate, 0.61–0.80 as good, and $0.81 - 1.00$ as very good agreement. As a note to the reader, be aware that Kappa statistics depend on the prevalence of each category and their number.

3   Training Procedure

Using our dataset, we built an ensemble of models for diagnosing Diabetic Retinopathy as follows. All the experiments detailed in this section were implemented using Pytorch, and have been trained thanks to the functionality of the FastAI library and using a GPU Nvidia RTX 2080 Ti.

First of all, we analysed the performance of 8 Deep Learning architectures (3 ResNet architectures [5], 2 Inception architectures [12], 2 EfficientNet architectures [13] and a HRnet architecture [15]) when trained with images of the dataset resized to 224×224—this allowed us to select an architecture for further experiments since training those Deep Learning architectures with the whole dataset and with images of bigger size might take several days. Namely, to train those 8 architectures, we used the transfer-learning method presented in [6]. This is a two-stage procedure that starts from a model pretrained in the ImageNet challenge, and can be summarised as follows. In the first stage, we replaced the head of the model (that is, the layers that give us the classification of the images), with a new head adapted to the number of classes of our particular dataset. Then, we trained these new layers (the rest of the layers stayed frozen) with the data of each particular dataset for two epochs. In the second stage, we unfreezed the whole model and retrained all the layers of the model with the new data for 100 epochs. In order to find a suitable learning rate for both the first and second stage, we used cyclical learning rates for optimisation [11]. Moreover, we employed early stopping based on monitoring the validation loss, and data augmentation [10] (using vertical and horizontal flips, rotations from $-180°$ to $180°$, zooms and lighting transformations) to prevent overfitting. The architecture that produced the best results when evaluated on the test set was ResNetRS [3], see Table 2.

The ResNetRS model obtained as explained previously was the basis for further experiments. Namely, using that model as a starting point, we trained a

Table 2. Preliminary results on the CatSalut dataset.

Architecture	Weighted kappa
Resnet50	0.5917
Resnet50d	0.6938
Resnet50RS	0.7112
Inceptionv4	0.6169
InceptionResnetv2	0.5688
EfficientNetB3	0.6884
EfficientNetv2	0
HRnetw40	0.6358

model with images of size 384×384 by applying the same techniques explained for training the first model. Subsequently, using the new model as a starting point, we repeated the training process with images of size 512×512. From such a model, we trained three different models using the same techniques explained previously, and using the following variants of the CatSalut dataset: (1) we applied undersampling to the images from the normal class, namely, we took 10000 random images of the normal class from the training set; (2) we applied undersampling to the images from the normal class (obtaining 10000 images), and oversampling to the images of the other classes (obtaining 10000 images per class); and, (3) we applied oversampling to the images of all the classes but the normal class (obtaining a dataset of approximately 600000 images).

4   Results

In this section, we present the results obtained by our ensemble of models with the test set of the CatSalut dataset. We analyse the results for rating the severity of Diabetic Retinopathy, and decide whether the case is derivable.

We start by analysing the multi-class case. With the test dataset from CatSalut (8227 images) labelled by three retina specialists, primary care physicians and our ensemble of models, we can compare their inter-rater reliability. The primary care physicians achieved a Kappa score of 0.75 showing a high consistency overall, although not as high as the internal consistency of the specialists ($\kappa = 0.86$).

The inter-rater reliability analysis between the retina specialists and the ensemble of our models is formatted on Table 3 as a confusion matrix. The Kappa score ($\kappa = 0.81$) shows a high consistency overall, higher than the consistency between the primary care physician and the specialists, although not as high as the internal consistency of the specialists ($\kappa = 0.86$). The most important misclassification in both the primary care physicians and the ensemble of models are the images from the proliferative class that are usually classified as normal. In any case, this class is underrepresented in this analysis, and it would be hasty to make any final judgement from such few samples.

Table 3. Confusion matrix of our ensemble of models for the Diabetic Retinopathy stage labels. The percentages are computed per row.

	Normal	Mild	Moderate	Severe	Proliferative	Treated
Normal	6935 (97.79%)	72 (1.02%)	83 (1.17%)	0 (0%)	1 (0.01%)	1 (0.01%)
Mild	149 (41.27%)	141 (39.06%)	71 (19.67%)	0 (0%)	0 (0%)	0 (0%)
Moderate	117 (18.31%)	47 (7.36%)	468 (73.24%)	5 (0.78%)	2 (0.31%)	0 (0%)
Severe	0 (0%)	0 (0%)	17 (70.83%)	7 (29.17%)	0 (0%)	0 (0%)
Proliferative	5 (71.43%)	0 (0%)	1 (14.29%)	1 (14.29%)	0 (0%)	0 (0%)
Treated	6 (6.82%)	0 (0%)	18 (20.45%)	1 (1.14%)	60 (68.18%)	3 (3.41%)

We focus now on analysing the binary case. On Table 4, we have the confusion matrix comparing both primary care physicians, and our ensemble of models against the retina specialists. We have designed two methods to obtain a binary prediction from our ensemble of models. First, it is worth noting that given an image, the output of each model of the ensemble is a distribution of the likelihood of each class for that image. From the three distributions produced by the models that form our ensemble, the binary class is computed using one of the following two methods:

1. The three distributions are added and divided by 3. The maximum value of the resulting distribution indicates the class of the image. If that class belongs either to the normal or mild class, the image is classified as non-derivable; otherwise, it is classified as non-derivable.
2. The three distributions are added and divided by 3. The values of the resulting distribution for the classes moderate, severe, proliferative and treated are added, and if the obtained value is over a fixed threshold, the image is classified as derivable; otherwise, it is classified as non-derivable. The threshold value was fixed by using the precision-recall curve of Fig. 2 and selecting the value that provides a better trade-off between precision and recall.

Table 4. Confusion matrix using the derivable Diabetic Retinopathy criteria. Percentages are computed per row. Predictions by primary care physicians and Deep Learning models are tested against the ground truth set by the specialists.

	Physicians ($\kappa = 0.648$)		Ensemble 1 ($\kappa = 0.757$)		Ensemble 2 ($\kappa = 0.761, \tau = 0.59$)	
	No	Yes	No	Yes	No	Yes
No	7371 (98.9%)	80 (1.1%)	7297 (97.6%)	175 (2.4%)	7354 (98.7%)	99 (1.32%)
Yes	324 (42.7%)	434 (57.3%)	156 (21.1%)	583 (78.9%)	208 (27.4%)	550 (72.6%)

Using this criteria the Kappa scores are 0.648 for the primary care physicians, 0.757 for the ensemble of models using the first approach, and 0.761 for the ensemble of models using the second approach. Immediately, we can see that our second approach for computing the binary class from the ensemble of models is above that of primary care physicians.

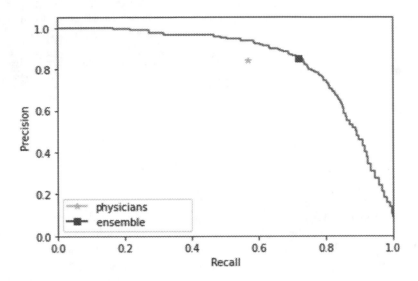

Fig. 2. Precision-recall curve for the ensemble of models.

We have also computed the precision and recall for each entry in Table 5. The ensemble of models using the second approach is slightly better in terms of precision than the primary care physicians. In addition, it obtains a considerably better recall than primary care physicians; but, the first ensemble approach produces the best recall. Finally, when weighing both precision and recall equally (f1-score), the second approach for ensembling the models obtains the best result.

Table 5. Metrics comparative table for existing algorithms and primary care physicians.

Metric	Physicians	Ensemble 1	Ensemble 2 ($\tau = 0.59$)
Precision	0.84	0.79	0.85
Recall	0.57	0.76	0.73
F1-score	0.68	0.77	0.78

5   Conclusions

In this paper, we have presented a successful approach to construct an ensemble of models for rating the severity of Diabetic Retinopathy from fundus digital images in a highly imbalanced dataset. In addition, we have compared the results against primary care physicians. At this stage of the clinical trial the agreement rate of our algorithm is above that of primary care physicians (κ of 0.81 vs. 0.75). In addition, the ensemble of models can be employed for determining if the fundus image belongs to a case derivable or non-derivable. This ensemble of models is also above primary care physicians (κ of 0.76 vs. 0.64).

References

1. Alyoubi, W.L., Shalash, W.M., Abulkhair, M.F.: Diabetic retinopathy detection through deep learning techniques: a review. Inform. Med. Unlocked **20**, 100377 (2020)

2. Authors not listed: Diabetic eye screening: guidance on camera approval (2020). https://www.gov.uk/government/publications/diabetic-eye-screening-approved-cameras-and-settings/diabetic-eye-screening-guidance-on-camera-approval

3. Bello, I., et al.: Revisiting resnets: improved training and scaling strategies. Adv. Neural Inf. Process. Syst. **34** (2021)

4. Dietterich, T.G.: Robust artificial intelligence and robust human organizations. Front. Comput. Sci. **13**(1), 1–3 (2019). https://doi.org/10.1007/s11704-018-8900-4

5. He, K., Zhang, X., Ren, S., Sun, J.: Deep residual learning for image recognition. In: IEEE Conference on Computer Vision and Pattern Recognition, pp. 770–778 (2016)

6. Howard, J., Gugger, S.: Fastai: a layered API for deep learning. Information **11**, 108 (2020)

7. Li, T., Gao, Y., Wang, K., Guo, S., Liu, H., Kang, H.: Diagnostic assessment of deep learning algorithms for diabetic retinopathy screening. Inf. Sci. **501**, 511–522 (2019)

8. Meijering, E.: A bird's-eye view of deep learning in bioimage analysis. Comput. Struct. Biotechnol. J. **18**, 2312–2325 (2020)

9. Nagpal, D., Panda, S., Malarvel, M., Pattanaik, P.A., Khan, M.Z.: A review of diabetic retinopathy: datasets, approaches, evaluation metrics and future trends. J. King Saud Univ.-Comput. Inf. Sci. **34**(9), 7138–7152 (2021)

10. Simard, P., Steinkraus, D., Platt, J.C.: Best practices for convolutional neural networks applied to visual document analysis. In: 12th International Conference on Document Analysis and Recognition, vol. 2, pp. 958–964 (2003)

11. Smith, L.: Cyclical learning rates for training neural networks. In: IEEE Winter Conference on Applications of Computer Vision, pp. 464–472 (2017)

12. Szegedy, C., et al.: Rethinking the inception architecture for computer vision. In: IEEE Conference on Computer Vision and Pattern Recognition, pp. 2818–2826 (2016)

13. Tan, M., Le, Q.V.: Efficientnet. rethinking model scaling for convolutional neural networks. In: International Conference on Machine Learning, vol. 97, pp. 6105–6114 (2019)

14. Vidal-Alaball, J., et al.: Artificial intelligence for the detection of diabetic retinopathy in primary care: protocol for algorithm development. JMIR Res Protoc. **1**(8), e12539 (2019)

15. Wang, J., et al.: Deep high-resolution representation learning for visual recognition. IEEE Trans. Pattern Anal. Mach. Intell. **43**(10), 3349–3364 (2020)

16. Zapata, M., et al.: Telemedicine for a general screening of retinal disease using nonmydriatic fundus cameras in optometry centers: Three-year results. Telemed. e-Health **23**(1), 30–36 (2017)

Gait Recognition Using 3D View-Transformation Model

Philipp Schwarz[1]([✉])[iD], Philipp Hofer[3][iD], and Josef Scharinger[2][iD]

[1] LIT Secure and Correct Systems Lab, Johannes Kepler University, Linz, Austria
philipp.schwarz@jku.at
[2] Institute of Networks and Security, Johannes Kepler University, Linz, Austria
josef.scharinger@jku.at
[3] Institute of Computational Perception, Johannes Kepler University, Linz, Austria
philipp.hofer@ins.jku.at

Abstract. When it comes to visual based gait recognition, one of the biggest problems is the variance introduced by different camera viewing angles. We generate 3D human models from single RGB person image frames, rotate these 3D models into the side view, and compute gait features used to train a convolutional neural network to recognize people based on their gait information. In our experiment we compare our approach with a method that recognizes people under different viewing angles and show that even for low-resolution input images, the applied view-transformation 1) preserves enough gait information for recognition purposes and 2) produces recognition accuracies just as high without requiring samples from each viewing angle. We believe our approach will produce even better results for higher resolution input images. As far as we know, this is the first appearance-based method that recreates 3D human models using only single RGB images to tackle the viewing-angle problem in gait recognition.

Keywords: 3D gait recognition · View-transformation model · Convolutional neural network

The research reported in this paper has been partly supported by the LIT Secure and Correct Systems Lab funded by the State of Upper Austria and by the Austrian Ministry for Transport, Innovation and Technology, the Federal Ministry of Science, Research and Economy, and the Province of Upper Austria in the frame of the COMET center SCCH. This work has been carried out within the scope of Digidow, the Christian Doppler Laboratory for Private Digital Authentication in the Physical World. We gratefully acknowledge financial support by the Austrian Federal Ministry for Digital and Economic Affairs, the National Foundation for Research, Technology and Development, the Christian Doppler Research Association, 3 Banken IT GmbH, Kepler Universitätsklinikum GmbH, NXP Semiconductors Austria GmbH & Co KG, Österreichische Staatsdruckerei GmbH, and the State of Upper Austria.

R. Moreno-Díaz et al. (Eds.): EUROCAST 2022, LNCS 13789, pp. 452–459, 2022.
https://doi.org/10.1007/978-3-031-25312-6_53

1   Introduction

In the past years, gait has become an increasingly important modality for person recognition. While there are various sensors that can capture gait information, predominantly visual-based data such as videos are used.

The human gait has some properties that make it very attractive for recognition purposes such as its long distance recognizability, not requiring physical contact or not requiring user cooperation. On the downside, there are a lot of factors which influence gait recognition negatively. For instance walking speed, viewing-angle, injuries, clothing variations or carrying objects. One of the biggest problems regarding visual based gait recognition is the variance introduced by different camera viewing angles. The similarity between two different persons viewed under the same viewing angle is often bigger than the similarity between two images of the same person under different viewing angles.

There exist several approaches that deal with the viewing angle problem. We differentiate between approaches based on view-invariant features and approaches based on View Transformation Models (VTM). The former attempts to compute features which are not or hardly affected by different viewing angles, while the latter seeks to reconstruct features of a different viewing angle. This work describes a VTM-based approach.

2   Proposed Method

We use low resolution RGB images of the commonly used CASIA-B [13] gait dataset as input for our approach. After preprocessing the images we compute a 3D model from a single RGB image for each image of this dataset by applying PIFuHD [10]. We rotate the 3D model into a $90\,°C$ view as it contains the most discriminating person information and project it onto a 2D plane. The projection is only a means to reduce the size of our features since 3D objects are generally too big to fit in memory when it comes to training a neural network. Based on these 2D representations we compute a feature similar to the well-known Gait Energy Image (GEI) [4] which serves as input to a Convolutional Neural Network (CNN). The last layer in the CNN classifies the input from which we compute the recognition accuracy.

Generating accurate 3D human models with PIFuHD requires high resolution images. Contrarily, one of the advantages of gait as a biometric modality is its recognizability under low resolution conditions. In order to close the gap between those contradicting requirements, we perform several preprocessing steps on our low resolution input data before we can create 3D human models. To increase recognition accuracy we also perform postprocessing steps on the projection of the 3D model before computing gait features. An overview of the whole processing pipeline can be viewed in Fig. 1. Each process is described in more detail in Sect. 2.2. To illustrate the improvements gained by our preprocessing measures Fig. 2 shows an unprocessed RGB image of the CASIA-B dataset as well as the resulting 3D model seen from the original perspective and from the front.

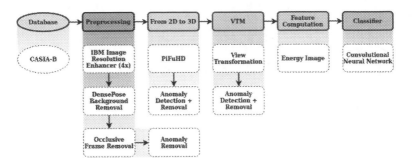

Fig. 1. Our proposed processing pipeline for 3D based Gait Recognition.

In the spirit of consistency and comparability we use the same frame for the following figures.

2.1 Dataset

In this work we use data from the publicly available dataset CASIA-B. It contains ten walking sequences for each of the 124 subjects. Six walks were recorded under normal conditions, two under carrying conditions and two under different clothing conditions. The walking sequences are captured by 11 cameras from 11 equidistant viewing angles. The images of this dataset have a resolution of 240 x 320px.

2.2 Preprocessing

To produce recognizable 3D models, the following processing steps are applied.

o **Image Resolution Enhancement**
   To artificially increase the resolution of our input images, we use IBM's Image

Fig. 2. Raw input image from CASIA-B dataset (left) with output of PIFuHD under same view (middle) and front view (right).

Resolution Enhancer [1]. It allows enhancing the resolution by a factor of up to four, which results in images of size 960x1280px. Fig. 3 shows the resolution enhanced image as well as the generated 3D model. Compared to Fig. 2 this preprocessing step does not seem to improve the quality of our model, unless combined with the next step in our pipeline.

Fig. 3. Upsampled RGB image (left) with output of PIFuHD under same view (middle) and front view (right).

o **DensePose Background Removal**
Removing only the background (without the previous resolution enhancement step) already visibly improves the quality of the 3D model as is shown in Fig. 4. We perform background subtraction using the silhouette estimated by the person detection framework introduced in [3]. We can generate even more

Fig. 4. Image with background removed (left) with output of PIFuHD under same view (middle) and front view (right).

accurate 3D models when we both enhance the resolution and remove the background. This is illustrated in Fig. 5.

Fig. 5. Image upsampled and background removed (left) with output of PIFuHD under same view (middle) and front view (right).

o **Occlusive Frame Removal**

Since we are not focusing on gait recognition under occlusion in this paper, we exclude frames that do not fully capture a persons silhouette. As we are working with data recorded under lab-conditions, we simply remove frames where a person 1) just enters or exits, 2) is too close to the camera or 3) is too far away to be recognized as such by the person detection framework mentioned above.

o **DensePose Anomaly Removal**

Since the DensePose person detection framework is not extremely precise, we have to deal with artifacts. Therefore, we implement a threshold-based mechanism that removes small pixel islands that are unrealistically far away from a person but have falsely been labeled as part of a person.

2.3   From 2D to 3D

We let PIFuHD [10] process the preprocessed images to obtain 3D human models which we have already displayed in the figures above. PIFuHD is based on PIFu [9], which is a framework that produces high-resolution 3D models from either single 2D images or multiple 2D images from different perspectives. PIFuHD extends the coarse encoder of PIFu with an additional encoder for fine details. This work only leverages the single input image capability of PIFuHD.

2.4   View Transformation and Feature Computation

We let a camera rotate around the center of the 3D human models until it reaches the 90 °C view. No viewing-angle estimation is done because the original viewing-angle is provided by CASIA-B. Rotating the 3D model can sometimes reveal artifacts which were not visible before, especially when the difference between the source view and the destination view (90 °C view) becomes larger. We differentiate between severe and non-severe artifacts. Accordingly, we implement an algorithm to get rid of the 3D model in case the artifacts are too severe and another algorithm to remove artifacts in the form of disconnected islands of pixel thereby preserving the 3D model.

From the person images, which are now viewed under a 90 °C angle, we compute a variation of the well-known GEI according to [11]. Additionally, no gait cycles are computed, we just take 20 consecutive frames which is roughly the same number of frames as one gait cycle.

3   Results

In our experiments, we only use the walking sequences recorded under normal walking conditions and disregard clothing and carrying variations. We partition the data according to [11] in training set and test set and perform six-fold cross-validation.

We use a custom shallow convolutional neural network and SGD as optimizer, similar to DPEI. In Table 1 we compare our approach with DPEI [11]. While DPEI can only accurately recognize persons that were seen under the same or a similar angle before (during training), our approach is not bound by this limitation, since we can transform a person under any viewing angle into any other viewing angle. Moreover, only a single frame of a person is required, even though more accurate 3D representations can be generated when multiple frames from different views are used [9].

Table 1. Comparison of Top-1 and Top-5 accuracies of our approach and DPEI.

		Top-1 Accuracy		Top-5 Accuracy	
Train walks	Test walks	DPEI	pifuhdEI	DPEI	pifuhdEI
01, 02, 03, 04	05, 06	**0.933**	0.847	0.969	**0.976**
02, 03, 04, 05	06, 01	**0.952**	0.931	0.969	**0.993**
03, 04, 05, 06	01, 02	0.955	**0.961**	0.982	**0.999**
04, 05, 06, 01	02, 03	**0.959**	0.942	0.986	0.996
05, 06, 01, 02	03, 04	0.953	**0.959**	0.994	**0.998**
06, 01, 02, 03	04, 05	**0.957**	0.884	**0.990**	0.981
Average		**0.951**	0.921	0.982	**0.991**

The Top-1 accuracy is on average slightly worse than that of DPEI and the average TOP-5 accuracy is slightly higher, despite the low resolution input images, anomalies introduced by PIFuHD and the low amount of training data in general (less than 60% of what was used in [11] due to stricter preprocessing methods).

Even though the quantitative results do not show a big increase in accuracy, we believe this approach in general bears much potential. Especially with the help of higher resolution cameras, we prognosticate more accurate 3D models and therefore higher accuracy in gait recognition.

4   Future Work

During this work, we already identified some starting points to improve this approach. Using gait data from higher resolution cameras is one improvement. A more accurate background subtraction algorithm might be useful, unless higher resolution data already suffices for accurately generating the 3D model. Adding gait data from cameras positioned at different angles improves the 3D model quality as already demonstrated in [9]. Viewing-angle estimation can be implemented to make this approach more applicable for real-world scenarios. Instead of computing hand-crafted features on which to train the neural net, either unprocessed 2D projections or compact 3D representations can be used as input to the neural net. More fine-tuned models as well as data-augmentation can also help in improving this approach.

5   Related Work

Various methods exist for acquiring 3D visual gait data. For instance, a setup of multiple calibrated cameras can be used [6,8,14]. Apart from multi-camera methods, there also exist RGBD-based single camera methods [2,5] and LiDAR-based methods [12]. Most recently machine learning methods have been used to generate 3D gait information, most notably PIFu and PIFuHD. A completely different approach is described in [7]. They morph 3D parametric human body models based on 2D silhouettes.

References

1. Ibm   image   resolution   enhancer.   https://github.com/IBM/MAX-Image-Resolution-Enhancer. Accessed 26 July 2021
2. Ahmed, F., Paul, P.P., Gavrilova, M.L.: DTW-based kernel and rank-level fusion for 3D gait recognition using Kinect. Vis. Comput. **31**(6-8), 915–924 (2015)
3. Güler, R.A., Neverova, N., Kokkinos, I.: DensePose: dense human pose estimation in the wild. In: Proceedings of the IEEE Computer Society Conference on Computer Vision and Pattern Recognition, pp. 7297–7306 (2018)
4. Han, J., Bhanu, B.: Individual recognition using gait energy image. IEEE Trans. Pattern Anal. Mach. Intell. **28**(2), 316–322 (2006)
5. Kondragunta, J., Jaiswal, A., Hirtz, G.: Estimation of gait parameters from 3D pose for elderly care. In: ACM International Conference Proceeding Series, pp. 66–72 (2019)

6. López-Fernández, D., Madrid-Cuevas, F.J., Carmona-Poyato, A., Muñoz-Salinas, R., Medina-Carnicer, R.: A new approach for multi-view gait recognition on unconstrained paths. J. Vis. Commun. Image Represent. **38**, 396–406 (2016)
7. Luo, J., Tjahjadi, T.: Gait recognition and understanding based on hierarchical temporal memory using 3D gait semantic folding. Sensors (Switzerland) **20**(6), 1646 (2020)
8. Muramatsu, D., Shiraishi, A., Makihara, Y., Uddin, M.Z., Yagi, Y.: Gait-based person recognition using arbitrary view transformation model. IEEE Trans. Image Process. **24**(1), 140–154 (2015)
9. Saito, S., Huang, Z., Natsume, R., Morishima, S., Li, H., Kanazawa, A.: PIFu: pixel-aligned implicit function for high-resolution clothed human digitization. In: Proceedings of the IEEE International Conference on Computer Vision, pp. 2304–2314 (2019)
10. Saito, S., Simon, T., Saragih, J., Joo, H.: PIFuHD: multi-level pixel-aligned implicit function for high-resolution 3D human digitization. In: Proceedings of the IEEE Computer Society Conference on Computer Vision and Pattern Recognition, pp. 81–90 (2020)
11. Schwarz, P., Scharinger, J., Hofer, P.: Gait recognition with densePose energy images. In: Rozinaj, G., Vargic, R. (eds.) IWSSIP 2021. CCIS, vol. 1527, pp. 65–70. Springer, Cham (2022). https://doi.org/10.1007/978-3-030-96878-6_6
12. Yamada, H., Ahn, J., Mozos, O.M., Iwashita, Y., Kurazume, R.: Gait-based person identification using 3D LiDAR and long short-term memory deep networks. Adv. Robot. **34**(18), 1201–1211 (2020)
13. Yu, S., Tan, D., Tan, T.: A framework for evaluating the effect of view angle, clothing and carrying condition on gait recognition. In: Proceedings - International Conference on Pattern Recognition, vol. 4, pp. 441–444 (2006)
14. Zhao, G., Liu, G., Li, H., Pietikäinen, M.: 3D gait recognition using multiple cameras. In: FGR 2006: Proceedings of the 7th International Conference on Automatic Face and Gesture Recognition 2006, pp. 529–534 (2006)

Segmentation and Multi-facet Classification of Individual Logs in Wooden Piles

Christoph Praschl[1(✉)] , Philipp Auersperg-Castell[3,4] ,
Brigitte Forster-Heinlein[4] , and Gerald Adam Zwettler[1,2]

[1] Research Group Advanced Information Systems and Technology,
Research and Development Department, University of Applied Sciences
Upper Austria, Hagenberg, Austria
{christoph.praschl,gerald.zwettler}@fh-hagenberg.at
[2] Department of Software Engineering, School of Informatics,
Communications and Media, University of Applied Sciences Upper Austria,
Hagenberg, Austria
[3] Bluedynamics Auersperg-Castell KG, Kritzing 31, Freinberg, Austria
phil@bluedynamics.com
[4] Faculty of Computer Science and Mathematics, University of Passau,
Passau, Germany
Brigitte.Forster@uni-passau.de

Abstract. The inspection of products and assessment of quality is connected with high costs and time effort in many industrial domains. This also applies to the forestry industry. Utilizing state-of-the-art deep learning models allows automizing the analysis of wooden piles in a vision-based manner. In this work, a parallel two-step approach is presented for the segmentation and multi-facet classification of individual logs, according to the wood type and quality. The present approach is based on a preliminary log localization step and like this allows determining the quality, volume and also the value of individual logs, respectively the whole wooden pile. Using a YOLOv4 model for wood species classification for douglas firs, pines and larches results in an accuracy of 74.53%, while a quality classification model for spruce logs reaches 86.58%. In addition to that, the trained U-NET segmentation model reaches an accuracy of 93%. In the future, the underlying data set and models will be further improved and integrated to a mobile application for the on site analysis of wooden piles by foresters.

Keywords: Wood log analysis · Log segmentation · Tree type classification · Quality classification · YOLO · U-Net

1 Introduction

Due to the steady improvement in the field of machine learning and computer vision, more and more visual areas of application are digitized. As a result, an increasing number of processes is performed in an automated, or at least semi-automated way and drives the topic of industry 4.0 forward. Especially when it comes to monitoring tasks in industrial [6,17,24] or agricultural [3,7, 22] areas, computer vision occupies an increasingly important part. Also in the scope of forestry, computer vision applications are expanding primarily in the field of tree analysis based on images from unmanned aerial vehicles [1,12,13]. However, the application of drones for analyzing forests and trees has limits, due to bureaucratic restrictions, but also in terms of the feasibility, since not every forest owner owns a drone. Depending on the application, aerial vehicles are also not the best choice according to the usability. For example, when it comes to on-ground analysis, e.g. of wooden piles in the context of log trading, smartphones can be preferred to drones. Especially since this area of application is currently done in a very time-consuming manual way it can be automated utilizing a smartphone app for assessing cross-sections of logs, as well as their quality and type of tree in a visual way. Like this it is possible to minimize time consumption and for this to reduce costs.

The methods in this work pick up the idea for digitizing parts of the forestry industry as described by Auersperg-Castell [2] and resume a preliminary publication of the authors [16] describing the utilization of neural networks for the localization of individual logs in wooden piles using a tiling process. The resulting regions of interests (ROI) of the preceding processing steps are the basis for the segmentation, as well as the type and quality classification of individual logs, resulting in a continuous system combining multiple aspects for the analyzation of wooden piles.

2   Related Work

There are related publications in the context of the individual proposed steps for the analyzation of wooden piles. For example, Decelle and Jalilian [8] compare different deep learning segmentation architectures in the context of wooden cross-sections. Like in the present work, the authors use among others an U-NET architecture for the separation of the logs' cut face from the remaining background. Next to that, also Schraml and Uhl [19] present a segmentation approach using a similarity based methodology instead of a neural network.

Also, in the context of the classification of the wood type and quality, recent approaches have been published. Kryl et al. [14] reviewed multiple methodologies in this area using classic approaches such as gray level covariance matrices or k-nearest neighbor, but also deep learning methodologies. This review, shows that previous publications differ from the present approach by carrying out the classification using images of the tree's bark [5,9], using cut out wooden boards instead of the raw cross-sections [21], based on macroscopic images of the wood [10,20,23] or utilizing infrared [4] and even x-ray images [15] instead of RGB images. To the best of the authors' knowledge, none of the related works have used deep learning approaches for the segmentation, tree type as well as quality classification of individual log cross-sections in wooden piles and for this differ from the present approach.

3   Material

The neural networks as presented in this work are trained using a base data set of 440 wooden pile images with 18521 logs. Currently, 23.8% of these logs are labelled according to the wooden type, which is connected to one of two forest types typical for Austria (**Group 1**: 15.3% spruces, 0.1% firs; **Group 2**: 1.9% douglas firs, 0.4% pines, 6.1% larches), and 23.3% according to the type dependent log quality classes AC, BR, CX and K (c.f. Table 1). Additionally, 2412 logs are segmented using binary masks. The mentioned quality classes are based on the classification system used in Austrian sawmills for construction work or product packaging. The original number of classes is reduced by combining the classes A to C to one class AC. Because of this situation, the proposed classification system may not be applicable for other countries and also not for other areas of applications as e.g. firewood, paper wood or pulp wood. The quality classes are used as follows:

- **AC:** These are the best qualities A through C with no or only few flaws and are usually paid the same price, so they are combined into one class.
- **BR:** This quality class contains logs of minor quality with partially rooted spots mostly due to fungus and for this generate lower revenues.
- **CX:** The class of CX contains logs of minor quality with cracks or irregular shape that are crooked or knotty. This class can be only partially classified from a photograph of the cutting area, since the crucial features can also occur along the whole remaining log and for this requires an additional post-classification step, which is not considered in this work.
- **K:** The last class contains wood that is infested by bark beetle and for this has a blue/gray shade at the rim on the cutting surface. However, the infestation has not progressed that far to impair the structural quality and is for this still sellable. Unsellable logs are already rejected, before stacking them to a wooden pile and for this don't have to be considered in the classification.

Table 1. The distribution of the log quality per type based on the manually classified logs.

Type of tree	AC	BR	CX	K
Spruce	1952 (68.8%)	241 (8.49%)	36 (1.2%)	598 (21.0%)
Fir	11 (73.3%)	0 (0%)	4 (26.7%)	0 (0%)
Douglas fir	270 (78.0%)	55 (15.9%)	2 (0.6%)	18 (5.2%)
Pine	74 (98.7%)	1 (1.3%)	0 (0%)	0 (0%)
Larch	972 (85.6%)	76 (6.7%)	35 (3.1%)	52 (4.6%)

4   Methodology

This section provides an overview of the project's over all process for estimating the value of wooden piles, with the focus of this work on utilizing neural networks for the segmentation of cutting surfaces with an U-Net model as introduced by Ronneberger et al. [18] and the classification of individual logs based on YOLO models [25].

4.1   Overview

Next to the fundamental image of the wooden pile, respectively the log ROIs, the proposed process presupposes additional user input. This meta information refers to (I) the distance between the camera and the pile shown in the image, (II) the forest type and (III) the pile's length. The distance is required for the transformation from pixel space to a metric space. Utilizing the forest type, the possible types of trees can already be pre-limited to a subset of the supported classes. The last of the three information can be seen as given, as it is defined by the harvester/lumberjack, when cutting the trees and stacking multiple logs to one pile and is required for the volume determination.

Based on this input, an approach with two parallel branches utilizing the results of a previous log localization step is proposed, as shown in Fig. 1. While the first branch utilizes one U-Net model for determining the exact log front faces, the second branch is based on multiple classification models. This second branch uses a YOLO model as a first step for the classification of the type of tree, within the known pile group. Based on the retrieved information, a second YOLO model is chosen, which is used to obtain the quality class of a log according to the determined type of tree.

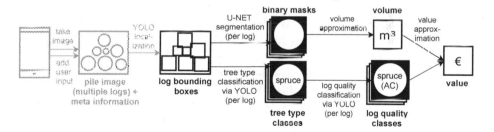

Fig. 1. The parallel approach for creating binary masks and classifications for individual logs. This process is based on the result of a previous localization approach and results in the volume of a wooden pile as well as log classes, and for this allows to approximate the pile's value.

4.2   Segmentation

The localization results of the YOLO network are used to create binary segmentation masks. For this task, the individual logs are clipped from the pile image. The log images extracted by utilizing the proposed strategy are then used as input of the U-Net model to create an instance segmentation of the logs. Finally, a post-processing step is performed by applying a threshold, for which in turn the biggest continuous contour growing from the image's center is extracted to get the actual cutting area. Afterwards the segmented result is in turn used to approximate the cutting area and with that the volume of the individual logs of the pile with respect to the user input in form of the pile length and the user's distance to the pile.

4.3 Multi-facet Classification

Next to the log segmentation, another execution branch utilizing neural networks is applied in the form of a multi-facet log classification. This classification process is also based on the localization results of the YOLO network and is separated into two individual steps using YOLO models. For this reason, logs are first classified based on their type of tree and in a second step regarding the actual wood quality using multiple models. The reason for this two-stage, multi-model approach is that the features that are crucial for the quality, are differently pronounced according to the type of tree, especially in terms of color differences. Since the type of the associated forest is known in the form of an user input, there are two different tree-type classification models, one used for the first pile group containing spruces and firs, and the second pile group containing douglas firs, pines and larchs. In addition to the pile group YOLO models, there are multiple quality classification models that are trained for the given type of tree.

5 Evaluation

The proposed process is evaluated using multiple scaled YOLOv4 models [25] and one U-Net segmentation model, which are trained using TensorFlow 2.3.1 and Python 3.7. The model trainings are done utilizing an Intel Core i9-10900K and a Gigabyte GeForce RTX 3070 with log images of 416×416 pixels for the classification and 256×256 for the segmentation. To the best of the authors' knowledge, there is neither a wooden pile nor a log data set publicly available, that is suitable for the evaluation of the proposed methodologies. There was the HAWKwood database, which is not available anymore [11]. For this reason, different images from the created training data set are randomly selected to evaluate the models. These images were not included in the training of the models.

5.1 Segmentation

The segmentation is evaluated using 90 individual logs, together with the associated ground truth masks. To these images, the trained U-NET model is applied. For the resulting model predictions in turn, the proposed post-processing methodology is executed to retrieve the final mask images. For the evaluation, the binarized results are compared with the ground truth. Figure 2 shows eight sample masks compared to the ground truth. On the one hand, red pixels indicate false positive values, with the U-NET falsely classifying the pixels as logs (foreground) and on the other hand blue pixels indicate wrongly detected background areas. All in all, the U-NET model is able to detect 55.84% of the pixels correctly as foreground and 37.5% of the pixels as background. Next to that, only 1.26% of the pixels are falsely classified as foreground and 5.39% as background. This results in an accuracy of 93.35%.

Fig. 2. Model predictions for eight sample log images of the evaluation data set. White pixels are showing the true positives, black pixels the true negatives, blue pixels are the false negatives and red pixels are the false positive values. (Color figure online)

5.2   Classification

Due to the highly unbalanced distribution of the manually classified logs in the wooden pile data set according to the types of tree, with 2837 spruces and 15 firs in the first pile group, the type of tree classification is currently only trained and evaluated for the second group. This evaluation was carried out using 231 randomly selected larch, pine and douglas fir logs. The associated results are shown in Table 2a, which can be summarized with an accuracy of 74.53%.

The evaluation of the log quality model is currently only carried out for spruce logs, due to the good availability of manually classified logs of this type of tree in the used wooden pile data set. This is done using 231 randomly selected logs from the created data set in combination with the associated ground truth quality class. Table 2b shows the confusion matrix comparing the detected classes with the associated ground truth. The evaluation results in an accuracy of 86.58%.

Table 2. Confusion matrices showing the distribution of the detected classes by (a) the trained type of tree and (b) the spruce quality YOLO models compared to the ground truth (GT) of the specific evaluation data set.

(a)

	Douglas Fir	Pine	Larch
Douglas Fir (GT)	32.18%	0	0
Pine (GT)	0	0	0
Larch (GT)	24.14%	0	41.37%

(b)

	AC	BR	CX	K
AC (GT)	75.75%	0.43%	0	4.76%
BR (GT)	3.03%	2.16%	0	0
CX (GT)	0.43%	0	0	0
K (GT)	4.76%	0	0	8.65%

6   Summary and Outlook

As shown in the results, the presented approach combining multiple deep learning models for the instance segmentation as well as classification of individual logs in wooden piles is promising for the utilization in forest industry in the context of analyzing logs. Next to that, the robustness of the classification approach is improved based on the separation in two forest groups, allowing to compensate the bias in the highly unbalanced training data set by focusing on a specific subset of the available data using specialized models. In the future, the trained models and especially the underlying data set should be further extended and improved. Additionally, the individual parts should be introduced to a mobile application allowing to assess the value of a wooden pile on site in the forest.

Acknowledgements. Many thanks to the local government of Upper Austria for facilitating this research initiative in the course of the *easy2innovate* funding program. Special thanks also to *Ulrich Hainberger* and *Luis Hainberger* from the Ulrich Hainberger e.U. forestry company for support in the cooperation, for providing thousands of precious heterogeneous test images and for invaluable input and valuable discussion.

References

1. Ângeorza, D.D., Rotar, I.: Evaluating plant biodiversity in natural and semi-natural areas with the help of aerial drones. Bull. Univ. Agric. Sci. Vet. Med. Cluj-Napoca Agric. **77**(2) (2020)
2. Auersperg-Castell, P.: Photooptische Holzpoltervermessung mittels Haar-Kaskaden. Bachelor's thesis, University of Passau, Germany (2018)
3. Bashir, S., Jabeen, A., Makroo, H., Mehraj, F.: Application of computer vision system in fruit quality monitoring. In: Sensor-Based Quality Assessment Systems for Fruits and Vegetables, p. 267 (2020)
4. Cao, J., Liang, H., Lin, X., Tu, W., Zhang, Y.: Potential of near-infrared spectroscopy to detect defects on the surface of solid wood boards. BioResources **12**(1), 19–28 (2017)
5. Carpentier, M., Giguere, P., Gaudreault, J.: Tree species identification from bark images using convolutional neural networks. In: 2018 IEEE/RSJ International Conference on Intelligent Robots and Systems (IROS), pp. 1075–1081. IEEE (2018)
6. Colucci, D., Morra, L., Zhang, X., Fissore, D., Lamberti, F.: An automatic computer vision pipeline for the in-line monitoring of freeze-drying processes. Comput. Ind. **115**, 103184 (2020)
7. da Costa, A.Z., Figueroa, H.E., Fracarolli, J.A.: Computer vision based detection of external defects on tomatoes using deep learning. Biosyst. Eng. **190**, 131–144 (2020)
8. Decelle, R., Jalilian, E.: Neural networks for cross-section segmentation in raw images of log ends. In: 2020 IEEE 4th International Conference on Image Processing, Applications and Systems (IPAS), pp. 131–137 (2020). https://doi.org/10.1109/IPAS50080.2020.9334960
9. Fiel, S., Sablatnig, R.: Automated identification of tree species from images of the bark, leaves or needles. NA (2010)

10. Gunawan, P., et al.: Wood identification on microscopic image with Daubechies wavelet method and local binary pattern. In: 2018 International Conference on Computer, Control, Informatics and Its Applications (IC3INA), pp. 23–27. IEEE (2018)

11. Herbon, C.: The HAWKwood database. arXiv preprint arXiv:1410.4393 (2014)

12. Kentsch, S., Lopez Caceres, M.L., Diez Donoso, Y.: Tree species classification by using computer vision and deep learning techniques for the analysis of drone images of mixed forests in Japan. In: EGU General Assembly Conference Abstracts, p. 197 (2020)

13. Kentsch, S., Lopez Caceres, M.L., Serrano, D., Roure, F., Diez, Y.: Computer vision and deep learning techniques for the analysis of drone-acquired forest images, a transfer learning study. Remote Sens. **12**(8), 1287 (2020)

14. Kryl, M., Danys, L., Jaros, R., Martinek, R., Kodytek, P., Bilik, P.: Wood recognition and quality imaging inspection systems. J. Sens. **2020**, 1–19 (2020)

15. Mu, H., Qi, D., Zhang, M., Yu, L.: Image edge detection of wood defects based on multi-fractal analysis. In: 2008 IEEE International Conference on Automation and Logistics, pp. 1232–1237. IEEE (2008)

16. Praschl, C., Auersperg-Castell, P., Forster-Heinlein, B., Zwettler, G.: Multi-resolution localization of individual logs in wooden piles utilizing yolo with tiling on client/server architectures. In: Proceedings of the 33rd European Modeling and Simulation Symposium (2021)

17. Roggi, G., Niccolai, A., Grimaccia, F., Lovera, M.: A computer vision line-tracking algorithm for automatic UAV photovoltaic plants monitoring applications. Energies **13**(4), 838 (2020)

18. Ronneberger, O., Fischer, P., Brox, T.: U-net: convolutional networks for biomedical image segmentation (2015)

19. Schraml, R., Uhl, A.: Similarity based cross-section segmentation in rough log end images. In: Iliadis, L., Maglogiannis, I., Papadopoulos, H. (eds.) AIAI 2014. IAICT, vol. 436, pp. 614–623. Springer, Heidelberg (2014). https://doi.org/10.1007/978-3-662-44654-6_61

20. Seng, L.K., Guniawan, T.: An experimental study on the use of visual texture for wood identification using a novel convolutional neural network layer. In: 2018 8th IEEE International Conference on Control System, Computing and Engineering (ICCSCE), pp. 156–159. IEEE (2018)

21. Shustrov, D., et al.: Species identification of wooden material using convolutional neural networks. Master's thesis, LUT University, Finland (2018)

22. Tian, H., Wang, T., Liu, Y., Qiao, X., Li, Y.: Computer vision technology in agricultural automation-a review. Inf. Process. Agric. **7**(1), 1–19 (2020)

23. Urbonas, A., Raudonis, V., Maskeliūnas, R., Damaševičius, R.: Automated identification of wood veneer surface defects using faster region-based convolutional neural network with data augmentation and transfer learning. Appl. Sci. **9**(22), 4898 (2019)

24. Villalba-Diez, J., Schmidt, D., Gevers, R., Ordieres-Meré, J., Buchwitz, M., Wellbrock, W.: Deep learning for industrial computer vision quality control in the printing Industry 4.0. Sensors **19**(18), 3987 (2019)

25. Wang, C.Y., Bochkovskiy, A., Liao, H.Y.M.: Scaled-YOLOv4: scaling cross stage partial network. arXiv preprint arXiv:2011.08036 (2020)

Drone Detection Using Deep Learning: A Benchmark Study

Ahmed Hashem[1] and Thomas Schlechter[2(✉)]

[1] Linz Center of Mechatronics GmbH, 4040 Linz, Austria
ahmed.hashem@jku.at
[2] University of Applied Sciences Upper Austria, 4600 Wels, Austria
thomas.schlechter@ieee.org
https://www.lcm.at/, https://www.fh-ooe.at/

Abstract. Since Unmanned Aerial Vehicles (UAVs) became available to the civilian public, it has witnessed dramatic spread and exponential popularity. This escalation gave rise to privacy and security concerns, both on the recreational and institutional levels. Although it is mainly used for leisure and productivity activities, it is evident that UAVs can also be used for malicious purposes. Today, as legislation and law enforcement federations can hardly control every incident, many institutions resort to surveillance systems to prevent hostile drone intrusion.

Although drone detection can be carried out using different technologies, such as radar or ultra-sonic, visual detection is arguably the most efficient method. Other than being cheap and readily available, cameras are typically a part of any surveillance system. Moreover, the rise of deep learning and neural network models rendered visual recognition very reliable [9,21].

In this work, three state-of-the-art object detectors, namely YOLOv4, SSD-MobileNetv1 and SSD-VGG16, are tested and compared to find the best performing detector on our drone data-set of 23,863 collected and annotated images. The main work covers detailed reportage of the results of each model, as well as a comprehensive comparison between them. In terms of accuracy and real-time capability, the best performance was achieved by the SSD-VGG16 model, which scored average precision (AP50) of 90.4%, average recall (AR) of 72.7% and inference speed of 58 frames per second on the NVIDIA Jetson Xavier kit.

Keywords: Drone detection · Neural network · Security · Artificial intelligence

1 Introduction

In 2013, after Amazon announced its plan to use drones for package delivery, hobby drones had become exponentially popular [5]. As per usual, legislative regulations were incapable of addressing the fast pace of advancements and inventions of technology. The widespread use of drones raised major privacy,

© The Author(s), under exclusive license to Springer Nature Switzerland AG 2022
R. Moreno-Díaz et al. (Eds.): EUROCAST 2022, LNCS 13789, pp. 468–475, 2022.
https://doi.org/10.1007/978-3-031-25312-6_55

security and safety concerns. These predicaments and safety concerns called for the need for drone, or rather anti-drone, surveillance systems that can detect drone intrusions and, if necessary, neutralize them.

In [21], Taha and Shoufan list and compare several drone detection modalities, namely RADAR, RF, IR and ultra-sonic, and compare their performance. Through that review, as well as many other papers, it can be concluded that visual detection, especially using recent advancements in Deep Neural Networks (DNNs) and Convolutional Neural Networks (CNNs), has become the most reliable and efficient method to achieve accurate and real-time object detection.

What makes drone detection a challenging task, however, is the characteristics of drone appearance and movement. There exists a myriad of drone models that can look very different from each other. From the number of rotors to the skeleton structure and color, drones constitute a real generalization challenge to detection algorithms. They can also come in a huge range of sizes, from a few centimeters to a couple of meters span. Finally, they have common shape characteristics with leafy branch endings of trees, birds and distant airplanes. In indoor environment, they can be hidden in complex backgrounds and can have similar appearance to other devices.

Drones have a very particular, yet very challenging, flight style as well. They can perform high acceleration and rotation movements in very small range. They can also fly at relatively high speeds for camera shutter to get clear resolution shots of them. This means they can appear in camera frames very small or very large, depending on the drone size and distance from the camera. They can also appear very blurred, depending on flight speed. Finally, they can stabilize in the air mimicking stationary objects.

In this work we utilize the recent advancements in deep learning and CNN to train state-of-the-art object detection models to detect drones. The paper sections are organized as follows: Sect. 2 presents a comprehensive review of the literature and related work with emphasis on the models tested in this work. In the third section, the methodology, a thorough description of the hardware setup, the software framework as well as the collected training data-set are presented. The results of training and testing of the models are presented and discussed in Sect. 4. Finally, Sect. 5 concludes the paper and presents its summary.

2   Related Work

Just like several other computer vision tasks, object detection can be carried out using DNNs or conventional computer vision algorithms. However, for drone detection, and due to the difficulties mentioned before, DNNs significantly outperform even the most sophisticated computer vision algorithms, such as Haar Cascades [17].

Take the YOLO (You Only Look Once) detector for instance; Version 4 of this detector has a "43.5% Average Precision (AP) (65.7% AP at 50% accuracy or AP50) on the MS COCO data-set at a real-time speed of 65 Frames Per Second (fps) on Tesla V100" [2]. YOLO was the first model of what is called

Single Shot Detectors. The name refers to the fact that these detectors can locate the object of interest and draw the bounding box around it in a single shot, as opposed to older models that had to do that on two stages with two different networks. This category of detectors gave hope in having real-time performance, which was previously unthinkable.

One year after the first version of YOLO was released, the Single Shot Multi-Box Detector (SSD) was published [11]. Although it was originally used with the "VGG-16" network as a "base network", the modularity of the framework allows for using other CNNs as base networks as well. In this paper, the YOLOv4 as well as the SSD-VGG-16 and SSD-MobileNet-v1 are tested and benchmarked on the collected data-set [6].

3   Methodology

The three state-of-the-art detectors, namely: YOLOv4, SSD-VGG-16 and SSD-MobileNet-v1, are all pre-trained on major detection datasets. YOLOv4 was pre-trained on the MS COCO data-set [10], while the other two networks were both trained on the PASCAL VOC data-set [3]. Here they are re-trained on the original drone data-set, that was manually collected and annotated during this work. The following sub-sections elaborate on the hardware and software framework that was used for training and testing, as well as the details of the dataset.

3.1   Hardware Setup

Three different drones, with different appearance, color and size, were chosen to be used in building the data-set. The Crazyflei drone [1] is the smallest of the three, just 6×6 cm. The Parrot Mambo Fly drone [16] is 18×18 cm, including the defenders. The biggest of the three is the black Syma X5SC drone [20], which spans 31×31 cm.

For our training, three different NVIDIA GPUs were used simultaneously to decrease the training time. They were used on separate machines and for training separate models though. The first is an NVIDIA GeForce RTX 2080-Ti with 11 GB GPU memory. The card is widely used for training DNNs and was used by the developers of YOLOv4 for their experiments [2]. Its relatively large memory and 4352 cores makes it a great choice for computer vision applications [13]. A training speed of 5 images/second was achieved using this card when training the YOLOv4 model with an input size of 512×512 and a minibatch size of 4.

The second GPU is the NVIDIA GeForce GTX 1060 with 6 GB of memory. Although this card is much less powerful than its 2080-Ti counterpart, it could still help with its 1280 cores [12]. The experiments that were performed on that card showed training speed half of that of the 2080-Ti but triple of that of the NVIDIA Jetson, which is our third and last GPU.

The NVIDIA Jetson AGX Xavier developer kit, was mainly used for inference. Being specifically designed to run AI and deep learning applications makes it a perfect choice for testing and implementing the chosen detectors [14]. As one of the most recent releases from NVIDIA, little research has been conducted using this powerful tool. This is why we present all the testing results using this card to evaluate its performance and limitations.

The 32-GB Jetson Xavier has a 512-core Volta GPU with a new technology called Tensor Cores [14]. Tensor Cores are GPU cores designed specifically for tensor multiplication. Tensor multiplication, which is the basic operation of almost all deep learning computations, is done instantly in chunks accumulating the results in high throughput registers. This results in significant speedup in performance [15]. The performance of the Jetson on drone detection is reported in the results section.

3.2   Software Framework

TensorFlow and PyTorch are arguably the biggest and strongest machine learning frameworks in Python. Both open libraries were developed by the tech giants Google and Facebook respectively. PyTorch, which was released in 2016 about a year after TensorFlow, was developed for machine learning and AI applications with emphasis on GPU utilization and optimization. Similar to TensorFlow, its paradigm enables lean and fast differential programming. However, PyTorch is more compliant with the Object Oriented Programming (OOP) paradigm and the familiar Python style [18]. The Tensor class, which enables handling multi-dimensional arrays and data-sets, is similar to the NumPy arrays data type with the additional capability to operate on GPUs [19].

Although TensorFlow is a very powerful library that enables great control over models and dataflow, the familiarity of PyTorch style renders it more attractive, especially that it also provides similar control and services. Overall, Tensor-Flow is still more widely used in industry and research than PyTorch. However, the trends show that PyTorch is becoming more and more popular and is forecasted to overtake TensorFlow in the near future, Fig. 1. For these reasons, and after the consultation of industry and research experts, PyTorch was the chosen platform for this project.

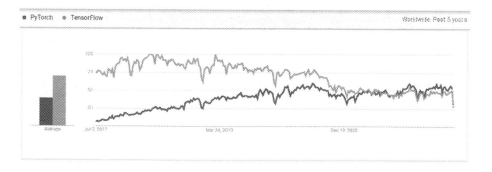

Fig. 1. Google search statistics for TensorFlow and PyTorch [4].

3.3   Data-Set

The data-set was recorded at first in videos using an Intel RealSense camera [7], and then filtered and converted to images. The final data-set, which consisted of 23,863 images was divided into training, validation and test subsets of 20,000, 1,863 and 2,000 images respectively. For annotation, Intel's image and video annotation tool, CVAT, was used to help accelerate the process [8].

Four out of the 22 videos that constituted the data-set included two drones instead of one to train the models on multiple detections. The videos were taken from different angles, elevations and lighting conditions to help the models generalize their training and avoid overfitting. The drones appear almost at every location in the image frame, including corners, and at different distances from the camera, from a few centimeters, to a few meters. Figure 2 shows a heat map for the statistical drone location in the image frame in the training set.

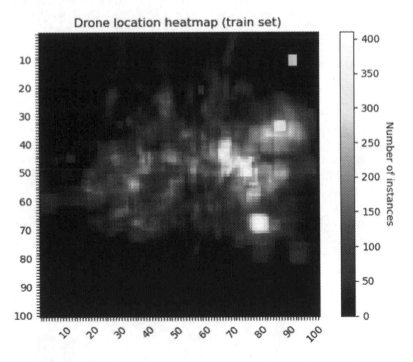

Fig. 2. A heatmap for the drone locations in the training set frames.

4   Results

Table 1 contains a summary of the main results of the three studied models. The first row refers to the size of the square images inputted to the models for training. Although YOLOv4 was tested for three different input sizes, only the results for the 416 input size are included. This is because it is the smallest size tested and the closest to the input size of the other two models.

The second row shows the Average Precision at 50% accuracy (AP50). As mentioned before, this refers to the average precision when the Intersection over Union (or IOU) of the generated bounding boxes is 50% minimum. This is a quite common and accepted standard for evaluating detection models. To be more precise, the mean AP (mAP) is also added in the third row of the table. In this figure, the AP values are evaluated and averaged for IoU values of [0.5:0.95]. In other words, the AP is evaluated at different IoU thresholds, from 0.50 to 0.95 with 0.05 steps, and then averaged to give more realistic values.

As the name suggests, recall refers to the portion of correct predictions relative to all the ground truth predictions that the model should have detected. In other words, while AP takes all model predictions as reference, recall takes all ground truth boxes as its denominator. AR is calculated by determining the recall at different IoU steps from 0.5 to 1 (regardless of the confidence) and then averaging those values [87].

Additionally, the F1 score for the models is computed and appended to the results. The F1 score is a suitable benchmarking metric as it is one number that represents precision and recall at the same time. Finally, the processing speed of the different models is added in the form of the number of frames processed per second on each of the used GPUs.

Table 1. Models' results summary.

Metric	YOLOv4	SSD-MobileNet1	SSD-VGG16
Input size	416	300	300
AP50	86.7%	88.1%	90.4%
mAP	53.0%	51.4%	62.1%
AR	70.3%	66.0%	72.7%
F1-Score	60.4%	57.8%	67.0%
Jetson fps	4	56	58
2080-Ti fps	21	143	170

Table 1 makes it clear that SSD-VGG is the best performance model. It surpasses the other models in every metric. The F1 overall score ranks it first as well. Not only does it possess the highest AP50 rate, but it also maintains formidable performance at more vigorous thresholds, i.e. AP75, mAP and AR. In addition, it is the fastest model with inference speed much higher than the real-time minimum requirement. Figure 3 shows a few samples of the drones from the testset detected by the model.

Fig. 3. A sample of the drone detections done by the SSD-VGG network on the testset.

5   Conclusion

In this work, an original drone detection data-set of 23,863 images is collected and annotated. Three DNN detection models, namely YOLOv4, SSD-MobileNetv1 and SSD-VGG16, are retrained and tested on the dataset. The goal was to train a high accuracy drone detection model that is to be used in real-time for surveillance or other purposes. This goal was achieved successfully by the SSD-VGG model, which scored an average precision (AP50) of 90.4%, average recall (AR) of 72.7% and inference speed of 58 frames per second on the NVIDIA Jetson Xavier kit.

References

1. Bitcraze: Home – Bitcraze. https://www.bitcraze.io/
2. Bochkovskiy, A., Wang, C.Y., Liao, H.Y.M.: YOLOv4: optimal speed and accuracy of object detection, April 2020. http://arxiv.org/abs/2004.10934
3. Everingham, M., Gool, L.V., Williams, C.K.I., Winn, J., Zisserman, A.: The PASCAL Visual Object Classes Homepage. http://host.robots.ox.ac.uk/pascal/VOC/
4. Google: Google Trends. https://trends.google.com/trends/?geo=US
5. Gruber, I.: The Evolution of Drones: From Military to Hobby & Commercial - Percepto. https://percepto.co/the-evolution-of-drones-from-military-to-hobby-commercial/
6. Howard, A.G., et al.: MobileNets: efficient convolutional neural networks for mobile vision applications, April 2017. https://arxiv.org/abs/1704.04861v1
7. Intel: Depth Camera D455 - Intel® RealSense™ Depth and Tracking Cameras. https://www.intelrealsense.com/depth-camera-d455/
8. Intel: openvinotoolkit/cvat: Powerful and efficient Computer Vision Annotation Tool (CVAT). https://github.com/openvinotoolkit/cvat
9. Lee, D.R., La, W.G., Kim, H.: Drone detection and identification system using artificial intelligence. In: Proceedings of the 9th International Conference on Information and Communication Technology Convergence: ICT Convergence Powered by Smart Intelligence, pp. 1131–1133, November 2018. https://doi.org/10.1109/ICTC.2018.8539442

10. Lin, T.Y., et al.: COCO - Common Objects in Context. https://cocodataset.org/#detection-eval

11. Liu, W., et al.: SSD: single shot MultiBox detector. In: Leibe, B., Matas, J., Sebe, N., Welling, M. (eds.) ECCV 2016. LNCS, vol. 9905, pp. 21–37. Springer, Cham (2016). https://doi.org/10.1007/978-3-319-46448-0_2. https://arxiv.org/abs/1512.02325v5

12. NVIDIA: GeForce GTX 1060 Graphics Cards – NVIDIA GeForce. https://www.nvidia.com/en-in/geforce/products/10series/geforce-gtx-1060/

13. NVIDIA: GeForce RTX 2080 TI-Grafikkarte – NVIDIA. https://www.nvidia.com/de-at/geforce/graphics-cards/rtx-2080-ti/

14. NVIDIA: Jetson AGX Xavier Developer Kit – NVIDIA Developer. https://developer.nvidia.com/embedded/jetson-agx-xavier-developer-kit

15. NVIDIA: Programming Tensor Cores in CUDA 9 – NVIDIA Developer Blog. https://developer.nvidia.com/blog/programming-tensor-cores-cuda-9/

16. Parrot: Parrot Mambo drone downloads – Parrot Support Center. https://www.parrot.com/us/support/documentation/mambo-range

17. Pawełczyk, M., Wojtyra, M.: Real world object detection dataset for quadcopter unmanned aerial vehicle detection. IEEE Access 8, 174394–174409 (2020). https://doi.org/10.1109/ACCESS.2020.3026192

18. PyTorch: PyTorch. https://pytorch.org/

19. PyTorch: PyTorch documentation - PyTorch 1.9.1 documentation. https://pytorch.org/docs/stable/index.html

20. Syma: SYMA X5SC EXPLORERS 2 - Drone - SYMA Official Site. http://www.symatoys.com/goodshow/x5sc-syma-x5sc-explorers-2.html

21. Taha, B., Shoufan, A.: Machine learning-based drone detection and classification: state-of-the-art in research. IEEE Access 7, 138669–138682 (2019). https://doi.org/10.1109/ACCESS.2019.2942944

Computer and Systems Based Methods and Electronic Technologies in Medicine

Continuous Time Normalized Signal Trains for a Better Classification of Myoelectric Signals

Philip Gaßner$^{(\boxtimes)}$ and Klaus Buchenrieder

Institut für Technische Informatik, Universität der Bundeswehr München,
85577 Neubiberg, Germany
{philip.gassner,klaus.buchenrieder}@unibw.de
https://www.unibw.de/technische-informatik

Keywords: EMG-signals · Classification · Hand prosthesis · Time normalized signal trains

1 Introduction

State-of-the-art hand prostheses differ from those of previous generations, in that more hand positions and programmable gestures are available [4]. As an example, consider multi-finger prostheses like the i-limb^{TM} ultra from Touch Bionics or the Bebionic^{TM} Hand from RSL Steeper. Both prosthetic effectors are primarily controlled by myoelectric signals, derived with two or more cutaneously applied sensors, placed atop residual muscles. After preprocessing and classification of these signals, three to five different movement states or hand positions can be accurately distinguished. Zardoshti-Kermani et al. [5] show that the classification becomes increasingly difficult as the number of gestures grows, because decision spaces and feature clusters overlap [3]. Since static separation becomes increasingly difficult, Hudgins et al. [3] and Attenberger [1] used time-dependencies inherent to electromyographic (EMG) signals to improve classification.

In this contribution, we bring forward a method to classify, for example, EMG signals before a motion or gesture is finished, by using continuously normalized EMG feature trains. Building on previous work [2], in which we classified EMG signal traces after the completion of a movement sequence, we here depart from established approaches.

2 Method

With previous solutions, recordings of an EMG signal are divided into individual independent sections, then preprocessed and finally classified. This leads to the loss of temporal dependence within a signal path. This procedure is called the standard method in the following. In previous work we showed that by time normalization for each gesture, signal-trains are formed, which are similar for

R. Moreno-Díaz et al. (Eds.): EUROCAST 2022, LNCS 13789, pp. 479–486, 2022.
https://doi.org/10.1007/978-3-031-25312-6_56

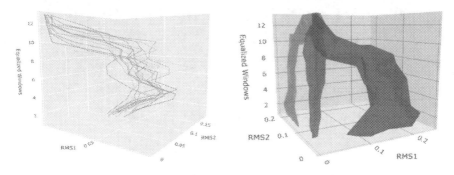

(a) Feature-trains of 15 repetitions of the gesture cocontraction.

(b) Body of normalized Gestures: Flexation, Extension and Fist

Fig. 1. Signal paths become enveloping bodies.

one gesture, but can be clearly distinguished from other gestures [2]. It was also explained that this improves the classification quality for a variety of classifiers. Figure 1(a), depicts 15 normalized RMS signal-trains, derived from two sensors for a hand-flexion, which obviously look very similar. If one combines several such EMG-feature-trains of a motion sequence into an enveloped body, the similarity of the individual signal courses become even more obvious. When building enveloped bodies, outlier points are detected by calculating a probability density function or by the Mahalanobis distance followed by select point removal. For the gestures: Extension, Flexation and Fist the enveloped bodys are pictured in Fig. 1(b). The three envelopes are clearly separated from each other for a large part. The strongest overlap occurs towards the end of the signal when it becomes weaker and the different envelopes start to merge. When a new signal-train is generated during the use-phase of the prosthesis, it is then very easy to determine whether it belongs to a certain body or not. The body represents hereby the training data and a single signal-train within relates to a single motion.

In previous work when only normalization was employed, the signal trains as well as the bodies could only be calculated on completion of a movement. This posed the main drawback. To take advantage of normalization before a gesture is finalized, we switched to building a body in discrete time-intervals for the classification. To achieve this, recorded samples are added at each time step until the gesture is complete. For each time step, the envelope can be formed analogously to the normalization. Therefore, classification can also be done after each time step. In the following examination, a time step is 100 ms long, thus the first envelope is formed during this time and a corresponding signal train can also be classified for the first time in this period. After further 100 ms the now newly recorded data are added. By this a data basis for the envelope of 200 ms and a signal train of the same length is created. These steps are repeated until a threshold value indicates the end of the movement of a gesture. This leads to the fact that the last envelope formed is identical with the envelope

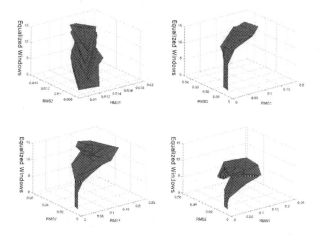

Fig. 2. Continuously forming body of a gesture. Shown in the frames is a body at the beginning of the gesture, after about 20% and 60% of the time, and at the end of the movement.

generated by the normalization as shown in Fig. 1(b) for, e.g., flexion-, extension- and fist-gestures. We call this second method continuous normalization. It is expected that the classification quality decreases with continuous normalization when compared to the initially used normalization method. Figure 2 presents four resulting envelopes of the gesture flexion at different times-steps. The first frame in the upper left corner shows the enveloped body after 100 ms. No clear structure has been established. The second frame in the upper right corner depicts the envelope after a just over 20% of the average movements. The first characteristic of a particular body can be identified. Like the clear bending and deflection in the direction of RMS1. The third frame shows the envelope after about 60%. It is loosing intensity and approaches low values. A characteristic body has been formed already at this point. The last frame shows the body after completion of the movement which is identical to the body created by the normalization.

Which shows that at the beginning of a movement, individual envelopes of gestures are very similar and differ only with increasing data volume, so that these are better distinguishable. An exception are envelopes of gestures, which are basically easy to discern, such as flexion and extension. These should be clearly separable at an early stage even with continuous normalization. During the use-phase of the prosthetic device, a continuous signal-train is generated from sensor-data, normalized and matched to the body envelopes of the training phase. In this research, all experiments were performed with a DELSYS® Bagnoli-4 EMG system and a National Instruments Ni USB-6229 16-bit data acquisition system^{TM} with two Sensors.

For the study five probands performed nine different gestures. Each gesture was repeated 15 times in one day. Data was collected on six days spread over three weeks. Thus, each gesture was repeated 90 times. Hence, 810 repetitions per person were performed. The evaluation thus covers a total of 4050 recorded movements. The following nine hand gestures were performed:

1. Cocontraction of the hand (Cocontraction).
2. Extension of the wrist (Extension).
3. Fist (Fist)
4. Flexation of the wrist (Flexation).
5. Extension of the indexfinger while flexing all other fingers (Index).
6. Performing an "OK" sign, by extension of the three fingers: pinky, ring finger and middle finger, while flexing the thumb and ring finger (OK).
7. Flexation of the four fingers, pinky, ring finger, middle finger and index finger while extending the thumb (Thumb Up).
8. Pronation of the wrist (Pronation).
9. Supination of the wrist (Supination).

For each execution of a gesture, four features were calculated for the EMG signal to enable classification:

1. Root mean Square (RMS).
2. Zero Crossing (ZC).
3. Approximate Entropy (ApEn).
4. Autoregressive coefficients of fourth-order (AR).

In order to investigate whether continuous normalization leads to an overall improvement in classification quality, 22 different classifiers were considered. The classifiers hereby belong to the four main groups: discriminant analytics, decision trees, support vector machines (SVM) and nearest neighbor algorithms (KNN). The F1 score is used as the classification metric and to assess of the methods, because the armonic mean of the precision and recall is more informative than the accuracy (ACC) measure, especially when there are many classes to distinguish. A comparison is made between the results of the standard method and the two normalization methods.

3   Results

The average F1 score is shown in Fig. 3 achieved by the different classifiers across all days, subjects and gestures, as a box plot. Clearly, the Normalized Method leads to an improvement in the F1 score, compared to the Standard Method for each classifier. This is because, the quantile 25 as well as the quantile 75 and the median are higher than the corresponding counterpart. When comparing the continuous normalization and the standard method, the F1 score is improved for 18 out of 22 classifiers compared to normalization. Note, that not every classifier improves. Three out of 22 classifiers deteriorate significantly due to continuous normalization. These are LinearDiscriminant, QuadraticDiscriminant and Supscpace Discriminant. This shows that the methods which use a discriminant to distinguish the gestures are not suitable for continuous normalization. In contrast, BaggedTree, SubSpaceKNN and SVMFineGaussian achieve significantly better results. The latter is particularly noteworthy, as it manages to increase the median F1 score of the standard method from 40% with normalization to 54% and to 70% with continuous normalization. The three classifiers which achieved the best F1 score are the BaggedTree, the SVMCubic and the SVMQuadratic, see Fig. 1. Further evaluations are performed with these three classifiers. The achieved quantiles of the classifiers are shown in Table 1. Here, we can see once again how all three quantiles improve when normalization methods are used. It is interesting to note, that this also applies to continuous normalization. Which improves the median by 13 percentage points (p.p.). The quantile 75 even reaches an average value of 94%. Therefore, it can be seen that these three classifiers not only succeed in achieving a higher F1 score than the standard method, but also perform better than normalization.

Table 1. The 25, 50, and 75 quantiles of the F1 score of the best three classifiers BaggedTree, SVMCubic and SVMQuadratic across all subjects, gestures, and days.

Method	Q_{25}	Q_{50}	Q_{75}
Standard	62%	74%	86%
Normalization	75%	84%	92%
Continuous normalization	80%	87%	94%

When considering individual gestures, F1 scores, as depicted in Fig. 4, result in an improved classification for eight out of nine gestures across all subjects. The sole exception is Extension, as the median remains almost unchanged, between 94% for normalization and 92% for continuous normalization. The Q_{75} is 96% for continuous normalization and reaches its maximum with normalization at 98%. The part that deteriorates the most for this gesture is Q_{25}. It falls from the standard of 85% to the minimum of 82% for continuous normalization and 85% for normalization only.

In conclusion, for an Extension the standard method is marginally better than continuous normalization method. The achieved values of the F1 score are on a quite high level with a median of 92%, Table 2. The gestures that benefited most from the new normalization method are Cocontraction, Index and Thumb-Up. Cocontraction's Q_{50} was improved by 27 percentage points. The improvement of the gesture is so significant that the Q_{25} of the continuous normalization at 82% is 10 p.p. higher than the Q_{75} of the standard method. Likewise, the Index gesture which improves by 22 p.p. at its median. The Q_{25} of the continuous normalization is also 74% and therefore 6 p.p. higher than the Q_{75} of the standard method, which reaches a value of 68%. The third strongest improvement is found in the Thumb-Up gesture. Which increases by 17 p.p. on median compared to the standard method. The Q_{25} of the continuous normalization is equal to the Q_{75} of the standard method at 76%, while the Q_{75} of the continuous normalization reaches a value of 91% and thereby is 15 p.p. higher than the counterpart of the standard method. Also worth mentioning are the improvements for the OK, Fist and Pronation gestures, as listed in Table 2.

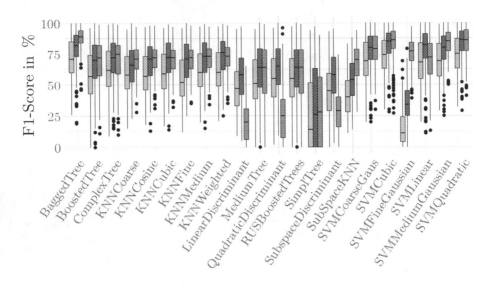

Fig. 3. Box plot of the average F1 score achieved across all subjects, days, and gestures, for the three methods standard, normalized, and continuous normalization.

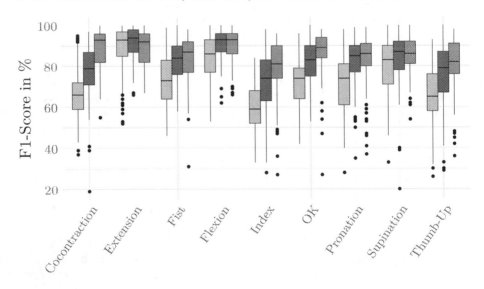

Fig. 4. Box plot of the F1 score of the three best classifiers for nine different gestures averaged over all subjects and recording days.

Table 2. Median F1 score of the best three classifiers comparing the standard and continuous Normalization method. Averaged across all subjects and days.

Method	Gesture	F1-Score in %	Δ in p.p.
Standard	Cocontraction	66	–
Standard	Extension	93	–
Standard	Fist	73	–
Standard	Flexion	86	–
Standard	Index	59	–
Standard	OK	74	–
Standard	Pronation	74	–
Standard	Supination	83	–
Standard	Thumb-Up	65	–
Continuous normalization	Cocontraction	93	27
Continuous normalization	Extension	92	−1
Continuous normalization	Fist	87	14
Continuous normalization	Flexion	93	7
Continuous normalization	Index	81	22
Continuous normalization	OK	89	15
Continuous normalization	Pronation	86	12
Continuous normalization	Supination	86	3
Continuous normalization	Thumb-Up	82	17

These range from 15 to 12 p.p. while, the median F1 score improves by more than 10 p.p. for six out of nine gestures. Which are in the range of 82% and 93%. This is a significant increase compared to the standard method.

4   Conclusions

In this work, it is demonstrated that the method for normalization of EMG signals can be improved by modification such that a classification is already possible before the movement is completed. With the new method of continuous normalization it is possible to greatly-improve the classification quality similar to the method of normalization and to separate numerous gestures in distinct classes. By the continuous normalization it comes to an increase of the dimensionality within the data. This leads to the situation that not all classification methods yield better results. Especially classifiers which use a discriminant are not suitable for this method. Decision trees, KNNs and SVMs have proven to be useful and achieve a considerably better classification quality with continuous normalization compared to the standard method. This study shows that the three classifiers which yield the best results for continuous normalization are

BaggedTree, SVMCubic and SVMQuadratic. For each of the nine gestures examined, on average, a higher F1 score resulted when continuous normalization is employed. This is particularly noteworthy since this method results in a median above 80% for each gesture. Three gestures even manage a median above 90%. The standard method manages this with only one gesture. The lowest median amounts to only 59% showing that continuous normalization can classify significantly more gestures with a higher accuracy in comparison to the standard method. Since this is now also possible during the movement of a gesture, the results clearly show that this method is suitable for the use in modern prostheses to appropriately control the large number of possible gestures a modern prosthesis can perform.

This research is funded by dtec.bw - Digitalization and Technology Research Center of the Bundeswehr - project VITAL-SENSE.

References

1. Attenberger, A.: Time analysis for improved upper limb movement classification. Doctoral thesis, Universität der Bundeswehr München (2016)
2. Gaßner, P., Buchenrieder, K.: Improved classification of myoelectric signals by using normalized signal trains. In: Moreno-Díaz, R., Pichler, F., Quesada-Arencibia, A. (eds.) EUROCAST 2019. LNCS, vol. 12014, pp. 372–379. Springer, Cham (2020). https://doi.org/10.1007/978-3-030-45096-0_46
3. Hudgins, B., Parker, P., Scott, R.N.: A new strategy for multifunction myoelectric control **40**(1), 82–94. https://doi.org/10.1109/10.204774. ISSN 0018-9294
4. van der Riet, D., Stopforth, R., Bright, G., Diegel, O.: An overview and comparison of upper limb prosthetics. In: 2013 Africon, pp. 1–8 (2013). https://doi.org/10.1109/AFRCON.2013.6757590
5. Zardoshti-Kermani, M., Wheeler, B.C., Badie, K., Hashemi, R.M.: EMG feature evaluation for movement control of upper extremity prostheses. IEEE Trans. Rehabil. Eng. **3**(4), 324–333. https://doi.org/10.1109/86.481972

A Comparison of Covariate Shift Detection Methods on Medical Datasets

Stephan Dreiseitl[(✉)] [iD]

Department of Software Engineering, University of Applied Sciences Upper Austria,
4232 Hagenberg, Austria
stephan.dreiseitl@fh-hagenberg.at

Abstract. The performance of machine learning models is known to deteriorate on datasets drawn from a different distribution from the one used in model building. In a supervised setting, this deterioration can be assessed by a decrease in the evaluation metrics of the models. When no gold standard information is available, and thus evaluation metrics cannot be determined, one may directly address the problem of detecting whether two datasets differ in distribution. Methods for assessing the difference of distribution from their samples are known as *covariate shift* detection algorithms.

We investigate the ability of the *maximum mean discrepancy* method, of univariate tests, and of a domain classifier trained to distinguish two datasets, to detect covariate shift in two datasets: one collected for predicting stroke, and one collected for predicting acute myocardial infarction. For this, we artificially perturb parts of the datasets, and check how well these modified datasets can be distinguished from the remaining portions of the original datasets. We observe that univariate tests compare favorably with the other two methods, that changes can be detected more easily in large datasets, that smaller changes are more difficult to detect than larger changes, and that dimensionality reduction is detrimental to detecting covariate shift.

Keywords: Covariate shift detection · Concept drift · Maximum mean discrepancy

1 Introduction

The validation of predictive models in healthcare is an important and necessary step in removing the deployment barrier of AI systems in these environments [5,17]. A central aspect of model validation, in particular in biomedical settings, is the so-called *external validation* of models with datasets different from those used during model development [9,14]. In external validation, the performance of predictive models is assessed on one or more datasets that were not used during original model building, not even in the validation part of this process. This means that a model makes predictions on patient data with possibly different characteristics, such as age distribution, prior case histories, or geographic origins. Only this kind of external validation allows researchers and practitioners

© The Author(s), under exclusive license to Springer Nature Switzerland AG 2022
R. Moreno-Díaz et al. (Eds.): EUROCAST 2022, LNCS 13789, pp. 487–495, 2022.
https://doi.org/10.1007/978-3-031-25312-6_57

to gauge the performance of a model on different datasets. The degree to which models perform well also on such external datasets is now being referred to as their *transportability* [11].

Evaluating a predictive model's transportability is most easily done by comparing the model's predictions on external validation data with known gold standard information. In healthcare environments, this seemingly easy task is often hindered by a temporary lack of ground truth information, as diagnostic information may only be available after some time. In these circumstances, model transportability can be rated by measuring to which degree the external validation data differs from the data used in model building.

To provide a framework for the following investigations, it is illustrative to make explicit the implicit assumption underlying all of supervised machine learning: that the distribution $P_t(x, y)$ of the training dataset is the same as the distribution $P_d(x, y)$ of the datasets processed by a model after deployment. Here, we consider $x \in \mathbb{R}^n$ to be the vector representation of a data item (its *covariates*), and y its corresponding gold standard target. For simplicity of terminology, we will in the following only consider classification problems, where y denotes a class label.

A predictive model may show decreased performance across various evaluation metrics for discrimination as well as calibration when it is applied to datasets with distributions differing from that of the training dataset. A *dataset shift* $P_t(x, y) \neq P_d(x, y)$, alternatively called *concept drift*, can be analyzed from a variety of angles [3,7]; note that most of these rely on the various ways of factoring a joint distribution as $P(x, y) = P(x \mid y)P(y) = P(y \mid x)P(x)$.

In this work, we restrict ourselves to empirically evaluating algorithms for detecting *covariate shift*, which occurs when $P_t(y|x) = P_d(y|x)$, but $P_t(x) \neq P_d(x)$ [8,15]. We are thus interested in whether the distribution $P(x)$ of covariates changed from one dataset to the next, without taking class labels into account.

We utilize the following methods to detect whether the underlying distribution of two datasets is different:

- *maximum mean discrepancy (MMD)* calculation, a kernel-based method for assessing the difference of two distributions via the distance of so-called *mean embeddings* of two samples from these distributions [4];
- a combination of Bonferroni-corrected univariate tests (Kolmogorov-Smirnov for numerical features, and binomial tests of proportions for binary features),
- a domain classifier that is trained to distinguish between the two datasets.

Furthermore, following [8], we also investigate the effects (if any) of first transforming the data via principal component analysis, and then performing all the tests above on the dimensionality-reduced datasets.

We use two different datasets from the medical domain in our experiments on covariate shift detection methods: a dataset on stroke prediction, publicly available on Kaggle [12], and a dataset on acute myocardial infarction [6] that we had previously analyzed in a different context [1]. Portions of each of these datasets are perturbed to different degrees, and the methods listed above are used to detect changes between the original (unperturbed) parts of the datasets, and the parts that had been altered.

2   Material and Methods

Algorithms for Detecting Covariate Shift. One of the premier tools for detecting covariate shift depends on the notion of *maximum mean discrepancy*, which will be outlined next. Fortet and Mourier [2] define the maximum mean discrepancy MMD of two distributions P and Q over a function class $\mathcal{F}$ as the largest difference between the average values that elements of that function class can take on the two distributions, i.e.,

$$\text{MMD}(P, Q, \mathcal{F}) := \sup_{f \in \mathcal{F}} |E_{X \sim P} f(X) - E_{Y \sim Q} f(Y)|.$$

It turns out that one can restrict oneself to a particular set of functions for answering the question whether two distributions are equal [10]:

$$P = Q \iff \text{MMD}(P, Q, \mathcal{F}_1) = 0,$$

where $\mathcal{F}_1 = \{f \mid \|f\|_{\mathcal{H}} \leq 1\}$ is the unit ball of functions in a reproducing kernel Hilbert space (RHKS) $\mathcal{H}$ with the additional technical constraint of being *universal* [13]. This constraint is satisfied by RIIKS with a wide variety of kernels, among others Gaussian kernels $k(x, y) = \exp(-1/(2\sigma^2)\|x - y\|^2)$ [13].

For two finite samples $\{x_1, \ldots, x_m\} \sim P$ and $\{y_1, \ldots, y_n\} \sim Q$, Gretton et al. [4] provide an unbiased estimate of $\text{MMD}^2(P, Q, \mathcal{F}_1)$ as

$$\text{MMD}^2(\{x_1, \ldots, x_m\}, \{y_1, \ldots, y_n\}, \mathcal{F}_1) = \frac{1}{m(m-1)} \sum_{i=1}^{m} \sum_{\substack{j=1 \\ j \neq i}}^{m} k(x_i, x_j) +$$

$$\frac{1}{n(n-1)} \sum_{i=1}^{n} \sum_{\substack{j=1 \\ j \neq i}}^{n} k(y_i, y_j) - \frac{2}{mn} \sum_{i=1}^{m} \sum_{j=1}^{n} k(x_i, y_j).$$

Here, $k(x, y)$ is a kernel function is a universal RKHS. For simplicity, this kernel is most often taken to be a Gaussian.

Testing the null hypothesis $H_0 : P = Q$ versus the two-sided alternative $H_1 : P \neq Q$ can be accomplished by a permutation test: For this, we combine the two finite samples into one dataset $U = \{x_1, \ldots, x_m\} \cup \{y_1, \ldots, y_n\}$. Drawing bootstrap samples $\{x_1', \ldots, x_m'\} \subset U$ and $\{y_1', \ldots, y_n'\} \subset U$ gives us in two samples from the same (combined) distribution, so that the null hypothesis holds. Calculating MMD^2 for these samples, and repeating the process, results in a distribution of the test statistic under H_0. Let eCDF denote the empirical cumulative distribution function obtained in this manner. A p-value for the hypothesis test can then be obtained as

$$p = 1 - \text{eCDF}\big(\text{MMD}^2(\{x_1, \ldots, x_m\}, \{y_1, \ldots, y_n\}, \mathcal{F}_1)\big),$$

because larger values of MMD^2 provide evidence against H_0.

Testing the difference between the distributions of univariate features via Kolmogorov-Smirnov (for numerical features) and binomial tests (for binary features) was adjusted for multiple testing via Bonferroni correction. Two distributions are different according to this criterion if at least one of the univariate tests for difference of features is significant after Bonferroni correction.

The third approach to detecting covariate shift was via a domain classifier. For this, we trained an SVM classifier (with Gaussian kernels) to distinguish two distributions based on samples from these distributions, and subsequently evaluated this classifier on additional disjoint samples from the two distributions. We used the equivalence of the area under the ROC curve (AUC) to Mann-Whitney U-statistics to statistically test the null hypothesis of the domain classifier not being able to distinguish between two datasets.

Characteristics of Datasets. The two datasets used in our investigations can be described as follows:

Stroke dataset. This dataset is publicly available from Kaggle [12]. It consists of 5110 case with 12 features each. Two of the features (id and stroke status) are irrelevant to detecting covariate shift, and were thus removed. Of the remaining ten features, three are quantitative, and seven are categorical.

Acute myocardial infarction dataset. This dataset had previously been used to derive an early prediction logistic regression model [6]. It contains 877 cases with 32 features, of which 3 are numerical, and 29 categorical.

Details of Experimental Setup. Both datasets were preprocessed by standardizing quantitative features, and one-hot encoding categorical features. All of the experiments described below were run on five different splits of the dataset into an original (unperturbed) part and a part that was altered in various ways to simulate covariate shift. This latter part always contained 400 cases, which were changed in one of three ways: a small change (defined as adding Gaussian noise with $\sigma = 0.1$ to quantitative features, and perturbing categorical features with probability $p = 0.05$), a medium change ($\sigma = 0.25$, $p = 0.1$) and a large change ($\sigma = 0.5$, $p = 0.15$). Additionally, we also ran experiments with no changes to check for type I errors.

All experiments were also performed on variants of the datasets that had been dimensionality-reduced by principal component analysis. For this, we elected to use the transformed features that combined to 80% of total variance in the datasets: this choice amounted to a reduction down to 6 features in the stroke dataset, and to 12 features in the myocardial infarction dataset.

The ability of statistical tests to detect changes also depends on the size of the datasets. We therefore ran our experiments with datasets containing 25, 50, 100, 200 and 400 perturbed cases. For all tests, we set the significance level to 0.05.

Two of the methods for detecting covariate shift require setting hyperparameter values: maximum mean discrepancy using Gaussian kernels requires choosing a particular kernel width σ; Gretton et al. [4] recommend the heuristic of setting it to the median of all pairwise distances between all points in the dataset. We follow this advice here. For the support vector machines used as domain classifiers (also with Gaussian kernels), we performed hyperparameter tuning via grid-search and five-fold cross-validation anew for each combination of dataset sizes and perturbation scales.

All experiments were run using Python 3.9 with the NumPy, SciPy and Pandas packages, and the alibi-detect implementation of maximum mean discrepancy [16].

3   Results

The settings outlined above were combined in all possible ways, summarized here as a Cartesian product:

dataset variant × fold number × change level

× dataset size × detection method.

For two dataset variants (original vs. dimensionality-reduced), five folds, four change levels, five dataset sizes and three detection methods, this resulted in 600 possible combinations for each of the two datasets. Since the *domain classifier* detection method uses a subset of the 400 perturbed cases in the training set, and the remainder in the test set, the largest *dataset size* setting of 400 for the test set is not possible. This reduces the number of valid combinations of settings to 560 for each of the two datasets.

Table 1 accumulates over the *fold number* and *change level* dimensions of the data cube representing the results of all experiments. One can observe the effect of the size of the perturbed datasets on being able to detect covariate shift: In all four subtables of this table, the probability of shift detection increases with increasing size of perturbed dataset. It can furthermore be seen that shift detection is easier on the original versions of the datasets, and harder on the PCA-reduced datasets. Of the three shift detection methods, univariate tests show the best performance.

As shown in Table 2, univariate tests also have the highest shift detection probabilities—except for the PCA-reduced version of the acute myocardial infarction dataset—when accumulating all experiments by the *fold number* and *dataset size* data dimensions. This table also includes *no perturbation* entries for determining the type 1 error rates, i.e., for checking how often methods flag a dataset as exhibiting covariate shift, when in fact there is none. One can observe that these type 1 error rates are at an acceptably low level.

Table 1. Concept shift detection results, accumulated over all perturbation levels (small/medium/large), for two datasets (both original and after dimensionality reduction via PCA). Numbers are relative frequencies of shift detection, stratified by shift detection method and size of dataset used to detect shift relative to a larger, unperturbed dataset. One combination of detection method and dataset size (indicated by ·) was not possible. The column header *classifier* denotes *domain classifier*.

original stroke dataset:

shift detection method

size of perturbed dataset		MMD	univ. tests	classifier
	25	0.40	0.67	0.67
	50	0.67	0.93	0.87
	100	0.80	1.00	1.00
	200	1.00	1.00	1.00
	400	1.00	1.00	·

PCA stroke dataset:

shift detection method

	MMD	univ. tests	classifier
0.27	0.27	0.67
0.47	0.67	0.67
0.73	0.80	0.87
0.67	1.00	0.93
0.67	1.00	·

original acute MI dataset:

shift detection method

size of perturbed dataset		MMD	univ. tests	classifier
	25	0.67	0.80	0.80
	50	0.93	1.00	1.00
	100	1.00	1.00	1.00
	200	1.00	1.00	1.00
	400	1.00	1.00	·

PCA acute MI dataset:

shift detection method

	MMD	univ. tests	classifier
0.40	0.20	0.60
0.67	0.47	0.80
0.67	0.67	0.80
0.67	0.67	1.00
0.87	0.80	·

Tables 1 and 2 also show that univariate tests perform no worse than the other two shift detection methods in the majority of cases; the exceptions are the two subtables of reporting on the *PCA acute MI dataset*, where the other methods perform better. We therefore chose the *univariate tests* shift detection method to compare the combined effects of perturbation level (no/small/medium/large) and dataset size (25/50/100/200/400) on shift detection probability. For a more fine-grained analysis, we re-ran all the univariate tests experiments for 100 folds. Table 3 gives the results of this setup. As expected, the larger the dataset sizes, the easier it is for the tests to detect even small levels of perturbation. Furthermore, as can already be seen in Tables 1 and 2, dimensionality reduction is detrimental to detecting covariate shift, as the numbers in the PCA subtables are consistently lower than the corresponding numbers in the other subtables.

Table 2. Concept shift detection results, accumulated over all sizes of datasets used for detecting shift (containing 25, 50, 100, 200, and 400 elements), for two datasets (both original and after dimensionality reduction via PCA). Numbers are relative frequencies of shift detection, stratified by shift detection method and level of perturbation. The column header *classifier* denotes *domain classifier*.

		original stroke dataset: shift detection method			PCA stroke dataset: shift detection method		
		MMD	univ. tests	classifier	MMD	univ. tests	classifier
level of perturbation	no	0.08	0.08	0.00	0.04	0.08	0.00
	small	0.52	0.66	0.55	0.08	0.56	0.35
	med.	0.80	1.00	1.00	0.64	0.76	1.00
	large	1.00	1.00	1.00	0.96	0.92	1.00

		original acute MI dataset: shift detection method			PCA acute MI dataset: shift detection method		
		MMD	univ. tests	classifier	MMD	univ. tests	classifier
level of perturbation	no	0.00	0.00	0.00	0.00	0.00	0.25
	small	0.76	0.88	0.85	0.12	0.08	0.45
	med.	1.00	1.00	1.00	0.84	0.68	0.95
	large	1.00	1.00	1.00	1.00	0.92	1.00

Table 3. Concept shift detection results, for the method of univariate testing and two datasets (both original and after dimensionality reduction via PCA). Numbers are relative frequencies of shift detection, stratified by shift detection method and dataset size.

		original stroke dataset: level of perturbation				PCA stroke dataset: level of perturbation			
		no	small	medium	large	no	small	medium	large
size of perturbed dataset	25	0.09	0.22	0.99	1.00	0.07	0.10	0.22	0.58
	50	0.15	0.60	1.00	1.00	0.10	0.14	0.59	0.99
	100	0.07	0.98	1.00	1.00	0.02	0.29	1.00	1.00
	200	0.07	1.00	1.00	1.00	0.05	0.91	1.00	1.00
	400	0.09	1.00	1.00	1.00	0.05	1.00	1.00	1.00

		original acute MI dataset: level of perturbation				PCA acute MI dataset: level of perturbation			
		no	small	medium	large	no	small	medium	large
size of perturbed dataset	25	0.06	0.80	1.00	1.00	0.08	0.08	0.16	0.82
	50	0.07	1.00	1.00	1.00	0.06	0.07	0.33	1.00
	100	0.05	1.00	1.00	1.00	0.04	0.09	0.94	1.00
	200	0.01	1.00	1.00	1.00	0.04	0.14	1.00	1.00
	400	0.03	1.00	1.00	1.00	0.06	0.48	1.00	1.00

4 Conclusion

We investigated the ability of three tests (MMD, univariate tests, and a domain classifier) to detect covariate shift on two datasets from the medical domain. Our findings are in line with those of Rabanser et al. [8], who also found that univariate tests work (surprisingly) well. We further observed that dimensionality reduction is mostly detrimental to detecting covariate shift, and that (unsurprisingly) larger sample sizes make it easier to detect covariate shift for all three methods. By making these observations on more than one dataset, we hint that the results and insights obtained in these experiments might be generalized to other scenarios as well.

References

1. Dreiseitl, S., Osl, M.: Testing the calibration of classification models from first principles. In: Proceedings of the AMIA Annual Fall Symposium 2012, Chicago, USA, pp. 164–169 (2012)
2. Fortet, R., Mourier, E.: Convergence de la réparation empirique vers la réparation théorique. Annales Scientifiques de l'École Normale Supérieure **70**, 266–285 (1953)
3. Gama, J.I.Z., Bifet, A., Pechenizkiy, M., Bouchachia, A.: A survey on concept drift adaptation. ACM Comput. Surv. **46**, 1–37 (2014)
4. Gretton, A., Borgwardt, K., Rasch, M., Schölkopf, B., Smola, A.: A kernel two-sample test. J. Mach. Learn. Res. **13**, 723–773 (2012)
5. Kelly, C., Karthikesalingam, A., Suleyman, M., Corrado, G., King, D.: Key challenges for delivering clinical impact with artificial intelligence. BMC Med. **17**, 195 (2019)
6. Kennedy, R., Burton, A., Fraser, H., McStay, L., Harrison, R.: Early diagnosis of acute myocardial infarction using clinical and electrocardiographic data at presentation: derivation and evaluation of logistic regression models. Eur. Heart J. **17**, 1181–1191 (1996)
7. Lu, J., Liu, A., Dong, F., Gu, F., Gama, J., Zhang, G.: Learning under concept drift: a review. IEEE Trans. Knowl. Data Eng. **31**, 2346–2363 (2019)
8. Rabanser, S., Günnemann, S., Lipton, Z.: Failing loudly: an empirical study of methods for detecting dataset shift. In: Proceedings of the 33rd Conference on Neural Information Processing Systems (NeurIPS 2019), pp. 1396–1408 (2019)
9. Riley, R., et al.: External validation of clinical prediction models using big datasets from e-health records or IPD meta-analysis: opportunities and challenges. Br. Med. J. **353**, i3140 (2016)
10. Smola, A., Gretton, A., Borgwardt, K.: Maximum mean discrepancy. Technical report NICTA-SML-06-001, National ICT Australia (2006)
11. Song, X., et al.: Cross-site transportability of an explainable artificial intelligence model for acute kidney injury prediction. Nat. Commun. **1**, 5668 (2020)
12. Soriano, F.: Stroke prediction dataset. https://www.kaggle.com/fedesoriano/stroke-prediction-dataset. Accessed 15 July 2021
13. Steinwart, I.: On the influence of the kernel on the consistency of support vector machines. J. Mach. Learn. Res. **2**, 67–93 (2002)
14. Steyerberg, E., Harrell Jr., F.: Prediction models need appropriate internal, internal-external, and external validation. J. Clin. Epidemiol. **69**, 245–247 (2016)

15. Takahashi, C., Braga, A.: A review of off-line mode dataset shifts. IEEE Comput. Intell. Mag. **15**, 16–27 (2020)
16. Van Looveren, A., Vacanti, G., Klaise, J., Coca, A., Cobb, O.: Alibi detect: algorithms for outlier, adversarial and drift detection. version 0.7.2. https://github.com/SeldonIO/alibi-detect. Accessed 10 July 2021
17. Yu, K.H., Beam, A., Kohane, I.: Artificial intelligence in healthcare. Nat. Biomed. Eng. **2**, 719–731 (2018)

Towards a Method to Provide Tactile Feedback in Minimally Invasive Robotic Surgery

Dema Govalla and Jerzy Rozenblit[✉]

Electrical and Computer Engineering, The University of Arizona, Tucson, USA
{demagovalla,jerzyr}@arizona.edu

Abstract. This paper proposes a concept to generate tactile feedback for surgeons during robot-assisted surgery. The prototype used to obtain such feedback consists of two strain gauges installed on the outer jaws of scissors' forceps. The prototype imitates the jaw of a robotic instrument grasper used in the state-of-the-art da Vinci Surgical System. Sensor data of the strain gauges are used to detect the deformation of an object during a series of experiments. The data is categorized into three attributes: Average, Range, and Most-Frequent. These attributes are used to develop a fuzzy classification system (FCS). The FCS classifies objects into five different deformation categories: very soft, soft, medium, hard, and very hard. The sensing prototype and FCS have been validated using a series of physical experiments with a variety of objects. The tests reveal that the proposed method is feasible.

Keywords: Tactile feedback · Robotic minimally invasive surgery · Strain gauge · Haptic feedback

1 Introduction

Robotics in the medical field domain, specifically in minimally invasive surgery (MIS), plays an essential role in today's surgical procedures. Robotic surgical systems have been researched since the 1980s [1]. Minimally invasive robotic surgery (MIRS) is performed by inserting surgical instruments through small incisions inside the patient's body while and the surgeon at the console controls the robot with several arms with the instruments attached to them. Using robotics in MIS has improved the quality of care for several surgical procedures [2]. Benefits include low blood loss, reduced post-operative pain, more precise surgeries, less risk of infection, and shorter patient recoveries [3].

We intend to add to these contributions by proposing a sensor-based deformation recognition system to improve a surgeon's tactile perception capabilities n MIRS. Current robotic systems do not provide such a function. Our hardware prototype design imitates a surgical instrument by installing strain gauge sensors on grasper jaws. Additionally, we designed a fuzzy classification system (FCS) to classify objects' deformations into a set ranging from very soft to very hard. The

R. Moreno-Díaz et al. (Eds.): EUROCAST 2022, LNCS 13789, pp. 496–503, 2022.
https://doi.org/10.1007/978-3-031-25312-6_58

hardware and software described in the paper investigate a potential solution to enable surgeons to recognize the softness or hardness of various anatomical structures such as tissue and vessels.

2   Background and Related Work

Minimally invasive surgery (MIS) began with the first cystoscopes in the early 19th century [4]. The surgical procedures in MIS are performed by making small incisions, using laparoscopes, endoscopes, and surgical instrument graspers. Researchers divide MIS into two categories: laparoscopic surgery and robotic surgery [4]. For this research, we focus on the latter. The primary goal of integrating medical robotics in surgery is to safely operate on patients at a site remote from the surgeon-the ability to transpose surgical and technical expertise from one location to a distant site [5]. A few benefits of minimally invasive robotic surgery (MIRS) include improvement in manual dexterity by using a controlled mechanical wrist, motion tremor removal and motion scaling, enhancement of three-dimensional (3D) vision, and intraoperative image guidance, which permits improved clinical uptake of the technology, ensuring better operative safety and consistency [6].

In MIRS, a system that can convert information to action by relying on sensors to gather information and transmitting it to the surgeon (e.g., via computer tomography, ultrasonography, magnetic resonance imaging) or by improving access to the area of the body that is difficult to access [6] is one of design requirements. Currently, using sensors for palpation is one of the main challenges of MIRS. Palpation is associated with using the hands to examine the body during surgical procedures. It is an essential part of physical examination, examining an organ's size, consistency, location, texture, and tenderness. The sense of touch (palpation) is as crucial as examine the patients with the sense of sight. In robot-assisted MIS, this sense of touch can be achieved with enhanced surgical instruments designed to compensate for the inability to palpate [6]. In this preliminary work, we focus on allowing surgeons in MIRS to recognize the deformation type in which the organ has. Deformation recognition in MIRS is the step forward towards methods for generating tactile feedback in robot-assisted surgery.

3   Tactile Detection: Design and Method

We designed a hardware prototype that uses two strain gauge sensors, a microprocessor with a bridge measurement circuit (amplifier and potentiometer on the board to adjust the measured results), and scissor forceps (SF). During experimentation, the forceps are open, and an object ready for detection is inserted between the SF's jaws. The user then presses a button to start measurement and grasps the object with the jaws. To have the same amount of force grasping the objects in this experiment, we consider a constant displacement of the forceps ratchets. Specifically, the displacement is from an open finger ring and squeezing until we reach the first step of the SF ratchet part. Depending on the object, the force that needs to reach the ratchet's first step will defer for very soft to rigid objects. For example, if nothing is in-between the forceps' jaws, little to no force is needed to get to the first ratchet level, while if we use a piece of wood in-between the forceps' jaws, an immense amount of force is required to get to the first ratchet level. A constant displacement point is to see how much stress the object exerts on the forceps. The more force we apply to get to the first ratchet level, the more stress is applied to the strain gauge. This is used to differentiate the object deformation.

Next, a microprocesor (e.g., Arduino) collects strain data from two strain gauges on the scissor forceps for one second (where the sampling frequency is 20 Hz). The collected raw data are processed to generate three attributes. The attributes consist of the Most-Frequent (MF), Average (A), and Range (R) of the strain gauge's measurements. The MF attribute is the most frequent strain gauge measurement value seen in the 20 samples, the Average attribute is the mean of the 20 samples, and the Range is calculated by subtracting the minimum value from the maximum value given the 20 samples. These attribute values are used to implement a proposed Multiple Input - Multiple Output (MIMO) Takagi-Sugeno-Kang fuzzy classification system (TSK-FCS), which has a fuzzy inference engine, a rule base, and a defuzzifier. Additionally, each attribute is characterized by Gaussian membership functions with linguistic terms. A linguistic term is a variable whose values are qualitative. For instance, two membership functions with linguistic terms LOW and HIGH are used for the Average and Range attributes, while three membership functions with linguistic terms LOW, MEDIUM, and HIGH are used for the MF attribute.

To generate each of the Gaussian membership functions, we determined two variables - the mean and the standard deviation based on the attribute data. For example, given multiple trials where we calculated the Average attribute, $A_n = \{A_1, A_2, ..., A_N\}$, we find the mean and the standard deviation of the set and use the Gaussian membership function formula, Eq. 1, to establish the linguistic term L.

$$L(A_n) = \exp\{-\frac{(A_n - A_n^{bar})^2}{2(A_n^\sigma)^2}\} \tag{1}$$

where A_n^{bar} and A_n^σ refer to the mean and standard deviation of the data set A_n, respectively. Similarly, we use Eq. 1 to find the linguistic terms for the Range and MF inputs given n trials. After determining the linguistic terms for the inputs, we can design a classifier that will tell us the deformation of the object we are experimenting with. Given that we will have two linguistic terms for Average, two for Range, and three for MF, the number of rules the system has is $12(2 \times 2 \times 3)$. In the TSK-FCS design, fuzzy IF-THEN rules are as follows:

R_k: If A is L_k^A and R is L_k^R and MF is L_k^{MF}, then deformation is D

where k is a rule number ranging from 1 to 12, A is the average, R is the range, MF is the most-frequent, $L_k^A, L_k^R \in \{$LOW, HIGH$\}$, $L_k^{MF} \in \{$LOW, MEDIUM, HIGH$\}$, and $D \in \{$Very Soft, Soft, Medium, Hard, Very Hard$\}$.

Let's consider the first rule:

R_1: If A is LOW and R is LOW and MF is LOW, then deformation is Very Soft

The antecedent part of R_1 is as follows:

$d_{VerySoft} = 1,\ d_{Soft} = 0,\ d_{Medium} = 0,\ d_{Hard} = 0,\ d_{VeryHard} = 0$

As shown, each $d_{deformation}$ gets assigned to a centered average value: 0 or 1. To find this value, we first use the following equation:

$$d_{deformation} = \frac{\sum_{k=1}^{12} z_k \tau_k}{\sum_{k=1}^{12} \tau_k} \tag{2}$$

where z_k is the rule output level and scaled to be 0 or 1 depending on the kth rule, and τ_k is the firing strength used to satisfy all antecedent clauses per each rule R_k. Next, the deformation type with the biggest centered average value gets assigned a 1, and the remaining deformations get assigned a 0. In the first rule instance, $d_{VerySoft}$ is greatest in value when Eq. 2 is considered, so it gets an output of 1, while the rest of the deformations get an output of 0.

To implement the system, we use MATLAB - Fuzzy Logic Toolbox to replicate the software design. It is a MIMO system that takes in three inputs (A, R, MF), the twelve set of rules we created, and has five outputs (VS, S, M, H, VH). We associate a singleton membership function to represent all five outputs. For example, depending on the attribute (input) values, each output gets assigned a 'Low (L)' and a 'High (H)' value; where L $= 0$ and H $- 1$. We do this because we want to assign a 1 to one of the five output and a 0 to the remaining outputs. Furthermore, these deformation outputs are intended to describe an object based on human tactile detection. For example, given a marshmallow, a sponge, and a piece of wood, humans can associate these three objects as a soft, medium, and hard.

4   Experimental Procedure and Results

The objective of our experiments was to assess the accuracy of the TSK-FCS when obtaining an object's deformation. The conducted research consisted of 130 trials. 100 of these trials were used to train the TSK-FCS. During the experimentation, the materials used were a ball of play dough, a marshmallow (wrapped in saran wrap), a sponge, a cardboard box (folded and taped), and a piece of wood. The objects were picked for the experiment because they represented a wide range of objects a human would consider as very soft, soft, medium, hard, and very hard. 20 trials were done with each object between the scissor forceps. Based on the observation given by the 100 trials, e.g., the attribute values given the different objects; we could separate each of the attributes into linguistic terms to obtain the desired output. Specifically, we can separate the Average value into two linguistic terms, if the Average is lower than 55, the object is most likely VS, and if the Average is greater than or equal to 55, the object is most likely S, M, H, or VH. Similar partitioning techniques are done for the Range and MF inputs. Table 1 shows precisely (e.g., the bold numbers) where the splitting was done for the input values. For Average, we did a split at 55. For Range, we did a split at 150 and for MF, we did two splits at 84 and 190.

Table 1. Rule base.

	Average	Range	MF
VS (play dough)	42	59	54
	53	93	59
S (marshmallow)	**57**	103	74
	70	137	**83**
M (sponge)	58	105	**85**
	94	**141**	103
H (cardboard)	94	**173**	145
	138	194	**189**
VH (wood)	131	188	**191**
	181	194	198

For the inputs, we generate a membership function for each linguistic term. For example, Average values lower than 55 have a membership function corresponding to a LOW linguistic term, and Average values higher than or equal to 55 are assigned as a High linguistic term. For the Range input, data from 59 to 141 is used to find the Range LOW, and data from 173 to 194 is used to find the High linguistic term. The MF data is split into three intervals: data from 54 to 83 is used to find the MF LOW linguistic term, data from 85 to 189 is used to find the MF Medium term, and data from 189 to 198 is used to find the MF High term. Each linguistic term of each attribute is represented by the Gaussian membership function equation (Eq. 1). The linguistic terms for each attribute act as an input for the TSK-FCS. Figure 1 shows the Gaussian membership function generated for all inputs.

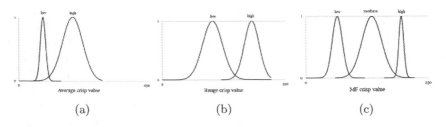

(a)   (b)   (c)

Fig. 1. (a) Average Linguistic Terms {LOW, HIGH}, (b) Range Linguistic Terms {LOW, HIGH}, (c) MF Linguistic Terms {LOW, MEDIUM, HIGH}.

Furthermore, using the set of rules generated from the training data set, we generated Table 2, where 12 ($2 \times 2 \times 3$) rules are considered. The table shows how we split the different objects into categories. For example, given that the Average is LOW, the Range is HIGH, and MF is LOW, the table associates those linguistic terms with a VS deformation. Another example would be: given that the Average is HIGH, Range is LOW, and MF is MEDIUM, the table associates those linguistic terms with an M deformation.

Table 2. Rule base.

Rule	Input 1	Input 2	Input 3	Output
	Average	Range	MF	Deformation
R_1	Low	Low	Low	Very soft
R_2	Low	Low	Medium	Medium
R_3	Low	Low	High	Medium
R_4	Low	High	Low	Very soft
R_5	Low	High	Medium	Hard
R_6	Low	High	High	Very hard
R_7	High	Low	Low	Soft
R_8	High	Low	Medium	Medium
R_9	High	Low	High	Medium
R_{10}	High	High	Low	Soft
R_{11}	High	High	Medium	Hard
R_{12}	High	High	High	Very hard

The remaining 30 trials were used as testing data to verify the functionality of the TSK-FCS. We selected meat as a means of imitating tissues in a human. Six different types of meats (beef and pork chorizo, ground beef, steak, pork meat, tripe, and cow feet) were used to test the system by replicating the deformations of objects in the human body. For example, steak and pork meats are used to represent human muscle. Ground beef, beef and pork chorizo represent soft tissue (fat, fibrous tissue, blood vessels, and nerves). The tripe represents the muscle wall of the stomach in most animals. The beef feet represent rigid objects (bones) in the human body.

Additionally, the testing trials are used to confirm that TSK-FCS works when determining the deformation of different objects. Given 30 trials, the TSK-FCS predicted the correct deformation for in 23 cases. The TSK-FCS predicted nine VS objects, three S objects, two M objects, four H objects, and five VH objects. The accuracy of the TSK-FCS determines how often the classifier is correct. In this case, the TSK-FCS has an accuracy of 76.66% (($23/30$) $\times$ 100). The result is shown in Table 3 using a confusion matrix.

True positives (TP) refer to the cases in which the TSK-FCS predicted the correct deformation in the matrix. For example, in row VS and column VS,

Table 3. Confusion matrix showing 76.66% accuracy.

TSK-FCS prediction					
Actual	VS	S	M	H	VH
VS	100%	0%	0%	0%	0%
S	40%	60%	0%	0%	0%
M	40%	20%	40%	0%	0%
H	0%	20%	0%	80%	0%
VH	0%	0%	16.6%	0%	83.3%

the TSK-FCS predicted nine total VS objects given nine very soft objects; this results in a TP of 100%. Conversely, the TSK-FCS has a misclassification rate which is how often the classifier is wrong. In this case, the TSK-FCS missed seven objects (2 S object, 3 M object, 1 H object, and 1 VH object). After testing was completed, the misclassification rate of the TSK-FCS was 23.33% ($(7/30) \times 100$). The accuracy of the TSK-FCS is acceptable for the prototype design. We deem it acceptable as at this stage we use to demonstrate the TSK-FCS in differentiating between the deformation types of an object.

5   Conclusion and Future Work

The paper proposed a method to enable tactile feedback when performing minimally invasive robotic surgery. Specifically, it is a proposed solution to allow surgeons to recognize an object's softness or hardness. We designed a hardware prototype that uses two strain gauge sensors attached to the exterior jaw of scissor forceps to replicate the grasper portion on a surgical instrument. The strain gauge measures the stress that is applied to the scissor forceps. The measurements are collected using an Arduino board to gather specific attributes. These attribute values are then used to implement a proposed TSK-FCS, which classifies the objects into one of five categories. The hardware and software designs are tested using different meats imitating human organs, tissues, and bones.

In the future, we will install force sensors on a robotic surgical instrument. By doing so, we can better improve the hardware design of the tactile feedback system. Next, more experiments using commercial artificial tissues (e.g., artificial muscle, bone, and fat tissue) will be done. Using artificial tissue will help replicate the objects in the human body and give more accurate data than the objects used in the experimental procedures of this pilot project. Lastly, a comparison between novices and experts using other palpation methods to detect tissue deformation versus using the proposed tactile feedback method will be made. By performing these additional experiments, we can further examine how the proposed method improves palpation in MIRS.

References

1. Kuo, C.-H., Dai, J.S.: Robotics for minimally invasive surgery: a historical review from the perspective of kinematics. In: International Symposium on History of Machines and Mechanisms, pp. 337–338 (2009). https://doi.org/10.1007/978-1-4020-9485-9
2. Peña, R., Smith, M.J., Ontiveros, N.P., Hammond, F.L., Wood, R.J.; Printing strain gauges on intuitive surgical da Vinci robot end effectors. In: IEEE/RSJ International Conference on Intelligent Robots and Systems (IROS), pp. 806–812 (2018). https://doi.org/10.1109/IROS.2018.8594517
3. Wottawa, C.R., et al.: Evaluating tactile feedback in robotic surgery for potential clinical application using an animal model. Surg. Endosc. **30**(8), 3198–3209 (2015). https://doi.org/10.1007/s00464-015-4602-2
4. Lee-Kong, S., Feingold, D.L.: The history of minimally invasive surgery. Semin. Colon Rectal Surg. **24**(1), 3–6 (2013). https://doi.org/10.1053/j.scrs.2012.10.003
5. Mack, M.J.: Minimally invasive and robotic surgery. J. Ame. Med. Assoc. **285**(5), 568–572 (2001). https://doi.org/10.1001/jama.285.5.568
6. Vitiello, V., Kwok, K.-W., Yang, G.-Z.: Introduction to robot-assisted minimally invasive surgery (MIS). Med. Robot., 1–P1 (2012). https://doi.org/10.1533/9780857097392.1
7. Drimus, A., Kootstra, G., Bilberg, A., Kragic, D.: Design of a flexible tactile sensor for classification of rigid and deformable objects. Robot. Auton. Syst. **62**(1), 3–15 (2014). https://doi.org/10.1016/j.robot.2012.07.021
8. Gandarias, J., Garcia-Cerezo, A., Gomez-De-Gabriel, J.: CNN-based methods for object recognition with high-resolution tactile sensors. IEEE Sens. J. **19**(16), 6872–6882 (2019). https://doi.org/10.1109/JSEN.2019.2912968
9. Jain, S., Hong, M., Rozenblit, J.W.: Proficiency based planner for safe path planning and applications in surgical training. In: 2019 Spring Simulation Conference (SpringSim), vol. 51, no. 5, pp. 1–12 (2019). https://doi.org/10.23919/SpringSim.2019.8732852
10. King, C.-H., et al.: Tactile feedback induces reduced grasping force in robot-assisted surgery. IEEE Trans. Haptics **2**(2), 103–110 (2009). https://doi.org/10.1109/TOH.2009.4
11. Kuncheva, L.: Fuzzy Classifier Design. Springer, Heidelberg (2000). https://doi.org/10.1007/978-3-7908-1850-5
12. Xu, D., Loeb, G.E., Fishel, J.A.: Tactile identification of objects using Bayesian exploration. In: IEEE International Conference on Robotics and Automation, pp. 3056–3061 (2013). https://doi.org/10.1109/ICRA.2013.6631001

Reference Datasets for Analysis of Traditional Japanese and German Martial Arts

Konrad Kluwak[1] , Ryszard Klempous[1] , Atsushi Ito[2] , Tomasz Górski[3] ,
Jan Nikodem[1(✉)] , Konrad Wojciechowski[7] , Jerzy Rozenblit[5] ,
Grzegorz Borowik[6] , Zenon Chaczko[4,8] , Wojciech Bożejko[1] ,
and Marek Kulbacki[7,8]

[1] Wrocław University of Science and Technology, Wroclaw, Poland
jan.nikodem@pwr.edu.pl
[2] Faculty of Economics, Chuo University, Tokyo, Japan
[3] Polish Naval Academy, Gdynia, Poland
[4] School of Electrical and Data Engineering, University of Technology,
Sydney, Australia
[5] Department of Electrical and Computer Engineering, The University of Arizona,
Tucson, USA
[6] SWPS University of Social Sciences and Humanities, Warsaw, Poland
[7] Polish-Japanese Academy of Information Technology, Warsaw, Poland
[8] DIVE IN AI, Wroclaw, Poland

Abstract. The study of Japanese fencing and German Longsword Mastercuts based on exact motion measurements in specialist labs is summarized in this work. Based on a streamlined measuring technique, the need for a more thorough study has been suggested that might apply to the observation and evaluation of movement during training in a real-world setting. The requisite data sets and domain knowledge must be available to create motion analysis methods of human sword combat. Such information helps compare several algorithms and techniques, and develop and test new computational methods. In 2020, we created one of the world's first reference databases of fencing actions, which included five master long sword strikes with kinetic, kinematic, and video modalities. We were able to assess these movements and suggest potential study directions thanks to the created methods and algorithms. This paper proposes to extend the presented registration technologies for long swords and swordsmanship to similar combat, such as Japanese Kendo sword fencing.

Keywords: Martial art analysis · German Longsword Mastercuts · Japanese fencing analysis · Human motion analysis · Reference datasets

1 Introduction

The study of motion is currently a popular research area in image analysis, computer vision, machine learning, and biomechanics. Motion analysis involves

ⓒ The Author(s), under exclusive license to Springer Nature Switzerland AG 2022
R. Moreno-Díaz et al. (Eds.): EUROCAST 2022, LNCS 13789, pp. 504–511, 2022.
https://doi.org/10.1007/978-3-031-25312-6_59

the detection, recognition, and tracking of moving objects, including humans [6]. Theoretically, motion capture systems can capture as many details as the human body can show. The gathered information includes facial and finger movements, estimation of body position, and activities performed. The problems with human motion analysis have been discussed in many academic works. Most of the relevant works are summarized in a recent compilation [15]. One of the oldest and most cited works on human motion analysis was written by J.K. Aggarwal and Q. Cai Human Motion Analysis: A Review [1]. It delineates three challenges in interpreting human movement research:

- analysis of movement including parts of the human body,
- tracking a moving person,
- recognition of human activities based on image sequences.

The well-known methods of movement analysis in sport [7,11,14] focus on the classification of movements that differ significantly from each other. Fencing is an example of a discipline where the detection and evaluation of similar body postures are essential. Authors [22] proposed a new repository called Martial Arts, Dance, and Sports dataset for 3D human pose estimation. To estimate human pose based on depth, they provided stereo depth images from a single viewpoint. They used five actors to collect data, with each actor performing one category of actions. Two martial arts masters performed a pre-arranged series of movements in Tai-chi and Karate. In paper [5], five master sword strokes were recorded by the MoCap system to determine the pattern of correct cutting and show the mistakes made by amateurs. Paper [16] proposed using the motion capture function from Microsoft Kinect, where the user can develop basic training and practice taekwondo using a virtual trainer. In recent years, there are also reviews [20] where researchers conducted a systematic study of scientific publications on martial arts and motion capture. In 2020, we created one of the world's first reference databases of fencing actions, which included five master

Fig. 1. The German and the Japanese Martial Arts. The figure on the left depicts german longsword strikes, and one is the Krumphau stroke (source: taken from the manual by Joachim, Meyer [13] from 1570). The left picture presents the fastest Naginata (source: taken from https://www.youtube.com/watch?v=yFgBxIxx4P4)

long sword strikes with kinetic, kinematic, and video modalities [9]. We were able to assess these movements and suggest potential study directions based on the developed analysis methods and algorithms. This paper proposes to extend those registration technologies for long swords and swordsmanship to similar combat, such as Japanese Kendo sword fencing (Fig. 1).

2   Five German Longsword Mastercuts Analysis

Fighting techniques from the late Middle Ages and Renaissance are the main emphases of the historical alliance of European Martial Arts [3,4]. We conducted groundbreaking research to automate the identification of particular German sword-cutting techniques [18,19] to popularize this craft and develop a reference dataset with data captured from expert and amateur performances [8]. The information about fencing needed to complete this study came from references, interviews with subject-matter experts, and recordings. The most representative movements of German Longsword Masterstrokes [11] were registered and studied:

1. *Zornhau* (Strike of Wrath) is a devastating above-the-shoulder diagonal blow. A strike to the opponent's left ear from the right shoulder.
2. *Schielhau* (Squinting Strike) is a false-edged strike. This blow hits the opponent's shoulder while deflecting his weapon.
3. *Zwerchhau* (Cross Strike) is a high, horizontal hit to the head that deflects the attack of the opponent.
4. A vertical attack from above to the opponent's wrists or sword is known as a *Krumphau* (Crooked Strike).
5. *Scheitelhau*. A high, vertical attack with a long edge directed at the top of the head or face while simultaneously retreating is known as a "crown strike".

The master, an expert fencer, performed reference movements that are examples of proper stroke patterns for blows captured by amateur fencing. The full-body plug-in gait configuration (39 markers), initially intended for medical applications, was used to record movements. In the measuring arrangement, 16 EMG electrodes (surface EMG) were employed to capture the activity of specific muscle groups during the cuts. All studies were conducted in the Human Motion Lab, R&D Center, Polish-Japanese Academy of Information Technology (bytom.pja.edu.pl) to create the first public database of German Longsword Mastercut. We recorded the movement of four subjects according to the assumed multimodal measurement protocol. The activity was recorded using 30 motion capture cameras (39 reflective markers on the body and five on the sword), 16 EMG electrodes, two ground reaction forces, and three hardware-synchronized video cameras [10]. The data was semi-automatically (manually) cleaned and saved in C3D and AVI formats. As a result of data recording, we obtained 404 modalities consisting of the positions of 3D markers, virtual markers, centers of gravity, angles, forces, moments, powers, electromyography, video, and generated markers of events. Most of the 3D data includes time series of positions

Fig. 2. Final positions of the master sword strokes. In sequence, from left: Strike of Wrath, Squinting Strike, Cross Strike, Crooked Strike, Crown Strike (source: own elaboration)

of subsequent markers or Euler angles of detection degrees of freedom of joints. The base sampling rate of the multimodal measurement system was 200 Hz. The dataset of five master longsword strikes reported in [9] had been created due to multimodal measurements. The ultimate poses for each of the five master strokes: Zornhau, Schielhau, Zwerchhau, Krumphau, and Scheitelhau, were chosen after analysis of the movements. Numerous illustrations of these positions were provided, drawn from 750 recordings made by 15 people who range in skill level when it comes to making sword strikes. The same mastercuts performed by various actors vary greatly. Both professional and amateur recordings are available in the established database. The fencer's finishing positions are visible in 3750 recognized frames from the motion recordings. Each item in the original database has more than 404 modalities to represent it.

2.1 Conclusions from HEMA

We have collected a reference database of chosen pieces of training using the Master Strikes of the German Longsword, thanks to the established algorithms and collaboration with an expert. This database contains three parts: B.M1 - registered position of 5 markers placed on the sword, B.M2 - registered position of 39 markers placed on the actor's body, and B.M3 - recorded angles of the actor's 26 joints. Of course, it is challenging to picture participant training in a recording studio identical to the one used for this project. The reference multimodal measuring methodology would then be replaced with monocular video in the next phase. We might also think about developing a base similar to this for additional fence types, such as saber, foil, and sword.

3 Japanese Fencing Analysis

Knowledge about Japanese fencing we have received from experts and literature sources such as [12,17]. Fencing knowledge from studies [2,21] also was essential for our research. Other researchers can apply the proposed and described registration technologies for both long sword and Japanese fencing to similar types of combat, such as Kendo (Japanese sword fencing), Naginata (Japanese stick fighting), and Jyojyutu (long stick fighting). Recognizing the dynamics of action in footwork in fencing seems crucial when considering movements in Kendo. The main focus can be on following fast movement, paying attention to even the most minor details, and learning movement patterns. For each of the five participants, ten captured recordings included T-pose position, cut in place, cut with a step forward, cut back, and cut with a step back. The starting position has the following body positioning: legs at shoulder width, right leg extended half a foot forward, left leg half a foot back. Right hand on top of the hilt, in a loose grip, left hand at the bottom; knuckles of the hand pointing down; elbows straight. The end of the sword is at the level of the sternum. The cut looks as follows: hands above the head, gently bent at the elbows, sword at an angle of 0-45°C to the ground; move the sword in a single line, not sideways; strike down to the height of one's sternum with the complete deceleration of the movement. The movement should always end at the same height. However, transitions with the step include the following actions: when raising the leg, raise the sword; the most important thing is to lower the sword at the same time as lowering the leg. When stepping, the cut should end at the exact moment as the step. Comparing the records of medieval sword strokes [13] with the released movements (strikes) of the Kamae of Japanese Kenjitsu [16], one can see a remarkable similarity. A more thorough analysis of these similarities is currently being conducted. The movement Forehead Strike (Fig. 3) is very similar to the movement (strike) Zornhau (Fig. 2 - graphics first on left) (Fig. 4).

In the Cyber-Physical Systems Laboratory, an OptiTrack system with passive markers was used for motion capturing. The system consists of eight Flex 13 cameras with 30–120 FPS at 1.3 MP resolution, OptiHub 2 synchronization devices, and Motive software for marker tracking. The OptiTrack system can track movements with a tolerance of less than 0.5 mm. Synchronization of the cameras is provided by connecting them to two OptiHub 2 devices and then connecting them to a computer. The Motive software uses standard sets of skeleton configurations. Using algorithms and collaboration with an expert, we have collected a reference database of chosen pieces of Japanese mastercuts training composed of 240 recordings of 6 performers (Fig. 5).

Fig. 3. Forehead strike (source: taken from [17])

Fig. 4. Downwoard strike (source: taken from [17])

Fig. 5. Process of laboratory set-up for mocap recordings. Cyber-Physical Systems Laboratory, Faculty of Information and Communication Technology, Wrocław University of Science and Technology (source: own elaboration)

4 Conclusions

Japanese fencing Kendo could use the registration technology proposed here for longsword mastercuts and fencing. Long weapons used in similar forms of combat include the naginata and stick. It appears to be quite helpful to recognize the action dynamics in fencing footwork when analyzing Kendo's moves. Based on publications and discussions with martial arts specialists, we will modify the fencing expertise from the papers that are foundational to this research. Our primary goals will be tracking quick motion, focusing on the minor details, and memorizing motion patterns. We suggest using augmented reality (AR) glasses to deliver real-time immersive feedback for performing blade work, visual cues, identifying action dynamics in fencing footwork, and practicing fencers. Therefore, fencers can correct their actions during training rather than after they receive feedback.

We propose to develop a simplified measurement protocol based on experiments from multimodal gait analysis reference laboratories and the results of the described experiments (Sects. 2 and 3). We intend to simplify the measurement configuration based on data registered from German Longsword and Japanese strikes. As a result, the target experiment will occur beyond the reference laboratories in real-world conditions. The steps that follow assume:

1. the use of prepared data from laboratories as reference data for kinematics and kinetics,
2. unification of the specification of cutting movements (both European and Japanese) for analysis in a simple measurement environment,
3. preparation of a simplified measurement protocol limited only to monocular camera recordings.

The next step is to perform video pose analyses, use accelerometer data for proper data analysis in a simplified environment, and refer to reference data recorded in motion laboratories. The extended procedures are based on the described steps for running video cameras outside the Laboratory with the possible support of local IMU sensors for real-world data recording. The ultimate goal is to develop correct mastercut recognition models solely from video data.

References

1. Aggarwal, J.K., Cai, Q.: Human motion analysis: a review. Comput. Vis. Image Underst. **73**(3), 428–440 (1999)
2. Czajkowski, Z.: Understanding Fencing: The Unity of Theory and Practice. SKA Swordplay Books, New York (2005)
3. Gassmann, J., Gassmann, J., Le Coultre, D.: Fighting with the longsword: modern-day HEMA practices. Acta Periodica Duellatorum **5**(2), 115–133 (2017)
4. Grant, N.: The Medieval Longsword. Bloomsbury Publishing, Oxford (2020)
5. Grontman, A., Horyza, L., Koczan, K., Marzec, M., Smiertka, M., Trybala, M.: Analysis of sword fencing training evaluation possibilities using motion capture techniques. In: 2020 IEEE 15th International Conference of System of Systems Engineering (SoSE) pp. 325–330 (2020)

6. Hu, W., Xie, N., Li, L., Zeng, X., Maybank, S.: A survey on visual content-based video indexing and retrieval. IEEE Trans. Syst. Man Cybern. Part C Appl. Rev. **41**(6), 797–819 (2011)
7. Kitagawa, M., Windsor, B.: MoCap for Artists: Workflow and Techniques for Motion Capture. CRC Press, Boca Raton (2020)
8. Klempous, R., et al.: Neural networks classification for training of five German longsword mastercuts-a novel application of motion capture: analysis of performance of sword fencing in the historical European martial arts (HEMA) domain. In: 2021 IEEE 21st International Symposium on Computational Intelligence and Informatics (CINTI), pp. 000137–000142. IEEE (2021)
9. Kluwak, K.J., Klempous, R.: Baza danych ruchu człowieka: 5 mistrzowskich uderzeń długim mieczem (5MUDM). Technical report 15, Politechnika Wrocławska, Wrocław (2020)
10. Kulbacki, M., Segen, J., Nowacki, J.P.: 4GAIT: synchronized MoCap, video, GRF and EMG datasets: acquisition, management and applications. In: Nguyen, N.T., Attachoo, B., Trawiński, B., Somboonviwat, K. (eds.) ACIIDS 2014. LNCS (LNAI), vol. 8398, pp. 555–564. Springer, Cham (2014). https://doi.org/10.1007/978-3-319-05458-2_57
11. Malawski, F., Kwolek, B.: Real-time action detection and analysis in fencing footwork. In: 2017 40th International Conference on Telecommunications and Signal Processing (TSP), pp. 520–523. IEEE (2017)
12. Masaaki, H.: Japanese Sword Fighting: Secrets of the Samurai. Nova Science Publishers, Inc., New York (2019)
13. Meyer, J.: Gründtliche Beschreibung der Kunst des Fechtens. https://www.wiktenauer.com/wiki/Gr%C3%BCndtliche_Beschreibung_der_Kunst_des_Fechtens_(Joachim _Meyer)
14. Noiumkar, S., Tirakoat, S.: Use of optical motion capture in sports science: a case study of golf swing. In: 2013 International Conference on Informatics and Creative Multimedia, pp. 310–313. IEEE (2013)
15. Prakash, C., Kumar, R., Mittal, N.: Recent developments in human gait research: parameters, approaches, applications, machine learning techniques, datasets and challenges. Artif. Intell. Rev. **49**(1), 1–40 (2018)
16. Sani, N.A., Hendrawan, M.A., Samopa, F.: Development of basic taekwondo training system application based on real time motion capture using Microsoft Kinect. In: ISICO 2015 (2015)
17. Suino, N.: Practice Drills for Japanese Swordsmanship. Weatherhill, New York (2008)
18. Thomas, M.G.: The Fighting Man's Guide to German Longsword Combat. SwordWorks, Timbo (2008)
19. Tobler, C.: Fighting with the German Longsword-Revised and Expanded Edition. eBook Partnership (2015)
20. Wan Idris, W.M.R., Rafi, A., Bidin, A., Jamal, A.A., Fadzli, S.A.: A systematic survey of martial art using motion capture technologies: the importance of extrinsic feedback. Multimed. Tools Appl. **78**(8), 10113–10140 (2019)
21. Williams, L., Walmsley, A.: Response timing and muscular coordination in fencing: a comparison of elite and novice fencers. J. Sci. Med. Sport **3**(4), 460–475 (2000)
22. Zhang, W., Liu, Z., Zhou, L., Leung, H., Chan, A.B.: Martial arts, dancing and sports dataset: A challenging stereo and multi-view dataset for 3D human pose estimation. Image Vis. Comput. **61**, 22–39 (2017)

A Novel Approach to Continuous Heart Rhythm Monitoring for Arrhythmia Detection

Jan Nikodem[1]([✉])[iD], Bruno Hrymniak[2][iD], Konrad Kluwak[1][iD],
Dorota Zyśko[2][iD], Ryszard Klempous[1][iD], Jerzy Rozenblit[3][iD],
Thomas A. Zelniker[4][iD], Andrzej Wytyczak-Partyka[1][iD],
Mateusz Bożejko[1,2,3,4,5], and Dariusz Jagielski[5][iD]

[1] Wrocław University of Science and Technology, Wroclaw, Poland
jan.nikodem@pwr.edu.pl
[2] Department of Cardiology, Centre for Heart Diseases, 4th Military Hospital,
Wroclaw, Poland
[3] Department of Electronics and Computer Engineering, University of Arizona,
Tucson, USA
[4] Division of Cardiology, Medical University of Vienna, Vienna, Austria
[5] Teaching Department for Emergency Medical Service, Wroclaw Medical University,
Wroclaw, Poland

1 Introduction

Wireless cardiac devices offer a novel method for remote monitoring of cardiac patients. Diagnosing the work of the heart, in the most basic approach, is mainly based on observing the hear rhythm. In the mid-twentieth century, the 12-lead electrocardiogram was developed and standardized by American Heart Association (AHA) [1, 20]. Since then, electrocardiography belongs to the first diagnostic steps in evaluating patients presenting with heart complaints. In particular, it plays an essential role as a non-invasive, inexpensive tool for assessing arrhythmias and ischemic heart disease.

A vital concept in electrocardiography is the idea of the Einthoven triangle, which allows the recording of heart rhythm and electrical activity from three limb leads. This idea of recording the voltage difference between electrodes, proposed 100 years ago, underlies all electrocardiogram (ECG) devices to this day and has also been used in our approach, but in a slightly changed form.

One of the frequent complaints of patients is arrhythmia, which can be detected with the help of the ECG device attached to the patient in a supine position. However, to obtain more diagnostic information, the examination should be carried out over an extended period (e.g., 24 h). Maintaining the patient's lying position over such a long period of time is burdensome and impractical. The ECG Holter devices are barely adequate to cope with patient physical activity requirements. Currently Holters allow for the daily recording of the heart activity, while allowing for patients' moderate activity during the recording period.

To increase the likelihood of recording an arrhythmia, a more extended ECG recording is often required [3, 9], sometimes even for a couple of weeks. The

R. Moreno-Díaz et al. (Eds.): EUROCAST 2022, LNCS 13789, pp. 512–519, 2022.
https://doi.org/10.1007/978-3-031-25312-6_60

implementation of such a solution creates new challenges. More specifically, the device must work for weeks and its use must be relatively well tolerated by the patient. Emerging technical problems, such as the long-term operation of the device on battery power or the stability of the electrodes, are accompanied by medical problems, such as allergy issues and abrasions to the skin. In addition, an extensive logged data set of 160–200 MB per day needs to be analyzed to detect potential heart rhythm abnormalities over a longer period of time. The volume of one or two weeks of ECG recordings increases sharply to a dozen gigabytes (GB) and, therefore, there is a need to automatically detect arrhythmic episodes in the ECG trace that may indicate pathologies. However, this requires the development of new algorithms for the initial analysis of ECG recordings. which will leads to the reduction of the analysis area from several GB to several hundred megabytes (MB) as is the case of a Holter monitor.

The device for continuous heart monitoring for arrhythmia detection should provide a reliable and convenient way of recording the ECG signal while maintaining daily activity. In addition, patients would benefit from a non-intrusive device, would not require active interventions such as closing the circuit with a finger, as in a needed in a smartwatch. It should also alert to the occurrence of different kinds of arrhythmias and conductance disorders.

2 Background and Objective

Atrial fibrillation (AF) is the most common type of cardiac arrhythmia [11]. It is estimated that AF occur in one in three, at index age of 55 years, people during their lifetime. The prevalence of AF in the adult population is between 2% and 4%, and due to the aging population, these numbers are expected to increase. AF is a risk factor for death and variety of cardiovascular diseases. It may lead to thromboembolic complications including stroke, heart failure and decompensation, myocardial ischaemia mainly due to excessive tachycardia [2]. Thromboembolic complications of AF can be prevented by anticoagulation therapy. However, antithrombotic treatment imposes the risk of bleeding complications. Therefore, this treatment is indicated if the presence of AF is confirmed by ECG recording. The most important factor that impedes the initiation of anticoagulant therapy is a delayed recognition of AF due to its paroxysmal nature and often asymptomatic occurrence. The most crucial component of preventing AF complications is early detection.

Another issue is the invasive approach to the treatment of AF, i.e., different ablation strategies [4]. The decision to use those methods can only be made in the case of an ECG-documented episode of AF. The obvious difficulty is that episodes of AF occur in various patients with different burdens, and even a few episodes in a year still increase the risk of thromboembolic complications.

Many strategies have been proposed to screen patients for AF. Education of the general population based on pulse regularity checking to select patients in whom ECG should be performed are the cheapest but also the least reliable means of recognizing existing arrhythmia [5]. The other approach is to determine the patient population at-risk of AF, based on the risk factor occurrence in whom prolonged ECG monitoring may reveal an illness. Awareness of the patients from the general population results in increased use of commonly available methods of ECG monitoring (standard 12-leads ECG, 24-h Holter monitoring) and the usage of wearables like hand watches with the function of the ECG recording. However, the watches or wristbands do not allow for continuous control of the heart rhythm. The existing medical devices for continuous rhythm recording can be classified based on the position of the electrodes: on or under the skin. The later system called an implantable loop recorder is the gold standard, however, its use is limited by the cost and the risk of the complications, including bleeding, bruising, and infections of this invasive procedure. Furthermore, a skin scar is an unavoidable remainder of the device insertion.

In turn, the external electrodes are not well tolerated when used for a prolonged period of time. The main problem is to obtain a stable position of the electrodes on the skin. Electrodes attached to the torso record best signals. This position's disadvantage is the need to use adhesive materials to attach them to the skin. This leads to dropping out of the electrodes, skin allergy issues and motion artefacts with prolonged registration. Localizing the electrodes on the limbs for continuous rhythm recording may simplify the procedure and increase their stability. The received ECG signal is a one bipolar lead and most frequently corresponds to the first limb lead of the Einthoven triangle. Nevertheless, the problem of motion and muscle artefacts remains to be resolved. The recording of ECG signals in a single-arm setting was proved to be feasible [10, 17, 19]. So far, there is no commercially available system using this method of ECG registration.

3   Proposed Solutions

As mentioned in the previous chapter, the 12-lead ECG as a standard test performed in the hospital and laboratory setting (recorded in a supine position) cannot be used for continuous, long-term recording of heart activity.

There are portable devices usable for monitoring ECG heart activity, which extend the recording time and are helpful for observing rare cardiac arrhythmias [13]. An excellent example of such devices may be a Holter monitor, a portable ambulatory device for cardiac 3–5–12 leads monitoring for 24 to 72 h. Nevertheless, the Holter recorder is limited by the constraints of the electrode placement and measurement time.

For patients with more transient symptoms (episodes), a cardiac event monitor worn for a month or more, should be used [3]. A more extended measuring period requires a device less restrictive of the patient's physical activity, and from this perspective, some smartwatch models capable of recording an ECG, seem like an exciting solution. These devices can be worn freely on the wrist for an extended period, but the recording is performed only with the measuring circuit closure by placing a finger from the other hand on the smartwatch. Thus, we obtain a measurement of the ECG potential difference between the upper limbs, which corresponds to *lead I* in a standard 12-lead ECG. Smartwatches can be worn for a long time. However, the timing of ECG recordings depends on the user's decision. Therefore, it does not meet the continuous monitoring requirements - it is an ECG recording based on the patient's request (usually of 30 s or so). Thus, a smartwatch is inappropriate because it requires the continuous closure of the measuring circuit through constant contact of the two hands with the device. As mentioned above, such devices are not good enough because they can provide only a snapshot in time of the patient's heart rhythm.

3.1 Proposed Wearable Device

The current state of the available electronics and IT technologies allows for the implementation of a wearable device. Moreover, as mentioned in the previous section, recording ECG signals in a single-arm setting proved to be feasible [10,17,19]. Therefore, our proposal focuses in on this direction of research and development. We designed the POLIBAND ECG armband for the detection of atrial fibrillation episodes. Technical details of the implementation of this wearable device can be found in [14], while in Fig. 1, its functional diagram is presented.

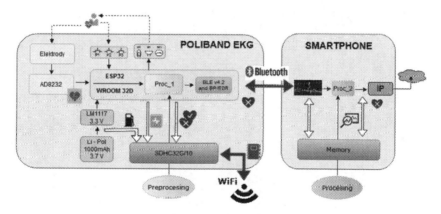

Fig. 1. Functional diagram of POLIBAND ECG communicating with a smartphone via Bluetooth.

The material technology (constantly being improved and tested) used to make the electrodes, in conjunction with the electronic input circuit, adjusts the impedance of the skin-electrode-device connections, ensuring the proper ECG signal conditioning and reduction of analog tract contamination. The two main aspects on which these activities focus are the fluctuation of electrode potential polarization and electrode-skin impedance fluctuation. Signal conditioning activities cannot be exaggerated, especially in terms of the use of filters. We are aware of avoiding the over-conditioning of the ECG signal because we are especially interested in the shape and periodicity of the signal, therefore, it does not need to be smoothed out too much.

3.2   ECG Signal Preprocessing

After conditioning, the electrodes' voltage signal is processed in a AC/DC converter (*AD 8232* chip) into a sequence of 12-bit digital samples. Then, it is recorded in the *SDHC32/10* memory card and preprocessed by *Proc_1*.

The preprocessing *Proc_1* routine consists of several sequential steps designed to cope with:

– baseline wandering,
– power line interferences (50/60 Hz, EU/USA),
– electromyogram noise,
    * day activity artefacts as changes in impedance electrode-skin, ESD discharges, patient mobility muscles potentials
    * physiological artefacts as spontaneous myographic activity of peripheral muscles,

The first three (*dashed*) steps which provide adequate filtrations are based on the selected digital filter implementations of recursive filters: high-pass, narrow pass-band and low-pass, respectively. This filtering is realized with software procedures that were designed to preserve the most significant ECG frequency components but at the same time suppress the noise frequencies [16]. These filters were conformed and implemented to the requirement for real-time SoC microprocessor operation. The results of their action are presented in Fig. 2.

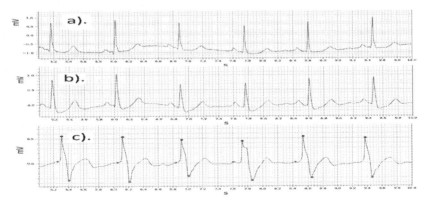

Fig. 2. ECG signals: a) original, b) without baseline wandering, c) without power line interferences but with fiducial points *R, S, P*.

The other two (*asterisked*) steps are more sophisticated, even for specialists who want to catch artefacts on the ECG. We worked on a relatively simple (implementable in a SoC microprocessor) binary classifier (artefact/non-artefact), but the results obtained were not satisfactory. Therefore, we use a dissimilar method in the last two steps when searching for artefacts and eliminate them from the ECG signal. Now, we search for QRS complexes and eliminate everything else (also artefacts) that is not useful for further ECG signal analysis.

We do not filter out what is wrong/unnecessary, i.e. artefacts from the signal because it is very difficult to define the concept of an artefact in the algorithm. In the provided ECG signal, we annotate the R-wave as a fiducial point (see Fig. 2c), then determine the Q-wave and S-wave, and as a result, we obtain the QRS-complex. We take out what is essential from the provided record, i.e., those fragments of the record, which are continuous sequences of many QRS complexes. We give up the remaining pieces of the record, however, within continuous sequences of many QRS complexes, we do not lose the PQ-segment, PQ-interval, ST-segment, and QT-interval records, which will used for further analysis.

4   Conclusion and Future Directions

The ECG signals obtained after the *Proc_1* preprocessing are filtered, thus distortions and noise are reduced. Next, only those parts of the ECG are selected that correspond to the morphology (QRS complex) of the ECG signal. Final waveforms are wirelessly transferred (Bluetooth) to the smartphone, where they will be further analyzed/classified, first in smartphone, second in cloud (Fig. 1).

Using the computing power of the smartphone, we plan the next stage of processing (*Proc_2* in Fig. 1). It will base on ECG signal classification in the scope of the occurrence of different kinds of arrhythmias. For this purpose, we plan to use spectral signatures, creating them for each form of arrhythmia, such as bradycardia, tachycardia, asystole, etc.

Spectral signatures will be created using methods as feature extraction as well as different transforms such as Fast Fourier, Discrete Wavelet or Stockwell [12,18]. These methods have been proven many times, both in the case of simple waveforms (capnography [15]) and more complex signals (audio signals). Hence, we expect that using them in the classification of the ECG signal will bring excellent results.

Having developed algorithms, we will work on digital signatures for selected abnormal states such as different kinds of bradycardias, tachycardia, asystole etc. In these studies, we will use the well-known [6–8] databases as well as the results collected on the basis of the POLIBAND ECG armband. Well-known [6–8] databases were created in hospital and laboratory conditions. Hence, using POLIBAND ECG data is crucial because this device works in much more demanding conditions than those that considered when creating previous devices.

The feasibility of collecting electrocardiograms from the arm described in the literature [17,19], was confirmed by experiments performed by us. It should be noted however, that in this approach the location of the electrodes drastically differs from the Einthoven triangle. We have not found any theoretical framework to explain this situation in the literature. Therefore, this should also be the subject of further research.

During our research, we were also unable to find a reasonable answer to the questions: how does the number of leads reduction affects the diagnostic information contained in the signal? We reduce the recording ECG signal from twelve to one bipolar lead. Is there such a considerable redundancy of information in 12-leads ECG recording that we really do not lose anything essential in this way? Of course, we do realize that there will be some losses. But it will be important to find out how widely and how crucially we will narrow the possibilities of a correct diagnosis.

Acknowledgement. We want to thank *Poliband Active Sp.z o.o.* for partial financing of the implementation of this publication. We want to thank *EMTEL Śliwa Sp.k.* for providing the software enabling the export of ECG records to CSV files.

References

1. AlGhatrif, M., Lindsay, J.: A brief review: history to understand fundamentals of electrocardiography, J. Community Hosp. Intern. Med. Perspect. **2**(1) (2012). https://doi.org/10.3402/jchimp.v2i1.14383. PMID: 23882360
2. Brugada J., et al.: 2019 ESC Guidelines for the management of patients with supraventricular tachycardia. The Task Force for the management of patients with supraventricular tachycardia of the European Society of Cardiology (ESC). Eur. Heart J. **41**(5), 655–720 (2020). https://doi.org/10.1093/EURHEARTJ/EHZ467
3. Bernstein, R.A., et al.: Effect of long-term continuous cardiac monitoring vs usual care on detection of atrial fibrillation in patients with stroke attributed to large- or small-vessel disease: the STROKE-AF randomized clinical trial. JAMA **325**(21), 2169–2177 (2021). https://doi.org/10.1001/JAMA.2021.6470
4. Charitakis, E., et al.: Comparing efficacy and safety in catheter ablation strategies for atrial fibrillation: a network meta-analysis. BMC Med. **20**(1), 193 (2022). https://doi.org/10.1186/s12916-022-02385-2. PMID: 35637488; PMCID: PMC9153169
5. da Costa, F.A., et al.: Awareness campaigns of atrial fibrillation as an opportunity for early detection by pharmacists: an international cross-sectional study. J. Thromb. Thrombolysis **49**(4), 606–617 (2019). https://doi.org/10.1007/s11239-019-02000-x
6. ECG Database: Lobachevsky University electrocardiography database. https://physionet.org/content/ludb/1.0.1/
7. ECG Database: MIT-BIH arrhythmia database. https://physionet.org/content/mitdb/1.0.0/
8. ECG Database: Mendeley, ECG signals. https://data.mendeley.com/datasets/7dybx7wyfn/3
9. Gladstone, D.J., et al.: Screening for atrial fibrillation in the older population: a randomized clinical trial. JAMA Cardiol. **6**(5), 558–567 (2021). https://doi.org/10.1001/JAMACARDIO.2021.0038
10. Gautham, A., Venkitaraman, K.R.: Designing of a single arm single lead ECG system for wet and dry electrode: a comparison with traditional system. Biomed. Eng. Appl. Basis Commun. **28**(03), 1650021 (2016). https://doi.org/10.4015/S1016237216500216

11. Hindricks G., et al.: 2020 ESC Guidelines for the diagnosis and management of atrial fibrillation developed in collaboration with the European Association for Cardio-Thoracic Surgery (EACTS), The Task Force for the diagnosis and management of atrial fibrillation of the European Society of Cardiology (ESC) Developed with the special contribution of the European Heart Rhythm Association (EHRA) of the ESC. Eur. Heart J. **42**(5), 373–498 (2021). Erratum. In: Eur Heart J. 2021 Feb 1;42(5):507. Erratum in: Eur Heart J. 2021 Feb 1;42(5):546–547. Erratum in: Eur Heart J. 2021 Oct 21;42(40):4194. https://doi.org/10.1093/eurheartj/ehaa612. PMID: 32860505

12. Kazemi, M., Krishnan, M.B., Howe, T.A.: Frequency analysis of capnogram signals to differentiate asthmatic and non-asthmatic conditions using radial basis function neural networks Iran. J. Allergy Asthma Immunol. **12**(3), 236–246 (2013). PMID: 23893807

13. Kim, N.H., Ko, J.S.: Introduction of wearable device in cardiovascular field for monitoring arrhythmia. Chonnam Med. J. **57**(1), 1–6 (2021). https://doi.org/10.4068/CMJ.2021.57.1.1

14. Klempous, R., Nikodem, J., Kluwak, K., Jagielski, D.: Electrocardiographic shoulder device and the method of measuring the electrocardiographic signal. Patent: PL439675, WIPO ST 10/C, November 2021. (in polish)

15. Koyama, T., Kobayashi, M., Ichikawa, T., Wakabayashi, Y., Abe, H.: Application of capnography waveform analyses for evaluation of recovery process in a patient with heart failure: a case report. Arch. Clin. Med. Case Rep. **4**(5), 779–787 (2020). https://doi.org/10.26502/acmcr.96550265

16. Mesin, L.: Heartbeat monitoring from adaptively down-sampled electrocardiogram. Comput. Biol. Med. **84**(5), 217–225 (2017). https://doi.org/10.1016/J.COMPBIOMED.2017.03.023

17. Raj, P.S., Hatzinakos, D.: Feasibility of single-arm single-lead ECG biometrics. In: Proceeding of 22nd European Signal Processing Conference (EUSPICO), vol. 2525 (2014)

18. Shdefat, A., Joo, M., Kim, H.: A method of analyzing ECG to diagnose heart abnormality utilizing SVM and DWT. J. Multimed. Inf. Syst. **3**(2), 35–42 (2016). https://doi.org/10.9717/JMIS.2016.3.2.35

19. Villegas, A., McEneaney, D., Escalona, O.: Arm-ECG wireless sensor system for wearable long-term surveillance of heart arrhythmias. Electronics **8**(11), 1300 (2019). https://doi.org/10.3390/electronics8111300

20. Wilson, F.N., et al.: Recommendations for standardization of electrocardiographic and vectorcardiographic leads. Circulation **10**(4), 564–573 (1954)

Indoor Positioning Framework for Training Rescue Operations Procedures at the Site of a Mass Incident or Disaster

Jan Nikodem[1]([✉])[ID], Gabriele Salvatore de Blasio[3][ID], Paweł Gawłowski[2][ID], Ryszard Klempous[1][ID], and Alexis Quesada-Arencibia[3][ID]

[1] Faculty of Information and Communication Technology,
Wrocław University of Science and Technology, Wrocław, Poland
{jan.nikodem,ryszard.klempous}@pwr.edu.pl
[2] Medical Simulation Center, Wrocław Medical University,
Wrocław, Poland
pawel.gawlowski@umed.wroc.pl
[3] Institute for Cybernetics, University of Las Palmas de Gran Canaria,
Las Palmas de Gran Canaria, Spain
{gabriel.deblasio,alexis.quesada}@ulpgc.es

Abstract. Modern IT technologies allow the construction of training systems related to exercising in the field of triage and rescue operation management. In proposed training system we use simulators of vital human signs based on mobile devices. These devices generate the victim's life cycle pattern, consisting of the values (heartbeats and respiratory rates, systolic and diastolic blood pressure, and capillary refill time) used as the basis for TRIAGE categorization.

The use of specially programmed smartphones as simulators was a temporary solution that facilitated system startup. Currently, these simulators are implemented on the basis of the ESP32 chip, which enables the connection of many types of environmental sensors. In the paper we will present new version of the victim simulator based on the ESP32 system on chip (SoC), and new functionalities such as heart rate monitoring and casualties positioning.

In the proposal presented in this work, a hybrid Wi-Fi/BLE positioning system is used to have a coarse positioning with the first technology, which has a longer range, and a finer positioning with the second, which has a shorter range.

1 Introduction

Contemporary professional and voluntary emergency services are perceived as competent and well-prepared units that help the injured in all types of health and life threats. Therefore, a medical staff advanced training process implemented already in the stage of studies and professional training is crucial. This results

R. Moreno-Díaz et al. (Eds.): EUROCAST 2022, LNCS 13789, pp. 520–527, 2022.
https://doi.org/10.1007/978-3-031-25312-6_61

in activities at the highest level of professionalism and one of the most effective modern forms of education is medical simulation.

The recent survey among professional paramedics in the city of Wrocław shows that paramedics with at least 10 years of experience performed on average only two preliminary triage procedures in situations where a large number of people were injured. Triage procedures are where life and death decisions are made, therefore, they should be based on the professional knowledge and experience of trained paramedic personnel [3].

In emergency medicine, simulations are an essential part of training. However, the skills and habits acquired during training slowly fade away if the consolidation exercises are not repeated regularly. Mass accidents and disasters involving a significant number of injured people are events that paramedics do not encounter in their daily practice. Therefore, simulation-based training must be performed repeatedly until the procedures become habitual.

At the site of a mass incident, during the rescue operation, knowledge of the location of rescuers and casualties is crucial. Therefore, in our training system, we propose equipment that enables the practical solution to position [4,5] the casualty and rescuers. We focus on indoor positioning, considering it more important (knowing the position of rescuers facilitates risk management in hazardous zones) and simultaneously more challenging to implement.

2   Background and Objective

Developing technology introduces medical computer simulation and phantoms based on IoT technology into education. Especially computer simulation supported by wireless, wearable devices is a rapidly growing area.

2.1   Training and Simulations in Paramedic Education

Nowadays, a lot of attention at medical universities focus on the study of medical procedures. However, an integral element of the actions of rescue services during mass accidents is crisis management. Analyzing the use of medical computer simulation during studies, we conclude that it is necessary to strive to develop didactic tools [6] for students to learn the procedures of crisis management in a mass incident.

The proposed simulation is to be complementary (as a second stage) in teaching disaster medicine with the already existing tool for segregating victims of a mass event using virtual reality. Its task is to build scenarios for managers of rescue operations at all levels. For this purpose, we use personal devices such as tablets or smartphones used by professional medical services at real work.

In the literature [2,7], simulation is described as a study, an action strategy, or an educational technique. The simulation consists in recreating or pretending to specific phenomena, situations, or models. They are presented similarly to the real ones in terms of construction and process flow. The simulation method enables shaping, improving, and assessing acquired skills in the field of individual activities or specific procedures and patterns of action. It is a kind of teaching technique carried out during a re-creative or interactive process.

After the introduction of advanced simulation techniques into the medical personnel education process, the focus was solely on the use of trainers of varying degrees of advancement. On their basis, three stages of the simulation were distinguished [1]. The low fidelity simulation is based on practice using medical equipment and a trainer/simulator. This equipment is helpful in achieving manual dexterity and gaining specific skills, e.g., learning how to install peripheral vascular access. Rooms for training in resuscitation or communication skills are examples of low-fidelity rooms.

The indirect fidelity simulation uses devices that can map essential life functions: pulse, heart rate, and breathing sounds. However, the simulator does not have functions such as speaking, chest movements, or eye activities. Indirect fidelity simulations are used as an introduction to simulations or to improve simulation skills.

The high fidelity simulation is a possibly faithful recreation of the learning environment, as well as the subject of work - a simulator (dressed in clothing, wig) for an actual workplace. Typical simulation rooms used in this technique look the same or almost identical to actual hospital rooms with advanced equipment and decor. In a high fidelity simulation, referred to as in situ simulation, the simulation room becomes a real workplace (e.g., Hospital Emergency Department), and the patient is replaced by a simulator or a simulated patient (actor).

Computer simulation programs are becoming more innovative. They use virtual reality to segregate people in a mass incident or to cooperate with the air ambulance service. All issues taught with medical computer simulation are designed to teach students to perform specific procedures or crisis management in various situations. However, it is impossible to technically learn specific medical techniques, for example, intravenous injections or endotracheal intubation. The low-fidelity medical simulation is designed to understand these activities which, under the conditions of an emergency team, are practiced by students at the high-fidelity level.

2.2   The Emergency TRIAGE Training System

The proposed training system [9,10] focuses on the management of rescue teams at the scene of a mass incident to improve the implementation of TRIAGE procedures, communication skills, coordination of actions of rescue teams, and the effectiveness of the team during difficult interventions in extremely stressful situations.

The training system allows to exercise the TRIAGE procedures at three levels of hierarchical command management chain (strategic, tactical, and executive). Provides connectivity at the scene based on Wi-Fi standard and the use of TCP/IP connection.

The paper [10] describes the proposed training system to practice emergency TRIAGE procedures in detail. Figure 1 shows its general structure consisting of

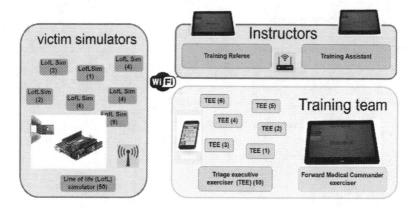

Fig. 1. General view of emergency TRIAGE training system.

three elements: victim simulators, instructors, and training team who communicate with each other using Wi-Fi connectivity.

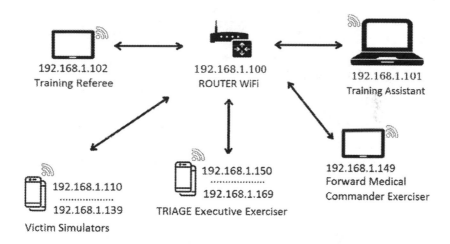

Fig. 2. The assignment of IP addresses in the local network.

For communication purposes, a Wi-Fi router operating in the 2.4 GHz ISM band is used, and the Internet Protocol version 4 (IPv4) is implemented, with the Transmission Control Protocol (TCP) in the ISO/OSI transport layer. Before starting the training, the Training Assistant prepares equipment for exercise using the previously configured Wi-Fi router. Possible assignment of IP addresses to the local network is shown in Fig. 2. A set of ten addresses 192.168.1.140-139 has been reserved for victim's and trainee's, indoor positioning systems.

3   Proposed Solution

3.1   Wi-Fi and BLE Technologies

The main advantage of using Wi-Fi technology is the presence of access points in virtually any indoor environment, and the relatively good positioning accuracy that the network provides [8,13,14]. BLE technology also offers many advantages, mainly due to its low power consumption, advanced services, and localisation capabilities [5,11,12]. A hybrid Wi-Fi/BLE indoor positioning provides the advantages of both technologies.

3.2   Methodology

Three access points (AP) are installed in the training environment to identify different zones, where several victims carrying Arduino One (AO) devices are located (Fig. 3). The victim's AO device $v_{i,j}$, where i denotes the zone and j identifies the victim, is connected to an HM-10 BLE module [16], each with a unique MAC address. The module will serve for victim positioning and will also allow the use of advanced services associated with BLE technology.

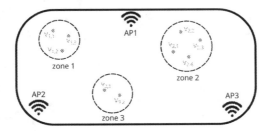

Fig. 3. Diagram of the training environment and the zones identified through of Wi-Fi technology, where each victim Arduino One device is symbolized by a red dot. (Color figure online)

Figure 4 shows schematically the procedure for the first phase: on a map of the training environment, the instructors will activate the victims' AO devices via their application. In the second phase, first responders use their application to access the training environment (Fig. 5). Each zone is delimited by the distance $R_{i,j,k}$ between the victim's AO device $v_{i,j}$ and the k-th AP: each zone within the environment, with its corresponding group of victims, can be identified by Wi-Fi technology and the Round Trip Time of Flight (RTOF) methodology [8]. Finally, first responders conduct a triage through their application and classify the status of that victim.

In a third phase, the first responders use their application to activate the HM-10 BLE module of AO (Fig. 6). In a fourth and final phase, medical teams access the previously identified zones knowing the severity of each victim. and locating them based on AO's MAC address and proximity estimation [15].

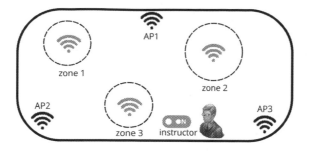

Fig. 4. First phase: instructors activate Arduino One devices.

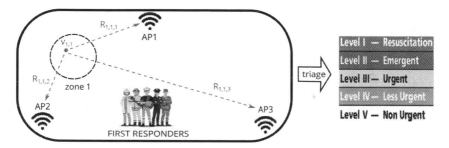

Fig. 5. Second phase: first responders access the training environment and perform triage.

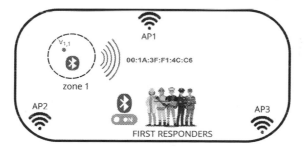

Fig. 6. Third phase: first responders activate victim's AO BLE modules.

4 Conclusions and Outlook

Knowing the actual locations of the victims and rescuers is crucial during emergency operations at the site of a mass incident or disaster. In the case of rescuers, this is especially important when they work in the danger zone. Then the Forward Medical Commander can effectively manage the action, coordinating rescue service activity, while ensuring the safety of its teammates.

Knowledge about victims' location is also very important. It allows the injured people to get help faster and, in the case of victims already assigned TRIAGE status, to monitor their activities.

The effectiveness of indoor positioning at the site of a mass incident or disaster depends on many factors, but does not affect the training conditions, process, and overall concept. Expanding the set of many already existing devices by a few devices supporting locations does not generate big technical problems and finds economic justification. Therefore, we are going to verify how the use of additional equipment, BLE, and Wi-Fi technologies can be an effective solution to position rescuers and casualties [4,5,12].

There are many modern IT technologies that support medical services in the field of triage and rescue operation management. We want to familiarize paramedic rescuers with them during training.

The victim's AO devices have a HM-10 BLE module connected, so that BLE packets can be read. In addition, the AO devices can in turn read Wi-Fi packets.

On the other hand, possible interference problems could be overcome by avoiding certain Wi-Fi channels and taking into account the fact that Bluetooth automatically uses FHSS (Frequency Hopping Spread Spectrum). The purpose of using a hybrid Wi-Fi/BLE positioning system is to have a coarse positioning with the former technology, which has a longer range, and a finer positioning with the latter, which has a shorter range.

Other technologies, such as Ultra Wideband (UWB), can be useful to apply to this type of systems.

References

1. Al-Elq, A.H.: Simulation-based medical teaching and learning. J. Fam. Community Med. **17**(1), 35–40 (2010). https://doi.org/10.4103/1319-1683.68787
2. Ayaz, O., Ismail, F.W.: Healthcare simulation: a key to the future of medical education - a review. Adv. Med. Educ. Pract. **13**, 301–308 (2022). https://doi.org/10.2147/AMEP.S353777
3. Bazyar, J., Farrokhi, M., Khankeh, H.: Triage systems in mass casualty incidents and disasters: a review study with a worldwide approach. Open Access Maced. J. Med. Sci. **7**(3), 482–494 (2019). https://doi.org/10.3889/oamjms.2019.119
4. de Blasio, G., Rodríguez-Rodríguez, J.C., García, C.R., Quesada-Arencibia, A.: Beacon-related parameters of Bluetooth low energy: development of a semi-automatic system to study their impact on indoor positioning systems. Sensors **19**(14), 3087 (2019)
5. de Blasio, G., Quesada-Arencibia, A., García, C.R., Molina-Gil, J.M., Caballero-Gil, C.: Study on an indoor positioning system for harsh environments based on Wi-Fi and Bluetooth low energy. Sensors **17**(6), 1299 (2017)
6. Czekajlo, M.: Medical simulation as a professional tool influencing patient safety used in the teaching process. Merkur Lekarski **XXXVII**, pp. 360–363 (2015)
7. Friedl, K.E., O'Neil, H.F.: Designing and using computer simulations in medical education and training: an introduction. Mil. Med. **178**(10 Suppl.), 1–6 (2013). https://doi.org/10.7205/MILMED-D-13-00209
8. Liu, H., Darabi, H., Banerjee, P., Liu, J.: Survey of wireless indoor positioning techniques and systems. IEEE Trans. Syst. Man. Cybern. Part C (Appl. Rev.) **37**(6), 1067–1080 (2007). https://doi.org/10.1109/TSMCC.2007.905750

9. Nikodem, J., Nikodem, M., Klempous, R., Gawłowski, P.: Wi-Fi communication and IoT technologies to improve emergency triage training. In: Zamojski, W., Mazurkiewicz, J., Sugier, J., Walkowiak, T., Kacprzyk, J. (eds.) DepCoS-RELCOMEX 2020. AISC, vol. 1173, pp. 451–460. Springer, Cham (2020). https://doi.org/10.1007/978-3-030-48256-5_44. ISSN 2194-5357. ISBN: 978-3-030-48255-8; 978-3-030-48256-5

10. Nikodem, J., Nikodem, M., Gawłowski, P, Klempous, R.: Training system for first response medical emergency groups to guide triage procedures. In: 8th International Workshop on Innovative Simulation for Health Care, IWISH, DIME Universitá di Genova; DIMEG University of Calabria (2019). ISBN: 978-88-85741-36-2; 978-88-85741-35-5. http://toc.proceedings.com/50560webtoc.pdf

11. Nikodem, M., Bawiec, M.: Experimental evaluation of advertisement-based Bluetooth low energy communication. Sensors **20**, 107 (2020)

12. Nikodem, M., Szeliński, P.: Channel diversity for indoor localization using Bluetooth low energy and extended advertisements. IEEE Access **9**, 169261–169269 (2021)

13. Torres-Sospedra, J., et al.: UJIIndoorLoc: a new multi-building and multi-floor database for WLAN fingerprint-based indoor localization problems. In: 2014 International Conference on Indoor Positioning and Indoor Navigation (IPIN), pp. 261–270 (2014). https://doi.org/10.1109/IPIN.2014.7275492

14. Debnath, S., Arif, W., Roy, S., Baishya, S., Sen, D.: A comprehensive survey of emergency communication network and management. Wirel. Pers. Commun. **124**(2), 1375–1421 (2022)

15. Saraiva, R., Lovisolo, L.: RF Positioning: Fundamentals, Applications and Tools. Artech House Publishers, Boston (2015)

16. IIM Bluetooth module datasheet, Datasheet V610, JNHuaMao Technology Company (2013)

Designing Sightseeing Support System in Oku-Nikko Using BLE Beacon

Atsushi Ito[1]([⊠])[iD], Haruto Kawakami[1], Haruka Nakayama[1], Yuko Hiramatsu[1], Madoka Hasegawa[2], Yasunari Harada[3], Kazutaka Ueda[4], and Akira Sasaki[5]

[1] Chuo University, 742-1 Higashinakano, Hachioji, Tokyo 192-039, Japan
{atc.00s,a20.8pj7,a19.y8d4}@g.chuo-u.ac.jp, susana_y@tamacc.chuo-u.ac.jp
[2] Utsunomiya University, 7-1-2 Yoto, Utsunomiya, Tochigi 321-8505, Japan
madoka@is.utsunomiya-u.ac.jp
[3] Waseda University, 1-104, Totsuka-cho, Shinjyuku-ku, Tokyo 169-8050, Japan
harada@waseda.jp
[4] University of Tokyo, 7-3-1 Hongo, Bunkyo-ku, Tokyo 113-8654, Japan
ueda@design-i.t.u-tokyo.ac.jp
[5] GClue Inc., 134-3 Ikkicyo Tsuruga Aza Kamiiai, Aizu-Wakamatsu, Fukushima 965-0006, Japan
akira@gclue.jp

Abstract. We are developing a tourism support application using BLE (Bluetooth Low Energy) beacons in Senjogahara, Oku-Nikko. There are several ways to supply power to a BLE beacon. We decided to use solar-powered since the Oku-Nikko area is on a mountain, and it is not easy to visit there frequently for maintenance. So, we developed a BLE beacon with a small silicon solar cell in 2018. However, during the summer, sunlight is blocked by the leaves of trees, and it is not easy to get enough electricity to drive a BLE beacon. Therefore, we redesigned the BLE beacon using dye-sensitized solar cells to generate electricity with weaker light than ordinary silicon solar cells. We replaced BLE beacons in Senjogahara with the new beacon in 2021. We confirmed that the new BLE beacons work stably even in an environment covered with forests. In this paper, we explain the design of the new BLE beacon and how it works under weak light.

Keywords: BLE beacon · Solar cell · Sightseeing support application · COVID-19 · Health tourism

1 Introduction

Because of the pandemic of COVID-19, the number of inbound tourists has become almost zero. Also, the number of domestic tourists has decreased. Many people are waiting to travel again and enjoy virtual experiences such as YouTube, VR, and websites for tourists. However, there are some things that we need to

Supported by JSPS Kakenhi (17H02249, 18K111849, 20H01278, 20H05702, 22K12598).

R. Moreno-Díaz et al. (Eds.): EUROCAST 2022, LNCS 13789, pp. 528–535, 2022.
https://doi.org/10.1007/978-3-031-25312-6_62

consider. The information that can be obtained from the Internet, YouTube, and other virtual experiences are limited to what is attractive to travelers. However, there is no information about the difficulty of access and danger in that area. In addition, the pandemic of covid-19 has changed people's lifestyles and made them more conscious of their health. Therefore, health tourism has become popular, incorporating the recovery, promotion, and maintenance of health into travel. Before the pandemic, there was much research on health tourism. According to the Global Wellness Tourism Economy - November 2018 by Global Wellness Institute (GWI), the global tourism market was approximately $639 billion in 2017 [1] as shown in Fig. 1. In 2018, the Japanese government launched the Health Tourism Certification System, evaluating and certifying health care based on three pillars: consideration of safety and security, provision of emotional value such as enjoyment and pleasure, and promotion of health awareness. In tourism after covid-19, UNWTO published "COVID-19 and Transforming Tourism" [2]. According to the report, worldwide tourist numbers will decrease by 58% to 78% in 2020, and tourist spending will decrease from $1.5 trillion in 2019 to $310–570 billion in 2020. Not only that, more than 100 million jobs in tourism are missing. The report recommends that a small number of tourists visit a region that also includes nature and that the tourism ecosystem is digitalized. In addition, Japan's Minister of the Environment, Koizumi, has proposed a Go-To National Park campaign, where people can enjoy nature while avoiding crowding [3]. We have developed a tourism support application using BLE beacons [4] in Nikko and Oku-Nikko (Nikko National Park [5]). We renewed our BLE beacon and smartphone application in 2021. However, we had some problems with BLE beacons since Senjogahara is covered with forest, and it is not easy to get enough sunlight. In this paper, we present the details of the newly designed beacon suitable for the mountain area. Section 2 describes the features of the new solar beacon, and in Sect. 3, we compare the new solar beacon with the solar beacon we used. Then, in Sect. 4. We mention the result of the evaluation, and the conclusion is described in Sect. 5.

2   Designing New Solar Beacon

A Bluetooth Low Energy (BLE) beacon is a device that transmits information such as ID by using the advertising function of BLE. BLE beacons are mainly used for indoor positioning. However, we have been using them to distribute tourism information outdoors. Doing this makes it possible to reduce power consumption compared to GPS in navigation applications. So, the BLE beacon is suitable for mountainous areas such as Senjogahara since it is difficult to charge a smartphone during walking. BLE beacon in mountain area has a problem. Usually, a BLE beacon uses a small battery, so it is required to change the battery once a year. It is not easy to visit the mountain area to check the battery status, so we developed a BLE beacon with solar cells. However, the BLE beacons with solar cells we used before had a problem. Senjogahara is covered with forest, and it is not easy to get enough sunlight, especially in summer. Usually, when solar

Wellness Tourism Growth Projections, 2017-2022

	Projected Expenditures (US$ billions)		Projected Average Annual Growth Rate
	2017	2022	2017-2022
North America	$241.7	$311.3	5.2%
Europe	$210.8	$275.0	5.5%
Asia-Pacific	$136.7	$251.6	13.0%
Latin America-Caribbean	$34.8	$54.7	9.5%
Middle East-North Africa	$10.7	$18.7	11.8%
Africa	$4.8	$8.1	11.1%
Total Wellness Tourism Industry	**$639.4**	**$919.4**	**7.5%**

Source: Global Wellness Institute estimates, based upon tourism industry data from Euromonitor International, economic data from the IMF, and GWI's data and projection model

Fig. 1. Global wellness tourism economy

Fig. 2. Appearance of the new beacon

Fig. 3. New BLE beacon circuit

cells are used in an urban area, the shortage of sunlight happens in winter. So, a solar cell must generate electricity even without direct sunlight. To solve this problem, we changed the solar cells from conventional polycrystalline solar cells to dye-sensitized solar cells (DSSC) [6]. DSSC can generate electricity at a higher efficiency in low-light environments. Figure 2 shows the exterior of the new BLE beacon with DSSC solar cells, and Fig. 3 shows its interior circuit. Figure 4 shows the newly placed beacon in Senjogahara, and Fig. 5 shows the pop-up information displayed on a smartphone application [7] in response to the beacon. The pop-up shows various information, such as the name of unique flowers, birds, mountains, legends, and the history of Okunikko. Furthermore, it displays the distance to the exits and the approximate walking time. Figure 6 shows the location of the beacon. The numbers in the figure are the serial numbers of the beacons.

3   Comparison

The following is a comparison of the old beacons and the new beacons.

Fig. 4. Beacon in Senjogahara

Fig. 5. Pop-up when a beacon finds a beacon

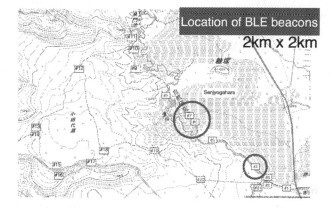

Fig. 6. Location of beacons

Fig. 7. Charging battery using silicon solar cell (Left: OK, Right: NG)

Fig. 8. Charging battery using DSSC (146 lx)

3.1   Old Beacon

The following are the specifications of the solar cells we have been used before [8].

- 10 × Polycrystaline solar cells.
- Rated output: 5 V @ 40 mA
- 55 mm diameter × 3 mm thick

Using Solar Lithium battery charger [9], the power generated by a solar cell is supplied to a lithium polymer battery and the beacon. This solar cell, however, needs to be exposed to a strong light to generate electricity. Figure 7 shows the approximate illuminance that can be charged and powered by this solar cell system. The measurements were performed to drive a beacon. The illuminance was measured by a smartphone application (Galactica [10]). The old solar beacon worked when the illuminance exceeded 340 Klux. This data is obtained during the daytime when there are a few clouds and direct sunlight. However, in Senjogahara, most footpaths are located in the forest, so the sunny places are limited to three locations, No. 4, 6, and 7 in Fig. 6. The beacons often stopped during the summer, which is the high season for hiking in Senjogahara.

3.2   New Beacon

The new beacon uses a Dye-Sensitized Solar Cell (DSSC) (FDSC-FSC4FGC). Size is 56.0×112.0 mm, Thickness 2.5 mm, and Effective power generation area is 48.2 cm^2. This solar cell can generate electricity even in dark places like a room with no lighting or on rainy evenings (less than 1K lx, Fig. 8). According to [11], a study on the power consumption of BLE beacons, the current power consumption is about 0.064 mAh when the beacon is driven by 3 V and sends only one Advertisement channel every 0.5 s. The charging circuit is equipped with a 3.7 V, 40 F capacitor, and when converted to battery capacity by referring to [12], it becomes 20 mAh. So that the device can work as $20/0.064 = 312$ h ($=13$ days) with a full charge. Using the energy balance calculation simulator [13], we can expect the beacon to work as long as there are no more than two hours of sunlight per day and almost no light.

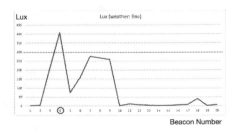

Fig. 9. Illuminance in sunny day (2021.8.29)

Fig. 10. Illuminance in rainy day (2021.9.4)

4   Evaluation

The new BLE solar beacon was placed at the end of June 2021. We checked the beacons several times, and they worked well in 2021 and 2022. Figure 9 and Fig. 10 show the measured results of illuminance at each beacon. Based on the results shown in both figures, the line plotted at 300K lx is the threshold of solar power to generate enough electricity to operate the old beacon. Tow measurement results show that the old beacon can only generate, charge, and operate at only three locations. In contrast, the new beacons will generate and charge power at any location, making them highly available. Figure 11 and Fig. 13 shows the Tx power of each beacon. The data varied considerably and was generally between −70 to −90 dBm. However, the cause of this variation is unclear, so we plan to continue our investigation. Figure 12 and Fig. 14 shows the advertising interval. Even though it is set to 0.5 s, the advertising interval varies a lot, so we plan to investigate the reason in the future.

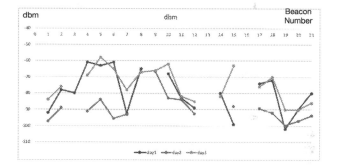

Fig. 11. Tx power of each beacon (dbm)

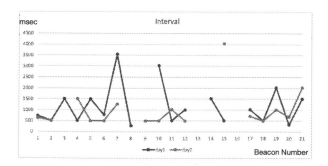

Fig. 12. Advertising interval of each beacon

534 A. Ito et al.

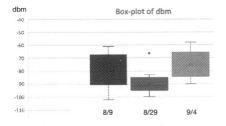

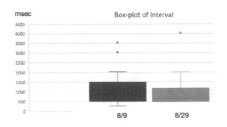

Fig. 13. Box-plot of dbm   **Fig. 14.** Box-plot of advertising interval

5 Conclusion

We have been using a solar BLE beacon in Senjogahara. Usually, standard poly-crystalline solar cells require relatively strong light to generate electricity. However, they did not work well in Senjogahara since a forest covers many areas. Therefore, we changed from polycrystalline solar cells to dye-sensitized solar cells that can generate electricity without intense light, such as in a dark room without lighting. We expected that the newly designed BLE solar beacon would be able to generate power stably even in Senjogahara. As a result of the measurements, the new beacon was found to be capable of generating and charging power at all locations where it was located.

Acknowledgements. The authors would like to express special thanks to Ms. Utsumi and Mr. Egashira of Nikko National Park Office of the Ministry of the Environment, Mr. Maehara of Tochigi Prefectural Government Office, and all members of the committee for increasing the satisfaction of tourists in Nikko. They provided us with information about Oku-Nikko and valuable advice. The authors also would like to express special thanks to Mr. Funakoshi, a Nikko Tourism Association manager. We also thank Mr. Takamura and Mr. Yoshida of Hatsuishi-kai, an association of shops in Nikko, Mr. Nakagawa of Kounritsuin Temple, and Mr. Nagai, a Professor Emeritus of Utsunomiya University.

References

1. Global Wellness Tourism Economy 2018. https://globalwellnessinstitute.org/wp-content/uploads/2018/11/GWI_GlobalWellnessTourismEconomyReport.pdf. Accessed 28 June 2022
2. COVID-19 and transforming tourism. https://www.unwto.org/news/un-policy-brief-on-tourism-and-covid-19. Accessed 28 June 2022
3. GoTo National Park, Interview of Mr. Koizumi, Minister of the Ministry of the Environment, 29 September 2020. https://www.env.go.jp/annai/kaiken/r2/0929.html. Accessed 28 June 2022
4. Sasaki, A., et al.: A study on the development of tourist support system using ICT and psychological effects. Appl. Sci. **10**, 8930 (2020). https://doi.org/10.3390/app10248930. Accessed 28 June 2022

5. Nikko National Park. https://www.env.go.jp/park/nikko/index.html. Accessed 28 June 2022
6. Dye Sensitized Solar Cell (DSSC). https://www.fujikura.co.jp/newsrelease/products/2062444_11541.html. Accessed 28 June 2022
7. Okunikko Navi. https://apps.apple.com/jp/app/%E5%A5%A5%E6%97%A5%E5%85%89%E3%83%8A%E3%83%93/id1620149411. Accessed 28 June 2022
8. Round Solar Panel Skill Badge - 5 V/40 mA. https://www.adafruit.com/product/700. Accessed 28 June 2022
9. USB/DC/Solar Lithium Ion/Polymer charger - v2. https://www.adafruit.com/product/390. Accessed 28 June 2022
10. Galactica.   https://apps.apple.com/us/app/galactica-luxmeter/id666846635. Accessed 28 June 2022
11. https://qiita.com/ksksue@github/items/0811fd62bd970fa93337 . Accessed 28 June 2022
12. Thomas, P.C., Mathai, V.J., Titus, G. (eds.) Emerging Technologies for Sustainability: Proceedings of the Annual International Conference on Emerging Research Areas (AICERA 2019), Kottayam, Kerala (English Edition), 18–20 July 2019
13. Energy balance calculation simulator. https://dsc.fujikura.jp/energy-balance-calculation.htm. Acccssed 28 June 2022

Systems in Industrial Robotics, Automation and IoT

Mixed Reality HMI for Collaborative Robots

Jakob Hörbst[1]($\boxtimes$) and Horst Orsolits[2]

[1] Division Robotics, ABB AG, Zürich, Switzerland
`jakob.hoerbst@at.abb.com`
[2] University of Applied Sciences Technikum Wien, Vienna, Austria
`orsolits@technikum-wien.at`

Abstract. Flexible production systems rely on simple reprogramming solution for the machines on the shop floor. Collaborative Robots play a crucial role in such manufacturing environments showing increasing potential for automation. Using digital twins for bidirectional communication show potential for improving the work between cobot and human. Therefore the development of a Mixed Reality HMI with a Microsoft HoloLens 2 for an ABB GoFa and to evaluate the benefits from such an application was the goal of this project. It was investigated which interfaces are shared by the robot and the HoloLens 2, which data from the robot can be displayed in which form in a mixed reality application and whether it is possible to control the robot with the HoloLens 2. The results show that it is possible to display data from the robot in near real-time and to control the robot with the gesture control of the glasses.

Keywords: Mixed Reality · HoloLens2 · Digital twin · Industrial robot

1 Introduction

For flexible manufacturing systems it is necessary to react quickly to changing products or processes. In order to achieve flexible, smart manufacturing systems one strategy of Industry 4.0 is towards the use of ditigal twins to enable smart decisions through real time communication between digital model and physical object [1]. Intuition often lets human workers solve different tasks faster than robots. When these human skills are combined with the repeatability and endurance of robots, full potential can be realized. Collaborative robots (cobots) serve this purpose and can work directly with humans. However, programming these cobots often still poses a high challenge to operators and simpler ways need to be researched. The goal of this work was to use Mixed Reality and a MS HoloLens 2 to interface with the robot (ABB GoFa) and thus simplify the collaboration between operators and robots. A mixed reality application created with Unity should enable visualization and simulation of the robot with a digital twin. Therefore a data model based on the available sensor data of the robot controller has to be developed. In addition, the digital twin will be used to control the real robot after a feasible and safe way could be determined throughout this study.

R. Moreno-Díaz et al. (Eds.): EUROCAST 2022, LNCS 13789, pp. 539–546, 2022.
https://doi.org/10.1007/978-3-031-25312-6_63

2   Problem and Task Definition

Programming robots often requires well-trained specialist personnel. The more flexible an application is to be, the more often changes have to be made in the program, which again results in personnel costs. In order to make programming robots easier, it is necessary to explore methods for simplifying programming.

A mixed reality application is to be developed for an MS HoloLens 2 that enables the robot to be programmed and controlled as intuitively as possible. For this purpose, it is to be determined which interfaces exist for this connection, which data can be read from the robot and visualized in the glasses and whether a bidirectional connection is possible in order to also control the robot via the glasses.

In the context of an evaluation and the analysis of the results from this, it is to be determined whether the use of Mixed Reality in comparison to conventional operation results in a time advantage, an improvement of the accuracy to time ratio can be achieved and how the workload behaves.

3   Materials and Methods

The hardware used for this work was an ABB GoFa colaborative robot and a MS HoloLens 2. Furthermore suitable networking hardware had to be identified to allow point to point communication using TCP/IP. A common interface had to be found and, if necessary, protocols used had to be acquired or defined. A software and necessary SDKs for creating the mixed reality app were chosen and a simulation environment for the app was set up. Finally, a switch was made from simulation to real hardware and an evaluation was performed. The implementation of this case study followed the V-Model starting with requirements engineering of all stake holders resulting in detailed work packages of each subdomain. Through each phase and development steps according verification and finally validation of the initial task definitions took place.

4   State of the Art

In a digital age, it is a challenge to unite the real and digital worlds. Augmented and mixed reality as described by [2] offer an approach for this. For the representation of complex content of real systems in augmented or mixed reality, digital twins [3] are very well suited. One goal of digital twins is to act bidirectionally as well. This is the topic [4] addresses and compares programming a robot with a 2D user interface and an app in Mixed Reality. When it comes to moving a robot intuitively, the focus is on kinesthetics, the possibility of hand guidance, which, however, imposes specific requirements on the robot's sensory system. For robots that do not have such sensor technology, research [5] possibilities to move the robot via gesture control in mixed reality. A different path was chosen by [6] for programming robots using AR. As part of their work, an augmented reality app for smartphones was developed to create robot paths. To do this, they use markers to complete the transformation from robot to get a smartphone. In addition, surface recognition is also used to capture the work table. This allows points to be projected directly onto the plane. In your application, points are first created on the surface and can then be placed in a desired height or orientation can be brought. Whether such technologies can also impact workload is being investigated by [7].

5   Practical Implementation

The practical implementation from the project (which was named GoHolo) can be divided into three parts, as three devices run programs as part of GoHolo (Fig. 1).

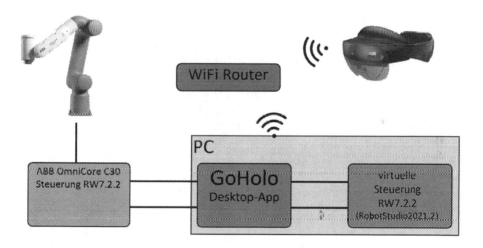

Fig. 1. Schematic representation of GoHolo

5.1   ABB GoFa

The robot itself can be considered like an actuator in this application, since most of the logic runs on the other two devices. The robot (programmed in RobotStudio) provides the data for the digital twin and responds to commands to run programs or for motion sequences sent by the MS HoloLens 2. An exact copy of the program additionally runs on a virtual controller on the PC and is used for simulations in MR.

5.2   Interface (PC)

A desktop application for PC was created in Microsoft Visual Studio and Windows Presentation Foundation. The program is the central part of the application and manages all commands and data coming from and going to the robot and virtual controller, respectively, and establishes communication with MS HoloLens 2. Various interfaces are used in this program. Socket messaging is used for communication with the HoloLens 2. The communication between the GoHolo interface and the robot controller is made up of different individual components. The Externally Guided Motion (EGM) option is used to stream data from the robot and also to guide the robot through the HoloLens. The PC-SDK can be used to access data from the robot and thus monitor the state of the robot or operate the individual operating modes. In addition to the axis angle, the moments and speeds in the robot are also streamed, for which socket messaging is used to transfer the data.

5.3   Microsoft HoloLens2

The application for the MS HoloLens 2 was programmed in Unity. The Mixed Reality Toolkit (MRTK) and the PTC Vuforia engine were used for this purpose. Interaction with the digital twin is done via gesture control. The MRTK offers many ready-made functions that can be used for this purpose and thus enables very user-friendly operation. For example, the main menu is always pinned to the flat hand (Fig. 2). Other windows and the robot itself can be moved freely. If the user does not want to position the robot freely in space, but wants to overlay it with the real robot, the position of the digital twin can be referenced to the real robot with a QR code. With Unity, it is also possible to display the robot itself in different ways. This makes it possible to make parts or the whole robot transparent and thus to see inside the robot or to display additional information directly on the robot.

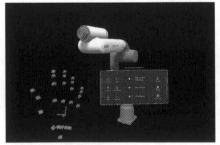

Fig. 2. Unity and real application showing hand menu

6   Results

It was possible to develop a comprehensive control system for the robot using MS HoloLens 2. With the MR application it is possible for the operator to get very fast and clear information about the current state of the robot. Two of these visualisations should be mentioned here. The display of dial gauges directly on the axes of the robot and thus enables a simple understanding of the current axis position. Figure 3 shows how these gauges are also coloured from the zero point (green) to the maximum axis position (red). For this feedback, the exact values can also be read out via a dashboard (Fig. 3 in the background).

The second point of the visualisation worth mentioning is the display of the current torques acting in the robot. For this purpose, the operator is given an X-ray view into the robot with MR. Figure 4 shows the motors of the robot which are also displayed with a colour scale. In the left picture, the robot is in a position in which hardly any torque is acting in the axes, whereas in the right picture it is clearly visible that a higher torque is acting in the second axis of the robot.

Fig. 3. Joint angle feedback displayed on the digital twin (Color figure online)

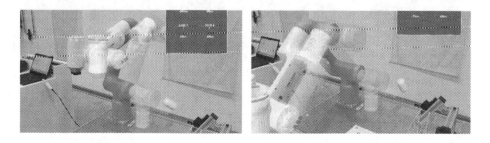

Fig. 4. Torque feedback shown on the digital twin

The control of the robot is very similar to the operation of a robot in manual mode. In the first step, the robot's axis jog was implemented. The robot's axes can be operated with sliders as shown in Fig. 5. First, the digital twin is brought into the desired position and then the movement of the real robot is started. Here, too, attention was paid to making the input as user-friendly as possible and so, only those axes of the robot are shown on the digital twin that are affected by the movement, all other axes are displayed transparently.

In practice, however, it happens much more often that a robot has to be moved cartesian or simply reoriented. This operation usually requires at least basic knowledge of robotics and is not self-explanatory. It is precisely at this point that MR and gesture control are intended to create a more intuitive option. By grasping a digital TCP and manipulating it in the digital world, the real robot can be moved live. The Cartesian position of the robot can be controlled by the position of the hand and the orientation can be controlled by turning the wrist. Figure 6 shows how the robot can be grabbed and moved by a digital laser beam.

Fig. 5. Joint control of the robot

Fig. 6. Digital lead through

To sum it up, GoHolo allows visualization of information, intuitive control by gestures, simulating movements while the real robot is still at standstill, axis-by-axis traversing, fading in the workspace, and creating waypoints in the MR.

In order to be able to make a statement as to whether and what advantages the GoHolo application brings an evaluation has been carried out. In the area of industrial robotics s a key success factor for the application is possible time savings with similar precision. In addition to the time factor, the workload for operators should also be determined and compared with conventional methods. The analysis of the evaluation showed that for the selected group of test persons (previous knowledge relevant to the subject) no temporal improvements could be measured, but that there is nevertheless great potential in the use of applications such as GoHolo in connection with robotics.

7   Summary and Outlook

Within the scope of this work, a mixed reality HMI for the robot could be created, which bidirectionally enables both the display of information on digital twins and the control of the robot via the digital twin. The subject group selected for evaluation, with significant prior knowledge of robotics and little experience with AR or MR, was unable to demonstrate any improvements. However, a steep learning curve was noted through self-performed experiments, resulting in faster success on all fronts after a short period of time. This should be taken up in further work.

It also turned out that Mixed Reality, in addition to being used with cobots, could also be a great advantage for larger industrial robots. Interaction with the robot through lead through is a great simplification for many, especially collaborative robots. However, this cannot be easily applied to larger industrial robots. With a mixed reality application like GoHolo, a bridge can be created here. In a short test on an ABB IRB 6700 (Fig. 7), it was determined how well the application can be applied to larger robots and the results show that the basic principle can also be scaled without any problems.

Fig. 7. GoHolo connected to an ABB IRB 6700

References

1. Zhong, R.Y., Xu, X., Klotz, E., Newman, S.T.: Intelligent manufacturing in the context of Industry 4.0: a review. Engineering **3**, 616–630 (2017)
2. Azuma, R.: A survey of augmented reality. Presence Teleop. Virtual Environ. **6**, 355–385 (1997)
3. Grieves, M.: Digital twin: manufacturing excellence through virtual factory replication (2014)
4. Gadre, S.Y., Rosen, E., Chien, G., Phillips, E., Tellex, S., Konidaris, G.: End-user robot programming using mixed reality. In: International Conference on Robotics and Automation (ICRA 2019), pp. 2707–2713 (2019)
5. Puljiz, D., Stöhr, E., Riesterer, K.S., Hein, B., Kröger, T.: Sensorless hand guidance using Microsoft Hololens. In: 2019 14th ACM/IEEE International Conference on Human-Robot Interaction (HRI), pp. 632–633 (2019)
6. Chacko, S.M., Armando, G., Vikram, K.: An augmented reality framework for robotic tool-path teaching. Procedia CIRP **93**, 1218–1223 (2020). 53rd CIRP Conference on Manufacturing Systems 2020
7. Stadler, S., Kain, K., Giuliani, M., Mirnig, N., Stollnberger, G., Tscheligi, M.: Augmented reality for industrial robot programmers: workload analysis for task-based, augmented reality-supported robot control. In: 2016 25th IEEE International Symposium on Robot and Human Interactive Communication (RO-MAN), pp. 179–184 (2016)

A Digital Twin Demonstrator for Research and Teaching in Universities

Mario Jungwirth[1]($\boxtimes$) (iD) and Wei-chen Lee[2] (iD)

[1] Research Group Smart Mechatronics Engineering, University of Applied Sciences Upper Austria, Wels Campus, Wels, Austria
mario.jungwirth@fh-wels.at

[2] Department of Mechanical Engineering, National Taiwan University of Science and Technology, Taipei, Taiwan, Republic of China
wclee@mail.ntust.edu.tw

Abstract. The importance of digitization in production and training was recognized and has found its way into many companies nowadays. Technologies such as IoT, rapid prototyping, and digital twins can be used to advantage in these fields. In order to show the numerous possibilities of such technologies, a digital twin demonstrator was built and extended to include virtual and augmented reality for control, data exchange, and data visualization. This demonstrator can be used for R&D topics as well as for teaching undergraduates and co-workers. A very flexible system configuration enables to adapt to many different tasks and can be easily reproduced. Future topics will be to exchange components, e.g., Python instead of MATLAB, alternatives to MQTT, etc., to increase the flexibility and check for the latency of the data connection via the internet. Research extended from the demonstrator is also presented in the paper to show how to use Node-RED installed Raspberry Pi to build an industrial IoT in a factory.

Keywords: Internet of Things · Rapid prototyping · Digital twin · Virtual reality · Augmented reality

1 System Configuration Digital Twin Demonstrator

As published in [1] a demonstrator was built in order to show the important characteristics of a digital twin on a simple system, which can be reproduced easily and cheaply. The physical system is a ducted fan driven by a DC motor with rotational speed, current, and temperature sensors connected to an Arduino, as shown in Fig. 1. Furthermore, a Programming Logic Controller (PLC) or microcomputer, e.g., a Raspberry Pi, could be used instead of an Arduino microcontroller. The digital twin is a virtual replica of the demonstrator incorporating data acquisition and processing, system modeling and control, condition monitoring, and a remaining useful life model, all built in MATLAB®. Digital twins can be used advantageously along the product development process in the design, build and operate phase as well as in production processes [2].

In this work, an extension of the digital-twin demonstrator using VR and AR technologies for human-machine-interaction and data visualization is presented. As shown

R. Moreno-Díaz et al. (Eds.): EUROCAST 2022, LNCS 13789, pp. 547–553, 2022.
https://doi.org/10.1007/978-3-031-25312-6_64

in Fig. 1, a CAD model of the real object is used within the AR-software tool Vuforia studio® to add effects animations (GIFs) for the rotational speed (RPM), current (Amp), and temperature (Temp) of the motor in real-time.

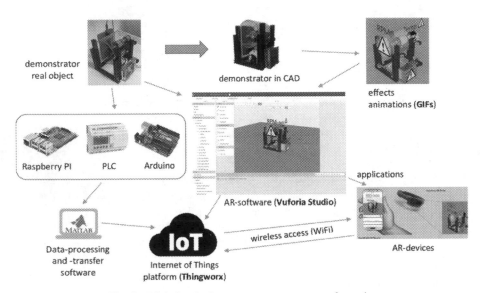

Fig. 1. Digital twin demonstrator - system configuration

The IoT platform Thingworx® is used as a data interface and IoT hub for the connected devices and the data-processing software.

2   Teaching Aspect by Using the Demonstrator

The demonstrator can be used for R&D as a very flexible system in retrofitting existing machines and production facilities, for small and medium enterprises (SMEs) who may not be the experts in this field, and for teaching low-skilled workers on new production systems as well.

Using the demonstrator for teaching students can be conducted in many different ways. What students learn from the simulation can be implemented in the real system for verification. In the meantime, the Internet of Things can be introduced through single-board computers such as Arduino or Raspberry Pi. For the Internet of Things software, in addition to using commercial Thingworx, we can also introduce students Node-RED, an open-source tool contributed by IBM. Node-Red can be installed on Raspberry Pi so that the Raspberry Pi becomes a lightweight IoT gateway. Students can learn how to communicate with OPC UA-based machine controllers or Modbus PLCs using Node-RED installed Raspberry Pi.

3   Research Aspect Extended from the Demonstrator

Suppose a factory wants to connect all the machines to a network to monitor the status of each machine. In that case, it most likely needs to rely on a commercial SCADA system. The small and medium-sized enterprises (SMEs) may not like this idea because it will increase the operation cost. The CNC controller manufacturers offer solutions for connecting to their devices. Annad et al. [3] used the Simatic Manager provided by Siemens to access the data of the Sinumerik 828D controller. Guo et al. [4] used VS2013 and the FOCAS library provided by FANUC to develop codes to collect the information on FANUC CNC machines. However, developing codes requires skilled programmers, which SMEs usually do not have.

Node-RED, an open-source software, has become a suitable development software to integrate machines in the factories of SMEs. Node-RED has built-in nodes of various communication protocols, which can save complicated programming. As a result, it has been used to build an industrial IoT architecture. For example, Newman et al. [5] selected the corresponding nodes of Node-RED to establish connections with different devices according to their communication protocols.

The objective of this extended research was to propose a technique to build an industrial IoT architecture in a factory based on Node-RED. The industrial IoT was used for communicating between the CNC controllers of Siemens and FANUC and the sensors through the PLC of Delta. We used Raspberry Pi 4 Model Bas the IoT gateway. The IoT system can allow us to monitor the controllers and sensors and present information such as the machining parameters and overall equipment efficiency (OEE) of each machine in a dashboard. In addition to accessing the data from the controllers and sensors, we also can upload the data and commands to the controllers to realize two-way communication.

The vertical five-axis milling CNC machine to be connected in this study was made by Dongtai Seiki, and its model number was CT-350. The controller installed on the machine is Sinumerik 840D sl, equipped with an OPC UA server inside. The data can be exchanged with the OPC UA communication protocol. This study will also connect the PLC device AH500 made by Delta. AH500 has RJ45 and RS485 communication ports and supports Modbus TCP communication protocol.

Node-RED is a powerful tool for building an IoT program. Its focus is to simplify the complexity of developing the program using a visual programming method, allowing developers to connect pre-defined nodes to build programs. Users can drag and drop nodes to create a flow. The program usually starts from the leftmost node of the flow and runs through the entire process to the right. Node-RED has nodes providing various communication protocols, such as OPC UA, Modbus, MQTT, etc.

In this study, the function of reading and writing Siemens controller information is established based on the OPC UA communication protocol. To establish the read/write function in the controller, we need to know which parameters the controller has captured. The parameter list can be found in the Siemens NC Variable Parameter Manual.

The structure of this research is illustrated in Fig. 2. We used communication protocols such as OPC UA and Modbus to connect with the equipment. The connected devices include a Siemens controller and a FANUC controller. In addition, the sensors and actuators without connection capability were connected to the IoT architecture using Delta PLC. The system uses Raspberry Pi as the IoT gateway and Node-RED software to integrate the data transmission of devices with different communication protocols, thereby completing applications such as data visualization, machine monitoring, and remote control of the machines.

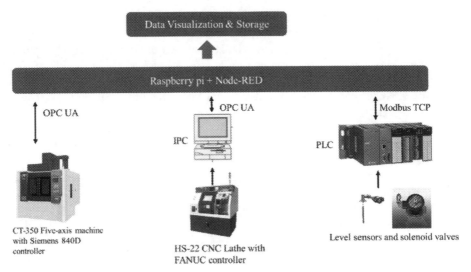

Fig. 2. The schematic illustrates the communication protocols and the connection for establishing the industrial IoT in the research.

The network connection architecture of this study is shown in Fig. 3. The five-axis milling machine, PLC and Raspberry Pi are connected to the network switch, while the lathe needs to be connected through an industrial PC connected to the switch. The Raspberry Pi system server controls all devices via the Ethernet connection.

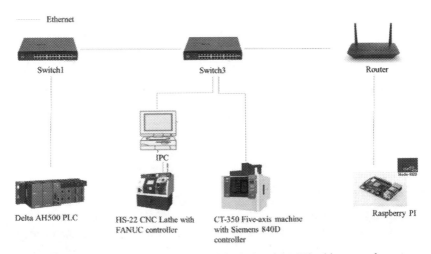

Fig. 3. The network connection of the industrial IoT in this research.

We would like to monitor the status of the connected machines remotely, so a dashboard for the machines was established. It includes machining data and other information. The machining data includes axis locations, tool information, feed rate, machining time, number of workpieces machined, program status, etc. We also developed the function so the operator can remotely upload the NC program, select the NC program to be executed, and start the operation.

This study uses the OPC UA protocol for communication with the CNC milling machine. The OPC UA has a server that can provide information to the client. The server installed in the CNC controller contains the information of the CNC machine in its nodes, and the NodeId of the node is required to know the data.

The machine data monitoring function is mainly established through the OPC UA client node in Node-RED. An example of the Node-RED program is shown in Fig. 4. The data flow is from left to right. There are three nodes in this program. The inject node is used to set up the NodeId for the OPC UA node to be read. Then the client node obtains the information from the server based on the received NodeId from the inject node. Finally, the dashboard node displays the information on the webpage.

Fig. 4. The Node-RED flow for accessing the data from the controller via OPC UA and displaying the data in a dashboard. (1): inject node; (2): node of OPC UA client; (3): dashboard node.

We also use Node-RED to connect Delta's AH500 PLC, a gateway for level sensors and solenoid valves. The level sensor was installed on the cutting fluid storage tank of the CNC machines, and the solenoid valve was installed on the water pipeline. When the cutting fluid is consumed to the set level, the solenoid valve will automatically open and make up enough cutting fluid. In this study, the PLC is connected to the Internet of Things architecture to monitor the fluid level. The communication protocol supported by the AH500 PLC is Modbus TCP. We used the Modbustcp node in Node-RED to establish the function of reading and writing PLC points. After the data is retrieved from the Modbustcp node, the data is processed separately. The Node-RED program for developing the function of the PLC AH500 is illustrated in Fig. 5.

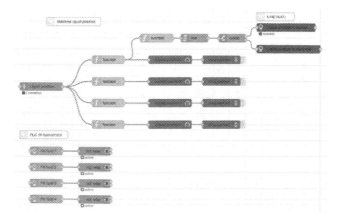

Fig. 5. The Node-RED program for developing the functions of the PLC AH500.

This research integrates different devices through the Raspberry Pi and Node-RED, captures the data, and makes it into a dashboard to display on the web page. The OPC UA Client node on Node-RED exchanges data with the machine controller to complete the real-time machine parameter monitoring, machine usage status, and remote operation functions. The dashboard displays the information about the machine, as shown in Fig. 6 [6]:

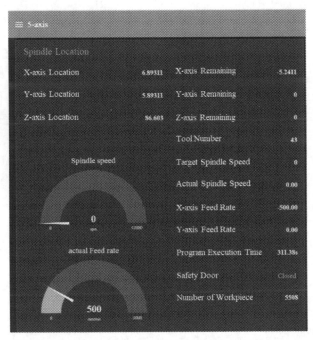

Fig. 6. The dashboard, created by using Node-RED, displays the machine parameters, such as the position of each axis, the spindle speed and the feed rate, etc.

(1) Machine parameters: This dashboard displays the position of each axis and the remaining distance from the target point. It also displays the machining information, including the target spindle speed, the actual spindle speed, the feed rate, the tool number, and the machining time.

(2) Program status: This dashboard displays the file name of the current NC program, the execution status, and the executing G-code. This dashboard also provides the remote operation function. The upload file name of the NC program can be input so that the file will be sent to the CNC machine. The three buttons in the middle can control the program execution. When the file upload is completed, pressing the start button can start the program execution. If an abnormality occurs, pressing the stop button can stop the machine. Pressing the reset button can allow the users to reselect the program to be executed.

4   Conclusive Remarks

In this paper, we described how to build a digital-twin demonstrator, which can be used as a teaching tool in universities. We also showed how to build an industrial IoT system integrating machines of different communication formats, using a low-cost Raspberry Pi as the IoT gateway and open-source Node-RED as the development software. Through the nodes provided by Node-RED, different machine controllers and sensors with various communication protocols were connected, and sensors without connection capability were connected using a PLC. All the captured information can be displayed through a dashboard on a webpage for easy access.

References

1. Jungwirth, M., Hehenberger, P., Merschak, S., Lee, W.C., Liao, C.Y.: Influence of digitization in mechatronics education programmes: a case study between Taiwan and Austria. In: 21st International Conference on Research and Education in Mechatronics, REM 2020, p. 7. Institute of Electrical and Electronics Engineers Inc. (2020)
2. Fuller, A., Fan, Z., Day, C., Barlow, C.: Digital twin: enabling technologies, challenges and open research. IEEE Access **8**, 108952–108971 (2020)
3. Anand, P., Philip, V.L., Eswaran, P.: Cost effective digitalization solution for Sinumerik CNC system to increase the transparency and utilization of the machine. Int. J. Recent Technol. Eng. **8**(2), 6–13 (2019)
4. Guo, Y., Sun, Y., Wu, K.: Research and development of monitoring system and data monitoring system and data acquisition of CNC machine tool in intelligent manufacturing. Int. J. Adv. Rob. Syst. **17**(2), 1–12 (2020)
5. Newman, D., Parto, M., Saleeby, K., Kurfess, T., Dugenske, A.: Development of a digital architecture for distributed CNC machine health monitoring. Smart Sustain. Manuf. Syst. **3**(2), 68–82 (2019)
6. Zeng, Y. J.: Design and Implementation of IIoT Using Node-RED. Master thesis, National Taiwan University of Science and Technology, Taipei, Taiwan (2022)

KI-Net: AI-Based Optimization in Industrial Manufacturing—A Project Overview

Bernhard Freudenthaler[1(✉)], Jorge Martinez-Gil[1], Anna Fensel[2], Kai Höfig[3], Stefan Huber[4], and Dirk Jacob[5]

[1] Software Competence Center Hagenberg GmbH, Softwarepark 32a, 4232 Hagenberg, Austria
{bernhard.freudenthaler,jorge.martinez-gil}@scch.at

[2] Department of Computer Science, Semantic Technology Institute (STI) Innsbruck, University of Innsbruck, Technikerstraße 21a, 6020 Innsbruck, Austria
anna.fensel@sti2.at

[3] Rosenheim Technical University of Applied Sciences, Hochschulstraße 1, 83024 Rosenheim, Germany
kai.hoefig@th-rosenheim.de

[4] Salzburg University of Applied Sciences, Urstein Süd 1, 5412 Puch/Salzburg, Austria
stefan.huber@fh-salzburg.ac.at

[5] University of Applied Sciences Kempten, Bahnhofstraße 61, 87435 Kempten, Germany
dirk.jacob@hs-kempten.de

Abstract. Artificial intelligence (AI) is a crucial technology of industrial digitalization. Especially in the production industry, a great potential is present in optimizing existing processes, e.g., concerning resource consumption, emission reduction, process and product quality improvements, predictive maintenance, and so on. Some of this potential is addressed by methods of industrial analytics beyond specific production technology. Furthermore, particular technological aspects in production systems address another part of this potential, e.g., mechatronics, robotics and motion control, automation systems, and so on. The problem is that the field of AI includes many research areas and methods, and many companies are losing the overview of the necessary and appropriate methods for solving the company problems. The reasons for this are, on the one hand, a lack of expertise in AI and, on the other hand, high complexity and risks of use for the companies (especially for SMEs). As a result, many potentials cannot yet be exploited. The KI-NET project aims to fill this gap, whereby a project overview is presented in this contribution.

Keywords: Artificial intelligence · Digital twin · Robotics · Systems engineering · Knowledge graphs · Manufacturing

R. Moreno-Díaz et al. (Eds.): EUROCAST 2022, LNCS 13789, pp. 554–561, 2022.
https://doi.org/10.1007/978-3-031-25312-6_65

1   Introduction

AI technologies bring significant advantages in analyzing complex data and supporting people in solving complex problems or relieving them of time-consuming and error-prone tasks. The strength of AI technologies lies in their ability to discover complex relationships, generalize, and independently extract information and policies from data without relying on explicit domain-specific knowledge.

Therefore, they are indispensable for evaluating data from a constantly growing number of sensors installed as part of the Internet of Things (IoT) and Industry 4.0, thus generating added value. At the same time, AI technologies can solve problems with a manageable number of algorithms and procedures, which cannot be solved with regular (i.e., requirements-driven) programming procedures.

Information and Communication Technologies (ICT) allow for more efficient and flexible industrial process design, leading to new products and expanding business areas and markets. AI is a critical technology for industrial digitalization with enormous potential for improving existing production processes, particularly in manufacturing and production. For example, AI can entirely automate the quality assurance of manufactured products, intelligently predict machine maintenance to save costly downtimes, and analyze complex data to optimize production processes and products.

However, digitalization is challenging for small and medium-sized enterprises (SMEs). It is widely assumed that the average level of digitalization among many SMEs in the manufacturing and production field can be notably improved. One significant problem is that AI frequently needs numerous other essential technologies (e.g., Big Data, Robotics, Digital Twins, and the Internet of Things). Often, finding the right expertise is far from a trivial task.

In the framework of the KI-NET project, a cross-border competence network has been formed as part of a project to explore, research, develop, and provide essential building blocks for AI-based optimization in industrial production. The goal was to help SMEs access targeted AI applications in production and maintenance processes. This paper is intended to give an overview of AI's applicability in manufacturing and production. The final goal is to help companies, especially SMEs, leverage the Industry 4.0 concept to bring breakthroughs in this context.

Therefore, the main contributions of this work can be summarized as follows:

- We introduce the KI-NET project that aimed to bring best practices in AI to the SMEs in the manufacturing and production sector.
- We show the results we obtained during the project's execution around prototypical solutions for systems engineering processes, digital twins and robotics, knowledge representation, and knowledge graphs.

The rest of this paper is structured as follows: Sect. 2 presents the state-of-the-art in digitalization of SMEs in the field of manufacturing and production. Section 3 presents the project objectives. Section 4 reports the main results derived from the KI-NET project. Furthermore finally, we end with conclusions and lessons that can be learned from this research project.

2   Related Works

Industry 4.0 is a term that expresses the fourth industrial revolution. This revolution brings an essential new aspect of the adaptive, dynamic, flexible individual manufacturing and production processes and its intelligent control based on an appropriate combination of data-driven and knowledge-driven technologies. This way, it is possible to use a transparent availability of a large amount of data, right down to the individual sensor on the machines. With the transition to Industry 4.0, a whole range of topics arises that are new aspects in this application area, such as AI, or that have been given a new status, such as security.

Furthermore, AI is a collective term for various subfields that pursue emulating human-like abilities (image recognition, language interaction, strategy development, situation assessments, etc.) in an algorithmic or information-processing manner. In other words, it aims to at least imitate the cognitive abilities of a human being to a certain extent. Many methods and techniques have great applicability in this context. For example, industrial maintenance [5], root cause analysis [8], optimization [4], time-series analysis [7], and so on.

It is important to note that the networking of heterogeneous objects, such as machines, sensors, actuators, and simulated components, has given rise to collective terms such as (Industrial) Internet of Things in the context of Industry 4.0. Other methods require a physical intervention of computing processes in industrial systems and thus form cyber-physical systems (CPS). Edge devices make it possible to connect individual hardware components and entire factories across geographical borders and outsource data, computing power, and user software to the cloud. The need for this global networking has led to the development of communication standards such as OPC Unified Architecture (OPC UA) and Time-Sensitive Networking (TSN), which enable secure, real-time, platform-independent, and manufacturer-independent data exchange. These basic technologies are being developed or further developed in the context of Industry 4.0 and are a prerequisite for using AI in the industrial environment.

Resource-rich organizations can afford to invest in tailor-made solutions to address some of their challenges. However, there is a clear gap in addressing this issue from a SMEs perspective. By the nature of their business, organizations cannot invest large sums in building solutions that meet their needs.

3   Project Objectives

The KI-Net aimed to bundle the main scientific and technological competencies of AI-based production and maintenance through the partners. The KI-Net project developed a cross-border competence network that explored, researched, and developed fundamental methods for AI-based optimizations in industrial manufacturing. This was intended to facilitate access for companies, especially SMEs, to the targeted use of AI in production and maintenance processes. The project aimed to identify which AI methods were the most suitable for industrial manufacturing tasks. The AI methods included, in particular:

- Systems engineering processes
- Digital twins and robotics
- Data analysis, optimization, and learning techniques
- Knowledge representation and knowledge graphs

The project partners pooled the necessary know-how to be the primary contact for industry, SMEs, and other institutions on this topic. Thus, the public can obtain information and knowledge from a single competence network and access the project partners' abilities.

4   Results

AI is a technology that will permanently change the field of production and maintenance. The presented use cases show the broad spectrum of possibilities for AI-based solutions. In order to develop and deploy AI methods, several requirements must be met. Development processes have to be adapted and extended to support data-driven development. At the same time, existing production facilities must be expanded to enable the development of solutions and integrate AI components into existing production facilities.

The cross-border approach has paved the way for a new research and innovation partnership in the program area (Interreg Austria-Bavaria)and the cooperation between science and industry in the field of AI-based production and maintenance, in line with regional strategies as well as the objective of the coordinated plan for artificial intelligence of the European Commission.

Individual use cases were explored, developed, and prepared in a suitable form for the public. These best-practice examples have been summarized as an application guideline for AI methods in industrial manufacturing and presented to the public at several knowledge transfer events. Furthermore, the results were made available online[1], and the developed knowledge was also integrated into the qualification modules of the project partners.

4.1   Systems Engineering Processes

A process for requirements analysis for AI algorithms has been developed to meet the typical qualitative properties such as precise formulation, quantifiability, allocability, traceability, and freedom from consistency. Furthermore, suitable quality assurance measures have been identified to demonstrate the reliability of AI algorithms specifically for the quality requirements of industrial manufacturing. The identified quality assurance measures have been investigated for their applicability in industrial manufacturing and combined to include quality requirements through a stepwise sample generation approach [2].

The rationale behind this approach is that AI algorithms are frequently used not only as pure software functions but are integrated into systems, such as image recognition methods. Therefore, the domain of systems engineering deals

---

[1] https://ki-net.eu/.

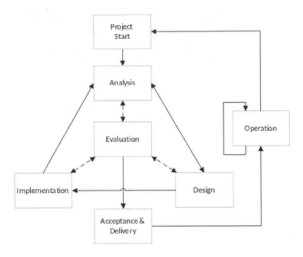

Fig. 1. Workflow example for user support that needs to implement AI in a software system

with integrating subsystems into an overall system. Here, many development mechanisms are based on requirements too. Therefore, suitable tools for system integration into industrial manufacturing processes have been evaluated. A holistic development process for AI-based processes in industrial manufacturing emerges from these activities, which have been made available to companies. Figure 1 shows an overview of this holistic development process.

4.2 Digital Twins and Robotics

This activity aimed to research and develop a software prototype for using digital twins and robotics in industrial manufacturing. Many methods of optimization and AI cannot work in a real operational environment (robot, machine, line, factory). The reason is that iterative search procedures repeatedly perform test runs, or a sufficient diversity of learning data cannot be achieved on a few real machines. In this activity, digital twins - i.e., digital surrogates - are to be developed for facilities, on the one hand, represent the real counterpart as good as possible and, on the other hand, are not subject to various limitations of the real counterparts, such as multiplicity and diversity, costs, space, energy, or simply physical real-time.

AI methods play a role in this activity on two levels: On the one hand, they serve for the modeling of the digital twins, and secondly, AI methods can be applied to the resulting digital twins themselves, such as the resulting digital twins themselves, e.g., the optimization of production steps (e.g., path and trajectory planning of robotics [6]) or the (sensor data-driven) prediction of production quality and maintenance indicators [9]. Figure 2 shows an overview of the prototype for Digital Twin that has been worked on.

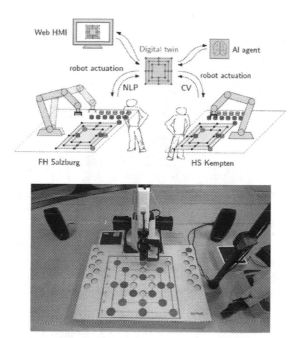

Fig. 2. Overview of the implemented prototype allowing bi-directional communication between Kempten and Salzburg

4.3   Knowledge Representation and Knowledge Graphs

The use of knowledge graphs (KGs) remains unexplored in the industrial domain [3]. However, this does not mean there are no knowledge-intensive approaches to address the problem. There are already strategies that make intensive use of structured information to perform several essential processes [1]. In these approaches, knowledge is usually provided by domain experts who have extensive experience in risk analysis. This approach defines all possible failures and their observable effects on the system. Among several strategies following this approach, the Failure Mode and Effects Analysis (FMEA) and Fault Tree Analysis (FTA) propose templates to collect this information.

In order to reduce production errors and increase overall quality, these processes must be analyzed in detail and improved. In order to illustrate how production errors can be minimized, a KG is developed. Firstly, a Bayesian Network (BN) maps the processes of a production line and uncovers complex dependencies. Bayesian structure learning automatically learns relationships by gathering data. To keep the workload for SMEs as low as possible, automated learning from data is essential. Figure 3 shows an example of a KG generated from the sensors of an assembly line.

In order to access a comprehensive and accurate analysis of complex systems, BNs are a data-driven technique that is widely used due to their flexible structure in the scope of uncertain knowledge representation and reasoning. Since

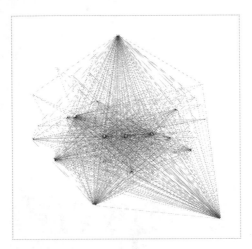

Fig. 3. Example of the kowledge graph generated to facilitate the interpretation of sensors on an assembly lines

structure learning for BNs is not easily interpretable, they cannot be sufficiently informative about dependencies between the variables. Thus, KGs enrich semantic interoperability and exchange information between humans or machines.

5   Conclusions

AI is a crucial technology for Industry 4.0. In fact, several AI-based solutions are already being used productively in production and maintenance. The number of use cases that can be solved with AI will increase continuously due to the rapid further development of AI methods and permanently changing system landscapes. The use cases presented in this paper demonstrate the broad spectrum of possibilities for AI-based solutions. In order to develop and deploy them, several requirements must be met. It is necessary to adapt and extend development processes to support data-driven development. At the same time, existing production facilities must be expanded to enable the development of solutions and integrate AI components into existing production facilities.

Within the INTERREG Austria-Bavaria 2014–2020, the KI-Net project has established a new research and innovation partnership in the program area that has been leveraged. Furthermore, the cooperation between science and industry in AI-based production and maintenance, according to the regional strategies and the objective of the coordinated plan for artificial intelligence of the European Commission, has been intensified. The project results are presented https://ki-net.eu/.

Acknowledgements. The research reported in this paper has been funded by the European Interreg Austria-Bavaria project "KI-Net (AB292)". It has also been partly funded by BMK, BMDW, and the State of Upper Austria in the frame of the COMET Program managed by FFG.

References

1. Alam, M., Fensel, A., Martinez-Gil, J., Moser, B., Recupero, D.R., Sack, H.: Special issue on machine learning and knowledge graphs. Future Gener. Comput. Syst. **129**, 50–53 (2022)

2. Bayeff-Filloff, F., Stecher, D., Höfig, K.: Stepwise sample generation. In: Proceedings of the 18th International Confernce on Computer Aided Syposium Theory (EUROCAST 2022), Las Palmas de Gran Canaria, Spain (2022)

3. Buchgeher, G., Gabauer, D., Martinez-Gil, J., Ehrlinger, L.: Knowledge graphs in manufacturing and production: a systematic literature review. IEEE Access **9**, 55537–55554 (2021)

4. Huber, S., Waclawek, H.: C^k-continuous spline approximation with tensorflow gradient descent optimizers. In: Proceedings 18th International Confernce on Comp. Aided Sys. Theory (EUROCAST 2022), Las Palmas de Gran Canaria, Spain (2022)

5. Kainzner, M., Klösch, C., Filipiak, D., Chhetri, T.R., Fensel, A., Martinez-Gil, J.: Towards reusable ontology alignment for manufacturing maintenance. In: Tiddi, I., Maleshkova, M., Pellegrini, T., de Boer, V., (eds.) Joint Proceedings of the Semantics co-located events: Poster& Demo track and Workshop on Ontology-Driven Conceptual Modelling of Digital Twins co-located with Semantics 2021, Amsterdam and Online, September 6–9, 2021, volume 2941 of CEUR Workshop Proceedings. CEUR-WS.org (2021)

6. Lehenauer, M., Wintersteller, S., Uray, M., Huber, S.: Improvements for mlrose applied to the traveling salesman problem. In: Proceedings of the 18th International Conference on Computer Aided System Theory (EUROCAST 2022), Las Palmas de Gran Canaria, Spain (2022)

7. Mahmoud, S., Martinez-Gil, J., Praher, P., Freudenthaler, B., Girkinger, A.: Deep learning rule for efficient changepoint detection in the presence of non-linear trends. In: Kotsis, G., et al. (eds.) DEXA 2021. CCIS, vol. 1479, pp. 184–191. Springer, Cham (2021). https://doi.org/10.1007/978-3-030-87101-7_18

8. Martinez-Gil, J., Buchgeher, G., Gabauer, D., Freudenthaler, B., Filipiak, D., Fensel, A.: Root cause analysis in the industrial domain using knowledge graphs: A case study on power transformers. In: Longo, F., Affenzeller, M., Padovano, A. (eds.) Proceedings of the 3rd International Conference on Industry 4.0 and Smart Manufacturing (ISM 2022), Virtual Event/Upper Austria University of Applied Sciences - Hagenberg Campus - Linz, Austria, 17–19 November 2021, volume 200 of Procedia Computer Science, pp. 944–953. Elsevier (2021)

9. Schäfer, G., Kozlica, R., Wegenkittl, S., Huber, S.: An architecture for deploying reinforcement learning in industrial environments. In: Proceedings of the 18th International Conference on Computer Aided System Theory (EUROCAST 2022), Las Palmas de Gran Canaria, Spain, Feb (2022)

Robot System as a Testbed for AI Optimizations

Marco Ullrich[✉], Christoph Saad, and Dirk Jacob

Kempten University of Applied Sciences, Bahnhofstraße 61, 87435 Kempten, Germany
{marco.ullrich,dirk.jacob}@hs-kempten.de,
christoph.saad@stud.hs-kempten.de

Abstract. As a part of the overarching project KI-Net, a robot cell is developed, which will act as a testbed for different software prototypes and AI-implementations. The application offers different interfaces to further instances and thus forms a modularity to the outside.

Keywords: Artificial intelligence · Reinforcement learning · Digital twin · Robotics

1 Introduction

As a part of the overarching project KI-Net, a demonstrator including two robot cells is developed, which will act as a testbed for different software prototypes (see Fig. 1). The robot cell of Kempten University of Applied Science forms the focus of this paper. The board game "Nine men's morris" serves as an application, which can be implemented with simple pick-and-place movements of the robot. This application offers different interfaces to further instances and thus forms a modularity to the outside. The two robot cells are geographically independent of each other. In such an interdisciplinary system, the platform-independent and service-oriented communication architecture OPC UA[1] [1] is used. The data, sent by the individual systems via OPC UA, are abstracted. Instead of robot axis positions, game field names of the new field positions are transmitted. This enables an addition of n robot cells. The demonstrator's general structure can be adapted to industrial plant settings, which are geographically independent.

The setup allows different game modes: human vs human, human vs AI, or AI vs AI. One way that moves can be made is by hand, in which case vision systems capture the progression of the game. By means of a web interface, a move can be made via a GUI, with the current state of play also displayed on the interface. Besides these real and digital means of making a move, a HoloLens 2 can also be used to move pieces in the sphere of mixed reality. In the second robotic system, which is located at the project consortium partner's site in Salzburg, the application can also be executed using natural language processing (NLP).

---

[1] Open Plattform Communications Unified Architecture.

© The Author(s), under exclusive license to Springer Nature Switzerland AG 2022
R. Moreno-Díaz et al. (Eds.): EUROCAST 2022, LNCS 13789, pp. 562–568, 2022.
https://doi.org/10.1007/978-3-031-25312-6_66

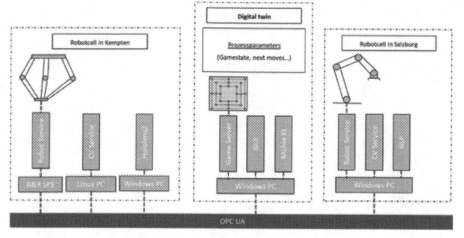

Fig. 1. Systematic structure of the whole demonstrator

2 Testbed's Hardware and Software Implementation

2.1 Robot Design

The design of the robot cell is based on the Plot-Bot-Project. [2] This offers a modular construction system, which enables educational institutions to develop a low-cost, but industrially suitable robot system. The hardware of the robot consists mostly of 3D-printed parts and is controlled by an industrial PLC by B&R Industrial Automation GmbH. The modular structure of the industrial controller's development environment allows the control parameters to be adapted to individual robot configurations. While in standard Plot-Bot configurations the actuation is realized with inexpensive stepper motors, servo motors are installed in this project so as to offer the opportunity for AI-based optimization of control parameters.

This robot is a parallel kinematic unit in the form of a delta kinematic system, with the special feature that the three drives do not move with the robot arms. This makes for a simple kinematic structure that can be operated at high speeds. The assembly plate is always parallel to the table top. The robot has three degrees of freedom and can be extended at will to include a rotation around "Z" on the table top.

2.2 Robot Trajectory

The robot's track is that travelled by the TCP[2] of the delta kinematic system between at least two points in its workspace. This track consists of Cartesian start and end coordinates, together with many interpolated intermediate points, the position of which is generally defined by the form of movement, such as linear (LIN) or point to point (PTP). If information about acceleration and speed is added to these individual points on the track, this is called the robot trajectory.

---

[2] The tool center point (TCP) is the point used for positioning the robot in any given robotic program. The TCP is defined as a transformation of the robot flange.

The form of movement in this application is pick and place. Basically, an object is picked up from its starting position and then placed at its target position. The complexity of this process can be determined individually in industry. In this robot cell, five different points are covered by the TCP (see Fig. 2). The first point is a waiting position. The robot then moves to position 2 (pre-pick position) before proceeding at a controlled speed to position 3 (pick position) and grasping the object. After that, the robot lifts the object and returns to position 2. The TCP subsequently moves on to position 4 (pre-place position) before depositing the object at position 5 (place position). The robot then goes back with its TCP to position 4 before either picking the next object or returning to the waiting position (pos. 1).

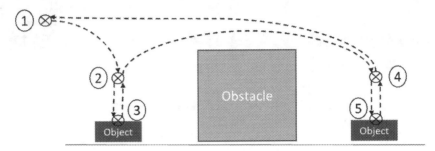

Fig. 2. Pick-and-place move with an obstacle

The robot trajectory described above is usually hard-coded. During the course of this project, a solution is sought to design the entire system as a kind of black box. The coordinates of the starting point (position 3) and the destination (position 5) are fixed. An intelligent system is supposed to generate the robot trajectory in between autonomously, avoiding any collisions with obstacles or between robots.

To generate an optimal trajectory for the pick-and-place motion of the robot, an off-policy reinforcement learning (RL) agent was developed. RL is a subset field of machine learning (ML) that aims to learn through interaction with an environment and a reward per episode.

Since the digital twin was not yet ready, a simple kinematic and dynamic mathematical model was developed and used as the training environment. The current state of the environment was described as a flat vector with the current and target positions and velocity for the TCP in all three dimensions. The environment could be also initialized with obstacle or collision zones that should be avoided. The robot will be controlled using the normalized acceleration values for each of the actuators. These are passed to the environment at each step as an action vector.

To implement the RL agent, the "brain" of the robot, the TensorFlow Agent library [3] was used. An actor-critic (AC) method was used for the learning algorithm. The actor network provides an action based on the current observation of the state of the environment. The critic estimates an error, which is used to calculate the loss and update the network's weights, using the environment observation state as well as the reward. The graphic in Fig. 3 illustrates how the AC algorithm generally works. Two algorithms were tested overall: Deep Deterministic Policy Gradient (DDPG) and Twin Delayed

DDPG (TD3). Each requires two artificial neural networks: one for the actor and one for the critic.

To quantify the progress of the robot and to enable the agent to learn, a reward-cost function must be defined to describe and lead the robot toward the goal and away from obstacles and unreachable poses. A few dozen experiments were run, with different simulation step sizes, reward-cost functions, and training algorithms. Each experiment was conducted with several sets of hypermeters for the neural networks. Each of the runs trained anywhere between several hundred to several hundred thousand episodes.

Due to changing reward-cost functions, the results of the experiments could not be directly compared with one another using only reward values. Therefore, the Euclidian distance to the goal position at the end of the episode as well as any collisions and whether the TCP left the working space was logged. An animation of the robot and the trajectory was also rendered at regular intervals.

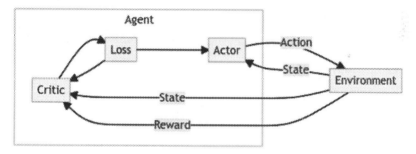

Fig. 3. Diagram of the working of an actor-critic reinforcement learning agent

While some of the agents did show a few promising results, none had a consistent and reliable result. It seemed as if the results depended more on the initial weights of the neural networks and the start-target position pairs rather than actual learning by the agents. This could be due to the inaccuracy of the simulation, the design of the architecture of the neural network, and/or the limited computing time and power available. For further experimentations, the use of a different simulation model for the environment, ideally with hardware acceleration for faster learning, is advised.

With this approach, only a static environment can be used and must be retrained for every change in obstacle or collision zone. This could be fixed by using additional sensors, such as proximity sensors or cameras that can sense or see these obstacles in all directions and actively avoid them. Additionally, the robot model uses a fixed load mass. This means that a new agent must be trained every time a new load is used. However, depending on how robust the agent ends up being, the same agent could still be used with small changes. In our case, the load change is so minimal that this should not be a problem.

With the current reward-cost function, only the time factor was optimized. For future developments, a factor could be added that takes the power consumption into account, which would allow a better balance, power consumption and pick-and-place cycle time.

Furthermore, before testing the agent on real hardware, a few additional points should be considered. Currently, it is assumed that the dictated actions can and will be achieved with no delays. This assumption cannot be made on real hardware. After finding good parameters and network architectures for the agent, delays as well as a small element of randomness can be added to the simulation to make the agent more robust and transferrable to real hardware.

2.3   Digital Twin

Different digital representations with individual characteristics serve in the project as simulation models, which interact in interrelations, even in real time with the real world. In this project, the use of digital representatives relates to the definition by Kritzinger et al. [4].

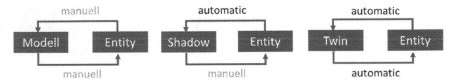

Fig. 4. Difference between a digital model, digital shadow and digital twin [4]

A distinction is made between three different systems, based on the way in which data flows between the real entity and the digital representation (see Fig. 4). If this is performed manually in both directions, this is known as a digital model. If the data flows automatically from the real entity to the digital representation, this is called a digital shadow. If the process occurs automatically in both directions, this is referred to as a digital twin [4].

The kinematic model used for the model-based RL agent described above is a model written with Python. It includes the direct and inverse kinematics as well as hardware restrictions due to e.g. bearings. A digital shadow with the Industrial Physics software serves as a monitoring model and will later substitute the self-developed kinematic model as a digital twin. Additionally, it offers possibilities as the interaction between the robot system and a HoloLens 2. Furthermore, the digital twin will be used as a hardware-in-the-loop (HIL) setup in further issues.

2.4   AI-Based Vision System

In order to record the ongoing process (in this case the state of play), a camera from the company IDS Imaging Development System GmbH was used. IDS describes this camera as a compact embedded-vision platform for industrial applications. Its integrated "deep ocean core" makes it possible to perform image processing tasks directly at the source of imaging, without the need for a PC. The camera is configured using IDS NXT Cockpit software [5].

Two systems with artificial neuronal networks were tested for processing the images – a detector and a classifier. As the classifier proved more stable (100%), this was the chosen option. The algorithm can be trained online using a vision app in the browser-based IDS

NXT Lighthouse cloud software and then uploaded into the camera. Fixed regions of interest (ROIs) are defined for the classifier. In addition, training images of the objects, or play pieces, are detected that might be found within the ROIs. The final algorithm can now also be used offline on the camera. Thanks to the OPC UA plugin, the camera can also directly host its own OPC UA server on board.

2.5 Human-Machine Interface (HMI) via HoloLens 2

The various advantages presented by a real system, such as a plant in industry, for example, for virtual modelling generate possibilities for accessing the spectrum of reality and virtuality. The intuitive and visual difference between human and machine communications in humans accessing the machine could be reduced by merging the real world with the virtual world. This would increase the machine's intuition in implementing human commands. Microsoft's HoloLens 2, supported by a natural user interface, offers an interactive means of presenting 3D projections in the immediate surroundings. Microsoft defines the work area of the goggles as mixed reality – a combination of augmented reality and augmented virtuality, so to speak [6].

With regard to the current state of technology, in comparison with monitoring, presentation and service, directly controlling mechatronic systems is a relatively small field. This project concerns a robot cell in the form of a delta kinematics system performing a simple pick-and-place movement. The robot demonstrates the process by playing the board game "Nine men's morris". A change in the state of play can be entered and performed conventionally "by hand" using a mouse and a keyboard. This human-machine interface is substituted by a HoloLens 2.

The project is divided into individual stages and implemented using Unity software. Among other things, a 3D model of the application is required – in our case, the game of "Nine men's morris". The playing field is modeled as a digital twin using Blender software, which is directly compatible with Unity. In addition, a rudimentary GUI is generated in the Hololens 2 with individual buttons and their logic. In order to be able to select individual playing fields, additional individual buttons must be generated over the model of the playing field, which exists purely as a hologram, and these must be selectable separately.

The generation and design of the virtual game board in the spatial real environment should function using a real-life QR code. One of the main points is communication and synchronization of the states of play with the main control, or the robot control. This is achieved using the OPC UA communication standard. The HoloLens 2 and the system network are connected via a separate modem supplying a Wi-Fi network.

3   Conclusion

The resulting testbed, consisting of the modular robot system, can be expanded as required. Further research should investigate the validity and extendibility of the model-based trajectory planning RL agent. Additionally, the testbed offers project opportunities for students and for follow-up research projects. On the one hand, the model-based RL agent could optimize the trajectory of the robot for energy efficiency implemented with a digital twin; on the other, a similar AI model could be used for servo-controller parameters, e.g. to improve jerk reactions.

Acknowledgement. The research reported in this paper was funded by the European Interreg Austria-Bavaria project "KI-Net (AB292)".

References

1. International Electrotechnical Commission: OPC Unified Architecture – Part 1: Overview and concepts. Standard IEC TR 62541–1:2020, International Electrotechnical Commission, Geneva, CH (2020). https://webstore.iec.ch/publication/61109
2. Jacob, D., Haberstroh, P., Neidhardt, D., Timmermann, B.: Modular 3D-printed robots for education and training for industrie 4.0. In: Moreno-Díaz, R., Pichler, F., Quesada-Arencibia, A. (eds.) EUROCAST 2017. LNCS, vol. 10671, pp. 214–219. Springer, Cham (2018). https://doi.org/10.1007/978-3-319-74718-7_26
3. Guadarrama, S.; et al.: TensorFlow: TF-Agents: a library for reinforcement learning in TensorFlow. https://github.com/tensorflow/agents (2018). Accessed 10 Nov 2021
4. Kritzinger, W., Karner, M., Traar, G., Henjes, J., Sihn, W.: Digital twin in manufacturing: a categorical literature review and classification. IFAC-PapersOnLine **51**(11), 1016–1022 (2018)
5. IDS Imaging Development Systems GmbH: IDS NXT. REDEFINING INDUSTRIAL CAMERAS. https://en.ids-imaging.com/ids-nxt.html (2022). Accessed 17 June 2022
6. Azuma, R.: A survey of augmented reality. Presence: Teleop. Virt. Environ. **6**, 355–385 (1997)

An Architecture for Deploying Reinforcement Learning in Industrial Environments

Georg Schäfer[⊠], Reuf Kozlica, Stefan Wegenkittl, and Stefan Huber

Salzburg University of Applied Sciences, Salzburg, Austria
{georg.schaefer,reuf.kozlica,stefan.wegenkittl,
stefan.huber}@fh-salzburg.ac.at

Abstract. Industry 4.0 is driven by demands like shorter time-to-market, mass customization of products, and batch size one production. Reinforcement Learning (RL), a machine learning paradigm shown to possess a great potential in improving and surpassing human level performance in numerous complex tasks, allows coping with the mentioned demands. In this paper, we present an OPC UA based Operational Technology (OT)-aware RL architecture, which extends the standard RL setting, combining it with the setting of digital twins. Moreover, we define an OPC UA information model allowing for a generalized plug-and-play like approach for exchanging the RL agent used. In conclusion, we demonstrate and evaluate the architecture, by creating a proof of concept. By means of solving a toy example, we show that this architecture can be used to determine the optimal policy using a real control system.

Keywords: Reinforcement learning · Industrial control system · Cyber physical system · OPC UA · Digital twin · Hardware-in-the-loop simulation

1 Motivation

In addition to supervised and unsupervised learning, RL represents a third large machine learning paradigm. In contrast to supervised and unsupervised learning, particular skills and knowledge are gained by an agent through an extensive trial and error process. Since it showed a potential of surpassing human level performance in various complex tasks [7], and without the need of pre-generated data in advance, RL is suited for applications in an industrial environment.

Through interaction with an environment, an agent can identify an optimal policy to autonomously execute complex control tasks [3]. Depending on the reward definition, productivity can be maximized, thereby lowering the cost

Georg Schäfer and Stefan Huber are supported by the European Interreg Österreich-Bayern project AB292 KI-Net and the Christian Doppler Research Association (JRC ISIA). Reuf Kozlica is supported by the Lab for Intelligent Data Analytics Salzburg (IDA Lab) funded by Land Salzburg (WISS 2025) under project number 20102-F1901166-KZP.

R. Moreno-Díaz et al. (Eds.): EUROCAST 2022, LNCS 13789, pp. 569–576, 2022.
https://doi.org/10.1007/978-3-031-25312-6_67

factor of the production. A RL agent is able to generate new data through exploration of its environment, helping to cope with lack of data typical for OT environments. Additionally, the agent is exploiting its environment, thus leading to early detection of unexpected behavior in simulations. This knowledge can be used to implement more realistic digital representations of the environment [3], supporting the creation of an industrial plant through different stages of its life cycle. Moreover, it has been shown to possess great potential for process optimization in Industrial Control Systems (ICS), allowing to cope with demands coming along with Industry 4.0, including: shorter time-to-market, mass customization of products, and batch size one production, cf. [7].

Although RL is a promising machine learning paradigm, there are still quite a few challenges to be overcome. One of those challenges is the deployment and integration of RL models into OT.

2   Introduction to Reinforcement Learning

RL aims to imitate the natural human learning behavior, especially in the early stage of human life, where exploration plays an important role. Thus, it is a computational approach to learning from interaction [10].

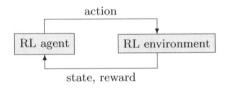

Fig. 1. Standard reinforcement learning setup.

The common RL setting is shown in Fig. 1. Its two main building blocks are the agent and the environment. The agent is in a specific state $s \in \mathcal{S}$ and can perform actions $a \in \mathcal{A}$, where each of those may be members of either discrete or continuous sets and can be multidimensional [3]. The action a performed by the agent is changing the state of the environment, and is being evaluated by the environment. For every step, the environment is sending the evaluation results in the form of a single scalar value, reward $\mathcal{R}$, to the agent. The goal of the agent is to maximize the accumulated reward over the long run. During the interaction with the environment, the agent is aiming to find a policy π, mapping states to actions, that maximizes the overall return [2]. The policy may be either deterministic or probabilistic. In the case of a deterministic policy, the same action is always used for a given state $a = \pi(s)$, whereas the probabilistic policy maps a distribution over actions when in a specific state $a \sim \pi(s, a)$ [10].

3   Challenges

Integration of RL algorithms into OT proves to be non-trivial, since there are some OT specific characteristics which do not fit into the regular RL setting. In our paper, we propose an OT-aware RL architecture that specifically addresses the following OT characteristics:

1. **Geographical distribution:** OT systems are often located across different sites, sometimes even in remote locations, where a visit is made difficult due to travel restrictions or inhospitable site conditions. Thus, OT systems are often geographically broadly dispersed. This fact impairs the regular RL setting, where the agent typically interacts with local environments.
2. **Platform independence:** OT systems are of a heterogeneous nature, many of them using proprietary technology, concerning hardware platform, operating system, or network protocols. On such systems, state of the art machine learning algorithms including RL models are hard to be integrated. This makes the integration of a RL agent into OT systems built by different manufacturers difficult.

Besides the above-mentioned OT-specific characteristics which impair the typical RL setting, we also consider the following requirements for the sake of general applicability of the architecture. This way, our architecture also addresses the needs of a framework for:

3. **RL agent agnosticism:** Being able to rely on generally available RL agent implementations[1] is important to reduce development effort. Therefore, the proposed architecture enables a plug-and-play like usage of different RL agents through definition of an OPC UA information model in Sect. 4.1.
4. **Digital representation:** A major challenge when working with RL algorithms is the sample inefficiency: an enormous amount of interaction data is required, which makes training expensive [6]. Moreover, this can result in unbearable cost for real-world applications. Our architecture addresses this issue through enabling the usage of digital representations in the initial training of the RL agent and seamless transition to the real system. This can lead to a significant reduction of overall training time and help to cope with real-time constraints of real control systems and the lack of real-world samples [3].

4   Proposed Architecture

Facing the requirements defined in Sect. 3, we propose an OT-aware OPC UA-based architecture. Figure 2 gives a simplified overview. Essentially, the standard RL setting [10] is extended by "OPC UA nodes". The nodes can be aggregated using n OPC UA servers, each of them described as a finite set $\mathcal{O}_i$, containing all nodes of a specific server, where $\mathcal{O} = \mathcal{O}_1 \times \mathcal{O}_2 \times ... \times \mathcal{O}_n$. In a certain sense, we combine the RL setting presented in Sect. 2 with that of digital twins as defined by [4].

With OPC UA, the communication can either occur via an optimized binary TCP protocol or using firewall-friendly Web Services by standards like SOAP

---

[1] E.g., https://www.tensorflow.org/agents.

and HTTP [5], fulfilling requirement 1. Regardless of the manufacturer, every TCP/IP enabled OT platform can implement OPC UA, hence meeting the 2nd requirement. OPC UA supports not only real hardware but also different types of simulations, thus allowing the architecture to fulfill requirement 4.

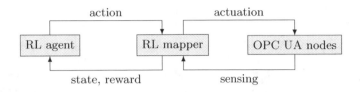

Fig. 2. Interaction between a RL agent and OPC UA nodes using a RL environment.

The RL action and state space is in a relationship with the OPC UA address space, and the corresponding translation is performed by the RL mapper. In particular, each agent's action $a \in \mathcal{A}$ is turned into an OPC UA call[2] using the function f in (1). This function sets the corresponding actuators using the OPC UA client-server model.

$$f : \mathcal{A} \to \mathcal{O} \tag{1}$$

Vice versa, the environment is notified using the OPC UA PubSub [8] on each sensor change, mapping OPC UA sensor nodes to states using the function g:

$$g : \mathcal{O} \to \mathcal{S} \tag{2}$$

After each sensor change, a reward evaluation is triggered and a state space transition occurs, which is forwarded to the agent. By preserving the standard RL setting, the agent can easily be substituted, fulfilling requirement 3.

4.1   Mapping Automation Using OPC UA Information Modelling

OPC UA is not only used for data transport, but also for information modelling. The information model defines the address space of an OPC UA server, which is used to navigate through the OPC UA nodes, providing information about the available data [9]. Throughout this section, we will use technical terms of the information modelling mechanisms of OPC UA as introduced by [5].

By creating custom *ObjectTypes* for nodes which should be accessible for the RL agent, the mapping from (1) and (2) can be automated. Therefore, multiple custom *ObjectTypes*, like *IntObservation, DoubleObservation, IntAction* and *DoubleAction*, have been created. These *ObjectTypes* require three variables with a corresponding *DataType* (e.g. *Int32* and *Double*):

---

[2] In this context an OPC UA call is a procedure call, which may contain a series of computational steps to be carried out.

1. **min**: The smallest possible value that can be assigned to a node, including the value specified.
2. **max**: The largest possible value that can be assigned to a node, including the value specified.
3. **step**: The step-size of the value, allowing a discretization.

By using a *HasProperty* reference, existing nodes having a *BaseDataVariable-Type* as *TypeDefinition*, e.g. variables, can be extended to automatically provide the RL agent with the required information, answering the following questions:

- Is the node relevant for the RL setting?
- Is the node used to define the action space $\mathcal{A}$?
- Is the node used to define the observation space $\mathcal{S}$?
- What are all the possible values the node might have?

Algorithm 1 shows how the required mapping f and g in (1) and (2) can be automated using pure information modelling.

Algorithm 1. Determining the action and observation space

Require: $\mathcal{O}$, the set containing all OPC UA nodes
1: Initialize $\mathcal{A} \leftarrow \varnothing$, $\mathcal{S} \leftarrow \varnothing$, $ActionSets \leftarrow \varnothing$ and $StateSets \leftarrow \varnothing$
2: **for each** $o \in \mathcal{O}$ **do**
3:     **if** o has property *ActionNode* **then**
4:         $ActionSets$.append(min(o):step(o):max(o))
5:     **end if**
6:     **if** o has property *ObservationNode* **then**
7:         $ObservationSets$.append(min(o):step(o):max(o))
8:     **end if**
9: **end for**
10: **for each** $actionSet \in ActionSets$ **do**
11:     $\mathcal{A} \leftarrow \mathcal{A} \times actionSet$
12: **end for**
13: **for each** $observationSet \in ObservationSets$ **do**
14:     $\mathcal{S} \leftarrow \mathcal{S} \times observationSet$
15: **end for**

---

5   Proof of Concept

To demonstrate and evaluate the proposed architecture, a proof of concept has been created. A sorting task on a material flow plant was chosen to be solved. Either a green or blue material may be released at the material outlet. Afterwards, it should be transported using the conveyor belts as well as the turntable to either the left or right side, depending on the color of the material, as shown in Fig. 3.

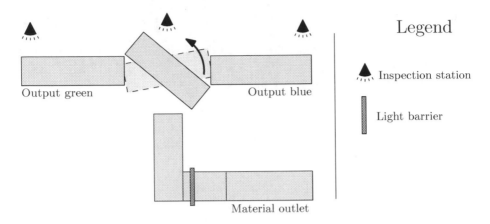

Fig. 3. Structure of the material flow plant

In order to evaluate the integration of a real control system, a Hardware-in-the-Loop (HiL) simulation [1] was used. Therefore, the integration of a real control system could be evaluated.

To not only show the deployment of a learned policy on a real control system, but also the learning of it within a reasonable time, the complexity regarding the action and state space A and S has been reduced to a minimum. Therefore, the action space A consists of four actions, determined by two boolean actuators to control the direction as well as the rotation of the turntable. The observation space S is determined by two sensors: one boolean light barrier and a color inspection station returning one of three possible values for the color green, the color blue as well as no detected material. This results in a total of six possible states, with two invalid states as long as there is no more than one material simultaneously on the material flow plant.

Figure 4 shows an excerpt of the OPC UA information model for the proposed sorting task, illustrating the used nodes comprising the state space S. The *Turntable* node is organized by the global *Objects* node, and it has an arbitrary amount of components. Each component having a *BaseDataVariableType* may be extended with a property introduced in Sect. 4.1 using a *HasProperty* reference. Using these properties enables an automatic generation of the action and state space A and S required by the RL agent by pure modelling.

To determine the reward $r \in \mathcal{R}$ additional sensors are needed. On each end of the material flow plant, a color inspection station is integrated. Additionally, a light grid is attached to the bottom of the plant, enabling a detection of dropped materials. To determine if a material got stuck, the passed time is logged and evaluated. This results in four possible rewards:

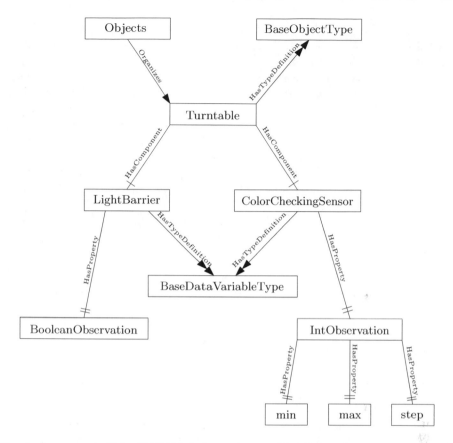

Fig. 4. An excerpt of the OPC UA information model defining the state space for the proposed sorting task.

$$r = \begin{cases} +5 & \text{if material is transported to the correct station} \\ -1 & \text{if material is transported to the wrong station} \\ -3 & \text{if material is dropped} \\ -5 & \text{if material gets stuck} \end{cases} \qquad (3)$$

Reducing the task to its bare minimum enables an identification of the optimal policy with a variety of RL agents. For this example, Q-learning [11] with a constant learning rate of $\alpha = 0.4$ and a discount factor of $\gamma = 0.9$ was chosen. To allow for exploration, a ϵ-greedy exploration strategy with $\epsilon = 0.1$ was used. The optimal policy could be identified within 80 min using a total of 150 episodes.

6   Conclusion and Discussion

Integrating RL into OT systems turns out to be challenging because of the characteristics of both worlds. To tackle these challenges, an OT-aware RL architecture has been proposed. In a proof of concept, we have demonstrated that an optimal policy was learned by the agent for a toy task, and we showed that the integration of a real programmable logic controller relying on real communication is possible. Using the proposed architecture in a proof of concept scenario, we showed that the challenges mentioned in Sect. 3 can be tackled. We have demonstrated that an optimal policy was learned by the agent for this task, and we showed that the integration of a real programmable logic controller relying on real communication is possible. Nevertheless, to support the development of an industrial system throughout the whole life cycle, we need to use different kinds of simulations, depending on the current development stage. To simplify the creation of industrial systems, we plan to create different simulations [1], and different digital representations [4].

References

1. VDI/VDE 3693 Blatt 1 - Virtuelle Inbetriebnahme - Modellarten und Glossar (8 2016). https://www.vdi.de/richtlinien/details/vdivde-3693-blatt-1-virtuelle-inbetriebnahme-modellarten-und-glossar
2. Kaelbling, L.P., Littman, M.L., Moore, A.W.: Reinforcement learning: a survey. J. Artif. Intell. Res. 4(1), 237–285 (1996)
3. Kober, J., Bagnell, J.A., Peters, J.: Reinforcement learning in robotics: a survey. Int. J. Robot. Res. 32(11), 1238–1274 (2013)
4. Kritzinger, W., Karner, M., Traar, G., Henjes, J., Sihn, W.: Digital twin in manufacturing: a categorical literature review and classification. IFAC-PapersOnLine 51(11), 1016–1022 (2018)
5. Mahnke, W., Leitner, S.H., Damm, M.: OPC Unified Architecture. Springer Science & Business Media (2009). https://doi.org/10.1007/978-3-540-68899-0
6. Mai, V., Mani, K., Paull, L.: Sample efficient deep reinforcement learning via uncertainty estimation. In: International Conference on Learning Representations (2022)
7. Nian, R., Liu, J., Huang, B.: A review on reinforcement learning: Introduction and applications in industrial process control. Comput. Chem. Eng. 139 106886 (2020)
8. OPC Foundation: IEC-62541, Part 14: PubSub (2020)
9. OPC Foundation: IEC-62541, Part 5: Information Model (2020)
10. Sutton, R.S., Barto, A.G.: Reinforcement learning: An introduction. MIT press, 2nd edn. (2018)
11. Watkins, C.J.C.H.: Learning from delayed rewards (1989)

$\mathcal{C}^k$-Continuous Spline Approximation with TensorFlow Gradient Descent Optimizers

Stefan Huber and Hannes Waclawek[✉]

Salzburg University of Applied Sciences, Salzburg, Austria
{stefan.huber,hannes.waclawek}@fh-salzburg.ac.at

Abstract. In this work we present an "out-of-the-box" application of Machine Learning (ML) optimizers for an industrial optimization problem. We introduce a piecewise polynomial model (spline) for fitting of $\mathcal{C}^k$-continuous functions, which can be deployed in a cam approximation setting. We then use the gradient descent optimization context provided by the machine learning framework TensorFlow to optimize the model parameters with respect to approximation quality and $\mathcal{C}^k$-continuity and evaluate available optimizers. Our experiments show that the problem solution is feasible using TensorFlow gradient tapes and that AMSGrad and SGD show the best results among available TensorFlow optimizers. Furthermore, we introduce a novel regularization approach to improve SGD convergence. Although experiments show that remaining discontinuities after optimization are small, we can eliminate these errors using a presented algorithm which has impact only on affected derivatives in the local spline segment.

Keywords: Gradient descent optimization · Tensorflow · Polynomial approximation · Splines · Regression

1 Introduction

When discussing the potential application of Machine Learning (ML) to industrial settings, we first of all have the application of various ML methods and models per se in mind. These methods, from neural networks to simple linear classifiers, are based on gradient descent optimization. This is why ML frameworks come with a variety of gradient descent optimizers that perform well on a diverse set of problems and in the past decades have received significant improvements in academia and practice.

Industry is full of classical numerical optimization and we can therefore, instead of using the entire framework in an industrial context, harness modern optimizers that lie at the heart of modern ML methods directly and apply them

Stefan Huber and Hannes Waclawek are supported by the European Interreg Österreich-Bayern project AB292 KI-Net and the Christian Doppler Research Association (JRC ISIA).

to industrial numerical optimization tasks. One of these optimization tasks is cam approximation, which is the task of fitting a continuous function to a number of input points with properties favorable for cam design. One way to achieve these favorable properties is via gradient based approaches, where an objective function allows to minimize user-definable losses. Servo drives like B&R Industrial Automation's ACOPOS series process cam profiles as a piecewise polynomial function (spline). This is why, with the goal of using the findings of this paper as a basis for cam approximation in future works, we want to lay the ground for performing polynomial approximation with a C^k-continuous piecewise polynomial spline model using gradient descent optimization provided by the machine learning framework TensorFlow. The continuity class C^k denotes the set of k-times continuously differentiable functions $\mathbb{R} \to \mathbb{R}$. Continuity is important in cam design concerning forces that are only constrained by the mechanical construction of machine parts. This leads to excessive wear and vibrations which we ought to prevent. Although our approach is motivated by cam design, it is generically applicable.

The contribution of this work is manifold:

1. "Out-of-the-box" application of ML-optimizers for an industrial setting.
2. A C^k-spline approximation method with novel gradient regularization.
3. Evaluation of TensorFlow optimizer performance for a well-known problem.
4. Non-convergence of optimizers using exponential moving averages, like Adam, is documented in literature [2]. We confirm with our experiments that this non-convergence extends to the presented optimization setting.
5. Algorithm to strictly establish continuity with impact only on affected derivatives in the local spline segment.

The Python libraries and Jupyter Notebooks used to perform our experiments are available under an MIT license at [5].

Prior work. There is a lot of prior work on neural networks for function approximation [1] or the use of gradient descent optimizers for B-spline curves [3]. There are also non-scientific texts on gradient descent optimization for polynomial regression. However, to the best of our knowledge, there is no thorough evaluation of gradient descent optimizers for C^k-continuous piecewise polynomial spline approximation.

2   Gradient Descent Optimization

TensorFlow provides a mechanism for automatic gradient computation using a so-called gradient tape. This mechanism allows to directly make use of the diverse range of gradient based optimizers offered by the framework and implement custom training loops. We implemented our own training loop in which we (i) obtain the gradients for a loss expression ℓ, (ii) optionally apply some regularization on the gradients and (iii) supply the optimizer with the gradients. This requires a computation of ℓ that allows the gradient tape to track the operations applied to the model parameters in form of TensorFlow variables.

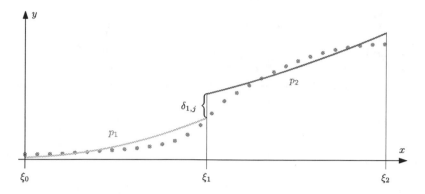

Fig. 1. Spline model derivative j consisting of two polynomial segments.

2.1   Spline Model

Many servo drives used in industrial applications, like B&R Industrial Automation's ACOPOS series, use piecewise polynomial functions (splines) as a base model for cam follower displacement curves. This requires the introduction of an according spline model in TensorFlow. Let us consider n samples at $x_1 \leq \cdots \leq x_n \in \mathbb{R}$ with respective values $y_i \in \mathbb{R}$. We ask for a spline $f : I \to \mathbb{R}$ on the interval $I = [x_1, x_n]$ that approximates the samples well and fulfills some additional domain-specific properties, like $\mathcal{C}^k$-continuity or $\mathcal{C}^k$-cyclicity[1]. Let us denote by $\xi_0 \leq \cdots \leq \xi_m$ the polynomial boundaries of f, where $\xi_0 = x_1$ and $\xi_m = x_n$. With $I_i = [\xi_{i-1}, \xi_i]$, the spline f is modeled by m polynomials $p_i : I \to \mathbb{R}$ that agree with f on I_i for $1 \leq i \leq m$. Each polynomial

$$p_i = \sum_{j=0}^{d} \alpha_{i,j} x^j \tag{1}$$

is determined by its coefficients $\alpha_{i,j}$, where d denotes the degree of the spline and its polynomials. That is, the $\alpha_{i,j}$ are the to be trained model parameters of the spline ML model. We investigate the convergence of these model parameters $\alpha_{i,j}$ of this spline model with respect to different loss functions, specifically for L_2-approximation error and $\mathcal{C}^k$-continuity, by means of different TensorFlow optimizers (see details below). Figure 1 depicts the principles of the presented spline model.

2.2   Loss Function

In order to establish $\mathcal{C}^k$-continuity, cyclicity, periodicity and allow for curve fitting via least squares approximation, we introduce the cost function

---

[1] By $\mathcal{C}^k$-cyclicity we mean that the derivative $f^{(i)}$ matches on x_1 and x_n for $1 \leq i \leq k$. If it additionally matches for $i = 0$ then we have $\mathcal{C}^k$-periodicity.

$$\ell = \lambda\ell_2 + (1 - \lambda)\ell_{\mathrm{CK}}. \tag{2}$$

By adjusting the value of λ in equation (2) we can put more weight to either the approximation quality or $\mathcal{C}^k$-continuity optimization target. The approximation error ℓ_2 is the least-square error and made invariant to the number of data points and number of polynomial segments by the following definition:

$$\ell_2 = \frac{m}{n} \sum_i |f(x_i) - y_i|^2. \tag{3}$$

We assign a value ℓ_{CK} to the amount of discontinuity in our spline function by summing up discontinuities at all ξ_i across relevant derivatives as

$$\ell_{\mathrm{CK}} = \frac{1}{m-1} \sum_{i=1}^{m-1} \sum_{j=0}^{k} \delta_{i,j}^2 \quad \text{with} \quad \delta_{i,j} = p_{i+1}^{(j)}(\xi_i) - p_i^{(j)}(\xi_i). \tag{4}$$

We make ℓ_{CK} in equation (4) invariant to the number of polynomial segments by applying an equilibration factor $\frac{1}{m-1}$, where $m-1$ is the number of boundary points excluding ξ_0 and ξ_m. This loss ℓ_{CK} can be naturally extended to $\mathcal{C}^k$-cyclicity/periodicity for cam profiles.[2]

2.3   TensorFlow Training Loop

The gradient tape environment of TensorFlow offers automatic differentiation of our loss function defined in equation (2). This requires a computation of ℓ that allows for tracking the operations applied to $\alpha_{i,j}$ through the usage of TensorFlow variables and arithmetic operations, see Listing 1.1.

```
for e in range(epochs):
    with tf.GradientTape(persistent=True) as tape:
        loss_l2 = calculate_l2_loss()
        loss_ck = calculate_ck_loss()
        loss = tf.add(tf.multiply(loss_l2, lambd),
                      tf.multiply(loss_ck, 1.0-lambd))
    gradients = tape.gradient(loss, coeffs)
    gradients = apply_regularization()
    optimizer.apply_gradients(zip(gradients, coeffs))
```

Listing 1.1. Gradient descent optimization loop in TensorFlow.

---

[2] In (4), change $m-1$ to m and generalize $\delta_{i,j} = p_{1+(i \bmod m)}^{(j)}(\xi_{i \bmod m}) - p_i^{(j)}(\xi_i)$. For cyclicity we ignore the case $j = 0$ when $i = m$, but not for periodicity.

In this training loop, we first calculate the loss according to equation (2) in a gradient tape context in lines 5 and 6 and then obtain the gradients according to that loss result in line 7 via the gradient tape environment automatic differentiation mechanism. We then apply regularization in line 8 that later will be introduced in Sect. 3.1 and supply the optimizer with the gradients in line 9.

3   Improving Spline Model Performance

In order to improve convergence behavior using the model defined in Sect. 2.1, we introduce a novel regularization approach and investigate effects of input data scaling and shifting of polynomial centers. In a cam design context, discontinuities remaining after the optimization procedure lead to forces and vibrations that are only constrained by the cam-follower system's mechanical design. To prevent such discontinuities, we propose an algorithm to strictly establish continuity after optimization.

3.1   A Degree-Based Regularization

With the polynomial model described in equation (1), terms of higher order have greater impact on the result. This leads to gradients having greater impact on terms of higher order, which impairs convergence behavior. This effect is also confirmed by our experiments. We propose a degree-based regularization approach, that mitigates this impact by effectively causing a shift of optimization of higher-degree coefficients to later epochs. We do this by introducing a gradient regularization vector $R = (r_0, \ldots, r_d)$, where

$$r_j = \frac{r'_j}{\sum_{k=0}^{d} r'_k} \quad \text{with} \quad r'_j = \frac{1}{1+j}. \tag{5}$$

The regularization is then applied by multiplying each gradient value $\frac{\partial \ell}{\partial \alpha_{i,j}}$ with r_j. Since the entries r_j of R sum up to 1, this effectively acts as an equilibration of all gradients per polynomial p_i.

This approach effectively makes the sum of gradients degree-independent. Experiments show that this allows for higher learning rates using non-adaptive optimizers like SGD and enables the use of SGD with Nesterov momentum, which does not converge without our proposed regularization approach. This brings faster convergence rates and lower remaining losses for non-adaptive optimizers. At a higher number of epochs, the advantage of the regularization is becoming less. Also, the advantage of the regularization is higher for polynomials of higher degree, say, $d \geq 4$.

3.2   Practical Considerations

Experiments show that, using the training parameters outlined in Sect. 4, SGD optimization has a certain radius of convergence with respect to the x-axis around the polynomial center. Shifting of polynomial centers to the mean of the respective segment allows segments with higher x-value ranges to converge. We can implement this by extending the polynomial model defined in equation (1) as

$$p_i = \sum_{j=0}^{d} \alpha_{i,j}(x - \mu_i)^j, \quad \text{where} \quad \mu_i = \frac{\xi_{i-1} + \xi_i}{2}. \tag{6}$$

If input data is scaled such that every polynomial segment is in the range $[0, 1]$, in all our experiments for all $0 \leq \lambda \leq 1$, SGD optimization is able to converge using this approach. With regards to scaling, as an example, for a spline consisting of 8 polynomial segments, we scale the input data such that $I = [0, 8]$. We skip the back-transformation as we would do in production code.

3.3   Strictly Establishing Continuity After Optimization

In order to strictly establish $\mathcal{C}^k$-continuity after optimization, i.e., to eliminate possible remaining ℓ_{CK}, we apply corrective polynomials that enforce $\delta(\xi_i) = 0$ at all ξ_i. The following method requires a spline degree $d \geq 2k + 1$. Let

$$m_{i,j} = \frac{p_i^{(j)}(\xi_i) + p_{i+1}^{(j)}(\xi_i)}{2} \tag{7}$$

denote the mean j-th derivative of p_i and p_{i+1} at ξ_i for all $0 \leq j \leq k$. Then there is a unique polynomial c_i of degree $2k + 1$ that has a j-th derivative of 0 at ξ_{i-1} and $m_j - p_i^{(j)}(\xi_i)$ at ξ_i for all $0 \leq j \leq k$. Likewise, there is a unique polynomial c_{i+1} with j-th derivative given by $m_j - p_{i+1}^{(j)}(\xi_i)$ at ξ_i and 0 at ξ_{i+1}. The corrected polynomials $p_i^* = p_i + c_i$ and $p_{i+1}^* = p_{i+1} + c_{i+1}$ then possess identical derivatives m_j at ξ_i for all $0 \leq j \leq k$, yet, the derivatives at ξ_{i-1} and ξ_{i+1} have not been altered. This allows us to apply the corrections at each ξ_i independently as they have only local impact. This is a nice property in contrast to natural splines or methods using B-Splines as discussed in [3].

4   Experimental Results

In a first step, we investigated mean squared error loss by setting $\lambda = 1$ in our loss function defined in equation (2) for a single polynomial, which revealed a learning rate of 0.1 as a reasonable setting. We then ran tests with available TensorFlow optimizers listed in [4] and compared their outcomes. We found that SGD with momentum, Adam, Adamax as well as AMSgrad show the lowest losses, with a declining tendency even after 5000 epochs. However, the training curves of Adamax and Adam exhibit recurring phases of instability every ~ 500 epochs. Non-convergence of these optimizers is documented in literature [2] and we can confirm with our experiments that it also extends to our optimization setting. Using the AMSGrad variant of Adam eliminates this behavior with comparable remaining loss levels. With these results in mind, we chose SGD with Nesterov momentum as non-adaptive and AMSGrad as adaptive optimizer for all further experiments, in order to work with optimizers from both paradigms.

The AMSGrad optimizer performs better on the $\lambda = 1$ optimization target, however, SGD is competitive. The loss curves of these optimizer candidates, as well as instabilities in the Adam loss curve are shown in Fig. 2. An overview of all evaluated optimizers is given in our GitHub repository at [5].

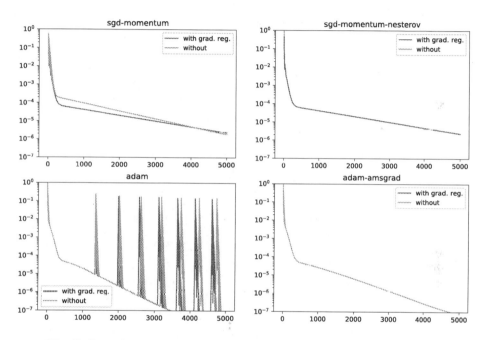

Fig. 2. Overview of optimizer loss curves for one polynomial with $\lambda = 1$.

With our degree-based regularization approach introduced in Sect. 3.1, SGD with momentum is able to converge quicker and we are able to use Nesterov momentum, which was not possible otherwise. We achieved best results with an SGD momentum setting of 0.95 and AMSGrad $\beta_1 = 0.9$, $\beta_2 = 0.999$ and $\epsilon = 10^{-7}$. On that basis, we investigated our general spline model, by we sweeping λ from 1 to 0. Experiments show that both optimizers are able to generate near $\mathcal{C}^2$-continuos results across the observed λ-range while at the same time delivering favorable approximation results. The remaining continuity correction errors for the algorithm introduced in Sect. 3.3 to process are small.

Using $\mathcal{C}^2$-splines of degree 5, again, AMSGrad has a better performance compared to SGD. For all tested $0 < \lambda < 1$, SGD and AMSGrad manage to produce splines of low loss within 10 000 epochs: SGD reaches $\ell \approx 10^{-4}$ and AMSGrad reaches $\ell \approx 10^{-6}$. Given an application-specific tolerance, we may already stop after a few hundred epochs.

5   Conclusion and Outlook

We have presented an "out-of-the-box" application of ML optimizers for the industrial optimization problem of cam approximation. The model introduced in Sect. 2.1 and extended by practical considerations in Sect. 3.2 allows for fitting of $\mathcal{C}^k$-continuos splines, which can be deployed in a cam approximation setting. Our experiments documented in Sect. 4 show that the problem solution is feasible using TensorFlow gradient tapes and that AMSGrad and SGD show the best results among available TensorFlow optimizers. Our gradient regularization approach introduced in Sect. 3.1 improves SGD convergence and allows usage of SGD with Nesterov momentum. Although experiments show that remaining discontinuities after optimization are small, we can eliminate these errors using the algorithm introduced in Sect. 3.3, which has impact only on affected derivatives in the local spline segment.

Additional terms in ℓ can accommodate for further domain-specific goals. For instance, we can reduce oscillations in f by penalizing the strain energy

$$\ell_{\text{strain}} = \int_I f''(x)^2 \, \mathrm{d}x \, .$$

In our experiments outlined in the previous section, we started with all polynomial coefficients initialized to zero to investigate convergence. To improve convergence speed in future experiments, we can start with the ℓ_2-optimal spline and let our method minimize the overall goal ℓ.

Flexibility of our method with regards to the underlying polynomial model allows for usage of different function types. In this way, as an example, an orthogonal basis using Chebyshev polynomials could improve convergence behavior compared to classical monomials.

References

1. Adcock, B., Dexter, N.: The gap between theory and practice in function approximation with deep neural networks. SIAM J. Math. Data Sci. **3**(2), 624–655 (2021). https://doi.org/10.1137/20M131309X
2. Reddi, S.J., Kale, S., Kumar, S.: On the convergence of adam and beyond. CoRR abs/1904.09237 (2019). https://doi.org/10.48550/arXiv.1904.09237
3. Sandgren, E., West, R.L.: Shape optimization of cam profiles using a b-spline representation. J. Mech. Trans. Autom. Design **111**(2), 195–201 (06 1989). https://doi.org/10.1115/1.3258983
4. TensorFlow: Built-in optimizer classes. https://www.tensorflow.org/api_docs/python/tf/keras/optimizers (2022), Accessed 28 Feb 2022
5. Waclawek, H., Huber, S.: Spline approximation with tensorflow gradient descent optimizers for use in cam approximation. https://github.com/hawaclawek/tf-for-splineapprox (2022), Accessed 31 May 2022

Stepwise Sample Generation

Florian Bayeff-Filloff[✉], Dominik Stecher, and Kai Höfig

Rosenheim Technical University of Applied Sciences, Rosenheim, Germany
{florian.bayeff-filloff,dominik.stecher,kai.hoefig}@th-rosenheim.de
https://www.th-rosenheim.de

Abstract. Increasingly more industrial applications incorporate artificial intelligence based systems, which require a lot of data, e.g. captured from real machines or digital twin simulations, to train their models. But the data sets available or captured are often small, imbalanced or for specific use cases only. The most used approach to solve this problem efficiently are virtual sample generators. This type of program is commonly used to artificially construct new data from a small original data set, but tend to ignore weak correlation between features or even introduce false new correlations.

Therefore, we propose a novel stepwise synthetic sample generation approach which allows engineers and domain experts to include their domain knowledge directly in the sample generation process. They can judge how features depend on each other, which value range is plausible or acceptable and which features aren't relevant at all for getting better AI model approximation results and generating suitable synthetic data samples. In addition, we propose using simple machine learning models, such as support vector machines, to verify the synthetic data.

Keywords: Artificial intelligence · Artificial data · Software development · Virtual sample generator

1 Introduction

The initial problem we attempt to solve is the large data requirement for currently applied, advanced Machine Learning (ML) methods such as deep learning, which often cannot be satisfied easily by Small and Medium Enterprises (SME) in cases such as rare defects, fault events, and low production volumes. Digital twins [3] can alleviate this issue, but tend to be complex to create and use, and come with increasing costs depending on the required fidelity of the simulation. However, useful information for the creation of a robust and effective AI model [10] are not only hidden inside captured samples - be that real-world measurements or digital twins data - but also in the minds of engineers and experts in the form of domain knowledge. To remedy this problem, we propose a virtual sample generator capable of including said knowledge and experience of

Supported by Interreg Österreich-Bayern 2014–2020 as part of the project KI-Net (AB292).

technical experts familiar with the system at hand in AI training data generation by letting them directly influence the generation process of artificial samples.

The remainder of this paper is organized as follows: We discuss related work in Sect. 2. In Sect. 3 we describe our Stepwise Sample Generation approach in detail. Section 4 describes our evaluation procedure and shows first evaluation result. A closing summary and outlook for future works is given in Sect. 5.

2   Related Work

It is well understood that larger data sets contain more useful information for the training of AI-based models and lead to an overall better model abstraction ability and quality [2,5]. However, most real-world data sets at hand for SMEs are small in size, strongly imbalanced or meant for specific use cases only. In the last years researchers developed different approaches to gain better insights from small sample data. Some of the related studies are listed in the following.

2.1   Data Augmentation

In image classification, data augmentation [12] is a well-established approach to generate more data by altering existing images in different ways and thus gaining more information. Methods include scaling, flipping, colour and hue changes, filter operations and many more. Figure 1 shows an example for classic image augmentations methods. However, such methods only work for image data, as rotating or flipping the measurements of a power meter results in nonsensical values.

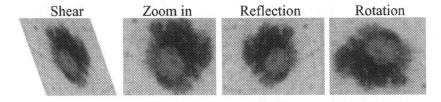

Fig. 1. Classic image augmentation provided by Mikolajczyk and Grochowski [7]

2.2   Virtual Sample Generator Methods

For industrial applications, where data sets mostly consist of sensor data, the most common and broadly used approach are Virtual Sample Generators (VSG). These are algorithms designed to generate a large Synthetic Data (SD) set based on a small Original Data (OD) set. The base concept was first proposed by Poggio and Vetter [8,9] as a method of sample augmentation, and has since then evolved and been applied in many fields such as chemistry [16], medicine [14] or food monitoring [4]. In general VSG techniques fall into one of three categories: (1) Sampling-based, (2) Deep Learning-based and (3) Information Diffusion-based. In the following we list a few examples. Zhang [16] proposed a VSG based on the Isomap Algorithm, where they aim to find sparse populated data regions and interpolate the OD there to generate new data points. Zhu did something similar based on Locally Linear Embedding [18] and Kriging [17]. Yang [15] and Wedyan [14] proposed the usage of Gaussian distributed features to sample new feature values from. Another way of generating virtual samples are Generative Adversarial Networks. Douzas [1] proposed to extend this base concept by using conditions, and Li [6] added histograms to the training step to better match the SD to the OD.

The main problem we found with previous VSGs is that they often use a general purpose algorithm for all features within a given data set, regardless of their actual real-world correlations. This can lead to new correlations between features that shouldn't exist or ignore weak correlations, either because the overall data volume is too small or their representation to few for the algorithm to detect them reliably. In the absence of a data set large enough to properly represent all correlations between individual features, it is up to engineers and experts to provide this knowledge during the data generation process as well as to remove unwanted correlations.

3   Approach Overview

In this section we describe our SD generation approach. It was developed in Python as part of the Data Analysis & Augmentation Toolkit (DAAT), our software contribution to the Interred KI-Net Project (AB292). This Toolkit currently consists of three parts: First, the Visual Analyser, for easy visual analysis of the given data set. Second, the Data Generator, which implements our data generation approach and several virtual sample generation algorithms. Third, the Verification Module, where simple ML models are trained and tested on OD and SD to verify the latter. We see this not only as a way to verify our approach, but as an integral part of the data generation process itself. In this paper we focus on our SD generation approach and the Verification Module.

The presented VSG can generate any number of synthetic samples based on a small OD set and improve the overall AI-model quality with limited data available. The flowchart of the general procedure employed by our approach is shown in Fig. 2. It consists of four main steps: (1) initializing the Generator, (2) selecting instructions for each feature defining dependencies and generation method, (3) executing the instructions in sequence, and lastly (4) verifying the generated data with the Verification Module.

3.1   Initialization

The first step is to initialize the Generator with the OD set and target label, if applicable. Currently only data sets consisting of numeric feature values are

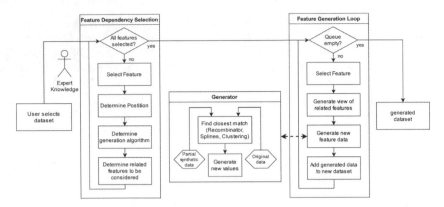

Fig. 2. Stepwise Sample Generation sequence

supported. The target feature can be defined as classification, regression, or none. This changes how the label is generated for the SD. For regression, the generated samples are matched with the n-nearest original samples, the mean is calculated and set as the new value. For classification, the data set is first separated by the target classes and the instructions are run on each class separately, setting the label as the current class. Otherwise, no label is generated. The support of other target labels and data set types, e.g., time series, is planed for future iterations.

3.2   Feature Dependency Selection

After initialization, instructions for each feature in the data set, except the target label, are defined and added to the generator pipeline. Each instruction tells the generator which of the available generation methods to use, which other features to use, as well as other method related settings, like the number of clusters to search for or lower and upper limits. Which features are dependent from each other and which generator method is the most fitting for each feature is considered domain knowledge. At this stage, the specific generation method can be chosen freely, but the instruction order is limited by the dependent features, as they must have been generated beforehand. This is because each generation method matches the partially generated SD to the OD set to generate values for the feature currently worked on.

Generation Methods. As a proof of concept, our prototype implementation includes five simple VSG methods: Distribution, Spline, Recombine, Cluster, KNN Mean. Additionally, the marker None can be set to skip a feature. Each of the methods is implemented as a base class extension. This structure enables the implementation and use of self specified algorithms within the generator by the user. In the following we briefly describe each included generation method. Distribution takes a feature, determines the mean and standard deviation and then samples new values according to the found distribution. Spline/Griddata is meant for feature combinations which can be described by functions. Recombine determines the k nearest original samples of the current partially generated synthetic sample and picks one value from them at random. Cluster runs a cluster algorithm on the OD set and determines the cluster the current synthetic sample lies within. It then samples a new random value from the cluster. KNN Mean is a simple interpolation algorithm, by taking the k nearest original samples and calculating the mean value.

3.3   Feature Generation Loop

Next, any number of synthetic samples can be generated and returned as a new SD set. For this the Generator runs trough the previously defined instructions in order. The values of the current feature are taken, a data set view of all specified dependent features is generated by filtering the OD set and the already partially generated SD set. These sub data sets are given to the selected generation method as parameters. Then the generation method is run and the resulting new values written in the partially generated SD set. After all instructions are run, the Feature Generation Loop (FGL) is finished, and the completed SD set can be retrieved from the Generator. Here we additionally give the option to retrieve the SD set combined with the OD seed.

Generator Setup Check. Additionally, before starting the final FGL, the instructions can be evaluated. This sub step is optional but recommended and not shown in Fig. 2. First, the instruction order is tested for inconsistencies and missing feature instruction definitions. Next, the instructions are executed on a small portion of the seed data set to generate an equally sized SD set. Finally, these data sets are given to the Verification Module, where they are evaluated against each other. The result is displayed as both table and graphs, providing an estimate on the instructions suitability and order validity in regards to the OD set. An example evaluation result is shown in Fig. 3, using the NASA KC1 (KC1) data set.

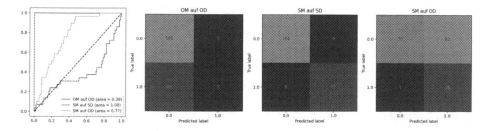

Fig. 3. KC1 data set - Setup Check using 30% OD

3.4 Verification Module

After the SD set is generated, it is advised to evaluate the new data set before proceeding with the time-consuming training of the final AI-model. For this, the DAAT includes a verification module using light-weight ML models such as Support Vector Machines (SVM) and Feed-Forward Artificial Neural Networks (FFANN).

For this purpose we split the OD and SD sets in training and test sets - typically 70:30. Next, we train two models with the exact same parameters on each training set and test each model on both test sets. This way, we can directly compare the performance of models trained on OD or SD sets. In a second step we train two new models each on the full data sets and use the other as test data. In both cases, we expect the SD-trained model to perform comparable or slightly better than the OD-trained model. We also expect the OD trained model to perform no worse on the synthetic test data.

4 Approach Evaluation

To demonstrate our proposed method, multiple experiments were performed on small data sets for classification problems. Using the KC1 data set [11] and Pima Indians Diabetes (PID) data set [13] we show our approach is capable of generating qualitative data samples - without trying to solve the actual problem such as fault detection - by comparing the performance and cross-evaluation results of ML methods on both OD and SD. The experiments were performed over 10, 100 or 1000 cycles, averaging the results to mitigate fluctuations introduced by random data sampling. While we acknowledge that better data sets exist, those typically lack the clear feature correlations or domain knowledge required.

Using PID, we generated two SD sets, one from 10% and one from 100% of the OD, labeled syn10 and syn100 respectively. Then three separate SVMs were trained on the resulting data sets and cross-evaluated over 1000 cycles. As shown in Table 1 our approach can generate well data points using less OD as a seed.

Table 1. PID data set - Evaluation over 1000 Cycles using 10% and 100% data as seed

Model	orig			syn10			syn100		
Data set	orig	syn10	syn100	orig	syn10	syn100	orig	syn10	syn100
Accuracy	0.780	0.843	0.724	0.709	0.997	0.886	0.638	0.883	0.978
Precision	0.686	0.978	0.995	0.555	0.996	0.952	0.475	0.829	0.975
Recall	0.615	0.711	0.590	0.669	0.999	0.875	0.866	0.991	0.993
F1	0.649	0.808	0.739	0.594	0.998	0.904	0.613	0.900	0.984

Using KC1, 10, 20 and 40% from the training data were randomly sampled and labeled as gen. From these, SD sets were generated, such that they, combined with their seed, were equally sized to the OD set and labeled as syn. Three simple FFANN were trained on the resulting data sets using class weights for balancing and evaluated using the original test data. As shown in Table 2, our approach can generate data of equal quality as the OD from different sized seed data sets.

Table 2. KC1 data set - Evaluation for different OD ratios

Data set	orig	gen			syn - 10CY			syn - 100CY		
Percentage	100%	10%	20%	40%	10%	20%	40%	10%	20%	40%
n OD	1475	148	295	590	148	295	590	148	295	590
Accuracy	0.686	0.601	0.621	0.664	0.773	0.753	0.734	0.752	0.764	0.762
Precision	0.269	0.239	0.224	0.254	0.359	0.274	0.289	0.339	0.347	0.331
Recall	0.638	0.748	0.598	0.645	0.537	0.489	0.602	0.564	0.496	0.500
F1	0.358	0.355	0.320	0.326	0.407	0.326	0.385	0.399	0.357	0.362

5   Conclusion and Future Work

In this paper we proposed a novel, modular and stepwise VSG approach. Our main goal was to provide an easy to understand example on how to incorporate domain knowledge within the data generation process. We tested our approach on the KC1 and PID data set and although the results are highly dependent on the instruction order, selected generation method and dependent features, our evaluations suggest that our approach can generate valid and qualitative SD.

For future iterations of our Toolkit, we plan to extend our approach. First, by support more data set types, like time series and non numeric sets, as well as the use of partially predefined data sets. Second, by extending the included five VSG methods with more sub types, e.g., Weibull and Poisson for Distribution, different cluster algorithms for Cluster, selection of different distance metrics etc., as well as more methods in general. We further plan to conduct case studies on actual data sets from industrial partners as well as university departments to assess the usefulness and scalability of our data generation approach on real world data.

References

1. Douzas, G., Bacao, F.: Effective data generation for imbalanced learning using conditional generative adversarial networks. Expert Syst. Appl. **91**, 464–471 (2018). https://doi.org/10.1016/j.eswa.2017.09.030
2. Hestness, J., Ardalani, N., Diamos, G.: Beyond human-level accuracy. In: Proceedings of the 24th Symposium on Principles and Practice of Parallel Programming. ACM (2019). https://doi.org/10.1145/3293883.3295710

3. Kaur, M.J., Mishra, V.P., Maheshwari, P.: The convergence of digital twin, IoT, and machine learning: transforming data into action. In: Farsi, M., Daneshkhah, A., Hosseinian-Far, A., Jahankhani, H. (eds.) Digital Twin Technologies and Smart Cities. IT, pp. 3–17. Springer, Cham (2020). https://doi.org/10.1007/978-3-030-18732-3_1

4. Khot, L.R., et al.: Evaluation of technique to overcome small dataset problems during neural-network based contamination classification of packaged beef using integrated olfactory sensor system. LWT - Food Sci. Technol. **45**(2), 233–240 (2012). https://doi.org/10.1016/j.lwt.2011.06.011

5. Kitchin, R., Lauriault, T.P.: Small data in the era of big data. GeoJournal **80**(4), 463–475 (2014). https://doi.org/10.1007/s10708-014-9601-7

6. Li, W., Ding, W., Sadasivam, R., Cui, X., Chen, P.: His-GAN: A histogram-based GAN model to improve data generation quality. Neural Netw. **119**, 31–45 (2019). https://doi.org/10.1016/j.neunet.2019.07.001

7. Mikolajczyk, A., Grochowski, M.: Data augmentation for improving deep learning in image classification problem. In: 2018 International Interdisciplinary PhD Workshop (IIPhDW). IEEE (2018). https://doi.org/10.1109/iiphdw.2018.8388338

8. Niyogi, P., Girosi, F., Poggio, T.: Incorporating prior information in machine learning by creating virtual examples. Proc. IEEE **86**(11), 2196–2209 (1998). https://doi.org/10.1109/5.726787

9. Poggio, T., Vetter, T.: Recognition and structure from one 2d model view: Observations on prototypes, object classes and symmetries. Tech. rep. (1992). https://doi.org/10.21236/ada259735

10. Russell, S., Norvig, P.: Artificial Intelligence, Global Edition A Modern Approach. Pearson Deutschland (2021). https://elibrary.pearson.de/book/99.150005/9781292401171

11. Sayyad Shirabad, J., Menzies, T.: The PROMISE Repository of Software Engineering Databases. In: School of Information Technology and Engineering, University of Ottawa, Canada (2005). http://promise.site.uottawa.ca/SERepository

12. Shorten, C., Khoshgoftaar, T.M.: A survey on image data augmentation for deep learning. J. Big Data **6**(1), 1–48 (2019). https://doi.org/10.1186/s40537-019-0197-0

13. Sigillito, V.: Pima indians diabetes database. National Institute of Diabetes and Digestive and Kidney Diseases, The Johns Hopkins University, Maryland (1990). https://raw.githubusercontent.com/jbrownlee/Datasets/master/pima-indians-diabetes.names

14. Wedyan, M., Crippa, A., Al-Jumaily, A.: A novel virtual sample generation method to overcome the small sample size problem in computer aided medical diagnosing. Algorithms **12**(8), 160 (2019). https://doi.org/10.3390/a12080160

15. Yang, J., Yu, X., Xie, Z.Q., Zhang, J.P.: A novel virtual sample generation method based on gaussian distribution. Knowl.-Based Syst. **24**(6), 740–748 (2011). https://doi.org/10.1016/j.knosys.2010.12.010

16. Zhang, X.H., Xu, Y., He, Y.L., Zhu, Q.X.: Novel manifold learning based virtual sample generation for optimizing soft sensor with small data. ISA Trans. **109**, 229–241 (2021). https://doi.org/10.1016/j.isatra.2020.10.006

17. Zhu, Q.X., Chen, Z.S., Zhang, X.H., Rajabifard, A., Xu, Y., Chen, Y.Q.: Dealing with small sample size problems in process industry using virtual sample generation: a kriging-based approach. Soft Comput.**24**(9), 6889–6902 (2019). https://doi.org/10.1007/s00500-019-04326-3
18. Zhu, Q.X., Zhang, X.H., He, Y.L.: Novel virtual sample generation based on locally linear embedding for optimizing the small sample problem: Case of soft sensor applications. Indust. Eng. Chem. Res. **59**(40), 17977–17986 (2020). https://doi.org/10.1021/acs.iecr.0c01942

Optimising Manufacturing Process with Bayesian Structure Learning and Knowledge Graphs

Tek Raj Chhetri[1]([envelope])[iD], Sareh Aghaei[1][iD], Anna Fensel[1,2][iD], Ulrich Göhner[3][iD], Sebnem Gül-Ficici[3][iD], and Jorge Martinez-Gil[4][iD]

[1] Semantic Technology Institute (STI) Innsbruck, Department of Computer Science, University of Innsbruck, Technikerstr. 21a, 6020 Innsbruck, Austria
{tekraj.chhetri,sareh.aghaei,anna.fensel}@sti2.at
[2] Wageningen Data Competence Center, Wageningen University and Research, Droevendaalsesteeg 2, 6708 PB Wageningen, The Netherlands
[3] Kempten University of Applied Sciences, Bahnhofstraße 61, 87435 Kempten, Germany
{ulrich.goehner,sebnem.guel-ficici}@hs-kempten.de
[4] Software Competence Center Hagenberg GmbH, Softwarepark 32a, 4232 Hagenberg, Austria
Jorge.Martinez-Gil@scch.at

Abstract. In manufacturing industry, product failure is costly, as it results in financial and time losses. Understanding the causes of product failure is critical for reducing the occurrence of failure and optimising the manufacturing process. As a result, a number of studies utilising data-driven approaches such as machine learning have been conducted to reduce the occurrence of this failure and to improve the manufacturing process. While these data-driven approaches enable pattern recognition, they lack the advantages associated with knowledge-driven approaches, such as knowledge representation and deductive reasoning. Similarly, knowledge-driven approaches lack the pattern-learning capabilities inherent in data-driven approaches such as machine learning. Therefore, in this paper, leveraging the advantages of both data-driven and knowledge-driven approaches, we present a strategy with a prototype implementation to reduce manufacturing product failure. The proposed strategy combines a data-driven technique, Bayesian structural learning, with a knowledge-based technique, knowledge graphs.

Keywords: Manufacturing product failure · Bayesian structural learning · Knowledge graphs · Structure learning

1 Introduction

Small and medium-sized enterprises (SMEs) as significant contributors in the manufacturing and production industry require ensuring a low failure rate of

© The Author(s), under exclusive license to Springer Nature Switzerland AG 2022
R. Moreno-Díaz et al. (Eds.): EUROCAST 2022, LNCS 13789, pp. 594–602, 2022.
https://doi.org/10.1007/978-3-031-25312-6_70

products to have a healthy production line [8]. Product failure leads to a loss of market share with the increasing competition and customer expectations in the current era of Industry 4.0. Thus, understanding the causes of product failure is essential in order to eliminate the failures or reduce their effects and optimise the manufacturing process.

While manufacturers have made efforts to reduce the occurrence of product failure in SMEs, analysis of the causes by manual inspections is becoming less efficient, expensive, time-consuming and difficult [7]. To address failures occurring at manufacturing with complex processes, diverse techniques can be employed, including data-driven and knowledge-based (or semantic-based) approaches.

In recent years, data-driven approaches have made progress using machine learning (ML) for monitoring, fault diagnosis, optimisation and control. As a data-driven technique, Bayesian networks (BNs) are widely used to access a comprehensive and accurate analysis of complex systems. BNs are probabilistic graphical models to characterise and analyse uncertainty problems through a directed acyclic graph (DAG). The task of learning the dependency graph from data is called structure learning [11]. Although the state-of-the-art solutions (e.g., using continuous optimisation) have achieved learning the structure of a BN with many variables, they are not easily interpretable and informative about dependencies between the variables. In contrast, semantic-based techniques (e.g., using knowledge graphs (KGs)) allow to define the basic concepts and primary semantic relationships in a domain and provide deductive reasoning.

In this paper, we propose and develop a hybrid model for evaluating and predicting product quality in SMEs' production lines and consequently reducing the failure rates. We utilise structure learning to find and represent probabilistic dependency relationships among the variables and then use KGs to enrich semantic interoperability and exchange information between humans or machines. The main contributions of our paper are summarised as follows: (i) we take advantage of structure learning in BNs to reflect the dependencies among variables in SMEs' manufacturing processes through identifying DAGs; (ii) to overcome the lack of semantic interoperability in the extracted DAGs, we employ the idea of KGs; (iii) we generate and annotate an OWL ontology based on the DAG obtained through the Bayesian structure learning process to create a KG.

The paper is organised as follows. Section 2 provides an overview on the related works. The methodology is discussed in Sect. 3, and Sect. 4 provides a detailed explanation about the implementation. The evaluation is discussed in Sect. 5. Section 6 concludes the paper and gives directions for future research.

2   Related Works

A number of studies, such as [3], [4] and [10], have been conducted on the use of semantic technologies and BNs, demonstrating the advantages of combining the two. Existing research focuses on either integrating BNs into existing ontologies or using ontologies to model BNs. For example, Riali et al. [10] extended the ontology (i.e., fuzzy ontology) with BNs to incorporate probabilistic knowledge present in real-world applications. On the other hand, Chen et al. [4] use ontology to model BNs to represent causal relationships between additive manufacturing. Cao et al. [4], similarly, use ontology and BN to investigate dynamic risk propagation on supply chains. A risk propagation ontology is created (or customised) according to the domain and then it is transformed into a BN.

In summary, the work described above presumes ontology to be existing, which can be viewed as a limitation given the dynamic nature of the settings. In an ontology, for instance, all concepts are predefined, and if there is a change in manufacturing steps, such as the addition or subtraction of certain steps, the ontology must be modified accordingly. Our proposed work can account for these dynamic circumstances, automatically generating the ontology and KG, thus helping industry, especially SMEs that are often limited in resources.

3   Methodology

In this paper, we describe our approach to manufacturing process optimisation in detail. Figure 1 summarises the approach taken in our study, with details provided in the following subsections.

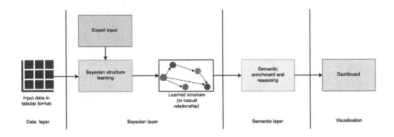

Fig. 1. Proposed methodology

3.1   Data Layer

The data layer is the first component to interact with the data. The data layer reads and preprocesses the input data. Preprocessing is used to ensure the data quality. For example, the input data for some features may be incomplete (i.e., it may contain missing values). Additionally, the data may include values on various scales. This is because missing values and inputs with varying scales result in suboptimal performance. The data layer's preprocessing performs imputation to fill in missing input and scaling values in different ranges to a common range.

3.2   Bayesian Layer

The Bayesian layer provides two major functionalities: learning the dependency graph of a BN from data, which is referred to as structure learning; and integrating expert inputs (or domain knowledge), a feature of BN [6]. The Bayesian layer yields the DAG as shown in Fig. 1 after performing the structure learning, which represents the learned relationships between the features. The Bayesian structure learning is based on [13] and [14], which perform structure learning by formulating combinatorial structure learning problem as continuous optimisation problems, thereby eliminating the combinatorial overhead.

3.3   Semantic Layer

The semantic layer enables capabilities such as reasoning and data enrichment inherent in semantic technology. Reasoning makes use of relationships and the deductive power of logic to generate new inferences (i.e., meaningfulness from the data). Additionally, the use of KG also enables interoperability, which is important when integrating with other external systems. To leverage semantic technology, the semantic layer converts the learned DAG to the corresponding semantic representation, specifically an ontology and a KG. Furthermore, the semantic layer provides reasoning via SPARQL queries.

Algorithm 1: OWL Ontology generator from DAG

Input: DAG graph G as an adjacency list
Result: OWL ontology O, ontology class mapper C_m, ontology object property mapper O_m, ontology data property mapper D_m
1 OWL Ontology ← initialise namespace;
2 **for** *each unique nodes in G* **do**
3 | create an OWL class as subclass of owl:Thing
4 **end**
5 **for** *each subgraph g in G* **do**
6 | **if** *g has child nodes* **then**
7 | | create an OWL ObjectProperty class with relation R ;
8 | | assign parent node as domain;
9 | | assign child node(s) as range;
10 | **end**
11 | **for** *each node n in child nodes* **do**
12 | | create OWL DataProperty class;
13 | | assign n as domain ;
14 | | assign data type as range ;
15 | **end**
16 **end**
17 Return O, C_m, O_m, D_m;

Algorithm 1 (and Algorithm 2) generates (and annotates) an OWL ontology based on the DAG obtained through Bayesian structure learning, in contrast to studies such as [12], which merge the BN into the existing ontology. This is especially advantageous when there is no ontology, which is frequently the case with SMEs. Additionally, this provides benefits, as one can take advantage of semantic technology's benefits without having any prior knowledge of it. Algorithm 1 takes the learned DAG graph G in an adjacency list format as an input. After creating the OWL class as a subclass of the *owl:Thing*, the object property is created, taking into account the connectivity of the nodes in G. In our study, the object property is defined as *isInfluencedByNode*. The *Node* in the object

---

Algorithm 2: Ontology Annotation

Input: DAG graph G as an adjacency list, OWL ontology O, ontology class mapper C_m,
         ontology object property mapper O_m, ontology data property mapper D_m
Result: Annotated OWL ontology

1 **for** *each subgraph g in G* **do**
2   **if** *g has child nodes* **then**
3   **for** *each nodes n in child nodes* **do**
4   create an instance i for node n;
5   create ObjectProperty restriction mapping O_m to C_m in O for instance i;
6   insert value to D_m for instance i;
7   **end**
8   **end**
9 **end**
10 Return Annotated OWL ontology;

---

property *isInfluencedByNode* represents the name of the influencing node (or
parent node). Our study consists of the two data properties, namely, *isOriginatedFromNode* and *hasInfluenceFactorOfNode*. *isOriginatedFromNode* is a data
property of type xsd:string that contains information about how the relationship
was discovered (i.e., based on expert input or learned via structure learning). The
hasInfluenceFactorOfNode property specifies the degree to which the child node
is influenced and is of type xsd:decimal. When the relationship is defined by a
domain expert, the *hasInfluenceFactorOfNode* has a weight of 1. Algorithm 2
uses ontology information such as class, object properties and data properties,
as well as the ontology itself and the graph G, to annotate the ontology and
create the KG.

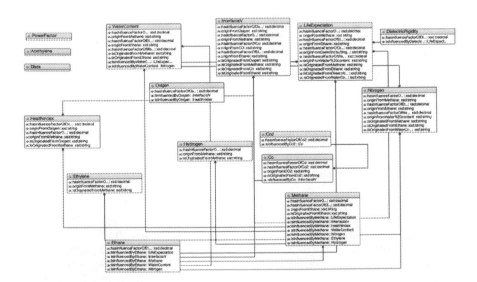

Fig. 2. Automatically generated OWL ontology based on DAG learned from Bayesian
structure learning.

Figure 2 shows the ontology generated using Algorithm 1. Each of the algorithms for annotation and ontology generation has a time complexity of $O(n^2)$. The ontology and KG instances that were generated are based on the power transformer dataset [1]. We can see in Fig. 2 (i.e., ontology) that some classes are not connected. The reason for this is, that structured learning was unable to establish a connection between those disjointed classes. This also demonstrates the inherent uncertainty of structure learning.

3.4 Visualisation

The visualisation component provides the user interface for interaction. For example, the visualisation component interactively displays the results of the semantic reasoning, assisting both experts and non-experts in comprehending the variables' relationships. Figure 3 shows the visualisation of the results of the semantic reasoning performed via SPARQL. The semantic reasoning in Fig. 3a shows all the KG instances having an influence factor (or weight) greater than or equal to 0.37 and Fig. 3b shows the nodes that are being influenced by $Co2$ nodes. Moreover, the visualisation also provides an interface that allows one to set the hyperparameters, such as DAG filter threshold, L1 and L2 regularisation, for the structure learning.

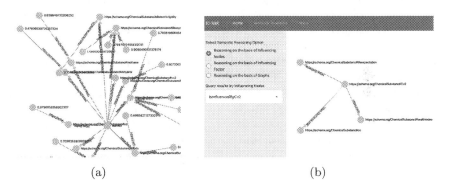

(a)   (b)

Fig. 3. (a) Visualisation of semantic reasoning results according to influencing factor (or weights). (b) Visualisation of the outcomes of semantic reasoning according to their influencing nodes (or class).

4   Implementation

Python version 3.7 and Streamlit version 1.7.0 were used for the implementation of the proposed work. For the implementation of the Bayesian structure learning algorithms discussed in Sect. 3.2, we use CausalNex [2] version 0.11.0. CausalNex is a Python library for Bayesian Networks and causal reasoning. Owlready2 version 0.37 [9] was used for ontology generation and annotation as discussed in

Sect. 3.3. Similarly, RDFLib version 6.1.1 was used for SPARQL queries in order to interact with the KG, and Streamlit agraph was used for the visualisation if the KG and the DAG. The other libraries scikit-learn version 1.1.1, NetworkX version 2.7.1 and pandas version 1.4.1 were used for handling data such as data preprocessing. The source code is available openly on GitHub[1].

5   Evaluation

When investigating a product failure, investigators would typically want to know the interdependence of the various manufacturing steps, as well as their relationships and effects on other steps. And since our work is focused on minimising product failure, we evaluated our work by evaluating if the generated KG would answer the question that would arise during the failure analysis. Table 1 presents the questions of interest for product failure analysis and their respective answers (i.e., how KG answers the raised questions).

Table 1. Competency questions pertaining to product failure analysis and the corresponding answers.

Questions	Answer
What are the interdependencies between the various manufacturing steps (or what are the interdependencies with step X)?	Interdependencies between various manufacturing steps are answered by the object property *isInfluencedByNode*
How does manufacturing step X influence manufacturing step Y, or what is the effect of manufacturing step X on step Y?	The effect of manufacturing step X on step Y data property *isInfluencedByNode*
How are the interdependencies between the various stages of production determined? Is it based on expert knowledge or independent data-driven learning?	The data property *isOriginatedFromNode* provides an answer to how the interdependencies were deduced

In addition, it is essential that the generated ontology is consistent and error-free. This is due to the fact that inconsistent ontology can lead to problems, such as erroneous inferences. We ran the Hermit[2] reasoner to evaluate the consistency of the generated ontology, which confirmed that the generated ontology had no consistency. The duration of the reasoner was roughly 60 ms.

6   Conclusion and Future Work

In this paper, we presented our work on manufacturing process optimisation using KG and BN, which, to the best of our knowledge, is among the first attempt

---

[1] Code: https://github.com/tekrajchhetri/ki-net.
[2] http://www.hermit-reasoner.com.

to bridge the gap in the industrial sector's usage of KGs in manufacturing. The use of the KG provides the interoperability, semantics (or meaning) of data and further allows for reasoning, which can be extremely beneficial when analysing failures in sectors such as manufacturing. In addition, the application of KG permits interpretability, a benefit that techniques such as deep learning lack.

Future work would consist of applying the proposed method to other domains or deploying it in industrial environments. In addition, one could extend the work by incorporating additional domain knowledge and applying machine learning to KG for improved results, as we demonstrated in our previous study [5].

Acknowledgements. The research reported in this paper has been funded by European Interreg Austria-Bavaria project KI-Net[3] (grant number: AB292). We would also like to thank Oleksandra Roche-Newton for her assistance in the manuscript preparation and Simon Außerlechner, system engineer at STI Innsbruck, for facilitating servers for experimentation([3] https://ki-net.eu).

References

1. Arias, R.: Data for: Root cause analysis improved with machine learning for failure analysis in power transformers (2020). https://doi.org/10.17632/RZ75W3FKXY. 1

2. Beaumont, P., et al.: CausalNex (2021). https://github.com/quantumblacklabs/causalnex. Last Accessed 25 Apr 2022

3. Cao, S., Bryceson, K., Hine, D.: An ontology-based bayesian network modelling for supply chain risk propagation. Indus. Manage. Data Syst. **119**(8), 1691–1711 (2019). https://doi.org/10.1108/IMDS-01-2019-0032

4. Chen, R., Lu, Y., Witherell, P., Simpson, T.W., Kumara, S., Yang, H.: Ontology-driven learning of bayesian network for causal inference and quality assurance in additive manufacturing. IEEE Robot. Autom. Lett. **6**(3), 6032–6038 (2021). https://doi.org/10.1109/LRA.2021.3090020

5. Chhetri, T.R., Kurteva, A., Adigun, J.G., Fensel, A.: Knowledge graph based hard drive failure prediction. Sensors **22**(3) (2022). https://doi.org/10.3390/s22030985

6. Heckerman, D.: A tutorial on learning with bayesian networks (2020). https://doi.org/10.48550/ARXIV.2002.00269

7. Kang, S., Kim, E., Shim, J., Chang, W., Cho, S.: Product failure prediction with missing data. Int. J. Prod. Res. **56**(14), 4849–4859 (2018)

8. Kang, Z., Catal, C., Tekinerdogan, B.: Product failure detection for production lines using a data-driven model. Expert Syst. Appl. **202**, 117398 (2022). https://doi.org/10.1016/j.eswa.2022.117398

9. Lamy, J.B.: Owlready: ontology-oriented programming in python with automatic classification and high level constructs for biomedical ontologies. Artif. Intell. Med. **80**, 11–28 (2017). https://doi.org/10.1016/j.artmed.2017.07.002

10. Riali, I., Fareh, M., Bouarfa, H.: A semantic approach for handling probabilistic knowledge of fuzzy ontologies. In: ICEIS (1), pp. 407–414 (2019)

11. Scanagatta, M., Salmerón, A., Stella, F.: A survey on bayesian network structure learning from data. Prog. Artif. Intell. **8**(4), 425–439 (2019)

12. Setiawan, F.A., Budiardjo, E.K., Wibowo, W.C.: Bynowlife: A novel framework for owl and bayesian network integration. Information **10**(3), 95 (2019). https://doi.org/10.3390/info10030095

13. Zheng, X., Aragam, B., Ravikumar, P., Xing, E.P.: DAGs with NO TEARS: Continuous Optimization for Structure Learning. In: Advances in Neural Information Processing Systems (2018)
14. Zheng, X., Dan, C., Aragam, B., Ravikumar, P., Xing, E.P.: Learning sparse nonparametric DAGs. In: International Conference on Artificial Intelligence and Statistics (2020)

Representing Technical Standards as Knowledge Graph to Guide the Design of Industrial Systems

Jose Illescas[ID], Georg Buchgeher[✉][ID], Lisa Ehrlinger[ID], David Gabauer[ID], and Jorge Martinez-Gil[ID]

Software Competence Center Hagenberg GmbH (SCCH), Hagenberg, Austria
{Jose.Illescas,Georg.Buchgeher,Lisa.Ehrlinger,
David.Gabauer,Jorge.Martinez-Gil}@scch.at
http://www.scch.at

Abstract. Technical standards help software architects to identify relevant requirements and to facilitate system certification, i.e., to systematically assess whether a system meets critical requirements in fields like security, safety, or interoperability. Despite their usefulness, standards typically remain vague on how requirements should be addressed via solutions like patterns or reference architectures. Thus, software architecture design remains a time-consuming human-centered process.

In this work, we propose an approach on how to use knowledge graphs for supporting software architects in the design of complex industrial systems. We discuss how project-generic knowledge (e.g., technical standards) and project-specific knowledge like the description of a concrete system can be modeled as knowledge graph. Making the architectural knowledge, which is currently present in technical standards and other resources, machine-readable, enables the support of the software architect through expert systems and therefore, improve the quality of the overall system design. However, since architectural knowledge is currently presented in many different formats, the transformation to a uniform, machine-readable form is required. We demonstrate the applicability of our approach with a representative example of an industrial client-server architecture and outline research challenges for future work.

Keywords: Knowledge graph · Ontology · Technical standard · System architecture · Architecture design · Architecture evaluation

1 Introduction

The design of industrial hardware and software systems involves expert knowledge of a broad spectrum of areas and fields, considering application domain knowledge (over general software engineering activities), system kind-specific application, and technology-specific expertise, among others. As systems evolve, the importance of meeting their quality (and functional) requirements, such as

R. Moreno-Díaz et al. (Eds.): EUROCAST 2022, LNCS 13789, pp. 603–610, 2022.
https://doi.org/10.1007/978-3-031-25312-6_71

safety, security, integrity, maintainability, etc., increases because they determine the foundation of the system [5]. Nevertheless, in practice, many of the fundamental quality requirements are not addressed due to the lack of knowledge, time, or expertise [1].

Thus, software architects are confronted with more demanding activities during the architecture design process as presented in [11] and have to work with many kinds of knowledge. Architectural knowledge generalizes explicit and implicit reusable knowledge, which can vary in form, type, degree of formality, etc., such as reference architectures, architectural styles, patterns, design patterns, technical standards, or guidelines.

Technical standards, developed and maintained by networks of international institutions (such as ISO, IEC, and ETSI) together with national organizations (such as NIST, DIN, and ANSI), contain relevant knowledge to be considered during the software architecture design as they reflect a global consensus of people with expertise in their subject of matter and who know the needs of the organizations they represent [2,13,14]. A technical standard contains a set of requirements and recommendations that are relevant for specific kinds of systems in a domain or for certain processes. To claim conformance to a standard all requirements defined by the standard must be fulfilled. Technical standards support software architects to identify relevant requirements and facilitate system certification. However, the adherence to such standards can be challenging, e.g., due to the vagueness of how to address provisions, or the expected familiarity with the standard that the architect requires to use it.

Recent advancements in artificial intelligence (AI) allow the development of novel kinds of systems and the automation of knowledge-intensive activities that previously had to be carried out manually by humans. Thus, the software engineering community researches how software engineering can be supported with AI-based technologies. Knowledge graphs (KGs) are an emerging technology for the development of explainable AI applications. KGs are used for semantically modelling a complex domain [9,19], and use reasoning- and AI-based methods for the development of knowledge-based systems like question-answering (QA) [15], decision support systems [18] and recommendation systems [7].

This work explores how KGs can be used to support software architects in designing complex industrial systems. The remainder of the paper is distributed as follows: we present our approach to build a KG for supporting software architects considering project-specific and generic knowledge in Sect. 2. Section 3 presents a representative example during the architecture design process supported by the KG and automated reasoning. Section 4 presents a short overview of the related work. Finally, we present research challenges and conclusions.

2   Approach

Architecture design is an incremental and iterative process, which makes it an exhaustive human-centered, resource-, time- and knowledge-intensive consuming activity [8]. Since software architects have a great impact on the quality of the system [4], it is important to support them with relevant knowledge that needs to be considered during architecture design and evaluation. Reusable architecture knowledge is therefore used to validate if the requirements have been met.

Such automated support would improve not only the quality, but the access of reusable knowledge gained by experience of the architect as well, two key factors of the continuous software evolution and development phases.

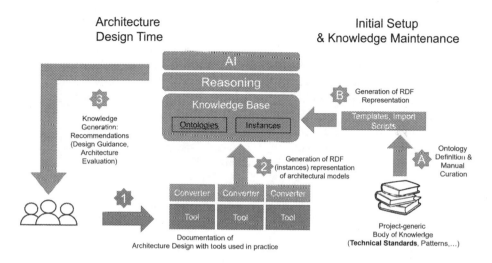

Fig. 1. Approach of the system for assisting and validating design decisions.

Figure 1 illustrates our approach of building KGs based on existing project-generic knowledge (such as technical standards) to support the software architecture design phase. As mentioned in [6], a KG is built by two main components, a knowledge base consisting of ontologies, describing the domain, and a reasoning component, which is used to perform inference and exploit non-obvious relations and derive new knowledge. Thus, several base ontologies are defined in a first step, e.g., a generic schema for technical standards which covers their main structure, relationships and main characteristics.

Software architects work with many kinds of architectural knowledge and tools which have different degrees of abstraction. The knowledge can be either project-generic or specific, tacit or explicit, and so forth. Certain kind of knowledge is also prone to the phenomena denoted vaporization of knowledge. Nevertheless, the implementation of such a KG, would support the main concept of knowledge management by capturing, sharing, using and reusing it, which also conforms greatly to the definition of an ontology.

On top of the KG, we intend to exploit reasoning and AI-based methods to automate the design process to find recommendations, alternatives, disregarded provisions that might be of great importance and be able to find and react to conflicting approaches, etc. Thus, enabling the KG to support the software architect during the architecture design process by providing design guidance and auto-mated architecture evaluation. As part of design guidance, context-dependent relevant architecture knowledge is derived and proposed. During automated architecture evaluation a candidate architecture solution structure is analyzed, e.g., to identify not or incorrectly addressed requirements and to suggest poten-tial improvements for an existing architecture design.

3   Exemplary Application to Industrial Control System

This chapter shows how to apply our approach from Sect. 2 to a client-server com-munication in an industrial setting, i.e., an industrial control system (ICS) that provides a remote maintenance API. The example considers only the security context of the system's communication, which can be evaluated to determine how secure it is. A technical standard whose scope considers cyber-security require-ments, could provide provisions that can be used to recommend and achieve a more secure communication, thus improving the security of the system.

On the one hand, we are provided with a system component structure, on the other hand we use a technical standard addressing cyber-security for com-ponents of industrial automation and control systems IACS. The system com-ponent structure, shown in Fig. 2, is comprised of two components, namely, the ICS component acting as the server and the remote maintenance component, which is a web application acting as the client. The ICS component provides a service port for accessing maintenance data. The remote maintenance compo-nent has a reference port for communicating with the port provided by the ICS system component. Both ports use a dedicated API, i.e., the *Remote Mainte-nance API* and support the communication protocols HTTP and HTTPS. The two components communicate over HTTP.

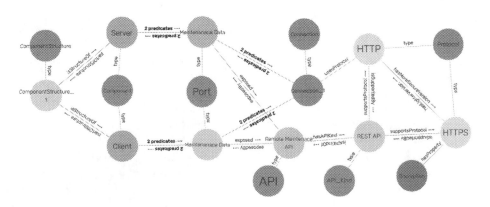

Fig. 2. Representation of the initial setup of the application (GraphDB visualization).

The IEC 62443, a standard series that address cyber-security for operational technology in automation and control systems, is considered. More specifically, in this example we refer to the IEC 62443-4-2 standard, titled Security for industrial automation and control systems - Part 4–2: Technical security requirements for IACS components, which will be further addressed as the base standard. The base standard provides a set of cyber security requirements for the components that compose an IACS. The document specifies security capabilities of those components with regards to the ability of mitigating security threats without the assistance of compensating countermeasures [12]. Among the relevant requirements we identified the following:

CR 3.1 Communication integrity. Capability to protect transmitted information, as the data being transmitted is a common target of manipulation.

CR 3.1 (Enhancement) Communication authentication. Components should be capable of verifying the authenticity of the received information.

CR 4.1 Information confidentiality. Components should be able to guarantee protection of confidentiality of data at rest and/or in transit.

Despite the simplicity of the example, more specific information is needed to answer questions like *Is the system solution tamper-proof?*, with respect to the data being transmitted. This question will be referred to as the example question. Notoriously, concepts such as *Components, Ports, API*, and their relationships, among others are needed to define system solutions, technical standards and their content. Those concepts and relationships are distributed in multiple ontologies that cover project-generic and project-specific information. The ontologies are classified as reusable solutions, system base, type specific instance ontologies, etc. For this example, the following base ontologies of our KG are used and further exploited by a reasoning engine that uses the OWL2 QL rule set:

Component Structures: Contains concepts relevant for component solution structures such as components, referenced and provided ports, exposed API and their respective attributes.

Standards Schema: A generic construct to define standards, provisions, their categories, enhancements and other kinds of supplemental information.

IEC 62443 Instances: Concrete instantiation of the base standard.

Protocol Instances: Instances of protocols with complementary properties and information.

We define an ontology based on the example description, mapping the description entities to the KG concepts. Then the system can check whether the proposed component solution has a partial conformance to the base standard. With partial conformance, we limit the scope to the three requirements mentioned above with respect to the data in transit.

To demonstrate the approach, we consider two scenarios. First, HTTP is used as communication protocol, which is not considered safe and does not conform to the base standard. In the second scenario, HTTPS is used. HTTPS is transmitted over TLS, which makes it a more secure, encrypted and robust variant of HTTP. Hence, a better recommendation can be proposed. The connection, as stated above, supports both protocols. This is a simple but relevant evaluation and assessment achieved with the help of the KG. After considering the suggestion of using HTTPS, the answer of the same example question shows a positive result, see Table 1.

Table 1. Result of the automated security evaluation for the two scenarios

ReferencePort	API	Protocol	isSafe
Maintenance data	Remote maintenance API	HTTP	FALSE
Maintenance data	Remote maintenance API	HTTPS	TRUE

The exemplary application in this section shows how a design decision can be supported by requirements obtained from a technical standard and how it can be complemented with more data.

4   Background and Related Work

There have been studies which expose the challenges that architects face due to the heterogeneity of the knowledge, as shown in [16], which analyzes how efficiently search engines can find AK to solve specific architectural tasks and stress how challenging the process of finding the required AK is.

Moreover, due to the growing amount of technical standards as an effect of Industry 4.0 (I4.0), the importance of technical KGs, based on technical content, to support engineering design activities is critical [10]. In [2] a KG, referred to as I40KG, for I4.0 related standards, norms, and reference frameworks is proposed. I40KG is intended to support newcomers, experts, and other stakeholders in understanding how to implement I4.0 systems by providing a Linked Data-conform collection of annotated, classified reference guidelines. The need to make such relevant knowledge accessible to system stakeholders and the semantic definition of standards and their relationships is considered. Nevertheless, our approach goes a step beyond. Besides classifying them and making their relationships clear, we want to use their content, especially the provisions and complementary information, to provide guidance and assistance during architectural evaluation, where a given system solution can be further analyzed and backed up by standards.

Furthermore, the application of AI methods in software engineering has been an exciting topic, as shown in [3] where a systematic review is presented. The different kinds and methods of AI applied at different stages of software engineering are reviewed with the conclusion that AI has successfully optimized many tasks related to the development cycle of software engineering. In [2], AI was used to create embeddings and find similarities between standards. However, we want to analyze to which extent we can use AI methods to explore and make more accessible the architectural knowledge silos within the KG.

Finally, [17] proposed a KG for bug resolution, showing some interesting results because the bug KG can provide more accurate and comprehensive information related to a bug issue. Due to the highly explainable content, we consider a KG for assisting software architects in a more complex process such as the design of industrial systems.

5   Conclusion

In this paper, we explained the idea of modeling a KG that covers project-generic knowledge, e.g., technical standards and project-specific knowledge for supporting software architects. Making architectural knowledge present in technical standards and other sources accessible in a more automated fashion can improve the quality of the industrial control systems as the architectural design process would be less demanding for such critical stakeholders.

Most of the available architectural knowledge is presented in natural language, thus, Natural Language Processing methods are required to automatically transform this data to a machine-readable form (e.g., a KG). The benefit of using KGs for representing architectural knowledge is the high expressiveness in contrast to classic data models (e.g., relational data model) [9]. Therefore, the highly explainable content of the KGs can support software architects during human-centric tasks of the architectural design process. The use of explainable AI like KGs is able to clarify the recommendations and analyses rather than relying on purely abstract black-box models.

Tools that interact with KGs in a more natural way are needed. Then arbitrary system context-relevant questions can be placed without the need of a query language like SPARQL. Such a demanding human-centered activity should support a flexible query composition mechanism to make the retrieval of required knowledge less demanding and more accessible.

Finally, defining a more robust and complete architectural knowledge domain to improve systems quality is essential. However, full automation might not be feasible. Manual curation, pre-, and post-preparation of the models and data are still required to improve the results.

Acknowledgements. This work was supported in part by the Interreg Österreich-Bayern 2014–2020 Programme funded under Grant (AB292) and in part by the FFG BRIDGE project AK-Graph (grant no. 883718).

References

1. Assal, H., Chiasson, S.: Security in the software development lifecycle. In: Proceedings of the Fourteenth USENIX Conference on Usable Privacy and Security, SOUPS 2018, pp. 281–296. USENIX Association, USA (2018)
2. Bader, S.R., Grangel-Gonzalez, I., Nanjappa, P., Vidal, M.-E., Maleshkova, M.: A knowledge graph for industry 4.0. In: Harth, A., et al. (eds.) ESWC 2020. LNCS, vol. 12123, pp. 465–480. Springer, Cham (2020). https://doi.org/10.1007/978-3-030-49461-2_27

3. Barenkamp, M., Rebstadt, J., Thomas, O.: Applications of AI in classical software engineering. AI Perspect. **2**(1), 1–15 (2020). https://doi.org/10.1186/s42467-020-00005-4
4. Capilla, R., Jansen, A., Tang, A., Avgeriou, P., Babar, M.A.: 10 years of software architecture knowledge management: practice and future. J. Syst. Softw. **116**, 191–205 (2016). https://doi.org/10.1016/j.jss.2015.08.054
5. Doukidis, G., Spinellis, D., Ebert, C.: Digital transformation - a primer for practitioners. IEEE Softw. **37**(05), 13–21 (2020). https://doi.org/10.1109/MS.2020.2999969
6. Ehrlinger, L., Wöß, W.: Towards a definition of knowledge graphs. In: SEMANTiCS (Posters, Demos, SuCCESS) (2016)
7. Engleitner, N., Kreiner, W., Schwarz, N., Kopetzky, T., Ehrlinger, L.: Knowledge graph embeddings for news article tag recommendation (2021). https://doi.org/10.13140/RG.2.2.12602.52161
8. Farshidi, S., Jansen, S., van der Werf, J.M.: Capturing software architecture knowledge for pattern-driven design. J. Syst. Softw. **169**, 110714 (2020). https://doi.org/10.1016/j.jss.2020.110714
9. Feilmayr, C., Wöß, W.: An analysis of ontologies and their success factors for application to business. Data Knowl. Eng. **101**, 1–23 (2016). https://doi.org/10.1016/j.datak.2015.11.003
10. Han, J., Sarica, S., Shi, F., Luo, J.: Semantic networks for engineering design: state of the art and future directions. J. Mech. Des. **144**(2) (2021). https://doi.org/10.1115/1.4052148
11. Hofmeister, C., Kruchten, P., Nord, R.L., Obbink, H., Ran, A., America, P.: A general model of software architecture design derived from five industrial approaches. J. Syst. Softw. **80**(1), 106–126 (2007). https://doi.org/10.1016/j.jss.2006.05.024
12. Security for industrial automation and control systems - part 4–2: Technical security requirements for iacs components. Standard, International Electrotechnical Commission (2019)
13. International Electrotechnical Commission: Understanding standards. https://iec.ch/understanding-standards
14. International Organization for Standarization: Standards. https://www.iso.org/standards.html
15. Lukovnikov, D., Fischer, A., Lehmann, J., Auer, S.: Neural network-based question answering over knowledge graphs on word and character level. In: Proceedings of the 26th International Conference on World Wide Web, pp. 1211–1220. International World Wide Web Conferences Steering Committee (2017). https://doi.org/10.1145/3038912.3052675
16. Soliman, M., Wiese, M., Li, Y., Riebisch, M., Avgeriou, P.: Exploring web search engines to find architectural knowledge (2021)
17. Wang, L., Sun, X., Wang, J., Duan, Y., Li, B.: Construct bug knowledge graph for bug resolution. In: 2017 IEEE/ACM 39th International Conference on Software Engineering Companion (ICSE-C), pp. 189–191 (2017). https://doi.org/10.1109/ICSE-C.2017.102
18. Wang, X., He, X., Cao, Y., Liu, M., Chua, T.S.: Kgat: knowledge graph attention network for recommendation. In: Proceedings of the 25th ACM SIGKDD International Conference on Knowledge Discovery & Data Mining, KDD 2019, pp. 950–958. Association for Computing Machinery, New York (2019). https://doi.org/10.1145/3292500.3330989
19. Yahya, M., Breslin, J.G., Ali, M.I.: Semantic web and knowledge graphs for industry 4.0. Appl. Sci. **11**(11) (2021). https://doi.org/10.3390/app11115110

Improvements for *mlrose* Applied to the Traveling Salesperson Problem

Stefan Wintersteller, Martin Uray$^{(\boxtimes)}$ ⓘ, Michael Lehenauer,
and Stefan Huber ⓘ

Salzburg University of Applied Sciences, Salzburg, Austria
{swintersteller.its-m2020,martin.uray,mlehenauer.its-m2020,
stefan.huber}@fh-salzburg.ac.at

Abstract. In this paper we discuss the application of Artificial Intelligence (AI) to the exemplary industrial use case of the two-dimensional commissioning problem in a high-bay storage, which essentially can be phrased as an instance of Traveling Salesperson Problem (TSP).

We investigate the *mlrose* library that provides an TSP optimizer based on various heuristic optimization techniques. Our focus is on two methods, namely Genetic Algorithm (GA) and Hill Climbing (HC), which are provided by *mlrose*. We present improvements for both methods that yield shorter tour lengths, by moderately exploiting the problem structure of TSP. That is, the proposed improvements have a generic character and are not limited to TSP only.

Keywords: Artificial intelligence · Traveling salesperson problem · Genetic algorithm · Hill Climbing · Commissioning · Material flow

1 Introduction

In this paper, we investigate the application of methods of AI to an industrial problem on the example of optimizing commissioning tasks in a high-bay storage. Our goal is not to improve on the state of the art in this task but instead shed light on this problem from an AI engineering point of view. From this point of view, we first have to translate this problem adequately to apply methods of artificial intelligence, then we would seek for established software implementations of these methods and evaluate these on the given task of high-bay storage commissioning.

The commissioning problem or order picking problem is the following: We are given a high-bay storage where goods are stored in slots arranged on a two-dimensional wall. An order comprises a finite set of places on that wall that need

---

Martin Uray is funded by the Science and Innovation Strategy Salzburg (WISS 2025) project "DaSuMa" (grant number 20204-WISS/140/572/3-2022) and Stefan Huber by the European Interreg Österreich-Bayern project AB292 "KI-Net". Both authors are also supported by the Christian Doppler Research Association (JRC ISIA).

R. Moreno-Díaz et al. (Eds.): EUROCAST 2022, LNCS 13789, pp. 611–618, 2022.
https://doi.org/10.1007/978-3-031-25312-6_72

to be visited to pick up the goods. We desire to do this as quickly as possible. Assuming a tapping point where the collection device starts and ends its job, we can interpret this as an instance of the TSP: Given a set of n locations $p_0, \ldots, p_{n-1}$ in the plane, we ask for the shortest closed tour on $\mathbb{R}^2$ that visits all points $p_0, \ldots, p_{n-1}$.

What we essentially ask for is the optimal order at which we visit the locations p_i. Furthermore, the way we measure distances between pairs of locations is relevant. To sum up, we consider $p_0, \ldots, p_{n-1}$ in a metric space (X, d) with a metric d, encode a tour as a permutation $\pi \colon \{0, \ldots, n-1\} \to \{0, \ldots, n-1\}$ and ask for a tour π that minimizes the tour length $\ell(\pi)$ with

$$\ell(\pi) = \sum_{i=0}^{n-1} d(p_{\pi(i)}, p_{\pi((i+1) \bmod n)}). \tag{1}$$

In this paper, we may interchangeably represent a permutation π as the sequence $(\pi(0), \ldots, \pi(n-1))$, when it fits better to the formal setting.

A natural choice for d is the Euclidean metric, which we use for experiments in this paper. However, the discussed methods work with any metric and in practice certain restrictions in the motion of the highbay storage may be reflected by a respective choice of d, such as the Manhattan metric.

1.1   Related Work

The GA is comprehensively described in [9]. Several improvements, modifications and adaption for the vanilla implementation for the problem of TSP have been proposed, like by employing Ant Colonies [5], Reinforcement Learning and supervised learning [3], or recurrent neural networks [10]. A recent and comprehensive overview on TSP using AI is given by Osaba et al. [6], covering the GA. This work highlights the most notable GA crossover variants.

Similarly, also the HC is comprehensively described in Russel and Norvig, including several modifications to overcome issues, like plateaus or ridges [9]. Additional extensions, like Simulated Annealing, Tabu Search, the Greedy Randomize Adaptive Search Procedure, Variable Neighborhood Search, and the Iterated Local Search support to overcome the local optima problem [2].

2   Experimental Setup

For all the experiments in this work a common setup is established. As there are already libraries for standard implementations for the GA and HC algorithm, we do not implement the algorithms from scratch, rather we use a library called $mlrose$[1] as a base and improve the above stated algorithm based on this library. This library already provides a mapping of the TSP to a set of implementations

---

[1] https://mlrose.readthedocs.io/.

of well-known AI methods, which makes it a favorable candidate for our commissioning task from an engineering point of view. For this work however, only the implementation of the GA and HC are used.

During experiments, an implementation error was discovered, which caused *mlrose* to consistently select unfit individuals when fitness can assume negative values, which is the case for mlrose's implementation for TSP[2]. The experiments presented in this paper in particular contain a comparison of the original and the fixed version of *mlrose*.

Our evaluations are based on the well-known precalculated data set *att48* from TSPLIB [7]. This data set contains 48 cities in a coordinate system with a known minimal tour length of 33523 (unit-less). All experiments are evaluated using the CPU clock, and were conducted on a Intel Core i7-7700K (4.20 GHz).

3   Genetic Algorithm (GA)

3.1   General Basics

The GA is an optimization and search procedure that is inspired by the maxim "survival of the fittest" in natural evolution. A candidate solution (individual) is encoded by a string over some alphabet (genetic code). Individuals are modified by two genetic operators: (i) random alteration (mutation) of single individuals and (ii) recombination of two parents (crossover) to form offsprings. Given a set of individuals (population), a selection mechanism based on a fitness function together with the two genetic operators produce a sequence of populations (generations). The genetic operators promote exploration of the search space while the selection mechanism attempts to promote the survival of fit individuals over generations. The GA as implemented in *mlrose* terminates after no progress has been made for a certain number of generations or a predefined maximum number of generations.

For GA to work well, it is paramount that a reasonable genetic representation of individuals is used. In particular, the crossover operator needs to have the property that the recombination of two fit parents produces fit offsprings again, otherwise the genetic structure of fit individuals would not survive over generations and GA easily degenerates to a randomized search. For further details on the GA, the reader be reffered to [9, Chapter 4].

3.2   Implementation in *mlrose*

The state vector representation is directly used by *mlrose* as genetic representation, i.e., an individual is encoded as a permutation sequence π of the integers $0, \ldots, n-1$, which are indices of the n locations to be visited. Recombination of a first parent π_1 and a second parent π_2 works as follows: The sequence π_1 is considered to be split at a random position, the prefix of π_1 is taken and the

---

[2] https://github.com/gkhayes/mlrose/issues/63.

missing locations in the genetic string are taken from π_2 in the order as they appear in π_2.

Note that TSP has the symmetry property that a solution candidate π and its reverse counterpart π^* can be considered to be the same solutions. Not only is $\ell(\pi) = \ell(\pi^*)$ but in some sense the structure of the solution is the same. The reason behind this is that the pairwise distances between locations in the Euclidean plane (or adequate metric spaces) are invariant with respect to reflection.

However, the recombination strategy does not take this symmetry property into account. This leads to the following problem: Consider the recombination of two parents, π_1 and π_2, that are reasonably similar and fit, however, their direction of traversal is essentially opposite. Then the offspring first traverses the locations like π_1 and then continues with π_2 that possesses the reversed direction, which likely destroys the fit solution structure displayed by π_1 and π_2. That is, two fit parents produce unfit offsprings.

As an illustrative extreme example, assume π_1 is a globally optimal solution of TSP and $\pi_2 = \pi_1^*$. For sake of argument, assume $\pi_1 = [0, 1, \ldots, 7]$ and $\pi_2 = [7, 6, \ldots, 0]$. Then the offspring π_3 that results from a split in the middle of the genetic string would be $\pi_3 = [0, \ldots, 3, 7, \ldots, 4]$, which is now typically far from globally optimal, i.e., $\ell(\pi_3) \gg \ell(\pi_1)$. This recombination would only not hurt if the middle of the fit tour π_1, where the split point of the recombination is located, would happen to be close to the start or end of π_1.

3.3   Modification

To mitigate the presented issue of the recombination strategy, we would like to have a natural notion of direction of traversal of a tour, so we could figure out whether we would need to reverse the parent π_2 before recombining it with π_1. But since we lack an adequate mathematical notion, we factor out the two possibilities of tour traversals of π_2 in a different way.

When recombining π_1 and π_2, we actually consider two candidate offsprings: offspring π_3 from π_1 and π_2 and offspring π_4 from π_1 and π_2^*. We then compare the fitness values of the two candidate offsprings, i.e., we compare $\ell(\pi_3)$ and $\ell(\pi_4)$, and keep only the better one as the recombination result. Following our observation from the previous section, we expect that one offspring of two fit parents results from a direction-conforming recombination and the other does not. (Of course, it still can happen that the two parents are bad mates for other reasons, i.e., they can still be structurally insufficiently compatible.)

This way we turn the original recombination operator into a reversal-invariant recombination operator. Note that our proposed recombination operator is beneficial not only for TSP, but generally for all problems with this reversal symmetry of the genetic encoding of individuals.

In literature other recombination methods, based on crossover [4,8] and mutation [1], can be found. These recombination operators work differently, but can all be applied additionally within the proposed method, instead of the implemented recombination operator.

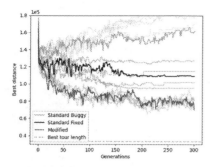 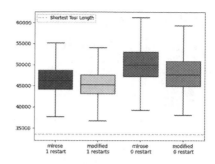

(a) Plots on the tour lengths for the experiments with the GA. The optimal solution is depicted by the red dashed line. Additional seeds are indicated transparent.

(b) The box plots on the tour lengths for the experiments with the HC algorithm. The optimal solution is depicted by the red dashed line.

Fig. 1. Results of the experiments on the GA (Fig. 1a) and HC (Fig. 1b).

3.4   Results

An experiment was carried out to measure the performance of the modified GA and the fixed version, in comparison with the default implementation by *mlrose*. All experiments algorithms use a shared parameter configuration of a population size of 100 and a maximum number of 300 generations, if not stated otherwise. While we would set a small positive mutation rate in practice, the higher the mutation rate is, the closer both implementations converge to a random search. Hence, for the sake of comparison, we set the mutation rate to 0.0 for our experiment. Carrying out all experiments 1000 times, the results visually look like Gaussian distributed (not shown in the paper) and hence the notation of (mean ± std. deviation) is used in the following discussion.

The tour lengths of the original implementation (buggy), the fixed, and modified version are shown over five different initial seed settings (Fig. 1a). The red dashed horizontal line marks the optimal solution at a tour length of 33523. The results over 1000 experiments show, that the modified GA (67961 ± 3602) is closer to the optimum than the original algorithm and the fixed version by *mlrose* (125019 ± 4438 and 110137 ± 6677, respectively) (however note, that the original version acts againts convergence to a minimum). The modifications pose a decrease in the mean tour lengths by a factor of 0.54 and 0.61 for the original and the fixed version, respectively.

The gain in the performance by the modified algorithm is at the expense of a higher computation time. The original algorithm by *mlrose* (18484 ± 111 ms) and its fixed version (18024 ± 100 ms) are faster than the modified GA (47988 ± 161 ms). The modification of the GA results in a mean computation slowdown by a factor of about 2.59 (original algorithm) and 2.66 (fixed algorithm), compared to the original implementation by *mlrose*.

4 Hill Climbing (HC)

4.1 General Basics and Implementation in *mlrose*

HC is a simple and most widely known optimization technique, cf. [9]. When phrased as a maximization (minimization, resp.) problem of a function ℓ over some domain, Hill Climbing moves stepwise upward (downward, resp.) along the steepest ascent (descent, resp.) until it reaches a local maximum (minimum, resp.) of ℓ. The domain is given by the transposition graph $G = (V, E)$ over the vertex set V of permutations π, where E contains an edge (π, π') between vertices π and π' iff we can turn π into π' via a single transposition, i.e., the tour π' results from the tour π by swapping two locations only.

In more detail, HC starts with a random tour π and calculates the cost $\ell(\pi)$ to be minimized. Then it considers all neighbors of π within G and their costs. If the neighbor π' with minimum costs has a lower cost than $\ell(\pi)$ then it moves to π' and repeats. Otherwise, π constitutes a local minimum and HC either terminates or restarts with a new random tour π, as implemented in *mlrose*. After a given maximum number of restarts, HC returns the best permutation found in all runs. For further details on the HC, the reader be reffered to [9, Chapter 4].

While vanilla HC is a simple optimization technique, various improvements are known in the literature to overcome different shortcomings, see [9] for an overview. First of all, HC gets stuck in local optima. To mitigate this issue, the *mlrose* implementation provides a restart mechanism. A second well-known issue for HC is the existence of plateaus, i.e., subregions of the domain where the fitness function is constant such that HC is no uphill direction. Allowing a certain number of sideways moves [9] would mitigate this issue, while no such mechanism is implemented in *mlrose*.

4.2 Modification

From the discussion in the previous section, we take away that local optima are the prominent issue for HC on TSP in *mlrose*.

Here a natural measure for the prominence of a local maximum is the number of steps in the transposition graph. A prominence of k means that we have to admit k downward steps from a local maximum until we can pursue an ascending path that allows us to escape the local maximum.

In the *mlrose* implementation, HC is already stuck at local maxima with a prominence of only 1, and it would resort to a restart. Our modification simply allows for a single downward step from local maxima to overcome local maxima of prominence 1. If the following step would lead us back to the old local maximum, we terminate this run and apply a restart as the original version. More generally, we simply keep a data structure of previously visited permutations to disallow cycles in the paths traced by HC.

This modification leads to another advantage: In the course of restarts, a series of Hill Climbing searches from randomly generated starting points is performed. After a restart, if the algorithm reaches a state that was visited in a previous trial, the Hill Climbing implemented by *mlrose* will take the same path again and will reach the very same local minimum again. The modified algorithm terminates after an already visited state is reached, which constitutes an early out optimization.

4.3   Results

An experiment over 1000 attempts was performed to measure the performance of the modified HC in comparison with the HC implementation by *mlrose*. The tour lengths of the modified algorithm and the HC implemented by *mlrose* using 0 and 1 restarts are shown in Fig. 1b. The results again look visually rather Gaussian distributed (not shown in the paper), such that we use the notation of (mean ± standard deviation) in the following. The red dashed horizontal line again marks the optimal tour length of 33523.

With 1 restart, the modified algorithm performs best (45420 ± 3340), while the implementation by *mlrose* has a slightly higher overall tour length (46438 ± 3427), which is expected since the modified version effectively extends the exploration.

For further comparison, the restarts parameter of both algorithms (standard HC implementation and modified) are limited to 0 to test the performance against the default configuration of *mlrose*. Here the improvement of the modified version (47944 ± 4348) (red) over the original version (50263 ± 4498) (green) becomes more significant.

The modification influences on the computing time as the modified algorithm is slightly slower (36588 ± 4243 ms) than the HC implemented by *mlrose* (34128 ± 3956 ms). Similar, the results for the experiments with 0 restarts. The modified algorithm has a higher computing time (18273 ± 2980 ms) than the HC implementation by *mlrose* (16701 ± 2551 ms). Increasing the number of restarts from 0 to 1 gives a slowdown of a factor of 1.9, for the modified and the original implementations likewise.

5   Conclusion and Final Remarks

This paper was motivated by the industrial application of AI to the industrial problem of optimizing commissioning tasks in a high-bay storage, which translates to the TSP.

For the experimental evaluation of the proposed approaches, we chose *mlrose* for a AI library that already provides optimization routines for TSP. With the experiments we had a closer look at two optimization techniques, namely GA and HC. After exploiting and fixing an implementation error within the library, the problem structure of TSP is analyzed: one improvement for the GA and one for the HC are introduced, respectively. The results show a reduction of 46%/39% for GA and 2.1%/4.6% for HC. The modifications we propose, however, have some generic character and are not only applicable to TSP.

For the GA, a significant improvement on the computed tour length can be shown based on our reversal-invariant crossover operator.

For the HC, the goal of the experiment was to show, that a problem-specific treatment is necessary for TSP. By altering the vanilla implementation towards the properties of the TSP, a clear improvement can be observed.

Finally, we would like to remark that to some extent our paper could be seen as a showcase that AI libraries should only carefully be applied as plug-and-play solutions to industrial problems and the specific problem structure of the industrial problem at hand likely provides means to improve the performance of the generic implementations. While the democratization through meta-learning facilities like AutoML relieve an application engineer from the tedious search for Machine Learning methods and their hyperparameters for a given problem at hand, we believe that in general, they do not make an understanding of the underlying methods obsolete.

References

1. Abdoun, O., Abouchabaka, J., Tajani, C.: Analyzing the performance of mutation operators to solve the travelling salesman problem. arXiv:1203.3099 (2012)
2. Al-Betar, M.A.: β-Hill climbing: an exploratory local search. Neural Comput. Appl. **28**(1), 153–168 (2016). https://doi.org/10.1007/s00521-016-2328-2
3. Gambardella, L.M., Dorigo, M.: Ant-Q: a reinforcement learning approach to the traveling salesman problem. In: Machine Learning Proceedings 1995, pp. 252–260. Elsevier (1995). https://doi.org/10.1016/B978-1-55860-377-6.50039-6
4. Hussain, A., Muhammad, Y.S., Nauman Sajid, M., Hussain, I., Mohamd Shoukry, A., Gani, S.: Genetic algorithm for traveling salesman problem with modified cycle crossover operator. Comput. Intell. Neurosci. **2017**, 1–7 (2017). https://doi.org/10.1155/2017/7430125
5. Mazidi, A., Fakhrahmad, M., Sadreddini, M.: Meta-heuristic approach to cvrp problem: local search optimization based on ga and ant colony. J. Adv. Comput. Res. **7**(1), 1–22 (2016)
6. Osaba, E., Yang, X.S., Del Ser, J.: Traveling salesman problem: a perspective review of recent research and new results with bio-inspired metaheuristics. In: Nature-Inspired Computation and Swarm Intelligence, pp. 135–164. Elsevier (2020). https://doi.org/10.1016/B978-0-12-819714-1.00020-8
7. Reinelt, G.: TSPLIB-a traveling salesman problem library. ORSA J. Comput. **3**(4), 376–384 (1991)
8. Roy, A., Manna, A., Maity, S.: A novel memetic genetic algorithm for solving traveling salesman problem based on multi-parent crossover technique. Decis. Mak. Appl. Manag. Eng. **2**(2) (2019). https://doi.org/10.31181/dmame1902076r
9. Russell, S., Norvig, P.: Artificial Intelligence: A Modern Approach. Prentice Hall, Upper Saddle River (2010)
10. Tarkov, M.S.: Solving the traveling salesman problem using a recurrent neural network. Numer. Anal. Appl. **8**(3), 275–283 (2015). https://doi.org/10.1134/S1995423915030088

Survey on Radar Odometry

Daniel Louback da Silva Lubanco[1]([✉]), Thomas Schlechter[2],
Markus Pichler-Scheder[1], and Christian Kastl[1]

[1] Linz Center of Mechatronics GmbH, 4040 Linz, Austria
{daniel.louback,markus.pichler-scheder,christian.kastl}@lcm.at
[2] University of Applied Sciences Upper Austria, 4600 Wels, Austria
thomas.schlechter@ieee.org
https://www.lcm.at/, https://www.fh-ooe.at/

Abstract. In this paper odometry approaches that use radar data are
analyzed. First, the importance of odometry is discussed along with
applications which usually require accurate odometry estimation. Moreover, sensors that are often used for odometry estimation are mentioned
as well as the possible drawbacks that these sensors may have. Finally,
the benefits of using radar as a source for odometry estimation are discussed. Furthermore, the approaches to perform radar odometry are categorized, and one categorization is evaluated as cardinal, namely the
division between the direct method and the indirect method. Therefore,
the direct method and the indirect method are investigated and their
characteristics are juxtaposed.

Keywords: Radar · Odometry · Navigation · Robotics

1 Introduction

This paper aims to discuss the recent developments in the radar odometry field.
It considers the motivation, advantages and drawbacks when using radar as
a source for odometry. Moreover, the different approaches for achieving radar
odometry are categorized and their principles are revealed.

Simultaneous Localization and Mapping (SLAM) consists of the problem of
an agent which is placed in an unknown environment and is able to create a representation of the environment, e.g. a map, while it localizes itself in that environment [6]. There is a huge variety of approaches to achieve SLAM including
[9,10]. Often, in order to achieve accurate results, the SLAM algorithm expects
that the provided odometry is as close as possible to be errorless. In mobile
robots and vehicles, odometry is usually calculated based on proprioceptive sensors, e.g. Inertial Measurement Unit (IMU) and wheel encoders. Nonetheless, it is
not always possible or meaningful to use wheel-encoders in robots, e.g. in drones;
also, IMU odometry estimations are affected by errors which are accumulated
over time; thus, a commercial IMU alone is often not enough for achieving highly

R. Moreno-Díaz et al. (Eds.): EUROCAST 2022, LNCS 13789, pp. 619–625, 2022.
https://doi.org/10.1007/978-3-031-25312-6_73

accurate estimations. Therefore, besides proprioceptive sensors, it is often sensible to include exteroceptive sensors for increasing the accuracy of the odometry estimation.

Exteroceptive sensors used for odometry estimation include camera, lidar, and radar. Even though, camera and lidar have advantages over radar, e.g. higher resolution from lidar, these two sensors have limitations with regards to their performance in several environments, e.g. environments which fog is present. See [19] for a performance comparison of lidar, radar and ultrasonic sensors with different materials. Therefore, due to its environmental robustness as well as its long measurement range capabilities, radars have recently received attention from researchers with regards to its use for odometry estimation [4].

Possibly, the most sensible categorization for radar odometry approaches is to divide them in direct and indirect methods [2]. In the former, the odometry estimation is calculated without the extraction of keypoints, e.g. by exploiting the Fourier-Mellin Transform (FMT) in order to register two radar images [3,16]. On the other hand, the latter performs the extraction of targets (keypoints) followed by data association between the consecutive measurements; in order to extract the keypoints, a Constant False Alarm (CFAR) detector can be used. CFAR is a widespread technique for detecting targets in radar signal processing; popular CFAR methods include Ordered-Statistic-CFAR and Cell-Averaging-CFAR [8].

Moreover, radar odometry methods may also be categorized by the type of radar which is used. For example, in [3] a scanning Frequency Modulated Continuous Wave (FMCW) radar was used, while in [11] a static FMCW radar was used.

Finally, radar odometry is often combined, or fused, with another source of odometry, commonly with an IMU, in order to obtain more accurate estimations. The fusion between radar and IMU is frequently denoted as Radar-Inertial odometry in the literature [14]. Radar and IMU data are often combined through a Kalman filter. Some of the radar odometry publications and their classifications can be seen in Table 1.

From the authors' point of view, the most significant distinction between radar odometry approaches is the one that divides them in direct and indirect methods. Therefore, this categorization will be the foremost highlighted in this paper.

This paper can be divided as follows: in the next section the direct method is explained, followed by a description of the indirect radar odometry approach. Finally, a conclusion is provided.

2   Direct Method

Direct radar odometry approaches in general consist of estimating the change in translation and change in orientation by using Fourier Transform (FT) properties along with correlation techniques. These allow one to find the local changes in translation and orientation which are converted to a global frame for odometry

Table 1. Some radar odometry publications.

Reference	Type of radar	Method	Sensor fusion
[3]	Scanning-Radar	Direct	No
[16]	Scanning-Radar	Direct	No
[15]	Scanning-Radar	Mixed	Yes (IMU)
[2]	Scanning-Radar	Indirect	No
[5]	MIMO FMCW Radar	Indirect	Yes (IMU)
[1]	MIMO FMCW Radar	Indirect	Yes (IMU)
[11]	MIMO FMCW Radar	Indirect	Yes (IMU)

estimation. See Fig. 1 for a diagram of how the direct method achieves relative motion estimation. Please notice that for direct methods, radar images are considered as 2-dimensional images in Cartesian coordinates formed by using radar range-azimuth data. To the best of the authors knowledge, all the publications which estimated the odometry with radar data using only the direct method were performed using a scanning-radar with 360-degrees field of view (FoV).

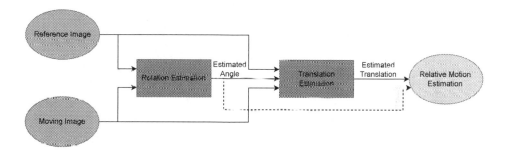

Fig. 1. Diagram for direct method.

The shift property states that if a signal $x(t)$ with its spectrum after the FT equal to $X(\omega)$ is shifted by t_0, the spectrum of this signal will be only affected on its phase:

$$\mathscr{F}\{x(t - t_0)\} = e^{-j\omega t_0} X(\omega) \tag{1}$$

2.1 Phase-Correlation

Among the correlation techniques for shift estimation, phase-correlation is a frequent choice for performing direct registration [3,18].

One of the advantages of the phase-correlation is that it can be implemented at reduced computational complexity by taking advantage of Fast Fourier Transform (FFT) and its inverse (IFFT).

Given two signals $s_1(x)$ and $s_2(x)$ such that $s_1, s_2 \in \mathbb{R}$. Suppose that s_2 is a shifted version of s_1, shifted by Δ_x. Then, s_2 can be written as:

$$s_2(x) = s_1(x - \Delta_x) \tag{2}$$

By using (1), we have that the spectra of the two signals will be related by:

$$S_2(u) = e^{-ju\Delta_x} S_1(u) \tag{3}$$

Consequently, their phase-normalized cross-spectrum $C(u)$ can be written as:

$$C(u) = \frac{S_2(u)S_1^*(u)}{|S_2(u)S_1^*(u)|} = e^{-ju\Delta_x} \tag{4}$$

After that, one can efficiently find the shift by using the IFFT on $C(u)$ leading in the 1d case to the Phase-Correlation Vector (PCV). Finally, one can find the shift Δ_x by finding the location of the highest peak in the PCV.

2.2   Rotation Estimation

Consider two radar images defined in the spatial domain in which the moving image $g_2(x,y)$ is rotated and translated with regards to the reference image $g_1(x,y)$. Let the rotation and translation components be θ_0, Δ_x, Δ_y respectively. Then, the moving image can be written as:

$$g_2(x,y) = g_1(x\cos(\theta_0) + y\sin(\theta_0) - \Delta_x, y\sin(\theta_0) - x\cos(\theta_0) - \Delta_y) \tag{5}$$

By observing (1) and (5) it is clear that the translation component will only affect the phase component of the spectrum. Hence, by defining $M_1(u,v)$ and $M_2(u,v)$ as the magnitude of the spectrum of $g_1(x,y)$ and $g_2(x,y)$ respectively, we have:

$$M_2(u,v) = M_1(u\cos(\theta_0) + v\sin(\theta_0), v\sin(\theta_0) - u\cos(\theta_0)) \tag{6}$$

Finally, one can then convert the two spectra to, e.g. polar or log-polar representation. For example, the resulting spectra of the two images in polar coordinates will have the following relationship:

$$M_1(\rho, \theta) = M_2(\rho, \theta - \theta_0) \tag{7}$$

Hence, by using phase-correlation, one finds the estimated change in orientation $(\hat{\theta}_0)$, i.e. the rotation component, between the two radar images.

2.3   Translation Estimation

After θ_0 is estimated, the next step consists of finding the translation components Δ_x and Δ_y. For that, one rotates either the reference or moving radar image by $-\hat{\theta}_0$ or $\hat{\theta}_0$ respectively. After this, phase-correlation may be used to find the estimated translation $(\hat{\Delta}_x, \hat{\Delta}_y)$ between the two radar images.

3   Indirect Method

In general, the indirect method works following these steps: (1) identifying targets within radar data. Along with that, the features from the targets are selected. (2) Finally, scan matching is used for local motion estimation which is often converted afterwards to a global frame for the odometry representation. The aforementioned steps used with the indirect method can have some variations, e.g. use of random sample consensus (RANSAC) [7] for removing outliers [17]. See Fig. 2 for a diagram showing how the indirect method estimates relative motion. The algorithms that use this method were tested with either scanning or non-scanning radar. Also, some of the algorithms were tested in a sensor fusion framework along with an IMU (see Table 1).

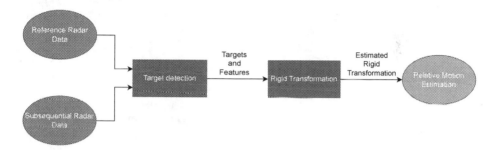

Fig. 2. Diagram for indirect method.

3.1   Target Identification and Features

In contrast with direct methods, indirect methods require the identification (detection) of targets or keypoints in radar data. Under the realm of possibilities for finding keypoints in radar data, a seemingly natural choice is to use CFAR because one is already widely employed for detection in radar systems. For example, radar odometry using CFAR for target detection can be seen in [1,5]. Nonetheless, research for finding a better detection model for radar data with the aim of performing odometry is still active. For example, in [2] a tailored approach to radar data was developed in order to find keypoints. Finally, some of the possible features used by indirect methods include: position, range, Doppler, angle of arrival (azimuth and/or elevation), and intensity.

3.2   Scan Matching

Scan matching consists of finding a rigid transformation (the change in translation and orientation in $2(x, y, \theta)$ or $3(x, y, z, \varphi, \theta, \psi)$ dimensions) which aligns two scans [12]. In the context of indirect radar odometry, each scan consists of the targets and their features. Therefore, scan matching focuses on finding the transformation which best associates two scans according to a criteria. In [2] a graph matching approach was employed which was based on global geometric constraints, while in [1] the normal distribution transform (NDT) [13] was used.

4   Conclusion

Odometry estimation using radar is an emerging field. The reason to select this sensor for performing motion estimation lies mainly on the robustness of radar with regards to environmental conditions. As discussed in the paper, one way to arrange radar odometry approaches is by dividing them between direct and indirect methods. While the direct method allows the estimation of odometry without having to perform the detection step, the indirect method was tested with a wider-array of radar types. To conclude, both methods are still under active research and developments that will either focus on one or another method, or even a combination of both are expected to come in the near future.

Acknowledgements. This work has been supported by the COMET-K2 Center of the Linz Center of Mechatronics (LCM) funded by the Austrian federal government and the federal state of Upper Austria.

References

1. Almalioglu, Y., Member, G.S., Turan, M., Lu, C.X., Trigoni, N., Markham, A.: Milli-RIO: ego-motion estimation with low-cost millimetre-wave radar. IEEE Sens. J. **21**(3), 3314–3323 (2021)
2. Cen, S.H., Newman, P.: Radar-only ego-motion estimation in difficult settings via graph matching. In: Proceedings of - IEEE International Conference Robotics and Automation, pp. 298–304 (2019). https://doi.org/10.1109/ICRA.2019.8793990
3. Checchin, P., Gérossier, F., Blanc, C., Chapuis, R., Trassoudaine, L.: Radar scan matching SLAM using the fourier-mellin transform. In: Howard, A., Iagnemma, K., Kelly, A. (eds.) Field and Service Robotics. Springer Tracts in Advanced Robotics, vol 62, pp. 151–161. Springer, Heidelberg (2010). https://doi.org/10.1007/978-3-642-13408-1_14
4. de Ponte Müller, F.: Survey on ranging sensors and cooperative techniques for relative positioning of vehicles. Sensors (Switzerland) **17**(2), 1–27 (2017). https://doi.org/10.3390/s17020271
5. Doer, C., Trommer, G.F.: An ekf based approach to radar inertial odometry. In: 2020 IEEE International Conference on Multisensor Fusion and Integration for Intelligent Systems (MFI), pp. 152–159 (2020). https://doi.org/10.1109/MFI49285.2020.9235254
6. Durrant-Whyte, H., Bailey, T.: Simultaneous localization and mapping: part I. IEEE Robot. Autom. Mag. **13**(2), 99–108 (2006). https://doi.org/10.1109/MRA.2006.1638022
7. Fischler, M.A., Bolles, R.C.: Random sample consensus: a paradigm for model fitting with applications to image analysis and automated cartography. Commun. ACM **24**(6), 381–395 (1981). https://doi.org/10.1145/358669.358692
8. Gamba, J.: Radar Signal Processing for Autonomous Driving, 1st edn. Springer, Heidelberg (2019). https://doi.org/10.1007/978-981-13-9193-4
9. Grisetti, G., Stachniss, C., Burgard, W.: Improving grid-based SLAM with Rao-Blackwellized particle filters by adaptive proposals and selective resampling. In: Proceedings - IEEE International Conference on Robotics Automation, vol. 2005, pp. 2432–2437 (2005). https://doi.org/10.1109/ROBOT.2005.1570477

10. Hess, W., Kohler, D., Rapp, H., Andor, D.: Real-time loop closure in 2D LIDAR SLAM. In: Proceedings - IEEE International Conference on Robotics and Automation, pp. 1271–1278 (2016). https://doi.org/10.1109/ICRA.2016.7487258
11. , Kramer, A., Stahoviak, C., Santamaria-Navarro, A., Agha-Mohammadi, A.A., Heckman, C.: Radar-inertial ego-velocity estimation for visually degraded environments. In: Proceedings - IEEE International Conference on Robotics and Automation, pp. 5739–5746 (2020). https://doi.org/10.1109/ICRA40945.2020.9196666
12. Lu, F., Milios, E.: Robot pose estimation in unknown environments by matching 2D range scans. J. Intell. Rob. Syst. **18**(3), 249–275 (1997). https://doi.org/10.1023/a:1007957421070
13. Magnusson, M., Lilienthal, A., Duckett, T.: Scan registration for autonomous mining vehicles using 3d-ndt. J. Field Rob. **24**, 803–827 (2007). https://doi.org/10.1002/rob.20204
14. Mohamed, S.A., Haghbayan, M.H., Westerlund, T., Heikkonen, J., Tenhunen, H., Plosila, J.: A survey on odometry for autonomous navigation systems. IEEE Access **7**, 97466–97486 (2019). https://doi.org/10.1109/ACCESS.2019.2929133
15. Monaco, C.D., Brennan, S.N.: Radarodo: ego-motion estimation from doppler and spatial data in radar images. IEEE Trans. Intell. Veh. **5**(3), 475–484 (2020). https://doi.org/10.1109/TIV.2020.2973536
16. Park, Y.S., Shin, Y.S., Kim, A.: PhaRaO: direct radar odometry using phase correlation. In: Proceedings - IEEE International Conference on Robotics and Automation, pp. 2617–2623 (2020). https://doi.org/10.1109/ICRA40945.2020.9197231
17. Quist, E.B., Niedfeldt, P.C., Beard, R.W.: Radar odometry with recursive-ransac. IEEE Trans. Aeros. Electron. Syst. **52**(4), 1618–1630 (2016). https://doi.org/10.1109/TAES.2016.140829
18. Reddy, B., Chatterji, B.: An fft-based technique for translation, rotation, and scale-invariant image registration. IEEE Trans. Image Process. **5**(8), 1266–1271 (1996). https://doi.org/10.1109/83.506761
19. Louback da Silva Lubanco, D., Kaineder, G., Scherhäufl, M., Schlechter, T., Salmen, D.: A comparison about the reflectivity of different materials with active sensors. In: 2020 5th International Conference on Robotics and Automation Engineering (ICRAE), pp. 59–63 (2020). https://doi.org/10.1109/ICRAE50850.2020.9310883

Systems Thinking. Relevance for Technology, Science and Management Professionals

On Modeling Complex Systems by Means of System Theory

Franz Pichler[✉]

Emeritus Systems Theory, JKU Linz, Linz, Austria
`telegraph.pichler@aon.at`

1 Preliminaries

Fifty years ago professor Mihajlo Mesarovic together with D. Macko and Y. Takahara, all from the "Systems Research Center", Case Western Reserve University, Cleveland, Ohio, USA, published 1970 the important book "Theory of Hierarchical, Multilevel, Systems". In this book for the first time a mathe-matical foundation for the modelling of complex systems has been given. However today this important scientific contribution seems to be forgotten and citations of it are rather seldom. This paper should help, that this important contribution of Mesarovic and his co-workers to the field of systems theory, there especially to mathematical systems theory, becomes again our attention. In the first part of this paper we discuss the field of systems theory in general. In the second and final part the concepts of "Multi Strata Models" and of "Multi-Echelon Models" are, as defined in their book of 1970, have our interest. Multilevel models of this kind have already found for a long time practical applications. However, Mesarovic and his group deserve the merit, to provide a general mathematical and systems theoretical framework for it. Finally we give an outlook to "holarchical models" as introduced by Arthur Koestler. Models of this kind can be considered as "intelligent multi-echelon models". Such models seem to be of specific interest for the automation ("digital transformation") of complex systems by the means of artificial intelligence.

2 Systems Theory as a Scientific Discipline

Each specific scientific discipline has developed on its own a number of insights and methods for the solving of the problems which are considered. This especially is true for the disciplines of natural science and engineering. There the results are often documented by models in mathematical or geometrical form which allow the application of theoretical methods for analysis and synthesis (design). Following the idea of "the economy of thinking" as introduced by the Austrian physicist and philosopher Ernst Mach, we may take for each specific discipline an abstract view of the existing models and related methods of problem solving. As result we get a collection of abstract models and methods which can be considered as a "Systems Theory" of the related discipline. In that way several specific "systems theories" have been developed in the

---

In memory of Professor Mihajlo Mesarovic.

R. Moreno-Díaz et al. (Eds.): EUROCAST 2022, LNCS 13789, pp. 629–634, 2022.
https://doi.org/10.1007/978-3-031-25312-6_74

past. As an early example the work of Karl Küpfmüller as documented by his book "Systemtheorie der elektrischen Nachrichtenübertragung" published in the year 1949 can be considered in Germanyas the birth of system theory for the field of communication engineering [1]. Another example is the work of Wilhelm Cauer as given in his "Theorie der linearen Wechselstromschaltung" of 1941 [2]. Besides of communication engineering the discipline of control engineering contributed in the past strongly in the development of system theory. As early American contribution the book of LeRoy, A. MacColl "Fundamental Theory of Servomechanism" from 1945 is an early example [3]. The book "Linear System Theory" written by Lotfi Zadeh & Charles A. Desoer in 1963 was again a fundamental contribution for the development of system theory for control engineering [4]. It introduced the "state space approach" as investigated earlier by Rudolf Kalman and others. Now in the addition to the already existing spectral methods by means of the Fourier-and Laplace-transform, computational methods could effectively be implemented on a computer.

All this examples are based on mathematical models and are as such contributions to mathematical system theory. Today the field of mathematical systems theory for communication- and control engineering is highly developed. An important type of model is given by the concept of an open dynamical system. Today the following different parts of mathematical systems theory can be considered:

Theory of linear systems.

Theory of finite state machines.

Theory of cellular automata.

Theory of abstract dynamical systems.

Theory of nonlinear systems.

Theory of general mathematical systems.

All this considered work was devoted to the field of engineering. However there were also efforts to establish systems thinking in other scientific fields. As an important contribution we mention the work on "General Sytems" by Ludwig Von Bertalanffy [5].

3   Contribution of Mihajlo Mesarovic to Mathematical Systems Theory

In the year 1958 Mihajlo Mesarovic came from the Institute Nikola Tesla, Belgrade for postdoctoral studies to the Massachusetts Institute of Technology (MIT). As a result of his studies he published his book on "The Control of Multivariable Systems" (1960) [6]. In 1960 he joined the Case Institute of Technology, Cleveland, Ohio where he became a professor at the Systems Research Center. In 1964 he edited the book "Views on General Systems Theory", proceedings of "The Second System Symposium at Case Institute of Technology", which included his fundamental paper "Foundations for a General Systems Theory" [7]. In the years of his stay at the Case Institute of Technology.

(today the "Case Western ReserveUniversity") Mesarovic together with members of his group published a number of papers in the field of General Mathematical Systems Theory and also several books [8]. We refer here especially to "Theory of Hierarchical, Multilevel Systems" (together with D. Macko and Y. Takahara) from 1970 [9] and "General Systems Theory: Mathematical Foundations" (together with Y. Takahara) of

1975 [10], both landmarks for the development of Mathematical Systems Theory. This work triggered also research and development at different European universities. We might refer here to the books of Pichler (1975, 1976) [13, 14], Locke (1984) [15] and Wunsch (1985) [16, 17].

The work of Mesarovic got internationally wide known by the results of the Club of Rome project on "World Modeling" which was performed at the "International Institute of Applied Systems Analysis" (IIASA) in Vienna-Laxenburg, Austria. For the general public the results have been published together with Eduard Pestel in 1975 by the book "Mankind at the Turning Point"[11].

In the following we restrict us to the discussion of two important architectural concepts for modelling complex systems which have been elaborated by Mihajlo Mesarovic and his group in his book of 1970. These are the concepts of "Multi Strata Models" and "Multi Echelon Models". Although both concepts are known in modelling complex systems for a long time, the book of Mesarovic deals with it in a satisfying mathematical manner for the first time.

4 Multi-strata Models

Mesarovic defines a multi-strata-model as a model which is presented by a number of systems specifications situated on different levels of description. Each one is a model of the considered overall complex system but taken from a specific viewpoint. The models, as described in the different levels are open, which means that they interact with the environment and interact also between it from level to level. Graphically such a model can be shown by a block-diagram, where the blocks are ordered vertically, from level n (the highest block) down to level 1 (the lowest block). Each block n, n-1, n-2, ..., 2 interacts with the relation "intervention" with the next block going down. Each block 1, 2, ... , n-1 is in relation "performance feedback" with the block above (Fig. 1).

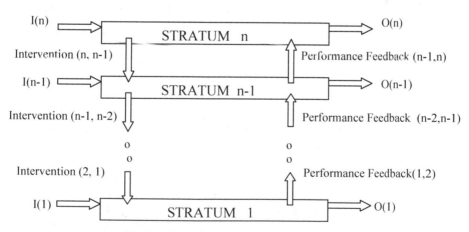

Fig. 1. Block-diagram of a multi-strata-model

Multi-strata models are useful for a proper documentation of complex systems. They allow the selection the right level of the presentation of the system for a given usage.

Take as an example a car. For the driver, the level which describes how to operate the car is the right one. For the mechanical technician a level where the different parts and their interconnections can be seen is important. For the electrical technician the electrical parts and their wiring are of interest. Today often manuals of complex technical systems do not use a multi-strata model. They often contain descriptions in detail which deal with the process of implementation and are so of little use to a general user. A well known example of multi-strata modeling is given by the ISO/OSI model for computer networks. Each of the seven levels is devoted to the hierarchical ordered tasks which have to be fulfilled in order to reach a proper network function.

Besides of their application for the analysis of complex systems multi-strata models can also be used for the design of a complex system. The design process might start on the n´th level which deals with a model which solves the designer/client problem. In this model the client states all features and functional requirements which the final system has to fulfill. The designer proves the feasibility under consideration of the non-functional requirements of the system. The next step is the design of the model on the (n-1)´th level. This model might show the architecture of the system consisting of the necessary components and the couplings between them. Each component has to fulfill the interventions which are stated by the model on top and all components together have to give the performance feedback for the top-model. This step has to be continued until at level 1 the final model is reached. Multi-strata models are per se of high multi-disciplinary nature. While model on the n´th level can be from the field of politics or economics. The model on level 1 can be a computer program. In addition to such a top-down approach in designing a complex system the question arise if a multi-strata model can also be used for bottom-up design. In principle this is possible. In this case we start with a complex system given at level 1 and look for emergent features which allow the design of a model on level 2. This is followed bottom-up until we reach on top at level n a model of a system fulfills the expectations of a client. Stephen Wolfram seems to follow such an idea in creating his "New Kind of Science". He started at level 1 with cellular automata and reached at level n by computation a result which is satisfying [18].

5 Multi-echelon Models

The second category of hierarchical models which is considered by Mihajlo Mesarovic in his monography of the year 1970, are multi-echelon models. Multi-echelon models, often also known as "multi-layer models", have also a multi-level description. However, contrary to multi-strata models where each level describes the whole system, the different levels of a multi-echelon are only models of a part of the system. To get the full description of the system by a model all components of the different levels are needed. Each component of a level n-1, n-2, ..., 1 has to fulfill a certain task which is assigned to him by a certain part of the level above. On the other hand each component of level n, n-1, ..., 2 has to assign a certain task to a component of the next level below. For any assignment of tasks there exists a feedback which reports the fulfillment of the assignment. The practical use of the concept of multi-echelon models is well known. For example such models are used to present the organizational structure of a company or to define the different steps of a production process. The important contribution of Mihajlo Mesarovic can be seen in the development of a mathematical systems theoretical framework which allows a theoretical treatment for such complex systems (Fig. 2).

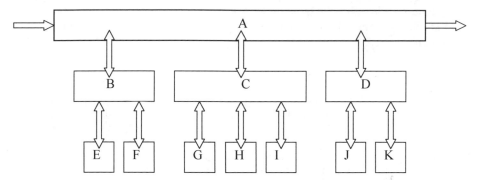

Fig. 2. Block-diagram of a multi-echelon model

6   On the Holarchical Models of Arthur Koestler

Arthur Koestler is maybe best known as a writer. However, after his emigration from France to England, he started a new career in Philosophy and Science and he published a number of books which are devoted to systems science. In the following we discuss his results and compare it with the work of Mihajlo Mesarovic on multi-echelon models.

Koestler´s books "The Ghost in the Machine" (1967) [19], "Beyond reductionism" (1968) [20] and "Janus" (1978) [21], deal with architectural models of complex intelligent systems with the goal to solve problems in brain research and for the understanding of the biological evolution. A central issue is for Koestler the concept of "holon", which is by defintion a "janus-faced" intelligent acting component of a hierarchical ordered model, called by Koestler a "holarchy". The exact definition of this concept is given by Koestler in verbal form by the "General Properties of Open Hierarchical Systems" (O.H.S.). It is easy to see that a holarchy in the sense of Koestler has the architecture of a multi-echelon model. The important additional feature of a holarchy is however, that the components have the ability to act in their decisions in a certain degree by their own intelligence. This means that they can learn and adapt to new local requirements. If we take for a holarchy as example the organization of a factory where the components are humans (from the top-management down to the individual workers) then each of the human-components has a certain degree of freedom and has the duty to fulfill his task in an intelligent manner. The author of this paper has in past tried to explain the concept of Koestler´s "Holons" and his concept of "Holarchy" in terms of System Theory and apply it for modeling complex systems [22–24].

Many organizations and processes function today as holarchies in the sense of Arthur Koestler. By the current trend of automation we can ask the question if a holarchy can be automated. For a positive answer this would mean that human intelligence which is available by the components can be successfully replaced by artificial intelligent acting machines. For certain holarchies which need little intelligence the recent available technology provided by a computer with artificial intelligence however might allow a good approximation. But for most of the practical existing holarchies, where professional acting humans determine the quality of work, such automation must fail. This means that the so called "digital transformation" of practical working systems can in general not be implemented.

References

1. Küpfmüller, K.: Die Systemtheorie Der Elektrischen Nachrichtenübertragung. Zürich (1949)
2. Cauer, W.: Theorie Der Linearen Wechselstromschaltungen. Leipzig (1941)
3. Maccoll, L.: Fundamental Theory of Servomechanism. New York (1945)
4. Zadeh, L., Desoer, C.: Linear System Theory. New York (1963)
5. Bertalanffy, L V.: General System Theory. New York (1968)
6. Mesarovic, M D.: The Control of Multivariable Systems. New York (1960)
7. Views on general system theory. In: Mesarovic, M. (ed.) Proceedings of the Second Systems Symposium at the Case Institute of Technology. New York (1964)
8. Mihajlo, D.: Mesarovic: mathematical theory of general systems. In: Hammer, P.C. (ed.) Advances in Mathematical Systems Theory, pp. 47–80. The Pennsylvania State University Press, University Park and London (1969)
9. Mesarovic, M., Macko, D., Takahara, Y.: Theory of Hierarchical Multi-Level Systems. Academic Press, New York (1970)
10. Mesarovic, M., Takahara, Y.: General Systems Theory: Mathematical Foundations. Academic Press, New York (1975)
11. Mesarovic, M., Pestel, E.: Mankind at the Turning Point. The Second Report to the Club of Rome, London (1975)
12. Mesarovic, M.D., Takahara, Y.: Abstract Systems Theory Lecture Notes in Control and Information Sciences, vol. 116. Springer, Berlin (1989)
13. Pichler, F.: Mathematische Systemtheorie: Dynamische Konstruktionen. Walter de Gruyter, Berlin (1975)
14. Pichler, F.: General dynamical systems: construction and realization. In: Marchesini, G., Mitter, S.K. (eds.) Mathematical Systems Theory Lecture Notes in Economics and Mathematical Systems, vol. 131, pp. 393–408. Springer, Berlin (1976)
15. Locke, M.: Grundlagen einer Theorie allgemeiner dynamischer Systeme. Akademie-Verlag, Berlin (1984)
16. Wunsch, V.G.: Geschichte der Systemtheorie. Akademie-Verlag, Berlin (1985)
17. Wunsch, G.: Grundlagen der Prozesstheorie. Teubner, Stuttgart (2000)
18. Wolfram, S.: A New Kind of Science. Wolfram Research, Champaign (2002)
19. Koestler, A.: The Ghost in the Machine. Hutchinson & Co Ltd., London (1967)
20. Koestler, A.: Beyond Reductionism: New Perspectives in the Life The Alpbach Symposium. Hutchinson & Co Ltd., London (1969)
21. Koestler, A.: Janus A Summing Up. Hutchinson & Co Ltd., London (1978)
22. Pichler, F.: Searching for Arthur koestler´s holons- a systems-theoretical perspective. In: Weibel, P. (ed.) Jenseits von Kunst. Passagen Verlag, pp. 452–455 (1997). ISBN 3–8165–254-1
23. Pichler, F.: Modeling complex systems by multi-agent holarchies. In: Kopacek, P., Moreno-Díaz, R., Pichler, F. (eds.) EUROCAST 1999. LNCS, vol. 1798, pp. 154–168. Springer, Heidelberg (2000). https://doi.org/10.1007/10720123_14
24. Pichler, F.: On the Construction of A. Koestler´s Holarchical Networks. Cybernetics and Systems Vol. 1 (ed. Robert Trappl), pp. 80–84 (2000). ISBN 3–85206–151-2

Crisis Management in a Federation – Cybernetic Lessons from a Pandemic

Markus Schwaninger[✉]

University of St. Gallen, St. Gallen, Switzerland
Markus.schwaninger@unisg.ch

Abstract. We aim to contribute to improving the management of pandemic crises. Our focus is on federal systems, as these are particularly powerful in dealing with environmental complexity. Through five waves of the pandemic, spanning a year and a half, we study the management of the crisis in the Swiss Federation. The purpose of this research is learning for how to deal with crises of the same type in the future. We apply the Viable System Model (VSM) as a framework for our inquiry, elaborating a diagnosis and a design for the management of epidemic or pandemic crises. The VSM is a conceptual tool that is particularly strong for analyzing federal systems. Hence substantial insights have surfaced to orientate a future crisis management.

Keywords: Crisis management · Complexity · Requisite variety · Variety engineering · Organization · Viable system model · Diagnosis · Design · Covid-19 pandemic · Resilience

1 Introduction

When the Covid virus hit the world in 2020, it was broadly treated as a virological, medical or epidemiological problem. Looking at the dynamics of events, I saw a need for studying the crisis from an organizational perspective. The focus of the study is on the federal republic of Switzerland. This small country would be demanding enough for such a study. It would also be gratifying, as it is a federation, which should have special capabilities for dealing with exceptional situations such as a pandemic. My co-researcher was Prof. Lukas Schoenenberger, a Swiss expert in the health system [1, 2].

As a framework for our project, Stafford Beer's Viable System Model appeared to be pertinent. We adopted a viewpoint of complexity, not complication, and a perspective of holism, not reductionism.

The purpose of our study was

- To diagnose the Covid-19 Pandemic from the cybernetic viewpoint of complexity absorption, and
- To draw lessons for the improvement of the state of crisis management as new crises are always imminent.

Our theoretical foundation was a very abstract one: the classic Law of Requisite Variety, which stems from the eminent cybernetician Ross Ashby [3]. It posits: "Only Variety can absorb Variety". This Law hinges on the concepts of Complexity and Variety.

We define Complexity as the ability of a system to assume many different states or behaviors. Variety is a technical term for Complexity. We conceive of it as the "amount of states or modes (or patterns) of behavior of a system". Variety can be calculated; it expounds the characteristics of an exponential function of the relationships and elements of the system under study [4]. Variety is also a synonym for Repertoire of Behaviors. The more complex the environment the higher the necessary variety to cope with it.

The Law of Requisite Variety implies: To maintain a system under control, the control system must have a Variety (repertoire of behavior) that matches the Variety of the system controlled. This law is universal and inexorable.

2 Case Study: The Covid-19 Crisis in a Federation

In this context, the system regulated is a social system in a crisis, and the regulator is the organization that has been created to manage this crisis. Our focus is on federal systems, as these are particularly powerful in coping with environmental complexity. Using the case of the Swiss Federation, we have studied the Covid-19 pandemic in that country for nearly two years, from March 2020 to January 2022.

The Swiss Federation has been chosen as a case study, - for two reasons: First, Switzerland has built an effective response system for coping with the crisis. Second, and more important, the form of state here is the Federation; the form of governance is democracy. Both are classical approaches to enabling the survival of social systems: Federal structure and democratic participation are two pillars of their viability.

In sum, we address the question of how the crisis organization within a country must be designed for mastering the crisis. This can only be achieved if the Variety of the organization equals the Variety of the environment, which in our case is the pandemic. In other words, that organization must develop Requisite Variety, i.e., a repertoire of behaviors that matches the repertoire of the pandemic, or more concretely, the destructive complexity of a virus going wild.

Speaking about complex social systems: If Ashby's Law is inexorable, then it must also be unachievable. Complexity can never be fully understood nor mastered in a literal sense. This contribution is not grounded in a technocratic hubris that assumes the possibility of total control of complex systems. Take a pandemic: If the virus seems under control, new mutants can emerge, which might call into question all previous successes. Yet, all that Ashby's Law does, is discern a condition under which control can occur. It does not assert that control can occur in any case. "Mastering the crisis" then is a relative term.

3   Methodology

We apply the Viable System Model (VSM) by Stafford Beer as a framework for our study [5–7]. That model is based on the Law of Requisite Variety. It has been widely used for both diagnosis and design of organizations. It also embodies the structural concept with the most rigorous theoretical claim: The assertion that it specifies the necessary AND sufficient structural preconditions for organizational viability. These preconditions are formulated in terms of necessary and sufficient *regulatory systems* (also *systems of management* or *systems of governance*):

"Systems 1": Basic operations with their managements
"System 2": Coordination
"System 3": Executive Management
"System 3*": Auditing
"System 4": Strategic Management
"System 5": Normative Management.

This set of prerequisites for viability holds for both, the Federation as a whole and the Cantons, i.e., member states, of which there are 26. Figure 1 shows these two plus further recursive levels of organization, with their respective units striving for viability.

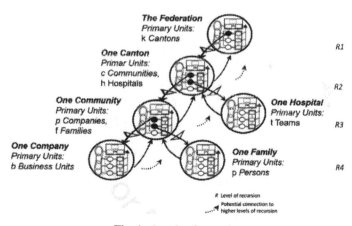

Fig. 1. Levels of recursion

We carefully elaborated a diagnosis and a design for the management of pandemic crises. Both the analysis and the synthesis of our study are based on Ashby's Law and the VSM. Substantial insights have surfaced to orientate a future crisis management. In a nutshell, the implication is what we call "Variety Engineering".

4   Trajectory of the Pandemic

The first wave of the pandemic came in February-March 2020. The first case of an infection in Switzerland occurred on 25 February, the first mortality on 5 March 2020. Figure 2 shows the daily new infections until early 2022. The 7-day averages of new cases (bold line), with the successive waves and the various Covid-variants triggering them, are visible in the graph.

Subsequently, both infections and deaths increased exponentially. The pandemic proved to be a threat due to the relentless, ferocious advance of the virus.

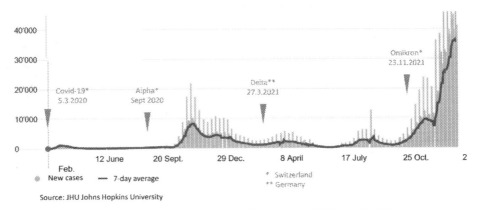

Source: JHU Johns Hopkins University

Fig. 2. New Covid infections - Switzerland 3/2020 to 2/2022

The Government – a Federal Council of Seven with a consensual mode of decision - took on the overall responsibility for a nationwide Covid crisis management. On the basis of emergency law [8], a drastic *shutdown* was imposed immediately (mid-March 2020) for three months. During the *shutdown*, far-reaching bans were imposed on the economy: closure of all businesses (except food and pharmacies), ban on all cultural and sporting events, temporary closure of all schools and universities, reduction of public transport to a minimum, suspension of air travel, practical ban on foreign travel. The economy and the education system functioned exclusively virtually, i.e., online (home office, distance learning). However, a lockdown, which would involve even more severe restrictions, e.g., curfews, was never inflicted.

Early on, the Government decided to provide financial help for companies and freelancers to alleviate the socio-economic consequences of the crisis, and enable their economic survival. Approximately 60 billion Swiss francs were allocated in March/April 2020 and distributed to the recipients, in an efficient and unbureaucratic manner. This way, many breakdowns were avoided.

Consequently, infections dropped almost to zero (July 2020). In summer, infections were low, and people became sloppier: the discipline of the population faltered. Also, too little testing was conducted in Switzerland and thus control of the epidemic was lost [9]. A second wave built up, which was much bigger than the first one. This cycle repeated itself, so that until early 2022 we had five waves of Covid infections (Fig. 1).

The same pattern was observable in many countries. A look at the behavior over time of deaths demonstrates that these react sensitively to the increases of the infections, during Waves I and II, after that the reactions are moderate, and have been running in counter direction since December 2021 [10]. This is the evidence that the Omicron variant of the virus is more infectious, but less deadly, and entails less severe disease courses than the earlier ones (Covid-19 initial, Alpha and Delta).

Due to this new situation, by 16th February 2022 the federal government abolished virtually all Covid-measures (except masks in public transport and in nursing homes).

5 Diagnosis

We must advance two things about the special nature of the Swiss state system. Federation is the form of state. A federation is a political entity characterized by a union of partially self-governing provinces, states, or other regions under a central federal government (federalism). The self-governing status of the component states, as well as the division of power between them and the central government, may not be altered by a unilateral decision of either party, the states or the federal political body. The system under study is a federation with three levels of recursion, municipal, cantonal, and federal. Our system-in-focus is the society of a federation.

Democracy the form of governance. Stemming from Greek *demos* and *kratein*— the rule of the people—, the concept of democracy implies bottom-up governance. The sovereign makes the final decision on substantive issues, as the holder of supreme power.

In Fig. 3 we have condensed the results of our diagnosis. The diagram represents the environment, to the left, and the organization, and to the right the operations with their management systems 1 (S1). These make the cantonal COVID operations and management.

The metasystem, i.e., the governance system that includes the higher management functions is constituted by:

- Coordination S2, made up of several components.
- Executive Management S3 – immediate and short-term orientation - with the Minister of Health and the Federal Office of Public Health.
- Strategy and Development S4, with the long-term orientation, namely embodied in a Scientific Task Force, which was established early on, already in March 2020.
- The Normative Function S5, which is the highest organ embracing the System's Identity and Ethos: The Swiss Identity, the Democratic Principles, The Constitution and ultimately Parliament and the Sovereign.

Across these functions we observe the following main diagnostic points or problems:

Problem 1: The role of the Federal Council in the crisis management was dominant throughout 2020 and 2021. The implementation of the measures, e.g., testing and vaccination, was the responsibility of the cantons. Often, the cantons were overwhelmed by the tasks and unable to fulfil them properly. The two following problems appear to be core (Fig. 4).

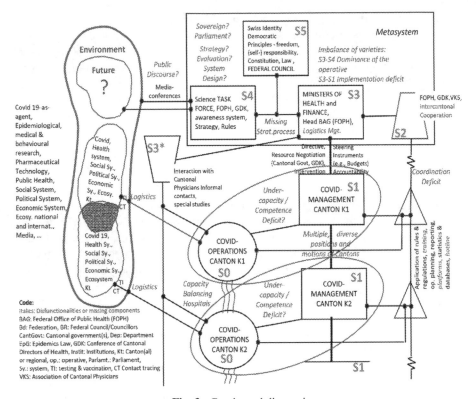

Fig. 3. Condensed diagnosis

Problem 2; see Fig. 4a. Vertically, in channel S3–S1 (Executive and Local Management), the power of the government to issue orders was offset by a lack of enforcement and sanctioning power. Thus, the potential behavioral repertoire of the Federal Council vis-à-vis cantonal claims and political pressure from interest groups was insufficient. The variety equation was out of balance.

Problem 3; see Fig. 4b, The Strategy Function S4: The long-term perspective tended to be neglected. As Pascal Strupler, former head of the FOPH, confessed recently: "We were so absorbed by the day-to-day business that the strategic part was neglected."

The long-term perspective (S4) was primarily embodied in the Scientific Task Force. That was a purely advisory body, and therefore it had no authority to make strategic decisions. The interaction S3 & S4 (Executive & Intelligence) showed a hypertrophy of the operative. There was a glaring lack of variety in S4—in the sense of too little power—and an excess of variety in S3 (Executive). The system was therefore not in equilibrium and problematically constellated.

Problem 4 refers to System 5, i.e., System Identity and Ethos/Normative Management, and the relationship of Systems (3 ↔ 4) ↔ 5. Switzerland's identity is expressed in its history as a confederation, the federalist and democratic form of government. These

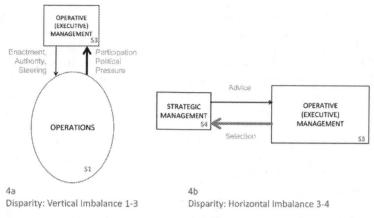

Fig. 4. Core problems of variety imbalance, vertical in 4a and horizonal in 4b

parameters shape culture in all its manifestations. The behavior of the population, groups and individuals is largely a function of this identity. The democratic principles and values unfold great power. The country's Covid management, especially the Federal Council, has consistently relied on the principles of freedom and responsibility, a sense of the common good and trust in institutions.

The normative basis for the decision-makers at this top level were thus clearly defined. But there was a lack of clarity about the responsibilities in S4 and S3 (Executive and Intelligence).

Problem 5 refers to the Information and Communication Systems. They fulfill an essential cross-function and play a crucial role in supporting most processes. These systems showed astonishing deficits. Most information and communication systems were outdated, some even inexistent. Essential tools did not function properly.

6   Lessons for Design

In our final report, suggestions for improvement were proposed. That was first in early 2021. We summarize them here in shorthand; further details are documented in publications [1] and [2].

Re Problem 1: Capacity & competence deficit of cantons. The focus was on the build-up of eigen-variety of the Cantons vis-à-vis the active virus. Attenuation of the complexity (foreign variety) of the virus' destructive potential. Improvement on vaccination campaigns and information. And: Leadership education and organization development to enhance qualification of cantonal politicians and staff.

Re Problem 2: The vertical variety imbalance. The way out of this conundrum is to reduce the time commitment to the operative S3 (Executive) for all members of the

Federal Council. According to the Epidemics Law, the Confederation is entitled to create a national operational body (type general staff) to manage enforcement in a special situation. However, such a body was never activated, and that took its revenge already in the fall of 2020, when the huge wave arose [11]. In other words, such an executive unit would enable a more effective realization of the strategy. In addition, the Federal Council would be relieved by the assignment of such a unit into Executive (S3), and thus would be free for the necessary commitment to Intelligence (S4).

Re Problem 3: Strategic blindness and debility. First, the variety of the Strategy function S4 needed to be expanded and the destructive variety of the active virus and of the antivaccinationists had to be attenuated. In this vein, the communication with the public needed to be strengthened (clarity, consistency, unity of doctrine). The second imperative was to establish a functioning strategic discourse of Executive S3 and Strategic S4, as a powerful absorber of complexity. Third, a long-term orientation and holistic system design was to be cultivated and supported by a permanent scientific body. These were ongoing concerns also after the abolishment of the measures of containment. Because the next pandemic will occur sooner or later.

Re Problem 4: The unclear distribution of tasks. Clarify the tasks and competencies of agents in the Metasystem, in the fight against the pandemic: federal and cantonal councils, and the crisis staff.

Re Problem 5: Information and communication. It was deemed important to establish a normative discourse about values, beforehand, not at the moment of actual crisis, namely in Parliament and in the public, involving education system and media. To mend the technical deficits, a comprehensive redesign of information systems was needed. This implied far-reaching reform.

So much for the diagnosis and design issues.

Over time, the quality of the Covid-management improved. Some of the deficits discussed here were mitigated, e.g., several shortcomings in the information and communication domain.

7   Final Reflection

Overall, how has Switzerland weathered the COVID-19 crisis? In answering this question, it would be insufficient to consider epidemiological criteria only. To achieve a more equilibrated view, we will consider four criteria in our assessment, even if some overlaps between them cannot be avoided. The balance is as follows. First, the death toll: on the record of cumulated, COVID-induced deaths per 100,000 population, Switzerland fared 34% better than the average of countries of the European Union, for the period March 2020 to June 2022 [12]. Second, the severity of restrictions: the Oxford Stringency Index [13] shows that the crisis management in Switzerland has given citizens more freedom than in all neighboring countries: No curfews, no loitering restrictions, low travel drawbacks, etc. The authorities hardly issued any commands, they always appealed to the self-responsibility of each individual towards society. The behavior of the citizens was crucial. They mostly complied with the recommendations of the authorities and adapted their behavior, notwithstanding resistances such as the antivaccinationist movement.

Third, the resilience against Corona: the Bloomberg Covid Resilience Ranking measures the resilience against Corona, of the 53 largest economies with a score consisting of 12 indicators, including the economic dimension. Switzerland received high marks from that ranking. Of the 53 countries monitored, it was second only to Norway in 2021. According to the report, Switzerland stands for mild measures that do not continually escalate; the virus is tackled where this can be done with the least social and economic disruption [14, 15]. Fourth, the socio-economic damages: the economy remained largely intact and showed rapid recovery as the crisis subsided [16]. The country pursued a unique path of crisis management that has proven effective.

In dealing with the crisis, what is the role of the complicated, complex, cumbersome, slow political processes, which are characteristic of the Swiss Federation? They seem to be a disadvantage. Yet, they prove highly effective in dealing with complexity. The diversity is much greater in this country than in many other countries, but the connecting elements are still stronger than the dividing elements. A landmark is that citizens here have to vote 3 to 4 times a year on federal, cantonal and local issues. That shapes culture. In the end, the complex political-organizational system warrants requisite variety.

To quote Karin Keller-Sutter, the Minister of Justice: "One must admit that it is difficult to forge alliances across language and party boundaries. But once something has been decided, it holds. With majority governments, such as in Germany or France, more mistakes happen there, because laws are rushed through – and when the government changes, everything is changed again. Our system is a bit slow, but it saves us from making bigger mistakes" [17].

Managers and professionals of all kinds are often in deep trouble when confronted with complex organizational issues, or when bad organization is the invisible cause of dysfunctional systems behavior and bad performance.

A way out of the predicament is shown by the Conant-Ashby theorem: "Every good regulator of a system must be a model of that system." In other words, the quality of a solution cannot be better than the goodness of the model on which it is based. That is the key to better performance. And this is the meaning of Systems thinking for professionals in Science, Technology and Management: to provide better theoretical models for the improvement of practical life.

References

1. Schwaninger, M., Schoenenberger, L.: Cybernetic crisis management in a federal system – insights from the Covid pandemic. Syst. Res. Behav. Sci. **39**, 3–20 (2022)
2. Schwaninger, M., Schoenenberger, L.: Krisenmanagement in der pandemie: eine organisationskybernetische Untersuchung auf den Ebenen Bund, Kanton, Gemeinde. In: Tuckermann, H., Schwaninger, M. (eds.) Wege aus der COVID-19-Krise. Anamnese, Diagnose und Design, pp. 73–109. Bern Haupt (2022)
3. Ashby, W.R.: An Introduction to Cybernetics. Chapman & Hall, London (1956)
4. Schwaninger, M.: Intelligent Organizations: Powerful Models for Systemic Management. Springer, Berlin (2009\2006)
5. Beer, S.: The Brain of the Firm. Wiley, Chichester (1981)

6. Beer, S.: The viable system model: its provenance, development, methodology and pathology. J. Oper. Res. Soc. **35**(1), 7–25 (1984)

7. Beer, S.: Diagnosing the System for Organizations. Wiley, Chichester (1985)

8. According to §7 Epidemics Law (Epidemiengesetz - EpG) of the Swiss Confederation, Schweizerische Eidgenossenschaft (2012)

9. Plattner, T., Meier, P., Luchetta, S., Broschinski, S.: So schlug sich die Schweiz gegenüber anderen Ländern, Tages-Anzeiger 11, pp. 2–3, Juni 2021

10. Data of Johns Hopkins University. https://coronavirus.jhu.edu/map.html. Accessed 12 June 2022

11. Zenger, C.: Der Bund handelt erratisch. Interview, St. Galler Tagblatt, p. 7, 20 November 2020

12. COVID-induced deaths per 100,000 population from March 2020 to June 2022 were 242 at average in the countries of the European Union and 158 in Switzerland. Calculus based on data from. https://www.bfs.admin.ch/bfs/de/home.html, https://www.ecdc.europa.eu/en/cases-2019-ncov-eueea, https://ec.europa.eu/eurostat/databrowser. Accessed 14 June 2022

13. Ritchie, H., et al.: COVID-19: Stringency index (2021). https://ourworldindata.org/covid-stringency-index. Accessed 17 June 2021. Our world in data

14. Chang, R., Varley, K., Munoz, M., Tam, F., Kaur Makol, M.: The Covid Resilience Ranking. The Best And Worst Places to Be as Reopening, Variants Collide (2021). https://www.bl00mberg.com/graphics/covid-resilience-ranking/. Accessed 5 Aug 2021

15. Oelrich, C., Trumpf, S.: Die Schweiz und Norwegen sind die Corona-Musterländer. St. Galler Tagblatt **5**(8), 2021 (2021)

16. Benz, M., Seliger, F.: "Wirtschaft in Echtzeit" - eine Corona-Bilanz, Neue Zürcher Zeitung 14. März **2022**, 22–23 (2022)

17. Keller-Sutter, K., Berset, A.: Doppel-Interview, Blick 1.6.2021. (translated by M.S.) (2021)

Using Archetypes to Teach Systems Thinking in an Engineering Master's Course

Meike Tilebein[1]([⊠]), Jan Wunderlich[1], and Ralf Tenberg[2]

[1] Institute for Diversity Studies in Engineering, University of Stuttgart, Pfaffenwaldring 9, 70569 Stuttgart, Germany
meike.tilebein@ids.uni-stuttgart.de
[2] Department of Technical Teaching and Learning, University of Darmstadt, Alexanderstraße 6, 64283 Darmstadt, Germany

Abstract. Systems Thinking can help to solve complex problems in different domains. For an engineering master's program, we designed a seminar course to teach Systems Thinking. For the seminar we use qualitative models known as archetypes as conceptual models and the Covid-19 pandemic as problem context. In this paper we describe the course design and report findings from running it. Based on students' evaluation and the materials they produced throughout the course, our findings (1) support our design assumptions regarding student motivation, (2) give hints on students' struggling with Systems Thinking and understanding and applying archetypes in particular. With this we want to contribute to the discussion of how to teach Systems Thinking in Higher Education.

Keywords: Systems Thinking · Qualitative modelling · Archetypes · Higher education · Motivation · Teaching

1 Introduction

Systems Thinking is widely seen to be a promising approach to complex problem solving. Roughly, it can be defined as "a paradigm for viewing reality based on the primacy of the whole and relationships" [1]. It is therefore strongly advocated that decision-makers (in business, politics etc.) are educated in Systems Thinking. The urging need for Systems Thinking skills is emphasized by a growing interest in this topic on the one hand while at the same time there seems to be a persistent lack of Systems Thinking skills on the other hand.

In their recent bibliometric study of scientific publications 1991–2018 in the field of Systems Thinking, [2] provide data stating that journal coverage of Systems Thinking has been exponentially growing over the past three decades. They also find that Systems Thinking is related to a wide range of applications.

Looking at the educational system and drawing from experience in engineering education in particular, [3] identifies seven distinct skills that combine to Systems Thinking: dynamic thinking, closed-loop thinking, generic thinking, structural thinking, operational thinking, continuum thinking, and scientific thinking that calls for rigorous

R. Moreno-Díaz et al. (Eds.): EUROCAST 2022, LNCS 13789, pp. 645–652, 2022.
https://doi.org/10.1007/978-3-031-25312-6_76

hypothesis-testing. However, when confronted with complex problems, individuals typically demonstrate a lack of Systems Thinking in the above sense. Decision-making in complex dynamic systems is often characterized by delays and misperceptions of feedback, difficulties in dealing with accumulation, and, in general, by inadequate mental models and barriers to learning [4]. Hence, the results of Sweeny and Sterman's Systems Thinking Inventory study [5] in the context of stock-and-flow thinking have been confirmed many times and in different domains and participants since it first appeared [6].

Different frameworks exist for the development and assessment of competencies towards proficiency in Systems Thinking (e.g. [7, 8]). While such development frameworks enable an in-depth skills assessment, they do not necessarily prescribe a path for teaching. [9] distinguishes two approaches to develop improved understanding of dynamically complex tasks: One is using models and the other is modelling. For each of them there is a corresponding teaching approach. Using models often relies on microworlds as interactive learning environments, whereas the modelling approach is typical of many System Dynamics courses. In this paper, we describe an engineering master's seminar course we designed around qualitative modelling only. For the seminar we take archetypes as conceptual models and the Covid-19 pandemic as problem context.

With this paper we want to contribute to the discussion of how to teach Systems Thinking in Higher Education. It is organized as follows: In the next section we present the design of our seminar course and explain our practical considerations and theory-based assumptions. In Sect. 3 we present our findings from running the course, both from teachers' and from students' perspectives. From matching results and observations with pre-course considerations, we derive lessons learnt that are briefly discussed in the concluding Sect. 4.

2   Course Design

2.1   General Aspects of Model-Based Teaching

Skills and learning outcomes related to modelling are important in each of the Systems Thinking assessment frameworks mentioned in Sect. 1. A distinction is made between qualitative modelling and quantitative modelling. Typically, both types of models are addressed in System Dynamics courses and textbooks.

For teaching with quantitative models, [10–12] provide teachers with a sequenced seven-step course framework: exploring existing models, copying models, adding structure, correcting or improving structure, modelling a "canned" model description, modelling problems with vivid, well-known structure and dynamics, and modelling personally chosen problems.

This process can carry learners from being novices to being experienced practitioners in quantitative modelling. While competences in quantitative modelling can support each of the Systems Thinking skills sketched above, there might be some considerations against intensive quantitative modelling exercises in teaching. Creating simulation models needs specific training in the respective software and is time-consuming, and students might turn to a gaming mode of using a model rather than developing a conceptual understanding of the underlying structure of the problem [9].

In order to improve the ratio of learning outcomes vs. student workload, one might want to turn to qualitative models. Qualitative models, and causal loop diagrams in particular, are often seen as a preparation or conceptual stage for more elaborated quantitative models, and as communication tools at the end of a quantitative modelling process [13], Hence, there is also an argument in favour of teaching with qualitative modelling, which can address a wide range of Systems Thinking skills. Examples of teaching based on qualitative modelling reported in the literature draw in particular on the value of archetypes, causal loop diagrams depicting widespread mechanisms as proposed by [14] or [15], such as e.g. the Success to the Successful archetype.

[16] describes a series of archetype-based MBA seminar courses with students without former exposure to System Dynamics. The author used archetypes as initial conceptual models and students were invited to extend and adapt the models. Findings included that learning outcomes exceeded the teachers' expectations and students showed outstanding motivation and commitment.

Similarly, [17] report on using causal loop diagrams and archetypes to facilitate Systems Thinking in business classes with no prior knowledge in Systems Thinking. The authors argue that, according to a study by [18], the main Systems Thinking skills driving performance in complex decision-making can be supported by qualitative modelling.

2.2 Curricular Embedding of the Course and Students' Prior Knowledge

The course is part of the optional specialization module Business Dynamics within the engineering master's program Technology Management (M.Sc.) at the University of Stuttgart, Germany. The program spans 4 semesters (2 years) during which students deepen their knowledge in core areas such as material sciences, construction design, manufacturing, energy and process engineering, and choose four additional specialization modules, one of the possible choices being Business Dynamics, which spans two semesters and is structured by two consecutive parts. Prerequisite for part 2 is a successful passing of part 1's written final test. The general Business Dynamics course (part 1) is to a large extent based on the textbook by [4]. The course covers causal loop diagrams and archetypes explicitly in 3 out of 15 lectures. The complete 15 weeks course is aimed at a student workload of 180 h. Part 2 is the 15 weeks/90 h workload seminar course in which students develop a model, hold a presentation and write a final essay. Part 2 is covered in this paper.

2.3 Practical Considerations for Course Organization

In the past we had run the seminar course several times based on quantitative modelling tasks within the context of a current research project of ours. Consequently, we had experienced some of the general disadvantages of quantitative modelling in teaching sketched in Sect. 2.1, plus the time needed for students to get familiar with the respective research project prior to modelling. This is why we decided for qualitative modelling.

Individual assignments are standard. Nevertheless, because we value intensive discussion in class as driver of learning processes, we wanted to enable intensive group interaction. Therefore, we looked for a common topical problem context that – in contrast to a research project – would be immediately accessible while of great interest to the students. Besides, availability of data on that problem would be required. For this reason, we chose the Covid-19 pandemic as a problem context.

2.4 Theory-Based Considerations on Student Motivation and Learning

Motivation is the central predictor for human learning. When we perceive learning and development requirements, it is due to our motivation whether and how we face these challenges [19]. Students' motivation to learn can be explained by the self-determination theory according to [20]. Based on this, [21] has developed a learning motivation theory in which a substantial distinction is made between controlled extrinsic motivation and autonomous extrinsic motivation. Extrinsic motivation is focused here, because intrinsic motivation – driven by pure interest – cannot be set as a premise for institutionalized learning processes, because human interests are fluctuating, selective and only partially rational. University learning, on the other hand, is about absorbing and understanding comprehensive knowledge, building interrelationships and expanding on that. Hence, to a certain extent, students are forced to learn something, but should do so on their own initiative, not as a direct result of an immediate compulsion and exclusively geared towards exam performance. It is precisely this combination of requirements that characterizes autonomous extrinsic motivation. Controlled extrinsic motivation is largely ruled out here, since the course is part of the portfolio of choice.

Within autonomous extrinsic motivation, [21] distinguishes further between identified and integrated extrinsic motivation. Identified extrinsic motivation is present when learners develop insight into the necessity of certain topics or content. Identified extrinsic motivation is therefore more of a long-term factor of students who are ready to learn, which can be less the product of individual teaching formats than of personal development and identification processes. Integrated extrinsic motivation is present when learners align their personal interests with topics or content. According to [20], this happens when they (1) perceive autonomy, (2) can experience their competencies and (3) are socially involved. The teaching format of the seminar course discussed here aims to promote autonomous extrinsic motivation among students in this sense:

To (1): In this course, the choice of specific applications is largely left to the students themselves. They have to search independently for a topic (or 2 topics respectively, at the beginning) in which to recognize archetypes. The following tasks must also be done relatively independently by the students, although teachers are always in the background to advise and support and repeatedly provide relevant input.

To (2): It goes without saying that Systems Thinking cannot be passed on as a simple information. A comprehensive implementation and transfer phase is therefore included in this teaching format, in which the theory can not only be learned, but also internalized in an active way. I. E. that competency development and implementation are cyclically linked to one another. Formative and summative evaluations in the teaching-learning process shall not only support the development of competencies. They can also support motivation, as they can positively confirm the perception of competencies. The overall approach of qualitative modelling is also intended to be beneficial for the perception of competencies. Compared to the time-consuming quantitative modelling approaches discussed above, in qualitative approaches, the students can receive feedback much earlier on how well they have worked or where there are still weak points.

To (3): Although the students have to work on their tasks individually, this is done in a community of practice. This community lives, on the one hand, through the tasks that have to be tackled in parallel, and, on the other hand, in particular through ongoing communication about the tasks during course and tutoring sessions. Instead of perceiving one-self as a lone warrior, the students can be certain that others are also working in the same problem context. This raises mutual interest in other students' experiences and results. In addition, formally, but also informally, a social comparison can always take place, which is very important for such an open and sometimes abstract development process, as uncertainties and fears can arise here, especially if students stagnate in their progress or encounter problems. So social inclusion helps the stronger students to get ahead and the weaker to not feel alone.

To sum up, the general design of our seminar course could support all three aspects of autonomous extrinsic motivation, i.e. "experiencing autonomy", "perception of competence" and "social inclusion", which in turn can generate high-quality motivation for high-performing students as well as for lower-performing students.

2.5 Course Description

As sketched above, in this seminar course students are asked to apply existing archetypes to aspects of their choice from the context of Covid-19. Given the limited number of archetypes and the need for individual assignments, we wanted to ensure that students do not accidentally work on identical problems. This is why we (1) excluded one of the most obvious problems at the time the course started (success-to-the-successful archetype as a conceptual model for governmental or external funding of vaccine development) by giving it as an example at the kickoff-session, and (2) asked the students to propose two different problems each in their first milestone presentation of which only one would be further elaborated.

Hence, students prepare two proposals each, one of which is to be elaborated further during self-study periods with intermittent feedback and class discussions, until final submission as an essay. Students are provided with reading materials reflecting and explaining the archetypes given in [14].

The seminar course encompasses nine stages, starting with a kick-off session where students are provided with the general course information. After preparing their proposals during a first self-study period, the students present their proposals in a plenary session followed by an immediate discussion and feedback from teachers and peers. At the end of this session one of each students' proposals is chosen for further elaboration during the second self-study stage, which contains another tutoring session and yields the intermediary results final presentations, where the final models and related work are presented and discussed, and feedback is given by peers and teachers. During the third and last self-study stage the students finish their essays and have the opportunity to partake in a last tutoring session, which focuses on structure and content of the final submissions.

3 Findings from Running the Course

3.1 Teachers' Observations

Three students were enrolled in the course. Table 1 summarizes the proposals presented by each student. The proposal chosen for elaboration is marked with a star.

Table 1. Students' first proposals, (*): proposals chosen for further elaboration

Student	Archetype	Proposed issue of reflection
1	Shifting the Burden*	"*Zombie Companies*": Companies which are not capable of surviving on their own, but which are kept in the market due to a suspension of insolvent company's obligation to apply for insolvency
	Success to the Successful	*Increased success of food-delivery*: Due to law-enforced lockdown of restaurants, the pandemic situation favors take-away and food delivery services over traditional catering on the premises of the hosts
2	Tragedy of the Commons*	*Economic necessities and compensational behavior*: Conflict between peoples' self-interest (e.g. earning money) and actions necessary for the common good (e.g. reduction of work and income in certain fields)
	Success to the Successful	*Tourism abroad vs. domestic tourism*: Due to travel bans and reluctance of the population to travel via public transportation, domestic tourism will be more successful than tourism relying on international public travel
3	Shifting the Burden*	*Effectiveness of governmental policies in Germany with regards to the pandemic*: Physical distancing and reduction of contacts as a symptomatic solution, vs. fundamental solutions
	Tragedy of the Commons	*Panic buying*: Fearing a shortage in an insecure immediate future during the beginning of the pandemic situation in Germany, the phenomenon of panic buying and a resulting shortage of some daily goods

3.2 Student Reactions and Feedback

The course was evaluated using the default evaluation instrument of the University of Stuttgart. While the quality of the students' models varied between students along the stages of the process and in the intermediate and final results due to varying understanding of system archetypes and their application, all participants of the seminar course rated unanimously:

- Pace and challenge of the seminar course have been regarded as most adequate.

- The individual learning effect is to be rated the highest possible.
- Two items related to student-teacher interaction earned highest rating, as well as peer participation, and that the amount of discussions was most adequate.
- Motivation to engage with course topics was highest.
- Compared to the lecture students invested more time into the seminar course.

The following statements summarize the free-text answers to the question what the students liked especially about the course:

- The creative freedom to work on a self-chosen problem was explicitly valued by all three students, with one explicit mention that this freedom increases motivation.
- Interaction between students and teachers was praised (thrice), as well as the plenary sessions and resulting interaction with and learning from other students (twice).
- A learning effect outlasting the duration of the course was mentioned.
- The combination of lecture and seminar course to apply theoretical knowledge was perceived as beneficial to understanding.
- The opportunity to transfer the System Dynamics methodology was valued.

4 Discussion and Conclusion

Our theory-based assumptions when designing the course were that model-based teaching using archetypes as conceptual problem descriptions, combined with the Covid-19 pandemic as a problem context, would motivate students and have a positive effect on their learning outcomes, rather than – given time/workload restrictions – letting them work with quantitative modelling on small detail problems. We now can match these assumptions with the results and observations reported in the previous section.

Regarding student motivation, the students' feedback reported above supports that the students were highly motivated. In line with our prior assumptions, the students' feedback can be related to experiencing autonomy as well as to perceiving their own competence, as well as to being socially involved.

Students also report a maximum in learning. Yet from the teachers' perspective, this has to be differentiated. Along the stages of the process we could see that there are still issues in Systems Thinking competence with regard to the full understanding of system archetypes. This emphasizes that the application of these methods in the face of complex real-world problems remains challenging.

In the specific seminar course presented here, the method of qualitative modelling as well as the topical reference to the corona pandemic was established in order to exploit the students' motivational force as far as possible. The aim was to create a direct projection space for students' living environment. You don't always have the chance to bring such intensity into teaching, but other topics can also work well here, because the world is (unfortunately) full of challenges even after the pandemic (e.g. the consequences of the climate catastrophe, the digitization of markets, etc.), which can generally be accessed via a Systems Thinking approach.

References

1. Maani, K.: System dynamics and organizational learning. In: Dangerfield, B. (ed.) System Dynamics. ECSSS, pp. 417–430. Springer, New York (2020). https://doi.org/10.1007/978-1-4939-8790-0_543
2. Hossain, N.U.I., Dayarathna, V.L., Nagahi, M., Jaradat, R.: Systems thinking: a review and bibliometric analysis. Systems **8**(3), 23 (2020)
3. Richmond, B.: Systems thinking: critical thinking skills for the 1990s and beyond. Syst. Dyn. Rev. **9**(2), 113–133 (1993)
4. Sterman, J.D.: Business Dynamics Systems Thinking and Modeling for a Complex World. Irwin/McGraw Hill, Boston (2000)
5. Sweeney, L.B., Sterman, J.D.: Bathtub dynamics: initial results of a systems thinking inventory. Syst. Dyn. Rev. **16**(4), 249–286 (2000)
6. Kapmeier, F., Happach, R.M., Tilebein, M.: Bathtub dynamics revisited: an examination of déformation professionelle in higher education: bathtub dynamics revisited. Syst. Res. Behav. Sci. **34**(3), 227–249 (2017)
7. Plate, R., Monroe, M.: A structure for assessing systems thinking. Creative Learn. Exch. Syst. Dyn. Syst. Think. K-12 Educ. **23**(1), 1–12 (2014)
8. Schaffernicht, M.F.G., Groesser, S.N.: A competence development framework for learning and teaching system dynamics. Syst. Dyn. Rev. **32**(1), 52–81 (2016)
9. Kunc, M.: Teaching strategic thinking using system dynamics: lessons from a strategic development course. Syst. Dyn. Rev. **28**(1), 28–45 (2012)
10. Richardson, G.P.: "Model" teaching. Syst. Dyn. Rev. **30**(1–2), 81–88 (2014)
11. Richardson, G.P.: "Model" teaching II: examples for the early stages. Syst. Dyn. Rev. **30**(4), 283–290 (2014)
12. Richardson, G.P.: "Model" teaching III: examples for the later stages. Syst. Dyn. Rev. **30**(4), 291–299 (2014)
13. Wolstenholme, E.: Using generic system archetypes to support thinking and modelling. Syst. Dyn. Rev. **20**(4), 341–356 (2004)
14. Senge, P.M.: The Fifth Discipline: The Art and Practice of the Learning Organization, 1st edn. Doubleday/Currency, New York (1990)
15. Wolstenholme, E.F.: Towards the definition and use of a core set of archetypal structures in system dynamics. Syst. Dyn. Rev. **19**(1), 7–26 (2003)
16. Schwaninger, M.: Modeling with archetypes: an effective approach to dealing with complexity. In: Moreno-Díaz, R., Pichler, F. (eds.) EUROCAST 2003. LNCS, vol. 2809, pp. 127–138. Springer, Heidelberg (2003). https://doi.org/10.1007/978-3-540-45210-2_13
17. Atwater, J.B., Pittman, P.H.: Facilitating systemic thinking in business classes. Decis. Sci. J. Innov. Educ. **4**(2), 273–292 (2006)
18. Maani, K.E., Maharaj, V.: Links between systems thinking and complex decision making: systems Thinking and Complex Decision Making. Syst. Dyn. Rev. **20**(1), 21–48 (2004)
19. Tenberg, R.: Was ist Lernkompetenz und wie kann sie gemessen werden? Theoretische Grundlagen und empirische Bilanzierung über Lernstrategien im beruflichen Lernen. Zeitschrift Für Berufs- Und Wirtschaftspädagogik **105**(4), 539–555 (2008)
20. Deci, E.L., Ryan, R.M.: Die Selbstbestimmungstheorie der Motivation und ihre Bedeutung für die Pädagogik. Zeitschrift Für Pädagogik **39**(2), 223–239 (1993)
21. Prenzel, M.: Selbstbestimmtes motiviertes und interessiertes Lernen bei angehenden Bürokaufleuten. Eine Längsschnittstudie. In: Krüger, H.-H., Olbertz, J.H. (eds.) Bildung zwischen Staat und Markt, pp. 47–50. Leske & Budrich, Opladen (1997)

Collecting VS Sharing Personal Data: Examining the Viability of the Concepts

Igor Perko(✉) (iD)

University of Maribor, Maribor, Slovenia
igor.perko@um.si

Abstract. The proposition of a data-sharing concept deals with governing the processes of personal biometrical data interchange. The data sharing concept proposes a set of mechanisms enabling individuals (data producers) to govern the data they produce. Data sharing concepts open a series of research questions: exploring the interactions between the society stakeholders and the sharing effect on their relations; invoking distributed data storing and analysis concepts; redefining the data governance processes; introducing AI-supported data negotiating mechanisms, to name a few. Data sharing can result in a new level of social dynamics, in which individuals and organisations negotiate on each data sharing interaction and thus dynamically redefine the relationship between society's transparency and individuals' privacy.

The proposed data sharing concept posts multiple implications for all stakeholders. Amongst them are individuals who provide new means for data self-governance, organisations and data researchers by adapting to the distributed data gathering strategies, and regulators for redesigning social frameworks and policy design processes.

As the proposal induces significant disruption to the fabric of society, it poses several challenges. For the data researchers and practitioners, the insights into distributed data and analysis software design and development are provided; for social researchers, the AI-supported transdisciplinary participative research; for the managers, insight on how to organise data negotiation processes into business processes.

Keywords: CyberSystemics · Data sharing · Data ownership · Artificial intelligence · GDPR

1 Introduction

CyberSystemics is a nearly borderless concept [1], ubiquitously present and at the same time ignored in all facets of society. Hybrid reality (HyR) [2], examining the co-existence of society and AI technology, was one of the four topics of the WOSC 2021 Congress [3]. HyR focus is on upholding the level of activity of all societal stakeholders by providing a safe digital environment.

In a situation where every smart device, every app, and every website streams detailed biometrical data, the variety of data interactions, some of them potentially conflicting,

© The Author(s), under exclusive license to Springer Nature Switzerland AG 2022
R. Moreno-Díaz et al. (Eds.): EUROCAST 2022, LNCS 13789, pp. 653–657, 2022.
https://doi.org/10.1007/978-3-031-25312-6_77

significantly exceeds the limited capacity of existing regulative frameworks and mecha-nisms [4]. Based on the dynamics of interactions in HyR, where the virtual and real-world interchange, we can safely assess that the currently used data collecting concepts will result in the development of serious pathological behaviour patterns by the organisations in possession of this data [2].

The proposition of a data-sharing concept in which data ownership and governance are assigned to the data producers instead of the data collectors is to be systemically examined. For this, the viable system model (VSM) diagnosis capacity is utilised. Data sharing concepts open a series of relevant research questions: What are the data sharing goals, boundaries, structures and processes [5]; what are the interactions between the society stakeholders, and how do they imply the emergence of their relations [6]; how to develop distributed data storing and analysis concepts [7]; how to redefine the data governance processes [8, 9], how to invoke AI-supported data negotiating mechanisms [10], to name a few.

By replacing data collecting with data sharing, we can foresee a new level of social dynamics, in which individuals and organisations negotiate on each and every data sharing interaction and thus dynamically redefine the relationship between society's transparency and individuals' privacy [11]. We provide new operational challenges for the data collectors and propose tools for developing dynamic regulation frameworks and policies.

The paper is structured as follows: in the second paragraph, data sharing concept backgrounds are elaborated; in the third paragraph method for data sharing examination is introduced; in summary, the discussion is provided.

2   Backgrounds

In HyR, Artificial intelligence (AI) models are considered as a system of self-evolving algorithms for reasoning, thus extracting useful and nonobvious patterns from data sets [12], connected with people by direct feedforward and feedback mechanisms [13]. Big data methods apply for preparing and organising the vast amounts of data required to drive AI reasoning processes.

IoT devices are and will produce constant flows of data to the data collecting systems, feeding the AI need for data. The collected data can include biometrical data on persons in the range of IoT sensors, capable of disclosing vital personal information, for instance, the state of the individual and its behavioural patterns [2].

Su, Perry, Bravo, Kase, Roy, Cox and Dasari [14] provide V&AR examples of how scientists and engineers can use advanced visualisation technologies to perform data analysis and assessment, thus transforming scientific discovery. At the same time, Fricker [15] researches new immersive co-design methodologies to introduce meaning-ful trajectories for participatory processes. Even though the data collecting concept is ethically problematic [16], adequate proposals for addressing the issue have not been proposed until the present time.

Data sharing-related problems and concepts are only marginally reported in the literature, even though the concepts provide strong implications for the communication exchange, the society and the asynchronous and federated artificial intelligence learning processes [17, 18].

Thoegersen and Borlund [19] explore the data sharing definitions among the research community. Savage and Vickers [20] report on the low researcher intentions to share data despite publication rules. Tenopir, Allard, Douglass, Aydinoglu, Wu, Read, Manoff and Frame [21] put the reasons on insufficient time and lack of funding, while Wallis, Rolando and Borgman [22] claim that data sharing occurs only through interpersonal exchanges. Data sharing barriers also exist inside national research communities; Zhou, Huang and Li [23] report on barriers in China, while Zhu [24] comments on the state in the UK.

Data sharing resides on data ownership and property rights, questioning the ethic of sharing non-proprietary data. The notion of data ownership was developed over time, where Anderson [25] discussed the data ownership at the level of research groups, identifying the emergence of data monetisation. The elaboration of data sharing concepts based on data ownership and property rights was not generalised and thus still lacks a requisitely holistic perspective.

The Viable System Model (VSM) [26] provides a standard system structure capable of surviving in its environment. There are variations in the VSM understanding and implementation [27, 28], but the general structure remains unchanged. The VSM consists of a recursive system of five subsystems in each viable system. Even though VSM has been often applied in the system's design, it can be used for diagnostic purposes [29], especially to identify potential systemic pathologies.

3 Methods

In the research, we are diagnosing the viability of data sharing and data collecting concepts by using the VSM model as a diagnostical framework, focusing on examining the following elements:

1. The concept goals
2. Operational processes
3. Internal and external communication channels and mechanisms
4. The Coordinators
5. The governors.

These elements for both concepts are examined from the viewpoint of multiple HyR stakeholders: data producers, consumers, and regulators.

The diagnostic process is conducted on a theoretical level, but more importantly, it is examined in a series of interactive situations, where data on interactions are collected using IoT devices. An obvious experimental environment is the Hybrid reality, in which biometrical Virtual reality (VR) goggles are used to examine user experience. In this environment, multiple individuals with diverse backgrounds can immerse themselves in an identical situation, measuring their situational behaviour using biometrical devices, such as eye-tracking, facial expression, cardio, and neuro signals. The experiment is focused on examining which data sharing strategy best aligns with the goals of the involved participant, either as the observed individual or a member of an organisational structure.

As a starting hypothesis, we assume that stakeholders may follow these goals in the HyR:

1. **Data producers:** exist in HyR and would like to augment their capacity to actively manage data interactions without putting additional effort into executing the management processes.
2. **Data consumers:** are using interaction data for intelligent optimising of their behaviour patterns to affect other HyR stakeholders.
3. **Regulators:** are developing adaptive behavioural frameworks and executing policies for their enforcement.

We expect that each stakeholder group follows its goals, which are divergent from the other stakeholder goals. The research is interdisciplinary since all should be considered in the research results. It invokes natural and social science research methods, combining personal individuality, technical optimisation, and adaptive governance. The research will provide novel, transdisciplinary research results.

4 Summary

The currently used data collecting concepts can lead to several pathologies, such as data misuse, manipulation, extortion, exploitation etc. The risk of misconduct in data governance expands in HyR by invoking new types of data in the analysis processes: biometric data streams, continuously feeding AI technology with detailed biometrical data, opening the capacity for successful behaviour predictions and prescriptions.

In our attempts to preserve the activity of all HyR stakeholders, the data sharing concept is proposed. On a conceptual level, it proposes frameworks and processes aimed at delivering data governance to the data producers based on a wide moral, ethical and legislative base of support.

In the proposed research, a VSM model is used to examine the viability of both concepts on a theoretical and practical level, using 2nd order cybernetics concepts [30] of self-observation in the examination process.

From the research, we expect to receive focus points for further research and development, such as intelligent data sharing negotiation concepts, capable of assessing if/how data can or cannot be shared in a particular interaction.

This research may significantly impact the design of intelligent dynamic data sharing negotiation protocols. Data sharing negotiating protocols can significantly impact the research processes in ethically ambiguous situations within the research laboratories, in the business environment and in personal communication.

References

1. Uranos. https://uranos.ch/index.php/research-menu/cybernetcis
2. Perko, I.: Hybrid reality development-can social responsibility concepts provide guidance? Kybernetes **50**, 676–693 (2021)
3. https://www.wosc2020.org/theme3

4. http://eur-lex.europa.eu/legal-content/EN/TXT/PDF/?uri=CELEX:32016R0679&from=en
5. Espejo, R., Bowling, D., Hoverstadt, P.: The viable system model and the Viplan software. Kybernetes **28**, 661–678 (1999)
6. Espejo, R., Lepskiy, V.: An agenda for ontological cybernetics and social responsibility. Kybernetes **50**, 694–710 (2021)
7. Zou, R.P., Lv, X.X., Zhao, J.S.: SPChain: blockchain-based medical data sharing and privacy-preserving eHealth system. Inf. Process. Manag. **58**, 18 (2021)
8. Reijers, W., O'Brolcháin, F., Haynes, P.: Governance in blockchain technologies & social contract theories. Ledger **1**, 134–151 (2016)
9. Bula, G., Espejo, R.: Governance and inclusive democracy. Kybernetes **41**, 339–347 (2012)
10. Perry, B., Uuk, R.: AI governance and the policymaking process: key considerations for reducing AI risk. Big Data Cogn. Comput. **3**, 17 (2019)
11. Merlec, M.M., Lee, Y.K., Hong, S.P., In, H.P.: A smart contract-based dynamic consent management system for personal data usage under GDPR. Sensors **21**, 24 (2021)
12. Martinez, I., Viles, E., Olaizola, I.G.: Data science methodologies: current challenges and future approaches. Big Data Res. **24**, 100183 (2021)
13. Guzman, A.L., Lewis, S.C.: Artificial intelligence and communication: a human-machine communication research agenda. New Media Soc. **22**, 70–86 (2020)
14. Su, S.M., et al.: Virtual and augmented reality applications to support data analysis and assessment of science and engineering. Comput. Sci. Eng. **22**, 27–38 (2020)
15. Fricker, P.: Virtual reality for immersive data interaction. Landsc. Archit. Front. **7**, 153–159 (2019)
16. Ioannou, A., Tussyadiah, I., Lu, Y.: Privacy concerns and disclosure of biometric and behavioral data for travel. Int. J. Inf. Manag. **54**, 15 (2020)
17. Liu, L., et al.: Blockchain-enabled secure data sharing scheme in mobile-edge computing: an asynchronous advantage actor-critic learning approach. IEEE Internet Things J. **8**, 2342–2353 (2021)
18. Lu, Y.L., Huang, X.H., Dai, Y.Y., Maharjan, S., Zhang, Y.: Blockchain and federated learning for privacy-preserved data sharing in industrial IoT. IEEE Trans. Ind. Inform. **16**, 4177–4186 (2020)
19. Thoegersen, J.L., Borlund, P.: Researcher attitudes toward data sharing in public data repositories: a meta-evaluation of studies on researcher data sharing. J. Doc. **17** (2021)
20. Savage, C.J., Vickers, A.J.: Empirical study of data sharing by authors publishing in PLoS journals. PLoS One **4**, 3 (2009)
21. Tenopir, C., et al.: Data sharing by scientists: practices and perceptions. PLoS One **6**, 21 (2011)
22. Wallis, J.C., Rolando, E., Borgman, C.L.: If we share data, will anyone use them? Data sharing and reuse in the long tail of science and technology. PLoS One **8**, 17 (2013)
23. Zhou, L.H., Huang, R.H., Li, B.Y.: "What is mine is not thine": understanding barriers to China's interagency government data sharing from existing literature. Libr. Infor. Sci. Res. **42**, 11 (2020)
24. Zhu, Y.M.: Open-access policy and data-sharing practice in UK academia. J. Inf. Sci. **46**, 41–52 (2020)
25. Anderson, G.C.: Data ownership - but what is the problem. Nature **345**, 8 (1990)
26. Beer, S.: The Heart of Enterprise. Willey, Chichester (1979)
27. Espejo, R.: The enterprise complexity model: an extension of the viable system model for emerging organisational forms. Syst. Res. Behav. Sci. **38**, 721–737 (2020)
28. Rios, J.N.: A self-organising network for the systems community. Kybernetes **33**, 590–606 (2004)
29. Schwaninger, M.: Design for viable organisations - the diagnostic power of the viable system model. Kybernetes **35**, 955–966 (2006)
30. Glanville, R.: The purpose of second-order cybernetics. Kybernetes **33**, 1379–1386 (2004)

Author Index

Printed in the United States
by Baker & Taylor Publisher Services